The **Rough Guide** to

New York City

written and researched by

Martin Dunford, Stephen Keeling
and Andrew Rosenberg

GRAND CENTRAL
TERMINAL

Contents

New York architecture colour section following p.208

Ethnic New York colour section following p.336

Colour maps following p.480

◀◀ Manhattan skyline ◀ Grand Central Terminal

Introduction to

New York City

An adrenaline-charged, history-laden place that holds immense romantic appeal for visitors, New York is the most enthralling city in the world. Its past is visible in the tangled lanes of Wall Street and tenements of the Lower East Side, while towering skyscrapers like the Empire State Building serve as monuments to the modern age. Street life shifts markedly from one area to the next. The waterfront, sometimes salty, sometimes refined, and the landscaped green spaces – notably Central Park – give the city a chance to catch its breath. Iconic symbols of world culture are always just a stone's throw away, if not outright staring you in the face. For raw energy, dynamism and social diversity, you'd be hard-pressed to top it; simply put, there's no place quite like it.

New York buzzes round-the-clock: not only can you find, buy or enjoy almost anything 24 hours a day, seven days a week, but there are also enough cultural attractions to fill months of sightseeing. That said, there are some key activities and sights that travellers simply should not miss. Take the city's patchwork of vastly different **neighbourhoods**: a stroll from Chinatown through Soho and Tribeca to the West Village reveals the variety of life wedged together in downtown Manhattan. Then there's the city's astonishing **architecture** – you can walk past glorious Art Deco skyscrapers on one block and rows of genteel brownstone houses on the next – as well as its excellent **museums**, both the celebrated, like the Met and the American Museum of Natural History, and the less well-known but equally worthy, such as the Frick Collection and the Brooklyn Museum.

As if the sights weren't enough, New York has an exhaustive selection of **shops**, and world-class **restaurants** and **bars** that cater to any taste, budget and schedule. It is justifiably famous for its diverse **theatre scene**, with dozens of venues offering everything from high-gloss Broadway musicals to scruffy avant-garde performance pieces. And if it's **nightlife** you're after, look no further: the city's throbbing, jam-packed clubs are known for their cutting-edge parties and music. In other words, plan on sleeping once you get home.

What to see

Though New York City officially comprises the central island of **Manhattan** and **four outer boroughs** – Brooklyn, Queens, the Bronx and Staten Island – for many, Manhattan simply *is* New York. Certainly, whatever your interests, you'll probably spend most of your time here. Understanding the intricacies of Manhattan's layout, and above all getting some grasp on its subway and bus systems, should be your first priority. Most importantly, note that New York is very much a city of neighbourhoods, and is therefore best explored on foot. For an overview of each district, plus what to see and do there, turn to the introduction of each chapter.

This guide starts at the southern tip of the island and moves north. **The Harbour Islands** – the Statue of Liberty and Ellis Island – were the first

So much to see, so little time...

As noted in our "20 Things not to miss" section (see p.10), you can't experience everything New York City has to offer on a single trip. Your best bet is to enjoy the city at your own pace, take in the attractions that interest you most and remember that you can always come back. The following suggested itineraries are based on what's possible in a day. They're mainly designed around key sights and neighbourhoods, and they include suggestions for where to have lunch. Don't be afraid to skip the major attractions, though – just wandering about can be an extremely fulfilling way to see the city.

Three days

- Ellis Island/Statue of Liberty; Financial District (lunch); Brooklyn Bridge; Brooklyn Heights.
- East Village; West Village (lunch); Empire State Building; Macy's; Times Square at night.
- Grand Central Terminal; Rockefeller Center (lunch); St Patrick's Cathedral; Museum of Modern Art; Fifth Avenue shops.

Five days

As above plus…

- Central Park; Metropolitan Museum of Art; Frick Collection; Upper East Side shops.
- Lower East Side; Tenement Museum; Chinatown (lunch); Soho shops.

Seven days

As above plus…

- Lincoln Center; Upper West Side (lunch); Museum of Natural History.
- Cathedral of St John the Divine; Columbia University; Harlem; the Cloisters.

glimpses of New York (and indeed America) for many nineteenth-century immigrants; the latter's history is recalled in its excellent Museum of Immigration. The **Financial District** encompasses the skyscrapers and historic buildings of Manhattan's southern reaches, including Ground Zero, the former World Trade Center site. Immediately east of here is **City Hall**, New York's well-appointed municipal centre, and the massive Gothic span of the **Brooklyn Bridge**, while to the west is swanky **Tribeca**, once a player in the city's art scene but now more of a loft-filled residential district. **Soho**, just to the north, was an even bigger centre for galleries in the 1970s and 80s; it's better known today for its shops, as well as some historic cast-iron buildings. East of here is **Chinatown**, Manhattan's most densely populated ethnic neighbourhood and a vibrant locale great for Chinese food and shopping. Now more a haven for pasta-and-red sauce tourist traps than Italians, **Little Italy** next door is slowly being swallowed by Chinatown's hungry expansion, while the **Lower East Side**, traditionally the city's gateway neighbourhood for new immigrants – whether German, Jewish or, more recently, Hispanic – is being gentrified by young urban professionals. The **East** and **West villages** are known for their bars, restaurants and shops that cater to students, would-be bohemians and, of course, tourists. **Chelsea** has displaced the West Village as the heart of Manhattan's gay scene, and scooped Soho for exciting gallery spaces; the area around **Union Square** and **Gramercy Park** features some lovely skyscrapers, including the Flatiron building, and some of the city's best restaurants. This is where the avenues begin their march north through the busy, regimented blocks of **midtown**, which is punctuated by some of the city's most impressive sights, including Times Square, the Empire State Building and the **Museum of Modern Art**.

▶ *Balthazar* restaurant

Beyond midtown, the character of the city changes quite rapidly. For more than a dozen blocks, the skyline is relentlessly high-rise, and home to some awe-inspiring architecture; this gives way to first-class museums and appealing stores as you work your way up Fifth Avenue as far as 59th Street. That's where the classic Manhattan vistas are broken by the broad expanse of **Central Park**, a supreme piece of nineteenth-century landscaping. Flanking the park, the **Upper East**

Navigating the city

Manhattan can seem a wearyingly complicated place to get around: its **grid-pattern** arrangement looks so straightforward on the map, but can be confusing on foot, and its many subway lines never meet up where you think they should. Don't be intimidated, though – with a little know-how you'll find the city's **streets** easy to navigate and its **subways and buses** efficient and fast. And if you're at all unsure, just ask – New Yorkers are accurate direction-givers and take pride initiating visitors into the great mysteries of their city.

There are a few simple terms that are important to learn. Firstly, "downtown Manhattan", "midtown Manhattan", and "upper Manhattan": **downtown Manhattan** runs from the southern tip of the island to around 14th Street; **midtown Manhattan** stretches from about here to the south end of Central Park; and **upper Manhattan** contains the park itself, the neighbourhoods on either side of it, and the whole area to the north. Direction-wise, whatever is north of where you're standing is **uptown**, while whatever's south is **downtown**. As for east and west, those directions are known as **crosstown** – hence "crosstown buses."

Downtown Manhattan is tricky to navigate because it was the first part of the city to be settled: streets here have names not numbers and are somewhat randomly arranged. The most fiendishly confusing part of downtown is the **West Village**, where the illogical tangle of streets is quaint but infuriating; for instance, somehow West 4th and West 11th streets, which should run parallel, intersect here. Things are much easier above Houston Street on the East Side and 14th Street on the West: the streets are numbered and follow a strict grid pattern. **Fifth Avenue**, the greatest of the big north–south avenues, cuts through the centre of Manhattan until it reaches Central Park, whereupon the avenue runs along its eastern flank; crosstown streets are flagged as East or West (eg W 42nd Street, E 42nd Street) from this dividing line, and building numbers also increase as you walk away from either side of Fifth Avenue.

Manhattan is about **thirteen miles long** from base to tip, and around **two miles wide** at its widest point: as a rule of thumb, allow five minutes to walk each east–west block between avenues, and one to two minutes for each north–south block between streets.

Side is wealthier and more grandiose, with many of its nineteenth-century millionaires' mansions now transformed into a string of magnificent museums known as "Museum Mile"; the most prominent of these is the vast **Metropolitan Museum of Art**. The residential neighbourhood here is staunchly patrician and boasts some of the swankiest addresses in Manhattan, as well as a nest of designer shops along Madison Avenue in the seventies.

On the other side of the park, the largely residential young-professional enclave of the **Upper West Side** is worth a visit, mostly for Lincoln Center, the American Museum of Natural History and Riverside Park along the Hudson River; studenty **Morningside Heights**, home to Columbia University, tops off the neighbourhood. Immediately north of Central Park, **Harlem**, the historic black city-within-a-city, has today a healthy sense of an improving community. Still farther north, past residential **Hamilton Heights** and **Washington Heights**, a largely Hispanic enclave that few visitors ever venture to visit, stands Inwood at the tip of the island. It's here you'll find the **Cloisters**, a nineteenth-century mock-up of a medieval monastery, packed with great European Romanesque and Gothic art and (transplanted) architecture – in short, one of Manhattan's must-sees.

It's an unfortunate fact that few visitors, especially those with limited time, bother to venture off Manhattan Island to the outer boroughs. This is a pity, because each of them – **Brooklyn**, **Queens**, **the Bronx** and **Staten Island** – has points of great interest, for both historical and contemporary reasons. More than anything, though, some of the city's most vibrant ethnic neighborhoods (and consequently best food) can be found in the outer boroughs: sample the Greek restaurants of the Astoria district in Queens, for example, or the Italian restaurants of the Bronx's Belmont section. If visitors do leave Manhattan, it's usually for Brooklyn, where you can hang out in hip Williamsburg, wander the brownstone-lined streets of Cobble Hill, ride a rickety roller coaster and soak up the old-world charm of Coney Island, or gorge on borscht in the Russian enclave of Brighton Beach.

On New York's menu

Don't come to the city on a diet or you'll miss out on one of its greatest pleasures: **food**. There's barely a country in the world whose cuisine isn't ably represented somewhere in the city, and you should do what you can to experiment with a little of everything; nevertheless, there are some types of cuisine in which New York particularly excels. There is **Jewish-American deli fare** on the Lower East Side, such as overstuffed brisket and pastrami sandwiches, smoked fish and bagels, latkes, knishes and chopped liver. All over town (especially in midtown) you can find traditional **steakhouses** serving massive porterhouses and tender sirloins. The city is littered with both throwback and nouveau **pizza places** serving pancake-flat pizzas topped with fresh tomatoes, homemade mozzarella and every other ingredient under the sun; Italian food, in general, is a real favourite. You'll find pearlescent **dim sum** in Chinatown, ramen noodles and pork buns in the East Village, and **sushi** pretty much everywhere, as fresh as you could ask for. Trends from the past few years include a greater focus on locally grown and sourced ingredients, and a proliferation of mobile food carts serving restaurant-worthy snacks and meals. Still, this doesn't really scratch the surface of what's on offer; for more details on our picks, see chapters 23, "Cafes and snacks", and 24, "Restaurants".

▲ Bryant Park

When to go

New York City's **climate** ranges from sticky, hot and humid in midsummer to very cold in January and February: be prepared to freeze or boil accordingly if you decide to visit during these periods. Spring is gentle, if unpredictable and often wet, while autumn is perhaps the best season, with crisp, clear days and warmish nights – either season is a great time to schedule a visit. Whenever you're visiting, plan to dress in layers, as it's the only way to combat overheated buildings in winter and overactive, icy air-conditioning come summertime. One of the joys of New York City's compact layout is the ease with which you can sightsee by foot, so make sure to pack a pair of comfortable, sturdy shoes, no matter the season.

Average monthly temperatures and rainfall

	Jan	Feb	Mar	Apr	May	Jun	Jul	Aug	Sep	Oct	Nov	Dec
New York City												
Max/min (C)	3/-3	4/-3	10/2	16/7	22/12	27/17	29/21	29/19	24/16	18/10	12/5	6/-1
Max/min (F)	38/26	40/26	50/36	60/44	72/54	80/62	84/70	84/66	76/60	64/50	54/40	42/30
Rainfall (mm)	89	79	102	97	112	91	112	104	102	86	112	97

things not to miss

It's not possible to see everything that New York has to offer in one trip, so what follows is a selective taste of the city's highlights: classic architecture, great food, scenic walks and plenty of high culture. They're arranged in colour-coded categories, which you can browse through to find the best things to see and do. All entries have a page reference to take you straight into the Guide, where you can find out more.

01 **Brooklyn Bridge** Page **70** • Take the less-than-a-mile walk across the bridge to see beautiful views of the downtown skyline and the Harbour Islands.

02 Opera at Lincoln Center Page **369** • Put on your glad rags for a night out at New York's spectacular Metropolitan Opera.

03 Baseball Page **413** • A summertime treat: enjoy a hot dog, a cold beer and America's pastime in the Yankees' or Mets' new homes – or for a more intimate experience, see a Cyclones game in Coney Island.

04 Statue of Liberty Page **46** • There's no greater symbol of the American dream than the magnificent statue that graces New York Harbor.

05 Shopping in Soho Page **75** • New York's most fashionable shopping district is home to landmark Prada, Apple and Top Shop stores, as well as a host of smaller fashion labels and designers.

07 The Frick Collection Page **175** • Though he may have been a ruthless coal baron, Henry Frick's discerning eye for art and the easy elegance of his collection's setting make this one of the city's best galleries.

06 Empire State Building Page **126** • Still the most original and elegant skyscraper of them all.

08 Halloween Parade Page **429** • One of the more inventive and outrageous of New York's many annual parades.

09 Museum of Modern Art Page **133** • Simply put, MoMA holds the most comprehensive collection of modern art in the world.

10 Ride Staten Island Ferry Page **59** • Savour Manhattan's skyline and the Statue of Liberty from a boat's-eye view – absolutely free.

11 Rockefeller Center Page **130** • If anywhere can truly claim to be the centre of New York, this stylish piece of twentieth-century urban planning is it.

12 Katz's Deli Page **314** • A slice of the old Lower East Side, with overstuffed sandwiches served up by a wisecracking counterstaff.

13 Fine dining and food trucks Pages **327** & **295** • After splashing out at a celebrity chef spot like *Le Bernardin*, save some cash – and still eat like a king – at one of the city's many mobile food trucks.

14 St John the Divine Page **197** • Still under construction more than a hundred years after its inception, St John's remains the largest and most imposing Gothic-style cathedral in the world.

15 **Metropolitan Museum of Art** Page **161** • You could easily spend a whole day (or week even) at the Met, exploring everything from Egyptian artefacts to modern masters.

16 **Central Park** Page **152** • The world's most iconic swathe of green: take a boat ride, watch Shakespeare in the park or enjoy a Conservatory Garden picnic after a morning spent in a museum.

17 **Live jazz** Page **361** • New York's jazz scene is particularly vibrant, with a host of small, intimate (and sometimes free) clubs competing with hallowed venues like the *Blue Note* and *Birdland*.

18 Grand Central Terminal Page **137** • Take a free lunchtime tour (Wed or Fri) of this magnificent building to learn the history of the station's majestic concourse.

19 The High Line Page **115** • It can get crowded, but this Chelsea walkway offers a unique perspective on the city below and on the power of progressive urban renewal.

20 A night out in Williamsburg

Page **356** • Dive bars with vintage jukeboxes, bowling alleys-cum-music halls, Williamsburg – verging on too hip for its own good – is still good fun for a drink or three.

Basics

Basics

Getting there

It's pretty easy to get to New York. The city is on every major airline's itinerary, and is also a regional hub for train and bus travel. Expressways surround Manhattan, making driving another viable option.

Flights from the US and Canada

From most places in North America, **flying** is the most convenient way to reach New York. There are **three international airports** (see Ⓦwww.panynj.gov) that serve the city: John F. Kennedy (JFK), LaGuardia (LGA), and Newark (EWR).

Airfares to New York depend on the season and can fluctuate wildly. The highest prices are generally found between May and September; you'll get the best prices by booking months in advance or flying during the low season, November to February (excluding late Nov until early Jan, the holiday season). The lowest **round-trip fares** from the West Coast tend to average around $300–400; from Chicago or Miami it's about $200–300. Nonstop flights from Canada are always more expensive; reckon on paying Can$325–400 from Toronto or Montréal and at least Can$500–600 from Vancouver.

Flights from the UK and Ireland

Flying to New York from the UK takes about seven hours; flights tend to leave Britain in the morning or afternoon and arrive in New York in the afternoon or evening, though the odd flight does leave as late as 8pm. Coming back, most flights depart in the evening and arrive in Britain early next morning; flying time, due to the prevailing winds, is usually a little shorter.

As far as **scheduled flights** go, Virgin Atlantic and British Airways offer the most direct services each day from London's Heathrow to JFK and Newark. American Airlines, Delta, Continental and United also fly direct on a daily basis; there is not much difference in the prices on the different airlines. Round-trip **fares** generally average £300–400 – buy as early as possible for the best rates. Continental flies nonstop to Newark from Birmingham, Manchester and Glasgow.

Aer Lingus, Continental and United all fly nonstop services to New York from Dublin, but these are always more expensive – expect to pay at least €500. Continental also flies nonstop from Belfast and Shannon Airport for about the same rates.

Flights from Australia, New Zealand and South Africa

It's not yet possible to take a nonstop flight between New York and **Australia or New Zealand**, though Qantas offers a direct service from Sydney, with a 2 hour 30 minute layover in Los Angeles (meaning you won't have to change planes). Most Aussies and Kiwis reach the eastern United States by way of LA and San Francisco (flying time is approximately ten hours to the West Coast, with another six-hour flight to New York). The best connections tend to be with United, Air New Zealand and Qantas; from Auckland, Air New Zealand connects with United flights in LA.

Fares from eastern Australian state capitals are generally the same: return flights for most of the year start at around Aus$1500 but can go up to more than Aus$2500 in December, when most Australians tend to visit; fares from Perth and Darwin can be up to Aus$500 more all year, and it's usually pricier from New Zealand (NZ$3000). If you intend to take in New York as part of a world trip, a **round-the-world ticket** offers the best value for money, working out just a little more than an all-in ticket.

There are no direct flights from South Africa; the cheapest routes from Johannesburg usually go through Dubai (Emirates), Frankfurt

(South African/Lufthansa or United/Continental) or Amsterdam and London. Rates start at around R11,000.

Trains

New York is connected to the rest of the continent by several **Amtrak train lines** (ⓣ1-800/USA-RAIL, ⓦwww.amtrak.com). The most frequent services are along the Boston-to-Washington corridor; there is also one daily train between Montréal and New York. Fares from Boston are about $120 round-trip, or $200 for the *Acela Express*, which saves 35 minutes. DC trains are about $150, considerably more on the *Metroliner* and *Acela Express*. Fares from Canada usually start around Can$130. Like planes, train fares are often based on availability; with the exception of peak travel times (ie Christmas), seats are much cheaper months in advance. Although it's possible to haul yourself long-distance from the West Coast, the Midwest, or the South, it's an exhausting trip (three days plus from California) and fares are expensive.

Buses

Going by **bus** is the most time-consuming and least comfortable mode of travel. The only reason to take the bus for more than a few hours is if you're going to make a number of stops en route; if this is the case, you might check out **Greyhound's Discovery Pass**, which is good for unlimited travel within a set period of time.

Unlike most parts of the country, where Greyhound is the only game in town, in the busy northeast corridor there is fierce competition between bus operators. One-way from either DC or Boston to New York can go for as little as $30 on one of the major lines. **Peter Pan Bus Lines** often has $25 one-way fares from New York to Boston and DC. Buses arrive in New York at the Port Authority Bus Terminal, Eighth Avenue and 42nd Street. Bolt Bus and Mega Bus offer the best buses and cheapest rates along the east coast (Mega Bus also runs buses to Toronto from around $40), while another cheap option (with the oldest buses) is **Fung Wah** bus, which runs nonstop between the Chinatowns of Boston and New York for $15 each way, and to Providence, Rhode Island for $30.

Airlines, agents, and operators

Airlines

Aer Lingus ⓦwww.aerlingus.com
Air Canada ⓦwww.aircanada.com
Air France ⓦwww.airfrance.com
Air Jamaica ⓦwww.airjamaica.com
Air New Zealand ⓦwww.airnz.co.nz
Alaska Airlines ⓦwww.alaskaair.com
Alitalia ⓦwww.alitalia.com
American Airlines ⓦwww.aa.com
British Airways ⓦwww.ba.com
Caribbean Airlines ⓦwww.bwee.com
Cathay Pacific ⓦwww.cathaypacific.com
Continental Airlines ⓦwww.continental.com
Delta ⓦwww.delta.com
El Al ⓦwww.elal.co.il
Emirates ⓦwww.emirates.com
Frontier Airlines ⓦwww.frontierairlines.com
Icelandair ⓦwww.icelandair.co.uk
JAL (Japan Air Lines) ⓦwww.jal.com
JetBlue ⓦwww.jetblue.com
KLM (Royal Dutch Airlines) ⓦwww.klm.com
Korean Air ⓦwww.koreanair.com
LanChile ⓦwww.lan.com
Lufthansa ⓦwww.lufthansa.com
Mexicana ⓦwww.mexicana.com
Midwest ⓦwww.midwestairlines.com
Qantas Airways ⓦwww.qantas.com
Singapore Airlines ⓦwww.singaporeair.com
South African Airways ⓦwww.flysaa.com
Southwest Airlines ⓦwww.southwest.com
United Airlines ⓦwww.united.com
US Airways ⓦwww.usair.com
WestJet ⓦwww.westjet.com
Virgin Atlantic ⓦwww.virgin-atlantic.com

Agents and operators

Amtrak Vacations US ⓣ1-800/654-5748, ⓦwww.amtrakvacations.com. Rail, accommodation and sightseeing packages.
Contiki US ⓣ1-888/CONTIKI, ⓦwww.contiki.com. 18- to 35-year-olds-only tour operator. Runs highly social sightseeing trips to New York that focus on major tourist attractions.
Delta Vacations US ⓣ1-800/654-6559, ⓦwww.deltavacations.com. Offers packages to New York that include mid-range to upscale accommodation, plus optional sightseeing and airport transfers.
International Gay and Lesbian Travel Association US ⓣ1-800/448-8550, ⓦwww.iglta.org. Trade group with lists of gay-owned or gay-friendly travel agents, accommodation and other travel businesses.

Six steps to a better kind of travel

At Rough Guides we are passionately committed to travel. We feel strongly that only through travelling do we truly come to understand the world we live in and the people we share it with – plus tourism has brought a great deal of **benefit** to developing economies around the world over the last few decades. But the extraordinary growth in tourism has also damaged some places irreparably, and of course **climate change** is exacerbated by most forms of transport, especially flying. This means that now more than ever it's important to **travel thoughtfully** and **responsibly**, with respect for the cultures you're visiting – not only to derive the most benefit from your trip but also to preserve the best bits of the planet for everyone to enjoy. At Rough Guides we feel there are six main areas in which you can make a difference:

- Consider what you're contributing to the **local economy**, and how much the services you use do the same, whether it's through employing local workers and guides or sourcing locally grown produce and local services.
- Consider the **environment** on holiday as well as at home. Water is scarce in many developing destinations, and the biodiversity of local flora and fauna can be adversely affected by tourism. Try to patronize businesses that take account of this.
- Travel with a purpose, not just to tick off experiences. Consider **spending longer** in a place, and getting to know it and its people.
- Give thought to how often you **fly**. Try to avoid short hops by air and more harmful night flights.
- Consider **alternatives to flying**, travelling instead by bus, train, boat and even by bike or on foot where possible.
- Make your trips **"climate neutral"** via a reputable carbon offset scheme. All Rough Guide flights are offset, and every year we donate money to a variety of charities devoted to combating the effects of climate change.

Maupintour US ⓣ1-800/255-4266, ⓦwww.maupintour.com. Luxury tours. Runs trips to New York, with city tours, show tickets and upscale meals.
New York City Vacation Packages US ⓣ1-888/692-8701, ⓦwww.nycvp.com. All sorts of short, reasonably priced New York vacations, from spa weekends to Broadway shows.
North South Travel UK ⓣ01245/608 291, ⓦwww.northsouthtravel.co.uk. Friendly, competitive travel agency, offering discounted fares worldwide. Profits are used to support projects in the developing world, especially the promotion of sustainable tourism.
STA Travel US ⓣ1-800/781-4040, UK ⓣ0871/2300 040; ⓦwww.statravel.com. Worldwide specialists in independent travel; also student IDs, travel insurance, car rental, rail passes and more. Good discounts for students and under-26s.
Trailfinders UK ⓣ0845/058 5858, Republic of Ireland ⓣ01/677 7888; ⓦwww.trailfinders.com. One of the best-informed and most efficient agents for independent travellers.
Viator US ⓣ1-866/648-5873 ⓦwww.viator.com. Books piecemeal local tours and sightseeing trips within New York.

Bus and rail contacts

Amtrak ⓣ1-800/872-7245, ⓦwww.amtrak.com.
Bolt Bus ⓣ1-877/265-8287, ⓦwww.boltbus.com.
Fung Wah Bus ⓣ212/925-8889, ⓦwww.fungwahbus.com.
Greyhound US ⓣ1-800/231-2222, Canada ⓣ1-800/661-8747, ⓦwww.greyhound.com.
Mega Bus ⓣ1-877/462-6342, ⓦwww.megabus.com.
Peter Pan us ⓣ1-800/343-9999, ⓦwww.peterpanbus.com.

Arrival

Most visitors to New York arrive at one of the three major international airports that serve the city: John F. Kennedy, LaGuardia and Newark. All three share a website at ⓦwww.panynj.gov. You can find general information about getting to and from the airports on the website or by calling ⓣ1-800/AIR-RIDE. Amtrak trains arrive at Penn Station, and most buses at the Port Authority Bus Terminal, both of which are in Midtown.

By air

Whichever airport you arrive at, one of the simplest ways into Manhattan is by **bus**. All airport bus services operate from one of two terminals in Manhattan: **Grand Central Terminal** (at Park Ave and 42nd St) and the **Port Authority Bus Terminal** (Eighth Ave at 34th St, ⓣ212/564-8484). Grand Central is more convenient for the east side of the island. The Port Authority Bus Terminal isn't as good a bet for Manhattan (as it entails carrying luggage from bus to street level), though you'll find it handy if you're heading for the west side of the city or out to New Jersey (by bus). Some airport buses also stop at **Penn Station** at 32nd Street between Seventh and Eighth avenues, where you can catch the Long Island Railroad (LIRR), as well as Amtrak long-distance trains to other parts of America.

Taxis are the easiest transport option if you are travelling in a group or are arriving at an antisocial hour. Ignore the individual cabs vying for attention as you exit the baggage claim; these "gypsy cab" operators are notorious for ripping off tourists. Any airport official can direct you to the taxi stand, where you can get an official New York City yellow taxi. A few car services have direct phones near the exits; they're competitive in price with taxis (they charge set rates). Remember to add a fifteen- to twenty-percent tip for the driver of any taxi.

If you're not so pressed for time and want to save some money, it is also possible to take the **train**, commuter or subway, from Newark or JFK, and a city bus from LaGuardia.

JFK

The **New York Airport Service** (ⓣ212/875-8200, ⓦwww.nyairportservice.com) runs **airport buses** from JFK to Grand Central Terminal, Port Authority Bus Terminal, Penn Station and midtown hotels every 15 to 20 minutes between 6.05am and 11pm. In the other direction, buses run from the same locations every 15 to 30 minutes between about 5.10am and 10pm. Journeys take 45 to 60 minutes, depending on time of day and traffic conditions. The fare is $15 one-way, $27 round-trip; discounts are available.

The **AirTrain** (ⓦwww.panynj.gov/airtrain) runs every few minutes, 24 hours daily, between JFK and the Jamaica and Howard Beach stations in Queens. The cost is $5 on a MetroCard (see p.25). The fastest onward connection into Manhattan is to take the LIRR (Long Island Rail Road) from Jamaica to Penn Station ($5.75 off-peak, $8 peak; 20min); buy tickets at the station, as fares are double if purchased on board. You can also take the subway (E, J, Z from Jamaica, and A from Howard Beach) for just $2.25 on MetroCard, anywhere in the city. In the daytime or early evening this is a cheap, viable option, although late at night it isn't the best choice – trains run infrequently and can be deserted. Travel time to Manhattan is usually a little under an hour.

Taxis charge a flat rate of $45 to anywhere in Manhattan from JFK (plus the new state tax surcharge of 50¢). There is no $1 peak time or 50-cent night surcharge for these trips. Tolls are payable however, and some drivers will try to increase the $45 rate by claiming you must take a toll route – even

the official taxi dispatchers may claim the amount will be "$50". Insist on $45; there are no toll roads between JFK and Manhattan, and all the bridges are **free**. The only toll is payable on the Midtown Tunnel ($5.50), but unless you are in a real hurry (if you are heading to Midtown the tunnel is slightly faster), you can insist on taking one of the bridges instead. All non-Manhattan destinations trips should be on the meter.

LaGuardia

The **New York Airport Service** (Ⓣ212/875-8200, Ⓦwww.nyairportservice.com) runs express **buses** from LaGuardia to Grand Central Station, Port Authority Bus Terminal and Penn Station every 15 to 30 minutes between 7.30am and 11pm. In the other direction, buses run from Grand Central 5am to 8pm, from Port Authority between 5.50am and 7.40pm, and from Penn Station between 7.40am and 7.10pm. Journey time is 45 to 60 minutes, depending on traffic. The fare is $12 one-way, $21 round-trip.

You can also travel from the airport by **city bus**. The best bargain in New York airport transit is the #M60 bus, which for $2.25 (exact change or MetroCard) takes you into Manhattan, across 125th Street and down Broadway to 106th Street. Ask for a transfer (see p.27) when you get on the bus and you can get almost anywhere. Journey time from LaGuardia ranges from 20 minutes late at night to an hour in rush-hour traffic. Alternatively, you can take the #M60 bus to Astoria Boulevard. There you can transfer to the N **subway**, which runs through midtown Manhattan and south to Brooklyn.

Taxis from LaGuardia use the meter; reckon on $25–30 into Manhattan plus tip and surcharges (Mon–Fri 4–8pm $1; daily 8pm–6am $0.50). Tolls are also extra, but you can insist on avoiding the Midtown Tunnel (see JFK, p.22).

Newark

Newark Airport Express (Ⓣ877/863-9275, Ⓦwww.coachusa.com) runs **buses** to Grand Central Station, Port Authority Bus Terminal and Penn Station every 15 minutes between 4am and 1am. In the other direction, buses run from the same locations just as frequently (about 4.45am to 1.45am). In either direction, the journey takes 30 to 45 minutes depending on the traffic. The fare is $15 one-way, $25 round-trip.

You can also take the short **AirTrain** ride to Newark Liberty International Airport Train Station and connect with frequent NJ Transit or Amtrak trains heading into Manhattan. The AirTrain runs 24 hours and nominally costs $5.50, but this is included when you buy a NJ Transit or Amtrak ticket from machines in the AirTrain terminals or at the main station – there's no need to pay separately for the AirTrain.

Heading into Manhattan the fare for NJ Transit is $15 (Amtrak trains are more expensive). If you really want to save a few dollars (and have plenty of time), take a NJ Transit train ($7.75) to Newark Penn Station (not to be confused with Penn Station in Manhattan) and transfer to the PATH system (Ⓣ1-800/234-7284, Ⓦwww.panynj.com), with connections to Downtown and midtown Manhattan for just $1.75. The PATH train runs 24 hours, but service is limited between midnight and 7am.

Taxis from Newark into Manhattan charge according to an expensive fixed schedule of rates, clearly listed at terminal taxi ranks – the dispatcher will confirm the rate before you get in. For points south of Central Park the rate is $50–55 ($60–70 further north), plus $5 for locations on the east side of the island and a $5 peak-time surcharge (Mon–Fri 6am–9pm & 4–7pm, Sat & Sun noon–8pm). On top of that you need to add $1 per suitcase, a tip and any **tolls** incurred; you can ask the driver to avoid toll roads in New Jersey but to get to Manhattan you'll need to take one of the toll tunnels ($8). Note, though, that this toll is only paid going into Manhattan, so even though you are obliged to pay "round-trip" tolls, the charge should only be $8.

By train, bus, or car

Amtrak trains arrive at **Penn Station**, at 32nd Street between Seventh and Eighth avenues, which is connected to the subway system and has plenty of taxis outside. If you come to New York by Greyhound or any other long-distance **bus** line (with the exception of the Chinatown buses, which arrive in Chinatown, and Mega Bus and Bolt Bus, which drop you off on Midtown streets), you arrive at the **Port Authority Bus Terminal** at 42nd Street and Eighth Avenue – this is also connected to the subway system and it's fairly easy to catch a taxi outside.

If you're coming from the East Coast (or if you don't mind long journeys), **driving** is an option, but note that you probably won't need (or want) a car once you're in the city. Major **highways** come in from most directions (I-87 and 95 from the north; I-95 from the south; and I-80 from the west). In terms of **tolls**, crossing the Hudson River costs $8, while bridges over the East River are free; the Midtown Tunnel is $5.50.

City transport

Public transit in New York is very good, extremely cheap and covers most conceivable corners of the city, whether by subway or bus. Don't be afraid to ask someone for help if you're confused. You'll no doubt find the need for a taxi from time to time, especially if you feel uncomfortable in an area at night; you will rarely have trouble tracking one down in Manhattan or on major Brooklyn avenues – the ubiquitous yellow cabs are always on the prowl for passengers. And don't forget your feet – Manhattanites walk everywhere.

By subway

The New York **subway** (☎718/330-1234, Ⓦwww.mta.info) is initially incomprehensible, but it's also the fastest and most efficient way to get from place to place in Manhattan and to the outer boroughs. Put aside your qualms: it's much safer and user-friendly than it once was, and it's definitely not as difficult to navigate as it seems. Nonetheless, it pays to familiarize yourself with the subway system before you set out. Study the map at the back of this book, or get a free map at any station or information kiosk. Though the subway runs daily 24 hours, some routes operate at certain times of day only; read any service advisories carefully.

The basics

• The subway costs **$2.25 per ride**, including all subway and most bus transfers (see p.27). In order to ride the subway, you must purchase a **MetroCard**, a card with an electronic strip, from a vending machine

Safety on the subway

By day the whole train is safe, but don't go into empty cars if you can help it. Some trains have doors that connect between cars, but do not use them other than in an emergency, because this is dangerous and illegal. Keep an eye on bags (and especially iPods, which can get snatched) at all times, especially when sitting or standing near the doors. With all the jostling in the crowds near the doors, this is a favourite spot for pickpockets.

At night, always try to use the centre cars, because they tend to be more crowded. Yellow signs on the platform saying "During off hours train stops here" indicate where the conductor's car will stop. While you wait, keep where the token booth attendants can see you if possible. For more information on safety, see "Crime and personal safety", p.36.

(in the subway station) or a subway teller. Vending machines accept all credit and debit cards, but keep some fresh bills on hand in case you have a problem.

• The **MetroCard** is available in several forms. It can be purchased in denominations between $2.25 and $80; a $20 purchase gives you $23 on your card. Unlimited-ride cards – almost always the best deal if you intend to be on the go – allow unlimited travel for a certain period of time: a daily "Fun Pass" for $8.25, 7-day pass for $27 and 30-day pass for $89.

• Prices for all cards, rides and passes are due to rise by a minimum 7.5 percent by May/June 2011.

• Most train routes run uptown or downtown in Manhattan, following the great avenues. Crosstown routes are few.

• Trains and their routes are identified by a number or letter (not by their colour).

• There are two types of train: the **express**, which stops only at major stations, and the **local**, stopping at every station. Listen to the conductor, who will usually announce the train's next stop.

• **Service changes** due to track repairs and other maintenance work are frequent (especially after midnight and on weekends) and confusing. Read the red-and-white Service Notice posters on bulletin boards throughout the system, and don't be afraid to ask other passengers what's going on. Listen closely to all announcements (though poor sound quality can make them hard to understand); occasionally, express trains run on local tracks.

• Don't hesitate to **ask directions** or **look at a map** on the train or in the station. If you travel late at night, know your route before you set out. Follow common-sense safety rules (see "Safety on the subway", p.25).

• If you are **lost**, go to the subway teller or phone ⓣ718/330-1234. State your location and destination; the teller or operator will tell you the most direct route.

By bus

The **bus system** (ⓣ718/330-1234, ⓦwww.mta.info) is simpler than the subway, as you can see where you're going and hop off at anything interesting. The bus also features many **crosstown** routes and most services run 24 hours. The major disadvantage is that buses can be extremely slow due to traffic – in peak hours almost down to walking pace.

Anywhere in the city the fare is **$2.25**, payable on entry with a **MetroCard** (the most convenient way) or with the correct change – no bills. Bus maps can be obtained at the main concourse of Grand Central Terminal or at visitor information centres, as well as in subway stations. There are routes on almost all the avenues and major streets. Most buses with an M designation before the route number travel exclusively in Manhattan; others may show a B for Brooklyn, Q for Queens, Bx for the Bronx or S for Staten Island. The crosstown routes are the most useful, especially the ones through Central Park. Also good are the buses that take you to east Manhattan where subway coverage is sparse. Most crosstown buses take their route number from the street they traverse, so the #M14 will travel along 14th Street. Buses display their number, origin, and destination up front.

There are three types of bus: regular, which stop every two or three blocks at five- to ten-minute intervals; limited stop, which travel the same routes but stop at only about a quarter of the regular stops; and express, which cost extra ($5.50) and stop hardly anywhere, shuttling commuters in and out of the outer boroughs and suburbs.

Bus stops are marked by yellow kerbstones and a blue, white and red sign that often (but not always) indicates which buses stop there. Once you're on board, to signal that you want to get off a bus, press the yellow or black strip on the wall; the driver will stop at the next official bus stop. After midnight you can ask to get off on any block along the route, whether or not it's a regular stop.

Transfers

If you're going to use buses a lot, it pays to understand the **transfer** system. A transfer allows a single fare to take you, one-way, anywhere in Manhattan; they're given free on request when you pay your fare. Because few buses go up and down and across, you can transfer from any bus to almost any other that continues your trip. (You can't use transfers for return trips.) The top of the transfer tells you how much time you have in which to use it – usually around two hours. If you're unsure where to get off to transfer, consult the map on the panel behind the driver, or ask the driver for help. If you use a MetroCard, you can automatically transfer for free within two hours from swiping the card.

By taxi

Taxis are always worth considering, especially if you're in a hurry or it's late at night. There are two types of taxis; in Manhattan, you'll generally be using **medallion cabs**, recognizable by their yellow paintwork and medallion up top. Before you hail a cab, work out exactly where you're going and if possible the quickest route there – a surprising number of cabbies are new to the job and speak little English. If you feel the driver doesn't seem to know your destination, point it out on a map. An illuminated sign atop the taxi indicates its availability. If the words "Off Duty" are lit, the driver won't pick you up.

The alternative is to take a **"gypsy cab"** (which looks like a regular car), further divided into two types: licensed gypsy cabs (identified by a "T" on the number plate), only permitted to pick up passengers on call by telephone, but that often illegally seek passengers on the street; and completely unlicensed, uninsured operators who tout for business wherever tourists arrive. Avoid these drivers like the plague – they will rip you off (and can be unsafe). Their main hunting grounds are outside tourist arrival points like Grand Central. If you're looking for a cab in Harlem or the outer boroughs at night however, you'll have little choice but to opt for a gypsy cab (preferably a licensed one); if you call ahead or pick one up on the street, always fix the fare in advance (ask someone before you head out for a rough idea).

Fares

Up to four people can travel in an ordinary medallion cab. Fares are $2.50 for the first fifth of a mile plus New York State Tax surcharge of 50¢ per ride, and 40¢ for each fifth of a mile thereafter or for each minute in

stopped or slow traffic. An additional surcharge of 50¢ is payable daily between 8pm and 6am, and $1 Monday to Friday 4 to 8pm. When you take a cab outside the city limits you must agree on a flat fare with the driver before the trip begins (metered fare rules only apply to New York City; drivers can set prices to other destinations as they see fit). Note that this does not apply to trips to Westchester and Nassau counties, for which there are previously determined fare rules. Trips to Newark Airport are on the meter plus $15 and tolls. Note also that all trips from Manhattan to JFK should be a flat $45 (plus the state tax surcharge of 50¢), though drivers sometimes try and use the meter.

Trips outside Manhattan can incur toll fees (which the driver will pay through E-Z Pass and which will be added to your fare); the only river crossings that cost money both ways are the Brooklyn-Battery Tunnel and Queens Midtown Tunnel ($5.50 each). Tolls for the Holland Tunnel, Lincoln Tunnel and George Washington Bridge (all $8) are paid coming into Manhattan only. All the other bridges are free.

The **tip** should be fifteen to twenty percent of the fare; you'll get a dirty look if you offer less. Drivers don't like splitting anything bigger than a $10 bill, and are in their rights to refuse a bill over $20.

Rules

Certain regulations govern taxi operators. A driver can ask your destination only when you're seated (this is often breached) – and must transport you (within the five boroughs), however undesirable your destination may be. You may face some problems, though, if it's late and you want to go to an outer borough. Also, if you request it, a driver must pick up or drop off other passengers, turn on the air conditioning, and turn the radio down or off. Many drivers use a cell phone while driving; this is common but prohibited, and while you can ask him or her to stop, don't expect compliance. If you lose something in a taxi, or you have a problem with a driver, get the license number from the right-hand side of the dashboard, or the medallion number from the rooftop sign or from the print-out receipt for the fare, and file a complaint at ⓣ311 or ⓦwww.ci.nyc.ny.us/apps/311.

By ferry

Manhattan is connected to New Jersey, Staten Island, Queens and Brooklyn by a web of **ferry** services. These generally serve commuters, but some routes are worth checking out for a relatively cheap opportunity to get onto the water. **New York Water Taxi** (ⓦwww.nywatertaxi.com) runs a weekend-only ferry service around Manhattan, linking West 44th Street with East 34th Street via stops all around the lower half of the island (May–Oct; day pass $20, kids $15). It also runs a handy year-round commuter service to DUMBO, Williamsburg and Hunters Point in Queens from various points in Manhattan; these tend to operate on weekdays 6.30 to 9am, and 3 to 7pm, and cost $3–5.50. Water Taxi now runs a daily shuttle from Wall Street's Pier 11 in Manhattan to Brooklyn's Ikea superstore in Red Hook (Mon–Fri 2–7.40pm, Sat & Sun 11am–8pm), an efficient way to reach this neighbourhood. The service is free on weekends, and $5 weekdays (if you spend over $10 in Ikea the ferry is free).

None of these options beats the bargain of the free **Staten Island Ferry** (ⓣ718/727-2508, ⓦwww.siferry.com), which leaves from its own terminal in Lower Manhattan's Battery Park and provides stunning views of New York Harbour around the clock. It's also a commuter boat, so avoid crowded rush hours if you can. Departures are every 15 to 20 minutes during rush hours (7–9am and 5–7pm), every 30 minutes during the day, and every 60 minutes late at night (the ferry runs 24hr) – weekends less frequently. Few visitors spend much time on Staten Island; it's easy to just turn around and get back on the ferry, although there's plenty to see if you stay. For info on visiting Staten Island, see p.264.

By car

Don't drive in New York. Even if you're brave enough to try dodging demolition-derby cabbies and jaywalking pedestrians, car rental is expensive and car parks almost laughably so (from $14/hour to $38/day). Legal street parking is nearly impossible to find.

If you really must drive, bear in mind these rules. Seatbelts are compulsory for everyone in front and for children in back. The city speed limit is 35mph. It's illegal to make a right turn at a red light. The use of hand-held mobile phones is illegal while driving. Bear in mind also that half the drivers around you will tend to bend or break these rules; that cars behind you (especially taxis) will blare their horns if you hesitate for more than a second; and that aggressive driving in general is the norm.

Read signs carefully to figure out **where to park** – if the sign says "No Standing", "No Stopping", or "Don't Even THINK of Parking Here" (yes, really), then don't. Watch for street-cleaning hours (when an entire side of a street will be off-limits), and don't park in a bus stop, in front of (or within several yards of) a fire hydrant, or anywhere with a yellow kerb. Private parking is expensive, but it makes sense to leave your car somewhere legitimate. If you park illegally and are towed, you must free your vehicle from the impound lot over on the West Side Highway (☎212/971-0770) – expect to pay a $185 cash tow fee and a $70 execution fee (plus $10–15 for each additional day they store it for you) and waste your day.

Car theft and **vandalism** are more of a problem in less-travelled parts of the city, but no matter where you park, never leave valuables in your car. For **foreign drivers**, any driver's licence issued by their country is valid in the US – for more information check the state DMV's website (Ⓦwww.nydmv.state.ny.us).

By bike

Cycling can be a viable, if somewhat dangerous, form of transportation around the city, but far more enjoyable if you stick to the city's 200 miles of bike lanes, as well as the cycle paths along the waterfront and in parks. Wear all possible **safety equipment** including pads and a helmet (required by law). When you park, double-chain and lock your bike (including wheels) to an immovable object if you'd like it to be there when you return.

Bike rental starts at about $10 per hour or $35 per day – which means opening to closing (9.30am to 6.30pm for instance). You need one or two pieces of ID (passport and credit card will be sufficient) and, in some cases, a deposit, though most firms will be satisfied with a credit-card imprint. Rates and deposits are generally more for racing models and mountain bikes. See Chapter 31, "Sports and outdoor activities," for more information on bicycle rental.

The media

Generally acknowledged as the media capital of the world, New York is the headquarters of just about all the country's major television news organizations and book and magazine publishers. This means that there is a newsstand on just about every corner selling a wonderful variety of newspapers and magazines, as well as frequent opportunities to take part in television-show tapings (see box, p.375).

Newspapers and magazines

Although it's still the most vibrant news market in the US, only four **newspapers** remain. The *New York Times* ($2; Ⓦwww.nytimes.com), an American institution, prides itself on being the "paper of record" – America's quality national paper (it has the third-largest circulation in the US). It has solid international coverage, and places much emphasis on its news analysis. The Sunday edition ($5) is a thumping bundle of newsprint divided into a number of supplements that take a full day to read.

It takes serious coordination to read the sizeable *Times* on the subway, one reason many turn to the *Daily News* and the *Post*. Tabloids in format and style, these rivals concentrate on local news. The *Daily News* (50¢; Ⓦwww.nydailynews.com) is a "picture newspaper" with many racy headlines. The *New York Post* (50¢; Ⓦwww.nypost.com), the city's oldest newspaper, started in 1801 by Alexander Hamilton, has been in decline for many years. Known for its solid city news and consistent conservative-slanted sermonizing, it also takes a fairly sensationalist approach to headlines.

The other New York-based daily newspaper is the *Wall Street Journal* ($2; Ⓦwww.wsj.com), in fact a national paper (with the largest circulation in the US) that also has strong, conservative national and international news coverage – despite an old-fashioned design that eschews the use of photographs.

Weeklies and monthlies

Of the **weekly** papers, the *Village Voice* (Tuesdays, free; Ⓦwww.villagevoice.com) is the most widely read, mainly for its comprehensive arts coverage and investigative features. It offers opinionated stories that often focus on the media, gay issues and civil rights. It's also one of the best pointers to what's on around town (including the most interesting, inexpensive cuisine and shopping). Its main competitor, the *New York Press* (Ⓦwww.nypress.com), is angrier, much more conservative and not afraid to offend. The listings are quite good; look for its "Best of Manhattan" special edition, published each September.

Other leading weeklies include *New York* magazine ($4.99; Ⓦwww.nymag.com), which has reasonably good listings and is more of a society and entertainment journal, and *Time Out New York* ($3.99; Ⓦwww.timeoutny.com) – a clone of its London original, combining the city's most comprehensive "what's on" listings with New York-slanted stories and features. The venerable *New Yorker* ($5.99; Ⓦwww.newyorker.com) has good highbrow listings, and features poetry and short fiction alongside its much-loved cartoons. The wackiest, and perhaps best, alternative to the *Voice* is *Paper* ($4; Ⓦwww.papermag.com), a monthly that carries witty and well-written rundowns on city nightlife and restaurants as well as current news and gossip. If you want a weekly with more of a political edge, there's the ironic *New York Observer* ($2; Ⓦwww.observer.com) and the *Forward* ($1; Ⓦwww.forward.com), a century-plus-old Jewish publication that's also published in Russian and Yiddish editions.

Many neighbourhoods and ethnic communities have their own weeklies, led by the politically oriented African-American *Amsterdam News* ($1; Ⓦwww.amsterdamnews.org), and the *Brooklyn Paper* (free every Fri; Ⓦwww.brooklynpaper.com).

International publications

British, European, Latin American and Asian newspapers are widely available, usually a day after publication – except for the *Financial Times*, which is printed (via satellite) in the US and sold on most newsstands. If you want a specific paper or magazine, try any Universal News or Hudson News, sprinkled throughout the city. Barnes & Noble superstores stock magazines and international newspapers, which you can peruse for **free** over coffee (not free).

Television

Any American will find on TV in New York mostly what they find at home, plus several multilingual stations and some wacky public access channels. Channels 13 and 21 are given over to **PBS** (Public Broadcasting Service), which has earned the nickname "Purely British Station" for its fondness of British drama series, although it excels at documentaries and educational children's shows. The 70-plus stations available on **cable** in most hotel rooms may be a bit more fascinating for foreign travellers; most cable channels are no better than the major networks (**ABC**, **CBS**, **NBC** and **Fox**), although a few of the specialized channels can be fairly interesting. **NY1** is the city's 24 hour local news channel, available exclusively on cable.

Radio

The FM dial is crammed with local stations of varying quality and content. The *New York Times* lists highlights daily; explore on your own and you're sure to come across something interesting.

Incidentally, it's possible to get BBC World Service programmes on WNYC (Ⓦwnyc.org) at 93.9FM or 820AM. **BBC** (Ⓦwww.bbc.co.uk/worldservice), **Radio Canada** (Ⓦwww.rcinet.ca) and **Voice of America** (Ⓦwww.voa.gov) list all their frequencies around the globe.

Tourist information

There is a veritable torrent of information available for visitors to New York City. Chances are, the answers to any questions you may have are readily accessible on a website or in a brochure.

General information

The official place for **information** is **NYC & Company**, at 810 Seventh Ave at 53rd Street (Mon–Fri 8.30am–6pm, Sat, Sun & holidays 9am–5pm; Ⓣ212/484-1222, Ⓦwww.nycgo.com). It has bus and subway maps, information on hotels and accommodation (including discounts), and up-to-date leaflets on what's going on in the arts and elsewhere. You'll find other small **tourist information centres** and kiosks all over the city, starting with the airports, Grand Central and Penn stations, and Port Authority Bus Terminal. For a list of kiosks in other areas see the box on p.34.

Maps

Other than our maps, the best **maps** of New York City are the free **bus maps** (ask any subway teller or librarian for one), as well as the huge, minutely detailed **neighbourhood maps** found fixed to the wall near the teller booth of subway stations. **Professional maps**, like *The Rough Guide Map of New York City*, which is rip-proof and waterproof, fill in the gaps. A great selection of New York City maps is available at Ⓦwww.randmcnally.com. Street atlases of all five boroughs cost around $10–15; if you're after a map of one of the individual outer boroughs, try those produced by Geographia or Hagstrom, on sale online and in bookstores for $5–15.

Tours

There are many different ways to take in the city. First-time visitors may be interested in taking a tour – they come in all kinds of lengths, themes and modes of transportation.

Bus tours

Bus tours can provide a good way to orient yourself with the city. Gray Line New York, Port Authority Terminal at 42nd Street and Eighth Avenue (Ⓣ800/669-0051 or 212/445-0848, Ⓦwww.newyorksightseeing.com), runs a large number of popular hop-on/hop-off bus tours that range from two hours ($44) to two-day passes ($54). Discounts are available for children under 12. Call or look at the website for complete information and to book a tour.

Helicopter tours

A more exciting option is to look at the city by **helicopter**. This is very expensive, but you won't easily forget the experience. **Liberty Helicopter Tours** (Ⓣ212/967-6464, Ⓦwww.libertyhelicopters.com), at the VIP Heliport (W 30th St and Twelfth Ave) and the Wall Street Heliport at Pier 6 (near the Staten Island Ferry), offers tours from around $135 per person for 6 to 8 minute, to $230 per

Information centres and kiosks

Brooklyn Tourism and Visitors Center Brooklyn Borough Hall, 209 Joralemon St ⓣ718/802-3846, ⓦwww.visitbrooklyn.org. Open Mon–Fri 10am–6pm.

Chinatown Visitor Information Kiosk Junction of Canal, Walker and Baxter sts. Open daily 10am–6pm, holidays 10am–3pm.

City Hall Information Kiosk Southern end of City Hall Park, Broadway at Park Row. Mon–Fri 9am–6pm, Sat & Sun 10am–5pm, holidays 9am–3pm.

Downtown Visitor Information Kiosks World Financial Center & Vesey St at Greenwich St ⓣ212/566-6700, ⓦwww.downtownny.com. Mon–Fri 9am–4pm, closed holidays.

Dairy Visitor Center & Gift Shop Central Park (mid-park at 65th St) ⓣ212/794-6564, ⓦwww.centralparknyc.org. Open daily 10am–5pm. Check also ⓦwww.nycparks.org, the official word on all of the obscure, famous and thrilling events in the city's parks.

East Village Visitor Center 61 E 4th St, between Bowery and Second Ave ⓣ212/228-4670, ⓦeastvillagevisitorscenter.com. Tues–Sat 1–6pm.

Federal Hall Information Center Federal Hall National Memorial, 26 Wall St. Open Mon–Fri 9am–5pm. Closed federal holidays.

Harlem Information Kiosk Studio Museum, 144 West 125th St between Powell and Malcolm X blvds. Mon–Fri 9am–6pm, Sat & Sun 10am–5pm, holidays 9am–3pm.

Lower East Side Visitor Center 54 Orchard St, between Hester and Grand sts ⓣ866/226-9010, ⓦwww.lowereastsideny.com. Mon–Fri 9am–5pm, Sat & Sun 10am–4pm.

Times Square Visitor's Center 1560 Broadway, between 46th and 47th sts ⓣ212/869-1890, ⓦwww.timessquarenyc.org. Mon-Fri 9am–7pm, Sat & Sun 8am–8pm.

person for 20 minutes. Helicopters take off regularly between 9am and 9pm every day unless winds and visibility are bad. Reservations are required; times and locations vary on Sundays and holidays. **New York Helicopter** offers slightly cheaper rates (around $140 for a 15min tour; ⓦwww.newyorkhelicopter.com).

Boat tours

A great way to see the island of Manhattan is to take one of many harbour cruises on offer. The **Circle Line** (ⓣ212/563-3200, ⓦwww.circleline42.com) sails from Pier 83 at West 42nd Street and Twelfth Avenue, circumnavigating Manhattan and taking in everything from the Statue of Liberty to Harlem, complete with a live commentary; the three-hour tour runs year-round ($34, seniors $29, under-12s $21). The evening two-hour Harbor Lights Cruise (March–Sept; $30, seniors $26, under-12s $19) offers dramatic views of the skyline. Thrill-seekers should try *The Beast* (May–Sept; $23, seniors $23, under-12s $17), a speedboat painted to look like a shark that will throw you around for thirty minutes at a wave-pounding 45 miles per hour.

Circle Line Downtown (ⓣ1-866/925-4631, ⓦwww.circlelinedowntown.com) runs harbour cruises from Downtown Manhattan's South Street Seaport; March to December on *Zephyr* (1hr; adults $27, seniors $23, children $16), and speedboat rides on the *Shark* May to September (30min; adults $23, seniors $20, children $16).

Alternatively, check out tours offered by **NY Waterway** (ⓣ800/533-3779, ⓦwww.nywaterway.com). Its 90-minute Harbor Cruises ($26, seniors $21, under-12s $16) leave the west end of Pier 78 at West 38th Street several times daily, year-round – check the website for a range of specialty cruises. You can also cruise the harbour in style aboard one of the historic yachts based at the South Street Seaport (p.62) or Chelsea Piers (see "Sports and outdoor activities", p.420).

Specialist tour companies

Big Apple Jazz Tours ⓣ212/439-1090, ⓦwww.bigapplejazz.com. Insider Gordon Polatnick offers a fabulous introduction to the Harlem jazz scene, with walking and bus tours that typically take in some of the lesser-known clubs and plenty of jazz history. Fri & Sat ($99; 4hr, 2 sets) and Sun ($49; 5hr & 3 clubs).

Big Onion Walking Tours ⓣ212/439-1090, ⓦwww.bigonion.com. Guided by history grad students from local universities, venerable Big Onion specializes in tours with an ethnic and historical focus: pick one, or take the "Immigrant New York" tour and learn about everyone. Cost is $15; the food-included "Multi-Ethnic Eating Tour" costs $20. These last about two hours.

Greenwich Village Literary Pub Crawl ⓣ212/613-5796. Local actors lead you to several of the most prominent bars in literary history and read from associated works. Tours meet every Sat at 2pm at the *White Horse Tavern*, 567 Hudson St (see p.351). Reservations are required: $20, students and seniors $15.

Harlem Heritage Tours ⓣ212/280-7888, ⓦwww.harlemheritage.com. Local Neal Shoemaker runs cultural tours of this historic neighbourhood, ranging from Spanish Harlem bus tours ($39) to Harlem Gospel ($39) and Civil Rights-themed walking tours ($25). The tours sometimes include food, a cultural performance, film clips and/or bus service.

Harlem is Home Tours ⓣ212/658-9160, ⓦwww.harlemonestop.com. The folks at Harlem OneStop manage these excellent walking tours of northern Manhattan, which include not just Harlem, but also Sugar Hill and Hamilton Heights – guides are always local characters (tours from $25).

Hush Hip Hop Tours ⓣ212/391-0900, ⓦwww.hushhiphoptours.com. Illuminating bus tours of the home of hip-hop, given by legends such as Kurtis Blow and DJ Kool Herc, from the South Bronx to Harlem and Brooklyn ($58–63).

Municipal Arts Society ⓣ212/935-3960, ⓦmas.org/tours. Opinionated, incredibly detailed historical and architectural tours in Manhattan, Brooklyn, Queens, and the Bronx. They also offer free ($10 donation suggested) tours of Downtown (Tues 12.30pm; from 55 Exchange Place, Suite 401) and Grand Central Terminal (Wed at 12.30pm; from the information booth). Walking tours cost $15.

NoshWalks ⓣ212/222-2243, ⓦwww.noshwalks.com. Weekend ethnic culinary tours of neighbourhoods in Manhattan, Queens, Brooklyn and the Bronx, incorporating local history and culture, by

Big Apple Greeter

If you're nervous about exploring New York, look into **Big Apple Greeter**, 1 Centre St, Suite 2035 (☎212/669-8159, Ⓦwww.bigapplegreeter.org), one of the best – and certainly cheapest – ways to see the city. This not-for-profit organization matches visitors with their active corps of trained volunteer "greeters". Specify the part of the city you'd like to see, indicate an aspect of New York life you'd like to explore, or plead for general orientation – whatever your interests, chances are they will find someone to take you around. Visits have a friendly, informal feel, and generally last a few hours. The service is free. You can call once you're in New York, but it's better to contact the organization as far in advance as possible.

the author of two NYC food guidebooks. $45 plus food. Reservations recommended.

Scott's Pizza Tours ☎212/222-2243, Ⓦwww.scottspizzatours.com. Yes, New York really does boast specialized pizza tours, and this is one of the best; Scott Wiener knows his slices and leads gut-busting bus tours ($55) or walks ($33) of the best pizza joints all over the city – slices included.

Wall Street Experience Ⓦwww.thewallstreetexperience.com. Edifying tours (2hr) of the Financial District from Wall Street insiders (founder Andrew Luan was a trader at Deutsche Bank). Local history is enhanced with easy-to-understand segments on the 2008 financial crisis, and traditional sights (like Federal Hall) are coupled with bank headquarters like Goldman Sachs. Mon, Wed & Fri $30–45.

Travel essentials

Costs

On a **moderate budget**, expect to spend at least $200 per night on accommodation in a mid-range, centrally located hotel in high season, plus $30–40 per person for a moderate sit-down dinner each night and about $15–20 more per person per day for takeaway and grocery meals. Getting around will cost $27 per person per week for unlimited public transportation, plus $10 each for the occasional cab ride. Sightseeing, drinking, clubbing, eating haute cuisine and going to the theatre have the potential to add exponentially to these costs. The combined New York City and State sales tax is 8.875 percent, payable on just about everything. Hotel rooms are subject to an additional 5.875 percent tax (for a total of 14.75 percent) and a $3.50 per night "occupancy tax" for rooms over $40 per night (you'll pay $2.50–3 if you can find a cheaper room).

You're expected to **tip** in restaurants, bars, taxicabs, hotels (both the bellboy and the cleaning staff) and even some posh restrooms. In restaurants in particular, it's unthinkable not to leave the minimum (15 percent of the bill) – even if you hated the service.

Crime and personal safety

In two words: don't worry. New York has come a long way in recent years. While the city can sometimes feel dangerous, the reality is somewhat different. As far as per capita crime rates go, New York is America's

Useful numbers

Police, fire, or ambulance ☎911
Non-emergency queries ☎311

safest city with a population over one million. Take the **normal precautions** and you should be fine; carry bags closed and across your body, don't let cameras dangle, keep wallets in front – not back – pockets, and don't flash money around. You should also keep a firm grip on your iPod/MP3 player on the subway (these are occasionally snatched just as the doors close). Mugging can and does happen, but rarely during the day. Avoid wandering empty streets or the subway late at night (especially alone). If you are unlucky enough to be mugged, try to stay calm and hand over the money. When the mugger has run off, hail a cab and ask to be taken to the nearest police station. You'll get sympathy and little else; file the theft and take the incident report to claim your insurance back home.

Note that possession of any "controlled substance" is absolutely illegal. Should you be found in possession of a very small amount of marijuana, you probably won't go to jail – but you can expect a hefty fine and, for foreigners, deportation.

Each area of New York has its own **police** precinct; to find the nearest station, call ⓣ646/610-5000 (during business hours only) or ⓣ311, or check the phone book. In emergencies, phone ⓣ911 or use one of the outdoor posts that give you a direct line to the emergency services. This information, plus crime stats, is available at ⓦwww.nyc.gov/nypd.

Electricity

US electricity is 110V AC and most plugs are two-pronged. Unless they're dual voltage (most mobile phones, cameras, MP3 players and laptops are), all Australian, British, European, Irish, New Zealand and South African appliances will need a voltage transformer as well as a plug adapter (hairdryers are the most common problem for travellers).

Entry requirements

Under the **Visa Waiver Program**, citizens of Australia, Ireland, New Zealand and the UK do not require visas for visits to the US of ninety days or less. You will, however, need to obtain **Electronic System for Travel Authorization** (ESTA) online before you fly (at ⓦwww.esta-uk.org). This is free and involves completing a basic immigration form in advance, on the computer. Once given, authorizations are valid for multiple entries into the US for around two years – it's recommended that you submit an ESTA application as soon as you begin making travel plans. You'll also need to present a machine-readable passport and a completed visa waiver form (I-94W) to Immigration upon arrival; the latter will be provided by your travel agent or by the airline (it's the green one, not the white one). Canadians now require a passport to cross the border, but can travel in the US for an unlimited amount of time without a visa. For visa information, visit ⓦwww.travel.state.gov. For customs information, visit ⓦwww.cbp.gov.

Consulates in New York City

Australia 34/F, 150 E 42nd St ⓣ212/351-6500, ⓦwww.australianyc.org.
Canada 1251 Sixth Ave, at 50th St ⓣ212/596-1628, ⓦwww.canadainternational.gc.ca/new_york.
Ireland 17/F, 345 Park Ave, between 51st and 52nd sts ⓣ212/319-2555, ⓦwww.consulateofirelandnewyork.org.
New Zealand 222 E 41st St, Suite 2510, between Second and Third aves ⓣ212/832-4038.
South Africa 333 E 38th St, between First and Second aves ⓣ212/213-4880, ⓦwww.southafrica-newyork.net/consulate.
UK 845 Third Ave, between 51st and 52nd sts ⓣ212/745-0200, ⓦwww.britainusa.com/ny.

Health

There are few health issues specific to New York City, short of the common cold. Pharmacies can be found every few blocks – CVS and Duane Reade are the city's major chains, many open 24hr (such as the Duane Reade at 1470 Broadway, near Times Square). If you do get sick or have an accident, things can get incredibly **expensive**; organize insurance before your trip, just in case. It will cost upwards of $100 to simply see a doctor or dentist, and prescription drugs can be very pricey – if you don't have US medical insurance (as opposed to overseas travel insurance), you'll have to cough up the money and make a claim when you get home.

Should you find yourself requiring a doctor or dentist, ask if your hotel has links to a local practice, or look in the Yellow Pages under "Clinics" or "Physicians and Surgeons". Doctors in Manhattan often have long waiting lists however, and will be reluctant to see a new patient at short notice – if you have an accident or need immediate attention head to the 24-hour emergency rooms at these and other Manhattan hospitals: St Vincent's, 170 West 12th St at Seventh Ave (ⓣ212/604-7000); New York Presbyterian (Cornell), East 70th Street at York Avenue (ⓣ212/746-5050); and Mount Sinai, Madison Avenue at 100th Street (ⓣ212/241-7171).

Should you be in a serious accident, a medical service will pick you up and charge later. Note that basic emergency care will cost at least $200, ranging to several thousand dollars for serious trauma – that's in addition to fees for drugs, appliances, supplies and the attendant physician, who will charge separately.

Insurance

You will want to invest in **travel insurance**. A typical travel-insurance policy usually provides cover for the loss of baggage, tickets, and – up to a certain limit – cash or cheques, as well as cancellation or curtailment of your journey. Many policies can be chopped and changed to exclude coverage you don't need – for example, sickness and accident benefits can often be excluded or included at will. Before you take out a new policy, however, it's worth checking whether you are already covered: some all-risks home-insurance policies may cover your possessions when overseas, and many private medical schemes include cover when abroad.

Internet

Wireless is king in New York, with free wi-fi hotspots in places like Times Square and Bryant Park, complimentary connections at cafés like *Starbucks* and most hotels offering it for no charge. If you're travelling without your own computer, accessing your email is still possible at internet cafés, though their numbers are dwindling. Try the Cyber Café, at 250 West 49th Street between Broadway and 8th Avenue (Mon–Fri 8am–11pm, Sat & Sun 11am–11pm; ⓣ212/333-4109, ⓦwww.cyber-cafe.com), which charges $12.80/hr, or Internet Cybercafé (daily 9am–12.30am; $12/hr, $8/hr from 8pm), at 277 Bleecker St and Jones Street in the West Village.

A great, free alternative is to stop by a branch of the New York City Public Library, where wi-fi and computer internet access are available. You first need to get a **guest pass** at the Stephen A. Schwarzman Building (the main library building; Mon & Thurs–Sat 10am–6pm, Tues & Wed 10am–9pm, Sun 1–5pm), at 42nd Street and Fifth Avenue. With the pass, you can reserve time slots at computers at any branch in person or via ⓦwww.nypl.org.

Laundry

Hotels do it but charge a lot. You're much better off going to an ordinary laundromat or dry cleaner, of which you'll find plenty listed in the *Yellow Pages* under "Laundries". Most laundromats also offer a very affordable drop service, where, for about $1 per pound or less, you can have your laundry washed, dried and tidily folded – often the same day (there's usually an $18–20 minimum though). Some budget hotels, YMCAs and hostels also have coin-operated washers and dryers.

Living and working in New York

It's not easy to live and work in New York, even for US residents. For anyone looking for short-term work, the typical urban employment options are available – temporary office work, waiting tables, babysitting, etc – as well as some quirkier opportunities, like artist's modelling in Soho or Tribeca. For ideas and positions, check the employment ads in the *New York Times*, *New York Press*, *Village Voice* and the free neighbourhood tabloids available throughout the city.

If you're a foreigner, you start at a disadvantage. Unless you already have family in the US (in which case special rules may apply), you need a **work visa**, and these can be extremely difficult to get. The US visa system is one of the world's most complex, with a bewildering range of visa types to suit every circumstance – most people hire a lawyer to do the paperwork ($2000 and up). Essentially, you'll need a firm offer of work from a US company; however, unless you have a special skill, few companies will want to go through the hassle of sponsoring you. Since tourists are not supposed to seek work, legally you'll have to apply for jobs from overseas. Plenty of foreigners do manage to work for short periods illegally in New York (typically cash-in-hand jobs, bar work or freelancing); be warned however that the penalties for doing so can be harsh (deportation and being barred from the US for up to ten years), and that if you repeatedly enter the country on a visa-waiver, you are likely to be severely questioned at immigration. For further visa information, go to ⓦwww.unitedstatesvisas.gov.

Finding a place to stay is tricky for everyone. A **studio apartment** – a single room with bathroom and kitchen – in a popular neighbourhood in Manhattan can go for upwards of $1800 per month. Many newcomers share studios and one-bedrooms among far too many people; it makes more sense to look in the outer boroughs or the nearby New Jersey towns of Jersey City and Hoboken. However, even some of these neighbourhoods are becoming expensive, and to find a real deal you must hunt hard and check out even the most unlikely possibilities. It frequently takes up to a month or two to find a place.

The best source for finding an apartment or room is **word of mouth**. Watch the **ads** in the *Village Voice*, the *New York Times* and on ⓦwww.newyork.craigslist.org (actually a great resource for all kinds of classified listings in New York). Try commercial and campus bulletin boards too, where you might secure a temporary apartment or sublet while the regular tenant is away.

Left luggage

The best place to leave luggage is with your hotel concierge, but you can also use Luggage Storage NY (Mon–Fri 8am–7.30pm, Sat 8am–6.30pm; ⓣ212/704-0386, ⓦwww.luggagestorageny.com; $6–10/day per item) at 48 West 46th St, between Sixth and Fifth avenues, or Schwartz Travel Services (daily 8am–11pm; ⓣ212/290-2626, ⓦwww.schwartztravel.com; $7–10/day per item) at 355 West 36th Street, near Penn Station.

Lost property

For things lost on buses or on the subway: NYC Transit Authority, at the West 34th Street/Eighth Avenue Station on the lower level-subway mezzanine (Mon, Tues & Fri 8am–3.30pm, Wed & Thurs 11am–6.30pm ⓣ212/712-4500). For things lost in a cab call ⓣ311 or file a report online (ⓦwww.nyc.gov/taxi); try to get the cab's medallion number (printed on your receipt).

Mail

Post offices in New York City are generally open Monday to Friday 9am to 5pm (though some open earlier) and Saturday from 9am to noon or later. The main post office in Midtown is at 421 Eighth Avenue, at West 33rd Street (ⓣ212/967-8585) and is open 24 hours, seven days a week. **Ordinary mail** within the US costs 44¢ for letters weighing up to an ounce, and 28¢ for postcards; addresses must include a **zip code** (postal code) and a return address in the upper left corner of the envelope. International letters and postcards will usually take about a week to reach their destination; rates are currently

75¢ for letters and postcards to Canada, and 98¢ to all other countries. To find a post office or check up-to-date rates, see Ⓦwww.usps.com or call Ⓣ1-800/275-8777.

Money

US currency comes in **bills** of $1, $5, $10, $20, $50 and $100, plus various larger (and rarer) denominations. The dollar is made up of 100 cents (¢) in coins of 1 cent (usually called a penny), 5 cents (a nickel), 10 cents (a dime), 25 cents (a quarter), 50 cents (a half-dollar) and one dollar. The $2 bill and the half-dollar and dollar coins are seldom seen. Change – especially quarters – is needed for buses, vending machines and telephones, so always carry plenty.

Most people on holiday in New York withdraw **cash** as needed from ATMs, which can be found at any bank branch and at many convenience stores and delis in the city, though the latter can charge fees of up to $3 for the service (in addition to bank charges). If you're visiting from abroad, make sure you have a personal identification number (PIN) that's designed to work overseas. A **credit card** is a must; American Express, MasterCard and Visa are widely accepted, and are almost always required for deposits at hotels. If you bring **travellers' cheques**, it's best to have them in US dollar denominations, as they can be changed in any bank and used as cash in many stores.

Most **banks** are open Mon–Fri 8.30am–5pm, and a few have limited Saturday hours (major Citibank branches tend to open Sat 9am–3pm). Major banks – such as Citibank and Chase – will exchange travellers' cheques and currency at a standard rate.

The value of the US dollar tends to vary considerably against other currencies; after remaining relatively weak for a number of years, it began to strengthen in 2009. At press time, one dollar was worth 0.64 British pounds (£), 0.77 euros, 1.03 Canadian dollars (Can$), 1.10 Australian dollars (Aus$), 1.36 New Zealand dollars (NZ$) and 7.31 South African Rand (R). For current exchange rates check Ⓦwww.xe.com.

Public holidays

New Year's Day Jan 1
Martin Luther King, Jr's Birthday Third Mon in Jan
Presidents' Day Third Mon in Feb
Memorial Day Last Mon in May
Independence Day July 4
Labor Day First Mon in Sept
Columbus Day Second Mon in Oct
Veterans' Day Nov 11
Thanksgiving Day Fourth Thurs in Nov
Christmas Day Dec 25

Opening hours

The **opening hours** of specific attractions are given throughout the Guide. As a general rule, most **museums** are open Tuesday to Sunday, 10am to 5/6pm, though most have one night per week where they stay open at least a few hours later. Government **offices** are open during regular business hours, usually 9am to 5pm. Store hours vary widely, depending on the kind of store and what part of town you're in, though you can generally count on them being open Monday to Saturday from around 10am to 6pm, with limited Sunday hours. Many of the larger chain or department stores will stay open to 9pm or later, and you generally don't have to walk more than a few blocks anywhere in Manhattan to find a 24-hour deli. On national **public holidays** (see box opposite), banks and offices are likely to be closed all day, and most shops will be closed or have reduced hours.

Phones

International visitors who want to use their **mobile phones** in New York will need to check with their phone provider to make sure it will work, and what the call charges will be. Unless you have a tri-band phone, it is unlikely that a mobile bought for use outside the US will work inside the States. You can rent mobile phones via Phonerental (US Ⓣ1-800/335-3705, international Ⓣ1-619/446-6980, Ⓦwww.phonerentalusa.com); rates are around $1.50 per day.

Public telephones are becoming harder to find due to the popularity of mobile phones. The cost of a local call (within New York) is 25¢ for three or four minutes, depending on the carrier (each phone

Calling home from the US

Note that the initial zero is omitted from the area code when dialling the UK, Ireland, Australia, and New Zealand from abroad. The US country code (which it shares with Canada) is 1.

Australia 011 + 61 + city code + local number.

Canada city code + local number.

New Zealand 011 + 64 + city code + local number.

UK 011 + 44 + city code + local number.

Republic of Ireland 011 + 353 + city code + local number.

company runs their own booths). Calls elsewhere within the US are usually 25¢ for one minute; overseas long-distance rates are pricier, and you're better off using a prepaid calling card ($5, $10 and $20), which you can buy at most grocery stores and newsstands.

There are five **area codes** in use in New York: ⓣ212 and ⓣ646 for Manhattan, ⓣ718 and ⓣ347 for the outer boroughs and ⓣ917 for (mostly) mobile phones. You must dial the area code, even if you're calling a number from a phone within the same area. For directory assistance, call ⓣ411.

Smoking

Since 2003 **smoking** has been banned in virtually all indoor public areas (including malls, bars, restaurants and most work places) in New York – fines start at around $100 for breaking this law, though it is rarely enforced in late-night bars and clubs (the onus is on the owner to stop you smoking).

Time

New York City is on **Eastern Standard Time** (EST), which is five hours behind Greenwich Mean Time (GMT), three hours ahead of Pacific Standard Time, fourteen to sixteen hours behind East Coast Australia (variations for Daylight Savings) and sixteen to eighteen hours behind New Zealand (variations for Daylight Savings).

Travellers with disabilities

New York City has had **disabled access** regulations imposed on an aggressively disabled-unfriendly system. There are wide variations in accessibility, making navigation a tricky business. At the same time, you'll find New Yorkers surprisingly willing to go out of their way to help you. If you're having trouble and you feel that passers-by are ignoring you, it's most likely out of respect for your privacy – never hesitate to ask for assistance.

For wheelchair users, getting around on the **subway** is next to impossible without someone to help you, and even then is extremely difficult at most stations. Several, but not all, lines are equipped with elevators, but this doesn't make much of a difference. The Transit Authority is working to make stations accessible, but at the rate they're going it won't happen soon. **Buses** are another story, and are the first choice of many disabled New Yorkers. All MTA buses are equipped with wheelchair lifts and locks. To get on a bus, wait at the bus stop to signal the driver you need to board; when he or she has seen you, move to the back door, where he or she will assist you. For travellers with other mobility difficulties, the driver will lower a special ramp to allow you easier access.

For wheelchair users, taxis are less of a possibility unless you have a collapsible chair, in which case drivers are required to store it and assist you; the unfortunate reality is that most drivers won't stop if they see you waiting. If you're refused, try to get the cab's medallion number and report the driver at ⓣ311. Most of the major hotels in New York have wheelchair accessible rooms, including roll-in showers.

Services for disabled travellers

Big Apple Greeter (see p.36).

FEGS 315 Hudson St ⓣ212/366-8400, ⓦwww.fegs.org. Formerly the New York Society for the Deaf, this is a good source of information on interpreter services, plus services for deaf individuals ranging from HIV-test counselling to kosher lunches.

The Lighthouse 111 East 59th Street ⓣ212/821-9200, ⓦwww.lighthouse.org. General services for the visually impaired.

The Mayor's Office for People with Disabilities 100 Gold St, 2nd floor ⓣ212/788-2830, ⓦwww.nyc.gov/html/mopd. General information and resources.

Traveler's Aid ⓣ202/546-1127, ⓦwww.travelersaid.org. Nonprofit organization with professional and volunteer staff who provide emergency assistance to disabled or elderly travellers at JFK airport: you can find volunteers at the Ground Transportation Counters in each terminal or via their main office in the arrivals area of Terminal 6 (daily 10am–6pm). They also operate at Newark airport.

Women travellers

Women travelling alone or with other women in New York City should attract no more attention than in any other urban destination in the US. As always, the usual precautions should suffice; a big part of visiting New York is to look as if you know what you're doing and where you're going. If someone's bugging you, either turn away, leave, or let him know your feelings loudly and firmly. Avoid getting noticeably intoxicated unless you are with a trusted friend. If you are being followed, turn around and look at the person following you, and step off the pavement and into the street; attackers hate the open. If you're unsure about the area where you're staying, ask other women's advice. However, don't avoid parts of the city just through hearsay – you might miss out on what's of most interest – and learn to expect New Yorkers (Manhattanites in particular, many of whom feel incorrectly that anywhere outside of the borough shouldn't be risked) to sound alarmist; it's part of the culture.

The City

The City

1 The Harbour Islands

The southern tip of Manhattan, together with the shores of New Jersey, Staten Island and Brooklyn, enclose the broad expanse of **New York Harbour**. When the Dutch arrived in 1624, it was teeming with fish, seals, whales and half of the world's oysters. With the water heavily polluted, the last oyster bed was closed in 1927, and though things are much improved (the harbour is officially clean enough to swim and fish), it will take many generations to recover its former glory. For now, the main attractions lie above water, where ferries provide dazzling views of New York's celebrated skyline. You can take a boat ride out to **Liberty**, **Ellis** or **Governors islands** – three highly compelling destinations – or, if you're feeling less purposeful, catch the Staten Island Ferry, which traverses the harbour.

Visiting Ellis and Liberty islands

The only way to get to any of the Harbour Islands is by **ferry**. Take the #1 train to South Ferry or the #4 or #5 train to Bowling Green, then walk to the boat pier in Battery Park. From the pier, **Statue Cruises** go to Liberty, then on to Ellis Island (daily, every 30–45min 9.30am–3.30pm; round-trip $12, seniors $10, children 3–12 $5; ⓣ877/523-9849, ⓦwww.statuecruises.com). Note that you must be at security thirty minutes before departure. You can **buy tickets** at Castle Clinton (see p.59), in the park, or in advance (highly recommended) with a credit card. If you want to visit the museum inside the Statue of Liberty, you need to buy a ticket with "monument access" (no extra charge). The best way to avoid the long wait (you must line up to buy tickets, and then again to clear security before boarding the ferry) is to buy tickets in advance, preferably reserving the 9am slot, and have them emailed to you; you can then go straight to the security line.

Give yourself at least half a day to see both Liberty and Ellis islands. Liberty Island needs at least one hour (that's only if you're walking around the island, and not going inside the statue – there is another long line to clear security for the interior), and Ellis requires at least two hours to do its museum justice. Start out as early as possible: keep in mind that if you take the last ferry of the day to Liberty Island, you won't be able to get over to Ellis.

Alternatively, the **Staten Island Ferry** (free; ⓦwww.siferry.com) departs every half-hour and shuttles between Manhattan and its namesake island. While it provides a beautiful panorama of the harbour and downtown skyline, it doesn't actually stop at any of the Harbour Islands (see p.59).

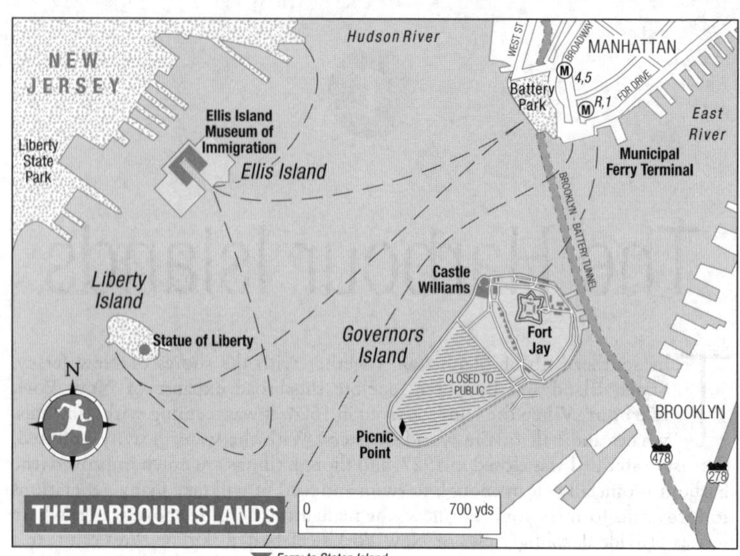

The Statue of Liberty

Of all America's symbols, none has proved more enduring than the **Statue of Liberty** (daily 9.30am–5pm; free; ⓣ212/363-3200, ⓦwww.nps.gov/stli), looming over the harbour from its pedestal on tiny **Liberty Island.** Indeed, there is probably no more immediately recognizable profile in existence than that of Lady Liberty, who stands with torch in hand, clutching a stone tablet. Measuring some 305ft from her pedestal base, she has acted as the figurehead of the American Dream for more than a century. When the first waves of European refugees arrived in the mid-nineteenth century, it was she who greeted them – the symbolic beginning of a new life.

These days, an immigrant's first view of the US is more likely to be the customs check at JFK Airport, but the statue nevertheless remains a stirring sight. **Emma Lazarus**'s poem *The New Colossus*, inspired by the new immigrant experience and inscribed on a tablet on the pedestal, is no less quotable now than when it was written in 1883:

"Give me your tired, your poor,
Your huddled masses yearning to breathe free,
The wretched refuse of your teeming shore.
Send these, the homeless, tempest-tost to me,
I lift my lamp beside the golden door!"

Some history

Native American shell middens found on Liberty Island date back hundreds of years, and in the early colonial period the abundance of shellfish nearby earned it the name Great Oyster Island. Sold by the British to Dutch merchant Isaac Bedloe in 1668, it was known as Bedloe's Island until 1956. Fort Wood was built here in 1812 as a defensive measure, and the War Department controlled much of the island well into the 1930s – the landscaped grounds you see today were created after the National Park Service assumed full ownership in 1937.

The **statue** itself, which depicts Liberty throwing off her shackles and holding a beacon to light the world, is the creation of French sculptor **Frédéric Auguste Bartholdi**, who crafted it a hundred years after the American Revolution, supposedly to commemorate the solidarity between France and America. (Actually, he originally intended the statue for Alexandria, Egypt.) Bartholdi built Liberty in Paris between 1874 and 1884, starting with a terracotta model and enlarging it through four successive versions to its present size of 151ft. The final product is a construction of thin copper sheets bolted together and supported by an iron framework designed by **Gustave Eiffel**.

Liberty had to be taken apart into hundreds of pieces in order to ship the statue to New York, where it was finally reassembled, although it was another two years before the figure could be properly unveiled. Only through the efforts of newspaper magnate Joseph Pulitzer, a keen supporter of the statue, were the necessary funds raised. **Richard Morris Hunt** built a pedestal around star-shaped Fort Wood, and Liberty was formally dedicated by President Cleveland on October 28, 1886, amid a patriotic outpouring that has never really stopped. Indeed, fifteen million people descended on Manhattan for the statue's centennial celebrations, and some three million people make the pilgrimage here each year.

The museum and statue interior

Three (free) **tour** options are available (reserved with the ferry ticket; see p.45): the basic ticket simply allows entry to Liberty Island, while a "monument access" ticket grants entrance to the museum at the base of the statue and the pedestal observation deck (168 steps up). In 2009, the **crown** of the statue was re-opened – to enjoy the cramped but spectacular views from here, you'll need to book a special ticket in advance and climb a total 354 steps. Note that you must go through another security screening before entry.

The **museum** is definitely worth a look, the downstairs lobby containing the original torch and flame (completed first and used to raise funds for the rest of the statue), and the small exhibition upstairs telling the story of Lady Liberty with prints, photographs, posters and replicas. At the top of the pedestal, you can look up into the centre of the statue's skirts – make sure you get a glance of her riveted and bolted interior, and her fire-hazard staircase. After you've perused the statue's interior offerings, take a turn around the balcony outside – the views are predictably superb. Informative and usually entertaining **ranger-guided tours** of the island's grounds are offered free of charge throughout the day (programme listings are posted at the island's information building).

Ellis Island

Just across the water from Liberty Island, and fifteen minutes further from Manhattan by ferry, sits **Ellis Island**, the former arrival point for over twelve million immigrants to the US. After $162 million was donated for its restoration, the main complex reopened in 1990 as the impressive **Ellis Island Museum of Immigration**.

Some history

The Dutch purchased the island from the Lenape Indians in 1630 (who had called it Kioshk or "Gull Island"), naming it Little Oyster Island after its famed beds of fist-sized shellfish. The English used it for hanging captured pirates and knew it as Gibbet Island, but the current name derives from Samuel Ellis, a New York merchant who bought the whole thing in the 1770s. Sold to the Federal government in 1808, Ellis Island was fortified during the war of 1812 but played a largely uneventful role in the history of the city for the next eighty years.

Up until the 1850s, there was no official **immigration process** in New York, but a surge of Irish, German and Scandinavian immigrants forced authorities to open an immigration centre at Castle Clinton in Battery Park. By the 1880s, millions of desperate immigrants (mostly southern and eastern Europeans) were leaving their homelands in search of a new life in America. The Battery Park facilities proved totally inadequate, and in 1892 Ellis Island became the new **immigration station**.

The main building was completed in 1903, and various additions were built in the ensuing years – hospitals, outhouses and the like, usually on bits of landfill. The immigrants who arrived here were all steerage-class passengers; richer immigrants were processed at their leisure on board ship. Though the processing centre had been designed to accommodate 500,000 immigrants per year, double that number arrived during the early part of the twentieth century; as many as 11,747 immigrants passed through the centre on a single day in 1907.

Once inside, each family was split up – men sent to one area, women and children to another – while a series of checks weeded out the undesirables and the infirm. The latter were taken to the second floor, where doctors would check for "loathsome and contagious diseases" as well as signs of insanity. Those who failed medical tests were marked with a white cross on their backs and either sent to the hospital or put back on the boat; only two percent of all immigrants were ever rejected, and of those, many jumped into the sea and tried to swim to Manhattan, or committed suicide. On average, eighty percent of immigrants were processed in less than eight hours, after which they headed either to New Jersey and trains to the West, or into New York City. After 1924, Ellis Island became primarily a detention facility (during World War II, some seven thousand German, Italian and Japanese people were detained here), before finally closing in 1954.

Ellis Island Museum of Immigration

Today, the main building serves as the **Ellis Island Museum of Immigration** (daily 9.30am–5.15pm; free; ⓣ212/363-3200, ⓦwww.nps.gov/elis), which eloquently recaptures the spirit of the place with artefacts, photographs, maps and personal accounts that tell the story of the immigrants who passed through Ellis Island on their way to a new life in America – some 100 million Americans can trace their roots through here. On the first floor, the excellent permanent exhibit "Peopling of America" chronicles four centuries of immigration, offering a statistical portrait of those who arrived at Ellis Island – who they were, where they came from and why they came. The huge, vaulted **Registry Room** on the second floor, scene of so much immigrant trepidation, elation and despair, has been left imposingly bare, with just a couple of inspectors' desks and American flags. In the side halls, a series of interview rooms recreates the process that immigrants went through on their way to naturalization; the white-tiled chambers are soberingly bureaucratic. Each room is augmented by recorded voices of those who passed through Ellis Island, recalling their experiences, along with photographs, explanatory text and small mementos – train timetables, toiletries and toys from home.

You can also watch thirty-minute-long re-enactments of immigrant experiences (April–Oct, usually around 7 times daily in the museum's theatre; $6; call ⓣ212/561-4500 for advance tickets) and a thirty-minute documentary film, *Island of Hope, Island of Tears*, shown throughout the day (free). If you turn up early

▲ Ellis Island Museum of Immigration

enough to get a place, you can get a free 45-minute **ranger-guided tour** (hourly) of the museum. **Audio tours** cost $8.

The museum's **American Family Immigration History Center** (same times as museum; Ⓦwww.ellisisland.org) holds a database of over 22 million immigrants who passed through New York between 1892 and 1924. Outside, the names of over 700,000 of these immigrants are engraved in copper; while the "Wall of Honor" (Ⓦwww.wallofhonor.com) is always accepting new submissions, it controversially requires families to pay $150 to be included on the list.

Governors Island

"Nowhere in New York is more pastoral", wrote travel writer Jan Morris of **Governors Island**, a 172-acre tract of land across from Brooklyn with unobstructed views of the Financial District and New York Harbour. Until the mid-1990s, this was the largest Coast Guard installation in the world, housing some 1600 service personnel and their families. Today, the island is being developed into a leafy historical park, its village greens and colonial architecture reminiscent of a New England college campus, making a dramatic contrast with the skyscrapers across the water.

Some history

The Lenape people referred to the island as Pagganck ("Nut Island") after its abundant chestnut, hickory and oak trees. When the Dutch arrived in 1624, they actually made camp here first before cautiously occupying Manhattan, and "purchased" what they called Noten Island from the Native Americans in 1637 (only to lose it to the British in the 1660s). Set aside for the "benefit and accommodation of His Majesty's Governors", Governors Island formally received its current name in 1784. Between 1794 and 1966, the US Army occupied the island, and for the following thirty years it was the US Coast Guard's largest and most extensive installation. It's hard to picture today, but the island was once two: tiny **Goverthing Island** was attached to the main island in 1909 by landfill, though a small community remained here (within the army base) until 1954. Subsequently

Visiting Governors Island

The only way to reach Governors Island (open June to mid-Oct; free) is by (free) **ferry** from the Battery Maritime Building at Slip 7 just northeast of the Staten Island Ferry Terminal (see p.59). There are free, two-hour **tours** on Wednesday and Thursday (ferries depart 10am & 1pm); on Friday (ferries hourly 10am–3pm; last ferry back 5pm), and Saturday and Sunday (ferries hourly 10am–5pm; last ferry back 7pm), you can visit the island independently. Access to the ferries is on a first-come, first-served basis, and limited to 400 people per trip (the weekday tours are limited to 60 people). Call ahead or check the websites for the schedule. Note that **food** options on the island are limited to a few food trucks and hot dogs and burgers at Water Taxi Beach.

submerged by sand, the village was excavated in 2009, buildings eerily frozen in the 1950s – ask at the visitor centre to see if it's been preserved.

In 2003, 22 acres of the island were sold to the National Park Service as the **Governors Island National Monument** (Ⓣ212/825-3045, Ⓦwww.nps.gov/gois), while the remaining 150 acres were purchased by the Governors Island Preservation and Education Corporation (GIPEC), jointly owned by the state and city of New York (Ⓦwww.govisland.com). In December 2007, GIPEC selected a design team to further develop the island's public spaces and historic district, an incredibly ambitious project that will take many years to complete. The plan is to bring in tenants for every one of the 52 historic buildings on the island, many converted into stores and art studios; in 2010, the **New York Harbor School** (a public high school) opened here.

The island

A visit to Governors Island makes for an intriguingly offbeat and bucolic day-trip. Ferries arrive at Soissons Dock, where you'll find the small **visitors' centre** (with maps and information about the island) and a gift shop. From here you can explore on foot or by bike (Bike and Roll; $10/hr, $20/day), or simply head to the tiny artificial **Water Taxi Beach** (to the right), which comes with food-and-drink tent, various events, live bands, volleyball and stupendous views.

It's a short stroll from the dock up to **Fort Jay**, completed in 1794. Reinforced in 1806, its dense stone walls helped to deter the British from attacking the city in 1812. Nearby, you can wander the shady lanes of **Nolan Park**, home to some beautifully preserved bright yellow Neoclassical and Federal-style mansions dating from 1857 to 1902 (occupied by officers during the army period), notably the Governor's House and Admiral's Mansion, site of the Reagan–Gorbachev Summit in 1988 – many of these are gradually being opened, or converted into art studios.

At the southern end of Nolan Park and facing the grassy **Parade Ground**, the grey stone Episcopalian **Chapel of St Cornelius & the Centurion** was completed in 1907. To the south, the humble white clapboard **Our Lady of the Sea Chapel** served as the Roman Catholic house of worship from 1942. The southern side of the Parade Ground is taken up by **Colonels' Row**, another collection of historic red-brick housing built between 1893 and 1917 (used for officers' housing) backed by the impressive bulk of **Liggett Hall**, a barracks completed in 1929. Heading back to the waterfront you'll see **Castle Williams** (under renovation till 2011), a circular fort completed in 1811 to complement the near-identical Castle Clinton in Battery Park. Used as a prison until 1966, the tiny cells inside held as many as 1000 Confederate soldiers during the Civil War.

The island also has plenty of green spaces in which to lounge in the sun, as well as a breezy promenade with stellar views of Manhattan – you can stroll right down to the southern tip, dubbed **Picnic Point**.

2

The Financial District

With its dizzying assemblage of skyscrapers, the **Financial District** has long been synonymous with the New York of popular imagination. This is where New Amsterdam was founded in the 1620s, and today the heart of the world's financial markets is still home to some of the city's most historic streets and sights. Over time, the area has seen more than its fair share of destruction and renewal; indeed, thanks to landfill, today's Financial District is double the size of that first Dutch colony, and many of the early colonial buildings burned down in either the Revolutionary War or the Great Fire of 1835. In September 2001, the character of the Financial District was altered radically once again when the attacks on the World Trade Center destroyed the Twin Towers (see box, p.56). Yet the regeneration of the area is startling: work is underway on the new One World Trade Center and a spate of ambitious projects from parks and office towers to transportation hubs and new hotels. Though some banks still maintain headquarters here, the most dramatic change is in the increase of residential development, as new condos and luxury conversions (many from former bank buildings) prove that the Financial District is once again in the process of integrating its present and future into its past. Begin your tour at Wall Street, accessible by the #2, #3, #4 and #5 trains.

Wall Street

Associated with money since the eighteenth century, **Wall Street** takes its name from the wooden stockade built by the Dutch in 1653 to protect themselves from the British colonies further north (the *wal* was dismantled in 1699). Though it remains the apex of the global financial system thanks to the Stock Exchange, most of the street was closed to traffic after 9/11, and fitness studios and condos have replaced almost all the banks that were once based here.

Trinity Church

Perched at Wall Street's western end on Broadway is **Trinity Church** (Mon–Fri 7am–6pm, Sat 8am–4pm, Sun 7am–4pm; free; Ⓣ212/602-0800, Ⓦwww.trinitywallstreet.org), a stoic onlooker of the street's dealings. The church held its first service in 1698, but this stern neo-Gothic structure – the third model – went up in 1846. It was the city's tallest building for fifty years, a reminder of how relatively recently high-rise Manhattan has sprung up. Trinity has the

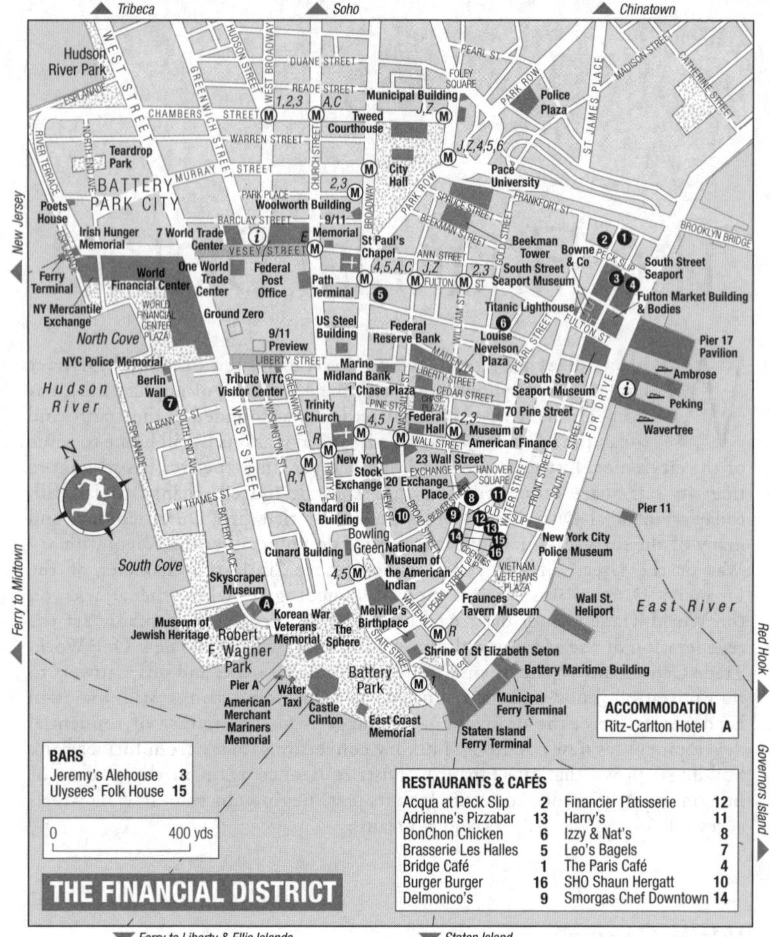

air of an English country church (hardly surprising, given its architect, Richard Upjohn, was English), especially in the sheltered **graveyard**, the resting place of many early Manhattanites: Alexander Hamilton (see box, p.212), famed diarist and lawyer George Templeton Strong, and steamboat king Robert Fulton among them. As you enter the church itself, note the ornate bronze doors designed by Richard Morris Hunt, a memorial to John Jacob Astor III. Inside, you'll find a small but enlightening **museum** (Mon–Fri 9am–5pm, Sat 9am–3.45pm, Sun 10–11am & 12.30–3.45pm; free) that explains the history of the church in more detail.

1 and 14 Wall Street

Opposite the church, the soaring Bank of New York building at **1 Wall Street** is an Art Deco wonder, topping out at 654ft in 1931. From the outside, you can just about make out the shimmering mosaic lobby interior (sadly closed to the public). On the other side of the street, the old Bankers Trust Company Building at

14 Wall Street (539ft) was completed in 1912 and is best known for its ostentatious step pyramid top, modelled on the Greek Mausoleum at Halicarnassus – wander down Broad Street for the best views.

New York Stock Exchange

The purse strings of the capitalist world are controlled behind the Neoclassical facade of the **New York Stock Exchange** (closed to the public; Ⓦwww.nyse.com) at the corner of Wall and Broad streets, where $50 billion changes hands on an average day. The main building at 18 Broad St, with its six mammoth Corinthian columns and monumental statues representing Integrity surrounded by Agriculture, Mining, Science, Industry and Invention, dates from 1903.

The origins of the exchange lie in the aftermath of the Revolutionary War when Secretary of the Treasury Alexander Hamilton offered $80 million worth of government bonds for sale. Not only did the public snap them up, but merchants also started trading the bonds, along with bills of exchange, promissory notes and other commercial paper. Trading became so popular that in 1792 a group of 22 stockbrokers and merchants gathered beneath a buttonwood tree on Wall Street, signing the **"Buttonwood Agreement"** and forming the initial trading group that would go on to be renamed the New York Stock Exchange in 1817. The event is commemorated by a tiny **buttonwood tree** on the pavement in front of 15 Broad St (it's not the original).

The rise and fall of Wall Street's merchant banks

Admired, feared and generally despised by most Americans at the time, J. P. Morgan is considered the godfather of US merchant banking (that is, banking for governments and big companies rather than individuals), presiding over New York's gradual replacement of London (largely bailed out by Morgan-led banks during World War I) as the world's biggest financial market from his base on Wall Street. Wall Street and its merchant banks (also "investment banks") boomed in the 1920s, survived the Great Depression and regulation of the 1930s and led the world with innovative products such as "junk bonds" and derivatives into the 1990s. Yet today, all the big investment banks have gone and most of Wall Street has been converted into condos – so where did it all go wrong?

A series of crashes, starting with the dot-com bust and 9/11 attacks in 2001, battered the markets and began the physical move away from the Financial District and Wall Street (as much for security as high rental costs). The 2008–2009 financial crisis proved the hardest blow. Investment banks had arranged hundreds of CDOs (Collateralized Debt Obligations), essentially bonds backed by sub-prime mortgages, since 1987; when over-extended borrowers began to default on their mortgages all over the US, the money dried up. Insurer AIG was bailed out by the US government to the tune of $186 billion, and one by one the investment banks failed, unable to cope with mind-boggling losses. Lehman Brothers, founded in 1850, collapsed with debts of over $700 billion (the largest bankruptcy in US history), and Bear Stearns and Merrill Lynch were sold to JP Morgan Chase and Bank of America respectively. Finally, Goldman Sachs and Morgan Stanley (the last heir to J.P.'s empire) converted to traditional bank holding companies (thus allowing them access to Federal funds), ending the era of merchant banks on Wall Street.

The financial sector remains a huge part of the New York economy, but these days hedge funds, not banks, tend to manage the biggest portfolios, and trading rooms are as likely to be based in Connecticut and New Jersey as Manhattan.

Federal Hall

Federal Hall, 26 Wall St (Mon–Fri 9am–5pm; free; free 30min tours 10am, 1pm, 2pm & 3pm; ⓣ212/825-6888, ⓦwww.nps.gov/feha), on the corner of Nassau Street, is one of the city's finest examples of Greek Revival architecture. Completed in 1842 as the US Customs House, it is best known today for the monumental **statue of George Washington** outside. The statue recalls the heady days of 1789, when Washington was sworn in as America's first president on a second-floor balcony here – elements of the US Constitution and Bill of Rights were also hammered out by Congress inside between 1785 and 1790, when New York was the de facto capital of the nation. Back then, this site was occupied by New York's second City Hall, built in 1703 and knocked down in 1812.

The documents and exhibits inside are worth a look, as is the main hall itself, with its elegant marble rotunda, Corinthian columns and Cretan maidens worked into the decorative railings. Displays cover the history of the building and pay tribute to the Washington connection (the Bible he used in the 1789 ceremony is on display), as well as the landmark libel case of German immigrant John Peter Zenger (1697–1746), who was arrested for libelling the British Crown in 1734, and was defended successfully by Andrew Hamilton. By 2011, the basement should be hosting a new exhibit, **The National Archives Vaults at Federal Hall**, containing important US documents such as the Bill of Rights, on permanent loan from Washington. It's also worth checking out the well-stocked **National Parks and NYC Information Center** at the back of the building.

23 Wall Street

Opposite Federal Hall at **23 Wall Street** is the unassuming building that once lay at the heart of the global financial system. In 1912, financier **J. P. Morgan** had his marble-clad headquarters built here; the extravagant use of what was then the most expensive real estate in the world (the building is only four storeys tall) epitomized the patrician aloofness of the period – the bank didn't even bother adding its name to the facade. J.P. Morgan had been based on this spot since 1873, taking his father's words to heart – "always be a bull on America". In 1920, a horse-drawn cart blew up out front, killing 38 and wounding over a hundred. The bombing has never been explained, though the most popular theory holds that the blast was planned by Italian anarchists taking revenge for the arrest of Sacco and Vanzetti. The marks on the building's wall have never been repaired, out of respect for the victims. In 2003, JP Morgan sold the building for $100 million, with part of the structure absorbed by the conversion of 15 Broad St into luxury condos by Philippe Starck.

Trump Building and the Museum of American Finance

Further along Wall Street, the former Bank of Manhattan Trust building at no. 40 was briefly the world's tallest skyscraper in 1930 (at 927ft), before being topped by the Chrysler Building (whose designers secretly increased the height of their tower after no. 40 was completed). Today, it's known as the **Trump Building** (closed to the public) after the flamboyant tycoon that bought it for just $1 million in 1995 (he claims its worth at least $400 million now).

Across William Street, the former Bank of New York building at 48 Wall St is home to the **Museum of American Finance** (Tues–Sat 10am–4pm; $8; ⓣ212/908-4110, ⓦwww.moaf.org). Housed in the fittingly opulent former main banking hall, this illuminating museum is the best place to gain an understanding of what's really going on outside: stocks, bonds and futures trading are demystified through multimedia presentations and a stack of rare artefacts that include a 1792 bond signed by Washington, an 1850s gold ingot and a stretch of ticker tape from the opening moments of 1929's Great Crash. Financial pioneer **Alexander Hamilton** (see box, p.212) is commemorated with his own room, while documentaries on Wall Street are shown throughout the day.

20 Exchange Place and Delmonico's

One block south of Wall Street on William Street, **20 Exchange Place** is a truly stupendous Art Deco tower (741ft), built for City Bank-Farmers Trust in 1931 and now a series of luxury apartments (Russian 'Spy' Anna Chapman was living here in 2010). The main entrance is adorned by eleven stone impressions of coins from the countries where the bank had offices, while the nineteenth floor is circled by fourteen "Giants of Finance", helmeted figures that look like classical Greek warriors.

Nearby, **Delmonico's**, 56 Beaver St at William Street, is technically the oldest restaurant in the country, although it's been closed for prolonged periods and has exchanged owners several times over the years. The Swiss-born Delmonico brothers built the original here in 1837 when eating options in New York were generally restricted to British-style taverns; in addition to the usual array of Astors and Morgans, Charles Dickens, French exile Louis-Napoléon and generals Grant and Sherman all dined here. The building is a bastion of opulence, with its grand portico supported by columns brought from the ruins of Pompeii and a menu that features many of the restaurant's culinary inventions (see p.307).

70 Pine Street

One block north of Wall Street on Pearl Street, **70 Pine St** (952ft) will remain the tallest skyscraper downtown until the completion of One World Trade Center. Completed in 1932 for Cities Services Company, it is one of New York's most graceful and iconic Art Deco towers, though it can be frustratingly hard to get a decent view – head down Cedar Street for the best glimpse. Insurance giant **AIG** bought the building in 1976, but as a consequence of the 2008 financial crisis sold it to Korean-American developer Youngwoo & Associates for around $150 million in 2009 – it looks like more luxury condos are on the way.

Federal Reserve Bank

Three blocks north of Wall Street lies the **Federal Reserve Bank of New York**, at 33 Liberty St near Nassau Street. Completed in 1924 and the largest of America's twelve reserve banks, there's good reason for the building's fortress-like exterior (based on Florentine *palazzos*): stashed 80ft below street level are ten percent of the world's gold reserves – 7000 tons of them (worth over $240 billion in 2010). Yet as impressive as all this sounds, gold has played a minor part in global finance since 1971 (when President Nixon ended trading gold at the fixed price of $35/ounce), and today the reserve is used primarily by foreign governments for book-keeping and reporting purposes.

You can enter the Fed to visit two multimedia **exhibitions** inside, housed in the vaulted former banking hall (both Mon–Fri 10am–4pm; first 20 visitors on the hour till 3pm): "**FedWorks**", naturally enough, explains how the Fed system works, allowing visitors to participate in monetary policy simulations and to identify counterfeit notes, while **the history of money** is highlighted through a priceless collection of coins loaned by the American Numismatic Society. This includes rare finds from the ancient Middle East, and the famous **1933 Double Eagle** (a $20 gold coin), thought to be worth $20 million today. You'll need a photo ID to pass through security.

Free **Gold Vault Tours** (1hr) are given Monday to Friday (9.30am, 10.30am, 11.30am, 1.30pm, 2.30pm & 3.30pm), but you must reserve these in advance. You'll see a couple of introductory videos then the vault itself, but only through the bars at the entrance; you'll only get close to one gleaming heap of gold bricks. Contact the Public Information Department, Federal Reserve Bank, 33 Liberty St, NY 10045 (Ⓣ212/720-6130, Ⓦwww.newyorkfed.org), preferably one month ahead. You'll need to arrive twenty minutes early with your passport; cameras or camera phones are not allowed.

Ground Zero and around

The former location of the Twin Towers, **Ground Zero** remains a vast construction site, with hundreds of workers labouring away at the new **World Trade Center**. Seven buildings in total were destroyed as a result of the 2001 terrorist attacks, but today the area is booming, invigorated by the huge surge of investment as part of the regeneration of Lower Manhattan.

The best **viewing points** are from inside the **World Financial Center** (see p.60) on the west side of Ground Zero; walk across busy West Street via the Liberty

September 11 and its aftermath

At 8.46am on September 11, 2001, a hijacked airliner slammed into the north tower of the **World Trade Center**; seventeen minutes later another hijacked plane struck the south tower. As thousands looked on in horror – in addition to hundreds of millions more viewing on TV – the south tower collapsed at 9.50am, its twin at 10.30am. All seven buildings of the World Trade Center complex eventually collapsed, and the centre was reduced to a mountain of steel, concrete and glass rubble. As black clouds billowed above, the whole area was covered in a blanket of concrete dust many inches thick; debris reached several hundred feet into the air. The devastation was staggering. While most of the 50,000 civilians working in the towers had been evacuated before the towers fell, many never made it out of the building; hundreds of firemen, policemen and rescue workers who arrived on the scene when the planes struck were crushed when the buildings collapsed. In all, **2995 people perished** at the WTC and the simultaneous attack on the Pentagon in Washington DC, in what was, in terms of casualties, the largest foreign attack on American soil in history. Radical Muslim Osama bin Laden's terrorist network, **al-Qaeda**, claimed responsibility for the attacks.

Dominating Lower Manhattan's landscape from nearly any angle, the 110-storey Twin Towers always loomed over their surroundings. The first tower went up in 1972 and the second a year later, and while becoming integral parts of the New York skyline, they also evolved into emblems of American power in the eyes of Islamic extremists.

In the days after the attack, downtown was basically shut down, and the seven-square-block area immediately around the WTC was the focus of an intense rescue effort. New Yorkers lined up to give blood and volunteered to help the

Street pedestrian bridge for the best panorama, then head north within the World Financial Center for views of the main tower. Work on the new site is slated for completion in 2014, but **One World Trade Center** is already towering above street level and glass-plated **7 World Trade Center** (741ft; also by David Childs) on the north side at 250 Greenwich St was completed in 2006. You can admire Jenny Holzer's intriguing lobby installation from the street outside; digital poetry text moving across wide plastic panels (the 65ft-long wall changes colour according to the time of day).

You can also visit the excellent **Tribute WTC Visitor Center** (Mon & Wed–Sat 10am–6pm, Tues noon–6pm, Sun noon–5pm; $10; ⓣ212/393-9160, ⓦwww.tributewtc.org), at 120 Liberty St (between Greenwich and Church sts), which arranges daily walking **tours** of the site's perimeter (Mon–Fri 11am, 1pm & 3pm, Sat & Sun noon, 1pm, 2pm & 3pm; $10; ⓣ212/422-3520), and self-guided audio tours for the same price. The centre houses five small galleries that commemorate the attacks of September 11, beginning with a model of the Twin Towers and a moving section about the day itself, embellished with video and taped accounts of real-life survivors. A handful of items found on the site – a pair of singed high-heel shoes, pieces of twisted metal – make heart-rending symbols of the tragedy.

St Paul's Chapel

Both the oldest church and the oldest building in continuous use in Manhattan, **St Paul's Chapel** (Mon–Sat 10am–6pm, Sun 7am–3pm; free; ⓣ212/233-4164, ⓦwww.saintpaulschapel.org), at Fulton Street and Broadway, dates from 1766, making it almost prehistoric by New York standards. The main attraction inside is **Unwavering Spirit**, a poignant exhibition on September 11. For eight months

rescue workers; vigils were held throughout the city, most notably in Union Square, which was peppered with candles and makeshift shrines. Then-Mayor **Rudy Giuliani** cut a highly composed and reassuring figure as New Yorkers struggled to come to terms with the assault on their city.

Moving forward

In 2003, Polish-born architect **Daniel Libeskind** was named the winner of a competition held to determine the overall design for the new World Trade Center, though his plans were initially plagued with controversy and he's had little subsequent involvement with the project. In 2006, a modified design, still incorporating Libeskind's original 1776ft-high **Tower of Freedom** (now One World Trade Center), was finally accepted and construction is well under way, supervised by architect **David Childs**. The whole $12 billion scheme, which also involves a Santiago Calatrava-designed transportation hub and four subsidiary towers conceived by Norman Foster, Richard Rogers, Fumihike Maki and the firm Kohn Pedersen Fox should be complete 2014–2015 (the target has been continually put back). In addition, the project includes the **National September 11 Memorial and Museum**, designed by Michael Arad and Peter Walker. The memorial, *Reflecting Absence*, will comprise two voids representing the footprints of the original towers, surrounded by oak trees and 30ft waterfalls tumbling into illuminated pools. The underground museum will use artefacts and exhibits to tell the story of September 11.

To get an idea what all this will look like, visit the **9/11 Memorial Preview Site** (Mon–Sat 10am–7pm, Sun 10am–6pm; free; ⓦwww.national911memorial.org) at 20 Vesey St and Church Street.

after the 9/11 attacks, St Paul's Chapel served as a sanctuary for the rescue workers at Ground Zero, providing food, a place to nap and spiritual support. The exhibit chronicles the church's role in these recovery efforts, with a moving ensemble of photos, artefacts and testimonies from those involved. The church itself was based on London's St Martin-in-the-Fields, with a handsome interior of narrow Corinthian columns and ornate chandeliers, though even **George Washington's pew**, preserved shrine-like from 1789–1790 (when New York was the US capital), forms part of the September 11 exhibition (it served as a foot treatment chair for firefighters). Outside, the historic cemetery is worth a wander, sprinkled with colonial headstones and the **Bell of Hope**, a gift from London in 2002; the bell is rung every September 11.

Bowling Green

Broadway ends at the city's oldest public garden, **Bowling Green**. This is supposedly the location of the most famous real-estate deal in history, when Peter Minuit, the newly arrived director general of the Dutch colony of New Amsterdam, bought the whole island from the Native Americans for a bucket of trade goods worth sixty guilders in 1626 (the figure of $24 was calculated in the 1840s). Though we don't know for sure who "sold" the island to Minuit (it was probably a northern branch of the Lenni Lenape), the other side of the story (and the part you never hear) was that the concept of owning land was utterly alien to Native Americans – they had merely agreed to support Dutch claims to *use* the land, as they did. The green was formally established in 1733, when it was used for lawn bowling by colonial Brits, on a lease of "one peppercorn per year". The encircling iron fence is an original from 1771, though the crowns that once topped the stakes were removed during the Revolutionary War, as was a statue of George III. The statue was melted into musket balls – little bits of the monarch that were then fired at his troops.

Just north of the green on the Broadway partition is a sculpture of a **Charging Bull** – not originally envisioned as a symbol of a "bull market" for Wall Street stocks, though that's how it is perceived by New Yorkers today. As the story goes, on December 15, 1989, Arturo Di Modica installed his sculpture in the middle of Broad Street. The city removed the sculpture the next day, but was forced to put it here when public support of the statue was surprisingly vocal. The bull stands opposite the former headquarters of John D. Rockefeller's **Standard Oil Company** at 26 Broadway. Originally constructed in 1885, when Rockefeller moved here from Cleveland, most of the elaborate, pyramid-topped building you see today was added in the 1920s, the pinnacle serving as a lighthouse for ships entering New York Harbour. You'll get the best views from Battery Park.

National Museum of the American Indian

Bowling Green sees plenty of office folk picnicking in the shadow of Cass Gilbert's US Custom House, home of the **National Museum of the American Indian** (daily 10am–5pm, Thurs till 8pm; free; ⓣ212/514-3700, ⓦwww.nmai.si.edu), an arm of the Smithsonian Institution in Washington DC. The main galleries lie on the second floor, where temporary exhibits focus on various aspects of Native American culture as well as shows by contemporary artists. Most exhibits last at least six months; **A Song for the Horse Nation**, a thought-provoking multimedia study of the relationship between Native Americans and horses, extends to July 2011 and includes some stunning objects, from hoof ornaments and Sioux beaded bags to hide robes and Cheyenne horse masks. On the first floor, the **Diker Pavilion** serves as an additional performance and exhibition space. Whatever's showing, you'll see artefacts from the Smithsonian's vast collection representing almost every Native American tribe; it was largely assembled by one man, George Gustav Heye (1874–1957), who travelled through the Americas picking up such works for over fifty years.

Completed in 1907 and in use till 1973, the Beaux Arts **Custom House** is itself part of the attraction; the facade is adorned with elaborate statuary representing the major continents (carved by Daniel Chester French) and the world's great commercial centres, while the spectacular marble-clad Great Hall and Rotunda inside are beautifully decorated; the sixteen murals covering the 135ft dome were painted by Reginald Marsh in 1937.

Battery Park and around

Due west of the Customs House, Lower Manhattan lets out its breath in **Battery Park**, a breezy, spruced-up space with monuments and fine views of the Statue of Liberty and the harbour.

Before landfill closed the gap in the 1850s, **Castle Clinton** (daily 8.30am–5pm), the red-brick fort on the west side of the park, was on an island. Built in 1811, it was ceded to the city in the 1820s, finding new life as a prestigious concert venue known as Castle Garden before doing service (pre-Ellis Island) as the drop-off point for arriving immigrants; from 1855 to 1890, eight million people passed through its walls. After serving as an aquarium, the squat fortress is now the place to buy **tickets for the Statue of Liberty and Ellis Island** (see p.45); it also contains a small exhibit on the history of the site. South of Castle Clinton stands the **East Coast Memorial**, a series of granite slabs inscribed with the names of all the American seamen who were killed in World War II.

Crossing the harbour

The **Staten Island ferry** (Ⓣ718/727-2508, Ⓦwww.siferry.com) sails from the modern Whitehall Ferry Terminal on the east side of Battery Park, built directly above the equally smart South Ferry subway station (at the end of the #1 line and accessible via R trains to Whitehall Street). The #4 and #5 trains to Bowling Green also let you off within easy walking distance. Weekday **departures** are scheduled every fifteen to twenty minutes during rush hours (7–9am & 5–7pm), every half-hour through the rest of the day and evenings, and every hour late at night (the ferry runs 24hr). On weekends, boats run every half-hour from Manhattan, but slightly less frequently on the return trip.

The twenty-five-minute ride is truly New York's best bargain: it's absolutely free, with wide-angle views of the city and the Statue of Liberty becoming more spectacular as you retreat. You also pass very close to Governors Island (near Manhattan, left of the boat) and the 1883 Robbins Reef Lighthouse (closer to Staten Island, off to the right). By the time you arrive on **Staten Island** (see p.264), the Manhattan skyline stands mirage-like: the city of a thousand and one posters, its skyscrapers almost bristling straight out of the water.

At the bottom of Broadway, the park entrance holds the city's first official memorial to the victims of **September 11**; its focal point is the cracked fifteen-foot steel-and-bronze sculpture *The Sphere* – designed by Fritz Koenig to represent world peace. The sculpture once stood in the WTC Plaza and survived the collapse of the towers, the only artwork on the premises not to be destroyed in the attack.

The Skyscraper Museum and the Museum of Jewish Heritage

Just behind the *Ritz-Carlton Hotel*, at 39 Battery Place facing Battery Park, is the **Skyscraper Museum** (Wed–Sun noon–6pm; $5; ⓣ212/968-1961, ⓦwww.skyscraper.org). The core display area is usually taken up with temporary exhibits, but always with skyscraper focus – recent displays have focused on Shanghai and Hong Kong. Permanent exhibits are dedicated to the Burj Khalifa (the world's tallest building), One World Trade Center and the Twin Towers, and hand-carved miniature wooden models of Downtown and Midtown Manhattan created by Michael Chesko.

Just opposite at 36 Battery Place, the **Museum of Jewish Heritage** (10am–5.45pm, Wed till 8pm, Fri till 5pm, closed Sat; Oct–March closes 3pm; closed Jewish holidays; $12 or $17 with audio guide, free Wed 4–8pm; ⓣ646/437-4200, ⓦwww.mjhnyc.org) was designed in 1997 by Kevin Roche as a memorial to the Holocaust; its six sides represent both the six million dead and the Star of David. The moving and informative collection, which covers three floors of permanent exhibits and multimedia installations, begins with the rituals and practical accoutrements of everyday Eastern European Jewish life pre-1930, before moving on to the horrors of the Holocaust and ending, more optimistically, with the establishment of Israel and subsequent Jewish achievements. Some of the more memorable installations include a fine hand-painted *Sukkah* cover from 1930s Hungary, and a heart-rending display commemorating the children murdered by the Nazis. Temporary exhibits also fill the upper floors, while the Zen-like "Garden of Stones" stands on the second-floor terrace. Be sure to also visit the innovative **Keeping History Center** on the third floor, where the "Voices of Liberty" exhibit features testimony from Holocaust survivors and immigrants via iPod-like audio guides.

Battery Park City

The hole dug for the foundations of the former World Trade Center threw up a million cubic yards of earth and rock, which was then dumped into the Hudson River to the west to form the 23-acre base of **Battery Park City**. This self-sufficient island of office blocks, apartments, chain boutiques and landscaped esplanade feels a far cry from the rest of Manhattan indeed. Battery Park City's southern end is anchored by **Robert F. Wagner Jr Park**, a refuge from the ferry crowds – you can follow the **Esplanade** up the Hudson from here as far as Chelsea. The centrepiece of the Battery Park development is the **World Financial Center** (ⓣ212/945-2600, ⓦwww.worldfinancialcenter.com), a rather grand and imposing fourteen-acre business, shopping and dining complex that looks down onto Ground Zero from just across West Street. Inside, the **Winter Garden**, a ten-storey, glass-ceilinged public plaza, brings light and life into a mall full of shops and restaurants. Decorated by sixteen 45ft-high Washingtonia palms from Florida, the plaza is a veritable oasis, and connects with the **North Cove** yacht harbour on the Hudson River side. Don't miss the small chunk of the **Berlin Wall** tucked away on the south side of the cove.

The Irish Hunger Memorial and Poets House

Just north of the World Financial Center, facing the Hudson at the end of Vesey Street, the **Irish Hunger Memorial** (daily 8am–6.30pm; free) is a sobering monument to the more than one million Irish people that starved to death during the Great Famine of 1845–1852. The tragedy sparked a flood of Irish immigration to the US, mostly through New York. An authentic famine-era stone cottage, one of many abandoned in the west of Ireland, was transported from County Mayo by artist Brian Tolle and set on a raised embankment overlooking the water. The passageway underneath echoes with haunting Irish folk songs, and you can follow the meandering path through the grassy garden and stones 25ft to the top.

To the north of the monument, at 10 River Terrace, the **Poets House** (Tues–Fri 11am–7pm, Sat 11am–6pm; free; ⓣ212/431-7920, ⓦwww.poetshouse.org) contains a fabulous reference library, reading room and audio collection dedicated to poets of every nationality (and free wi-fi) – a relaxing place to end an afternoon.

State Street

State Street curves along Battery Park's east side. A rounded, red-brick facade identifies the **Shrine of St Elizabeth Ann Seton** at 7 State St (daily 7am–5pm; ⓣ212/269-6865, ⓦwww.setonshrine.com), honouring the first native-born American to be canonized. The shrine comprises a working Catholic chapel, the Church of Our Lady of the Rosary, built in 1965 in Georgian style with a small room at the front containing a statue of the saint and rather pious illustrations of her life. Before moving to Maryland to found a religious community, St Elizabeth lived briefly (1801–03) in a small house on this site. You enter through the adjacent porticoed building, completed in 1793 and known as Watson House, one of only a few old buildings in the area that has survived the modern onslaught. Seton (1774–1821) was canonized in 1975, principally in recognition of her work establishing the Sisters of Charity and schools for poor women and children.

Cut through the buildings to Pearl Street from here and you'll see the small memorial (set into the wall) marking the site of **Herman Melville's birthplace**; the author of *Moby Dick* was born in a small townhouse on this spot in 1819, now long gone.

North along Pearl Street

For a window into eighteenth-century Manhattan, check out the **Fraunces Tavern Museum**, 54 Pearl St at Broad Street (Tues–Sat noon–6pm; $10; ⓣ212/425-1778, ⓦwww.frauncestavernmuseum.org). The ochre-and-red-brick building was constructed in 1719 and became the *Queen's Head Inn* after Samuel Fraunces purchased the property in 1762; having survived extensive modifications, several fires and a brief stint as a hotel in the nineteenth century, the three-storey Georgian house was almost totally reconstructed by the Sons of the Revolution in the early part of the twentieth century to mimic how it appeared on December 4, 1783. It was then that a weeping George Washington took leave of his assembled officers, intent on returning to rural life in Virginia: "I am not only retiring from all public employments," he wrote, "but am retiring within myself." With hindsight, it was a hasty statement – six years later he was to return as the new nation's president. The **Long Room** where the speech was made has been faithfully decked out in the style of the time, while the adjacent Federal-style **Clinton Room** is smothered in rare and florid French wallpaper from 1838. The tavern's upper floors contain a permanent exhibit tracing the site's history, a room with over two hundred flags and an expansive collection of Revolutionary War artefacts; look out for a lock of Washington's hair, preserved like a holy relic. Fascinating temporary exhibits are also held here, usually on related themes (such as the influence of the Magna Carta on the Revolution).

On the other side of Pearl Street (in the shadow of 85 Broad St, Goldman Sachs' old headquarters), are the oldest remnants of colonial New York. This was the site of the city's first tavern, transformed into the **Stadt Huys** or City Hall in 1653 when New Amsterdam was officially incorporated – the city government still dates its foundation from this year. Nothing remains from that period, but archeologists have uncovered the foundations of **Governor Lovelace's Tavern**, a British pub dating from the 1670s, preserved under glass panels just off the street; the outlines of where both buildings once stood are marked by coloured bricks. At Coenties Slip you can turn left to reach historic **Stone Street**, a narrow cobbled lane of 1830s rowhouses packed with restaurants (see p.307), or turn right to the **Vietnam Veterans Memorial**, a modern assembly of glass blocks etched with troops' letters home. The mementos are sad and often haunting, but the place is a peaceful spot for contemplation.

Continue up South Street to Old Slip, where you'll find the small but ornate building that once housed the **First Precinct Police Station**, now home to the **New York City Police Museum** (Mon–Sat 10am–5pm; $7; ⓣ212/480-3100, ⓦwww.nycpolicemuseum.org). Three floors of exhibits showcase the history of New York's Finest, a force established in 1845; as well as historic uniforms, guns and vehicles such as a 1972 Plymouth patrol car, special displays cover weapons used by the likes of Al Capone and his mentor Frankie Yale, and Lieutenant Petrosino, one of the first and most successful Italian-American officers to tackle the "Black Hand" gangs of the early 1900s (see p.87). A special multimedia exhibit commemorates the NYPD's role in **September 11**, when 23 officers were killed, and the Hall of Heroes honours all officers who have died in the line of duty. Finally, a display documents how the NYPD has reduced crime levels in the city by over fifty percent since the 1990s.

Just to the north on Pearl Street, **Hanover Square** is home to the **British Memorial Garden**, dedicated to the 67 British citizens killed on 9/11, and the majestic **India House**, completed in 1853 for Hanover Bank and subsequently used by the New York Cotton Exchange (1870–1885). It's now an exclusive club for august financial types, and houses the more accessible *Harry's Café* (see p.307).

South Street Seaport

New York's original dockyards were located on Manhattan's southern tip between Battery Park and Fulton Street, and today a tiny part of this heritage is preserved as the touristy **South Street Seaport**. Created by the Dutch in the 1620s, the port boomed in the nineteenth century, favoured by sea captains for providing shelter from the westerly winds and the ice that floated down the Hudson River during winter. **Robert Fulton** started a ferry service from here to Brooklyn in 1814, leaving his name for the street and then its market, New York's largest (the fish market moved to the Bronx in 2006). After World War II, containers came to dominate shipping, and Manhattan effectively ceased being a port in the 1970s; ships were handled in New Jersey and Staten Island, and the docks were left as

▲ South Street Seaport

rotting eyesores. Beginning in 1966, a private initiative rescued some of the remaining warehouses, creating the historical seaport you see today; a mix of attractively restored buildings and ships, with fairly standard main-street stores and cafés. Since 2009, there's also been a **Water Taxi Beach** here every summer (Mon–Wed & Sun 11am–10pm, Thurs 11am–midnight, Fri & Sat 11am–2am; free); a small strip of imported sand with tables, drinks and weekend dance parties.

The South Street Seaport Museum

Housed in a series of painstakingly restored warehouses, the **South Street Seaport Museum**, 12 Fulton St (Jan–March Mon & Fri–Sun 10am–5pm, Mon Schermerhorn Row Galleries only; April–Dec daily 10am–6pm; $12, $8 ships only; Ⓣ212/748-8600, Ⓦwww.southstreetseaportmuseum.org), offers illuminating maritime art and trades exhibits and a spread of refitted ships and chubby tugboats (the largest collection of sailing vessels – by tonnage – in the US). The main ticket office and galleries lie on Fulton Street, housed in **Schermerhorn Row**, a unique ensemble of Federal-style warehouses dating to about 1811. The interiors have been hollowed out to accommodate the galleries, with exposed brick and ceiling timbers sensitively restored – recent temporary exhibitions have focused on the SS *Normandie* and New Amsterdam. There's also a **permanent exhibition** of plans, models and memorabilia associated with luxury ocean liners in the Walter Lord Gallery, around the corner at 209 Water St. Next door is **Bowne & Co., Stationers** (Wed–Sun 10am–5pm; Ⓣ212/748-8651), a gaslit nineteenth-century shop producing wonderfully authentic letterpress printing.

Your ticket also includes a look around the *Ambrose* (a 1908 lightship) and *Peking* (a 1911 barque), moored at nearby Pier 16. **The Ambrose** remained in service till 1964, spending much of its working life in New York Harbour. Exhibits tackle the history of the boat, navigation and the role of lightships in general – you can also view the engine room and sailors' quarters. **The Peking** is massive in comparison – wander the aft deck to appreciate its scale. Built as a German merchant ship, it became a British training boat in the 1930s and ended up here in 1975. The midship rooms have been restored, and exhibits describe life at sea. The *Wavertree*, a graceful tall-ship built in 1885, is still being restored and is expected to open in 2012.

The museum runs **cruises** around the harbour on the *Pioneer*, an 1885 schooner that accommodates up to forty people (May–Sept; $25, students and seniors $20, under-12s $15; reservations on ⓣ212/748-8786). Cruises normally last two hours and depart on both weekdays (3–5pm, 7–9pm & 9.30–11.30pm) and weekends (1–3pm, 4–6pm, 7–9pm & 9.30–11.30pm), though you'll pay an extra $10 at peak times (4–6pm & 7–9pm). Call in advance for the latest information. More leisurely excursions up the Hudson are available on the museum's 1893 fishing schooner *Lettie G. Howard* ($100 day-trips, $500 for the weekend; ⓣ212/748-8757) and the tug *W.O. Decker*, which coasts around the harbour ($100; ⓣ212/748-8786); check the museum website for the schedule.

Pier 17 and the rest of the Seaport

The Seaport is slated for a major expansion in the next few years, but until then the **Pier 17 Pavilion** will remain the focal point of the district, created from the old fish-market wharf that was demolished and then restored in 1982. The three-storey glass-and-steel pavilion houses all kinds of restaurants and shops; a bit more interesting is the outdoor promenade, where you'll find the museum ships and booths selling cruise and water-taxi tickets. Circle Line Downtown (ⓣ1-866/925-4631, ⓦwww.circlelinedowntown.com) runs **harbour cruises** from March to December on *Zephyr* (1hr; $25, seniors $23, children $15), and speedboat rides on the *Shark* from May to September (30min; $21, seniors $19, children $15). The views of the Brooklyn and Manhattan bridges from the promenade are fantastic (and free) at any time of year.

Just across South Street, the old Fulton Market Building contains the ever-popular **Bodies** exhibition (Mon–Thurs & Sun 10am–7pm, Fri & Sat 10am–9pm; $26.50, weekend/holiday $27.50; ⓣ1-888/926-3437, ⓦwww.bodiesny.com), with its presentation of 20 real human bodies and 260 organs, polymer-preserved in fascinating but slightly disturbing detail. Opening in 2005, the exhibition has been extended indefinitely, though a 2007 *New York Times* article claimed that such displays have created "a ghastly new underground mini-industry" in China, the origin of the preserved cadavers.

3

City Hall Park and the Brooklyn Bridge

Since 1812, **City Hall Park** has been the seat of New York's municipal government. Within the park's borders is stately **City Hall**, with **Tweed Courthouse** just to the north; the towers of **Park Row** and the **Woolworth Building** stand nearby; the **Municipal Building** watches over Police Plaza and the city's courthouses; and the **Brooklyn Bridge**, a magnificent feat of engineering, soars over the East River. In stark contrast, the **African Burial Ground National Monument** is a poignant and powerful reminder of the city's early African population. Coming to the park by subway, take the #2 or #3 train to Park Place; the #4, #5 or #6 train to Brooklyn Bridge–City Hall; or the R train to City Hall.

City Hall

Towards the northern end of City Hall Park sits **City Hall** itself, a gleaming white marble palace with Neoclassical columns, arches and furnishings virtually unchanged since it was completed in 1812. It's the oldest city hall in the US to retain its original government function; the **mayor's office** and the chambers of the New York City Council are inside, while official receptions and press conferences are also held here. Increased security means the building is fenced off from the rest of the park, and the only way you can see the magnificent interior is to take a **free guided tour** offered by Art Commission experts, well worth your time. Tours are offered twice a week: Thursdays at 10am (reserve in advance at Ⓣ311 or 212/639-9675, Ⓦwww.nyc.gov/html/artcom); and Wednesdays at noon (sign up at the NYC information kiosk, opposite the Woolworth Building, open Mon–Fri 9am–6pm, Sat & Sun 10am–5pm). Both tours take just over one hour and are identical.

Tours begin in the elegant triple-arcaded lobby, which opens up to the **Rotunda**, one of the most sensational pieces of architecture in the city; the all-white coffered dome (topped with a skylight and invisible from the outside), is ringed by ten Corinthian columns and a floating marble staircase that spirals up to the second floor. Up here you'll see the **Council Chamber**, where the city council meets once a month and the ceiling is covered in a giant allegorical mural

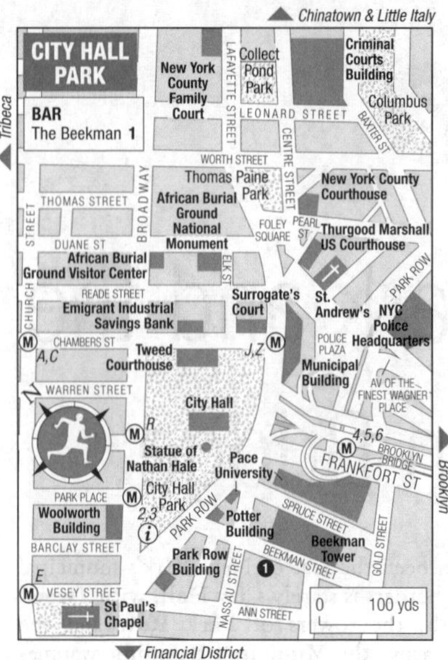

representing New York. Most of the decor dates back to 1898, when the chamber was re-designed to take in the newly expanded city boroughs. An 1825 portrait of the Marquis de Lafayette by Samuel Morse (later of Morse Code fame), sits on the wall.

More nineteenth-century portraits by John Trumbull adorn the **Governor's Room**, an immaculate French Regency-style reception room containing George Washington's writing desk and a rare mahogany table from 1814. The room hosted President-elect Abraham Lincoln in 1861 (who shook hands for eight hours straight), and served as the backdrop in 1865 when Lincoln's body lay in state for 120,000 sorrowful New Yorkers to file past.

Park Row and the Woolworth Building

City Hall Park is flanked on either side by impressive early twentieth-century skyscrapers. **Park Row**, the eastern edge of the park, was once known as "Newspaper Row". From the 1830s to the 1920s, the city's most influential publishers, news services and trade publications had their offices on this street or surrounding blocks. The *New York Times* operated from no. 41, a Romanesque structure that grew from five storeys to sixteen to accommodate the booming paper until it relocated uptown in 1904 (Pace University moved here in 1952). The wildly ornamented **Potter Building** at no. 38 dates from 1886, when it was a pioneer in fireproofing, thanks to its iron-clad lower floors and durable terracotta trim. Today, as with much of downtown, it's being converted into high-end apartments (with a *Starbucks* on the first floor). The **Park Row Building**, at no. 15, was completed in 1899; at 391ft, it was the tallest office building in the world. Behind the elaborate limestone-and-brick facade were the offices of the Associated Press as well as the headquarters of the IRT subway (investor and gambler August Belmont financed both this tower and the transit system). The Park Row Building towered over its surroundings until 1908, when the Singer Building, at 165 Broadway (now demolished), surpassed it – it's now primarily filled with expensive apartments.

Contrast this Gilded Age opulence with Frank Gehry's contemporary masterpiece, towering over Park Row at 8 Spruce St; his 77-storey **Beekman Tower** (867ft) topped out in 2009, its rippling stainless steel curtain wall containing nine hundred luxury rentals and a new public school at its base.

In 1913, the tallest building in the world was on the opposite side of City Hall Park: the **Woolworth Building** (792ft) at 233 Broadway, held the title until the Chrysler Building pipped it in 1929. Cass Gilbert's "Cathedral of Commerce" oozes money and prestige. The soaring, graceful lines are covered in white terracotta tiles and fringed with Gothic-style gargoyles and decorations that are more whimsical than portentous. Frank Woolworth made his fortune from his "five and dime" stores – everything cost either 5¢ or 10¢, strictly no credit. True to his philosophy, he paid cash for the construction of his skyscraper, and reliefs at each corner of the ornate lobby (sadly, now closed to sightseers) show him doing just that: counting out the money in nickels and dimes.

Tweed Courthouse

If City Hall is the acceptable face of New York's municipal bureaucracy, the spectacular **Tweed Courthouse**, just to the north with its entrance at 52 Chambers St, is a reminder of the city government's infamous corruption in the nineteenth century. The man behind this former county courthouse, **William Marcy "Boss" Tweed**, worked his way up from nowhere to become chairman of the Democratic Central Committee in 1856. Tweed embezzled the city's revenues (even the courthouse's budget, which rolled up from $3 million to $12 million during its construction between 1861 and 1881), until political cartoonist Thomas Nast and the editor of the *New York Times* (who'd refused a $500,000 bribe to keep quiet) turned public opinion against him in the early 1870s. Fittingly, Tweed was finally tried in an unfinished courtroom in his own building in 1873, and died in 1878 in Ludlow Street Jail – a prison he'd had built while he was Commissioner of Public Works.

Tweed's monument to greed, which now houses the Department of Education and a kindergarten, looks more like a mansion than a municipal building, especially after the lavish $85 million restoration completed in 2001. To get a look at its fabulous interior, you need to take a **free guided tour**, arranged by the Art Commission (Fri noon; 1hr; reserve in advance at Ⓣ311 or 212/639-9675, Ⓦwww.nyc.gov/html/artcom), which begin in the 75ft monumental **rotunda**, soaring upward to the stained-glass skylight. Here it's easy to spot the contrasting styles of the two architects that worked on the building; the cast-iron floors, doors and stairways have been skilfully blended with a series of exposed red-and-white brick Romanesque arches – indeed, this is the most developed cast-iron interior in the city. The jarring Roy Lichtenstein moulded fibreglass installation **Element E** dominates the space, emphasizing that this is also a modern place of work – offices now occupy all the old courtrooms. The tour takes in one of these high-ceilinged halls with ornate plasterwork and giant chandeliers, as well as the remarkable southern **annexe**, a confection of polished granite columns, white marble and English ceramic tile floors; the upper floors feature elaborate exposed-brick vaulting.

The Municipal Building and around

At the east end of Chambers Street, across Centre Street, stands the 25-storey **Municipal Building**, looking like an oversized chest of drawers 580ft tall. Built between 1908 and 1913, it was the first skyscraper constructed by the well-known architectural firm McKim, Mead, and White, although it was actually designed by one of the firm's younger partners, William Mitchell Kendall. At its top, an extravagant "wedding cake" tower of columns and pinnacles, including the

▲ The Municipal Building

frivolous 25ft gilt sculpture *Civic Fame*, attempts to dress up the no-nonsense home of public records and much of the city government's offices. The shields decorating the moulding above the colonnade represent the various phases of New York as colony, city and state: the triple-X insignia is the Amsterdam city seal, and the combination of windmill, beavers and flour barrels represents New Amsterdam and its first trading products, images used on the city seal today. There's little to see inside, but the **City Store** (Mon–Fri 9am–4.30pm) at the base sells New York City maps, books and souvenirs.

To the north lies New York's court district, dominated by the grandiose 590ft tower of the **Thurgood Marshall US Courthouse**, at 40 Centre St. Designed by Cass Gilbert and completed in 1933, the building is undergoing a massive restoration that should be complete by the end of 2010. The adjacent building, at 60 Centre St, is the **New York County Courthouse** (daily 9am–5pm), one of the state's supreme courts. A massive hexagonal Neoclassical structure completed in 1927, it merits a quick peek into the lobby to see its elaborate rotunda, decorated in the 1930s with storybook murals illustrating the history of justice (you'll have to pass through security to get a good look, but as it's a public building you are allowed to go in). The columned facades of the courthouses look onto **Foley Square**, named for the sheriff and saloonkeeper Thomas "Big Tom" Foley, one of the few admirable figures in the Tammany Hall era. The focal point of the wide concrete plaza is Lorenzo Pace's three-hundred-ton black granite sculpture, *The Triumph of the Human Spirit*, a tribute to the many thousands of enslaved Africans who died on American soil – particularly those whose bodies were discovered in the African burial ground just off the west side of the square (see below).

African Burial Ground National Monument

In 1991, construction of a federal office building at 290 Broadway uncovered one of the most important US archeological finds of the twentieth century, the remains of 419 skeletons in what was once a vast African burial ground. Today, the **African Burial Ground National Monument** (daily 9am–5pm; free; Ⓦwww.nps.gov/afbg) on Duane Street occupies a tiny portion of a cemetery that covered five blocks between the 1690s and 1794. Then outside the city boundary, this was the only place Africans could be buried. After being examined at Howard University, the skeletons, along with artefacts (such as beads) buried with them, were re-interred at this site in 2003, marked by seven grassy mounds and a highly polished black granite monument. The soaring **Ancestral Chamber** in the centre is a symbolic counterpoint to the infamous "Gate of No Return" on Gorée Island

The Notorious Five Points

East of Foley Square is the area once known as **Five Points**, named for the intersection of Mulberry, Worth, Park, Baxter and Little Water streets, the last of which no longer exists. A former pond here known as the Collect was filled in as part of a public-works project around 1812, but the fetid, damp location soon became a massive slum as a relentless influx of immigrants, sailors and criminals sought refuge here, and toxic industries were shunted to this unlovely side of town. In 1829, the local press started using the Five Points moniker, and by 1855, when immigrants formed 72 percent of the population, its muddy streets – called Bone Alley, Ragpickers' Row and other similarly inviting names – were lined with flimsy tenements. Diseases such as cholera skipped easily from room to overcrowded room.

The neighbourhood was further marred by vicious pitched battles among the district's numerous Irish **gangs**, including the Roach Guards, the Plug Uglies and the Dead Rabbits (depicted with flair in Martin Scorsese's *The Gangs of New York*). After the Civil War, when the area's Irish majority gave way to the new waves of Italian and Chinese immigrants, the gangs consolidated to form the Five Pointers. The group acted as a strong arm for Tammany Hall, effectively training the top names of organized crime, including Al Capone.

Upper-class sightseers like Charles Dickens (who came here in 1842), both fascinated and repelled by Five Points, invented the concept of "slumming" in their tours of the neighbourhood. They made lurid note of the crime, filth and other markers of obvious moral depravity, but most New Yorkers were not gravely concerned until 1890, when police reporter and photographer Jacob A. Riis published *How the Other Half Lives*, a report on the city's slums. In particular, his gripping images, which retained his subjects' dignity while graphically showing the squalor all around them, helped convince readers that these people were not poor simply due to moral laxity. The book was remarkably successful in its mission to evoke sympathy for the plight of this troubled community, and it's in large part thanks to Riis that Five Points was razed by 1895, eventually replaced by a park and a towering courthouse.

in Senegal, through which slaves would leave Africa for the New World. Instead of captivity and departure, this gateway represents spiritual freedom and return, facing east towards Africa. The spiral path into the **Ancestral Libation Court**, 4ft below street level, is engraved with signs and symbols of the African Diaspora, inspired by the discovery of what might be one symbol, the *sankofa*, on the coffin of a former slave – heart-rending evidence that despite their situation, slaves maintained spiritual links with their homeland (the *sankofa* symbolized "returning to your roots"). Despite its relatively small size, the curving walls and mystical symbols create a meditative, temple-like atmosphere, in utter contrast to its skyscraper-bound surroundings.

To learn more about the burial ground, walk around the corner to 290 Broadway and the new **visitor centre** (Mon–Fri 9am–5pm, closed federal holidays; free; ⓣ212/637-2019), which opened in 2010; look for the dedicated entrance just along from the main building entrance. A twenty-minute video (played throughout the day) introduces the site, while an interactive exhibition with touch-screen computers and replicas of the artefacts found here trace not just the history of the cemetery but of slavery in New York. Experts believe as many as 15,000 free and enslaved blacks were buried here, and examination of the bones revealed a cycle of back-breaking toil that began in childhood. One of the reasons the site is considered so significant is that slavery (and the cruelty that went with it) is something many people associate with the Deep South. In reality, New York had the second largest enslaved population outside of South Carolina in 1776, and slave labour built much of the colonial city. Maya Angelou alluded to this misconception at the emotional re-interment ceremony: "You may bury me in the bottom of Manhattan. I will rise. My people will get me. I will rise out of the huts of history's shame". Slavery was abolished in New York State in 1827.

From here, if you retrace your steps to Foley Square and down Centre Street, you'll see the footpath that runs over the Brooklyn Bridge.

The Brooklyn Bridge

One of several spans across the East River, the **Brooklyn Bridge** is today dwarfed by lower Manhattan's skyscrapers, but in its day, the bridge was a technological quantum leap, its elegant gateways towering over the brick structures around it. For twenty years after its opening in 1883, it was the world's largest and longest suspension bridge, and – for many more years – the longest single-span structure. To New Yorkers, it was an object of awe, the concrete symbol of the Great American Dream. Italian immigrant painter Joseph Stella called it "a shrine containing all the efforts of the new civilization of America". Indeed, the bridge's meeting of art and function, of romantic Gothic and daring practicality, became a sort of spiritual model for the next generation's skyscrapers. On a practical level, it expanded the scope of New York City, paving the way for the incorporation of the outer boroughs and the creation of a true metropolis.

The bridge didn't go up without difficulties. Early in the project, in 1869, architect and engineer John Augustus Roebling crushed his foot taking measurements for the piers and died of tetanus less than three weeks later. His son Washington took over, only to be crippled by the bends after working in an insecure underwater caisson; he subsequently directed the work from his sickbed

▲ Brooklyn Bridge

overlooking the site. Some twenty workers died during the construction, and a week after the opening day, twelve people were crushed to death in a panicked rush on the bridge's footpath. Despite this tragic toll (as well as innumerable suicides over the years), New Yorkers still look to the bridge with affection, celebrating its milestone anniversaries with parades and respecting it as a civic symbol on a par with the Empire State Building.

The **view** from below (especially on the Brooklyn side) as well as the top is undeniably spectacular. You can **walk across** its wooden planks from Centre Street, but resist the urge to look back till you're at the midpoint, when the Financial District's giants stand shoulder to shoulder behind the spidery latticework of cables. You can follow the pedestrian path straight to its end, at the corner of Adams and Tillary streets in **Downtown Brooklyn** (see p.219), behind the main post office. More convenient for sightseeing, however, is to exit the bridge at the first set of stairs: walk down and bear right to follow the path through the park at Cadman Plaza. If you cross onto Middagh Street, you'll be in the core of **Brooklyn Heights** (see p.223); or follow Cadman Plaza West down the hill to Old Fulton Street and the **Fulton Ferry District** (see p.221).

If you're not up to walking over the bridge (though it really is the most interesting way), a **taxi** from the City Hall area to Brooklyn Heights costs about $7.

4

Tribeca and Soho

The adjoining neighbourhoods of **Tribeca** and **Soho** encompass the area from Ground Zero north to Houston Street (pronounced HOW-ston) and east from the Hudson River to Broadway. Acting as a sort of segue between the businesslike formality of the Financial District and the relaxed artiness of the West Village, the district is home to wealthy New Yorkers with a taste for retro-industrial cool and the stores that cater to them. Nineteenth-century warehouses have been converted into vast lofts overlooking cobblestone streets, and the area's cast-iron buildings (and their enormous ground-floor windows) make it a perfect spot for purveyors of fine art, antiques and luxury goods.

The art scenes that flourished here in the 1970s and 1980s have, for the most part, moved on to Chelsea and the outer boroughs, but there are still plenty of reasons to visit the area. Tribeca feels more residential, its streets populated by stylish moms and their hip tots, as well as the occasional celebrity. Soho is also the haunt of young and fashionable Hollywood types, with rents that have now eclipsed the West Village, though the focus here is on dining and, especially, shopping.

Tribeca

Tribeca (try-BECK-a), the Triangle below Canal Street, is a former wholesale-food district that has become an enclave of urban style; its old industrial buildings house the spacious loft apartments of the area's gentry. Less a triangle than a crumpled rectangle, the neighbourhood is bounded by Canal and Murray streets to the north and south, and Broadway and the Hudson River to the east and west. The name is a mid-1970s invention of real-estate brokers who thought it better suited to the neighbourhood's increasing trendiness; rapper Jay-Z, Mariah Carey, Gwyneth Paltrow and novelist Patrick McGrath are among a long list of celebrities that own apartments here. Another big name in the neighbourhood is Robert De Niro, who helped found both the **Tribeca Film Center**, a state-of-the-art building catering to producers, directors and editors, and the **Tribeca Film Festival** in 2002. Most visitors who trek to Tribeca do so for its **restaurants** (see p.308). The area is accessible via the #1 train to Canal Street (for the north edge), Franklin Street (centre), and Chambers Street for the south side (the #2 and #3 also stop here).

Chambers Street to the Hudson River

Heading west along Chambers Street from City Hall Park, you'll get a taster of Tribeca's historic roots at the triangular intersection with West Broadway.

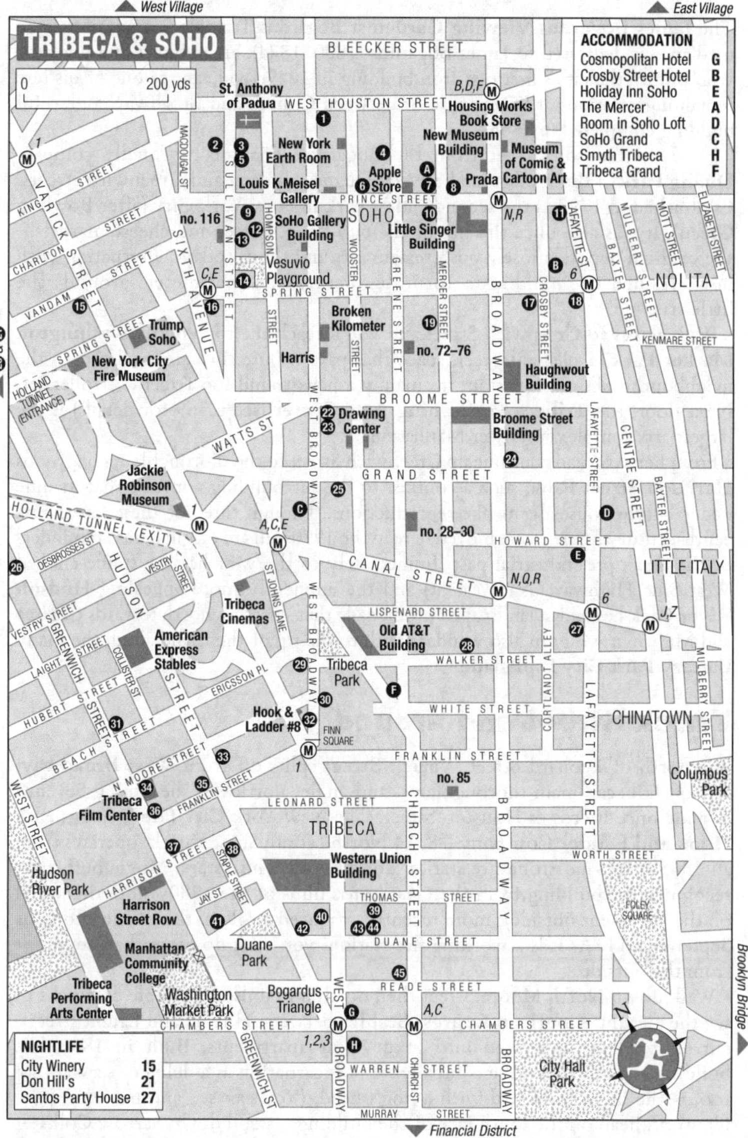

RESTAURANTS & CAFÉS

Aquagrill	16
Balthazar	17
Balthazar Bakery	17
Blaue Gans	43
Blue Ribbon Sushi	13
Bouley	42
Bubby's	33
Calexico Carne Asada	6
City Hall	44
Corton	30
Cupping Room Café	23
Dos Caminos	1
Duane Park Patisserie	41
Grandaisy Bakery	29
Hampton Chutney	11
Harrison	37
Kelley and Ping	4
L'Ecole	24
Locanda Verde	34
Lure Fishbar	8
Megu	39
Mercer Kitchen	7
Mezzogiorno	14
Nobu	35
Omen	12
Once Upon a Tart	5
Pakistan Tea House	45
Pepe Rosso To Go	3
Petite Abeille	40
Raoul's	9
Spring Street Natural Restaurant	18
Tribeca Grill	36
Turks & Frogs	26

BARS

Bar 89	19
Bubble Lounge	32
Church Lounge	F
Ear Inn	20
Fanelli's Café	10
Greenwich Street Tavern	31
Kenn's Broome Street Bar	22
M1-5 Lounge	28
Puffy's Tavern	38
The Room	2
Toad Hall	25

The **James Bogardus Viewing Garden** at Bogardus Triangle – more of a large median – is dedicated to James Bogardus (1800–1874), an architect and inventor who put up the city's first cast-iron building in 1849. You can see one of his few remaining creations at 85 Leonard St between Church and Broadway, a graceful building completed in 1868.

Head up Hudson Street from the Bogardus Triangle to equally compact **Duane Park**, a sliver of green between Duane, Hudson and Greenwich streets. Established in 1797 as the second-oldest park in New York City (after Bowling Green), it was also once the site of the city's egg, butter and cheese markets – the original depots (mostly posh restaurants and shops today), alternating with new residential buildings, form a picturesque perimeter around the little triangle.

Walk across to Greenwich Street and you'll reach the top end of **Washington Market Park**, a pleasant green space that pays tribute, in name at least, to the neighbourhood's old function; it's mainly a playground for Tribeca's stroller set. Next door, the **Tribeca Performing Arts Center** (see p.369 for details) is the largest arts complex in Lower Manhattan.

From here you can continue up Greenwich Street to the thoroughly incongruous **Harrison Street Row**, such a contrast to the surrounding concrete that its nine Federal-style houses seem like reproductions. Though three of these late eighteenth-century homes were moved here in the 1970s, all are original, rare reminders of the area's pre-industrial past. Immediately to the west lies the traffic-choked West Side Highway (aka West St) and the eminently more appealing **Hudson River Park** beyond, a landscaped promenade that stretches north towards Chelsea and Midtown; you can also wander south to the tip of the island along the shady **Battery Park City Esplanade**.

Varick Street and around

Just north of Leonard Street, **Varick Street** splits off from **West Broadway**, one of Tribeca's main thoroughfares, and angles northwest, becoming Seventh Avenue once it crosses Houston Street. The New York City Fire Department's **Hook and Ladder Company #8**, 14 North Moore St, at Varick, operates from an 1865 brick-and-stone fire station dotted with white stars. Movie buffs may recognize the building from the *Ghostbusters* films of the 1980s (note the mural on the pavement outside); more recently, it played a role in the rescue efforts of September 11. As it is a working fire station, you can't do more than admire it from the outside.

Walk down North Moore Street then north up Hudson a couple of blocks to see the elegant **American Express Stables** between Hubert and Laight streets, currently being converted into luxury loft apartments. Built in 1867, the building is a relic from the company's first incarnation as a delivery service; so, too, is the high-relief seal with a dog's head. (You can see another, not quite identical, head on the south face of the building – stroll down narrow Collister to Hubert St.)

Keep walking north to Spring Street and you'll come to the **New York City Fire Museum** (Tues–Sat 10am–5pm, Sun 10am–4pm; $5; ⓣ212/691-1303 ⓦwww.nycfiremuseum.org) at no. 278. Housed in a 1904 Beaux Arts fire station, the museum displays old fire trucks dating back to the 1840s and plenty of art and NYFD memorabilia, but also acts as a touching memorial to the 343 firefighters that died on September 11. The NYFD lost 778 men in the line of duty between 1865 and September 10, but the devastating losses of the following day drew worldwide sympathy. Photos, videos and artefacts found at the site record the disaster, and tiles commemorate those lost. Walking east along Spring Street from here brings you right into central Soho.

Note that the long-anticipated **Jackie Robinson Museum**, commemorating the famous African-American baseball player, should be open at Canal and Varick streets by early 2011 (see Ⓦwww.jackierobinson.org).

Soho

Like Tribeca, **Soho** (short for *So*uth of *Ho*uston) has also undergone a series of transformations in the past few decades. In the 1980s, Soho was the centre of New York's art scene, but today a mostly non-resident crowd uses the area between Houston and Canal streets and Sixth Avenue and Lafayette Street as an enormous outdoor shopping mall. By day a place to buy khakis or trendy trousers, at night the neighbourhood becomes a playground for gangs of well-groomed bistro- and bar-goers.

▲ Shopping break, Spring Street

Despite the commercialism, Soho's artistic legacy hasn't been completely eradicated. If anything, it has been incorporated into the neighbourhood's new character. You can still visit a couple of permanent installations tucked away on upper floors, or just cruise the visionary **Prada boutique** (Mon–Sat noon–8pm, Sun 11am–7pm), designed by Dutch architect Rem Koolhaas. The store, at Prince Street and Broadway, acts as a sort of gatekeeper to the area's myriad shopfronts, which showcase everything from avant-garde home decor to conceptual fashion. The R and N trains to Prince drop you at Prada's front door; the B, D or F to Broadway–Lafayette deposits you a block north at Houston. For access to the west side of the neighbourhood, take the C or E to Spring Street.

Broadway

Any exploration of Soho's streets entails crisscrossing and doubling back, but an easy enough starting point is the intersection of Houston Street and Broadway. **Broadway** reigns supreme as downtown's busiest drag, and numerous storefronts, most of them jazzed-up chain shops trying to compete with Soho's pricey designer boutiques, make it easy to get swept up in the commercial frenzy. For more visual stimulation, pop upstairs to the **Museum of Comic and Cartoon Art**, on the fourth floor at 594 Broadway (Tues–Sun noon–5pm; $5, under-12s free; ⓣ212/254-3511, ⓦwww.moccany.org), where you may catch a themed exhibit on anything from World War II propaganda to contemporary *anime*.

Broadway is also the place to start a tour of Soho's distinctive **cast-iron architecture**, best appreciated from the outside – many are now shops, but the interiors have usually been substantially remodelled. The stately **New Museum Building** (previously Astor Building), 583 Broadway, was built in 1896 on the site of the house where John Jacob Astor, America's original tycoon, died in 1848 – it's now occupied by condos with an Esprit store on street level (which has at least

Soho's cast-iron architecture

In vogue from around 1860 to the turn of the twentieth century, the **cast-iron architecture** that is visible all over Soho initiated the age of prefabricated buildings. With mix-and-match components moulded from iron, which was cheaper than brick or stone, a building of four storeys could go up in as many months. The heavy iron crossbeams could carry the weight of the floors, allowing greater space for windows.

The label can be confusing at first, as you won't see any obvious sign of metal (other than fire escapes); another major appeal for architects was that it was easy to disguise the iron with remarkably **decorative facades**. Almost any style or whim could be cast in iron, painted or plastered and pinned to the front of an otherwise dreary building to resemble marble: instant face-lifts for Soho's existing structures, and the birth of a whole new generation of beauties. Glorifying Soho's sweatshops, architects indulged themselves in Baroque balustrades and forests of Renaissance columns. But as quickly as the trend took off, it fell out of favour. Stricter building codes were passed in 1899, when it was discovered that iron beams, initially thought to be fireproof, could easily buckle at high temperatures. At the same time, steel proved an even cheaper building material.

With nearly 150 structures still standing, Soho contains one of the largest collections of cast-iron buildings in the world, and the **Soho Cast-Iron Historic District**, from Houston Street south to Canal Street and from West Broadway to Crosby Street on the east, helps preserve the finest examples; the district is to expand a couple of blocks east and west in 2010.

maintained the original columns inside). One of the later examples of the form is the **Little Singer Building**, 561 Broadway, which is actually an L-shape building with a second front at 88 Prince St. The twelve-storey terracotta-tiled office and warehouse of the sewing-machine company was erected in 1904 by architect Ernest Flagg, who went on to build the record-breaking Singer Tower in the Financial District in 1908, thus rendering this earlier creation "little" in comparison. Here, Flagg used wide plate-glass windows set in delicate iron frames, a technique that pointed the way to the glass curtain wall of the 1950s. Today, the first floor is a Mango fashion store while the rest is a residential co-op – units were selling for $5–6 million in 2010. A block and a half south, on the northeast corner of Broome and Broadway, stands the magnificent 1857 **Haughwout Building**, the oldest cast-iron structure in the city, as well as the first building of any kind to boast a passenger elevator – the lift, designed by Elisha Otis, was steam-powered. The facade of the former housewares emporium (it's now a Bebe fashion store) is mesmerizing; 92 colonnaded arches are framed behind taller columns and the whole building looks more like an elaborate sculpture. Diagonally opposite and equally impossible to ignore, the ostentatious wedding-cake exterior of the **Broome Street Building**, 487 Broadway, was completed in 1896. By the turn of the century, this was known as the Silk Exchange, but the building is mostly residential today – Britney Spears owned the penthouse till 2006.

Greene Street and the Cast-Iron Historic District

If you continue down Broadway to Grand Street and turn right (west), you'll be in a prime position to appreciate a couple of architectural gems on **Greene Street**. First dip south to **no. 28–30**, the building known as the "**Queen of Greene Street**". Architect Isaac Duckworth's five-storey French Second Empire extravagance dates from 1873 and was tastefully renovated in 2010 by trendy Swiss-based USM Modular Furniture. Retrace your steps and head north across Broome to see more of Duckworth's artistry at **no. 72–76** Greene St. Thanks to its mass of columns and peaked cornice, this creation, completed just prior to no. 28–30, has naturally been given the title "**King of Greene Street**". Today, the first floor is a fittingly swanky Droog fashion boutique (Mon–Sat 11am–7pm, Sun noon–6pm), worth a look in its own right (more art installation than shop).

One block west, at 35 and 40 Wooster St, between Grand and Broome streets, the **Drawing Center** (Wed & Fri–Sun noon–6pm, Thurs noon–8pm; free; ⓣ212/226-7547, ⓦwww.drawingcenter.org), shows contemporary and historical drawing exhibits. Masters including Marcel Duchamp and Richard Tuttle, as well as emerging and unknown artists, are shown together.

Farther north, beyond Spring Street, you enter the heart of the **Cast-Iron Historic District**, where you'll see vivacious facades, as well as curlicue bishop's-crook cast-iron lampposts. None is quite as splendid as Duckworth's, but all are beautifully preserved and make excellent display cases for the high-end retail offerings inside. Wander north of Prince Street to see **The New York Earth Room**, 141 Wooster St (Wed–Sun noon–3pm & 3.30–6pm; closed July & Aug; free; ⓦwww.earthroom.org), a permanent installation by land artist Walter de Maria. Since 1980, this second-floor loft has been some of the most squandered real estate in NYC, as it is covered in almost two feet of moist brown earth, all of which weighs some 280,000 pounds. Commissioned and maintained by the Dia Art Foundation, the dirt is periodically aerated and cleaned, to keep mushrooms and bugs from flourishing. The entrance is easy to miss; press the buzzer and walk up to the second floor.

The busiest shop in this area is one of the few not devoted to fashion, cosmetics or high-end art (and is not cast iron): the landmark **Apple Store** (daily 9am–9pm, Sun till 7pm), occupying the former post office on the corner of Greene and Prince streets.

West Broadway and the South Village

The north–south avenue of **West Broadway**, lined on either side with stately buildings, is the edge of the cast-iron district and was once the traditional boundary of Soho, though these days the blocks to the west are usually considered part of the area. Smaller and more residential, this section was once known as the **South Village**, its primarily Italian residents an extension of the Greenwich Village community until Robert Moses' brutal widening of Houston Street in 1940 effectively split them in two. The change in architecture is obvious, as the high-rise cast-iron warehouses give way to older Federal and Greek Revival rowhouses and cafés. At the top of Sullivan Street, **St Anthony of Padua Church** was built in 1888 by the oldest Italian congregation in the US. The church hosted the 2005 funeral of local resident and mafioso Vincent Gigante, better known as "The Oddfather" because he feigned mental illness for years to avoid prison. Walk back down to **116 Sullivan Street** to find one of the oldest homes in the neighbourhood, an elegant Federal-style townhouse completed in 1832 and particularly noted for its carved wooden doorway.

Back on West Broadway, the deceptively plain **Soho Gallery Building** at no. 420 was the home of the most influential art galleries in the city between the 1970s and 1990s. In 1971, art dealers Leo Castelli, André Emmerich and John Weber, along with Castelli's ex-wife Ileana Sonnabend, moved here from their offices uptown. Perhaps the most over-the-top exhibition occurred in 1991 in Sonnabend's gallery, when Jeff Koons debuted his *Made in Heaven* collection, a series of sexually explicit photos and sculptures featuring his Italian porn-star wife, La Cicciolina. The art-market bubble burst a year later, and the galleries started to leave Soho; though all the original dealers have since died, their galleries remain in the Upper East Side and Chelsea (Koons still lives and works in the Upper East Side). Today, the Soho Gallery Building is occupied by a DKNY store and luxury apartments.

At 393 West Broadway, about a block south, you can find **Broken Kilometer**, another installation by Walter de Maria (Wed–Sun noon–3pm & 3.30–6pm; free; Ⓦwww.brokenkilometer.org). This collection of five hundred carefully arranged brass rods is a slightly disorienting study in scale and perspective, as well as a testament to the sturdiness of cast-iron buildings – the collected rods weigh more than eighteen tons.

5

Chinatown, Little Italy and Nolita

With several Chinese newspapers, a dozen Buddhist temples and around five hundred restaurants, **Chinatown** is Manhattan's most densely populated ethnic neighbourhood. Over the last twenty years, it has pushed across its traditional border on Canal Street into the smaller enclave of **Little Italy**, and today it has begun to sprawl east across Division Street and East Broadway into the periphery of the Lower East Side. On the northern fringes of Little Italy, the hip quarter known as **Nolita** is home to a number of chic restaurants, bars and boutiques. Together, these three bustling neighbourhoods can make for a diverting side-trip away from Manhattan's more ordered districts.

Chinatown and Little Italy are best reached by taking the #6, J, M, N, Q, R or Z train to Canal Street. The Spring Street stop on the #6 is the most direct to Nolita.

Chinatown

Walk through the crowded streets of **Chinatown** at any time of day and you'll find every shop doing a brisk trade. Restaurants are packed full; storefronts display heaps of shiny squid, clawing crabs and fresh lobsters; and street markets offer overflowing piles of exotic green vegetables, garlic and ginger root. Beneath the neighbourhood's prosperous facade, however, is a darker legacy. Since 9/11, some of the most regrettable institutions associated with the area – namely non-union sweatshops – have closed, or at least moved (rising rents in Manhattan have forced these factories out to satellite Chinatowns in Queens and Brooklyn), but other sharp practices continue to flourish. Organized crime is prevalent, illegal immigrants are commonly exploited, and living conditions can be abysmal for poorer Chinese.

Outsiders, however, won't see anything sinister. The neighbourhood is a melange of vintage storefronts, modern Chinese graffiti and tourist-oriented kitsch, like pagoda roofs on phone booths. Lined with tacky shops and frequently a pedestrian traffic jam, the unappealing east–west thoroughfare of **Canal Street** is unfortunately often all visitors ever see of Chinatown – perhaps along with the inside of a *dim sum* palace on Mott Street. Explore the narrow sidestreets, though,

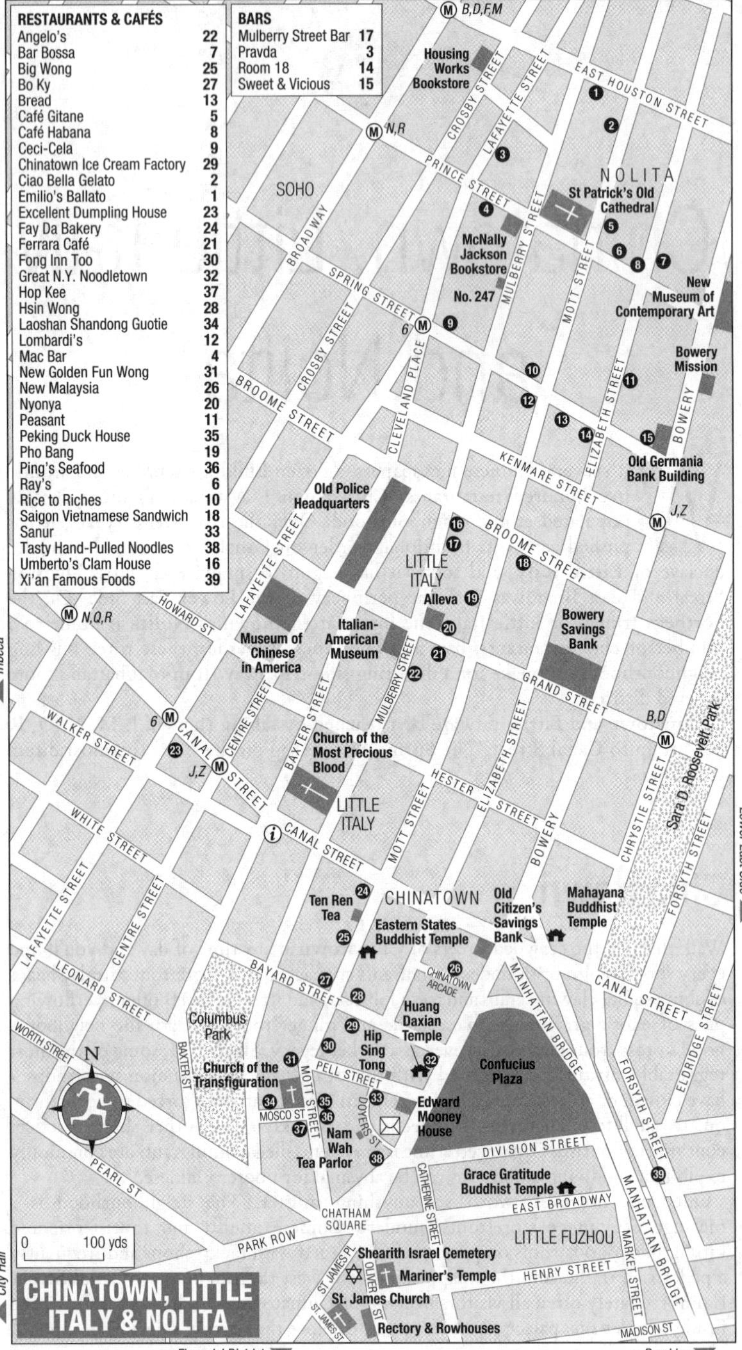
RESTAURANTS & CAFÉS
Angelo's 22
Bar Bossa 7
Big Wong 25
Bo Ky 27
Bread 13
Café Gitane 5
Café Habana 8
Ceci-Cela 9
Chinatown Ice Cream Factory 29
Ciao Bella Gelato 2
Emilio's Ballato 1
Excellent Dumpling House 23
Fay Da Bakery 24
Ferrara Café 21
Fong Inn Too 30
Great N.Y. Noodletown 32
Hop Kee 37
Hsin Wong 28
Laoshan Shandong Guotie 34
Lombardi's 12
Mac Bar 4
New Golden Fun Wong 31
New Malaysia 26
Nyonya 20
Peasant 11
Peking Duck House 35
Pho Bang 19
Ping's Seafood 36
Ray's 6
Rice to Riches 10
Saigon Vietnamese Sandwich 18
Sanur 33
Tasty Hand-Pulled Noodles 38
Umberto's Clam House 16
Xi'an Famous Foods 39
BARS
Mulberry Street Bar 17
Pravda 3
Room 18 14
Sweet & Vicious 15
East Village
Tribeca
Lower East Side
City Hall
Financial District
Brooklyn
B,D,F,M
N,R
6
J,Z
B,D
N,Q,R
Housing Works Bookstore
McNally Jackson Bookstore
No. 247
St Patrick's Old Cathedral
New Museum of Contemporary Art
Bowery Mission
Old Germania Bank Building
Old Police Headquarters
Alleva
Bowery Savings Bank
Museum of Chinese in America
Italian-American Museum
Church of the Most Precious Blood
Ten Ren Tea
Eastern States Buddhist Temple
Old Citizen's Savings Bank
Mahayana Buddhist Temple
Chinatown Arcade
Huang Daxian Temple
Hip Sing Tong
Church of the Transfiguration
Edward Mooney House
Nam Wah Tea Parlor
Confucius Plaza
Grace Gratitude Buddhist Temple
Shearith Israel Cemetery
Mariner's Temple
St. James Church
Rectory & Rowhouses
Columbus Park
Sara D. Roosevelt Park
SOHO
NOLITA
LITTLE ITALY
CHINATOWN
LITTLE FUZHOU
Chatham Square
East Houston Street
Prince Street
Spring Street
Broome Street
Kenmare Street
Grand Street
Hester Street
Canal Street
Howard St
Walker Street
White Street
Leonard Street
Worth Street
Bayard Street
Pell Street
Mosco St
Doyers St
Division Street
East Broadway
Henry Street
Madison St
Park Row
Pearl St
Broadway
Crosby Street
Lafayette Street
Mulberry Street
Mott Street
Elizabeth Street
Bowery
Cleveland Place
Centre Street
Baxter Street
Baxter St
Chrystie Street
Forsyth Street
Eldridge Street
Catherine Street
Market Street
Oliver St
St James Pl
St James St
Manhattan Bridge
N
0 100 yds
CHINATOWN, LITTLE ITALY & NOLITA

and you will be rewarded with a taste of a Chinatown that functions more for its residents than for tourists and retains many of its older traditions. **Mott Street** is the main north–south avenue, although the streets around it – Pell, Bayard, Doyers and the Bowery – also host a glut of restaurants, tea-and-rice shops and grocery stores that are fun to browse. Nowhere in this city can you **eat** so well, and so much, for so little – for restaurant recommendations, see p.311. You can pick up additional maps, brochures and coupon booklets at the **information kiosk** (daily 10am–6pm) at Canal and Baxter streets.

Some history

The first known **Cantonese** immigrant to New York arrived in 1858, and settled on Mott Street. He was not joined by significant numbers of his countrymen – and they were virtually all men – until the 1870s. By 1890, the census recorded about 12,000 Chinese. Most of these men had previously worked out West on the trans-continental railroad or in gold mines, and few intended to stay in the US. Their idea was simply to make a nest egg, then return to their families and (hopefully) a far easier life in China; as a result, the neighbourhood around the intersection of Mott and Pell streets became known as the "bachelor society". Inevitably, money took rather longer to accumulate than expected, and though some did go back, Chinatown soon became a permanent settlement. Residents made their livings as cooks, cigar vendors, sailors and operators of *fan-tan* parlours and opium dens.

By the end of the nineteenth century, the quarter was notoriously violent, in large part due to its Triad-like "tongs". These Chinese organized-crime operations

Before Chinatown was Chinatown

As is true for many of the neighbourhoods in New York City, the area that is now known as Chinatown has undergone several transformations. The first trace of another culture is the **cemetery of Congregation Shearith Israel**, just south of Chatham Square on St James Place. The oldest Jewish congregation in North America, Shearith Israel was established in New York in 1654 by a small group of Sephardim from Brazil, descendants of Jews who had fled the Spanish Inquisition. This small graveyard was in use from 1683 to 1833, but all that remains today is a collection of seventeenth- and eighteenth-century headstones. The cemetery is opened every year around Memorial Day, when a special ceremony pays tribute to those Jews interred here who died in the Revolutionary War, but at other times you can just peer through the iron railings.

Just around the corner on St James Street, the **St James Church** marks the arrival of the Irish in the mid-nineteenth century. A big Greek Revival brownstone, the church was the gathering place of the first American division of the Irish-Catholic brotherhood, the Ancient Order of Hibernians in 1836. True to the cultural mixing that is characteristic of Manhattan's slums, St James Church was founded with the help of a Cuban priest, Félix Varela, who was also instrumental in the early Catholic period of the Church of the Transfiguration on Mott Street. If you walk around the corner from St James Church to Oliver Street, you'll see the former church rectory in a row of tenement-style homes, as well as the much-worse-for-wear **Mariner's Temple**, established in 1845 and the oldest Baptist church in Manhattan (both churches tend to open only for services).

Perhaps the most overlooked anachronism is the **Edward Mooney House**, a tiny Georgian-style brick building at the corner of the Bowery and Pell Street that looks very out of step with its plastic-facade neighbours. Built in 1785, it's the oldest surviving rowhouse in New York City, erected by a merchant who saw this neighbourhood's future as a centre for commerce – today, it's occupied by a mortgage brokers.

doubled as municipal-aid societies and thrived on prostitution, gambling and the opium trade. Beginning in the waning years of the nineteenth century, the **Tong Wars** raged well into the 1930s in the form of intermittent assassinations.

Growing resentment led to the Chinese Exclusion Act of 1882, which completely forbade entry to Chinese workers for ten years, and in the early twentieth century, additional **immigration quotas**, particularly the 1924 National Origins Provision (NOP), further restricted the flow of Asians to America. In 1965, the Immigration Act did away with the NOP, and some 20,000 new Chinese immigrants, many of them women, began to arrive in Chinatown. Local businessmen took advantage of the declining midtown garment business and made use of the new, unskilled female workforce to open garment factories of their own.

The early 1990s saw another major shift, as large numbers of illegal immigrants from the Fujian province of China arrived. Unlike the established Cantonese, the **Fujianese** were largely uneducated labourers who spoke their own dialects and Mandarin. Cultural and linguistic differences made it difficult for them to find work in Chinatown, and a large number turned to more desperate means. By 1994, Fujianese-on-Fujianese violence comprised the majority of Chinatown's crime, prompting local leaders to break the neighbourhood's traditional bond of silence and call in city officials for help. Today, Cantonese is still the *lingua franca* of Chinatown; though many well-off Cantonese have moved to the outer boroughs, they remain the district's most important customers, and businesses remain largely Cantonese-owned. This combined with high rents has led many Mandarin-speaking "mainlanders" (immigrants from mainland China) to settle in Brooklyn's Sunset Park, though the southern half of **East Broadway** remains a Fujianese enclave.

Columbus Park

The southern limits of Chinatown begin just a few blocks north of City Hall Park at the intersection of Worth and Baxter streets, once the centre of the Five Points slum (see p.69). From here, **Columbus Park** stretches north, a green sward away from Chinatown's hectic consumerism. It's favoured by the neighbourhood's elderly, who congregate for morning *t'ai chi* and marathon games of *xiangqi* (Chinese chess). The park was laid out by Calvert Vaux, of Central Park fame, but little of his original plan remains – ball fields take up one end, while craggy rock-gardens are the backdrop on the north side. Facing Bayard Street, an open-air concert pavilion is a relic of the late nineteenth century.

Chatham Square and Little Fuzhou

Southeast of the park Worth Street ends at **Chatham Square**, really a concrete triangle hemmed in by traffic, where Fujianese civic organizations have erected a statue of **Lin Zexu**, a Qing-dynasty official who is revered in China for cracking down on the opium trade. Lin arrested thousands of Chinese opium dealers, destroyed 2.6 million pounds of the drug and kicked out the British opium merchants in 1839, thereby precipitating the Opium Wars. The Fujianese have cast their hero as a "pioneer in the war against drugs", according to the inscription. Also in Chatham Square is a small arch that pays tribute to Chinese-Americans killed in World War II. Just to the north looms **Confucius Plaza**, a 1970s housing complex that's still considered some of the best living quarters in Chinatown; a statue of the Chinese philosopher was erected outside in 1976.

East from Chatham Square is the "new" Chinatown – the district expanded by the Fujianese and other mainland immigrants in the past few decades. East Broadway, often dubbed **Little Fuzhou**, is the main commercial avenue, an earthy, authentic blend of bakeries, restaurants and markets. Founded in 1974 by revered Chinese monk Master Fayun, the **Grace Gratitude Buddhist Temple** (daily 10am–5pm; free; ⓣ212/925-1335) at 48 East Broadway is one of the oldest Chan (Zen) Buddhist temples in the city, a serious place of worship maintained by resident monks. The architecture is typically modern, but there's a shrine to Buddhist bodhisattva Guanyin (known as the "Goddess of Mercy") in the lobby, and the main hall is dominated by gold statues representing three incarnations of Buddha.

Pell and Doyers streets

Just to the north of Chatham Square, on the corner of **Pell Street** and the Bowery, you'll find the **Huang Daxian Temple** (daily 9am–6pm; free; ⓣ212/349-6221), one of Chinatown's few Taoist temples and, like most of them, a converted shopfront. This one is dedicated to Huang Daxian, a quasi-historical figure who is said to have lived in China in the fourth century, worshipped today for his supposed powers of healing. Better known as Wong Tai Sin in Cantonese, he remains one of the most popular Taoist deities in Hong Kong. On the other side of Pell Street stands the venerable **Edward Mooney House** (see box, p.81).

Further along Pell Street itself, no. 16 is the headquarters of the United in Victory Association, aka the **Hip Sing Tong**, where some seventy people were killed when the rival On Leong group raided the building in 1924 (the doorway is next to the Foot Rub place). Halfway along Pell is crooked **Doyers Street**. Once known as the "Bloody Angle" for its role as a battleground during the Tong Wars, there's little more malicious than barber shops operating here now.

North along Mott Street

At first glance, **Mott Street**, the "dragon's spine" of Chinatown, is a strip of tacky gift shops and countless modern teashops. Look past the kitsch, though, and you'll also find herbal-medicine vendors, traditional furniture dealers and barely renovated tenements – this is the oldest section of Chinatown. At 25 Mott St (at the corner of Mosco St), the green-domed **Church of the Transfiguration** (Sat 2–5pm, otherwise services only; free; ⓣ212/962-5157, ⓦwww.transfigurationnyc.org), is an elegant Georgian building known as the "church of immigrants" for good reason. Established here in 1801 as a Lutheran parish, it was sold to Irish Catholics fifty years later; the plaque honouring those killed in World War I lists primarily Italian names, while today, Mass is said daily in Cantonese, English and Mandarin.

Further north, the **Eastern States Buddhist Temple**, 64 Mott St (daily 8am–6pm; ⓣ212/966-6229), is the oldest temple on the East Coast. Established in 1962 by the Ying family (originally from Ningbo, China), the room's linoleum floors and dropped ceiling make it more functional than fancy. The main deity here is Sakyamuni Buddha, but note also the glass-encased gold statue of the "four-faced Buddha", a replica of the revered image in Bangkok's Erawan Shrine. Tea lovers should cross the street to **Ten Ren Tea**, 75 Mott St (daily 10am–8pm; ⓣ212/349-228), the lauded Taiwanese tea merchant, which sells everything from cheap green tea to expensive oolongs.

Canal and Grand streets

Say "Canal Street" to most New Yorkers, and they'll think not of a real canal (which this busy thoroughfare was until 1820), but of counterfeit handbags, which you'll see on sale in nearly every shop you pass. A casual stroll here is impossible;

▲ Buddha images for sale, Canal Street

the streets are lined with food vendors, souvenir stalls and hawkers talking up their knock-off bargains – foot traffic often grinds to a halt.

Toward the east end of Canal, at the junction with the Bowery, the former **Citizen's Savings Bank** is something of a local landmark, its neo-Byzantine bronze dome looming majestically above the chaotic streets. Completed in 1924, it now functions as a branch of HSBC (Mon–Fri 8.30am–5pm, Sat & Sun 10am–2pm); enter on Canal Street to take a look at the interior of the dome and its four surviving murals: Thrift, Success, Safety and Wisdom (no photography allowed).

Chinese influence is more obvious at the gilded **Mahayana Buddhist Temple**, at 133 Canal St opposite (daily 8am–6pm; free; ⓣ212/925-8787), much more lavish than its counterpart on Mott Street (it was established in 1997 by the same family). Candlelight and blue neon glow around the giant gold Buddha on the main altar, while along the walls are 32 plaques that tell the story of Buddha's life. Despite the assault of red and gold, it's a surprisingly peaceful place. The entrance hall contains a smaller shrine to Guanyin (p.83), and the small shop upstairs sells books and statues.

Canal Street channels its eastbound traffic onto the **Manhattan Bridge**, which crosses the East River to Brooklyn, completed in 1909. The grand Beaux Arts arch over the centre lanes (modelled on the Porte St-Denis in Paris), looks a bit out of place compared to the neon signs and abandoned Chinese cinemas gathered around the piers below, but it's in good company with the regal **Bowery Savings Bank**, two blocks north of Canal on the Bowery, at the corner of Grand Street (the city's main east–west avenue in the 1800s). Designed by Stanford White in 1894, today the building is a posh location for private dinners and functions known as Capitale, and sadly off-limits to casual visitors.

Museum of Chinese in America

The slickly presented **Museum of Chinese in America** (Mon & Fri 11am–5pm, Thurs 11am–9pm, Sat & Sun 10am–5pm; $7, free Thurs; ⓣ212/619-4785, ⓦwww.mocanyc.org) moved into new premises at 215 Centre St (just south of Grand St) in 2009. Designed by Maya Lin (best known for her Vietnam Veterans Memorial in Washington DC) in an old red-brick warehouse, its core exhibition provides an historical overview of the Chinese-American experience from 1784 to the present, through an evocative blend of multimedia displays, artefacts and filmed interviews of real people. Some of the issues tackled are the Chinese Exclusion Act of 1882, the emergence of "Chop-Suey" restaurants and bigoted "Yellowface" movies in the 1930s, and the identity of second-generation Chinese-Americans since the 1960s. Galleries are arranged around a sunlit courtyard reminiscent of a traditional Chinese house, and include temporary exhibitions of Chinese and Chinese-American art.

Little Italy

Bounded roughly by Canal Street to the south, Houston Street to the north, Mulberry Street to the east and Broadway to the west, **Little Italy** is light years away from the solid ethnic enclave of old, but it's still fun for a stroll and a decent cappuccino on the hoof. The area was settled in the latter half of the nineteenth century by a huge influx of Italian immigrants, who supplanted the district's earlier Irish inhabitants and, like their Chinese and Jewish counterparts, clannishly cut themselves off to recreate the Old Country; even streets were claimed by different regions, with settlers from Campania and Naples on Mulberry, Sicilians on Elizabeth, and Mott Street divided between Calabrians (south end) and immigrants from Puglia (north end). After World War II, the Italians started moving out of the city (though Robert De Niro roamed the area in the 1950s), and the neighbourhood is much smaller and more commercial than it once was, with Chinatown encroaching on three sides – Mulberry Street is the only Italian territory south of Broome Street.

If you walk north on Mulberry from Chinatown to get here, the transition from the throngs south of Canal to the kitsch of today's Little Italy can be a little difficult to stomach. The red, green and white tinsel decorations along Mulberry Street and the suited hosts who aggressively lure out-of-town visitors to their restaurants are undeniable signs that the neighbourhood is little more than a tourist trap. Few Italians still live here, though a number still visit for a dose of nostalgia, some Frank Sinatra and a plate of fully *Americano* spaghetti with red sauce. For a more vibrant, if workaday, Italian-American experience, you'll want to head to Belmont in the Bronx (see p.257).

This is not to advise missing out on Little Italy altogether. Some original bakeries and *salumerias* (Italian specialty food stores) do survive, and there, amid the imported cheeses, sausages and salamis hanging from the ceiling, you can buy sandwiches made with slabs of mozzarella or eat slices of fresh focaccia. In addition, you'll still find plenty of places to indulge with a cappuccino and a pastry, not least of which is *Ferrara's*, 195 Grand St, the oldest and most popular café. Another establishment of note is the belt-defying *Lombardi's*, 32 Spring St, which is not only the city's oldest pizzeria but also one of its finest. For more on Little Italy's comestibles, see p.288 and p.312.

Along Mulberry Street

Little Italy's main strip, **Mulberry Street** is an almost solid row of restaurants and cafés – and is therefore filled with tourists. The street is particularly lively, if a bit like a theme park, at night, when the lights come on and the streets fill with restaurant hosts who shout menu specials at passers-by. If you're here in mid-September, the eleven-day **Festa di San Gennaro** (see p.428) is a wild and tacky celebration of the patron saint of Naples. Italians from all over the city converge on Mulberry Street, and the area is filled with street stalls and numerous Italian fast-food and snack vendors. The festivities centre on the 1892 **Church of the Most Precious Blood**, 109 Mulberry St (main entrance on Baxter St), providing visitors with a chance to see the inside of this small church, which is normally closed.

None of the eating places around here really stands out, but 129 Mulberry at Hester Street, the former site of *Umberto's Clam House* (now relocated two blocks north), was quite notorious in its time: in 1972, it was the scene of a vicious gangland murder when "Crazy Joey" Gallo was shot dead while celebrating his birthday with his wife and stepdaughter. Gallo, a big talker and ruthless businessman, was keen to protect his interests in Brooklyn; he was alleged to have offended a rival family and so paid the price. Today, the space is occupied by run-of-the-mill *Da Gennaro* restaurant. For a more tangible Mafia vibe, you can't beat the 1908 *Mulberry Street Bar*, at no. 176 1/2, where the back room, all fogged mirrors and tile floors, has been the setting for numerous Mob movies and episodes of *The Sopranos*. Incidentally, the very real Gambino crime family ran operations from the **Ravenite Social Club**, 247 Mulberry St, between Prince and Spring (now a posh shoe shop); boss John Gotti went to jail in 1992 (his son John Gotti Jr claims to have renounced crime).

At the corner of Mulberry and Grand streets, **Alleva Dairy** (Mon–Sat 8.30am–6pm, Sun 8.30am–3pm; free; ⓣ212/226-7990, ⓦwww.allevadairy.com) was established in 1892 and claims to be the oldest cheese-maker in the US – perhaps true if the definition of cheese is limited to mozzarella and ricotta.

Italian-American Museum and Old Police HQ

To learn more about the historic roots of the area, stop by the **Italian-American Museum** (Wed–Sun 11am–6pm, Fri until 8pm; July–Sept Fri–Sun only; donation $5; ⓣ212/965-9000, ⓦwww.italianamericanmuseum.org), housed in the former Banca Stabile, at 155 Mulberry St, opposite Alleva. The bank opened in 1885 and offered services to immigrants, including translation, letter writing, wire transfers and travel booking. The building still contains the old vault and banking machines, enhanced by small but enlightening exhibits on the old neighbourhood and Stabile family business – though the bank closed in 1932, the family maintained their other businesses here until the 1960s. Look out for a brutal extortion note from 1914, written by a member of the "Black Hand" to a local business owner, and the display about Giuseppe Petrosino, one of the first Italian-American NYPD officers, who was murdered working a case in Sicily in 1909 (see also p.62). The museum hopes to expand into the adjacent buildings over the next few years.

Wander one block west of Mulberry on Grand Street to see the grandeur of the **Old Police Headquarters** (closed to the public), a palatial 1909 Neoclassical construction between Baxter and Centre streets. Meant to cow would-be criminals into obedience with its high-rise copper dome and lavish ornamentation, it was more or less a complete failure: the blocks immediately surrounding the edifice were some of the most corrupt in the city in the early twentieth century. Police headquarters moved to a bland modern building near City Hall in 1973, and the overbearing palace was converted in 1987 into luxury condominiums. Residents have included Calvin Klein, Winona Ryder and Christy Turlington; one-bedroom apartments were selling for $4 million in 2010.

Nolita

The blocks surrounding St Patrick's Old Cathedral, particularly north to Houston and east to the Bowery, were rechristened **Nolita** ("North of Little Italy") by savvy real estate developers in the late 1990s. Stylish shop-owners are the newest variety of immigrant here, as numerous tiny boutiques have taken over former Italian haunts. Most are above Spring Street, but the trendiness has spread south, too. Although this district is not cheap by any means, it is a bit more personal and less status-mad than much of neighbouring Soho. The shops showcase handmade shoes, custom swimwear and items with vintage flair, often sold by the designers themselves, or at least by obsessive buyers who have strong affection for the goodies they've collected from elsewhere.

If you're not interested in shopping, you should definitely check out the **New Museum of Contemporary Art** on the Bowery, a stylish showcase for the latest trends in multimedia art. Nolita is also an appealing place to put up your feet after a long walking tour. Choose from any of the numerous restaurants (p.312), or head to the café inside the **McNally Jackson** bookstore, 52 Prince St (Mon–Sat 10am–10pm, Sun 10am–8pm), or the **Housing Works Bookstore Café**, 126 Crosby St (Mon–Fri 10am–9pm, Sat & Sun noon–7pm).

St Patrick's Old Cathedral

St Patrick's Old Cathedral (daily except Wed 8am–6pm; free; ⓣ212/226-8075, ⓦwww.oldcathedral.org) at the corner of Mott and Prince streets, is the spiritual heart of Little Italy and the oldest Catholic cathedral in the city. When it was consecrated in 1815, it served the Irish immigrant community and hosted the Roman Catholic archdiocese in New York. Catholic leadership has moved uptown to a newer St Patrick's Cathedral on Fifth Avenue at 50th Street, relegating "old St Pat's" to the status of a parish church. It now serves English-, Spanish- and Chinese-speaking worshippers. Designed by Joseph-François Mangin, the architect behind City Hall, the building is grand Gothic Revival, with an 85ft vault, a gleaming gilt altar and a massive pipe organ that was installed in 1868, when the church was restored following a terrible fire.

Equally notable is the **cemetery** behind the church, which is ringed with a brick wall that the Ancient Order of Hibernians used as a defence in 1835, when anti-Irish rioters threatened to burn down the church. The cemetery is almost always locked, but try to peek through one of the gates – you may recognize the view from a scene in Martin Scorsese's *Mean Streets* (one of the few parts of the movie actually shot here, even though the film was set in Little Italy).

The Bowery

Forming the boundary between Nolita and the Lower East Side, **the Bowery** was until relatively recently a byword for poverty and destitution, America's original **skid row**. At its peak in 1949, around 14,000 homeless people could be found here, most dossing down in hostels known as flophouses. Today, only a few flophouses remain, and these mostly cater to Chinese labourers at the southern end of the Bowery. The street runs north from Chatham Square in Chinatown to Cooper Square in the East Village, where it is increasingly lined with smart, contemporary buildings (see p.99).

The current gentrification of this wide thoroughfare is just the latest of many changes over the years: the street takes its name from *bouwerie*, the Dutch word for farm, when it was the city's main agricultural supplier. In the nineteenth century, it was flanked by music halls, opera houses, vaudeville theatres, hotels and middle-market restaurants, drawing people from all parts of Manhattan – including opera lover **Walt Whitman** (see box, p.222). The good times did not last, and by the early twentieth century the street was becoming associated with crime and poverty, attracting religious and social welfare institutions like the **Bowery Mission**, which opened in 1880. The Bowery's notoriety immortalized it in literature, with many writers making use of its less than stellar reputation. Theodore Dreiser closed his 1900 tragedy *Sister Carrie* with a suicide in a Bowery flophouse, while fifty years later William S. Burroughs alluded to the area in a story that complained of bums waiting to "waylay one in the Bowery". The Great Depression signalled a low-point in the Bowery's fortunes, and between the 1940s and 1980s the whole strip was synonymous with bums, alcoholics and the homeless. Those days are largely gone, and though pockets of the old Bowery remain (check out the graffiti-smothered walls of the 1899 **old Germania Bank Building**, at no. 190, at the corner of Spring Street, actually the home of photographer Jay Maisel), wine stores, galleries and high-end apartments are becoming far more prevalent.

New Museum of Contemporary Art

Two blocks east of St Patrick's Old Cathedral, the **New Museum of Contemporary Art** (Wed, Sat & Sun noon–6pm, Thurs & Fri noon–9pm; $12, free after 7pm Thurs; Ⓣ212/219-1222, Ⓦwww.newmuseum.org) is a powerful symbol of the Bowery's rebirth. The building itself, at 235 Bowery opposite Prince Street, is as much the attraction as the avant-garde work inside, a stack of seven shimmering aluminium boxes designed by Tokyo-based architects Kazuyo Sejima and Ryue Nishizawa.

An industrial elevator glides between the four main floors, each holding one exhibition space. The warehouse-like galleries, all brilliant white with shiny concrete floors, are spacious but still small enough to digest without overdosing on the often thought-provoking and diverse range of temporary exhibits inside. The **shop** in the lobby has a fabulous book section and café, while the **Sky Room** on the 7th floor opens at weekends for rare views across the Lower East Side and Nolita. Lively guided **tours** (free) take place at 12.30pm Wednesday to Sunday, and also 3pm on Saturday and Sunday; free iPod audio tours are also available at the visitor desk in the lobby.

6

The Lower East Side

Historically the epitome of the American ethnic melting pot, the **Lower East Side** – bordered to the north by Houston Street, the south by East Broadway, the east by the East River and the west by the Bowery – is one of Manhattan's most enthralling downtown neighbourhoods. A fair proportion of its inhabitants are working-class Dominicans and Chinese, but among them you're also likely to find small Jewish communities, students, moneyed artsy types, and hipster refugees from the more gentrified areas of Soho and the East Village. Many visitors come for the shopping; most of the city's best vintage-clothing and furniture stores are here, which has in turn attracted a number of emerging designers as well. The plethora of drinking, dancing and food options also draws large crowds every night of the week.

To begin your tour of the neighbourhood, take the #F train to Lower East Side–Second Avenue or Delancey Street. For information about local events and tours, visit the **Lower East Side Visitor Center** at 54 Orchard St, between Hester and Grand streets (Mon–Fri 9am–5pm, Sat & Sun 10am–4pm; Ⓣ212/226-9010, Ⓦwww.lowereastsideny.com). For **tours** of the neighbourhood's Jewish heritage (and to gain entrance into some of the otherwise private synagogues), contact the **Lower East Side Conservancy** (Ⓣ212/374-4100, Ⓦwww.nycjewishtours.org).

Some history

Most of this area was owned by the pro-British DeLancey family until 1787, when it was confiscated and sold off by the new American government (Delancey St is named after James DeLancey, and Orchard St recalls his farm). The first tenement buildings in the city were constructed on the Lower East Side in 1833, and the development of **Kleindeutschland** (Little Germany) along the Bowery followed closely behind in 1840. By 1860, Irish immigrants had started to dominate the neighbourhood, and by the end of the nineteenth century it was attracting international humanitarian attention as an insular slum for over half a million **Jews**, the most densely populated spot in the world. Mainly from Eastern Europe, these refugees came to America in search of a better life, but instead found themselves scratching out a living in a free-for-all of textile sweatshops and pushcarts. By the 1880s, the area had become America's **garment capital**, and by 1900, seventy percent of the nation's women's clothing was manufactured here – today, there are still over 100 small garment factories in the Lower East Side. For many Jews, the entertainment industry was the only way out; comedian George Burns, composer Ira Gershwin and William Fox, founder of the Fox Film Corporation, all grew up here.

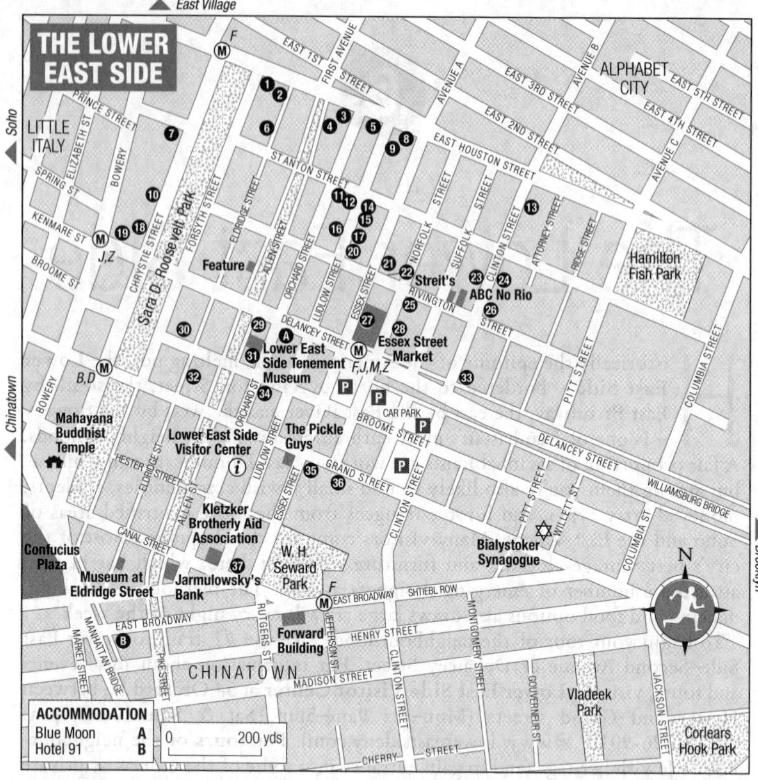

RESTAURANTS & CAFÉS			
Cibao Restaurant	26	Sammy's Roumanian Steakhouse	18
Congee Village	29	Schiller's Liquor Bar	25
DessertTruck Works	13	Shopsin's	27
Doughnut Plant	36	Stanton Social	12
Il Laboratorio del Gelato	31	Sugar Sweet Sunshine	22
Katz's Deli	5	Vanessa's Dumpling House	32
Kossar's	35	WD-50	24
Les Enfants Terribles	37	Yonah Schimmel Knish Bakery	1
Mikey's Burger	20		
Russ & Daughters	3		

BARS		NIGHTLIFE	
Back Room	28	Arlene's Grocery	11
Barramundi	23	bOb Bar	6
Barrio Chino	34	Bowery Ballroom	19
The Delancey	33	Cake Shop	17
Happy Ending Lounge	30	The Living Room	15
Kush	10	Mercury Lounge	8
Libation	16	Pianos	14
Magician	21	Rockwood Music Hall	4
Max Fish	9	Sapphire Lounge	2
		Stanton Public	7

Low standards of hygiene and abysmal housing made disease rife and life expectancy low: in 1875, the infant mortality rate was forty percent, mainly due to cholera. It was conditions like these that spurred reformers like Jacob Riis and Stephen Crane to record the plight of the city's immigrants in writing and photographs, thereby spawning not only a whole school of journalism but also some notable changes in urban planning.

The **Chinese** and **Dominicans** moved into the area in the 1980s, but it wasn't until the 1990s that the Lower East Side saw high-end development when retro clubs, chic bars, gourmet restaurants and unique boutiques sprouted up all over. Despite the changes, the area clings to its immigrant roots; about forty percent of the people living here were born in another country, with a quarter of residents Spanish-speaking, and around twenty percent from China and other parts of East Asia.

Houston Street to Grand Street

South of Houston Street, **Jewish** immigrants indelibly stamped their character on the Lower East Side with their shops, delis, restaurants and synagogues. Even now, with Chinatown overflowing into the neighbourhood, the area exhibits remnants of its Jewish past: on Houston itself, you'll find *Katz's Deli* at no. 205, at the corner of Ludlow; *Russ & Daughters* at no. 179, at the corner with Orchard; and venerable knish-maker *Yonah Schimmel*, farther west at no. 137 (see p.289 for reviews).

Ludlow and Orchard streets

When a few artsy types discovered the then run-down, shabby **Ludlow Street** in the early 1990s, it sparked a hipster migration south from the East Village. Between 1992 and 1997, Aaron Rose ran the **Alleged Gallery** at 172 Ludlow St between Houston and Stanton streets, a dynamic focal point for urban artists involved with skateboarding, graffiti and independent film dubbed "**The Beautiful Losers**". The artists are long gone, and today the street is home to fashion boutiques (no. 172 is the Marmalade vintage clothing store), cafés and bars.

Walking south, the southwest corner of Ludlow and Rivington Street is where the cover for **Paul's Boutique**, the 1989 Beastie Boys album, was shot (it's now the *Three Monkeys* café, with photos of the group and the album cover inside). The musical connections continue south of Grand Street at 56 Ludlow, where **The Velvet Underground** lived and recorded in 1965.

Running parallel to Ludlow south of Houston is **Orchard Street**, centre of the so-called **Bargain District**. This area is at its best on Sundays, when the street is closed to traffic between Houston and Delancey, and it's filled with stalls and store-fronts hawking discounted designer clothes and accessories.

Lower East Side Tenement Museum

Even if you don't have the time to tour the Lower East Side extensively, make sure you visit the **Lower East Side Tenement Museum** (Ⓣ212/431-0233, Ⓦwww.tenement.org), an 1863 tenement building at 97 Orchard St, restored

▲ Lower East Side Tenement Museum

by the museum founders in the 1990s (it had been abandoned since 1935). If you've visited Ellis Island (p.47), this museum continues the immigrant story: guides do a brilliant job bringing to life the building's (and the neighbourhood's) past and present, aided by documents, photographs and artefacts found on site, concentrating on the area's multiple ethnic heritages. This will probably be your only chance to see the claustrophobic, crumbling interior of a tenement, with its deceptively elegant, though ghostly, entry hall and two communal toilets for every four families. Various apartments inside have been renovated with period furnishings to reflect the lives of its tenants, from the mid-nineteenth century when there was no plumbing (or indoor toilets), electricity or heat, to the mid-twentieth century when many families ran cottage industries out of their apartments.

The tenement is accessible only by various themed **guided tours** (every 15–30min, 10.30am–5pm; 1hr; $20); for tickets, go to the museum's **visitor centre** at 108 Orchard St (daily 10am–6pm), where you can also watch a couple of introductory videos (20min, on permanent loop) and peruse the bookshop. Plans are afoot to open a new centre across the road at 103 Orchard St, and an 1870s German saloon at no. 97 in late 2010.

Tours include "Getting By: Weathering the Great Depressions of 1873 and 1929", which focuses on a German-Jewish family and an Italian family; "The Moores", which examines the grim life of an Irish family 1868–69; and the kid-friendly "Confino Living History Tour" (Sat & Sun 1pm & 3pm only). The museum also offers a 1hr 30min **walking tour** of the neighbourhood (April–Dec 1pm & 3pm; $20); this is designed to complement the tenement tours, so it's best to do it second. For all tours, come early or book in advance.

Delancey and Essex streets

Orchard Street bisects **Delancey Street**, once the horizontal axis of the old Jewish Lower East Side, now a tacky boulevard leading to the **Williamsburg Bridge** and Brooklyn. Two blocks east, at Delancey and Essex, sprawls the **Essex Street Market** (Mon–Sat 8am–6pm; Ⓦwww.essexstreetmarket.com), erected under the aegis of Mayor LaGuardia in 1939, when pushcarts were made illegal. Here you'll find all sorts of fresh fruit, fish and vegetables, along with artisan chocolates, cheese and *Shopsin's* restaurant (p.314). Two blocks south of Delancey, 49 Essex St is home to **The Pickle Guys** (Mon–Thurs & Sun 9am–6pm, Fri 9am–4pm; Ⓣ212/656-9739, Ⓦwww.pickleguys.com), where people line up outside the store to buy fresh home-made pickles, olives and other yummy picnic staples from huge barrels of garlicky brine.

Rivington Street

One block north of Delancey Street on Essex, **Rivington Street** epitomizes the fashionable face of the Lower East Side, with a string of hip bars and restaurants – it's supposedly Lady Gaga's favourite place for a drink (the fashion-forward singer got her start in the Lower East Side).

Walking east beyond Suffolk Street takes you to **Streit's** (Mon–Thurs 9am–4.30pm; Ⓦwww.streitsmatzos.com), 148 Rivington St, maker of fine matzo (a cracker-like flatbread) and kosher foods for Passover on this spot since 1925 – another survivor of the old Jewish neighbourhood.

Next door, the welded gate composed of old gears and scrap metal distinguishes **ABC No Rio**, 156 Rivington St (Ⓣ212/254-3697, Ⓦwww.abcnorio.org). This long-downtrodden but still vibrant community arts centre has hosted gallery shows, raucous concerts, a 'zine library, art installations and the like since 1980. Despite an extensive and ongoing renovation, the centre still runs Hardcore/Punk Matinees every Saturday at 3.30pm, and the Sunday Open Series of poetry readings at 3pm each week, featuring new works by local neighbourhood poets and writers.

Canal Street and around

Though the southern part of the Lower East Side has largely been absorbed by Chinatown, the area used to be an important hub for the Jewish community. To get a feel for the old quarter, start on **Canal Street** at Eldridge Street, two blocks west of Orchard. Just south of Canal, at 12 Eldridge St (opposite a row of bustling noodle joints), you'll find the thoroughly absorbing **Museum at Eldridge Street** (Mon–Thurs & Sun 10am–5pm by tour only; $10, free Mon 10am–noon; ⓣ212/219-0888, ⓦwww.eldridgestreet.org). Completed in 1887 as the first **synagogue** constructed by Eastern European Orthodox Jews in the US, the painstakingly restored site opened as a museum in 2007. It's still one of the neighbourhood jewels: the facade is a grand brick and terracotta hybrid of Romanesque, Moorish and Gothic influences, but the real highlight is the **main sanctuary** upstairs, a gasp-inducing space with rich woodwork, painted ceiling, giant chandelier and original stained-glass windows, including the west-wing rose window – a spectacular Star of David roundel. The **women's balcony** offers a closer view of the artwork, while displays show just how dilapidated the synagogue had become by the early 1970s. The synagogue is a functioning house of worship, but you can visit the interior on half-hourly **guided tours** (last tour 4pm; 1hr), which also provide plenty of entertaining stories about the neighbourhood. Tours begin at the lower level, where the **Bes Medrash** or "House of Study" also serves as a synagogue, and there's a shop and the Limud Center; the interactive computer displays here offer further insights into the history of the building.

East on Canal Street at nos. 54–58, above the row of food and electrical stores, is the ornate facade of **Sender Jarmulowsky's Bank**, dwarfing the buildings around it. Founded in 1873 by a Russian-Jewish peddler who made his fortune reselling ship tickets, the bank catered to the financial needs of the area's non-English-speaking immigrants. Jarmulowsky, who was dubbed the "East Side J.P. Morgan", and became the first president and key benefactor of the Eldridge Street Synagogue (see above), died less than a month after the current building was completed in 1912. As the threat of war in Europe grew, the bank was plagued by runs and riots, and in 1917 it finally collapsed; on its closure, thousands lost what little savings they had accumulated. The building is currently vacant but may end up as apartments or a hotel.

At the corner of Canal and Ludlow streets, the **Kletzker Brotherly Aid Association** building at 41 Canal St is a relic of a time when Jewish towns set up their own lodges (in this case, the town was Kletzk, in modern-day Belarus) to provide community healthcare and Jewish burials, assistance for widows and other similar services. Today, it's a Chinese funeral home, though if you walk around the corner, the second entrance at 5 Ludlow St still displays the Kletzker name and establishment date of 1892. The once-prominent Star of David here has been removed by the new owners, but look closely and you can still see its faded outline.

East Broadway

Canal Street ends at **East Broadway**, now almost exclusively a Fujianese enclave but once a thriving Jewish neighbourhood. At the junction between the two streets, the handsome **Forward Building** at 175 East Broadway became the headquarters of the influential Jewish daily *The Forward* in 1912, with adjacent Straus Square a hangout for radicals and activists (the building features carved bas-relief portraits of Karl Marx and Friedrich Engels).

The section of East Broadway between Clinton and Montgomery streets is known as **Shtiebl Row**, once home to dozens of storefront *shtieblach* (small congregations) but now lined by ugly housing projects on the north side. Several remain in the historic rowhouses on the south side of the street, however, often marked by small signs in Hebrew; the **Congregation Beth Hachasidim De Polen**, a branch of Agudath Israel of America, a leading Orthodox organization, is at 233 East Broadway. The best way to see inside any of the *shtieblach* is to contact the Lower East Side Conservancy (p.89).

The **Bialystoker Synagogue** (Ⓦwww.bialystoker.org), near the junction of Grand and East Broadway at 7 Willett St, was built in 1826 as a Methodist Church and purchased by the Beth Haknesseth Anshe Bialystok Congregation in 1905. Sombre grey stone on the outside, hemmed in by grim housing projects, the synagogue's sanctuary is a trove of stained glass, gold leaf and exuberant murals of zodiac signs, all beautifully restored. There's also a balcony door that was used to hide slaves as part of the Underground Railway, and a memorial plaque to the gangster Bugsy Siegel (aka Benjamin Siegel), who worshipped here as a child. To get a **tour** inside (Mon–Thurs 7–10am; free), you'll have to call Hondo Abramowitz in advance at Ⓣ212/475-0165 – unless there's a service, it's usually locked up.

The East Village

Like the Lower East Side to the south, **the East Village**, which extends east from Broadway to the East River and north from Houston Street to 14th Street, was once a solidly working-class refuge for immigrants. In the middle part of the twentieth century, rents began to rise in Greenwich Village, sending New York's nonconformist intelligentsia scurrying here, and by the 1960s the East Village was at the height of its irreverent, creative and often lawless period.

Since the 1990s, however, the area's panoply of restaurants and bars, never mind its proximity to NYU, have ensured that rents here are almost – although not quite – as insane as those in the neighbouring West Village, and the East Village is now no longer the hotbed of dissidence and artistry it once was. You're likely to see a pretty standard cross section of boutiques, thrift stores and record shops patronized by more tourists, students and uptowners than authentic bohemians these days, but thoughtful resistance to the status quo can still be found, and the neighbourhood is home to some of the cheapest bars and restaurants downtown (see p.315).

The East Village's cultural heritage

Over the years, the East Village has been home to its share of **famous artists**, **politicos** and **literati**: W.H. Auden lived at 77 St Mark's Place between 1953 and 1972; years earlier, the Communist journal *Novy Mir* operated from the basement, numbering among its contributors Leon Trotsky, who lived for a brief time in New York. In the 1950s, the East Village became one of the main New York haunts of the **Beat poets** – Kerouac, Burroughs, Ginsberg – who, when not riding trains across the country, would get together at Ginsberg's house on East 7th Street for declamatory readings; Ginsberg wrote *Kaddish* at 170 East 2nd St in 1961, as tribute to his mother, Naomi. Later, Andy Warhol debuted the Velvet Underground at the *Fillmore East*, which played host to just about every band you've ever heard of – and forgotten about – before becoming *The Saint* (also now defunct), a gay disco famous for its three-day parties. In 1973, Puerto Rican artists established the **Nuyorican Poets Café** on East 3rd Street (p.378), a haven for up-and-coming New York poets and writers. By the 1980s, the East Village was best known for its **radical visual artists**, including Keith Haring, Jeff Koons and Jean-Michel Basquiat, while gay icon **Quentin Crisp** lived at 46 East 3rd St from 1981 till his death in 1999.

Toward the end of the 1980s, the neighbourhood was the centre of a different kind of attention: the city evicted the homeless from Tompkins Square Park, and the neighbourhood's many dead-broke squatter artists were forced out, a story memorialized in the hit Broadway musical **Rent**. With suitable irony, the show has made millions of dollars since its debut in 1996, and was successfully adapted for the big screen in 2005 – its Broadway run finally ended in 2008.

EAST VILLAGE

ACCOMMODATION

Bowery Hotel	B
East Village Bed and Coffee	A
Whitehouse Hotel of New York	C

NIGHTLIFE

Louis 649	18
Pyramid Club	42

BARS

7B	41
Angel's Share	24
Bar Veloce	6
Bourgeois Pig	38
Burp Castle	35
Cozy Café Hookah Lounge	62
Croxley Ales	56
d.b.a.	55
Decibel	22
Grassroots Tavern	29
Hi Fi	11
Holiday Cocktail Lounge	26
KGB Bar	50
Lakeside Lounge	12
The Lobby Bar	B
Manitoba's	43
McSorley's Old Ale House	34
The Sunburnt Cow	28
Temple Bar	63
Von	59
Zum Schneider	39

RESTAURANTS & CAFÉS

Angelica Kitchen	5
Artichoke	1
B & H Dairy	31
Boca Chica	61
Bond Street	54
Brick Lane Curry House	46
Caracas Arepa Bar	36
Crif Dogs	27
Curry-Ya	13
De Robertis	9
DBGB Kitchen & Bar	64
Dok Suni	33
Dos Toros Taqueria	2
Five Points	52
Frank	48
Graffiti Food & Wine Bar	14
Hasaki	19
Haveli	45
Hecho en Dumbo	51
Il Buco	58
Il Posto Accanto	57
Ippudo	15
Jack's Luxury Oyster Bar	44
Lavagna	49
Liquiteria	7
Luke's Lobster	37
Mama's Food Shop	53
Mamoun's Falafel	30
Momofuku Milk Bar	3
Momofuku Noodle Bar	10
Otafuku	21
Pommes Frites	32
Porchetta	40
Prune	60
Robataya NY	16
Rhong-Tiam	47
Sarita's Mac & Cheese	4
Spot Dessert Bar	25
This Little Piggy Had Roast Beef	17
Tsampa	20
Veniero's Pasticceria & Café	8
Veselka	23

0 500 yds

The East Village can best be reached by taking the #6 train to Astor Place, or the R and N trains to the 8th Street station. Information and walking tours ($25) are provided by the **East Village Visitor Center**, 61 East 4th St, between Bowery and Second Avenue (Tues–Sat 1–6pm; Ⓣ212/228-4670, Ⓦeastvillage visitorscenter.com).

Noho

Squashed between Astor Place, the Bowery, Broadway and Houston Street, **Noho** (*No*rth of *Ho*uston) was considered part of the East Village until the name was invented by a group of local activists in the 1970s. All that's left to hint that this might once have been more than a down-at-heel gathering of industrial buildings is **Colonnade Row**, a strip of four 1833 Greek Revival houses just south of Astor Place on Lafayette Street. Originally over twice as long, the row was constructed as residences for the likes of Cornelius Vanderbilt; it now contains the Astor Place Theater (longtime home to The Blue Man Group; see p.367). The stocky brownstone-and-brick building across Lafayette was once the **Astor Library**. Built with a bequest from John Jacob Astor between 1853 and 1881 (in a belated gesture of *noblesse oblige*), it was the first public library in New York. It became the **Public Theater** in 1967, under the direction of Joseph Papp, founder of Shakespeare in the Park (see p.368).

A quick detour east onto East 4th Street takes you to the **Merchant's House Museum** at no. 29 (Mon & Thurs–Sun noon–5pm; $8; Ⓣ212/777-1089, Ⓦwww.merchantshouse.com). Constructed in 1832, this elegant Federal-style rowhouse offers a rare and intimate glimpse of domestic life in New York during the 1850s. The house was purchased by Seabury Tredwell in 1835, a successful metal merchant. Remarkably, much of the mid-nineteenth-century interior remains in pristine condition, largely thanks to Seabury's daughter Gertrude, who lived here until 1933 – it was preserved as a museum three years later. Folders loaded with information provide ample material for a self-guided tour of the house, providing fascinating background, anecdotes and quotes from the family, their servants and neighbours. Highlights include furniture fashioned by New York's best cabinet-makers, the mahogany four-poster beds upstairs (where both Gertrude and Seabury passed away) and the tiny brass bells in the basement, used to summon the servants.

From here, the site of the legendary underground music club **CBGB** is just a few blocks south, at 315 Bowery. The New York **punk-rock** scene began here in the 1970s, famously hosting bands such as **the Ramones**, **Blondie**, **Patti Smith** and the **Talking Heads**. In 2003, the city renamed the corner of East 2nd Street and the Bowery "Joey Ramone Place", in honour of the late punk legend. The club finally closed in 2006, and in a sign of the times has become a John Varvatos fashion boutique (Mon–Sat noon–9pm, Sun noon–7pm); designer clothes and vinyl records are displayed in the original, dimly lit interior, with walls plastered with punk memorabilia.

Another vestige of the East Village's radical past lies across the Bowery at 9 Bleecker St, where the **Yippie Museum and Café** (daily 10am–10pm, depending on events; Ⓣ212/677-5918, Ⓦwww.yippiemuseum.org) hosts informal concerts and readings at the weekends. The museum moniker is slightly misleading, but it's still an interesting place to visit, with the cheapest coffee (organic) in the area ($0.75), free wi-fi and a cosy lounge loaded with radical magazines and flyers. The counterculture/anti-war group, led by Abbie Hoffman (who died in 1989), has been based here since 1973, despite being regularly faced with eviction. Some of the old characters that staff the café run tours of Yippie-related sights in the area (Thurs 1pm; $10).

Astor Place

At Third Avenue and East 8th Street lies **Astor Place**, named for real-estate tycoon John Jacob Astor. Infamous for his greed, Astor was the wealthiest person in the US at the time of his death in 1848 (worth $115 billion in modern terms). Beneath the replicated old-fashioned kiosk of the Astor Place subway station, the platform walls sport reliefs of beavers, recalling Astor's first big killings – in the fur trade. The teen hangout here is the balancing black steel cube *Alamo* (1967) by Tony Rosenthal, which dominates the centre of the intersection.

Astor Place Opera House (now gone) was erected on the corner of Astor Place and East 8th Street in 1847, infamous as the site of the **Astor Place Riot** just two years later. Ostensibly the result of a dispute between English Shakespearean actor William Macready and local stage-star Edwin Forrest, the riot exposed the bitter class divisions of the time; Macready was supported by Anglophile, upper-class theatre lovers, while Forrest was backed by the predominantly Irish working class in the area, who were fervently anti-British. Protestors tried to stop Macready's performance, and in the resulting clashes 22 people died.

▲ *The Alamo*, Astor Place

Cooper Square

Just east of Astor Place is **Cooper Square**, a busy crossroads formed by the intersection of the Bowery, Third and Fourth avenues and St Mark's Place/East 8th Street, where students, tourists and teenagers mill around, wolfing pizza, drinking cheap beer or skateboarding. Despite the construction of several glitzy contemporary buildings nearby, the focus of the square remains the brownstone mass of the Foundation Building of the **Cooper Union for the Advancement of Science and Art** (Ⓣ212/353-4100, Ⓦwww.cooper.edu), a college for the poor established in 1859 by the wealthy entrepreneur Peter Cooper (1791–1883). Today, Cooper Union is a prestigious art, engineering and architecture school, whose nineteenth-century glory is evoked with a statue of the benevolent Cooper by Augustus Saint-Gaudens just in front. From the entrance hall, the guards will normally allow you to walk downstairs to the **Great Hall**, where historical exhibits are displayed in the gallery outside. The hall itself is not particularly exciting, though it's where, in 1860, Abraham Lincoln wowed an audience of New Yorkers with his "right makes might" speech, criticizing the pro-slavery policies of the Southern states – before going to *McSorley's* on East 7th Street (see p.350) to quench his thirst. In 1909, it was also the site of the first open meeting of the NAACP, chaired by W.E.B. Du Bois. You should also check out the gleaming **New Academic Building** at 41 Cooper Square across the street, completed in 2009 with a contemporary, environmentally friendly design; it's closed to the public during term, but tours are offered at other times and you can also visit the art gallery inside (check the website for details).

St Mark's Place

East from Cooper Square, between Third Avenue and Avenue A, East 8th Street is known as **St Mark's Place,** lined with souvenir stalls, punk and hippie-chic clothiers and newly installed chain restaurants, signalling the end of the gritty atmosphere that had dominated this thoroughfare for years. **St Mark's Comics** at no. 11 between Third and Second avenues is one of the few iconic stores to have survived (see p.395), while rock fans often make the pilgrimage to no. 96–98, east of First Avenue, which featured on the cover of the 1975 **Led Zeppelin** album *Physical Graffiti*. To the north and south of St Mark's Place, East 7th and 9th streets also boast used-clothing stores as well as several original boutiques, while 6th Street between First and Second avenues is known as "Indian" or **"Curry" Row** after the preponderance of restaurants here from the Subcontinent, most with a Bengali slant.

Little Ukraine and the Yiddish Theater District

Just behind Cooper Square is an area long inhabited by New York's Ukrainian community, most evidenced by the lavishly adorned exterior of St George's Catholic Church on East 7th Street, and the **Ukrainian Museum**, 222 East 6th St (Wed–Sun 11.30am–5pm; $8; Ⓣ212/228-0110, Ⓦwww.ukrainianmuseum.org), primarily a collection of Ukrainian folk costumes and modern art, and examples of the country's famous painted eggs, known as *pysanky*. You can buy them at the **Surma Ukrainian Shop** at 11 East 7th St (Mon–Fri 11am–6pm, Sat 11am–4pm), along with Ukrainian music, newspapers, cards and icons.

Across on Second Avenue, between East 5th and 6th streets, the apartment on the second floor of no. 91 was the childhood home of the **Gershwin** brothers, one of the greatest musical partnerships in history. George and Ira grew up in the heart of the **Yiddish Theater District**, centred on Second Avenue, which by World War I rivalled Broadway in scale and quality. The Immigration Act of 1924 signalled the end, however, and today all that remains of this once exuberant art form is the **Yiddish Walk of Fame**, like the stars on Hollywood Boulevard, at the corner of East 10th Street.

St Mark's Church-in-the-Bowery

Opposite the Yiddish Walk of Fame is **St Mark's Church-in-the-Bowery**, the second oldest church building in the city. **Peter Stuyvesant**, the last Dutch Director-General of the New Netherlands, who arrived in what was then New Amsterdam in 1647 and surrendered the city to the English in 1664, built a small chapel here in 1660. The chapel was close to his farm, and he was laid to rest inside twelve years later. The box-like Episcopalian house of worship that currently occupies this space was completed in 1799 over his tomb, and sports a Neoclassical portico that was added fifty years later – Stuyvesant's tombstone is now set into the outer walls. Nearby is a bust of the Director-General donated by the Dutch in 1915, looking far nobler than the crude early English caricatures of "Peg-leg Pete" suggest.

The church is still used for services and is normally locked – walk up to the office on the second floor (via a side door) and someone will let you in to see the vivid stained-glass windows inside. In the 1960s, the **St Mark's Poetry Project** (Ⓣ212/674-0910, Ⓦwww.poetryproject.com) was founded here to ignite artistic and social change. Today, it remains an important cultural rendezvous, with poetry readings Monday, Wednesday and Friday evenings at 8pm ($8), dance performances by the Danspace Project (Ⓦwww.danspaceproject.org), and plays from the Ontological-Hysteric Theater (Ⓦwww.ontological.com).

Tompkins Square Park

Fringed by avenues A and B and East 7th and 10th streets, **Tompkins Square Park** was once part of the estate of New York Governor (and later US vice-president) Daniel D. Tompkins (1774–1825), before passing to the city in 1834. The park has long been a focus for the Lower East Side/East Village community as well as one of New York's great centres for political protest. The late Yippie leader Abbie Hoffman lived nearby, and residents like him, along with the many incidents in the square, are what have given the East Village its maverick reputation. In recent years, Tompkins Square Park has evolved from its former identity as a place of protest, squatters and riots (see box opposite) to a desirable

The Tompkins Square riots

Until 1991, Tompkins Square Park was more or less a shantytown (known locally as "Tent City"). Hundreds of homeless people slept on benches or under makeshift shelters between the paths. In the winter, only the really hardy or truly desperate lived here, but when the weather got warmer the numbers swelled, as activists, anarchists and all manner of statement-makers descended upon the former army barracks. Things came to a head in the 1988 **Tompkins Square Riots**, when massive demonstrations against a 1am curfew for the previously 24-hour park led the police, badges covered and nightsticks drawn, to attempt to clear the square of people. In the ensuing battle, 44 demonstrators and bystanders were hurt; the investigation that followed heavily criticized the police for the violence. It wasn't the first disturbance here – a far larger riot occurred in **1874**, when police crushed a demonstration involving thousands of unemployed. In 1991 the park was temporarily closed and dozens of homeless people who had been living there were relocated. The park was eventually overhauled, its winding pathways and playground restored; the changes are enforced by an 11pm lock-up and police surveillance.

outdoor space that appeals to everyone, from local families to drag queens. The cleaned-up park features handball courts, a dog run and a farmers' greenmarket on Sundays (8am–6pm), as well as free concerts, a regular summer pastime for locals.

One of the few things to see in the area is the **Slocum Memorial Fountain** (1906), a nine-foot pink marble monument showing two children gazing forlornly out to sea (just inside the brick enclosure on the north side of the park). In 1904, the local community, then mostly made up of German immigrants, was devastated by the burning and sinking of a cruise ship, the *General Slocum*, in Long Island Sound. In the aftermath, most of the traumatized German-Americans in the neighbourhood moved away, many to Yorkville (see p.182). The monument commemorates the 1021 lives lost, mostly women and children, with a moving quote from Shelley's poem *Revolt of Islam*. Near the centre of the park is the **Prabhupada elm tree**, the site of the Hare Krishna movement's first ceremony outside of India, held in 1966, and named after the founder Swami Prabhupada (Allen Ginsberg was also in attendance that day).

At 151 Avenue B, on the east side of the park, is the famous saxophonist and composer **Charlie Parker's house** (Ⓦwww.charlieparkerresidence.net), a simple whitewashed 1849 structure with a Gothic doorway. Bird, as he was know to colleagues, friends and fans, lived here from 1950 until his death in 1954. The house is privately owned (and closed to the public) by jazz photographer Judy Rhodes, who led the campaign to have the house listed as an historic landmark in the 1990s. The free **Charlie Parker Jazz Festival** features concerts in the park every last weekend in August (see Ⓦwww.CityParksFoundation.org).

Alphabet City

East of Tompkins Square Park and north of Houston Street is **Alphabet City**, one of the most dramatically revitalized areas of Manhattan. Deriving its name from the grid of avenues lettered A–D, Alphabet City is also known to its remaining Puerto Rican residents as **Loisaida** (a Spanglish rendering of "Lower East Side"). Like Tompkins Square Park, this used to be a notoriously unsafe corner of town run by drug pushers and gangsters; today, the crime rate

Community gardens

In the 1970s, huge parts of the East Village burned to the ground after cuts in the city's firefighting budget closed many of the local firehouses. Since then, **Green Thumb** (ⓦwww.greenthumbnyc.org), founded in 1978 on the back of work by local (mostly female) activists, has helped the community transform these neglected and empty lots, turning the rubble-filled messes into some of the prettiest and most verdant spaces in lower Manhattan. In 1995, NYC Parks & Recreation began managing the programme, but a dramatic reversal in city policy in 1998 – to convert garden land into real estate – almost scuppered the whole project. Despite a last-minute agreement that ensured the safety of 114 of the neighbourhood's 600-plus gardens in 1999, the battle reached fever pitch in February 2000, when **El Jardin de la Esperanza** (Hope Garden) on East 7th Street between avenues B and C was bulldozed to make way for market-priced housing. Around thirty local residents were arrested while protesting the action; the city began to bulldoze the garden while the last resister was being removed – a mere forty minutes before an injunction was issued to prevent the city from destroying any further community gardens. The final 2002 agreement guaranteed the preservation of an additional 200 community gardens.

The fight seems to have been well worth it. There is no nicer way to spend a summer evening or a Sunday afternoon than by picnicking among the lush trees and carefully planted foliage of these spaces. Of particular note is the **East 6th Street and Avenue B** (Sat & Sun 1–6pm) affair, overgrown with wildflowers, vegetables, trees and roses. The garden also provides a space for yoga classes in the morning and performance art in the evening during the summer, as well as a forum for bake sales, sing-alongs and other community events. Other gardens include the very serene **6 B/C Botanical Garden** on East 6th Street between B and C; **Miracle Garden** on East 3rd Street between A and B; **Loisaida Garden** on East 4th Street between B and C; the **Parque de Tranquilidad** on East 4th Street between C and D; and the **Lower East Side Ecology Center Garden** on East 7th Street between B and C. Note that most gardens are open only at the weekends.

is way down, many of the old buildings have been renovated, and the streets are increasingly the haunt of twenty-somethings and edgier tourist youth. Comestibles aside, it's worth wandering around this part of town just to see some of the murals and **public art**, as well as the numerous **community gardens** (see box above).

8

The West Village

Greenwich Village (now commonly called the **West Village** or just "**the Village**") has been the artistic, Bohemian heart of New York since the 1920s, and though still one of the more progressive neighbourhoods in the city, it has attained a moneyed status over the last four decades and is definitely the place for those who have Arrived. Celebrities seem to snap up properties left, right and centre, and the historic enclave is booming with development. These famous residents – the likes of Nicole Kidman, Philip Seymour Hoffman, Ethan Hawke and Cameron Diaz, for example – have come for the same reasons that the intelligentsia did a century ago: quaint sidestreets, charming brownstones and brick townhouses unrivalled elsewhere in Manhattan. It's quiet and residential, but with a busy streetlife that keeps humming later into the night than in many other parts of the city.

Bounded by 14th Street to the north, Houston Street to the south, the Hudson River to the west and Broadway to the east, the West Village is easily reached by the #1 train to Christopher Street or the A, C, E, F or M to West 4th Street.

Some history

Greenwich Village was originally designed as a rural retreat away from the frenetic nucleus of early New York City. During the yellow fever epidemic of 1822, it became highly sought-after as a wealthy refuge from infected downtown streets, and before long it had sprouted elegant Federal and Greek Revival terraces and lured some of the city's highest society names.

At the close of the nineteenth century, German, Irish and Italian immigrants swarmed to jobs in breweries, warehouses and coal yards along the Hudson River, causing the once-genteel veneer of New York City's refined "American Ward" to disappear. As the immigrants moved in, rents plummeted and the neighbourhood took on a much more working-class atmosphere. The area's large houses proved a fertile hunting ground for struggling artists and intellectuals on the lookout for cheap rents, and by the end of World War I, the Village had become **New York's Left Bank**; writer E.E. Cummings, playwright Eugene O'Neill, dancer Isadora Duncan and famous eccentrics such as Joe Gould made their home here.

In the 1950s, the Village became a hub for the **Beat Movement**, a loose collection of writers, poets, artists and students (later known as the Beats or Beatniks) – Jack Kerouac and William S. Burroughs among them. Meanwhile, the neighbourhood's cafés, clubs and off-Broadway theatres came to define Village life, laying the path for rebellious, countercultural groups and activities in the 1960s, particularly **folk music**, with **Bob Dylan** resident here for much of his early career. The mystique and allure of a freethinking activist Greenwich Village was further enhanced over the years by radicals such as the **Weather Underground** (see box, p.108), history-changing events like the **Stonewall Riots** (see box, p.112) and

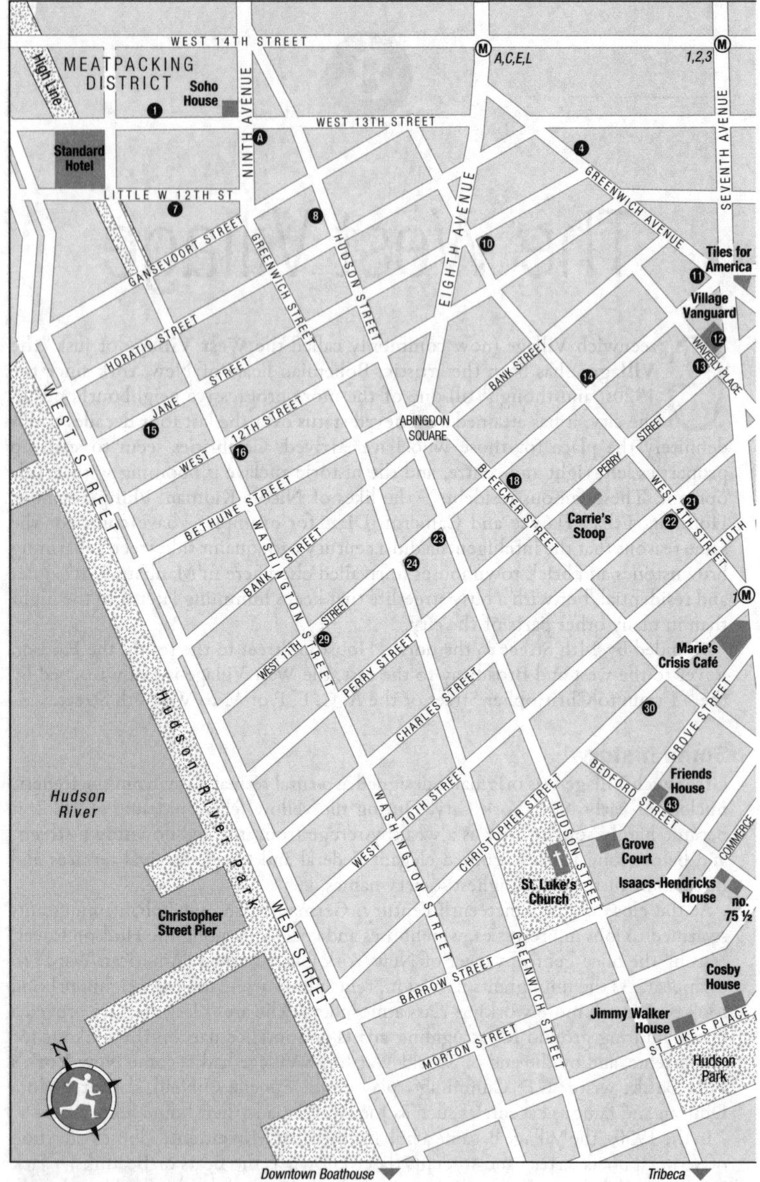

RESTAURANTS & CAFÉS

Babbo	27	Di Fiore Marquet	5	'ino	56	Moustache	43
Baoguette	30	Doma	13	Joe's Pizza	45	Num Pang	6
Blue Hill	28	Faicco's Pork Store	44	John's Pizzeria	37	Peanut Butter & Company	47
Caffè Dante	53	Fatty Crab	8	Kesté Pizza & Vino	38	Pearl Oyster Bar	31
Caffè Reggio	41	Gotham Bar & Grill	9	Lupa	55	Sevilla	21
Cones	42	Gray's Papaya	17	Magnolia Bakery	18	Souen	3
Cornelia Street Café	32	Grey Dog's Coffee	51	Marys Fish Camp	22	Tartine	14
Corner Bistro	10	Home	36	Minetta Tavern	46		

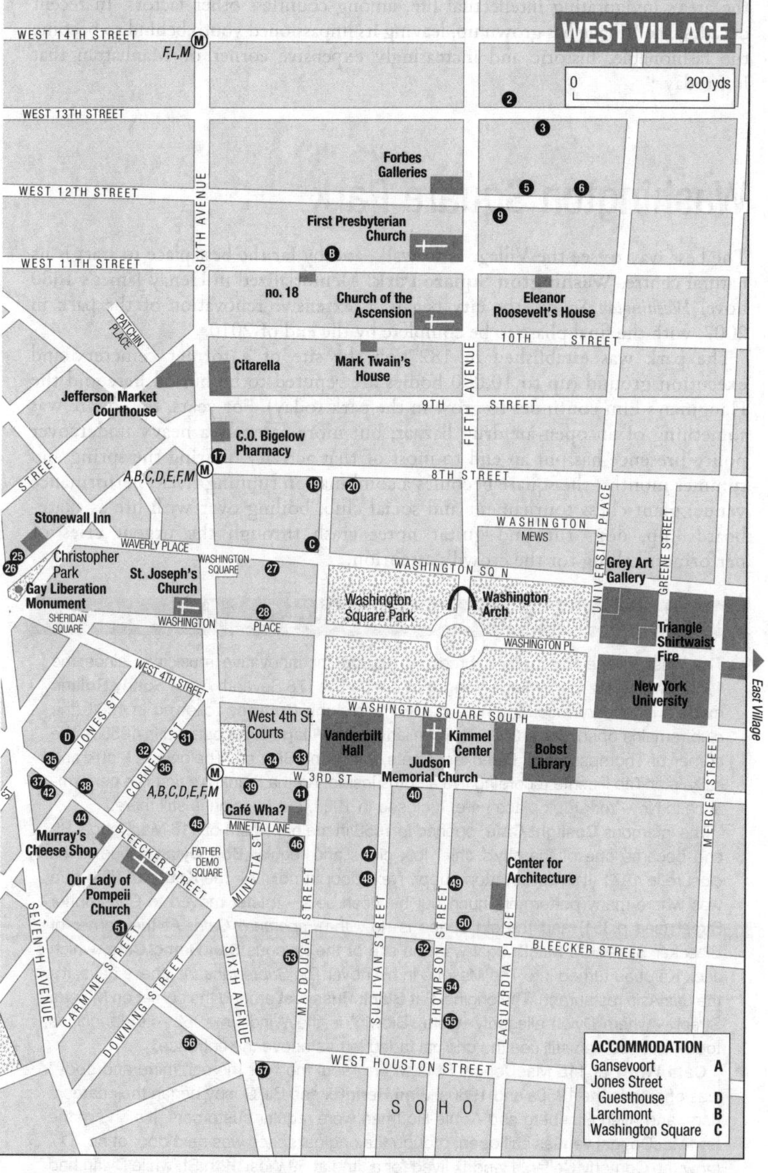

		BARS		NIGHTLIFE			
Tea & Sympathy	4	55 Bar	25	Apt	1	SOB's (Sounds of Brazil)	57
The Spotted Pig	24	8th St Winecellar	20	Bar Next Door	33	Sullivan Room	48
Thé Adoré	2	Blind Tiger Ale	35	The Bitter End	50	Village Underground	39
Tomoe Sushi	54	The Dove Parlour	49	Blue Note	34	Village Vanguard	12
Tortilla Flats	16	Fat Black Pussycat	39	Cielo	7	Zinc Bar	40
Two Boots to Go West	11	Jane Ballroom	15	(Le) Poisson Rouge	52		
Wallsé	29	Kettle of Fish	26	Love	19		
		White Horse Tavern	23				

the area's invigorating intellectual life, among countless other factors. In recent decades, the Village has grown up, leaving its impassioned youth behind to become the fashionable, historic and increasingly expensive corner of Manhattan that it is today.

Washington Square Park

The best way to see the Village is to walk, and by far the best place to start is its natural centre, **Washington Square Park**. Memorialized in Henry James's 1880 novel *Washington Square*, the city began an extensive renovation of the park in 2007, with the final phase to be complete by the end of 2010.

The park was established in 1827 on the site of a former cemetery and execution ground (up to 10,000 bodies are reputed to be buried here and the Hangman's Elm continues to grow in the park today). For years, the square was something of an open-air drug bazaar, but more recently a heavy undercover police presence has put an end to most of that activity. During the spring and summer months, the square becomes a combination running track, performance venue, giant chess tournament and social club, boiling over with life as skateboards flip, dogs run and guitar notes crash through the urgent cries of performers calling for the crowd's attention.

Musical landmarks of the West Village

The West Village has been a breeding ground for innovative musicians since the 1930s, when jazz club **Village Vanguard** opened at 178 Seventh Ave – **Sonny Rollins** made a legendary recording here in 1957 and **John Coltrane** followed in 1961 (the club remains open; see p.362). The similarly feted **Village Gate** opened in 1958 at the corner of Thompson and Bleecker streets, with Nina Simone, Thelonious Monk and salsa star Tito Puente recording live albums inside; Aretha Franklin's first live performance in New York took place here. It closed in 1993, but the sign is still there.

The infamous **Gaslight Café**, opened in 1958 in the basement of 116 MacDougal St, and became one of the city's chief folk clubs and regular **Bob Dylan** venue till its closure in 1971 (it's now a tattoo shop). Next door at no. 114, the **Kettle of Fish** pub was where many performers hung out between sets – it later moved to Christopher Street (see p.351) and the old space is now the *Esperanto Café*. At the corner of Bleecker Street, 93 MacDougal was the site of the raucous **San Remo Café**, which Jack Kerouac turned into *The Masque* in his novel *The Subterraneans* (these days, it's the *Ritz Asia* restaurant). The original **Fat Black Pussycat** around the corner on Minetta Street – where Dylan allegedly wrote "Blowin' in the Wind" in 1962 – is *Panchito's* today, but you can still see the original faded letters above the entrance.

Café Wha? at 115 MacDougal St is where "soul food for the ear, mind and body" was offered in the 1950s and 1960s. **Jimi Hendrix** and Bill Cosby began their careers here, and Allen Ginsberg and Abbie Hoffman were regular customers. It's one of the few MacDougal venues still open, though the original space was next door at no. 117 (now the Comedy Cellar). Hendrix lived for a time at 59 West 12th St, while Dylan had digs at 161 West 4th St and later at 92–94 MacDougal St.

By the 1970s, new musical genres such as disco, punk, salsa and hip-hop were emerging elsewhere in New York and the importance of the Village faded, though there are still several **jazz clubs** (see p.362), and venues such as the **Bitter End** at 147 Bleecker St (see p.359) occasionally nurture future stars: **Lady Gaga** was a struggling regular here in 2007.

The Triangle Shirtwaist Fire

One of New York's most infamous tragedies occurred on March 25, 1911, at the corner of Washington Place and Greene Street, when a fire started on the eighth floor of the **Triangle Shirtwaist garment factory**, one of the city's notorious sweatshops. A terrible combination of flammable fabrics, locked doors, collapsing fire escapes and the inability of fire-truck ladders to reach higher than the sixth floor, resulted in the deaths of 146 workers – almost entirely women, primarily immigrants, and some only 13 years old – in less than fifteen minutes. The fire led to legislation requiring improved safety standards, and helped spur the growth of the International Ladies' Garment Workers' Union. The site is now known as the Brown Building and forms part of NYU, with flowers left in front of the plaque commemorating the disaster on March 25 each year.

The most imposing monument in the park itself is Stanford White's **Washington Arch**, built in 1892 to commemorate the centenary of George Washington's presidential inauguration. On the northern side of the park, only the row of elegant Greek Revival mansions – the "solid, honourable dwellings" that James described – remind visitors of the area's more illustrious past. The author based much of the novel on his grandmother's house at **no. 19**, while James himself was born around the corner on Washington Place (the house had already been torn down when he returned to the city in 1906, much to his disgust). Further along Washington Square North, **no. 11** served as Will Smith's home in the 2007 movie *I am Legend* (much of it shot in the area), while Edith Wharton lived at **no. 7** in 1882. Later, **no. 3** became known as the "studio building", home to artists such as William Glackens, Guy Pène du Bois and Edward Hopper, who lived here from 1913 until his death in 1967. Today, all these buildings, like much of the property around the square, belong to New York University (NYU).

NYU and south of the square

The south and east sides of the square are lined with bulky **New York University** buildings, although even non-students will be interested in the university's innovative **Grey Art Gallery**, 100 Washington Square East (Tues, Thurs & Fri 11am–6pm, Wed 11am–8pm, Sat 11am–5pm; suggested admission $3; ⓣ212/998-6780, ⓦwww.nyu.edu/greyart). The space hosts top-notch travelling exhibitions, which rotate every three months and feature a wide range of media, including sculpture, painting, photography and provocative video shows. On the south side of the square, only the elaborate **Judson Memorial Church** (ⓦwww.judson.org) stands out amid a messy blend of modern architecture, one of Stanford White's most elegant Italianate creations. Built as a Baptist church in 1892, the Judson is a hub of local activism today, particularly in the areas of immigration, Fair Trade and anti-war protest, but it's also worth a look inside for its seventeen gorgeous stained-glass windows by John La Farge and small baptistery designed by Augustus Saint-Gaudens. The church is only open before and after services (Wed 6–8pm & Sun 10.30am–1.30pm).

MacDougal Street

From the southwest corner of the park, **MacDougal Street** cuts south towards Soho; from the 1920s to the 1970s, this was the dynamic heart of Village cultural life (see box opposite), and though it remains clogged with bars and cafés, its patrons these days are more likely to be NYU students looking for cheap drinks than aspiring artists. No. 133–139 was once the home of the **Provincetown**

Playhouse established here by the Provincetown Players in 1918; Eugene O'Neill, Edna St Vincent Millay and Djuna Barnes were all key members. Despite vociferous local opposition, NYU demolished most of the building in 2009 to extend its Law School; at the time of writing, a new playhouse was being constructed on the same site, incorporating parts of the original.

Continuing south brings you to venerable *Caffè Reggio* at 119 MacDougal St, one of the first and most atmospheric Village coffeehouses, dating back to 1927 (see p.292). The brick rowhouse opposite at no. 130–132 is where **Louisa May Alcott** lived between 1867 and 1870; it's thought she wrote most of *Little Women* (1868) here.

Center for Architecture

Two blocks south of the park, at 536 LaGuardia Place, the innovative **Center for Architecture** (Mon–Fri 9am–8pm, Sat 11am–5pm; free; ⓣ212/683-0023, ⓦwww.aiany.org) hosts temporary exhibitions highlighting every aspect of architectural design, from Modernism to specific shows on New York themes (like the 1964 World's Fair). The centre itself, operated by the American Institute of Architects, is a bright and stylish hub for evening programmes, conferences, lectures, film screenings and off-site tours (check the website for details).

North of Washington Square Park

Running between University Place and Fifth Avenue just north of the park, the small cobblestone street and old pastel buildings of **Washington Mews** seem out of place amid the grand brownstones that abut the square. This alley was used to stable horses until it was redesigned in 1916 to stable humans, and most recently NYU professors.

If you head north up Fifth Avenue, you'll pass a couple of imposing churches. On the corner of West 10th Street stands the Episcopal **Church of the Ascension** (Mon–Sat noon–1pm; free; ⓦwww.ascensionnyc.org), built in 1841 by Richard Upjohn (the Trinity Church architect), where a vast but gracefully toned La Farge altar painting and some fine stained glass are on view. Continuing the Gothic theme, Joseph Wells's bulky, chocolate-brown **First Presbyterian Church**

The Weathermen

In 1969, disillusioned by the failure of peaceful protest to stop the Vietnam War, a militant faction of pressure group Students for a Democratic Society set up a bomb factory in the basement of the Henry Brevoort–designed house at 18 West 11th St. Known as the **Weathermen** (after the Bob Dylan lyrics, "you don't need a weatherman to know which way the wind blows"), the group aimed to bomb a military ball to be held at Fort Dix, New Jersey, but the plan backfired disastrously. On March 6, 1970, the house's arsenal exploded, killing three of the group (two escaped). The organization went into hiding soon after, becoming the **Weather Underground** and evading capture by the FBI, despite being on their Most Wanted List. Whilst the group was responsible for several bombings in the 1970s, the loss of life was studiously avoided – though buildings in New York and Washington DC, were damaged, the group's most notorious exploit was busting counterculture guru Timothy Leary out of prison in 1970. By 1980, most of the group had surrendered to the authorities, though few were ever charged; the FBI had broken so many laws trying to catch them, most evidence was inadmissible.

Incidentally, the Weathermen's neighbour at the time of the 11th Street bomb was actor Dustin Hoffman, whose home at no. 16 suffered extensive damage from the blast.

(Mon–Fri noon–12.30pm; free; services Sun 11am; Ⓦwww.fpcnyc.org), just across 11th Street, was completed in 1845 with a crenellated tower modelled on the one at Magdalen College in Oxford, England. Inside, you'll find carved black-walnut pews, a soaring altarpiece and a fabulous Tiffany Rose Window.

One block north is one of the city's quirkiest small museums, the **Forbes Galleries**, 62 Fifth Ave, at 12th Street (Tues, Wed, Fri & Sat 10am–4pm; free; Ⓣ212/206-5548, Ⓦwww.forbesgalleries.com), which contain a rather whimsical collection of treasures assembled by the Forbes family, owners of the publishing empire. The 10,000-strong host of tin soldiers, over 500 model boats and early Monopoly boards will appeal primarily to aficionados and kids, though the galleries also hold temporary exhibitions of a diverse range of art work, from cartoons to rare Art Deco gems.

Walk west on West 10th and 11th streets and you'll find some of the best-preserved early nineteenth-century townhouses in the Village, with the exception of the rebuilt facade of **18 West 11th St** (see box below). **Mark Twain** lived at 14 West 10th St between 1900 and 1902, while poet **Emma Lazarus** lived at no. 18. **Eleanor Roosevelt** kept an apartment at 20 East 11th St between 1933 and 1942, but since this period coincided with her husband's presidency, it's probable that she spent more time talking domestic and foreign policies than playing bridge with her West Village neighbours.

Sixth Avenue and around

Although **Sixth Avenue** is for the most part lined with mediocre stores, restaurants and modern buildings, there are some exceptions, like the unmistakable clocktower of the nineteenth-century **Jefferson Market Courthouse** (Mon & Wed 9am–8pm, Tues & Thurs 9am–7pm, Fri & Sat 10am–5pm; free) at West 10th Street. Completed in 1877 by Central Park co-designer Calvert Vaux on the site of a former market, this imposing Victorian Gothic edifice served as a district courthouse until 1945; the murderer of architect Stanford White (see p.124) was tried here in 1906, as was Mae West, arrested for appearing in an "immoral" play (*Sex*) in 1927. It's been a public library since 1967, and is worth a quick peek inside; stroll up to the second floor via the spiral stone staircase to see the original ceiling and stained-glass windows, still reminiscent of a Gothic church despite the rows of books.

Across the street from the courthouse and opening onto West 10th Street, **Patchin Place** is a tiny mews constructed in 1848 (you can only peer through the gate). The rowhouses were home to the reclusive author Djuna Barnes for more than forty years; supposedly, Barnes's long-time neighbour E.E. Cummings used to call her "just to see if she was still alive". Patchin Place has also been home to Marlon Brando, Ezra Pound and Eugene O'Neill. Heading south, look out for **C.O. Bigelow Pharmacy**, at 414 Sixth Ave, just north of West 8th Street, founded in 1838 and probably the city's oldest drugstore, and a few blocks further on (at Sixth Avenue and 3rd Street), the **West 4th Street Courts**. Known as "The Cage" for the physical style of basketball typically on display here, the courts attract amateur players from all over the city and regularly host high-quality street tournaments.

Bleecker Street and St Luke's Place

Off Sixth Avenue's west side are some of the Village's prettiest residential streets, where you can easily spend a couple hours strolling and soaking up the neighbourhood's charms. To start exploring, cross Father Demo Square on Sixth

▲ Residential street in the Village

Avenue and walk up **Bleecker Street**, past the Italian Renaissance-style **Our Lady of Pompeii Church** (Mon, Tues, Thurs & Fri 7am–5.30pm, Wed & Sun 7am–7pm, Sat 7am–6pm; free), built in 1929 – check out the florid interior, replete with marble columns, stained glass and murals that evoke the spirit, if not quite the artistry, of classical Italy. Until the 1970s there was an Italian open-air marketplace on this stretch, and it's still lined by a few Italian stores and cafés, notably **Faicco's** (see p.293) and **Rocco's** (best known for its nut-sprinkled *cannoli*), as well as celebrated deli **Murray's Cheese Shop** (see p.407). If folk music is your thing, **Bob Dylan** lived for a time at 161 West 4th St, and the cover of his 1963 *Freewheelin'* album was shot a few paces away on Jones Street, just off Bleecker, a scene faithfully recreated in the Cameron Crowe movie *Vanilla Sky*.

If you turn down Leroy Street, and continue west across Seventh Avenue, you'll come to St Luke's Place; no. 10 was used as the exterior of the **Cosby house**, while no. 6 (recognizable by the two gas lamps at the bottom of the steps) is the ex-residence of **Jimmy Walker**, mayor of New York in the 1920s. Walker was for a time the most popular of mayors, a big-spending wisecracker who gave up working as a songwriter for politics and lived an extravagant lifestyle that rarely kept him out of the gossip columns – he resigned in 1932, accused of corruption.

Bedford and Grove streets

Just north of St Luke's Place, **Bedford Street** runs west off Seventh Avenue to become one of the quietest and most desirable Village addresses. Edna St Vincent Millay, the young poet and playwright, lived at no. 75 1/2 in the 1920s; at only 9ft wide, it is one of the narrowest houses in the city – and still fetched over $2 million in 2010. The brick and clapboard structure next door at no. 77 is the **Isaacs-Hendricks House**, built in 1799 and the oldest house in the Village.

The building at no. 90, right on the corner of **Grove Street** (above the *Little Owl*), served as the exterior for Monica's apartment in *Friends*, though the TV series was shot entirely in L.A. studios. Opposite is **17 Grove St**, built in 1822 and one of the most complete wood-frame houses in the city. Turn left here down Grove Street and you'll find **Grove Court** just off the road, one of the neighbourhood's most attractive and exclusive little mews (again, you have to peer through the gate).

Heading back to Seventh Avenue on Grove Street, *Marie's Crisis Café* at no. 59 was the site of the rented rooms where English revolutionary writer and philosopher **Thomas Paine** died in 1809. Paine, who was reviled in England for his support of both the American and French revolutions, was the author of the eighteenth century's three best-selling pamphlets, his *Common Sense* of 1776 generally credited for turning public opinion in favour of US independence. Cantankerous and conceited to the end, Paine made plenty of enemies, and after the publication of the *Age of Reason*, many Americans assumed he was an atheist (he was actually a deist). By the time he died here, he was poverty stricken and abandoned by his former friends. The current building dates from 1839, the café named in part after Paine's masterful essay *The American Crisis*.

Christopher Street

Christopher Street runs west from Jefferson Market Courthouse past **Christopher Park**, the traditional centre of the city's gay community. Confusingly, the park contains a pompous-looking statue of Civil War cavalry commander General Sheridan, though Sheridan Square is actually the next space down, where West 4th Street meets Washington Place. Historically, the area is better known as the scene of one of the worst and bloodiest of New York's **Draft Riots** (see Contexts, p.441), when a marauding mob assembled here in 1863 and attacked members of the black community, several of whom were lynched. Violence also erupted in 1969, when the **gay community** wasn't as readily accepted as it is now (see box, p.112). The riots are commemorated by George Segal's **Gay Liberation Monument** in the park, four life-size white-painted figures (two males, two females), unveiled in 1992. Nowadays, however, the gay community is fairly synonymous with Village life; for complete listings of gay bars and clubs, see p.382 and p.383.

Stonewall Riots

On June 27, 1969, police raided the **Stonewall gay bar** and started arresting its occupants – for the local gay community, simply the latest occurrence in a long history of harassment. Spontaneously, word got around to other bars in the area, and before long the *Stonewall* was surrounded by hundreds of angry protestors, resulting in a siege that lasted the better part of the night and ended with several arrests and a number of injured policemen. Though hardly a victory for their rights, it was the first time that gay men had stood up en masse to police persecution and, as such, formally inaugurated the gay-rights movement. The event is honoured by the Annual Lesbian, Gay, Bisexual and Transgender March (often just referred to as the **Gay Pride March**). Typically the last Sunday in June, this parade is one of the city's most exciting and colourful (see p.427).

The Far West Village

The area northwest of Sixth Avenue, dubbed the **Far West Village** by those ever-creative realtors, contains some of the most appealing and expensive residential streets in the city. Most of the gorgeous townhouses here are owned, not rented, and a bevy of unique stores, coffee bars and restaurants cater to its upwardly mobile and moneyed residential community – including plenty of Hollywood stars. Much to the chagrin of locals, you'll probably see small groups of excited fans taking photos at **66 Perry St**, between Bleecker and West 4th Street, used as the exterior of Carrie's apartment in *Sex and the City* ("Carrie's Stoop"), while almost constant lines form outside lauded **Magnolia Bakery** at Bleecker and West 11th Street (see p.292). The historic **White Horse Tavern** (see p.351), over at West 11th Street and Hudson, was frequented by Norman Mailer and Hunter S. Thompson among others, and is where legend claims Dylan Thomas had his last drink – you'll see a portrait of the poet and various memorabilia in the wood-panelled room named after him. The area has its rock connections, too; between 1971 and 1973, John Lennon and Yoko Ono lived in relative obscurity at **105 Bank St**, a block from the *White Horse* at Greenwich Street, before moving uptown (see p.192). And in 1979, a 21-year-old Sid Vicious took a lethal dose of heroin at **63 Bank St**, between Bleecker and West 4th streets. These days, a stroll along leafy **Hudson River Park** is more likely to reveal joggers and pushchairs than punks, though **Pier 45** (aka the Christopher St. Pier) remains a lively hangout for gay youth, especially at night. For a closer look at the water, head over to the **Downtown Boathouse** at Pier 40, at the end of Houston Street (see p.420), which offers free **kayaking** at the weekends; you can only paddle around the piers in the immediate vicinity, but the sensational views, fresh air and chance to work off all those cupcakes make this a fabulous deal.

9

Chelsea

A squat grid of renovated tenements, rowhouses and warehouses, **Chelsea** lies west of Broadway between 14th and 30th streets, though the area between 14th and 23rd streets is the heart of the neighbourhood. For years, these dreary, overlooked buildings and bare streets gave Chelsea an atmosphere of neglect. Over the past few decades, however, Chelsea has become quite commercial, influenced by the arrival of a large gay community in the late 1980s and early 1990s and the decamping of the art scene from Soho to Chelsea's western reaches. Today, it's filled with affluent townhouses and newish condos, while stores and restaurants pepper the scene, along with cutting-edge **art galleries**.

To begin your visit to Chelsea, take the #1, #2 or #3 train to 14th Street and Seventh Avenue, or the #A, #C or #E to 14th and Eighth.

Some history

The neighbourhood, developed on former farmland, began to take shape in 1830 thanks to **Clement Clarke Moore**, famous as the author of the surprise poetic hit *A Visit from St Nick* (popularly known as *'Twas the Night Before Christmas*), whose estate comprised most of what is now Chelsea. That year, Moore, anticipating Manhattan's movement uptown, laid out his land for sale in broad lots. However, stuck as it was between the ritziness of Fifth Avenue, the hipness of Greenwich Village and the poverty of Hell's Kitchen, the area never quite made it onto the shortlist of desirable places to live. Manhattan's chic residential focus leapfrogged over Chelsea to the East 40s and 50s, and the arrival of the slaughterhouses, an elevated railroad, and working-class poor sealed Chelsea's reputation as a rough-and-tumble no-go area for decades.

The last few decades have seen a totally new Chelsea emerge. New York's drifting art scene has been extremely significant in the neighbourhood's transformation. In the early 1990s, a number of respected **galleries** began making use of the large spaces available in the low-rise warehouses in far west Chelsea, securing the area's cultural bent. This influx has been counterbalanced by the steadily expanding presence of retail superstores, especially along **Sixth Avenue**, the building of the **Chelsea Piers** mega-sized sports complex and high-rise apartments and hotels springing up north of 23rd Street. For years now, the neighbourhood has been crowded with shoppers, restaurant-goers and the like, and it shows no signs of quietening down.

Meatpacking District

Creating a buffer between the West Village and Chelsea proper, the **Meatpacking District** between Gansevoort Street and West 15th Street, west of Ninth Avenue, has seen the majority of its working slaughterhouses converted to French bistros,

CHELSEA

0 500 yds

CAFÉS

Amy's Bread	21
Billy's Bakery	8
Eleni's Cookie's	20
Rafaella on Ninth	9

CLUBS & LIVE MUSIC

APT	25
Cielo	27
High Line Ballroom	19

BARS

El Quinto Pino	3
Half King	6
Hiro Ballroom	18
Hogs & Heifers	26
Peter McManus Café	13

RESTAURANTS

Bottino	2
Cafeteria	17
Co.	4
Cookshop	10
El Quijote	7
Gascogne	15
La Lunchonette	14
La Nacional	24
La Taza de Oro	23
Moran's	12
The Old Homestead	22
Paradou	28
Park	16
Red Cat	5
Rocking Horse	11
Txikito	1

ACCOMMODATION

Chelsea Center Hostel	A
Chelsea International Hostel	D
Chelsea Lodge	E
Chelsea Savoy Hotel	C
Gansevoort	F
Hotel Chelsea	B

Midtown West
Union Square
West Village
CHELSEA GALLERY DISTRICT
Chelsea Park
FLOWER MARKET
FIT Museum
Garage Antiques Market
West 25th Street Market
BROADWAY
West Street
High Line
Hudson River Park
CHELSEA HISTORIC DISTRICT
London Terrace Gardens
General Theological Seminary
Chelsea Art Museum
IAC Building
Cushman Row
Oldest House in Chelsea
Chelsea Piers
Joyce Theater
Chelsea Market
Rubin Museum of Art
Chelsea Outdoor Flea Market
MEATPACKING DISTRICT
Standard Hotel
Hudson River
ELEVENTH AVENUE
TENTH AVENUE
NINTH AVENUE
EIGHTH AVENUE
SEVENTH AVENUE
SIXTH AVENUE
W 29TH ST
W 28TH ST
W 27TH ST
W 26TH ST
W 25TH ST
W 24TH ST
W 23RD ST
W 22ND ST
W 21ST ST
W 20TH ST
W 19TH ST
W 18TH ST
W 17TH ST
W 16TH ST
W 15TH ST
W 14TH ST
W 13TH ST
W 12TH ST
LITTLE W 12TH ST
GANSEVOORT ST
HUDSON ST
HORATIO ST
JANE ST
GREENWICH AVE
59 60 61 62 63 64

after-hours clubs, wine bars and fancy galleries. Though a few wholesale meat companies remain, the area is now very much designer territory, with Stella McCartney and Helmut Lang among the fashion boutiques lining the cobblestone streets. The opening of the **High Line** has added much to the area's appeal, providing a tranquil greenway right into the heart of Chelsea.

The High Line

An ambitious urban renewal project that spans the Meatpacking District and West Chelsea, the **High Line**, which runs from Gansevoort Street to 30th Street (daily: mid-March to mid-Dec 7am–10pm, mid-Dec to mid-March 7am–8pm; Ⓦwww.thehighline.org), opened in the summer of 2009 to big crowds and rave reviews. It's a stunning transformation of a disused railway, constructed between 1929 and 1934, that once moved goods and produce around lower Manhattan, then spent a number of years rusted, overgrown and threatened with demolition. Concerned activists fought to stave off what seemed inevitable, but it wasn't until two locals formed the Friends of the High Line in 1999 that the tide improbably began to turn. Construction began in 2006.

Basically an elevated promenade-cum-public park some thirty feet in the air, it pays proper homage to its history – steel rails peek out from the ground; smooth pavement and wood echo the lines of train tracks and sometimes slope right up onto the benches; it cuts through the middle of buildings (like the *Standard Hotel*) and many wild growth patches have been left as is.

The first completed stretch runs from Gansevoort to 20th street. It's at its most untamed at the southernmost end, becoming a bit more elegant and organized above 14th Street. All along you can gaze out west over the river for a nice view, or look east to the city to get a real scale of the old meatpacking plants and factories in lower Chelsea.

The portion between 20th and 30th streets was being completed after this book went to press; in addition, the Whitney is planning a museum annexe at the Gansevoort Street entrance, to be designed by **Renzo Piano** (see Morgan Library, p.136 & New York Times Building, p.148).

▲ The High Line

West Chelsea

As you head north up **Ninth Avenue**, the red-brick **Chelsea Market** fills an entire block between 15th and 16th streets. This high-class food temple is housed in the old National Biscuit Company (aka "Nabisco") factory, where legend has it the Oreo cookie was created. Many of the factory's features remain, including pieces of rail track used to transport provisions. The handpicked retailers inside sell fresh fruit, fish, bread, wine, brownies and flowers (for more details, see "Shopping", p.406).

Farther north, on West 20th, 21st and 22nd streets between Ninth and Tenth avenues, is the **Chelsea Historic District**, which boasts a picturesque variety of predominantly Italianate and Greek Revival rowhouses. Dating from the 1830s to the 1890s, they demonstrate the faith some early developers had in Chelsea as an up-and-coming New York neighbourhood. The **oldest house** in the area, at 404 West 20th St (just off Ninth Ave), stands out with its 1829 wood siding, predating as it does the all-brick constructions of James Wells, Chelsea's first real-estate developer. The ornate iron fencing heading west along this block, known as **Cushman Row**, is original and quite impressive. Closer to Tenth Avenue, Jack Kerouac lived at 454 20th St with his wife Joan Haverty in 1951 while he wrote *On the Road* (mostly at the *Hotel Chelsea*, see opposite).

General Theological Seminary

Across the road, the block bounded by 20th and 21st streets between Ninth and Tenth avenues contains one of Chelsea's secrets, the 1817 **General Theological Seminary** (entrance on 21st Street; Mon–Fri 10am–5pm, Sat 10am–3pm; free; Ⓦwww.gts.edu). Clement Clarke Moore donated this island of land to the institute, and today the harmonious assembly of ivy-clad Gothic structures surrounding a green feels like part of a college campus. Though the buildings still house a working Episcopal seminary – the oldest in the United States – it's possible to explore the site as long as you sign in and keep quiet. You'll need to arrange for a special pass to check out their collection of Latin Bibles, one of the largest in the world.

London Terrace

Just north of the historic district at 435 West 23rd St is one of New York's premier residences for those who believe in understated opulence. **London Terrace**, two rows of apartment buildings a full city block long, sit between Ninth and Tenth avenues and surround a private interior garden (the corner Towers and interior Gardens units are managed separately). The building had the misfortune of being completed in 1930 at the height of the Great Depression, and despite a swimming pool and other posh amenities, many of the 1670 apartments stood empty for several years. The first management, wanting to evoke thoughts of Britain, made the doormen wear London-style police uniforms, thereby giving the building its name. The apartments were later nicknamed "The Fashion Projects" because of their designer, photographer and model residents (including Isaac Mizrahi, Debbie Harry and Annie Leibovitz).

Chelsea's gallery district

Tenth Avenue serves as a dividing line between Chelsea's more historic and quainter side to the east and its industrial past to the west. For years there was not much to see or do along this stretch – that is, until the galleries started swarming in. Along 22nd Street between Tenth and Eleventh avenues, as well as farther north up to West 29th, lie the **galleries** and **warehouse spaces** that house one of New York's most vibrant art scenes. (See "Commercial galleries," p.387, for more details on the best of Chelsea's 150-odd galleries.) Even the ovular entryway to **Comme des Garçons** – the store is just west of Tenth Avenue at 520 West 22nd St – masquerades as art in this part of town. The buildings used by Chelsea's galleries are especially imposing above West 23rd Street, and in some cases even stretch for a whole block.

You could get your bearings at the **Chelsea Art Museum**, 556 West 22nd St (Tues–Sat 11am–6pm, Thurs until 8pm; $8, free for 16 and under; Ⓦwww.chelseaartmuseum.org), which shows rotating exhibits over three floors in a historic red-brick building.

Chelsea Piers and around

At West 23rd Street and the West Side Highway, you'll find **Chelsea Piers** (Ⓦwww.chelseapiers.com), a glitzy, family-friendly, and somewhat incongruous entertainment development stretching from piers 59 to 62. First opened in 1910, this was where passengers would disembark from the great transatlantic liners (it was en route to the Chelsea Piers that the *Titanic* sank in 1912). By the 1960s, however, the piers had fallen into decay through disuse, and as late as the mid-1980s an official report condemned them as "shabby, pathetic reminders of a glorious past". Since then, money and effort have been poured into the revival of the area. Reopened in 1995, the new Chelsea Piers, whose commercial aura begs comparison with South Street Seaport (see p.62), is primarily a huge sports complex, with ice rinks and open-air roller rinks, as well as a skate park, bowling alley and a landscaped golf driving range (for more details, see "Sports and outdoor activities", p.420).

Just north are the latest instalments in the continuation of **Hudson River Park** (see p.74), which have added large green spaces, a carousel, art displays and a skate park to Piers 62, 63 and 64.

Across from Chelsea Piers, at the end of 19th Street, warehouses and car parks have given way to the billowing, fluid walls of Frank Gehry's **IAC Building**, one of New York's most fanciful examples of contemporary architecture. It's right next to Jean Nouvel's similarly striking **100 Eleventh Avenue**, a glittering patchwork of glass that holds luxury condos.

Eighth Avenue

Double back east along 23rd Street to Chelsea's main drag, **Eighth Avenue**, where the more laidback vibe of the West Village, below 14th Street, segues into a stretch of vibrant retail energy. Along here, dozens of trendy bars, restaurants, health-food stores, gyms, bookstores and clothes shops cater to Chelsea's large, out and proud gay population.

Hotel Chelsea

Just beyond Eighth Avenue, at 222 East 23rd St, is one of the neighbourhood's major claims to fame – the **Hotel Chelsea**. Originally built as a luxury cooperative apartment building in 1884 and converted to a hotel in 1903, the building has been the undisputed residence of the city's harder-up literati and its musical vagabonds. Mark Twain, Tennessee Williams, Dylan Thomas and Thomas Wolfe all spent time here, and in 1951 Jack Kerouac, armed with a specially adapted typewriter (and a lot of Benzedrine), typed the first draft of *On the Road* nonstop onto a 120-foot roll of paper. William Burroughs (in a presumably more relaxed state) completed *Naked Lunch* at the *Chelsea*, and Arthur C. Clarke wrote *2001: A Space Odyssey* while in residence.

In the 1960s, the *Chelsea* entered a wilder phase. Andy Warhol and his doomed protégées Edie Sedgwick and Candy Darling holed up here and made the film *Chelsea Girls*. In probably the hotel's most infamous moment, Sid Vicious stabbed Nancy Spungen to death in 1978 in their suite, a few months before he fatally overdosed on heroin. The photographer Robert Mapplethorpe and Patti Smith also lived here in the late 1960s and early 1970s, and the hotel inspired Joni Mitchell's song *Chelsea Morning* and Leonard Cohen's *Chelsea Hotel No.2*. More recently, the late Dee Dee Ramone roamed its halls and wrote a barely received novel about the place.

With a pedigree like this it's easy to forget the hotel itself, which has a down-at-heel Edwardian grandeur all of its own. The lobby, with its famously phallic wall-mounted sculpture *Chelsea Dogs*, and plastered with more respectable work by Larry Rivers, is worth a gander. To see anything else, you'll need to either stay here (see p.274 for review) or take one of the monthly cultural tours (usually last Tues of month; $40), during which select residents open their doors to visitors.

East Chelsea

Sandwiched between infinitely more interesting blocks, the eastern edge of Chelsea has become a buzzing strip of commerce, concentrated mostly along **Sixth Avenue** between West 17th and 23rd streets. In the last few years, a crush of discount emporiums like Best Buy, along with mediocre national chain restaurants, have mostly driven out the mom-and-pop businesses, and the trend only seems to be accelerating. On weekends especially, Sixth Avenue teems with bargain hunters lugging oversized bags from places like Bed, Bath and Beyond, the Container Store and the Sports Authority, while the weekend flea markets have been steadily disappearing (or moving to Hell's Kitchen; see p.406) – though a few indoor markets do remain.

Rubin Museum of Art

For a brief escape from the commercialism, visit the **Rubin Museum of Art** (Mon & Thurs 11am–5pm, Wed 11am–7pm, Fri 11am–10pm, Sat & Sun 11am–6pm, closed Tues; $10, free on Fri 7–10pm; Ⓦwww.rmanyc.org) at 150 West 17th Street, between Sixth and Seventh avenues. The serene museum is one of the city's lesser-visited gems, a collection of two thousand paintings, sculptures and textiles from the Himalayas and surrounding regions. The permanent exhibits on the second and third floors are organized and labelled with great care and thought, essential for a subject that will be familiar to few. While a few pieces manage to stand out, the thrust is less about individual artists and objects and more about understanding how and why art is created. A stylish ground-floor bar, the *K2 Lounge*, hosts regular performances.

Flower Market and FIT

The area around West 28th Street is Manhattan's **Flower Market** – not really a market as such, more the warehouses and storefronts where potted plants and cut flowers are stored before brightening offices and atriums across the city. The district, which has atrophied against a tide of gentrifications, still manages to surprise, its greenery bursting out of the drab blocks in a welcome touch of life.

West 28th Street's historical background couldn't be more at odds with its present incarnation: from the mid-1880s until the 1950s, the short block between Sixth Avenue and Broadway was the original **Tin Pan Alley**, where music publishers would peddle songs by the likes of Irving Berlin and George Gershwin to artists and producers from vaudeville and Broadway. The name came from the piano-playing racket coming out of the publishing houses here at any time of the day, a sound that one journalist compared to banging on tin pans.

A block west, the **Museum at the Fashion Institute of Technology (FIT)**, Seventh Ave at 27th Street (Tues–Fri noon to 8pm, Sat 10am–5pm; Ⓦwww.fitnyc.edu; free), covers two levels; you'll find exhibits on contemporary design and fashion history.

10

Union Square, Gramercy and the Flatiron District

Sandwiched between the bohemian chic of the East Village and the opulence of midtown, the knot of close-knit neighbourhoods east of Fifth Avenue might seem rather bland in comparison. Yet this part of town is equally dynamic, with a spate of new construction projects, some of the city's best restaurants and stores, and several of New York's most historically significant buildings and landmarks. Chief among the latter is **Union Square**, between 14th and 17th streets, a bustling open space that breaks up Broadway's pell-mell dash north. To the northeast is the posh neighbourhood of **Gramercy**, with its private clubs and members-only park. Straddling Broadway northwest of Union Square and running up to 23rd Street, the **Flatiron District** was once the centre of Manhattan's fine shopping and still retains a certain elegance and energy, while foodies should make the pilgrimage to revitalized **Madison Square Park** to sample the celebrated burgers at *Shake Shack* and some of the surrounding eateries – among the best in the city. It is here, as you head north in the blocks between Third, Park and Fifth avenues, that midtown Manhattan's skyscrapers begin to rise from downtown's generally low-lying buildings.

Union Square and around

Located at the confluence of Broadway, Fourth and Park avenues between 14th and 17th streets, **Union Square** is an inviting public space. Among the statues here are George Washington as equestrian; Gandhi; a Lafayette by Bartholdi (more famous for the Statue of Liberty); and, at the centre of the green, a massive flagstaff base whose bas-reliefs symbolize the forces of Good and Evil in the American Revolution. Opened as a park in 1839, the square is surrounded by a crush of commerce and serves as a welcome respite from crazed taxi-drivers and rushed pedestrians on 14th Street. Mostly, however, Union Square is beloved for its **Greenmarket** – the largest in Manhattan (see p.409) – that sells all sorts of seasonal goods and non-edible products, like hand-spun wools and flowers.

Like the generally more rambunctious Washington Square in the West Village, Union Square Park is also often the site of civil demonstrations. After September 11, hundreds of vigils were held here, and the entire square became a makeshift memorial to the victims until it was finally ordered dismantled by then-Mayor Rudy Giuliani. The park's southern boundary serves as the informal centre of Manhattan protest against miscellaneous causes, everything from the war in Iraq to legalized marijuana, with raggedly dressed protesters brandishing megaphones at passers-by day and night.

Around the Square

The square is flanked by a range of excellent restaurants, as well as by buildings in a mismatched hodgepodge of architectural styles, not least of which is the old **American Savings Bank** at 20 Union Square East – now the **Daryl Roth Theatre**

▲ Union Square

– of which only the grandiose columned exterior survives, completed in 1923. The pedimented Union Square Theater just north of here at 17th Steet became the second **Tammany Hall** in 1929, once headquarters of the Democratic Party and a fine example of Colonial-Revival architecture. The **Consolidated Edison** (or ConEd) building, one block east on 14th Street, is home to the company responsible for providing the city with both energy and steaming manholes. The majestic Warren & Wetmore-designed tower, completed in 1929, is topped by a 38-foot-high bronze lantern, a memorial to employees killed in World War I. The narrow **Decker Building** on the other side of the park at 33 Union Square West was where Andy Warhol moved his **Factory** in 1968, occupying the sixth floor until 1973; the artist was shot by Valerie Solanas here shortly after the move. The building itself, completed in 1893, is a lavish, Moorish-inspired skyscraper.

Irving Place

East of Union Square, the six graceful blocks of **Irving Place** head north towards Gramercy Park. Irving Place was named for Washington Irving, the early nineteenth-century writer best known for his creepy tale of the Headless Horseman, *The Legend of Sleepy Hollow*, and also for supposedly being the first American to earn a living from his writing. The claims that he lived for a short time at no. 49 (trumpeted in a plaque outside the quaint house) are spurious; he did, at the least, frequently visit his nephew's house on East 21st, and a bust of Irving stands in front of the early nineteenth-century Washington Irving High School at East 17th Street.

Another celebrated author, Pulitzer Prize-winning short-story writer O. Henry, did live at no. 55 (opposite *Cibar*) between 1902 and 1910. Again in the mythmaking vein, O. Henry reputedly dreamed up and wrote *The Gift of the Magi* at **Pete's Tavern**, at 18th Street and Irving Place, one of New York's oldest bars. The legend serves the place and its atmosphere well.

Stuyvesant Square

The area between Irving Place and the East River is something of a no-man's-land, with a clutch of nondescript apartment buildings and businesses. It is, however, a good place for a stroll, even if only to hop off the beaten path and to check out the neighbourhood's few historical points of interest. The land that makes up **Stuyvesant Square**, between East 15th and 17th streets, was gifted to the city in

1836 by **Peter Gerard Stuyvesant**, a descendant of the last Director-General of New Amsterdam (see Contexts, p.440). The park contains Gertrude Vanderbilt Whitney's bronze statue of the Director-General (replete with peg-leg), unveiled in 1941, and a sculpture of Czech composer **Antonín Dvořák** who lived nearby on East 17th Street in the 1890s.

Though framed by the buildings of Beth Israel Medical Centre and bisected by bustling Second Avenue, the park still retains something of its secluded quality, especially on the western side. Here you'll find the **Friends' Meeting Houses and Seminary** (1860), whose austere Greek Revival facade contrasts with the grand Romanesque brownstone of **St George's Episcopal Church** next door, completed in 1856. The most famous member of the congregation was J.P. Morgan, who lived just up the road (see p.54). Remembered as the most powerful and ruthless banker of the Gilded Age, Pierpont, as he was commonly known, was also a devout Episcopalian; in St George's, says Morgan biographer Ron Chernow, "he seemed mesmerized by ritual and lapsed into reveries of mystic depth". His funeral, held here in 1913, was more akin to that of a head of state, and was conducted by an unprecedented three bishops (the tycoon is buried in Hartford, Connecticut). The church is normally open for services only (Sun 9.30 & 11.15am), but you can schedule a weekday tour with the parish office (Ⓣ646/723-4178); it's worth a quick peek for its soaring wood-beam roof, monument to Henry Bacon (designer of the Lincoln Memorial in Washington DC) and the carved pulpit, dedicated to J.P.

Gramercy Park and around

Irving Place comes to an end at the ordered open space of **Gramercy Park**. This former "little crooked swamp" (which is what the Dutch called it before the name was Anglicized) between East 20th and 21st streets is one of the city's prettiest squares. It is beautifully manicured and, most noticeably, completely empty for much of the day – principally because it is the city's last private park and the only people who can gain access are those rich or fortunate enough to live here. Famous past key-holders have included Mark Twain, Uma Thurman and Julia Roberts, as well as a host of Kennedys and Roosevelts. Despite the park's exclusivity, it's well worth a walk around the edge for a glimpse of the trim, historic area that was once the city's main theatre district.

Inside the park gates stands a statue of the actor **Edwin Booth** (brother of Lincoln's assassin, John Wilkes Booth) in the guise of Hamlet, one of his most famous roles. (Ironically, Edwin rescued Lincoln's son, Robert, from a train accident years before John's fatal action.) In 1887, aided by architect (and Gramercy Park resident) Stanford White, Booth turned his home at 16 Gramercy Park South into the private club **The Players**. The porch railings on this rather forbidding building are decorated with distinctive figures representing Comedy and Tragedy. In the nineteenth century, actors and theatre types were not accepted in general society, so Booth created the club for play and socializing – neglecting, however, to admit women, who were not allowed in until 1989. Later members included the Barrymores, Frank Sinatra and (oddly) Sir Winston Churchill, while more recent inductees are Morgan Freeman and Liv Ullmann. These days it seems to be the club that is trying to keep regular society out rather than vice versa.

Next door at no. 15 is the equally patrician **National Arts Club** (Ⓣ212/475-3424, Ⓦwww.nationalartsclub.org), fittingly located in the rather grand Tilden Mansion. Built in 1840, the mansion was Victorianized in the 1870s by Central Park co-designer Calvert Vaux at the request of owner Governor Samuel Tilden, and is studded with terracotta busts of Shakespeare, Milton and Franklin, among others. Charles de Kay, a *New York Times* art critic, founded the club in 1898 to create a meeting place for artists, patrons and audiences of all the arts; it moved here in 1906. Non-members are permitted to visit the temporary art exhibitions inside, usually open Monday to Friday 10am to 5pm, but call or check the website to confirm. On the other side of The Players is the **Visual Arts Foundation** at no. 17, occupying the former home of Joseph Pulitzer, while at no. 38 on the northeast corner of the square is the mock-Tudor building in which John Steinbeck, then a struggling reporter for the now defunct *New York World*, lived from 1925 to 1926 (it took getting fired from that job to plunge him into fiction). The brick-red structure at no. 34 was one of the city's very **first building cooperatives**.

At 2 Lexington Ave and Gramercy Park North is the imposing 1920s bulk of the **Gramercy Park Hotel** (see "Accommodation," p.274), whose elite early residents included Mary McCarthy, a very young John F. Kennedy and Humphrey Bogart. Lastly, lining Gramercy Park West is a splendid row of brick Greek Revival townhouses from the 1840s with ornate wrought-iron work; James Harper, of the publishing house Harper & Row, lived at no. 4 until his death in 1869.

The Flatiron District

The small district north and northwest of Union Square, between Fifth and Park avenues up to 23rd Street, is generally known as the **Flatiron District**, taking its name from the distinctive early skyscraper on the southwest corner of Madison Square Park (see front cover). This area is a nice enough place to stroll around in, though there's little to see. This stretch of Broadway was once the heart of the so-called **"Ladies' Mile"**, which during the mid-nineteenth century was lined with fancy stores and boutiques. The area started losing its lustre around the turn of the twentieth century, and by World War I, Ladies' Mile had all but disintegrated due to the department stores' uptown migration. However, a few sculpted facades and curvy lintels remain as mementos of that gilded age, including Lord & Taylor's Victorian wedding-cake of a building at 901 Broadway at 20th Street (the store is now at 424 Fifth Ave, at 38th St).

Theodore Roosevelt's Birthplace

Standing apart from its rather commercial surroundings at 28 East 20th St is **Theodore Roosevelt's Birthplace** (Tues–Sat 9am–5pm, tours on the hour 10am–4pm; free; ⓣ212/260-1616), or at least a reconstruction of it, viewable on an obligatory guided tour. In 1923, the house was rebuilt as it would have been when Roosevelt was born there in 1858, the rooms restored to reflect their appearance between 1865 and 1872. The rather sombre mansion contains mostly original furnishings: a brilliant chandelier in the parlour, obelisks from a family trip to Egypt, young "Teedie's" crib and more. A room at the top of the house holds some of TR's hunting trophies; a gallery on the ground floor exhibits photos and documents from the life of the 26th president – still the only one born in New York City.

The Flatiron Building

The lofty, elegant and decidedly anorexic **Flatiron Building** (originally the Fuller Construction Company, later renamed in honour of its distinctive shape) is set on a narrow, triangular plot of land at the manic intersection of Broadway, Fifth Avenue and 23rd Street. It is one of the city's most famous buildings, evoking images of

Edwardian New York. Though it's hard to believe today, the Flatiron was the city's first true skyscraper (a fact hotly debated by architectural-history buffs), hung on a steel frame in 1902 with its full twenty storeys dwarfing all the other buildings around. Its uncommonly thin, tapered structure creates unusual wind currents at ground level, and years ago policemen were posted to prevent men gathering to watch the wind raise the skirts of women passing on 23rd Street. The cry they gave to warn off voyeurs – "23 Skidoo!" – has passed into the language. Such behaviour would presumably have horrified **Edith Wharton**, who was born in 1862 at 14 West 23rd St, just around the corner. Her parents' townhouse has been altered many times since then, and is currently occupied by a *Starbucks*.

Madison Square Park and around

Just northeast of the Flatiron Building, between Park and Fifth avenues, lies **Madison Square Park**. Though enveloped by a maelstrom of cars, cabs, buses and dodging pedestrians, because of the stateliness of the surrounding buildings and its peaceful green spaces, it possesses a grandiosity and neat seclusion that Union Square has long since lost – be sure to grab a burger at *Shake Shack* in the middle (see p.294).

On the park's east side, at 5 Madison Ave, stands the tiered, stately **Metropolitan Life Tower**, which at 700ft was the world's tallest building between 1909 and 1913 (when it was surpassed by the Woolworth Building, see p.66). The tower was sold to a developer in 2007 for $200 million, and, like much of the area, is expected to be converted into either residential apartments or a hotel.

Met Life also once owned **11 Madison Ave**, across East 24th Street (it now houses Credit Suisse), connected to the tower building by a sky-bridge. Completed in 1929, the onset of the Great Depression quashed MetLife's plans to make this section a mind-blowing hundred storeys high – viewed from the park, you can see how it was designed to be the base for something much bigger. On the other side of 25th Street, at 27 Madison Ave, the **Appellate Division** of the **New York State Supreme Court** boasts a marble facade, resolutely righteous with its statues of Justice, Wisdom and Peace. The chamber inside where arguments are heard (open to the public Tues–Thurs 2pm; free) is almost rococo in its detail.

The grand structure opposite is the **New York Life Building**, the work of Cass Gilbert, creator of the Woolworth Building downtown. It went up in 1928 on the site of the original **Madison Square Garden** (see box opposite), renowned scene

Stanford White and the former Madison Square Garden

Stanford White, a partner in the illustrious architectural team of McKim, Mead, and White, which designed many of the city's great Beaux Arts buildings, including the General Post Office and the old Penn Station, as well as the second incarnation of Madison Square Garden (at 26th St and Madison; now demolished), was by all accounts something of a rake. His dalliance with millionaire Harry Thaw's future wife, Evelyn Nesbit, a Broadway showgirl (who was unattached at the time), had been well publicized – even to the extent that the naked statue of the goddess Diana on the top of the Madison Square Garden building was said to have been modelled on her. Violent and possessive, Thaw could never accept his wife's past, and one night in 1906 he burst into the roof garden of White's Madison Square Garden tower apartment, found the architect surrounded, as usual, by doting women and admirers, and shot him in the head. Thaw was carted away after trial to a mental institution, which he was subsequently in and out of for around a third of his remaining years, while his wife's show-business career took a tumble: she resorted to drugs and prostitution, dying in 1967 in Los Angeles.

of drunken and debauched revels of high and Broadway society. Some believe that the junction nearby, at Madison and West 27th Street, is the birthplace of baseball, as the members of the country's first ball club, the New York Knickerbockers, started playing in a vacant sandlot here in 1842.

Museum of Sex

One of the city's more provocative institutions, the **Museum of Sex**, at 233 Fifth Ave (daily 11am–6.30pm, Sat until 8pm; $16.25, ages 18 and over only; Ⓣ212/689-6337, Ⓦwww.museumofsex.org), attempts to bring serious study to its subject but is only of passing interest. The first floor has temporary exhibitions on subjects like pornography and the sex lives of animals, while upstairs features a mishmash of items from the permanent collection (much of which has been donated), such as early vibrators, sex dolls and so forth.

Church of the Transfiguration

The lone reminder of the time when the area was New York's theatreland is the **Church of the Transfiguration**, just off Fifth Avenue at 1 East 29th St (chapel open daily 8am–6pm). Built in 1849, this dinky, rusticated church, made of brown brick, topped with copper roofs, and set back from the street, has long been a traditional place of worship for showbiz people and various social misfits. It was not until 1870, though, that members of the theatre profession started coming here to pray. That year, the place was tagged with the name "The Little Church Around the Corner" after a devout priest from a larger, stuffier church had refused to officiate at the funeral of an actor named George Holland, sending the bereaved here instead. Since then, the church has been a haven for actors, and there is even an Episcopal Actors' Guild. The chapel itself is an intimate little building in a gloriously leafy garden, providing comfort and solace away from the skyscrapers on Fifth Avenue. Its interior is furnished in warm wood and lit with soft candlelight. The figures of famous actors (most notably Edwin Booth as Hamlet) are memorialized in the stained glass.

Lexington Avenue

Two blocks east of Madison, **Lexington Avenue**, which begins its long journey north at Gramercy Park, passes the lumbering **69th Regiment Armory** at 26th Street. The site of the famous Armory Show of 1913, which brought modern art to New York, and was a very early home to the Knicks' basketball team, it retains its original function as the headquarters of the National Guard's "Fighting Sixth-Ninth", though its drill hall is still used for events and exhibitions.

Just west of the Armory, on the corner of Park Avenue, 104 East 26th St was once the brownstone home of **Herman Melville**, long since replaced with a modern office building but remembered with a small plaque. The author moved here in 1863, working on the unfinished *Billy Budd* before dying in the house in 1891. The nearby intersection is named Herman Melville Square in his honour.

North of the Armory lies what is sometimes dubbed **Curry Hill**, a collection of Indian restaurants and stores along Lexington Avenue between East 27th and 30th streets – blink and you might miss it altogether. Most of New York's Indian population lives in Queens, but the cluster of businesses here (many of them Tamil) just about warrants the moniker.

11

Midtown East

Largely corporate and commercial, and anchored by **Grand Central Terminal**, Cornelius Vanderbilt's Beaux Arts transportation hub, the area known as **Midtown East** rolls north from the 30s through the 50s, and east from Sixth Avenue. Some of the city's most determinedly modish boutiques, richest Art Deco facades and most sophisticated Modernist skyscrapers are in this district, primarily scattered along **Fifth**, **Madison** and **Park avenues**. This is where you'll find the **Empire State Building**, the soaring symbol of New York City; the **Seagram Building**; the Art Deco, automobile-inspired **Chrysler Building**; the rambling, geometric bulk of the **United Nations** complex; and the renovated **Museum of Modern Art**.

Fifth Avenue

For the last two centuries, an address on **Fifth Avenue** has signified prosperity, respectability and high social standing. Whether around Washington Square or far uptown around the Harlem River, the boulevard has traditionally been the home to Manhattan's finest mansions, hotels, churches and stores. Thanks to its show of wealth and opulence, Fifth Avenue has always drawn crowds, nowhere more than on the stretch between 34th and 59th streets, home to grand institutions like **Rockefeller Center** and the **New York Public Library**. The streets nearly reach a standstill at Christmas, with shoppers stalled at elaborate window displays; at other times, it plays host to some of the city's biggest processions (see Chapter 32, "Parades and festivals", for more details).

The Empire State Building

The city's tallest skyscraper, the **Empire State Building**, at 350 Fifth Ave, between 33rd and 34th streets, has easily been the most potent and evocative symbol of New York since its completion in 1931. The building occupies what has always been a prime piece of real estate, originally the site of the first *Waldorf-Astoria Hotel*, built by William Waldorf Astor and opened in 1893 (its current Art Deco home lies on Park Ave; see p.138).

Wall Street visionary John Jacob Raskob and his partner Alfred E. Smith, a former governor, began compiling funds in October 1929, just three weeks before the stock market crash. Despite the ensuing Depression, the Empire State Building proceeded full steam ahead and came in well under budget after just fourteen months. Since the opening, the building has seen its share of celebrity and tragedy:

RESTAURANTS					
'21' Club	10	Four Seasons	13	Oyster Bar	27
2nd Avenue Deli	31	Hatsuhana	21	Quality Meats	1
Aquavit	4	La Bonne Soupe	6	Smith & Wollensky	20
Caffe Linda	19	La Grenouille	11	Szechuan Gourmet	28
Cho Dang Gol	30	Menchanko Tei	3 & 23	Zarela	17
db Bistro Moderne	26	The Modern	8		
El Rio Grande	29	Naples 45	24		
Emporium Brasil	22	New York Kom Tang	32		

BARS	
Campbell Apartment	27
Casa Lever	9
King Cole Bar	7
Le Colonial	2
P.J.Clarke's	5

CAFÉS	
Algonquin Hotel lobby	N
Buttercup Bake Shop	15
Ess-a-Bagel	16
Fresco by Scotto on the Go	12
La Maison du Chocolat	18
Oms/b	25
Prime Burger	14

King Kong clung to it while grabbing at passing aircraft; in 1945, an actual B-25 bomber negotiating its way through heavy fog crashed into the building's 79th storey, killing fourteen people; and in 1979, two Englishmen parachuted from its summit to the ground, only to be carted off by the NYPD for disturbing the peace. The darkest moment in the building's history came in February 1997, when a man opened fire on the observation deck, killing one tourist and injuring seven others; that's but one reason there is tight security upon entrance, with metal detectors, package scanners and the like.

From toe to TV mast, the building is 102 storeys and 1454 feet tall, but its height is deceptive, rising in stately tiers with steady panache. Indeed, standing on Fifth Avenue below, it's quite easy to walk right by without even noticing it's there. From elsewhere in the city it can seem ubiquitous, especially at night, when lit in various colours until the wee hours of morning (you can look up the lighting schedule online at Ⓦwww.esbnyc.com/tourism/tourism_lightingschedule.cfm).

Currently being retrofitted to make it more energy efficient, the Empire State is filled with Art Deco touches: the restored grand ceiling in the lobby with its cosmic gold murals, the elevator doors, the chandeliers in the new cocktail lounge, the *Empire Room*, in the space that once held a post office. On the second floor is the **New York Skyride**, a pricey, eight-minute simulated flight over the city's landmarks (daily 8am–10pm; for tickets bought online, $25.50, youths and seniors $18.50; $4 more at box office; Ⓣ212/279-9777 or 1-866/SKY-RIDE, Ⓦwww.skyride.com). Of course most people come for the trip to the top, rather than to mill about or try the Skyride.

Getting to the top

A first set of elevators takes you to the 80th floor, where you transfer to get up to the main observatory on the **86th floor**. The views from the outdoor walkways here are as stunning as you'd expect; on a clear day visibility can be up to eighty miles, but, given the city's air pollution, on most it's more likely to be between ten and twenty. You get a great vantage point on the Chrysler Building, completed not long before the Empire State, and on the surprisingly elegant Queensboro Bridge beyond that. For an additional $15, a second set of elevators will take you to the glassed-in **102nd-floor observatory**, the base of the radio and TV antennas; all things considered it's unnecessary, unless you want to be able to say you've been as far up as you can go. (Daily 8am–2am, last trip 1.15am; $20, children ages 6–12 $14, children 5 and under and military personnel free; combined tickets for New York Skyride and the Observatory $45; audio tour $8; Ⓣ212/736-3100, Ⓦwww.esbnyc.com).

The New York Public Library and around

Several unexceptional blocks north of the Empire State Building on Fifth Avenue is one of midtown Manhattan's most striking buildings: the **New York Public Library** (Mon & Thurs–Sat 10am–6pm, Tues & Wed 10am–9pm, Sun 1–5pm; Ⓣ212/930-0800 or 917/275-6975, Ⓦwww.nypl.org), which stretches between 40th and 42nd streets. Beaux Arts in style and faced with white marble, it is the headquarters of the largest public-library system in the world. To explore the library, either walk around yourself or take one of the **free tours** (Mon–Sat 11am and 2pm, Sun 2pm), which last an hour and give a good all-round picture of the building, including the **Map Room** and evocative Periodicals Room, with its stunning faux-wood ceiling and paintings of old New York. Tours start at the information desk in Astor Hall (the main lobby). The undisputed highlight of the library, however, is the large, coffered 636-seat **Reading Room** on the third floor. Authors Norman Mailer and E.L. Doctorow worked here, as did Leon Trotsky during his brief sojourn in New York just prior to the 1917 Russian Revolution. It was also here that Chester Carlson came up with the idea for the Xerox copier and Norbert Pearlroth searched for strange facts for his "Ripley's Believe It or Not!" cartoon strip in the famed research library – the largest with a circulating stock in the world. Its 88 miles of books are stored beneath the reading room on eight levels of stacks, which run the half-acre length of Bryant Park (behind the library; see below).

Bryant Park

The restoration of **Bryant Park** (hours vary but roughly 7am–10pm, closes earlier in Feb, March & Oct; ⓣ212/768-4242, ⓦwww.bryantpark.org), just behind the library to the west between 40th and 42nd streets, is one of the city's resounding success stories. A seedy eyesore until 1992, it is now a beautiful, grassy block filled with trees, flowerbeds and inviting chairs (the fact that they aren't chained to the ground is proof enough of revitalization).

Summertime brings life to the park – there are free dance and yoga classes, as well as various performances throughout the week, free wi-fi and free outdoor movies on Monday evenings. Games, lectures and rallies also take place in the park, and you can even rent a portion of it for your own event (see website).

North to Rockefeller Center

The **Chase Bank**, on the southwest corner of West 43rd Street and Fifth Avenue, is an eye-catcher. An early glass'n'gloss box, it teasingly displays its vault (no longer in use) to passers-by. Around the next corner, West 44th Street contains several old-guard New York institutions. The Georgian-style **Harvard Club**, at no. 35 (ⓣ212/840-6600, ⓦwww.hcny.com), has an interior so lavish that lesser mortals aren't even allowed to enter (you must be a Harvard alumnus/a). Built in 1894, the Harvard Club was the first of several elite associations in the neighbourhood.

The **New York Yacht Club**, at 37 West 44th St (ⓣ212/382-1000, ⓦwww.nyyc.org), chartered in 1844, is just next door. In its current location since 1901, this playfully eccentric exterior of bay windows is moulded as ships' sterns; waves and dolphins complete the effect of tipsy Beaux Arts fun. For years this has been the home of the America's Cup, a yachting trophy first won by the schooner *America* in 1851. Across the street the 225-year-old **General Society for Mechanics and Tradesmen** occupies a late nineteenth-century building; step inside to peruse the library (Mon–Fri 11am–7pm, Fri 10am–5pm; free) and examine their amazing collection of locks (by appointment ⓣ212/840-1840; $10 admission).

The Round Table

All across the globe, the period between World War I and World War II saw an incredible outpouring of creative energy. In America, one of the groups involved in this burst of productivity was the so-called **Round Table**, which originated at the **Algonquin Hotel**. Several writers, many of whom had worked together for the Army newspaper *Stars and Stripes*, met in June 1919 at the hotel to roast *New York Times* drama critic Alexander Woollcott. They had so much fun that they decided to return the following afternoon; it wasn't long before their meeting became a ritual. At the heart of the group were Dorothy Parker, Robert Benchley, Robert Sherwood, Irving Berlin, Harold Ross (founder of *New Yorker* magazine), George Bernard Shaw and George S. Kaufman, among others. Outspoken and unafraid to comment on the state of the postwar world, they wielded an increasing influence on social issues through the 1920s; when the Round Table spoke, the country listened. Then the Great Depression arrived, and a decade after its inception, it finally faded from the scene.

"Dammit, it was the twenties and we had to be smarty," said Dorothy Parker of the sharp-tongued wits known as the Round Table (see box, p.129), whose members lunched and drank regularly at the **Algonquin Hotel**, at 59 West 44th St (☎212/840-6800). The bar, the *Oak Room*, is still one of the most civilized in town and hosts an acclaimed cabaret series.

West 47th Street, or the **Diamond District** (marked by the diamond-shaped lamps mounted on pylons at the Fifth- and Sixth-avenue ends of the street), is a diverting side-trip from Fifth Avenue, a strip of wholesale and retail shops chock-full of gems and jewellery first established in the 1920s. These shops are largely managed by Hasidic Jews, who impart much of the street's workaday vibe, making the row feel less like something just off ritzy Fifth Avenue and more like the Garment District, by way of the Middle East. Come here to get jewellery fixed at reasonable prices.

Before heading down there, it's worth ducking into the **Fred F. French Building** at 551 Fifth Ave. The colourful mosaics near the top of the building's exterior are a mere prelude to the combination of Art Deco and Middle Eastern imagery on the vaulted ceiling and bronze doors of the lobby.

Rockefeller Center

Taking up the entire block between Fifth and Sixth avenues and 49th and 50th streets, **Rockefeller Center** (☎212/332-6868 or 632-3975, ⓦwww.rockefellercenter.com) is one of the finest examples of urban planning in New York. Built between 1930 and 1939 by John D. Rockefeller, Jr, son of the oil magnate, its offices, cafés, theatre, underground concourse and rooftop gardens work together with an intelligence and grace rarely seen. Just across 50th Street on the corner of Sixth Avenue stands the similarly Art Deco-style **Radio City Music Hall**, arguably the most famous theatre in the United States.

The GE Building ("30 Rock")

You're lured into the Center from Fifth Avenue down the gentle slope of the **Channel Gardens** to the focus of the Center – the **GE Building** (formerly the RCA Building), nicknamed "30 Rock" by entertainment insiders aware of the television studios in its towers. Rising 850ft, its monumental lines echo the scale of Manhattan, though they are softened by symmetrical setbacks to prevent an overpowering expanse of wall. At the foot of the building, the **Lower Plaza** holds a sunken restaurant in the summer months – a great place for afternoon cocktails – linked visually to the downward flow of the building by **Paul Manship**'s sparkling sculpture *Prometheus*. In winter this recessed area becomes an **ice rink** (hours and prices vary; call ☎212/332-7654) and following a New York tradition that dates to 1931, a huge tree is displayed at Christmas time, drawing hordes of gawkers, especially the night it's first lit (first week of Dec).

Inside, the GE Building is no less impressive. **José Maria Sert**'s lobby murals, *American Progress* and *Time*, are faded but still in tune with the 1930s ambience – presumably more so than the original paintings by Diego Rivera, which were removed by John D.'s son Nelson Rockefeller when the artist refused to scrap a panel glorifying Lenin. A leaflet available from the lobby desk details a self-guided tour of the Center (also available online).

NBC Studios

Among the GE Building's many offices is **NBC Studios** (70min behind-the-scenes tours Mon–Thurs 8.30am–4.30pm, Fri & Sat 9.30am–5.30pm, Sun 9.30am–4.30pm; reservations at the NBC Experience Tour Desk; $19.25, children 6–12 $16.25; call ☎212/664-3700 to reserve or buy a combination ticket with

Rockefeller Center tour, $24.95) on 49th Street between Fifth and Sixth avenues, which produces, among other things, the long-running sketch-comedy hit *Saturday Night Live* and the popular morning programme the *Today Show*. To become part of the throng that appears (and waves frantically) when the anchors step outside, all one has to do is show up – the earlier the better. This is especially true on summer Fridays when the *Today Show* hosts concerts, which begin at 7am (for information on other show tapings visit Ⓦwww.nbc.com/tickets or call the ticket line at Ⓣ212/664-3056; see also p.375).

Top of the Rock

The observation deck on the top of Rockefeller Center, first opened in 1933, fell into disuse and was closed in the 1980s. The owners returned to John D.'s original vision by restoring the platform on the structure's 70th floor in November 2005. And in contrast to the Empire State Building, **Top of the Rock** (daily 8am to midnight, last elevator at 11pm; $21; Ⓣ212/698-2000, Ⓦwww.topoftherocknyc.com) offers completely unobstructed views, and the timed-entry scheme, multiple observation decks and decent square footage of the viewing platforms make a visit seem less like a cattle call. The panorama allows you to examine the layout of Central Park, how built-up downtown Manhattan is compared to the north and offers a vertiginous look at St Patrick's Cathedral below. A "Sunrise Sunset" ticket option ($30) allows particularly dedicated visitors to scale the building twice in one day and experience the city in two different veils of sunlight.

Radio City Music Hall

On the northeast corner of Sixth Avenue and 50th Street is **Radio City Music Hall** (see p.359 for venue review), a sweeping and dramatic Art Deco jewel box that represents the last word in 1930s luxury. The staircase is positively regal, the chandeliers are the world's largest, and the auditorium looks like an extravagant scalloped shell: "Art Deco's true shrine", as critic Paul Goldberger rightly called it. You're unlikely to be taking in a show here – with a couple of exceptions, the venue

▲ Radio City Music Hall

rarely books the type of acts that once made it such a hot ticket – so to explore, take one of the hour-long "Stage Door" walking tours (daily 11am–3pm; $18.50; for tickets call ⓣ212/307-7171, tour info ⓣ212-247-4777, ⓦwww.radiocity.com). In addition to the behind-the-scenes look at the building, the tour includes a brief meeting and photo-op with a Rockette (the "house" dancers that are part of the Christmas Spectacular, the big annual event at RCMH).

North to Central Park

Fifth Avenue has another sumptuous Art Deco component in the Rockefeller Center, the **International Building**. The lobby looks out on **Lee Lawrie**'s bronze *Atlas*, which rules the space – a thorough cleaning in the summer of 2008 returned its lustre – and the muscleman gazes toward **St Patrick's Cathedral** across the avenue. Designed by James Renwick and completed in 1888, St Patrick's sits on the corner of 50th Street amid the glitz like a misplaced bit of moral imperative, painstakingly detailed yet – notwithstanding the mysticism of **Lady Chapel** to the rear – spiritually lifeless. Despite its shortcomings, St Patrick's is still an essential part of the midtown landscape, a foil for Rockefeller Center and one of the most important Catholic churches in America.

Across the street from St Patrick's are the striped awnings of **Saks Fifth Avenue** at no. 611, one of the last of New York's premier department stores to relocate to midtown from Herald Square. With its columns on the ground floor and graceful pathways through high-end fashion collections, Saks is every bit as glamorous today as it was when it opened in 1924.

Paley Center for Media

If your body needs the kind of rejuvenation only an hour in front of a television can offer, visit the **Paley Center for Media**, at 25 West 52nd St between Fifth and Sixth avenues (Wed & Fri–Sun noon–6pm, Thurs noon–8pm; $10; ⓣ212/621-6800, ⓦwww.paleycenter.org). Formerly known as the Museum of Television & Radio, the space was renamed in 2007 with a nod to the eventual inclusion of digital media. In a building designed by Philip Johnson, the organization preserves an archive of 140,000 mostly American TV shows, radio broadcasts and commercials, accessible via an excellent computerized reference system. Regular screenings and panel discussions take place in the downstairs theatre, and the year-round lunch-hour programme *Food for Thought* calls the centre home: marquee-name actors perform one-act plays, and advance booking is highly recommended (shows once a week on Mon, Wed, Thurs or Fri; show 2pm, lunch precedes it; $65; ⓣ646/366-9340, ⓦwww.foodforthoughtproductions.com).

The '21' Club and the American Folk Art Museum

Right next door to the Paley Center is the **"21" Club**, at 21 West 52nd St (ⓣ212/582-7200, ⓦwww.21club.com), which has been providing food (and drink) since the early days of Prohibition, and remains an Old Boys institution. Founded by Jack Kriendler and Charlie Berns, the club quickly became one of the most exclusive establishments in town, a place where the young socialites of the Roaring Twenties could spend wild nights dancing the Charleston and enjoying wines and spirits of the finest quality. Although *'21'* was raided more than once, federal agents were never able to pin anything on Jack and Charlie. At the first sign of a raid, they would activate an ingenious system of pulleys and levers, which would sweep bottles from the bar shelves and hurl the smashed remains down a chute into the New York sewer system.

The next block up, and steps away from the **Museum of Modern Art**, is the excellent **American Folk Art Museum**, at 45 West 53rd St (Tues–Thurs, Sat & Sun 10.30am–5.30pm, Fri 10.30am–7.30pm; $9, free Friday 5.30–7.30pm; ⓣ212/265-1040, ⓦwww.folkartmuseum.org), which exhibits multicultural folk art from all over America, with a permanent collection that includes over 3500 works and is highlighted by Henry Darger's watercolours and Ralph Fasanella's dizzying urban commentaries. Friday evenings feature free musical performances, and the affiliated Folk Art Institute runs courses, lectures and workshops.

The Museum of Modern Art

New York City's **Museum of Modern Art – MoMA** to its friends – offers the finest and most complete collection of late nineteenth- and twentieth-century art anywhere, with a permanent collection of more than 150,000 paintings, sculptures, drawings, prints and photographs, as well as a world-class film archive. Despite its high admission price, it's an essential stop for anyone even remotely interested in the world of modern art.

Founded in 1929 by three wealthy women, including Abby Aldrich Rockefeller (wife of John D., Jr), as the very first museum dedicated entirely to modern art, MoMA moved to its present home ten years later. Philip Johnson designed expansions in the 1950s and 1960s, and in 1984 a steel-pipe and glass renovation by Cesar Pelli doubled gallery space. The latest renovation was completed in 2004 by Japanese architect Yoshio Taniguchi, doubling the exhibition space yet again and creating new and vibrant public areas; another is already in the works – gallery space in a soaring new skyscraper next door that will be one of the city's tallest structures.

The building is quite clever: it's easy to navigate, but it also constantly and deliberately gives glimpses of other levels, like the sculpture garden, the lobby, and the spacious second-floor landing where large canvases or installations are often displayed. The core collection – at least in the Painting and Sculpture galleries – is arranged more or less in chronological order and while pieces do go in and out (to and from the archive, out on loan etc), it tends to stay relatively stable. The substantial collections of photography, drawings, architectural design and contemporary art each have their own galleries on the third and second floors and they usually rotate, so it's hard to guarantee exactly what you'll see; temporary exhibitions are also afforded their own dedicated areas. Despite all this space, the main galleries in MoMA can still feel very crowded, especially during weekends and holidays, and queues can be long at the entrance, cloakroom, cafés and for audio guides. Buy tickets in advance, and get here early or late in the afternoon, to avoid the worst of it.

MoMA practicalities

The Museum of Modern Art (ⓣ212/708-9400, ⓦwww.moma.org) is located at 11 West 53rd St, just off Fifth Avenue. Take the E train to 5th Avenue–53rd Street, or the B, D, or F train to 47–50th streets/Rockefeller Center. **Hours** are Mon and Wed–Sun 10.30am–5.30pm, Friday until 8pm (and Thurs until 8.45pm in the height of summer); it is **closed Tuesdays** throughout the year, as well as Thanksgiving Day and Christmas Day. **Admission** is $20, free for children 16 and under. Thanks to corporate sponsorship, the **museum is free** for everyone on Fridays from 4 to 8pm – predictably, the lines are extremely long at this time, so get there by 3.30pm at the latest, or after 6.30pm, when the initial rush has (usually) died down. At other times, you can avoid waiting in line by **booking tickets in advance** on the website. Note also that you must check in large shopping bags and backpacks of any size – don't bring them if you want to avoid another wait for the cloakroom.

Painting and Sculpture I

The core of the collection is the Painting and Sculpture galleries, numbered from 1 to 25. Most visitors head directly for the fifth floor – to **Painting and Sculpture I**, which covers 1880 to 1940. Gallery 1 opens with the **Post-Impressionists** of the late nineteenth century, with works by **Cézanne**, **Seurat**, **Van Gogh** and **Gauguin** mixed in with vivid early paintings by **Munch** and **James Ensor** that already hint at a more Modernist perspective. This is developed in the next gallery by **Picasso**, most notably with his seminal *Demoiselles d'Avignon*, as well as by some of his later, more Cubist pieces. More works by Picasso and **Léger** follow in Gallery 3, and, beyond them, the big swirling colours of **Boccioni** and the Italian Futurists, highlighted by Severini's fractured *Dynamic Hieroglyphic of the Bal Tabarin*. Gallery 5 is an explosion of colour, with paintings by **Chagall**, **Kandinsky** and **Kirchner**, while Gallery 6 is entirely devoted to **Matisse**. Featured are the flat, almost primitive *Dance I*, his *Red Studio* and other paintings, as well as his lumpy series of sculpted heads of *Jeanette*. After Matisse is a so-called **"Crossroads" gallery** (Gallery 7), which houses some of the most recognizable works of the modern age – Picasso's *Three Women at the Spring*, the same artist's *Three Musicians* and Léger's *Three Women*, all painted the same year (1921), as well as some haunting works by **de Chirico**. The adjoining galleries are devoted to the paintings of the Dutch De Stijl movement. **Malevich** is heavily featured in Gallery 8, and you can trace the development of the movement's leading light, **Mondrian**, in Gallery 9, from his tentative early work to the pure colour abstract of *Broadway Boogie Woogie*, painted in New York in 1943. Gallery 10 features artists of the German Neue Sachlichkeit school, **Otto Dix** and **Max Beckmann**, while Gallery 11 holds the big names in Mexican modern art – Rivera, Siqueiros, Orozco and Kahlo. Gallery 12 is devoted to the Surrealists, and many of the works here will be familiar from popular reproductions: the vivid creations of **Miró**, **Magritte**'s *The Menaced Assassin* and the famously drooping clocks of **Dalí**'s *Persistence of Memory*, though the latter is often on loan to other galleries. Finally, tiny Gallery 13 features Jacob Lawrence's *Migration Series*, a shorthand history of the African-American shift from the rural south to the urban north.

Painting and Sculpture II

Painting and Sculpture II, the next floor down, displays work from the 1940s to 1960s and inevitably has a more American feel, starting with works by **Rothko** in Gallery 15. In Gallery 16, **Dubuffet**'s challenging paintings sit with **Giacometti**'s stick-like figures and paintings by **Bacon** – *Study of a Baboon* – and **Picasso**, while Gallery 17 is devoted to **Pollock**'s large splattered canvases. Beyond here the **Abstract Expressionists** hold sway, with the "zips" of **Barnett Newman** (18) and "multiforms" of Rothko (18 and 19) – both working at the height of their influence in the 1950s, when these paintings were done; Gallery 19 also has de Kooning's fierce *Woman I*. Later galleries contain lots of work familiar from the modern canon – **Jasper Johns**' *Flag* and **Robert Rauschenberg**'s mixed-media paintings (20), **Warhol**'s soup cans and *Marilyn Monroe*, **Lichtenstein**'s cartoons and **Oldenburg**'s soft sculptures (21).

Photography, Architecture and Design, Drawings

The other sections of the museum's collection are just as impressive and shouldn't be missed. On the third floor, the **Photography** galleries are devoted to a rotating selection of exceptional work from visiting artists and the museum's permanent collection – everything from the candid street photos of Paris by **Cartier-Bresson** and **Richard Avedon**'s penetrating portraits of well-known figures to **Helen Levitt**'s colourful shots of unwitting New York characters.

MoMA refreshments

If you need to take a break during your tour of the museum, the popular second-floor café, *Café 2*, does very good, slickly presented **Italian-style food**, though you'll often have a long wait at lunchtime. *Terrace 5*, on the fifth floor, is a more formal option, and provides soothing views of the **sculpture garden**. A very swanky full-service restaurant (also open to non-museum guests), *The Modern*, sits on the ground floor, serving the **Alsatian-inspired cuisine** of lauded chef Gabriel Kreuther (see p.326 for review). The *Bar Room* is a slightly less formal section of the restaurant. You can also grab coffee and ice cream from the bar in the sculpture garden (usually open May–Sept).

Architecture and Design, on the same floor, hosts revolving exhibits showcasing every aspect of design from the mid-nineteenth century to the present; illustrations of buildings, interior design, lots of glass and ceramics, and a series of neat large-scale objects like vintage cars, bikes and even helicopters.

The **Drawing** galleries, also on the third floor, show revolving exhibitions by a glittering array of twentieth-century artists, including **Pollock**, **Rauschenberg**, **de Kooning**, **Warhol**, **Jasper Johns** and **Roy Lichtenstein**. Finally, the second-floor galleries give MoMA the chance to show its **Contemporary art** in all media, and usually show works from the 1970s onward, including pieces by **Bruce Nauman**, **Jeff Koons** and other stellar names from the world of contemporary art.

53rd Street to Grand Army Plaza

Northward from MoMA, the avenue's ground floors shift from mundane offices to an elegant stretch of exclusive shops and art galleries. Taking ostentatious wealth to the extreme is **Trump Tower**, no. 725 at 56th Street. Perfumed air, polished marble panelling and a five-storey waterfall are calculated to knock you senseless with expensive "good taste". The building itself is clever: a neat little outdoor garden is squeezed high in a corner, and each of the 230 apartments above the atrium provides views in three directions; members of the hyper-rich crowd who have homes here include New York Yankee captain Derek Jeter.

The stores on these blocks are as much sights as shops, with **Cartier**, **Gucci**, **Tiffany & Co**, **Bergdorf Goodman** and **Harry Winston Jewelers** among the gilt-edged names (see "Shopping", Chapter 30, for more on this area's stores). At 59th Street, Fifth Avenue reaches **Grand Army Plaza** and the fringes of Central Park, where a golden statue of William Tecumseh Sherman stands guard amid all the highbrow shopping, and the copper-edged 1907 **Plaza Hotel** lords over the plaza's western border. One of Manhattan's most beloved institutions, the hotel's reputation was built not just on looks, but on lore: it boasts its own historian, keeper of such anecdotes as when legendary tenor Enrico Caruso, enraged by the loud ticking of the hotel's clocks, stopped them all by throwing a shoe at one (they were calibrated to function together). The management apologized with a magnum of champagne.

The *Plaza* was sold for $675 million in August 2004 to the El-Ad Group, which then announced that the space would be converted to high-end condominiums. After outrage and worry about the loss of jobs and changes to its old-school elegance, El-Ad scaled back its plans and reintroduced hotel rooms into the mix. After a $400 million update, the hotel reopened on its centenary. Preservationists had nothing to be afraid of; everything was in its right place, refreshed and as indulgent as ever. The famed *Oak Bar* and *Palm Court* have returned as well, but aside from those establishments, access is a bit limited for casual gawkers.

Madison Avenue

Madison Avenue parallels Fifth with some of the grandeur but less of the excitement. In the East 30s, the avenue runs through the heart of the mundane and residential **Murray Hill** neighbourhood, an area distinguished mostly by the presence of the **Morgan Library & Museum**. Heading north to the East 40s and the Upper East Side, you encounter the Madison Avenue of legend, the centre of the international advertising industry in the 1960s and 1970s. Today, this section of town is a major upscale shopping boulevard.

Murray Hill and the Morgan Library

Madison Avenue is the main artery of **Murray Hill**, a tenuously tagged residential area (no commercial building was allowed until the 1920s) of statuesque, canopy-fronted buildings bounded by East 34th and 40th streets, and lacking any real centre or sense of community. Indeed, you're likely to pass through without even realizing it.

When Madison Avenue was on a par with Fifth as the place to live, Murray Hill was dominated by the Morgan family, including the crusty old financier J.P. and his offspring, who at one time owned a clutch of properties here. Morgan Junior lived in the brownstone house on the corner of 37th Street and Madison (now headquarters of the American Lutheran Church), his father in a house that was later pulled down to make way for an extension to his library next door. The uplifting **Morgan Library & Museum**, 225 Madison Ave at East 36th St (Tues–Thurs 10.30am–5pm, Fri 10.30am–9pm, Sat 10am–6pm, Sun 11am–6pm; $12, free Fri 7–9pm; ⓣ212/685-0008, ⓦwww.themorgan.org), housed in a mock-Roman villa, still stands here though. Morgan would often come to his library to luxuriate among the art treasures he had acquired on his trips to Europe: manuscripts, paintings, prints and furniture. A stunning piazza-style gathering space, designed by Pritzker Prize-winner Renzo Piano, brings together the villa and the McKim building where Morgan stored his collection. Piano's renovation, completed in 2006, also doubled the exhibition space and added several new features to the building, including an entrance on Madison Avenue, a subterranean performance hall and a naturally lit reading room.

The collection of nearly ten thousnd drawings and prints by such greats as Da Vinci, Degas and Dürer is augmented by rare literary manuscripts by Dickens, Austen and Thoreau as well as handwritten correspondence between Ernest Hemingway and George Plimpton, and musical scribblings by everyone from Haydn to Dylan. There's also a copy of the 1455 Gutenberg Bible (the museum owns three out of the eleven that survive; another rests in the New York Public Library, see p.128). Morgan's personal library and study are also on view.

North of Murray Hill

Leaving behind the relative quiet of Murray Hill, Madison Avenue becomes progressively more commercial the further north one goes. Several good stores – some specializing in men's haberdashery, shoes and cigars – still cater to the needs of the more aristocratic consumer. Brooks Brothers, traditional clothiers of the Ivy League and inventors of the button-down collar, occupies a corner of East 44th Street. Between 50th and 51st streets the **Villard Houses**, a replica collection of Italian *palazzos* (ones that didn't quite make it to Fifth Ave) by McKim, Mead, and White, merit more than a passing glance. The houses have been surgically incorporated into the *Helmsley Palace Hotel*, and the interiors polished up to their original splendour.

Madison's most interesting sight come in a four-block strip above 53rd Street. The tiny, vest-pocket-sized **Paley Park** is on the north side of East 53rd between Madison and Fifth avenues. Its soothing mini-waterfall and transparent water tunnel are juxtaposed with a haunting five-panel section of the former Berlin Wall. Around the corner, the **Continental Illinois Center** looks like a cross between a space rocket and a grain silo, but the **Sony Building** (formerly the AT&T Building), at no. 550 between 55th and 56th streets, has grabbed more headlines. A Johnson–Burgee collaboration, it follows the postmodernist theory of borrowing from historical styles: a Modernist skyscraper is sandwiched between a Chippendale top and a Renaissance base. The **IBM Building**, at no. 580–590, between 56th and 57th streets, has a far more user-friendly plaza than the Sony Building. In the calm, glass-enclosed atrium, tinkling music, tropical foliage, a coffee bar and comfortable seating make for a livelier experience. Across East 57th Street at no. 41–45 is the eye-catching **Fuller Building**. Black-and-white Art Deco, it has a fine entrance and tiled floor. Cut east on 57th Street to no. 57 to find the **Four Seasons Hotel**, notable for sweeping marble and limestone design by I.M. Pei.

Park Avenue

In 1929, author Collinson Owen wrote that **Park Avenue** is "where wealth is so swollen that it almost bursts". Things have changed little since. The focal point of the avenue is the hulking **Grand Central Terminal**, at 42nd Street. South of Grand Central, Park Avenue narrows in both width and interest, but to the north of the building it becomes an impressively broad boulevard. Built to accommodate elevated rail tracks, the area quickly became a battleground, as corporate headquarters and refined residences jostled for prominence. Whatever your feelings about conspicuous wealth, from the 40s north, Park Avenue is one of the city's most awesome sights. Its sweeping expanse, genteel facades and sculpture-studded medians capture both the gracious and grand sides of New York in one fell swoop.

Grand Central Terminal

Park Avenue hits 42nd Street at Pershing Square, where it lifts off the ground to make room for the massive **Grand Central Terminal** (Ⓦwww.grandcentralterminal.com). More than just a train station, the terminal is a full-blown destination in itself. When it was constructed in 1913 (on the site of the original station built by Cornelius Vanderbilt), the terminal was a masterly piece of urban planning. After the electrification of the railways made it possible to reroute trains underground, the rail lines behind the existing station were sold off to developers and the profits went toward the building of a new terminal – built around a basic iron frame but clothed with a Beaux Arts skin. While Grand Central soon took on an almost mythical significance, today its traffic consists mainly of commuters speeding out to Connecticut, Westchester County and upstate New York, and any claim to being a gateway to an undiscovered continent is purely symbolic.

The most spectacular aspect of the building is its **size**, though the MetLife building (see p.138) dwarfs it in height. The station's main concourse is one of the world's finest and most imposing open spaces, 470ft long and 150ft high. The **barrel-vaulted ceiling** is speckled like a Baroque church with a painted representation of the winter night sky, its 2500 stars shown back to front – "as God would have seen them", the French painter Paul Helleu reputedly remarked. Stand in the middle and you realize that Grand Central represents a time when stations were seen as miniature cities. Walking around the marble corridors and feeling the subtle shifts in dynamics, mood and pace is an elegant and instructive experience you're unlikely to forget. You can explore Grand Central on your own or take the excellent **tour** run by the Municipal Arts Society (every Wed 12.30pm, 90min; $10 suggested donation; Ⓦwww.mas.org); the Grand Central Partnership runs a lunchtime tour as well (Fri 12.30pm, 90–120min; free; Ⓦwww.grandcentralpartnership.org), which meets across 42nd Street in the Sculpture Court of the Whitney Museum at Altria.

In addition to its architectural and historical offerings, there are fifty shops here, including the tantalizing Grand Central Market, which sells every gourmet food imaginable, and more than thirty restaurants, many of which are on the terminal's lower concourse. Chief among the eateries is the *Grand Central Oyster Bar* (review on p.326), which is located in the vaulted bowels of the station and is one of the city's most celebrated seafood spots. Just outside of the restaurant is something that explains why the *Oyster Bar*'s babble is not solely the result of the people eating there: two people can stand on opposite sides of any of the vaulted spaces and hold a conversation just by whispering, an acoustic fluke that makes this the loudest eatery in town.

For a civilized cocktail, stop into the *Campbell Apartment* (see p.352). The grand one-time home of the terminal's architect, it is found near the terminal's west-side taxi stand.

Around Grand Central

Across East 42nd Street to the south, the former **Bowery Savings Bank**, now one of Harry Cipriani's upscale eateries, echoes Grand Central's grandeur. **The Grand Hyatt Hotel**, meanwhile, next to Grand Central Terminal on the south side of 42nd Street, is another notable instance of excess, and perhaps the best (or worst) example in the city of all that is truly vulgar about contemporary American interior design. The thundering waterfalls, lurking palms and gliding escalators represent plush-carpeted bad taste at its most meretricious.

Just north of Grand Central on 200 Park Ave stands the Bauhaus bulk of the **MetLife Building**, built in 1963 as the Pan Am Building and impressive more for its size than its grandeur. Bauhaus guru Walter Gropius had a hand in designing the structure; the critical consensus is that he could have done better. As the headquarters of the now-defunct international airline, the building, in profile, was meant to suggest an airplane wing. The blue-grey mass certainly adds drama to the cityscape, although it robs Park Avenue of its southern views, sealing off 44th Street and sapping much of the vigour of the surrounding buildings.

The Helmsley Building, the Waldorf–Astoria and north

Standing astride the avenue at 46th Street at no. 230 is the high altar of the New York Central Building (built in 1928 and years later rechristened the **Helmsley Building**). A delicate construction with a lewdly excessive Rococo lobby, it rises up directly in the middle of the avenue; twin tunnels allow traffic to pass beneath it. In its mid-twentieth-century heyday it formed a punctuation mark to the avenue, but its thunder was stolen in 1963 by the completion of the Met Life Building, which looms above and behind it.

Wherever you placed the solid mass of the **Waldorf-Astoria Hotel**, at no. 301 (see p.278), a resplendent statement of Art Deco elegance between 49th and 50th streets, it would more than hold its own. Even if not staying here, duck inside to stroll through a block of vintage grandeur, sweeping marble and hushed plushness where such well-knowns as Herbert Hoover, Cole Porter and Princess Grace of Monaco have bunked. The grand circular bar of the *Bull and Bear* is downstairs.

Crouching just across 50th Street, **St Bartholomew's Church** is a low-slung Byzantine hybrid with portals designed by McKim, Mead, and White; it adds an immeasurable amount of character to the area, lending the lumbering skyscrapers a much-needed sense of scale. The church fought against developers for years, and ultimately became a test case for New York City's landmark preservation law. Today, its congregation thrives and its members sponsor many community-outreach programmes.

Directly behind St Bartholomew's, the spiky-topped **General Electric Building** seems like a wild extension of the church, its slender shaft rising to a meshed crown of abstract sparks and lightning strokes that symbolize the radio waves used by its original owner, RCA. A New York-designated landmark, the building is another Art Deco delight, with nickel-silver ornamentation, carved red marble and a lobby with a vaulted ceiling (entrance at 570 Lexington Ave).

Among all this architectural ostentation it's difficult at first to see the originality of the **Seagram Building**, at 375 Park Ave between 52nd and 53rd streets. Designed by Mies van der Rohe and Philip Johnson, and built in 1958, this was the seminal curtain-wall skyscraper: deceptively simple and cleverly detailed, with floors supported internally rather than by the building's walls, allowing a skin of smoky glass and whiskey-bronze metal. Although the facade has now weathered to a dull black, it remains the supreme example of Modernist reason. The **plaza**, an open forecourt designed to set the building apart from its neighbours and display it to advantage, was such a success as a public space that the city revised the zoning laws to encourage other high-rise builders to supply similar plazas.

Across Park Avenue between 53rd and 54th streets is **Lever House**, at no. 390, the building that set the Modernist ball rolling on Park Avenue when it was constructed in 1952. Back then, the two right-angled slabs that form a steel-and-glass book end seemed revolutionary when compared with the surrounding buildings. Its vintage appeal helps to make *Casa Lever*, the Italian restaurant on the ground floor (and one with some funky design touches itself), a welcome spot for a drink or meal.

Lexington Avenue

One block east of Park Avenue, **Lexington Avenue** marks a sort of border between East Side elegance and the everyday avenues closer to the East River. It roars into life around 42nd Street and the Chrysler Building, and especially through the mid-40s, where commuters swarm around Grand Central Terminal. From there, Lexington lurches northward past 53rd Street and the towering aluminum and glass **Citigroup Center**, to the bulk of **Bloomingdale's** department store at 59th Street, which marks the end of the avenue's midtown stretch of highlights.

The Chrysler Building and around

The Chrysler Building, at 405 Lexington Ave, dates from 1930, a time when architects married prestige with grace and style. For a fleeting moment, this was the world's tallest building; it was surpassed by the Empire State Building in 1931, and is currently tied with the new Times building (p.148) for no. 3. However, since the rediscovery of Art Deco, it has become one of Manhattan's best-loved structures. The golden age of motoring is evoked by the building's car-motif friezes, hood-ornament gargoyles, radiator-grille spire, and the fact that the entire building is almost completely fashioned from stainless steel. Its designer, William Van Alen, indulged in a feud with an erstwhile partner, H. Craig Severance, who was designing a building at 40 Wall St at the same time. Each was determined to have the higher skyscraper. Van Alen secretly built the stainless-steel spire inside the Chrysler's crown, and when 40 Wall St finally topped out a few feet higher than the Chrysler, Van Alen popped the 185-foot spire out through the top of the building and won the day.

The Chrysler Corporation moved out decades ago, and for a while the building was allowed to decline by a company that didn't wholly appreciate its spirit. The current owner has pledged to keep it lovingly intact, and it was renovated in 2000 by Philip Johnson. The lobby, once a car showroom, is all you can see, but that's enough in itself. The opulent walls are covered in African marble; the ceiling shows a realistic, if rather faded, study of airplanes, machines and brawny builders who worked on the tower; and the lift doors have magnificent inlaid-wood designs.

On the south side of 42nd Street flanking Lexington Avenue are two more noteworthy buildings. The **Chanin Building**, at 122 East 42nd St, on the right, is another Art Deco monument, cut with terracotta carvings of leaves, tendrils and sea creatures. Also interesting is the design of the weighty **Mobil Building** across the street at no. 150. Built in 1956, it was the first metal-clad office building in the world at the time. Made with seven thousand panels of chromium-nickel stainless steel, it was designed to enable the wind to keep it clean.

Citigroup Center and around

Just as the Chrysler Building dominates the lower stretches of Lexington Avenue, the chisel-topped **Citigroup Center** (better known by its former name of Citicorp Center), at 153 East 53rd St, between 53rd and 54th streets, towers above northern midtown. Opened in 1978, the building, now one of New York's most conspicuous landmarks, looks as if it is sheathed in shiny graph paper. Its slanted roof was designed to house solar panels and provide power, but the idea was ahead of the technology and Citicorp, as the company was previously called, had to satisfy itself by adopting the distinctive top as a corporate logo.

Hiding under the Center's skirts at 619 Lexington Ave is **St Peter's Lutheran Church**, known as "the Jazz Church" for being the venue of many a jazz musician's funeral; it's also host to a long-running jazz-tinged vespers service at 5pm (there are Wednesday lunchtime jazz performances and the occasional evening concert as well). The tiny church was built to replace the one demolished to make way for Citicorp, and part of the deal was that the church had to stand out from the Center – which explains the granite material. The thoroughly modern interior includes sculptor Louise Nevelson's white-walled Erol Beker Chapel of the Good Shepherd. Another Nevelson sculpture (*Night Presence IV*) can be seen at East 92nd Street, on the median running down Park Avenue.

One block north on Lexington Avenue, and in direct contrast to the simple, contemporary St Peter's, stands the Reformed **Central Synagogue**, 652 Lexington Ave, at East 55th Street. Striking because of its Moorish appearance, this landmark structure was built in 1870–72 by German immigrant Henry Fernbach. The oldest continually used Jewish house of worship in the city, it was heavily damaged in a blaze in 1998 and repairs were unable to fully restore all the site's features, though services are still held as usual.

Third, Second and First avenues

The construction of the Citigroup Center spurred the development of **Third Avenue** in the late 1970s. One 1980s postmodern entry on that stretch, the so-called **Lipstick Building** at no. 885, is a tiered, oval-shaped steel tower created by Philip Johnson and John Burgee; it also holds the former offices of disgraced (and incarcerated) Ponzi-scheme broker Bernie Madoff. Nightlife, however, congregates on **Second Avenue**, which also has some architectural attractions lying on or around 42nd Street. The stone facade of the sombre yet elegant former **Daily News Building**, at 220 East 42nd St, fronts a surprising Art Deco interior. The most impressive remnant of the original 1929 decor is a large globe encased in a lighted circular frame (with updated geography), made famous by Superman movies when the Daily News Building appropriately housed the *Daily Planet*. The tabloid after which the building is named has since moved to 450 West 33rd St, and the building is not open on weekends.

Just north and around the corner from the Daily News, at 320 East 43rd St, between First and Second avenues, is one of the city's most peaceful (if surreal) spaces – the **Ford Foundation Building**. Built in 1967, the building featured the first of the atria that are now commonplace across Manhattan. Structurally, the atrium is a giant greenhouse, gracefully supported by soaring granite columns and edged with two walls of offices visible through the windows. This subtropical garden, which changes with the seasons, was one of the first attempts to create a "natural" environment inside a building, and it's astonishingly quiet. Forty-second Street is no more than a murmur outside, and all you can hear is the burble of water, the echo of voices, and the clipped crack of feet on the brick walkways. The indoor/outdoor experience here is one of New York City's great architectural coups.

At the east end of 42nd Street, steps lead up to the 1925 **Tudor City**, which rises behind a tiny tree-filled park. With coats of arms, leaded glass and neat neighbourhood shops, this area is the very picture of self-contained residential respectability. It's an official historic district to boot. Head down the steps here and you'll be plum opposite the **United Nations**.

The United Nations

Some see the **United Nations complex** – built after World War II, when John D. Rockefeller, Jr donated $8.5 million to buy the eighteen-acre East River site – as one of the major sights of New York. Others, usually those who've been there, are not so complimentary. Despite the symbolism of the UN, few buildings are quite so dull to walk around. What's more, as if to rationalize the years of UN impotence in international war and hunger zones, the (obligatory) guided tours emphasize that the UN's main purpose is to promote dialogue and awareness rather than enforcement. The organization itself moves at a snail's pace – bogged down by regulations and a lack of funds – which is the general feel of the tour as well.

For the determined, the complex consists of three main buildings – the thin, glass-curtained slab of the **Secretariat**; the sweeping curve of the **General Assembly Building**, whose chambers can accommodate more than 191 national delegations; and the low-rise **Conference Wing**, which connects the other two structures. Construction on the complex began in 1949 and finished in 1963, the product of a suitably international team of architects that included Le Corbusier – though he pulled out before the construction was completed. Guided tours (Mon–Fri 9.45am–4.45pm; tours last 45min; $16; bring ID; ⓣ212/963-8687,

Ⓦwww.un.org) take in the UN conference chambers and its constituent parts; make sure to call ahead to see if anything is off-limits that day.

Even more revealing than the stately chambers are its thoughtful exhibition spaces and artful country gifts on view, including an intricate ivory carving from China and a huge (12ft by 15ft) stained-glass window by artist Marc Chagall, commissioned in 1964 as a memorial to Dag Hammarskjold, the second Secretary-General of the United Nations. Council chambers visited on the tour include the **Security Council**, the **Economic and Social Council** and the **Trusteeship Council** – all of which are similarly retro (note the clunky machinery of the journalists' areas) and sport some intriguing Marxist murals. Once you've been whisked around all these sites and have seen examples of the many artefacts that have been donated to the UN by its various member states, the tour is more or less over and will leave you in the basement of the General Assembly Building. Where the UN has real class is in its beautiful **gardens**, with their modern sculpture and views of the East River.

Beekman Place and Sutton Place

Outside of the environs of the UN, **First Avenue** has a certain rangy looseness that's a relief after the concrete claustrophobia of midtown. **Beekman Place** (49th to 51st sts between First Ave and the East River) is quieter still, a beguiling enclave of garbled styles. Similar, though not quite as intimate, is **Sutton Place**, which stretches from 53rd to 59th streets between First Avenue and the river. Originally built for the lordly Morgans and Vanderbilts in 1875, Sutton Place increases in elegance as you move north and, for today's *crème de la crème*, **Riverview Terrace** (off 58th St at the river) is a (very) private enclave of five brownstone houses. The UN Secretary-General has an official residence on Sutton Place, and the locals are choosy about whom they let in: disgraced ex-president Richard Nixon was refused on the grounds he would be a security risk.

12

Midtown West

Between West 30th and 59th streets and west of Sixth Avenue, much of midtown Manhattan is enthralling, noisy and garish, packed with attractions meant to entertain the legions of tourists staying in the area's many hotels. The heart of **Midtown West** is **Times Square**, where jostling crowds and huge neon signs assault the senses at all times of the day. It's here that the east side's more sedate approach to capitalism finally overflows its bounds and New York City reaches its commercial zenith. South of Times Square is the bustling, business-oriented **Garment District**, home to Madison Square Garden and Macy's department store, while just north of the once "naughty, bawdy 42nd Street" is the **Theater District**, which offers the most impressive concentration of live theatre in the world.

For glimpses of vintage seediness, head west beyond Eighth Avenue to **Hell's Kitchen** – though keep in mind that the buzzing forces of gentrification are hard at work in this part of town, and shiny open-air eateries are far more common than peep-show pavilions these days. There aren't many tourist attractions per se in this direction, though if you hike all the way over to the Hudson River, you'll come upon the massive **Intrepid Sea, Air & Space Museum**, which is housed in a retired aircraft carrier. Back over in the centre of the island, **Sixth Avenue**, its architecture melding cultural and corporate New York, is good for a stroll, while **57th Street** has some of the city's most distinctive shops and steadfast clusters of galleries, many of which display some of the world's greatest works of art.

The Garment District

Squeezing in between Sixth and Eighth avenues from West 30th to 42nd streets, the **Garment District**, home to the twin modern monsters of Penn Station and Madison Square Garden and sometimes referred to as the Fashion District, offers little of interest to the casual tourist.

With the rise in foreign production, fewer and fewer garments are put together in this tiny (and ever-diminishing) quarter, though it's still responsible for a high percentage of American-made clothing. Walking around, you might just think nothing at all is going on: outlets are almost entirely wholesale and don't bother to woo customers, and the only visible evidence of the industry is the racks of clothes shunted around on the street and occasional bins of off-cuts that give the area the look of an open-air rummage sale.

RESTAURANTS

Ariana Afghan Kebab	11
Aureole	35
Becco	25
Carnegie Deli	8
Chez Napoleon	18
Churrascaria Plataforma	22
Hallo Berlin	28
Hell's Kitchen	24
Landmark Tavern	27
Le Bernardin	16
Pam Real Thai	21
Petrossian	1
Ruby Foo's	20
Russian Tea Room	4
Stage Deli	9
Sugiyama	6
Thalia	19
Trattoria dell'Arte	3
Uncle Vanya Café	7
Virgil's Real BBQ	32
West Bank Café	36
Yakitori Totto	6

BARS

Ardesia	12
Jimmy's Corner	33
Kashkaval	5
P.J. Carney's	2
Rudy's	30
Russian Vodka Room	14
Stout	39

CAFÉS

Brasserie Maison	10
Café Edison	23
Café Forant	15
Cosmic Diner	13
Cupcake Café	37
Little Pie Company	34
Poseidon Bakery	29

CLUBS & LIVE MUSIC

Birdland	31
Hammerstein Ballroom	38
Iridium Jazz Club	17
Pacha	26

One of the benefits of walking through this part of town, though, is taking advantage of the designers' **sample sales**, where floor samples and models' castoffs are sold to the public at cheap prices (see p.404 for more on sample sales).

Greeley and Herald squares

Sixth Avenue collides with Broadway at West 34th Street at an unremarkable triangle given the somewhat overblown title **Greeley Square**, in honour of Horace Greeley, founder of the *New York Tribune* newspaper. One could make the case that Greeley deserves better: known for his rallying call to the youth of the nineteenth century ("Go West, young man!"), he also supported the rights of women and trade unions, denounced slavery and capital punishment, and commissioned a weekly column from Karl Marx.

The somewhat more interesting **Herald Square** faces Greeley Square in a continuation of the battle between the *New York Herald* newspaper and its archrival, Horace Greeley's *Tribune*. (The two papers merged in 1924 to form the *New York Herald Tribune*, which was published until 1967.) During the 1890s this was the Tenderloin area, with dance halls, brothels and rough bars like *Satan's Circus* and the *Burnt Rag* thriving beside the elevated railway that ran up Sixth Avenue. These days its streets are congested with consumers, many heading for the massive Macy's department store adjacent to the square.

Macy's

Macy's, at 151 West 34th St (Ⓣ212/695-4400, Ⓦwww.macys.com), bills itself as "the world's largest store", which is not overly hyperbolic, considering the building takes up an entire city block and offers about two million square feet of selling space. Founded in 1858, the store moved to its current location in 1902 although it wasn't until the 1980s that Macy's went fashionably upmarket, with designers – such as Tommy Hilfiger – building their own shops in store. Macy's fortunes declined dramatically, however, when the economy went into a tailspin in 1990, but scrambled out of its 1992 bankruptcy in the nick of time, complete with a debt-restructuring plan that allowed it to continue financing its famed annual Thanksgiving Day Parade (see Chapter 32, "Parades and festivals").

Madison Square Garden and Penn Station

The most prominent landmark in the Garment District, the **Pennsylvania Station and Madison Square Garden complex** takes up the whole block between Seventh and Eighth avenues and 32nd and 33rd streets. It's a combined box-and-drum structure: at the same time its train-station belly swallows up millions of commuters, its above-ground facilities house Knicks basketball and Rangers hockey games, as well as professional wrestling and boxing matches (for ticket details, see p.418).

There's nothing memorable about the train station; its grimy subterranean levels are an example of just about everything that's wrong with the subway. The original 1910 Penn Station, which brought an air of dignity to the neighbourhood and set the stage for the ornate General Post Office and other elaborate *belle époque* structures, was demolished in 1963 to make way for this monstrous structure. One of McKim, Mead, and White's greatest designs, the station's original edifice reworked the ideas of the Roman Baths of Caracalla to awesome effect: the floors of the grand arcade were pink marble, the walls pink granite. Glass floor tiles in the main waiting room allowed light from the glass roof to flow through to the trains and platforms below. Architectural historian Vincent Scully lamented the differences in the two structures in the 1960s, saying, "Through it one entered

Old Penn Station and the Landmarks Preservation Law

When the old **Penn Station** was demolished in 1963 to expand the Madison Square Garden sports complex, the notion of conservation was only a gleam in the eye of its middle-class supporters, at the time few and far between but ten years later a broad-based power group. Despite the vocal opposition of a few, "modernization" was the theme of the day – so much so that almost nothing of the original building was saved. A number of the carefully crafted statues and decorations actually became landfill for New Jersey's Meadowlands complex just across the Hudson River.

At around the same time, the Singer Building, an early, graceful skyscraper in the Financial District, was demolished to make way for the hulking US Steel Building. In the end, it was public disgust with the wanton destruction of these two buildings that brought about the passing of the **Landmarks Preservation Law**. This act ensures that buildings granted landmark status – a designation based on aesthetic value or historical importance – cannot be destroyed or even altered. The law goes beyond protecting buildings, and also applies to districts, such as Fort Greene and Soho, as well as "scenic" landmarks, including Verdi Square at Broadway and West 73rd Street.

the city like a god... One scuttles in now like a rat." Some of Penn Station's lost lustre may be restored when – or rather, if – an expanded station opens in the General Post Office building; that long-standing plan finally looks set to happen but it's seemed that way before.

Glimpses of the original structure are visible in photos hanging in the Amtrak waiting area of today's Penn Station, as well as in the four-faced clock on display in the Long Island Railroad (LIRR) ticket area on 34th Street and Seventh Avenue. Andrew Leicester's 1994 *Ghost Series* lines the walls, including terracotta wall murals saluting the Corinthian and Ionic columns of the old Penn Station. Also look for a rendering of Adolph A. Weinman's sculpture *Day & Night*, an ornate statue surrounding a clock that welcomed passengers at the old station's entrance. Be sure to look above your head in the LIRR ticket area for Maya Lin's *Eclipsed Time*, a sculpture of glass, aluminum and fibre optics that alludes to the immeasurability of time with random number patterns.

The General Post Office

Immediately behind Penn Station at 421 Eighth Ave, the **General Post Office** (aka the James A. Farley Post Office) is a 1913 McKim, Mead, and White structure that survived the push for modernization, and stands as a relic from an era when municipal pride was all about making statements – the block-and-a-half-long building is fronted by twenty Corinthian columns and steps spanning the length of the colonnade. There's still a working post-office branch here, although the main sorting stations have moved into more modern spaces farther west; a few scattered displays on postal history flesh things out. That said, the building is no architectural dinosaur: a new Penn Station for Amtrak was to be built inside, keeping the original exterior preserved, but it's uncertain if that will ever come to pass (see the section on Madison Square Garden above). Originally set to open in 2011, the redevelopment, to be named Moynihan Station after the late New York State Senator Daniel Patrick Moynihan, looks more like it will just begin to be constructed around then.

Port Authority Bus Terminal

One of midtown's more reviled landmarks, the **Port Authority Bus Terminal Building** crouches on Eighth Avenue between West 40th and 42nd streets (for practical details see p.25). Not long ago, the Port Authority served as a magnet for down-and-outs, but it is spruced up and remarkably safe now, even if some of the blocks around it remain grotty. Greyhound buses leave from here, as do several other regional services.

Times Square and around

Forty-second Street meets Broadway at the southern outskirts of **Times Square**, the centre of the Theater District (see box, p.148), where the constantly pulsating neon conjures up the notion of a beating heart for Manhattan. The area is certainly always alive with activity. Traditionally a melting pot of debauchery, depravity and fun, for decades the quarter was a place where out-of-towners provided easy pickings for petty criminals, drug dealers and prostitutes. Most of Times Square's legendary pornography and crime are long gone, replaced by sanitized superstores, high-rise office buildings and boutique hotels that have killed off the square's historically greasy appeal. This doesn't mean, though, that the area is without charm, and hundreds of thousands of people still mass here every New Year's Eve, when a giant sparkling ball drops from the top of Times Tower on the stroke of

▲ Times Square

midnight. If you have never seen Times Square, plan your first visit for after dark. Without passing through the square, take a taxi to 57th and Broadway and start walking south. The spectacle will open out before your eyes, slowly at first, and then with a rush of energy and animation.

Like nearby Greeley and Herald squares, Times Square took its name from a newspaper – the *New York Times* built its offices here in 1904. While the *Herald* and *Tribune* fought each other in ever more vicious circulation battles, the *Times* stood on more restrained ground under the banner "All the news that's fit to print", a policy that has enabled both its survival and its current status as most powerful newspaper in the country. The newspaper's old headquarters, **Times Tower**, is at the southernmost end of the square on a small block between 42nd and 43rd streets. Originally an elegant building modelled on Giotto's campanile in Florence, the famous zipper sign displaying the news of the world was added in 1928. In 1965, the building was "skinned" and covered with the lifeless marble slabs visible today. The paper's offices have long since moved, most recently to a newly constructed 52-storey Renzo Piano tower across from Port Authority, and most of the printing is done in New Jersey.

Not actually a square at all, Times Square is formed by the intersection between arrow-straight Seventh Avenue and left-leaning Broadway; the latter more or less follows true north through much of the island, which tilts to the northeast. So narrow is the angle between these two thoroughfares that Broadway, which meets Seventh Avenue at 43rd Street, does not begin to strike off on its own again until 48th Street, just above the traffic island of **Duffy Square**. That stretch has been made into a pedestrianized plaza in an effort to improve traffic flow; there's seating along the way as well. On and off the street are the theatres that host big plays and musicals (see box, p.366), as well as the **Discovery Times Square Exposition**, at 224 West 44th St (Mon–Wed 10am–8pm, Thurs & Fri 10am–9.30pm, Sat 9.30am–9.30pm, Sun 9.30am–8pm; $27.50,

The Theater District

Though many of the **theatres** hosting big-budget musicals and dramas considered to be "Broadway shows" are not technically on that avenue, they are, for the most part, located within a couple blocks of it in the West 40s (concentrated on 44th and 45th sts). Sadly, the majority of New York's great theatres have been destroyed to make way for office buildings. However, some of the old grandeur still survives in the forty venues that remain. The **New Amsterdam**, at 214 West 42nd St, and the family-oriented **New Victory**, at 209 West 42nd St, both between Seventh and Eighth avenues, were refurbished by Disney some years ago, two of the truly welcome results of the massive changes here. The **Lyceum**, at 149 West 45th St, retains its original facade, while the **Shubert Theater**, at 225 West 44th St, which hosted *A Chorus Line* during its fifteen-year run, has a magnificent landmarked interior that belies its simple outward appearance. The modest **Helen Hayes Theater**, at 240 West 44th St, is the smallest of the Broadway houses; down the street at the **Actors Studio**, at 432 West 44th St, Lee Strasberg taught the principles of "method-acting", a technique invented by Russian actor Constantin Stanislavski to help actors "live the part".

The famous **neon**, so much a signature of Times Square, was initially confined to the theatres and spawned the term "the Great White Way". Today the illumination is not limited to theatres. Myriad ads, forming one of the world's most garish nocturnal displays, promote hundreds of products and services. Businesses that rent offices here are actually required to allow signage on their walls – the city's attempt to retain the square's traditional feel, paradoxically enough, with the most advanced technology possible.

kids 4–12 $17.50; ⓦwww.discoverytsx.com), which puts on large-scale, crowd-pleasing exhibits covering subjects like King Tutankhamun and the *Titanic*. Not much to look at itself, Duffy Square offers an excellent view of Times Square's lights, megahotels, theme stores and restaurants. A glass "stairway to nowhere", modest in comparison, is balanced on the renovated **TKTS booth**, which sells half-price, same-day tickets for Broadway shows (whose exorbitant prices these days make a visit to TKTS a necessity; see p.366 for details). A lifelike statue of Broadway's doyen **George M. Cohan** looks on, while at eye level you can find enough gifts in the souvenir shops for your five hundred closest friends.

Hell's Kitchen

Sprawling across the blocks west of Times Square to the Hudson River between 30th and 59th streets lies **Clinton** (named for nineteenth-century Governor Dewitt Clinton), more famously known as **Hell's Kitchen**, an area centred on the restaurants, bars and ethnic delis of **Ninth Avenue** – the staging set for the excellent Ninth Avenue International Food Festival (ⓦwww.ninthavenuefood festival.com) each May.

Head to Hell's Kitchen from Eighth Avenue by walking west on 46th Street along so-called **Restaurant Row** – the area's preferred haunt for pre- and post-theatre dining, even though most of the strip's eateries are mediocre at best. The Gothic red **St Clement's Episcopal Church**, at 423 West 46th St (ⓦwww.stclementsnyc.org) doubles as a community theatre, very much in keeping with the neighbourhood vibe.

Among New York's most violent and lurid neighbourhoods at one time, Hell's Kitchen was rumoured to be named for a tenement at 54th Street and Tenth Avenue. More commonly, the name has been attributed to a veteran policeman who went by the sobriquet "Dutch Fred the Cop". In response to his young partner's comment – while watching a riot – that the place was hell, Fred reportedly replied, "Hell's a mild climate. This is Hell's kitchen." The area originally contained slaughterhouses and factories that made soap and glue, with sections named "Misery Lane" and "Poverty Row". Irish immigrants were the first inhabitants; Greeks, Puerto Ricans and African-Americans soon joined them. Amid the overcrowding, tensions rapidly developed between (and within) ethnic groups – the rough-and-tumble neighbourhood was popularized in the musical *West Side Story* (1957). A violent Irish gang, the Westies, claimed the streets in the 1970s and early 1980s, but the area has since been cleaned up and is far less dangerous than it ever has been – though as ever you should still keep your wits about you. Trim residential streets counter the odd tatty block, and construction and renovation of luxury apartments and hotels occurs at sometimes breakneck speed. Along with other gentrifiers, there's now a substantial gay community, with nearly as many gay bars and nightspots as in Chelsea or the East Village.

The Intrepid Sea, Air & Space Museum

If you continue west to the river from Times Square, you will reach the **Intrepid Sea, Air & Space Museum**, 46th Street and Twelfth Avenue at Pier 86 (April–Sept Mon–Fri 10am–5pm, Sat & Sun 10am–6pm, Oct–March Tues–Sun 10am–5pm; $19.50, ages 3–17 $11.50; ⓣ212/245-0072, ⓦwww.intrepidmuseum.org). This huge (900ft-long) old aircraft carrier has a distinguished history: it picked up capsules from the Mercury and Gemini space missions and made several trips to Vietnam. It holds an array of modern and vintage air- and sea-craft, including the A-12 Blackbird, the world's fastest spy plane, and the USS *Growler*, the only guided-missile submarine open to the public. Interactive exhibits and simulators dominate the interior, but make sure to explore further into the bowels of the carrier, where you can see the crew's dining and sleeping quarters, the anchor room and a lot of navigational gadgets. The retired Concorde, formerly operated by British Airways, is also on hand, though the stats about the aircraft are more remarkable than an inspection of the craft. If you're visiting at the end of May, **Fleet Week** (the week leading up to Memorial Day) is a big deal here, and deservedly so, with ships visiting from all corners of the globe, as well as military demonstrations and competitions.

Sixth Avenue

Back east of Times Square, **Sixth Avenue** is officially named **Avenue of the Americas** but no New Yorker ever calls it that. While there's little of the ground-floor glitter of Fifth or the razzmatazz of Broadway, the street does more or less separate the business side of Midtown East from the theatre side of Midtown West (even though Fifth Ave is where the east–west addresses switch).

International Center of Photography

Just north of Bryant Park, the **International Center of Photography**, 1133 Sixth Ave at 43rd Street (Tues–Thurs, Sat & Sun 10am–6pm, Fri 10am–8pm; $12; Ⓣ212/857-0000, Ⓦwww.icp.org), was founded in 1974 by Cornell Capa (brother of war photographer Robert Capa). This exceptional museum and school sponsors around twenty exhibits a year dedicated to "concerned photography", avant-garde works and retrospectives of modern masters. Many of the shows focus on holdings from their own extensive permanent collection, which contains basically all of Robert Capa's photography, as well as that of New York sensationalist Weegee.

Rockefeller Center Extension and the Equitable Center

The **Rockefeller Center Extension** defines the Sixth Avenue stretch from 47th to 51st streets and gives it whatever visual excitement exists. Following the **Time & Life Building** at 50th Street, three near-identical buildings went up in the 1970s. Though they have none of the romance or style of their predecessor, they at least possess the monumentality. Backing onto Rockefeller Center proper (see p.130), the repeated statement of each building comes over with some power.

Occupying the block bordered by Sixth and Seventh avenues and 51st and 52nd streets, the **AXA Equitable Center** has plenty for the eye in the form of its public art. At 1290 Sixth Ave, the financial offices display Thomas Hart Benton's *America Today* murals. This creation (1931) was celebrated for its representation of ordinary pre-Depression-era Americans from a variety of classes, shown both at work and at leisure. It spurred an interest in murals as public art, and lent momentum to the Federal Arts Project (which provided both employment for artists suffering through the decade, and a morale boost for the rest of the public) in the 1930s. The mid-block galleria is highlighted by a series of Sol Lewitt murals, and Roy Lichtenstein's *Mural with Blue Brushtroke* provides a rush of colour for the atrium at 787 Seventh Ave.

While Sixth Avenue proceeds grandly and placidly north for several blocks before reaching the green expanse of Central Park, it's the **Ed Sullivan Theater**, a block north and west on 1697 Broadway between 53rd and 54th streets, that attracts the most people in this neighbourhood. Queues wrap around 53rd Street for standby tickets to see the *Late Show* with David Letterman, just as they might have fifty years ago for the Ed Sullivan variety show shot on the same stage.

57th Street

The area just around 57th Street from Broadway over to Fifth Avenue competes with Soho and Chelsea as a centre for **upmarket art sales**. Galleries here are noticeably snootier than their downtown relations, and some require appointments for viewings. One that provides something other than a quick, uncomfortable browse is the **Art Students League**, at 215 West 57th St (ⓦwww.theartstudentsleague.org), built in 1892 by Henry J. Hardenbergh (who later built the *Plaza Hotel*) to mimic Francis the First's hunting lodge at Fontainebleau. Besides offering inexpensive art classes to the public, the League allows visitors the chance to observe the instructors and students in action. (For more on galleries in this area, see Chapter 29, "Commercial galleries".)

Carnegie Hall and around

At 154 West 57th St is stately **Carnegie Hall**, one of the world's greatest concert venues, revered by musicians and audiences alike. The Renaissance-inspired structure was built in the 1890s by steel magnate and self-styled "improver of mankind" Andrew Carnegie, and the still-superb acoustics ensure full houses most of the year. Tchaikovsky conducted the programme on opening night and Mahler, Rachmaninov, Toscanini, Frank Sinatra and Judy Garland have all performed here (not to mention Duke Ellington, Billie Holiday, the Beatles, Spinal Tap and Lady Gaga). Tours are available September to June only (Mon–Fri 11.30am, 2pm & 3pm, Sat 11.30am & 12.30pm, Sun 12.30pm; $10; tours ⓣ212/903-9765, tickets ⓣ212-247-7800, ⓦwww.carnegiehall.org); they finish up in a small, second-floor gallery of memorabilia that's open to the public for free.

A few nearby apartment buildings are worth a gander on the way to Central Park. An absolute riot of terra cotta embellishments cover the facade of **Alwyn Court**, at 180 West 58th St, though unfortunately you can't enter the building to see the mural and skylight in the courtyard. Around the corner is the **Gainsborough Studios** building, at 222 Central Park South, between Broadway and Seventh Avenue. Built in 1905, it became an official city landmark in 1988 and is notable for the Moravian tiles that dominate the top two floors, as well as the double-storey windows that peer onto Central Park. Note the bust of the building's namesake, English artist Thomas Gainsborough, which hovers above the entrance on the facade.

If instead you head west from Carnegie Hall on 57th Street, at the intersection with Eight Avenue you'll hit the **Hearst World Headquarters**, which had its 597ft tower completed in June 2006. The tower, designed by Lord Norman Foster, is incongruously attached atop a multi-style six-storey base of precast limestone. It is certified as one of the most environmentally friendly high-rise buildings ever constructed, employing technologies to reduce pollution and energy consumption, while fully utilizing renewable energy resources.

13

Central Park

"All radiant in the magic atmosphere of art and taste", raved *Harper's* magazine on the occasion of the opening of **Central Park** in 1876. A slight overstatement, perhaps, although today few people could imagine New York City without the park. Devotedly used by locals and visited by nearly everyone who spends a few days here, it serves purposes as varied as the individuals who take advantage of it: it's an environmental haven, a beach, a playground, a running track, a venue for pop music, opera, theatre and street entertainers, and much more.

Some history

Poet and newspaper editor **William Cullen Bryant** is credited with first publicizing the idea for an open public space in Manhattan in 1844; seven years later, City Hall finally agreed to carry out his plan, paying $5 million for 840 acres north of the (then) city limits at 38th Street, a desolate swampy area occupied at the time by scattered shantytowns whose residents were evicted as planning began to pick up speed.

In 1857, after a fierce design contest, **Frederick Law Olmsted** and **Calvert Vaux** were chosen to create the rural paradise they called "Greensward", an

Park practicalities

The **Central Park Conservancy** (☎212/310-6600 or 212/360-1311, ⓦwww.centralparknyc.org), founded in 1980, is a nonprofit organization dedicated to preserving and managing the park. It runs four **Visitor Centers**, which have free maps and other helpful literature, as well as feature special events. All are open year-round Tues–Sun 10am–5pm: The **Dairy** (65th St at mid-park; ☎212/794-6564); **Belvedere Castle** (79th St at mid-park; ☎212/772-0210); the **North Meadow Recreation Center** (mid-park at 97th St; ☎212/348-4867); and the **Charles A. Dana Discovery Center** (110th St off Fifth Ave; ☎212/860-1370).

Restrooms are available at Hecksher Playground, the Boat Pond (Conservatory Water), Mineral Springs House (northwest end of Sheep's Meadow), Bethesda Terrace, Loeb Boathouse, the Delacorte Theater, the East 85th Street Playground, the Tennis House (94th St mid-park), the North Meadow Recreation Center, the Conservatory Garden, the Robert Bendheim Playground (East 100th St at Fifth Ave), the Great Hill and the Charles A. Dana Discovery Center.

Urban Park Rangers (☎212/628-2345, ⓦwww.nyc.gov/parks/rangers) are in the park to help; they lead walking tours, give directions, provide necessary first aid, even organize camping trips. In case of emergency, use the **emergency call boxes** located throughout the park and along the park drives (they provide a direct connection to the Central Park Precinct), or dial ☎911 at any payphone.

illusion of the countryside smack in the heart of Manhattan. The sparseness of the existing terrain didn't just attract builders; it also provided Olmsted and Vaux with the perfect opportunity to plan the park according to the precepts of classical English landscape gardening. They designed 36 elegant bridges, each unique, and planned an ingenious system of four sunken transverse roads to segregate different kinds of traffic.

It took sixteen years and $14 million ($270 million in today's money) to construct the entire park, though the sapling trees planted here didn't reach their full height for five decades. Central Park opened to the public in 1876. So great was the acclaim for Olmsted and Vaux that they were soon in demand as park architects all over the United States. Locally, they went on to design Riverside and Morningside parks in Manhattan, as well as Prospect Park in Brooklyn.

At its opening, the powers that be emphasized that Central Park was a "people's park", available to all. Though most of the impoverished masses for whom it was allegedly built had neither the time nor the money to travel up to 59th Street from their downtown slums and enjoy it, people eventually started flooding in as the city grew in size and wealth.

Robert Moses, a relentless urban planner and the power behind some of the city's largest building projects in the mid-twentieth century, tried hard to put his imprint (concrete) on Central Park while he served as parks commissioner from 1935 to 1960. Happily, public opinion kept damage from his

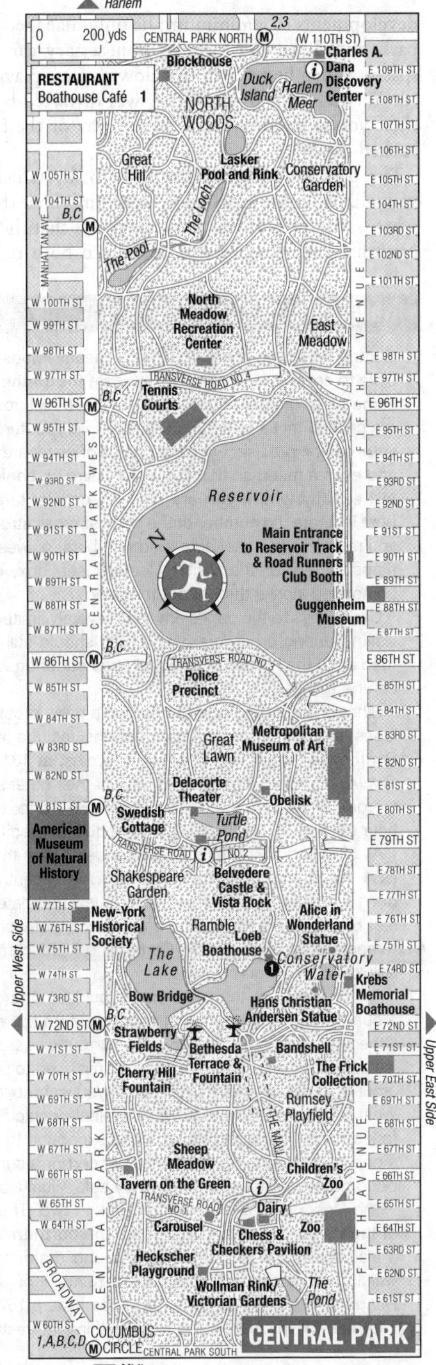

developments to a minimum; he only managed to pave over a small portion of the park, mostly in the form of unnecessary car parks (since reconverted to green space). When he tried to tear down a park playground in 1956 to build a car park for *Tavern on the Green*, Moses was thwarted by outraged citizens – mothers and their young children stood in the way of the bulldozers, and the city sheepishly backed down.

The park hit rock bottom in 1973, by which point it had degenerated into a vandalized, crime-infested eyesore on which the bankrupt city had no money to spare (see p.443). It was only the threat that the park would be turned over to the National Park Service that mobilized both politicians and local citizens to find

Navigating the park

Central Park is so enormous that it's nearly impossible to miss entirely and as impossible to cover in one visit. The intricate **footpaths** that meander through the park are some of its greatest successes. If you've lost your way among them, though, there are several tricks to finding it again. Every feature has a name in order that rendezvous can be precise. Even the bodies of water are differentiated (a loch, a pool, a lake and even a meer) so that there can never be confusion. But if you do need **to figure out exactly where you are**, find the nearest **lamppost**. The first two digits on the post indicate the number of the nearest cross street, while the last two show whether you're nearer the east side (odd numbers) or west side (even). You can pick up free maps at any of the Visitor Centers (see box, p.152) or two dozen freestanding unmanned kiosks throughout the park.

Car access to the park's drives is severely limited outside rush hours. Even if you're visiting during a car-free period, you should still keep a watchful eye: crossing the road amid the hordes of goggled and headphoned rollerbladers, cyclists and joggers can be trying.

Since there are no bus routes in the park, most people either walk or don rollerblades and glide there. Other options include **renting a bicycle** from the Loeb Boathouse (see p.156) or Metro Bicycles, at 1311 Lexington Ave (Ⓣ212/427-4450, Ⓦwww.metrobicycles.com; ask about their other shops, since another may be closer to you). Bikes from the Boathouse are $9–15 for the first hour, and from Metro $9 an hour (or $45–55 for the day); both require a credit card or refundable cash deposit.

All of the above options are better deals than the famed **horse and carriage rides** ($34 for 30min; Ⓣ212/736-0680, Ⓦwww.centralparkcarriages.com). Incidentally, don't worry about the horses: a 1994 law mandates that they must get fifteen-minute rest breaks every two hours, and they cannot work more than nine hours a day or in temperatures above 90°F. Carriage drivers can get their licences suspended or revoked for non-compliance.

As for **safety** in the park, you should be fine during the day everywhere except around the Blockhouse on the northwestern tip, which is best visited only on a tour. Otherwise, just stay alert to your surroundings and try to avoid being alone in an isolated area; after dark, it's safer than it used to be, but it's still not advisable to walk around, especially not by yourself. If you want to look at the buildings of Central Park West lit up, as they were in Woody Allen's iconic film *Manhattan*, the best option is to fork out for a carriage ride. The one exception to the after-dark rule is in the case of a public evening event such as a concert or a summertime Shakespeare in the Park performance; these events are very safe – just leave when the crowds do.

The **Reservoir** divides Central Park in two. The larger **southern park** holds most of the attractions (and people), but the **northern park** (above 86th St) is well worth a visit for its wilder natural setting and dramatically quieter ambience. Organized walking tours are available from a number of sources, including the Urban Park Rangers and the Visitor Centers (see box, p.152), but almost any stroll, formal or informal, will invariably lead to something interesting.

funds to refit it. That ongoing effort is now overseen by a feisty nonprofit group called the **Central Park Conservancy** (see box, p.152), which works in conjunction with the city government to maintain the park, increase its policing and restore areas like Bethesda Terrace.

Despite the advent of motorized traffic, the idea of nature-as-disorder intended by Olmsted and Vaux largely survives. (About two-thirds of the park is either identical or quite similar to the original design.) Cars and buses cut through the park in the sheltered, sunken transverses originally intended for horse-drawn carriages, and remain mostly unseen from the park itself. The skyline, of course, has drastically changed, but the buildings that menacingly thrust their way into view are kept at bay by a fortress of trees, adding to the feeling that you're on a green island in the centre of a magnificent city.

The southern park: 59th to 86th streets

Many visitors enter the park at Grand Army Plaza (Fifth Ave and 59th St; see p.135). From here, **The Pond** lies to the left, and a little further north is the **Wollman Memorial Rink**, on 63rd Street at mid-park (ice skating Nov–Mon & Tues 10am–2.30pm, Wed & Thurs 10am–10pm, $10.25; Fri & Sat 10am–11pm, Sun 10am–9pm, $14.75; Ⓣ212/439-6900, Ⓦwww.wollmanskatingrink.com). Don blades for some of the city's most atmospheric ice skating; you're surrounded by onlookers, trees and, beyond that, a brilliant view of Central Park South's skyline. In summers, the rink becomes **Victorian Gardens** (Ⓦwww.victoriangardensnyc.com), a small amusement park with rides and carnival-style entertainment.

Central Park Zoo

East of the skating rink, at 64th Street and Fifth Avenue, lies the small **Central Park Zoo** (April–Oct Mon–Fri 10am–5pm, Sat, Sun & holidays 10am–5.30pm, Nov–March daily 10am–4.30pm; $10, children ages 3–12 $5, children under 3 free; Ⓣ212/439-6500, Ⓦwww.centralparkzoo.com). This welcoming wildlife centre has over a hundred species on view in mostly natural-looking homes. The animals are as close to the viewer as possible: the penguins, for example, swim around at eye level in Plexiglas pools. Other highlights include giant polar bears, a humid tropical zone filled with exotic birds, and the sea lions, which cavort in a pool right by the zoo entrance. This complex also boasts the **Tisch Children's Zoo**: there's a petting area, interactive displays and a musical clock just outside the entrance that draws rapt children at the start of each hour. The zoo is a charming stopoff for an hour or two, but if you're a dedicated animal-lover or have older children, you're better off heading to the Bronx Zoo (see p.258).

The Dairy and the Carousel

Close to the zoo stands the **Dairy** (65th St at mid-park), a cutesy yellow neo-Gothic chalet built in 1870 as a café. Despite local lore, there were never any cows here, though it did sell milk for children. It's now one of the park's Visitor Centers (see p.152). Weekend walking tours often leave from here – check Ⓦwww.centralparknyc.org for times and routes. You can also pick up pieces here for the **Chess and Checkers Pavilion** near the zoo.

Just west of the Dairy, you will see the octagonal brick building that houses the Carousel, on 64th Street at mid-park (daily 10am–6pm weather permitting; $2; Ⓣ212/439-6900). Built in 1903 and moved to the park from Coney Island in 1951, this is one of the park's little gems. There are fewer than 150 such vintage handmade carousels left in the country (others in the city are in Prospect Park, Dumbo, Flushing-Meadows Park, Forest Park and Coney Island, though the latter is in storage). A ride on it is a magical experience: its wood-carved, colourfully painted jumping horses are accompanied by the music of a military-band organ.

The Mall and Sheep Meadow

Heading north from the Dairy, you'll pass through the avenue of trees known as **The Mall.** The trees, whose branches tangle together to form a "roof" (hence its nickname, "The Cathedral"), are elms, a rarity in America. The statues that line the avenue are all literary and artistic greats: Shakespeare arrived first, and others from across the world soon followed, often privately funded by the appropriate immigrant groups – hence Italy's Mazzini and Germany's Beethoven. At the base of the Mall is one of only two acknowledgements to either park architect: a small memorial garden in Frederick Law Olmsted's name. Poor Calvert Vaux wasn't commemorated anywhere until April 2008, when the 72nd Street transverse was rechristened "Olmsted & Vaux Way".

To the west lies the **Sheep Meadow** (between 66th and 69th sts), fifteen acres of commons where sheep grazed until 1934, when they were banished to Brooklyn's Prospect Park. In the summer, the meadow is crowded with picnickers, sunbathers and Frisbee players. Two grass bowling and croquet lawns are maintained on a hill near the Sheep Meadow's northwest corner; to the southeast are a number of very popular volleyball courts (call ⓣ212/360-8133 for information on lawn bowling; call ⓣ212/408-0209 for volleyball and other ball-field permit information). On warm weekends, an area between the Sheep Meadow and the north end of the Mall is usually filled with rollerbladers dancing to funk, disco and hip-hop – one of the best free shows in town.

Bethesda Terrace and around

At the northernmost point of the Mall lie the **Bandshell** and **Rumsey Playfield**, the sites of the free SummerStage performance series (see box, p.159). There's also the **Bethesda Terrace and Fountain** (72nd St at mid-park), one of the few formal elements planned by Olmsted and Vaux. The crowning centerpiece of the fountain is the nineteenth-century *Angel of the Waters* sculpture, the only statue included in the original park design. Its earnest puritanical angels were recently made famous again by Tony Kushner's Pulitzer Prize-winning play *Angels in America*, of which the last scene is set here. The subterranean arcade is the subject of a series of major renovations aimed at restoring the intricate Minton tiling that once covered the ceiling. The fountain overlooks **The Lake**, where you can go for a Venetian-style gondola ride or rent a rowboat from the **Loeb Boathouse** on the eastern bank (April–Oct daily 10am until dusk, weather permitting; rowboats $12 for the first hour, $2.50 each 15min thereafter, $20 refundable cash deposit; gondola rides available 5–9pm, $30/30min/group, requires reservations; ⓣ212/517-2233, ⓦwww.thecentralparkboathouse.com). You can also rent bikes here.

The narrowest point on the lake is crossed by the elegant cast-iron and wood **Bow Bridge**. Take this bridge if you want to amble to **The Ramble** on the lake's northern banks, a 37-acre area of unruly woodland, filled with narrow winding paths, rocky outcrops, streams and an array of native plant life. Once a favourite spot for drug dealers and anonymous sex, it is now a great place to watch for one of the park's 54 species of birds or take a quiet daytime stroll. Clean-up notwithstanding, steer clear of this area at night.

▲ The Boat Pond, Central Park

To the west of Bethesda Terrace, along the 72nd St Drive, is the **Cherry Hill Fountain**. Originally a turnaround point for carriages, it was designed to have excellent views of the Lake, the Mall and the Ramble. One of the pretty areas paved by Moses in the 1930s for use as a car park, it was restored to its natural state in the early 1980s.

Back to the east of Bethesda Terrace is the **Boat Pond** (72nd St and Fifth Ave), where model-boat races are held every Saturday in the summer; you can participate by showing up at the kiosk and renting a craft from Central Park Sailboats. The fanciful *Alice in Wonderland* statue at the northern end of the pond was donated by publisher George Delacorte and is a favourite climbing spot for kids. During July the New York Public Library sponsors Wednesday-morning (11am) storytelling sessions for children at the *Hans Christian Andersen* statue on the west side of the pond (Ⓣ212/340-0906 for more information). A storyteller from the Central Park Conservancy also appears here at 11am on Saturdays throughout the summer.

Strawberry Fields

Strawberry Fields (72nd St and Central Park West) is a peaceful area dedicated to John Lennon, who was murdered in 1980 in front of his home at the Dakota Building, across the street on Central Park West. (See box, p.192 for more on the death of John Lennon.) Strawberry Fields is always crowded with those here to remember Lennon, at no time more so than December 8, the anniversary of his murder. Near the West 72nd Street entrance to the park is a round Italianate mosaic with the word "Imagine" at its centre, donated by Lennon's widow, Yoko Ono, and frequently covered with flowers. This is also a favourite spot for picnickers.

The Great Lawn and around

Behind the **Metropolitan Museum of Art** (see p.161) stands the **Obelisk**, the oldest structure in the park, which dates from 1450 BC. It was a gift to the city from Egypt in 1881, and, like its twin on the Thames River in London, is

Picnicking in the park

Central Park has ample **picnicking opportunities**, the most obvious of which is the hectic, perpetually crowded expanse of the Sheep Meadow. For (a very) little more peace and quiet, you might try one of these other fine locations: the western shore of the Lake, near Hernshead; the lawn in front of Turtle Pond, which has a nice view of Belvedere Castle; the Conservatory Garden; the lawn immediately north of the Ramble; Strawberry Fields; the Arthur Ross Pinetum; Cherry Hill; and the areas around the Delacorte Theater.

nicknamed "Cleopatra's Needle". Immediately west of the needle is the **Great Lawn** (81st St at mid-park). It was the site of the park's original reservoir from 1842 until 1931, when the water was drained to create a playing field. Years later, the lawn became a popular site for free concerts and rallies (Simon and Garfunkel, Elton John, Garth Brooks, Sting and the Pope, who celebrated mass here in 1995, have all attracted crowds numbering over half a million), but it was badly overused and had serious drainage problems. Reopened in 1998 after a massive two-year, $18 million reconstruction, the lawn's engineering and sandy soil now mean that even if there's a heavy downpour at lunchtime, the grass will be dry by evening. Rebuilt, reseeded and renewed, it will hopefully stay that way by only hosting the more sedate free New York Philharmonic and Metropolitan Opera concerts (see box opposite). The lawn features eight softball fields and, at its northern end, new basketball and volleyball courts and an eight-mile running track.

The refurbished **Turtle Pond** is at the southern end of the Lawn, with a new wooden dock and nature blind designed for better views of the aquatic wildlife (yes, there actually is wildlife here, including ducks, fish and frogs). Note the massive statue of fourteenth-century Polish king **Wladyslaw Jagiello** on the southeast corner of the pond, donated by the Polish government as a Holocaust memorial.

Southwest of the Lawn is the **Delacorte Theater**, the venue of the annual free Shakespeare in the Park festival (see box opposite). In another of the park's Shakespearean touches, the theatre features Milton Hebald's sculptures of Romeo and Juliet and *The Tempest*'s Prospero, while the tranquil **Shakespeare Garden** next door claims to hold every species of plant or flower mentioned in the Bard's plays. East of the garden is **Belvedere Castle**, a mock medieval citadel erected on top of Vista Rock in 1869 as a lookout on the highest point in the park. It's still a splendid viewpoint, and houses the New York Meteorological Observatory's weather centre; there's also a handy Visitor Center here (see p.152). For more plays of the puppet kind, check out the **Swedish Cottage Marionette Theater** (79th St at mid-park) at the base of Vista Rock, which holds fun shows aimed at young kids (most of the year Tues–Fri 10.30am & noon, Sat & Sun 1pm; $8, kids $5; ⓣ212/988-9093 for reservation).

The northern park

There are fewer attractions, but more open spaces, above the Great Lawn. Much of the northern park is taken up by the **Reservoir** (86th–97th sts at mid-park, main entrance at 90th St and Fifth Ave), a 107-acre, billion-gallon reservoir originally designed in 1862 and no longer active. It's a favourite for active uptown residents: the raised 1.58-mile track is a great place to get breathtaking 360-degree views of the skyline. North of the reservoir are a tennis-court complex and the soccer fields of the **North Meadow Recreation Center** (97th St at mid-park; ⓣ212/348-4867; for tennis permits and info, call ⓣ212/316-0800). The landscape north of here, in the aptly named North Woods, feels more like upstate New York than Manhattan: the 90-acre area contains man-made but natural-looking stone arches plus the **Loch**, which is now more of a stream, and the **Ravine**, which conceals five small waterfalls.

Conservatory Garden

If you see nothing else in the park above 86th Street, don't miss the **Conservatory Garden** (daily 8am–dusk; East 104th–106th sts along Fifth Ave with entrance at 105th). Filled with flowering trees and shrubs, planted flowerbeds, fanciful fountains and shaded benches, the space actually houses three gardens, each landscaped in a distinct style. You'll first walk through the Italian garden, a reserved oasis with neat lawns and trimmed hedges. To the south is the English area, enhanced by the Burnett Fountain, which depicts the two children from F.H. Burnett's classic book *The Secret Garden*. The French garden, the northernmost of the three, hosts sculptor Walter Schott's *Three Dancing Maidens*. Visit the French garden for the flowers – twenty thousand tulips in spring and two thousand Korean chrysanthemums in autumn. North of this green space is the

Seasonal events and activities

SummerStage and **Shakespeare in the Park** are two of the most popular cultural summer programmes in Manhattan. Both activities are free and help to take the sting out of New York's infamous hazy, hot and humid summers. In 1986, **SummerStage** presented its inaugural Central Park concert with Sun Ra performing to an audience of fifty people. When he returned with Sonic Youth six years later, the audience numbered ten thousand. The musical acts are of consistently good quality, and cover pretty much every genre during the festival's mid-June to mid-August run. Located at the Rumsey Playfield near 72nd Street and Fifth Avenue, concerts here are crowded and sticky, but unbeatable. Dance performances, DJ sets and (paid admission) benefit shows also share the stage. More information: ⓣ212/360-2756 or 2777, ⓦwww.summerstage.org.

Shakespeare in the Park takes place at the open-air Delacorte Theater (see opposite). Pairs of free tickets are distributed daily at 1pm for that evening's performance, but you'll have to get in line well beforehand, as a crowd often starts to gather by 7am. You can also pick them up at the Public Theater, 425 Lafayette St (see p.368), from 1pm on the day of the performance, though again, expect to wait. Alternatively, you can try for a ticket via their online draw-register on the website below. Performances are Tues–Sun at 8pm, early June to early August. More information: ⓣ212/539-8750 or ⓦwww.publictheater.org.

New York Philharmonic in the Park (ⓣ212/875-5709, ⓦwww.nyphil.org) and **Metropolitan Opera in the Park** (ⓣ212/362-6000, ⓦwww.metoperafamily.org) hold several evenings of classical music in the summer, usually on the Great Lawn and often with a booming fireworks display to usher the crowds home.

Horseback-riding is available by special arrangement with the Riverdale Equestrian Center (ⓣ914/633-0303, ⓦwww.riverdaleriding.com). Rides are $100 per person per hour, and can be done year-round, weather permitting.

The Harlem Meer Performance Festival (110th St between Fifth and Lenox aves; ⓣ212/860-1370) offers fairly intimate and enjoyable free performances of jazz and salsa music outside the Charles A. Dana Discovery Center on Sundays from June to September from 2 to 4pm.

stand-alone **Robert Bendleim Playground** for disabled children, at 108th Street near Fifth Avenue, where youngsters can play in "accessible" sandboxes and swings, or work out their upper bodies on balance beams.

Charles A. Dana Discovery Center, Harlem Meer and around

At the top of the park is the **Charles A. Dana Discovery Center**, an environmental education centre and visitor centre (see box, p.152). Crowds of locals fish in the adjacent **Harlem Meer**, an eleven-acre pond stocked with more than fifty thousand fish. The Discovery Center provides free bamboo fishing poles and bait.

In the extreme northeast corner of the park, at 110th Street and Fifth Avenue, is a 1997 monument to **Duke Ellington**, the esteemed musician and composer of such classics as *Mood Indigo*. On top of the three columns that summon the nine muses, the Duke stands before his grand piano, symbolically looking toward Harlem for the next generation of musical vanguards. In the park's northwestern corner stands the **Blockhouse**, one of the few landmarks still to be awaiting renovation: one of several such houses built as a lookout over pancake-flat Harlem during the war of 1812, it's the only one which remains. Now a ruin, it's a picturesque but iffy place to visit even during the daytime – stick to seeing it from one of the park's scheduled tours.

14

The Metropolitan Museum of Art

The **Metropolitan Museum of Art**, or the **Met**, as it's usually called, is the foremost art museum in America. It started in 1870 in a brownstone downtown before decamping to its present site in Central Park, a Gothic Revival building designed by Jacob Wrey Mould and Calvert Vaux in 1880. Over time, various additions to the site have completely surrounded the original structure; the museum's familiar multi-columned, wide-stepped facade on Fifth Avenue was conceived by Richard Morris Hunt and completed in 1902, while the north and south wings were added by McKim, Mead, and White between 1911 and 1913.

The museum's collection includes over two million works of art from the Americas, Europe, Africa and the Far East, as well as the classical and ancient worlds. The **main entrance** to the museum leads to the **Great Hall**, a deftly lit Neoclassical cavern where you can consult floor plans, check tour times and pick up info on the Met's excellent lecture listings. Straight across from the entrance is the Grand Staircase, which leads to, for many visitors, the museum's single greatest attraction – the European Paintings galleries. Make sure you pick up the detailed room-by-room gallery **maps** for the European Paintings and Nineteenth-Century Paintings collections, available at the **main information desk** in the Great Hall.

Met practicalities

The Met (Tues–Thurs & Sun 9.30am–5.30pm, Fri & Sat 9.30am–9pm; ⓣ212/535-7710, ⓦwww.metmuseum.org) is at 1000 Fifth Ave at 82nd Street, set into Central Park. Take subway #4, #5 or #6 to 86th St–Lexington Avenue. There is **no set admission price**, but the suggested donation is $20, $15 for senior citizens and $10 for students (includes admission to the Cloisters on the same day; see p.215). These suggested amounts are exactly that: whether you pay 12¢ or $12, the cashier won't flinch, so if you can, spread out your exploration over several days. Recorded **audio tours** of the major collections are $7. The museum also runs **free guided tours** daily. Call or check the website for schedules. Be aware that the collection is regularly reorganized and galleries can be **closed**, so call ahead to confirm if there are particular pieces you want to see. Note also that mobile-phone use is only allowed in the Great Hall, and that flash photography and video cameras cannot be used anywhere. All backpacks must be left at the coat-check.

METROPOLITAN MUSEUM OF ART

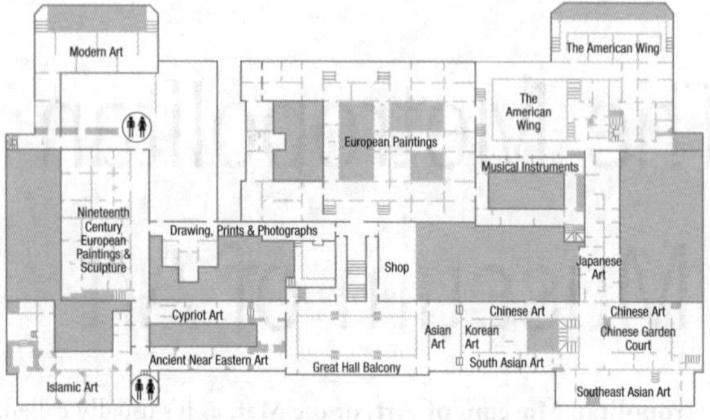

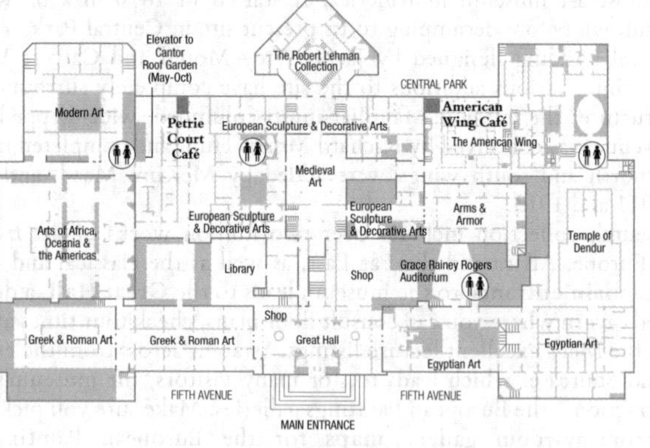

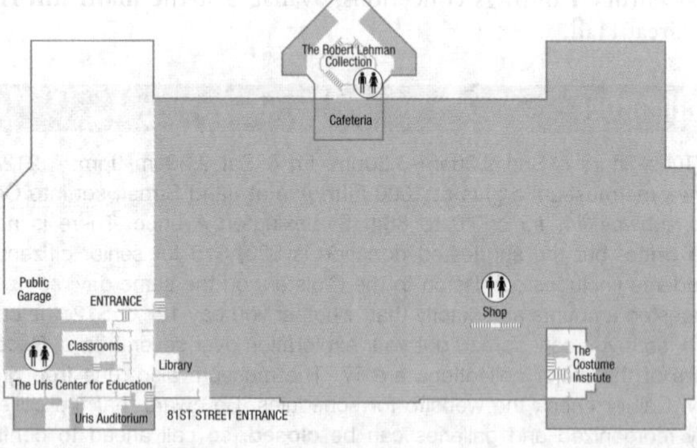

The Met is so big that at least some sections are likely to be closed for renovation when you visit. The painting galleries in the American Wing and the Islamic Art galleries will be off-limits until 2011/2012.

European Paintings

The Met's **European Paintings galleries**, located on the second floor at the top of the Grand Staircase, are organized roughly by nationality and period. They begin with huge works by **Tiepolo** (Gallery 1) and a room full of eighteenth-century French portraits by the likes of Elizabeth Vigée-Lebrun, Marie-Denise Villers and Jacques-Louis David (Gallery 2).

Spanish paintings

In the current layout, turning right at Gallery 2 brings you to the **Spanish** section; highlights include **Goya**'s widely reproduced portrait of a toddler in a red jumpsuit, *Don Manuel Osorio Manrique de Zuniga*, in Gallery 21; **Velázquez**'s piercing and sombre *Portrait of Juan de Pareja* in Gallery 16; and a room of freaky, dazzling canvases by **El Greco** (Gallery 17) each of which underscores the jarring modernism of his approach. In solitary contrast is his wraith-like *View of Toledo*, one of the best of his works displayed anywhere in the world.

Italian paintings

The central galleries contain **Italian paintings**, with **Duccio**'s sublime *Madonna and Child* currently holding court in Gallery 3. Described by the Met as "one of the great single acquisitions of the last half century", the delicately crafted painting is an extremely rare example of early Renaissance art, acquired by the Met in 2004 for around $45 million. The collection continues with the Sienese school before moving into the High Renaissance, with **Botticelli**'s *Last Communion of St Jerome* one of the few high points (Gallery 4B); other standouts include works by **Mantegna** and **Carlo Crivelli**, as well as an outstandingly preserved chunk of **Ghirlandaio fresco**, *St Christopher and the Infant Christ*, in Gallery 6. As for later pictures, there's Mannerist master **Bronzino**'s dapper but haughty *Portrait of a Young Man* and a showy **Raphael**, *Madonna and Child Enthroned with Saints*, which features his signature, pin-up-pretty Virgin Mary (both in Gallery 7). There are also rooms filled with massive works by **Titian** and **Tintoretto**, though it's **Veronese**'s raunchy and artfully composed *Mars and Venus United by Love* that's especially appealing among the Venetians (Gallery 8).

Northern European paintings

Galleries dedicated to northern European schools surround the Italian rooms, with **Vermeer** particularly well represented. Most haunting of all is the *Study of a Young Woman* in Gallery 14A; she's an odd-looking creature with huge doleful eyes and twinkly earrings, her enigmatic expression making her Vermeer's own Mona Lisa. While Vermeer's paintings focused on stillness and light, the portraits of **Hals** and **Rembrandt** burst with life. At first, galleries 13 and 14 simply seem full of men in jaunty hats and ruffles, but the personalities of the sitters emerge on closer inspection, from the heavy-lidded world-weariness of Rembrandt's *Portrait of a Man* to his deeply reflective *Aristotle with a Bust of Homer* (both in Gallery 13).

Other highlights include Flemish Painting from the fifteenth and sixteenth centuries. Particularly prominent are the paintings of **Jan Van Eyck**, who is usually credited with beginning the tradition of North European realism. The freestanding panels of *The Crucifixion* and *The Last Judgement* in Gallery 23 were painted early in his career and are full of scurrying, startled figures, tightly composed with expressive and even horrific detail. Another great Northern Gothic painter, **Gerard David**, used local settings for his religious scenes; the background of his exquisite *Virgin and Child with Four Angels* is medieval Bruges and *The Rest on the Flight to Egypt* features a forest glade, again with the turrets of Bruges visible down below (both in Gallery 24). Head to adjacent Gallery 25 and **Pieter Bruegel the Elder**'s *Harvesters* to see how these innovations were assimilated. Made charming by its snapshot ordinariness (check the sprawling figure napping under a tree), this is one of the Met's most reproduced pictures.

The Met's elegant collection of **English pictures**, usually in Gallery 15, is also worth seeking out. **Sir Thomas Lawrence**'s study of actress *Elizabeth Farren*, which he painted at the precocious age of 21, is impressive, as much for how well it conveys her spirited personality as for its technical mastery. Look out also for **Thomas Gainsborough**'s *Wood Gatherers*, one of his most famous paintings.

Nineteenth-Century European Paintings and Sculpture

Most visitors to the Met head directly to the **Nineteenth-Century European Paintings and Sculpture galleries,** following the left-hand corridor at the top of the Grand Staircase. This passage leads to another hall, which is littered with stunning **Rodin** sculptures in white marble and bronze. Twenty rooms branch off from here, leading to an array of Impressionist and Post-Impressionist paintings.

Impressionists

To the far left, you'll find the precursors of the **Impressionists** such as **Delacroix** and **Ingres**, while the central section is devoted to **Degas**, where fans will find studies in just about every medium, from pastels to sculpture. Many examine one of his favourite themes: dancers.

To the right, the Annenberg Collection houses galleries dedicated to all the big names; several works by **Manet**, the Impressionist movement's most influential predecessor, whose early style of contrasting light and shadow with modulated shades of black can be firmly linked to the traditions of Hals, Velázquez and Goya. *Boating* evokes a vividly fresh, spring morning, while the striking *Young Lady in 1866* is a realistic portrayal of a girl in her peignoir.

Monet was one of the Impressionist movement's most prolific painters, returning again and again to a single subject in order to produce a series of images capturing different nuances of light and atmosphere. The Met's hoard runs like Monet's Greatest Hits: the museum has a canvas from almost every major sequence by the artist, including *Water Lilies*, *Rouen Cathedral (The Portal)*, *The Houses of Parliament (Effect of Fog)*, and *Haystacks (Effect of Snow and Sun)*.

Cézanne's technique was very different. He laboured long to achieve a painstaking analysis of form and colour, an effect clear in the *Landscape of Marseilles*. Of his few portraits, the jarring, almost Cubist angles and spaces of the rather plain

Mme Cézanne in a Red Dress seem years ahead of their time: she looks clearly pained, as if she'd rather be anywhere than under her husband's gaze. Take a look, too, at *The Card Players*, whose dynamic triangular structure thrusts out, yet retains the quiet concentration of the moment. Though there's also work here by every Impressionist name from **Berthe Morisot** to **Pissarro**, it's **Renoir** who's perhaps the best represented. Sadly, most of his works are from after 1878, when he began to move away from the techniques he'd learned while working with Monet and toward the chocolate-boxy soft focus that plagued his later work. Of these, *Mme Charpentier and Her Children* is a likeable enough piece, one whose affectionate tone manages to sidestep the sentimentality of this period.

Post-Impressionists

Paintings of the **Post-Impressionists**, logically enough, lie beyond these first galleries. One of the highlights of the collection is **Gauguin**'s masterly *La Orana Maria*. This Annunciation-derived scene, a Renaissance staple, has been transferred to a different culture in an attempt to unfold the symbolism, and perhaps voice the artist's feeling for the native South Sea islanders.

In the same room, there are also more than a half-dozen canvases by **Van Gogh**, including his *Self-Portrait with Straw Hat*, famed *Irises* and the twisty, thrashing trees of *Cypresses*, and two Pointillist pictures by the master of the technique, **Georges-Pierre Seurat**. The sparkling night-time scene *Circus Sideshow* was the first attempt to replicate artificial light using multicoloured dots; there's also a small canvas that was the final study for Seurat's masterpiece *Sunday Afternoon on the Island of La Grande Jatte*.

Asian Art

Also on the second floor are the **Asian Art** galleries, an impressive, schizophrenic collection that includes works in various media from most major Asian civilizations. From the **Great Hall Balcony**, turning right leads to art from Central Asia, Cyprus and the Near East, with some exceptional silver and gold pieces from Iran as well as some huge carvings from the Palace of Assyrian king Ashurnasirpal II, in Nimrud.

Turning left at the balcony takes you to a collection of stone works arranged around a serene, twenty-foot-high Buddha and equally large Bodhisattva from China's Northern Qi Dynasty (550–577). The focal point, however, is the enormous (and exquisite) fourteenth-century mural, *The Pure Land of Bhaisajyaguru* (also known as the "Medicine Buddha"). This piece was carefully reconstructed after being severely damaged in an earthquake and is a study in calm reflection – it was created in China during the Yuan Dynasty (circa 1319).

Take the right fork from this gallery for **Korean Art** and **South Asian Art**. There's a vast, if rather monotonous, range of **statues** of Hindu and Buddhist deities here, alongside numerous pieces of friezes, many of which still possess exceptional detail despite years of exposure. *The Great Departure and the Temptation of the Buddha*, carved in the third century, is particularly lively: Siddhartha sets out on his spiritual journey, chased by a harem of dancing girls and grasping cherubs.

Beyond a pristine reproduction of a Jain Meeting Hall lies **Southeast Asian Art** and **Chinese Art**, yet the real highlight in this area is the **Chinese Garden Court**, a serene, minimalist retreat enclosed by the galleries, and the adjacent **Ming Room**, a typical salon decorated in period style with wooden lattice doors.

Assembled by experts from China, the naturally lit garden is representative of one found in wealthy Chinese homes of the Ming Dynasty: a pagoda, small waterfall and stocked goldfish pond landscaped with limestone rocks, trees and shrubs conjure up a sense of peace.

Japanese Art

After meditating in the garden, head into the section dedicated to **Japanese Art.** It contains objects from the prehistoric to the present, ordered not chronologically but thematically, with rotating exhibits divided by medium: ceramics, textiles, paintings and prints. The undeniable showstoppers here are the seventeenth- and eighteenth-century hand-painted **Kano screens**, often elaborate scenes of historical allusion and divine fervour. Since all the exhibited paintings, calligraphy, and scrolls of Asian art are rotated every six months or so, the scenes change, but their beauty remains constant. Make sure you check out the view of the Temple of Dendur (see p.168) from the **Japanese Reading Room** (first gallery on the right).

The American Wing

Close to being a museum in its own right, the **American Wing** is a thorough introduction to the development of fine art in America, with a vast collection of paintings, period furniture, glass, silverware and ceramics. The spectacular **courtyard** re-opened in 2009, studded with sculpture from the likes of Daniel Chester French and Augustus Saint-Gaudens – you can also grab a snack at the **café** here.

Twelve of the Wing's twenty **period rooms**, dating from 1680 to 1810, were also re-opened in 2009 after renovation, allowing visitors to tour American interiors and decorative arts in chronological order, ending with the Frank Lloyd Wright Room (1912–14). Note, though, that the American Painting galleries on the second floor are likely to be closed for renovation until early 2012; many pieces remain on view on the mezzanine level, crammed into glass cases. Sadly, *Washington Crossing the Delaware* by **Emanuel Leutze**, the celebrated image of Washington escaping across the river in the winter of 1776, is unlikely to be on show until the renovation is complete.

American Painting

Much of the **American Painting** collection is worth seeking out, though the mezzanine display areas – in use until the renovation is complete – are hardly ideal; ask one of the guards if you are looking for a specific piece. There are several works by **Benjamin West**, who worked in London and taught or influenced many of the American painters of his day – *The Triumph of Love* is typical of his Neoclassical, allegorical works. Look out, too, for the painters of the **Hudson Valley School**, who glorified the landscape in their vast lyrical canvases; **Thomas Cole**, the school's doyen, is represented by *The Oxbow*, while his pupil **Frederic Church** has the immense *Heart of the Andes*, which combines the grand sweep of the mountains with minutely depicted flora. **Albert Bierstadt** and **S.R. Gifford** concentrated on the American West – their respective works *The Rocky Mountains, Lander's Peak* and *Kauterskill Falls* have a near-visionary idealism, bound to a belief that the westward development of the country was a manifestation of divine will.

Winslow Homer is also well represented, from his early illustrations of the Civil War to his late, quasi-Impressionistic seascapes, of which *Northeaster* is one of the

The Cantor Roof Garden

From May to October, you can ascend to the **Cantor Roof Garden**, located on top of the Lila Acheson Wallace Wing (see Modern Art, p.169). The leafy garden is an outdoor gallery, and each summer it's used to showcase contemporary sculpture (Jeff Koons has been a recent subject); it's also nominally a bar, though the mediocre drinks and pricey snacks aren't the reason to come here. The views are what draw most visitors – from this height, you can grasp how vast Central Park truly is; you're also within close view of Cleopatra's Needle. By far the best time to come for a cocktail is October, when the weather's cooler and the foliage has begun to turn.

To reach the garden, head for the southwest elevators on the first floor, just outside the Modern Art gallery – you'll find them if you head left of the main marble stairs in the entrance hall.

finest. Highlights of American art of the late nineteenth and early twentieth centuries include **J.W. Alexander**'s *Repose*; **Thomas Eakin**'s subdued, almost ghostly *Max Schmitt in a Single Scull*; and **William Merritt Chase**'s *For the Little One*, an Impressionist study of his wife sewing. The collection is crowned with a selection of works by the best-known American artist of the era: **James Abbott McNeill Whistler**. The standout is *Arrangement in Flesh Color and Black: Portrait of Theodore Duret*, a realist portrait of one of the Impressionists' most supportive patrons – it's a tribute to Whistler's mastery of his technique that despite labouring on the painting for a long time, it retains the spontaneity of a sketch.

Medieval Art

Although you could move straight to **Medieval Art** from the American Wing, you'd miss out on the museum's carefully planned approach. Instead, enter these galleries via the corridor from the western end (or rear) of the Great Hall on the left of the main staircase. There you'll see displays of the sumptuous Byzantine metalwork and jewellery that financier **J.P. Morgan** donated to the museum in its early days. At the end of the corridor is the **main sculpture hall**, piled high with religious statuary and carvings; it's divided by a 52ft-high *reja* – a decorative open-work, iron altar screen – from Valladolid Cathedral. If you're here in December, you'll see a highlight of New York's Christmas season: a beautifully decorated, 20ft-high Christmas tree lit up in the centre of the sculpture hall. The **medieval treasury** to the right of the hall has an all-encompassing display of objects religious, liturgical and secular.

Egyptian Art

The Met hogs a collection of more than 35,000 objects from **Ancient Egypt**, most of which are displayed to their full potential. Brightly efficient corridors steer you through the treasures of the museum's own digs during the 1920s and 1930s, as well as other art and artefacts from 3000 BC to the Byzantine period of Egyptian culture.

Prepare to be awed as you enter from the Great Hall on the first floor: the large **statuary**, **tombs** and **sarcophagi** in the first few rooms are immediately striking. As you move into the interior galleries, arranged chronologically, the smaller, quieter sculptural pieces are also quite eye-catching. Don't miss the finely crafted models of ships, a brewery and a cattle stable in Gallery 4, offerings found in the **Tomb of Meketre**. Incredibly well preserved, they look as if they were made yesterday, not 4000 years ago, and offer a rare insight into everyday Egyptian life. Look, too, for the dazzling collection of **Princess Sithathoryunet jewellery** in Gallery 8, a pinnacle in Egyptian decorative art from around 1830 BC.

The Temple of Dendur

At the end of the collection sits the **Temple of Dendur**, housed in a vast airy gallery lined with photographs and placards about the temple's history and its original site on the banks of the Nile. Built by the Emperor Augustus in 15 BC for the goddess Isis of Philae, the temple was moved here as a gift from the Egyptian government during the construction of the Aswan High Dam in 1965 – otherwise, it would have drowned. Though you can't walk all the way inside, you can go in just far enough to get a glimpse of the interior rooms, their walls chock-full of hieroglyphs and the scrawls of nineteenth-century **graffiti** artists (though "J Livingston" is no relation to the famous explorer). The entire gallery is glassed-in on one side, and looks out onto Central Park; the most magical time to view the temple is when it's illuminated at night and the gallery seems to glow, lending it an air of mystery that's missing during the day.

Greek and Roman Art

Thanks to a magnificent renovation completed in 2007, one of the largest collections of ancient art in the world occupies some of the most attractive wings of the museum. Enter from the southern end of the Great Hall, and you'll find yourself in the wonderfully bright **Greek Sculpture Court**, a fittingly elegant setting for sixth- to fourth-century BC marble sculptures. The adjacent galleries display Greek art

▲ Chariot, Leon Levy and Shelby White Court

from the prehistoric era through to the fourth century BC. Look out for the tiny but fanciful **Minoan vase** in the shape of a bull's head from around 1450 BC (first gallery on the right, at the back) and the **Marble Statue of a Kouros** (second gallery on the left) – one of the earliest examples of a funerary statue (*kouros* means "youth") to have survived intact. Dating from 580 BC and originally from Attica, it marked the grave of the son of a wealthy family, created to ensure he would be remembered.

Beyond here, the hefty **Sardis Column** from the Temple of Artemis marks the entrance into the stunning **Leon Levy and Shelby White Court**, a soaring two-storey atrium of **Roman sculpture** from the first century BC to the second century AD, with mosaic floors, Doric columns and a glass ceiling – take a moment to soak up your surroundings at the fountain in the centre. Highlights include the incredibly detailed *Badminton Sarcophagus* towards the back, and beyond this a small but enigmatic bust of the Emperor **Caracalla** from the third century.

Arts of Africa, Oceania and the Americas

Michael C. Rockefeller, son of Governor Nelson Rockefeller, disappeared during a trip to West New Guinea in 1961. In 1969, Nelson donated the entire contents of his missing son's **Museum of Primitive Art** – over 3300 works, plus library and photographic material, much of it collected by his son – to the Met. This wing, on the first floor past the Greek and Roman galleries, stands as a memorial to Michael. It includes many Asmat objects, such as carved *mbis* (memorial poles), figures and a canoe from Irian Jaya, alongside the Met's comprehensive collection of art from **Africa**, **Oceania** and **the Americas**.

It's a superb set of galleries, the muted, understated decor throwing the exhibits into sharp and often dramatic focus. The **African exhibit** offers an overview of the major geographic regions and their cultures, though West Africa is better represented than the rest of the continent. Particularly awe-inspiring is the display of art from the Court of Benin (in present-day Nigeria) – tiny carved ivory figures, created with astonishing detail.

The **Pacific collection** covers the islands of Melanesia, Micronesia, Polynesia and Australia, and contains a wide array of objects, including wild, somewhat frightening wooden masks with all-too-realistic eyes. Sadly, **Mexico**, **Central America** and **South America** get somewhat short shrift, though there is a respectable collection of pre-Columbian jade, Mayan and Aztec pottery and Mexican ceramic sculpture; the best part by far, however, is the **Jan Mitchell Treasury**, an entire room filled with South American gold jewellery and ornaments – particularly the exquisite hammered-gold nose ornaments and earrings from Peru and the richly carved, jewelled ornaments from Colombia.

Modern Art

The Met's **Modern Art** collection – housed over two floors in the Lila Acheson Wallace Wing (named in honour of the founder of *Reader's Digest*), directly to the rear of the Rockefeller Wing – is another fine hoard that includes several stunning individual works, from mid-century experimental and abstract canvases to contemporary sculpture.

1905 to 1940

Work on the first floor is arranged roughly by school and period, covering **American and European art from 1905 to 1945**. The first galleries on the right side are dedicated to American art, beginning with the mural-like images of Broadway and Wall Street by **Florine Stettheimer**, and including the paintings of **Arthur Dove**, **Charles Sheeler** and **Georgia O'Keeffe**, whose moody *From the Faraway, Nearby* resembles a progressive rock album cover.

Beyond here, the European galleries begin with the Surrealists, with work from **Miró** and **Dalí** giving way to **Picasso**, **Bonnard**, **Braque** and **Modigliani**. Picasso is particularly well represented, his work sprinkled throughout the first floor, from his Blue Period, through his Cubist Period, to more familiar skewed-perspective portraits; his sombre *Girl Asleep at a Table*, *Woman in an Armchair* and *Still Life with Pipes* are considered Cubist masterpieces. Following small rooms dedicated to **Matisse** and **Paul Klee**, the galleries end with the Fauvism of **Derain** and **Soutine** and more Cubism from Picasso, Braque and **Gris**. Note that some of the most famous pieces in the collection – **Modigliani**'s firm-breasted *Reclining Nude*, for example – are often moved around or on loan elsewhere.

1945 to the present

The mezzanine and second floors contain **European and American art from 1945 to the present**, from installations to vast abstracts. The mezzanine level displays the work of **Chuck Close**, whose *Lucas* has the characteristic intense stare of his giant portraits, as well as **Andy Warhol**'s monumental *Mao* and his camouflage-patterned *Last Self-Portrait*. The second floor is filled with giant, abstract canvases from artists such as **Mark Rothko**, with an entire room devoted to grumpy Abstract Expressionist **Clyfford Still** who once "repossessed" a picture by knifing it from its frame when he fell out with the owner. You'll also find **Jackson Pollock**'s swirling *Autumn Rhythm (No. 30)* here; if you stand up close, the painting seems to suck you in, and you'll spot far more colours than at first glance.

European Sculpture and Decorative Arts

Most people pass right through the **European Sculpture and Decorative Arts** section on their way between the Modern and Medieval art galleries, but there are a couple of reasons to pause. The **European Sculpture Court** is a gorgeous sunlit courtyard studded with grand marble statues, notably *Andromeda and the Sea Monster* (1694) by **Domenico Guidi** and the agonizing *Ugolino and his Sons* (1867) by **Carpeaux**, depicting the Pisan traitor from Dante's *Inferno*. There's also a copy of **Rodin**'s *Burghers of Calais*, an impressive bronze ensemble recalling the Hundred Years' War. The decorative arts section – furniture, ceramics, glassware and the like – is less appealing, but displayed in some opulent Baroque- and Rococo-style rooms reminiscent of a French palace.

The Lehman Pavilion

Another of the Met's many gems, the two-floor **Lehman Pavilion** was tacked on to the rear of the museum in 1975 to house the holdings of Robert Lehman, a relentless collector and scion of the Lehman Brothers banking family. Lehman bequeathed his entire collection with the stipulation that the galleries retain the appearance of a private home, and parts of this extension – an octagonal building centred on a brilliantly lit atrium – do resemble rooms in his former mansion. The walls around the atrium are lined with mostly uninteresting **Impressionist** works from **Derain**, **Cézanne**, **Renoir** and **Edouard Vuillard**, though **Balthus**'s creamy and disturbing *Nude with a Mirror* at the entrance to the inner galleries is worth a longer look.

Italian Renaissance art

Lehman's artistic interests fill important gaps in the Met's collection, notably the **Italian Renaissance**. This period was his passion, and his personal hoard includes some standout works such as the tiny, easily missed *Annunciation* by **Botticelli**; it's stashed in a glass cabinet in the second room. More impressive are the Venetian works, including a glassy *Madonna and Child* by **Bellini** in which Mary looks like a 1920s screen goddess, and cartoonish wooden icons by **Carlo Crivelli** featuring a grumpy St Peter.

Other Old Master paintings

As for **non-Italian art**, Lehman evidently liked **Ingres**, whose languid, sculptural portrait of the *Princesse de Broglie* in her bright-blue dress sparkles on the wall; similarly impressive is **Goya**'s *Countess of Altamira and Her Daughter*, the soft pink of her outfit contrasting sharply with her plain features. One picture stands out from them all, though: **Rembrandt**'s unflinching *Portrait of Gerard de Lairesse*, his bug eyes and snout-like nose evidence of the ravages of congenital syphilis.

The final galleries house more Italian and **Northern European works**, from the likes of **Hans Holbein the Younger** and **Petrus Christus**, as well as collections of exquisite porcelain, vases, glasswork and other glittering bits and pieces.

The Upper East Side

The defining characteristic of Manhattan's **Upper East Side** – a two-square-mile grid that runs from 59th to 96th streets between Fifth Avenue and the East River – is wealth. Despite the lowering of rents in recent years and an influx of young professionals, this area has been an enclave of New York's upper class since the 1890s, when dynasties such as the Rockefellers, Whitneys and Astors built mansions here. Today, Martin Scorsese, artist Jeff Koons, Spike Lee, long-time resident Woody Allen and Madonna call the Upper East Side home, a world aptly portrayed in movies such as *Breakfast at Tiffany's* and *Manhattan*, and more recently in TV shows *Sex and the City* and *Gossip Girl*.

Scattered between the luxurious apartments are some of the city's finest **museums** and upscale shops, while farther east, in the middle of the East River, sits **Roosevelt Island**, an area distinctly different from the rest of the city, and one that many Manhattanites frequently forget is there.

Upper East Side Historic District

Encompassing 59th to 78th streets, between Fifth and Lexington avenues, the **Upper East Side Historic District** has been the haughty patrician face of Manhattan since the late nineteenth century. Wealthy families built their fashionable residences on **Fifth Avenue** overlooking Central Park, lavish Neoclassical mansions cluttered with columns and classical statues.

Today, the area is jam-packed with museums; Henry Clay Frick's mansion at East 70th Street, marginally less ostentatious than its neighbours, is now the intimate and tranquil home of the **Frick Collection**, one of the city's must-see spots, while the modern exhibits at the **Whitney** are across at 74th Street and Madison.

The Grolier Club

North of **Grand Army Plaza**, Fifth Avenue and its opulent sidestreets are dotted with **private clubs** that served, and still cater to, the city's wealthy (see box, p.174). One of the few open to the public (at least partly) is the relatively modest **Grolier Club** (Mon–Sat 10am–5pm; closed Aug; free; ⓣ212/838-6690, ⓦwww.grolierclub.org), 47 East 60th St, just off Park Avenue. There are four public art shows a year in the main ground-floor gallery, usually with a literary or artistic theme utilizing paintings, books and sculpture; recent displays have focused on Samuel Johnson, the Mississippi River and English novelist Mary Webb. Established in 1884 as a literary club, the Grolier's current premises date from 1917.

UPPER EAST SIDE
0 500 yds
RESTAURANTS & CAFÉS
Alice's Tea Cup 33
Barking Dog Luncheonette 2
Beyoglu
Café Boulud 16
Café Sabarsky in the Neue Galerie 7
Caffè Buon Gusto 20
Candle Café 23
Cascabel Taqueria 17
Daniel 30
Donguri 11
E.A.T. 15
FC Chocolate Bar 32
Flex Mussels 14
Heidelberg 8
JG Melon Restaurant 25
Jojo 34
King's Carriage House 12
Le Refuge 13
M. Rohrs' 9
Maya 31
Mitchel London Foods 29
Naruto Ramen 3
Neil's Coffee Shop 28
Paola's A
El Paso Taqueria 1
Pastrami Queen 18
Persephone 36
Persepolis 26
Pig Heaven 17
Rectangles 24
Serendipity 3 38
Taco Taco 4
Tal Bagels 6
Viand 35
ACCOMMODATION
Franklin B
Mark C
Pierre D
Wales A
BARS
American Trash 21
Auction House 5
Balcony Bar 10
Bar Pléiades 22
Bemelmans Bar 19
Roof Garden Café 10
Stir 27
Subway Inn 37
NIGHTLIFE
Café Carlyle 19
Harlem
Museo del Barrio
Museum of City of New York
Mount Sinai Hospital
Metro North
EL BARRIO
Islamic Cultural Center
Jewish Museum
Otto and Addie Kahn Mansion
Cooper-Hewitt Museum
CARNEGIE HILL
Ruppert Park
National Academy of Design
Guggenheim Museum
Gracie Mansion
Church of the Holy Trinity
Henderson Place
Schaller and Weber
Carl Schurz Park
Neue Galerie
Institute for the Study of the Ancient World
YORKVILLE
Metropolitan Museum of Art
Alexander Calder Sidewalk
Cherokee Apartments
Orwasher's Handmade Bread
John Jay Park
Whitney Museum of American Art
St James Church
Asia Society
Sotheby's
Frick Collection
Union Club
Hunter College
Park Avenue Armory
Park East Synagogue
Central Park
Roosevelt House
Temple Emanu-El
St. Vincent's
Cosmopolitan Club
Museum of American Illustration
Colony Club
Mount Vernon Hotel Museum & Garden
Knickerbocker Club
Metropolitan
Grolier Club
Christ Church United Methodist
Roosevelt Island Tram
Harmonie Club
Bloomingdale's
Plaza Hotel
GRAND ARMY PLAZA
QUEENSBORO BRIDGE
East River
Harlem River Drive
FDR Drive
Transverse Road No. 2
Transverse Road No. 1
East Drive
Central Park South
Fifth Avenue
Madison Avenue
Park Avenue
Lexington Avenue
Third Avenue
Second Avenue
First Avenue
York Avenue
East End Avenue
Midtown West
Midtown East
Queens & Roosevelt Island

Christ Church United Methodist

On the corner of 60th Street at 520 Park Ave, **Christ Church United Methodist** (Mon–Fri 7am–6pm; Sun services only; ⓣ212/838-3036, ⓦwww.christchurchnyc.org) looks relatively plain from the outside, but the interior is one of the most striking in New York. Ralph Adams Cram started work on this Romanesque masterpiece in 1931, but the lavish Byzantine interior wasn't completed until 1949. The apse and vaulted ceiling are smothered in dazzling gold-leaf mosaics – parts of the choir screen date from 1660 and were once owned by Tsar Nicholas II of Russia. The altar itself is carved from Spanish marble, with the nave columns hewn from veined, purple Levanto marble.

Museum of American Illustration

If you'd rather spend time dawdling over cartoons, head two blocks east to the **Museum of American Illustration**, housed in an 1875 carriage house at 128 East 63rd St between Park and Lexington avenues (Tues 10am–8pm, Wed–Fri 10am–5pm, Sat noon–4pm; free; ⓣ212/838-2560, ⓦwww.societyillustrators.org). Rotating selections from the museum's permanent collection of more than 2000 illustrations include everything from wartime propaganda to contemporary ads. Exhibitions are based on a theme or illustrator; designed primarily for aficionados, they are nonetheless accessible, well presented and topical.

Members only

The traditional **gentlemen's club** originated in London in the eighteenth century but was quickly transported to North America, becoming especially popular among the burgeoning wealthy classes of nineteenth-century New York. Founded in 1836, the **Union Club**, 101 East 69th St at Park Avenue, is the second oldest in the nation (the current building opened in 1933), its 135 founders very much the city's social elite; **J.P. Morgan**, Cornelius Vanderbilt, William Randolph Hearst and **John Jacob Astor IV** would all become members. Equally exclusive is the still-male-only **Knickerbocker Club**, a handsome Federal-style structure on the corner of Fifth Avenue and 62nd Street, founded in 1871 by Union Club members who thought the club's standards of admission had dropped (the building dates from 1915), and attracting a bevy of Astors, Roosevelts and Rockefellers.

Indeed, in the 1890s established society still looked askance at bankers and industrialists – the city's new money. When Union Club member J.P. Morgan proposed his friend Frank King, the latter was blackballed because he had done manual labour in his youth. Not one to be slighted, Morgan resigned and commissioned Stanford White to design a club for him – one that would be bigger, better and grander than all the rest. Such was the birth of the **Metropolitan Club**, 1 East 60th St at Fifth Avenue, an exuberant construction completed in 1894 with a marvellously outrageous gateway: just the thing to greet its affluent members (both then and now).

Another group of New Yorkers unwelcome in the elite clubs, prosperous German Jews, founded the elegant **Harmonie Club** in 1852, hiring Stanford White to build a new home at 4 East 60th St (across the road from the Metropolitan Club) in 1905.

All the clubs, both restrictive and lax, refused to open their doors to women. In 1903, with the opening of the **Colony Club**, 564 Park Ave at 62nd Street, the ladies fought back, founding the first social club for members of their sex. The ornate **Cosmopolitan Club**, with its New Orleans-style balconies at 122 East 66th St between Lexington and Park avenues, also opened as a women's institution in 1909 (the building dates from 1932, and is unmarked).

Park Avenue Armory

The **Park Avenue Armory** (ⓣ212/616-3930, ⓦwww.armoryonpark.org), further north at 643 Park Ave, dominates the block between East 66th and 67th streets. Completed in 1881 for the National Guard's Seventh Regiment, the exterior features pseudo-medieval crenellations, and the interior a grand double staircase and spidery wrought-iron chandeliers. The most reliable way to get a peek at the lavish rooms inside is to attend one of the frequent art and antique shows staged here (it's normally closed otherwise); you'll usually have to pay to attend the shows (which showcase the enormous **drill hall**), but the period rooms on the first floor will be open for free **self-guided tours**. Highlights include the incredibly opulent **Veterans Room** and **Library**, designed by Stanford White and decked out with Tiffany interiors and stained glass – the fireplace in the former is particularly fine, framed with blue glass tiles and murals. Check out also the portraits in the **Colonel's Reception Room**, where George Washington and compatriot Marquis de Lafayette would no doubt be mortified to find themselves on display with a very regal George VI. The website is the best place to find out about upcoming exhibitions.

Roosevelt Houses

The two blocks between the Armory and Fifth Avenue are a trim mix of luxury apartment buildings and elegant townhouses, while East 65th Street holds a decidedly presidential air: the **Roosevelt Houses** at no. 47–49, at Madison Avenue, were a wedding gift from Sara Delano Roosevelt to her son FDR and Eleanor Roosevelt in 1908. The couple lived at no. 49 until 1938, while Sara stayed on at no. 47 until her death in 1941, when the two townhouses were sold to Hunter College. Today, it houses the college's Roosevelt House Public Policy Institute, while a museum should be open to the public by 2011.

Temple Emanu-El

One block west of the Roosevelt Houses, **Temple Emanu-El**, stands on the corner of 65th Street and Fifth Avenue (Mon–Thurs 10am–4.30pm; free; ⓣ212/744-1400). Completed in 1929 and still America's largest Reformed Jewish synagogue, this awe-inspiring Romanesque-Byzantine cavern – a vast, moody and contemplative place – manages to feel much bigger inside than it looks from the outside (you can only take a quick look, escorted by a member of staff). The entrance is on 65th Street, where there's also the **Herbert & Eileen Bernard Museum** on the second floor (same hours; free); its three rooms hold both temporary exhibits on religious themes like the Kabbalah as well as an artefact-heavy history of the temple itself.

The Frick Collection

A spectacular feat of acquisitive good taste, the **Frick Collection**, 1 East 70th St at Fifth Avenue, is one of New York's finest sights (Tues–Sat 10am–6pm, Sun 11am–5pm; $18, pay what you wish Sun 11am–1pm; ⓣ212/288-0700, ⓦwww.frick.org). The collection comprises the art treasures amassed by **Henry Clay Frick** (1849–1919), one of New York's most ruthless robber-barons, and is housed in the sumptuous mansion he had built in 1914. The legacy of his ill-gotten gains – he spent millions on the best of Europe's art – is a superb assembly of work.

Opened in 1935, for the most part the museum has been kept as it looked when the Fricks lived here. What sets it apart from most galleries is that it strives hard to be as unlike a museum as possible. There is no wall text describing the pictures, though you can dial up info on most pieces using the hand-held guides available in the lobby (included with the price of admission). There are few ropes, fresh flowers on every table, and chairs provided for weary visitors, even in the most lavishly decorated rooms. Make sure you pay a visit to the enclosed central **Garden Court**, where marble floors, fountains and greenery, all simply arranged, exude serenity.

Start your visit with the **introductory film** (22min) shown every hour in the **Music Room**, which provides background on Frick's coke and steel empire and his ravenous appetite for acquiring art, which really got going in the 1890s.

The South Hall to Fragonard Room

With its magnificent array of Old Masters, the collection rivals to a certain extent the much larger holdings of the Met, especially in the quality of Italian Renaissance pieces, an area in which the Met is comparatively weak. Don't rush; even the initial corridors beyond the entrance hold some exceptional pieces. The **South Hall** contains Renoir's beguiling *Mother and Children* and two fabulous Vermeers: *Girl at Her Muse* and *Officer and Laughing Girl*, the latter in particular a masterful play on light. Look out, too, for the elegant French Rococo furniture here – though paintings take the limelight, Frick also collected antique tables, chests and chairs, spread liberally throughout the mansion.

Keep an open mind as you enter the eighteenth-century **Boucher Room**. With its flowery walls, overdone furniture and Boucher's Rococo representations of the arts and sciences in gilded frames, it is not to modern tastes. More reserved English paintings pack the **Dining Room**: giant portraits by Romney and Gainsborough, whose *St James's Park* is a study in social mores – there isn't a woman walking under the trees who isn't assessing the competition. The nearby **Fragonard Room** contains the French painter's typically florid *Progress of Love* series, painted for Louis XV's mistress Madame du Barry but discarded by her soon afterwards.

The Living Hall

The **Living Hall** houses one of the most impressive Renaissance pictures anywhere in America: Bellini's sublime *St Francis in the Desert*. Stunningly well preserved, the picture suggests Francis's vision of Christ. This canvas unfairly overshadows the rest of the pieces in the room, although also notable are a couple of knockout portraits by Hans Holbein the Younger: his masterpieces *Thomas Cromwell* and *Sir Thomas More*, Tudor adversaries that now seem to stare at each other. More's world-weariness is graphically evidenced by the bags under his eyes and his five-o'clock shadow, while the two are separated by El Greco's restrained *St Jerome*.

Library and North Hall

Move into the **Library** to see more English pictures, such as Turner's *Fishing Boats entering Calais Harbour*, Reynolds' *Lady Taylor*, who's dwarfed by her huge blue ribbon and feather hat, and one of Constable's *Salisbury Cathedral* series; there's also a portrait of Frick himself here, as a white-bearded old man, and one of Frick's rare American paintings, a portrait of George Washington by Gilbert Stuart. Across in the **North Hall**, look for the gorgeous but chill-inducing *Vétheuil in Winter* by Monet, and a classic Degas, *The Rehearsal*.

The West and East galleries

The **West Gallery** is another important space: the long, elegant room is decorated with dark-green walls, a concave glass ceiling and ornately carved wood trim. There's a clutch of snazzy Dutch pictures here, including Rembrandt's enigmatic

Polish Rider and his most magnificent self-portrait, regal robes contrasting with his sorrowful, weary expression. Look out for a couple of uncharacteristically informal portraits of Frans Snyders and his wife by Van Dyck, Frick's favourite artist, and Turner's vast canvases of Dieppe and Cologne. This gallery is also the location of the last picture Frick himself bought before his death in 1919: Vermeer's seemingly unfinished *Mistress and Maid*, a gripping snapshot of an intimate moment.

At the far end of the West Gallery is the tiny **Enamel Room**, named for the exquisite set of mostly sixteenth-century Limoges enamels on display. There's also a collection of small altarpieces by Piero della Francesca; it's another sign of Frick's good taste that he snapped up work by this artist, who is now one of the acknowledged Italian masters but was little regarded in the nineteenth century. The **Oval Room** at the other end of the West Gallery is filled with a quartet of pretty portraits by James McNeill Whistler, the only US painter admired by Frick, as well as the incredibly detailed "Fraga Philip", a portrait of Spain's King Philip IV by Velázquez. Finally, the **East Gallery** displays a mishmash of styles and periods; highlights are Reynolds' bug-eyed but dashing *General Burgoyne*, the vigorous *Forge* by Goya, and Manet's unusually cropped *Bullfight*.

The modern **basement gallery** displays temporary exhibits from other museums; accessible only by a steep spiral staircase just to the left beyond the entry hall, it's easy to miss unless you're looking for it.

St James' Church and the Asia Society

One block east of the Frick is the stately and elaborate neo-Gothic facade of **St James' Church**, 865 Madison Ave at East 71st Street (Tues–Sun 8am–8pm; free; Ⓣ212/288-4100, Ⓦwww.stjames.org). First constructed in 1885, what you see today dates mostly from the 1920s, including the graceful, gilded reredos above the marble altar, designed by Ralph Adams Cram.

A prominent educational resource founded by John D. Rockefeller III, the **Asia Society**, one block east at 725 Park Ave and East 70th Street (Tues–Sun 11am–6pm, Fri until 9pm; $10, free Fri 6–9pm; Ⓣ212/517-ASIA or 288-6400, Ⓦwww.asiasociety.org), offers two floors of small but nevertheless enthralling exhibition spaces dedicated to both traditional and contemporary art from all over Asia. In addition to the usually worthwhile temporary exhibits, ranging from Japanese lacquerware to ancient Buddhist sculpture, a variety of intriguing performances, political roundtables, lectures, films and free events are frequently held here.

Whitney Museum of American Art

In a grey, arsenal-like building designed in 1966 by Marcel Breuer, the **Whitney Museum of American Art** (Wed, Thurs, Sat & Sun 11am–6pm, Fri 1–9pm; $18, Fri 6–9pm pay what you wish; Ⓣ1-800/WHITNEY, Ⓦwww.whitney.org), 945 Madison Ave at East 75th Street, has – from the outside at least – a suspiciously institutional air. Once inside, though, first impressions prove wildly off-base: not only does the Whitney incorporate some of the best-designed exhibition space in the city, but the intelligent, challenging shows, designed from its eminent collection of twentieth-century American art, are outstanding.

Gertrude Vanderbilt Whitney (1875–1942), a sculptor and champion of American art, founded the Whitney Studio in 1914 to exhibit the work of living American artists who could not find support in established art circles – she was the first to exhibit Edward Hopper, in 1920. By 1929, she had collected more than 500 works by various artists, all of which she offered, with a generous endowment, to the Met. When her offer was refused, she set up her own museum in Greenwich Village in 1930, with her collection as its core exhibit, relocating to its current spot in 1966. The Brutalist building was initially a controversial addition to the neat townhouses of the Upper East Side, but it's a sign of how beloved the structure has become that plans to wreck its integrity with a Neoclassical addition were shouted down in the late 1990s. Forced to find more space, the Whitney kicked its administrative offices off site and transformed the fifth floor into additional galleries.

The Whitney is best known for its superb **temporary exhibitions**, to which it devotes most of its time and space (even stairwells). Many of these exhibitions are retrospectives of established artists or debuts of their lesser-known counterparts: Jasper Johns, Cy Twombly and Cindy Sherman were all given their first retrospectives here, and hipster photographer Ryan McGinley also had a solo show. The most thought-provoking exhibitions, however, push the boundaries of art as a concept – strong showings of late have been in the realms of video installations (incorporating names such as Bill Viola and Nam June Paik) and computer and digital technology.

Without a doubt, though, the Whitney is most famous for its **Biennial**, which was first held in 1932 and continues to occur between March and June in even-numbered years. Designed to give a provocative overview of what's happening in contemporary American art, it's often panned by critics, sometimes for good reason. Nonetheless, the Biennial is always packed with visitors, so catch it if you can.

The collection

The museum owns more than 12,000 paintings, sculptures, photographs and films by almost 2000 artists such as Calder, Nevelson, O'Keeffe, de Kooning, Rauschenberg and LeWitt. For an overview of its holdings, see **The Whitney's Collection**, a somewhat arbitrary pick of the Whitney's best on display on the fifth floor. Work is rotated here, but the collection is particularly strong on **Edward Hopper** (2000 of his works were bequeathed to the museum in 1970), and several of his best paintings are usually on show. The eerie *Early Sunday Morning* is a typical example: it focuses on light and shadow, a bleak urban landscape, uneasily tense in its lighting and rejection of topical detail. The street could be anywhere (in fact it's Seventh Ave); for Hopper, it becomes universal. Look out also for **Joseph Stella**'s Futurist *Brooklyn Bridge*; **Jackson Pollock**'s explosion of colour, *Number 27*; and **Jasper Johns**' celebrated *Three Flags*, which erases the emblem of patriotism and replaces it with ambiguity.

As if to balance the figurative works that formed the nucleus of the original collection, more recent purchases have included an emphasis on abstract art. **Marsden Hartley**'s *Painting Number 5* is a jarring work painted in memory of a German officer friend killed in the early days of World War I. **Georgia O'Keeffe**'s *Abstraction* is gentler, though with its own darkness: it was suggested by the noises of cattle being driven to slaughter.

The **Abstract Expressionists** are also a strong presence, with great works by masters **Pollock** and **de Kooning**. **Mark Rothko** and the **Color Field** painters are also well represented – though you need a sharp eye to discern any colour in **Ad Reinhardt**'s *Black Painting*. In a different direction, **Warhol**, **Johns** and **Oldenburg** each subvert the meaning of their images. Warhol's silk-screened *Coke Bottles* fade into motif; and Oldenburg's light-hearted *Soft Sculptures*, with its toilets and motors, falls into line with his declaration, "I'm into art that doesn't sit on its ass in a museum."

Museum Mile and Carnegie Hill

Upper Fifth Avenue is nicknamed **Museum Mile**, home to New York's greatest concentration of museums, several of which are housed in the area's few remaining mansions. North of the Met (covered in Chapter 14), the neighbourhood is known as **Carnegie Hill** after steel magnate Andrew Carnegie, who constructed his mansion on Fifth Avenue and 91st Street (it's now the Cooper-Hewitt National Design Museum; see p.181). As you wander between museums, look out for some eye-popping architecture and public art: **East 79th Street** contains some of the finest turn-of-the-century Beaux Arts and neo-Renaissance mansions in the city, while the **Alexander Calder Sidewalk** outside 1018 Madison Ave between 78th and 79th streets was installed in 1970, a series of striking black-and-white parallel and diagonal lines and crescents. Note that the Museo del Barrio and the new Museum for African Art are covered in the Harlem chapter (see p.210).

Institute for the Study of the Ancient World

Primarily a cutting-edge research facility, NYU's **Institute for the Study of the Ancient World** (Tues–Thurs, Sat & Sun 11am–6pm, Fri 11am–8pm; free; ⓣ212/992-7843; ⓦwww.nyu.edu/isaw), 15 East 84th St (near Madison Ave), also hosts thought-provoking exhibitions on prehistory – anything from mysterious Central European objects dating back five thousand years to ancient grave goods from the Republic of Georgia. Exhibitions usually last five months, but sometimes there are gaps between shows, so check in advance.

Neue Galerie

Dedicated to early twentieth-century art from Austria and Germany, the small but fabulous **Neue Galerie**, 1048 Fifth Ave at 86th Street (Mon & Thurs–Sun 11am–6pm; $15, free first Fri of the month 6–8pm; ⓣ212/628-6200, ⓦwww.neuegalerie.org), occupies an ornate Georgian-style mansion on the corner of 86th Street, completed in 1914. The house was built by industrialist William Starr Miller but was later occupied by the formidable New York socialite Grace Vanderbilt between 1944 and 1953, after the death of her millionaire husband, Cornelius Vanderbilt III. In 2001, it was transformed into the museum, thanks largely to the work of New York art collectors Serge Sabarsky and Ronald S. Lauder.

The exhibits tend to rotate, but the collection contains some real gems. The galleries begin on the wood-panelled second floor, where the undoubted star is **Gustav Klimt**'s *Portrait of Adele Bloch-Bauer I* (1907), a resplendent portrait from Klimt's "Golden Period". The Bloch-Bauers were one of Vienna's richest Jewish families; the painting was looted by the Nazis in 1938 but descendants sued the Austrian government and had the painting returned in 2006 – the gallery is said to have paid $135 million for it soon after. On this floor, dedicated to art from Vienna circa 1900, you'll also find exceptional work by **Egon Schiele** and **Max Oppenheimer**, while the third floor is usually reserved for rotating German work from various movements of the early twentieth century: look out for Paul Klee (of the Blaue Reiter and Bauhaus movements), Ernst Ludwig Kirchner (of the Brücke) and Otto Dix (of the Neue Sachlichkeit). At the Neue's *Café Sabarsky* (see p.297), you can pause for exquisite Viennese pastries before heading back to Museum Mile.

Guggenheim Museum

Multistorey parking garage or upturned beehive? Whatever you may think of the collection, it's the **Guggenheim Museum** building, 1071 Fifth Ave at 89th Street, that steals the show (Mon–Wed, Fri & Sun 10am–5.45pm, Sat 10am–7.45pm; $18, Sat 5.45–7.45pm pay what you wish; ⓣ212/423-3500, ⓦwww.guggenheim.org). The structure, designed by **Frank Lloyd Wright** specifically for the museum, caused a storm of controversy when it was unveiled in 1959, bearing, as it did, little relation to the statuesque apartment buildings of this most genteel part of Fifth Avenue. Reactions ranged from disgusted disbelief to critical acclaim – "one of the greatest rooms erected in the twentieth century", wrote Philip Johnson, himself no slouch in the architectural genius stakes. Time has been kinder than his contemporaries were – nearly half a century later, the museum is now a beloved New York landmark.

The institution's namesake, **Solomon R. Guggenheim** (1861–1949), was one of America's richest men, thanks to his silver and copper mines. Although abstract art was considered little more than a fad at the time, Guggenheim, always a man with an eye for a sound investment, began collecting modern paintings with fervour. He bought wholesale the canvases of **Kandinsky**, then added works by **Chagall**, **Klee** and **Léger**, among others, and exhibited them to a bemused American public in his suite of rooms in the *Plaza Hotel*. The Guggenheim Foundation was created in 1937; after exhibiting the collection in various rented spaces, it commissioned Wright to design a permanent home. The museum's holdings have been bolstered since Guggenheim's day via acquisitions and donations. A significant gift came in 1976 when collector **Justin K. Thannhauser** handed over more works by Cézanne, Degas, Gauguin, Manet, Toulouse-Lautrec, Van Gogh and Picasso, among others, greatly enhancing the museum's Impressionist and Post-Impressionist holdings. The Foundation now includes museums in Berlin, Bilbao and Venice (which is named for Solomon's niece Peggy, another art-collecting magpie).

▲ Guggenheim Museum

The building

Collection of art aside, it's the **structure** that dominates – it's not hard to theorize that the egomaniacal Wright engineered it that way. Most visitors find it difficult to not be impressed (or sidetracked) by the tiers of cream concrete overhead, an uplifting interior space designed so that the public could experience the spiral of the central rotunda from top to bottom. The circular galleries rise upward at a not-so-gentle slope, so you may prefer to start at the top of the museum and work your way down; most of the temporary exhibits are designed to be seen that way.

The collection

Magnificent **temporary exhibitions** take up most of the museum, but you'll always see plenty of **Kandinsky**'s exuberant work (most temporary shows are linked, albeit tenuously, to pieces in the permanent collection); look out for the jarring *Komposition 8*, and the abstract *Blue Mountain*. The Level 2 and 3 annexes also contain **permanent displays**: it's almost overwhelming to walk into the Level 2 annexe and immediately see **Picasso**'s haunting *Woman Ironing* and *Le Moulin de la Galette*. Next in line are a **Degas**, *Dancers in Green and Yellow*; **Monet**, with *The Palazzo Ducale Seen from San Giorgio*; works by **Van Gogh** including his vivid *Roadway with Underpass, Landscape with Snow* and *Mountains at Saint Remy*; **Cézanne**'s hazy *Bibémus* and the wonderful *Man with Crossed Arms*; and **Picasso**'s recognizable *Woman with Yellow Hair*. Note, though, that even the permanent displays get moved around, so you may not see all of the above.

National Academy of Design

In 1825, a group of artists including Samuel Morse founded the little-known **National Academy of Design**, 1083 Fifth Ave at East 89th Street (Wed & Thurs noon–5pm, Fri 1–9pm, Sat & Sun 11am–6pm; $10; Ⓣ212/369-4880, Ⓦwww.nationalacademy.org). Intended to ape London's prestigious Royal Academy, it is today housed in the bow-fronted, Beaux Arts Huntington townhouse next to the Church of the Heavenly Rest. The house was substantially re-built by millionaire Archer Huntington in 1913 (Archer's father made a fortune in San Francisco overseeing early American railways), and in 1939 he donated the building to the Academy.

Its doors are usually open to the public for three or four **shows** a year, starting with the **Academy's Annual** in the spring, featuring work selected from members of the Academy, a list that has included big names like **Richard Diebenkorn**, **Chuck Close**, **Robert Rauschenberg** and **Jasper Johns**. Each artist – famous, notorious or neither – is required to donate a picture to the place when they join. On alternate years, work is supplied by a juried invitational group of exclusively non-academicians. The rest of the year, the Academy hosts thematic exhibitions with work from its permanent collection. When the galleries are closed between shows (check the website before you go), you can still peruse the shop.

Cooper-Hewitt National Design Museum

The **Cooper-Hewitt National Design Museum** (Mon–Thurs 10am–5pm, Fri 10am–9pm, Sat 10am–6pm, Sun noon–6pm; $15; Ⓣ212/849-8400, Ⓦwww.cooperhewitt.org), 2 East 91st St at Fifth Avenue, was established in 1897 by the granddaughters of Peter Cooper (see p.99) and became part of the Smithsonian network in 1967. Its displays are housed in a mansion completed for millionaire industrialist **Andrew Carnegie** in 1902, a spacious building with dark wood-panelled walls, glass conservatory, carved ceilings and parquet floors – the interior is as much a draw as the exhibits. An ambitious redevelopment project ("Re:Design") will see the property restored and expanded to house a permanent exhibition dubbed "**What is Design?**" on the first floor, drawing on the museum's collection of 200,000 items, and two higher floors of temporary exhibits. These shows are almost always worth checking out and include a diverse roster of subjects from modern car design to high fashion. The nearby townhouses at 7–11 90th St will host the elegant **National Design Library**, expected to open in late 2010. The museum itself will be **closed between 2011 and 2013** while the main work is completed.

15 Jewish Museum

Given how Jewish culture has flourished in New York, it is fitting that the **Jewish Museum**, 1109 Fifth Ave at East 92nd Street, is the largest museum of Judaica outside Israel (Tues & Thurs–Sun 11am–5.45pm; $12, Sat free; Ⓣ212/423-3200, Ⓦwww.jewishmuseum.org). Housed in the French Gothic **Felix Warburg Mansion** (built for the famous Jewish banker in 1908), the top two floors house "Culture & Continuity: The Jewish Journey", a permanent exhibition that traces the development of Judaism from 1200 BC to the modern day. Pivotal events such as the Babylonian exile in 586 BC, the destruction of the Temple in 70 AD, and the development of the Jewish diaspora are highlighted with films and some rare artefacts, including ancient pottery, ageing Hanukkah lamps, Roman burial stones and precious Torahs. After tackling anti-Semitism and the establishment of Israel in 1948, the exhibition concludes with a thoughtful study of modern Jewish identity. The lower floors host temporary exhibits, usually of famous Jewish artists such as Man Ray.

Museum of the City of New York

The small but oddly appealing **Museum of the City of New York**, 1220 Fifth Ave at East 103rd Street, is housed in a grand neo-Georgian building, purpose-built in 1930 (Tues–Sun 10am–5pm; $10; Ⓣ212/534-1672, Ⓦwww.mcny.org). The museum displays an eclectic mix of exhibits highlighting aspects of the city and its history; more recently, its facade has served as the posh high school in the cult TV series *Gossip Girl*. Only the audiovisual presentation (25min; every 30min) on the second floor tackles the history of the city in a conventional way, from the Lenape Indians to the 9/11 attacks. The rest of the museum is filled with temporary exhibits and three main permanent collections: New York Toy Stories, which includes motion toys, board games, sports equipment, and dollhouses from the 1800s; Trade, which focuses on New York's role as a port from the 1600s to the 1970s; and New York Interiors, with six ornately furnished period rooms behind glass, from a Dutch home of the seventeenth century to a 1906 drawing room. The galleries will remain open while the museum undertakes a major renovation, to be complete by 2012.

North and east of here, the neighbourhood rather joltingly transitions from blocks of quiet, moneyed apartment buildings to **El Barrio**, or **Spanish Harlem** (for the nearby Museo del Barrio, see p.210).

Yorkville and around

It's only in **Yorkville** that the Upper East Side displays minute traces of New York's European immigrant history: around 1900, this was a German–Hungarian neighbourhood that spilled out from East 79th to 96th streets between Lexington and the East River.

Lexington Avenue itself was only gentrified in the 1960s, as the western stretches of the Upper East Side increased in value, and money-savvy property developers rushed in to snap up real estate farther east. Only forty years later, the signs of its economic heyday are already long gone, and this is now one of the cheaper residential areas in the city. The proliferation of small apartments (as well as a generous number of hip restaurants and sports bars) means that the East 70s and 80s are home to a number of young, unattached and upwardly mobile professionals.

Amid all the DVD stores and fast-food joints, there are a few hints of the old neighbourhood, notably traditional German delicatessens and cafés: look for lauded sausage-maker **Schaller and Weber**, 1654 Second Ave at East 86th Street (Mon–Fri 9am–6pm, Sat 8.30am–6pm), established in 1937; **Heidelberg**, next door at no. 1648 (see p.331 for review), which is one year older; and **M. Rohrs'**, around the corner at 310 East 86th St, a coffee shop with roots in 1896 (see p.297). **Orwasher's Handmade Bread**, 308 East 78th St near Second Avenue (Mon–Sat 8am–7pm, Sun 9am–4pm), was founded in 1916 and claims to have invented raisin pumpernickel bread during World War II.

Gracie Mansion

One of the reasons that riverside Carl Schurz Park, at the end of East 86th Street, is so exceptionally well maintained is the high-profile security that surrounds **Gracie Mansion**, East End Avenue at 88th Street (45min tours Wed 10am, 11am, 1pm & 2pm; $7, reservations required; ⓣ212/570-4751). Built in 1799 by Scottish-born merchant Archibald Gracie, it is one of the best-preserved Federal-style buildings in New York. Appropriated by the city in 1896 (in lieu of unpaid taxes), Gracie Mansion has been the official residence of the mayor of New York City since 1942, when Fiorello LaGuardia set up house here; the name's a misnomer, since it's more a large wood-frame cottage than a grand residence. The mansion was meticulously restored in 2002, but other than a few antiques and the bold murals in the dining room, the house itself isn't particularly compelling, and

▲ Gracie Mansion

the tours are most interesting for the effusive guides and the stories associated with past mayors.

Current billionaire mayor **Michael Bloomberg** has opted not to live at Gracie Mansion (though he does hold meetings and functions here) – a far cry from the **Rudy Giuliani** era when, thanks to an acrimonious split, he and his wife continued to live in the same home even when his new partner was visiting.

Henderson Place

Across from the park and just below Gracie Mansion, at East 86th Street and East End Avenue, is **Henderson Place**, a set of 24 old servants' quarters now transformed into a "historic district" of luxury cottages. Built in 1882 by John Henderson, a fur importer and real-estate developer, the small and sprightly Queen Anne-style dwellings were intended to provide close and convenient housing for servants working in the palatial old East End Avenue mansions, most of which have now been torn down. Ironically, these servants' quarters now represent some of the most sought-after real estate in the city, offering the space, quiet and privacy that much of the city lacks.

Mount Vernon Hotel Museum

Further south along the East River is the **Mount Vernon Hotel Museum and Garden**, 421 East 61st St between First and York avenues (Tues–Sun 11am–4pm, June & July Tues until 9pm, closed Aug; $8; Ⓣ212/838-6878, Ⓦwww.mvhm.org), a fine schist stone house squashed between modern tower blocks. Inside, you'll find a series of 1820s period rooms, meticulously restored since 1924 when the house was saved by the Colonial Dames of America (an association of women that can trace their ancestry back to colonial times). The Dames were attracted by a connection with Abigail Adams Smith (daughter of President John Adams), though recent research has revealed this to be rather tenuous; the property was indeed once part of an estate bought by Abigail and her husband in 1795 (when this area was lush countryside), but the family soon went bankrupt, and it was only completed as a carriage house in 1799 by the new owner. It served as a hotel between 1826 and 1833 before reverting to a private residence. Visits are by guided tours only (provided on demand until 3.15pm).

Roosevelt Island

An aerial **tramway** (every 15min 6am–3am, Fri & Sat until 3.30am; every 7.5min during rush hours; $2.25 one-way; Ⓣ212/832-4555, Ⓦwww.rioc.com) near the Queensboro Bridge connects Manhattan with **Roosevelt Island** in the middle of the East River, an odd little corner of New York that's home to around 13,000 people (you can also take the F train here). While the modern tower blocks and new-town layout can seem a little soulless, there is a languid, small-community vibe on the island that can be appealing – it also makes for an easy outdoor break from midtown, with a breezy promenade and fabulous views of the city. Get **information** at the Roosevelt Island Historical Society Kiosk, situated across from Tram dock (Ⓣ212/688-4836, Ⓦwww.rihs.us); call ahead, as opening times vary. You'll find a *Starbucks* and a couple of restaurants near the subway station.

Some history

Only two miles long and no more than 800ft wide, the island was known as **Minnahannock** by the local Native Americans. In 1686, ownership passed to English farmer Robert Blackwell, who imaginatively renamed it **Blackwell Island**. In 1828, the city of New York snapped up the land for $32,000 and assigned it for use as a **quarantine site** for criminals, lunatics and smallpox victims; in 1843, Charles Dickens came to expose conditions of the chronically ill, insane and destitute who were crowded into the eight hospitals and asylums built here. By 1921, it was officially known as **Welfare Island**, but by the 1950s much of the island was deserted, forgotten and unloved. Forward-thinking city mayor John Lindsay enlisted architects John Burgee and Philip Johnson to demolish most of the old buildings and create a master plan for new residential living areas. Duly rechristened Roosevelt Island in 1973, the island received its first new inhabitants two years later. Today, locals are fiercely protective of their hidden enclave: to snag one of the cheap apartments here, you'll have to join the years-long official waiting list.

North island

Arriving via the tramway or subway, stroll north along Main Street to see the white clapboard **Blackwell House**, built in 1796 by James Blackwell; the exterior has been lovingly restored, but you can't go inside. From here you can take the Roosevelt Island bus (25¢), which loops from Tramway Plaza north to the new Octagon development and back, or wander up the west promenade soaking up the views of the Upper East Side. At the north end of the island, **Octagon Tower** was built in 1839 as the admin centre of New York's first municipal asylum (most of it was demolished in the 1970s), and is now incorporated into the new Octagon Development; you can take a peek at the magnificent domed lobby and spiral staircase inside. At the northern tip itself, **Lighthouse Park** affords excellent views of the upper reaches of the East River, and is also home to a 50ft-high Gothic lighthouse, dating back to 1872.

South island

The southern end of the island is encompassed by **Southpoint Park**, currently being converted into a garden and memorial to Franklin Roosevelt. You can wander along the riverside path here to see a ghostly reminder of the island's past: the ruins of the **Smallpox Hospital**, completed in 1856 by architect James Renwick, Jr. It almost collapsed in 2007, and is currently being restored. Nearby, the **Strecker Laboratory**, the city's premier laboratory for bacteriological research when it opened in 1892, was restored in the early 1990s and houses subway electrical infrastructure.

16

The Upper West Side and Morningside Heights

While the Upper East Side has always been a patrician stronghold, the Upper West Side, only minutes away on the other side of the park, has grown into its position as a somewhat younger, somewhat hipper, but nonetheless affluent counterpart. Later to develop, it has seen its share of struggling actors, writers and opera singers come and go over the years. In the 1990s, the Upper West Side was the neighbourhood of choice for upwardly mobile dot-commers, and though those days seem long gone, young professionals and their stroller-bound children still make up a sizeable part of the population.

This isn't to say it lacks glamour; the lower stretches of **Central Park West** and **Riverside Drive** are quite fashionable, while the network of performing spaces at **Lincoln Center** makes the neighbourhood New York's de facto palace of culture. And as you move north, gorgeous – and occasionally landmarked – blocks pop up in the 80s, 90s and 100s, especially off and along Riverside Drive and the West End. In general, though, the neighbourhood loses some of its lustre along the way, culminating in **Morningside Heights**, home to **Columbia University** at the edge of Harlem, as well as the monolithic **Cathedral of St John the Divine**.

The Upper West Side

North of 59th Street, the somewhat tawdry Midtown West becomes decidedly less commercial and garish, and then morphs into the largely residential **Upper West Side**. The neighbourhood stretches along Central Park, running west from the park to the Hudson River, and north from Columbus Circle at 59th Street to 110th Street and the beginning of Morningside Heights. Its main artery is **Broadway** and its twin pinnacles of prosperity are the historic apartment houses

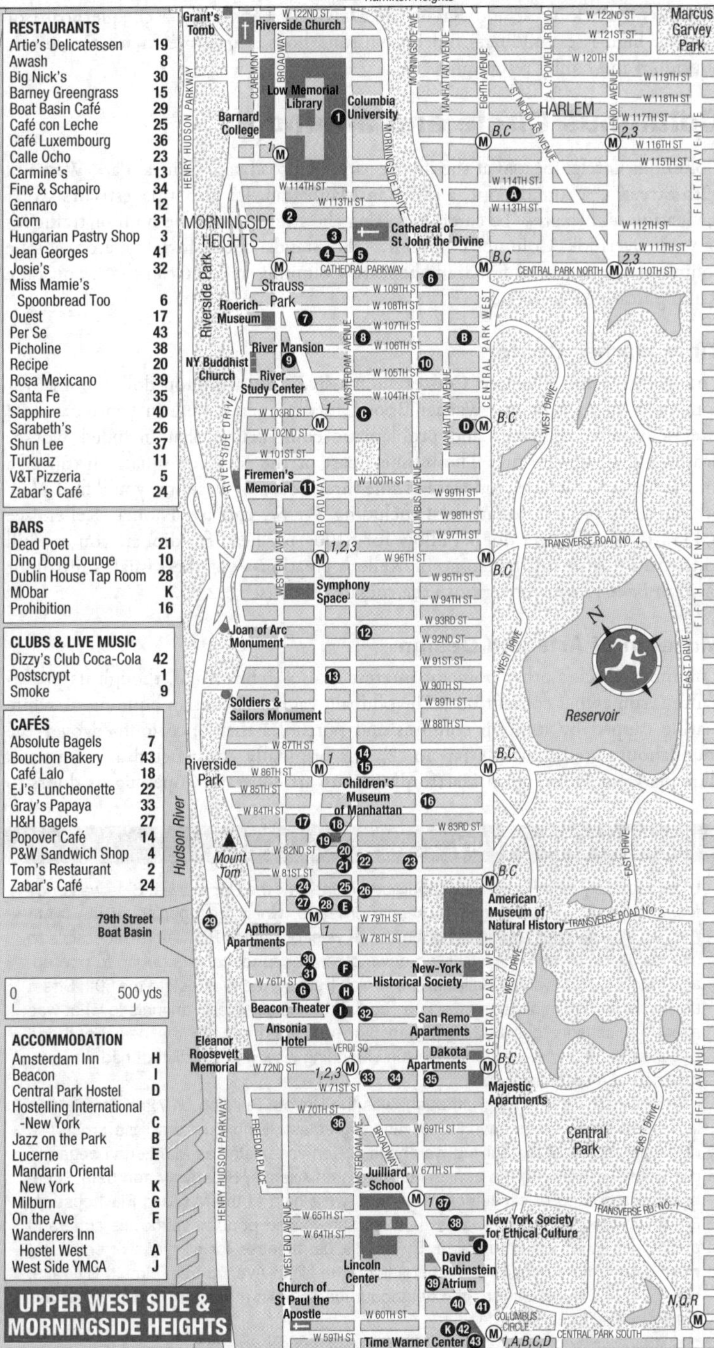
Hamilton Heights
RESTAURANTS
Artie's Delicatessen 19
Awash 8
Big Nick's 30
Barney Greengrass 15
Boat Basin Café 29
Café con Leche 25
Café Luxembourg 36
Calle Ocho 23
Carmine's 13
Fine & Schapiro 34
Gennaro 12
Grom 31
Hungarian Pastry Shop 3
Jean Georges 41
Josie's 32
Miss Mamie's Spoonbread Too 6
Ouest 17
Per Se 43
Picholine 38
Recipe 20
Rosa Mexicano 39
Santa Fe 35
Sapphire 40
Sarabeth's 26
Shun Lee 37
Turkuaz 11
V&T Pizzeria 5
Zabar's Café 24
BARS
Dead Poet 21
Ding Dong Lounge 10
Dublin House Tap Room 28
MObar K
Prohibition 16
CLUBS & LIVE MUSIC
Dizzy's Club Coca-Cola 42
Postscrypt 1
Smoke 9
CAFÉS
Absolute Bagels 7
Bouchon Bakery 43
Café Lalo 18
EJ's Luncheonette 22
Gray's Papaya 33
H&H Bagels 27
Popover Café 14
P&W Sandwich Shop 4
Tom's Restaurant 2
Zabar's Café 24
0 500 yds
ACCOMMODATION
Amsterdam Inn H
Beacon I
Central Park Hostel D
Hostelling International -New York C
Jazz on the Park B
Lucerne E
Mandarin Oriental New York K
Milburn G
On the Ave F
Wanderers Inn Hostel West A
West Side YMCA J
UPPER WEST SIDE & MORNINGSIDE HEIGHTS
Grant's Tomb
Riverside Church
Low Memorial Library
Columbia University
Barnard College
HARLEM
Marcus Garvey Park
MORNINGSIDE HEIGHTS
Cathedral of St John the Divine
Strauss Park
Roerich Museum
River Mansion
NY Buddhist Church
River Study Center
Firemen's Memorial
Riverside Park
Symphony Space
Joan of Arc Monument
Soldiers & Sailors Monument
Children's Museum of Manhattan
Mount Tom
Hudson River
79th Street Boat Basin
Apthorp Apartments
American Museum of Natural History
New-York Historical Society
Beacon Theater
San Remo Apartments
Ansonia Hotel
Eleanor Roosevelt Memorial
Dakota Apartments
Majestic Apartments
Reservoir
Central Park
Juilliard School
New York Society for Ethical Culture
David Rubinstein Atrium
Lincoln Center
Church of St Paul the Apostle
Time Warner Center
COLUMBUS CIRCLE
CENTRAL PARK SOUTH
CENTRAL PARK NORTH (W 110TH ST)
CATHEDRAL PARKWAY
TRANSVERSE ROAD NO. 4
TRANSVERSE ROAD NO. 2
TRANSVERSE RD. NO. 1
HENRY HUDSON PARKWAY
RIVERSIDE DRIVE
CLAREMONT
BROADWAY
AMSTERDAM AVENUE
MORNINGSIDE DRIVE
MORNINGSIDE AVE
MANHATTAN AVENUE
EIGHTH AVENUE
ST NICHOLAS AVENUE
A.C. POWELL JR BLVD
LENOX AVENUE
FIFTH AVENUE
WEST END AVENUE
COLUMBUS AVENUE
CENTRAL PARK WEST
WEST DRIVE
EAST DRIVE
FREEDOM PLACE
VERDI SQ

of **Central Park West** and **Riverside Drive**. In between is a chequerboard of modern high-rise buildings, old brownstone houses, gourmet markets, upscale boutiques and family restaurants.

Columbus Circle and around

Columbus Circle, located at the intersection of Broadway, Central Park West and 59th Street, is a roundabout, a rarity in Manhattan. It's also a pedestrian's worst navigation nightmare – be careful crossing the street. Amid the hum of traffic it's easy to overlook Columbus himself, who stands uncomfortably atop a lone column in the centre island. Stand beneath Columbus and you can check out some striking nearby architecture.

Time Warner Center

The glitzy **Time Warner Center**, a massive, multi-million-dollar home for companies like CNN and Warner Books, finally opened here in February 2004 after a highly publicized and problematic construction that included worker deaths and an on-site fire. The business part of the complex squats on top of a multistorey mall where, aside from some three dozen or so shops, you'll find a few of the city's priciest restaurants, including *Per Se*, run by Thomas Keller (see p.333). If your budget doesn't allow for $100+ per head for dinner, you can kill some time – and still try some of Keller's creations – at the casual, third-floor *Bouchon Bakery*, which overlooks the ruckus below (see p.298).

Museum of Arts and Design

Columbus Circle's other point of interest is also architectural, though its provenance is somewhat contentious. The oddball, vaguely Venetian building of white marble capped by lollipop columns and portholes that once loomed over the roundabout's southern side (at no. 2) was originally constructed as a museum showplace for Huntington Hartford's private art collection, opening its doors to

Upper West Side history

Like practically every other neighbourhood in the city, the Upper West Side was once fecund farmland. That began to change in 1879, when the opening of the Ninth Avenue elevated train made the open space west of Central Park more accessible to city residents, who mainly still lived downtown. Cheap tenements began to pop up, and the New York Central Railroad line, which transported livestock to the 60th Street stockyards, went in about a year later, adding the smell of farm animals to what was already a sensory overload. Between 59th and 65th streets, the neighbourhood became home to more warehouses than anything else, and the district had the early makings of a soulless slum.

One diamond in the rough, though, was the Dakota Building on 72nd Street, built in 1884. Slowly, other townhouses and high-class living quarters rose around it, displacing some of the hulking warehouses. Ten years later, as Manhattan began to grow north in earnest, the confluence of Eighth Avenue, Broadway and 59th Street became a hotbed of excitement. Concerts were held at the Majestic Playhouse on Broadway and 60th Street, area theatres showcased popular vaudeville acts, and quality watering holes multiplied. By the 1920s, theatres for all types of entertainment (some more risqué than others) lined the Ninth Avenue train circuit. By 1929, shopping had taken over as the neighbourhood's main attraction, and the area has hardly looked back since.

the public in 1964. As a misjudged counter to his contemporaries' funding of expressionist art, however, the museum lasted only five years, while the building itself was considered by some New York residents to be one of the city's grand follies, a sentiment that resonated for years afterwards.

Despite this, and after years of vacancy and disrepair, preservationists were furious when the **Museum of Arts & Design** (Tues–Sun 11am–6pm, Thurs until 9pm; $15; ⓣ212/299-7777, ⓦwww.madmuseum.org) chose the place for the relocation of its collection. The battle was fought over whether or not the museum's practical needs should take precedence over the building's architectural importance to the city. In the end, with lawsuits flying all around, the museum won out. The Museum of Arts & Design moved in after $90 million worth of renovations had converted the former gallery into a sleek tower with random cutaways that allow light to penetrate the building and which tripled the exhibition space. The eclectic collection, featuring everything from blown-glass objets d'art to contemporary jewellery, is now displayed to full effect spread over half the building's twelve floors, which also contain a small theatre and artist-in-residence studios. Changing exhibits cover a wide array of media (from paper to porcelain to metal to glass) and are often accompanied by lectures and workshops. A modern American restaurant, *Robert*, occupies the top floor and offers extravagant views, if only mediocre food.

Around Columbus Circle

Opposite Columbus Circle, on the park side, stands the **Maine Monument**, a large stone column with the prow of a ship jutting out from its base, erected in 1913 and dedicated to the 260 seamen who died when the battleship *Maine* inexplicably exploded in Havana Harbor in 1898, propelling forward the Spanish-American War. Across the street, at the junction of Broadway and Central Park West, are the glittering **Trump International Hotel** and condos.

For aesthetic relief, go west a few blocks and contemplate the **Church of St Paul the Apostle**, at Columbus Avenue and 60th Street (ⓣ212/265-3495, ⓦwww.stpaultheapostle.org), a beautiful Old Gothic structure housing Byzantine basilica features, including a high altar by Stanford White. A few steps north is the **New York Society for Ethical Culture**, 2 West 64th St at Central Park West (ⓣ212/874-5210, ⓦwww.nysec.org), "a haven for those who want to share the high adventure of integrating ethical ideals into daily life". Founded in 1876 (though the building itself wasn't built until 1902), this distinguished organization also helped to found the NAACP (National Association for the Advancement of Coloured People) and the ACLU (American Civil Liberties Union). It holds regular Sunday meetings and organizes occasional recitals and lectures on social responsibility, politics and other related topics.

Lincoln Center

One of the boulevards that lead out from Columbus Circle, Broadway, continues north to the **Lincoln Center for the Performing Arts**, an imposing group of six marble-and-glass buildings arranged around a large plaza between 63rd and 66th streets. It's not, as most assume, named for President Abraham Lincoln; rather, it honours the name of the surrounding area in Manhattan's early times, probably named Lincoln for a tenant farmer who tilled the land here. Robert Moses came up with the idea of creating a cultural centre here in the 1950s as a way of "encouraging" the area's gentrification, one of his rare exercises in urban renewal that has been extremely successful. A number of architects worked on the plans, and the complex was finally built in the mid-1960s on a site that formerly held some of the city's poorest slums. In a case of life imitating art imitating life, once the slums were emptied and their residents moved to ghettos farther uptown, the deserted area became a movie set: before construction began in 1960, the run-down buildings served as the open-air location for *West Side Story*, which was based on the stage musical set here.

Home to the world-class **Metropolitan Opera**, the **New York City Ballet** and the **New York Philharmonic**, as well as a host of other smaller companies, Lincoln Center is worth seeing even if you're not catching a performance; the best way is on an **organized tour** – otherwise you'll only be allowed to peek into the ornate lobbies of the buildings. Hour-long tours leave from the airy, pleasant **David Rubinstein Atrium**, Broadway between 62nd and 63rd streets, and take in the main part of the Center (3–5 tours daily 10.30am–4.30pm, 60–90min; $15; ⓣ212/875-5350). Be warned that tours can get booked up and times vary each day; it's best to phone ahead to be sure of a place. Backstage tours of the Met are also available; see p.191 for more information.

If your budget's tight, you may want to stop by here for the **free entertainment** that is often offered: there's the Autumn Crafts Fair in early September, folk and jazz bands at lunchtime, Thursday evening concerts in the Atrium and dazzling fountain and light displays every evening in the summer. In addition, Lincoln Center hosts a variety of affordable summertime events, including July's Midsummer Night Swing – a dance series that allows you to swing, salsa, hustle and ballroom dance on an outdoor bandstand at the Lincoln Center Plaza Fountain – and August's multicultural Out of Doors festival. Contact **Lincoln Center Information** (ⓣ212/875-5000, ⓦnew.lincolncenter.org) for specifics.

Visitors these days will find Lincoln Center in the throes of a fiftieth anniversary overhaul. Besides the new Atrium noted above, Alice Tully Hall (see p.191), virtually unchanged since its opening in 1969, has benefited from a recent makeover that brings the theatre up to date with new seats and furnishings, enhanced staging capabilities and a stunning three-storey glass-enclosed foyer; the David H. Koch Theater has also been renovated. It's not all indoors, either: the plaza walkways and entrances are also being redesigned and the celebrated **fountain**, a popular meeting spot at the centre of it all, has been given *Bellagio*-style effects that mimic the Las Vegas hotel.

The David H. Koch Theater and Avery Fisher Hall

Philip Johnson's spare and elegant **David H. Koch Theater**, on the south side of the plaza, is home to both the New York City Ballet (including its famed annual performances of the *Nutcracker* in December) and the New York City Opera. Its enormous foyer is ringed with balconies embellished with delicate bronze grilles and boasts an imposing, four-storey ceiling finished in gold leaf. The ballet season runs from late November to February and early April to June; the opera season starts in mid-March and runs to mid-November. Call ⓣ212/870-5570 for ticket information.

Johnson also had a hand in **Avery Fisher Hall**, opposite the theatre on the north side of the plaza, where the New York Philharmonic plays; he was called in to refashion the interior after its acoustics were found to be below par. More changes began to take place in the 2010 summer, again with an emphasis on improved acoustics. The Philharmonic performs here from late September into June, while Mostly Mozart, the country's first and most popular indoor summer chamber-music series, takes place in July and August. Call ⓣ212/875-5030 for performance information.

The Metropolitan Opera House

In contrast to the surrounding Modernist starkness, the plaza's focal point, the **Metropolitan Opera House** (aka "the Met"), is gushingly ornate and oozes opulence, with enormous crystal chandeliers and red-carpeted staircases, designed for grand entrances in evening wear. Behind two of the high arched windows hang **murals by Marc Chagall**. The artist wanted stained glass, but at the time it was felt that glass wouldn't last long in an area still less than reverential toward the arts, so paintings were hung behind square-paned glass to give a similar effect. These days, they're covered for part of the day to protect them from the sun; the rest of the time they're best viewed from the plaza outside. The mural on the left, *Le Triomphe de la Musique*, is cast with a variety of well-known performers, while *Les Sources de la Musique* is reminiscent of Chagall's renowned scenery for the Met production of *The Magic Flute*: the god of music strums a lyre while a Tree of Life, Verdi and Wagner all float down the Hudson River. You can learn more about the Opera House on one of the **backstage tours** of the building (Sept–June Mon–Thurs 3.30pm, Sun 10.30am & 1.30pm; reservations required; $16; Ⓣ212/769-7020). For performance information, see p.369.

The rest of Lincoln Center

Two piazzas flank the Met. To the south there is **Damrosch Park**, a large space facing the Guggenheim Bandshell, where chairs are set up in the summer so you can catch free lunchtime concerts and various performances. To the north you will find a lovely, smaller plaza facing the **Vivian Beaumont Theater**, designed by Eero Saarinen in 1965 and home to the smaller **Mitzi E. Newhouse Theater**. The **New York Public Library for the Performing Arts** (Mon & Thurs noon–8pm, Tues, Wed & Fri 11am–6pm, Sat 10am–6pm; free; Ⓣ212/870-1630, Ⓦwww.nypl.org/lpa) is located behind the Vivian Beaumont and holds over eight million items (everything from performing-arts ephemera to scores and manuscripts), plus a museum that exhibits costumes, set designs and music scores.

At the corner of Broadway and 65th Street is **Alice Tully Hall**, a recital hall that houses the Chamber Music Society of Lincoln Center, and the **Walter E. Reade Theater**, which features foreign films and retrospectives and, together with the Avery Fisher and Alice Tully halls, hosts the annual New York Film Festival in September (see p.429). The celebrated **Juilliard School of Music** is in an adjacent building (the best way to check it out is via one of the regular concerts by its students; see p.369 for details).

The smallish **Dante Park**, an island on Broadway across from the main Lincoln Center Plaza, features a statue of its namesake; the American branch of the Dante Alighieri Society put it up in 1921 to commemorate the 600th anniversary of the writer's death. But the park's *pièce de résistance* is a piece of art dating from 1999: *Time Sculpture*, a bronze and stone masterwork featuring a series of large clocks, was designed by Philip Johnson and dedicated to the patrons of Lincoln Center.

Central Park West

Central Park West stretches north from Columbus Circle to 110th Street along the western edge of the park. Home to some of the city's most architecturally distinguished apartment buildings, like the **Dakota** and **Majestic**, as well as the enormous **American Museum of Natural History**, Central Park West bustles with taxis and tour buses. In contrast, the sidestreets between Central Park West and Columbus Avenue in the upper 60s and 70s are quiet, tree-lined and filled with beautifully renovated brownstone houses, many of which are single-family homes.

Most of the monolithic, mansion-inspired apartment complexes in this area date from the early twentieth century and rim the edge of the park, hogging the best views. The southernmost of these is the Hotel des Artistes, at 1 West 67th St at Central Park West. It was built in 1917 especially for artists (hence the name), and

The death of John Lennon

The Dakota Building, at 1 West 72nd St, is most famous as the former home of **John Lennon** – and present home of his widow, **Yoko Ono**, who owns a number of the building's apartments. It was outside the Dakota, on the night of December 8, 1980, that the ex-Beatle was murdered – shot by a man who professed to be one of his greatest admirers.

His murderer, **Mark David Chapman**, had hung around outside the building all day, clutching a copy of his hero's latest album, **Double Fantasy**, and accosting Lennon for his autograph, which he received. This was nothing unusual: fans loitered outside the building and hustled for a glimpse of the singer. But when the couple returned from a late-night recording session, Chapman was still there, and he pumped five .38 bullets into Lennon as he walked through the Dakota's 72nd Street entrance. Lennon was picked up by the doorman and rushed to the hospital in a taxi, but he died on the way from blood loss. A distraught Yoko issued a statement immediately: "John loved and prayed for the human race. Please do the same for him." No one really knows the reasons behind Chapman's actions. Suffice it to say his obsession with Lennon had obviously unhinged him. Chapman was given a sentence of twenty years to life in prison; he has since been denied parole on five separate occasions – Ono told the parole board she wouldn't feel safe with Chapman walking the streets. He's expected to remain behind bars for the foreseeable future.

Fans of Lennon may want to light a stick of incense across the road in **Strawberry Fields** (see p.157), a section of Central Park that has been restored and maintained in his memory through an endowment by Ono. Its trees and shrubs were donated by a number of countries as a gesture toward world peace. The gardens are pretty enough, if unspectacular, though it would take a hard-bitten cynic not to be a little bit moved by the **Imagine** mosaic on the pathway.

was once the Manhattan address for the likes of Noel Coward, Norman Rockwell, Isadora Duncan and Alexander Woollcott. The building now consists of expensive co-op apartments.

Four blocks north, between 71st and 72nd streets, you'll find the fittingly named **Majestic**. This gigantic, pale yellow, Art Deco landmark was thrown up in 1930 and is best known for its twin towers and avant-garde brickwork. The next block north houses one of New York's more illustrious residences: the **Dakota Building**, at 1 West 72nd St, one of the earliest co-ops in the city. The rather hoary story of its name is that when construction finished in 1884, its uptown location was considered as remote as the Dakota territory by Manhattanites. Whatever the case, this grandiose hulk of German Renaissance masonry is undeniably impressive. Its turrets, gables and other odd details were all included for one reason: to persuade wealthy New Yorkers that life in an apartment could be just as luxurious as in a private house. For the large part, the developers succeeded: over the years, few of the residents here haven't had some sort of public renown, from Lauren Bacall and Judy Garland to Leonard Bernstein; of course, it's best known as the home of the late John Lennon (see box above).

North of here is **San Remo**, at 145–146 Central Park West on 74th Street. Another apartment complex, this one dates from 1930 and is one of the most significant components of the skyline here: its ornate twin towers, topped by columned, mock-Roman temples, are visible from most points in Central Park. Architecture aside, the residents' board here is known for its snooty exclusiveness: they rejected Madonna as a buyer of a multi-million-dollar co-op, though her former boyfriend Warren Beatty did live here with Diane Keaton. A block further north is the **Central Park West–76th Historic District**, from 75th to 77th streets on Central Park West, and on 76th Street toward Columbus Avenue, home to a number of small, late nineteenth-century rowhouses, as well as the **Kenilworth Apartments**, at 151 Central Park West on 75th Street, notable for its mansard roof and carved limestone exterior.

The New-York Historical Society

The oft-overlooked **New-York Historical Society**, at 170 Central Park West (Tues–Thurs & Sat 10am–6pm, Fri 10am–8pm, Sun 11am–5.45pm; $12, free Fri 6–8pm; Ⓣ212/873-3400, Ⓦwww.nyhistory.org), houses a permanent collection of books, prints and portraits, as well as a research library; it also hosts unusual travelling exhibitions. Note that the museum is in the midst of renovations and portions will be closed through 2011; call or check the website ahead of time. The holdings are highlighted by illustrations by **James Audubon**, the Harlem artist and naturalist who specialized in lovingly detailed paintings of birds: remarkably, the Historical Society holds all 433 existing original watercolours of Audubon's landmark *Birds of America*. Elsewhere is a broad cross section of **nineteenth-century American painting**, principally portraiture and Hudson River School landscapes, among them Thomas Cole's famed and pompous *Course of Empire* series. On the fourth floor, the Henry Luce Center contains cultural and historical odds-and-ends that make the museum seem more one of American than New York history; besides advertising ephemera, Tiffany lamps and political buttons, look out for the highly decorative ceramic jug, snakes with human heads crawling up its side, made for Thomas Nast, who exposed Boss Tweed's corruption. Don't miss the museum **library** either, which contains manuscripts, maps, the original Louisiana Purchase document and the correspondence between Aaron Burr and Alexander Hamilton that led up to their deadly duel (see p.212).

The American Museum of Natural History

The **American Museum of Natural History**, at Central Park West on 79th Street (daily 10am–5.45pm, Rose Center open until 8.45pm on first Fri of month; $16, kids 2–12 $9, with additional cost for IMAX films, certain special exhibits and

▲ Dinosaur exhibit, American Museum of Natural History

Hayden Planetarium shows; ⓣ212/769-5100, ⓦwww.amnh.org), is one of the best museums of its kind in the world, an enormous complex of buildings full of fossils, gems, taxidermy and other natural specimens. This elegant giant fills four blocks with a strange architectural melange of heavy Neoclassical and rustic Romanesque styles – it was built in several stages, the first of which was overseen by Central Park designer Calvert Vaux. Founded in 1869, it is one of the oldest natural-history museums in the world, with four floors of exhibition halls and 32 million items on display.

The collection

The museum's vast marble front steps on Central Park West are a great place to read or soak up the sun. An appropriately haughty statue of museum co-founder Theodore Roosevelt looks out toward the park from his perch on horseback, flanked by a pair of Native Americans marching gamely alongside. This entrance (which opens onto the second floor) leaves you well positioned for a loop of the more interesting halls on that level: principally the **Hall of Asian Peoples** and **Hall of African Peoples**, both of which are filled with fascinating, often beautiful, art and artefacts, and backed up with informal commentary and indigenous music. The Hall of Asian Peoples begins with relics from Russia and Central Asia, moves on to pieces from Tibet – including a gorgeous recreation of an ornate, gilded Tibetan Buddhist shrine – and then on to China and Japan, with displays of some fantastic textiles, rugs, brass and jade ornaments. The Hall of African Peoples displays ceremonial costumes, musical instruments and masks from all over the continent. Another highlight of this floor is the lower half of the **Hall of African Mammals**, a double-height room whose exhibits continue on to the third-floor balcony: don't miss the life-size family of elephants in the centre of the room (it's fairly difficult to do so). Once you're on the third floor, stop by the mildly creepy **Reptiles and Amphibians Hall**, filled with samples of almost any species in the category. A little less interesting is the **Eastern Woodlands and Plains Indians** exhibit, a rather pedestrian display of artefacts, clothing and the like.

The wildly popular **Dinosaur Exhibit**, the first stop for many, dominates the fourth floor; early vertebrates and mammals can be found here too. The museum houses the largest dinosaur collection in the world, with more than 100 specimens on display. Here, you can touch fossils, watch robotic dinosaurs and walk on a transparent bridge over a 50ft-long Barosaurus spine. Interactive computer programmes supplement the multi-level exhibits.

Downstairs on the first floor is the **Hall of Gems and Minerals**, which includes some strikingly beautiful crystals – not least the Star of India, the largest blue sapphire ever found. The enormous, double-height gallery dedicated to **Ocean Life** includes a 94ft-long (life-size) Blue Whale disconcertingly suspended from the ceiling. The Hall of **North American Mammals** hasn't changed in ages – the dark corridors, marble floors and illuminated diorama cases filled with stuffed specimens have seen over fifty years' worth of children on school trips. The greatest draw on this floor, however, is the **Hall of Biodiversity**. It focuses on both the ecological and evolutionary aspects of biodiversity, with multimedia displays on everything from the changes humans have wrought on the environment (with examples of solutions brought about by local activists and community groups in all parts of the world) to a walkthrough of a simulated rainforest. The **Lefrak Theater**, also located on this floor, presents some interesting nature-oriented IMAX films (there is an additional charge).

The Rose Center for Earth and Space

Across from the Hall of Biodiversity is the **Rose Center for Earth and Space**, including the **Hall of Planet Earth**, a multimedia exploration of how the earth works, with displays on a wide variety of subjects such as the formation of planets, underwater rock formation, plate tectonics and carbon dating. Items on display include a 2.7-billion-year-old specimen of a banded iron formation and volcanic ash from Mount Vesuvius. One of the newer displays is an earthquake monitoring system; a three-drum seismograph and colour screen work together to show real-time seismic activity from around the globe. The centrepiece of the room is the Dynamic Earth Globe, where visitors are able to watch the earth go through its full rotation via satellite, getting as close as possible to the views astronauts see from outer space.

The Hall of Planet Earth links visitors to the rest of the Rose Center, which is made up of the **Hall of the Universe** and the **Hayden Planetarium**. The centre boasts an enormous sphere, 87ft in diameter, which appears to be floating inside a huge cube above the main entrance to the Center. The sphere actually houses the planetarium, which includes two theatres, as well as research facilities and classrooms, and is illuminated rather eerily at night. Inside, the state-of-the-art **Space Theater** uses a Zeiss projector to create sky shows with sources like the Hubble telescope and NASA laboratories.

On the planetarium's second floor, the **Big Bang Theater** offers a multi-sensory recreation of the "birth" of the universe, while the **Cosmic Pathway** is a sloping spiral walkway that takes you through thirteen billion years of cosmic evolution via an interactive computerized timeline. It leads to the Hall of the Universe, which offers exhibits and interactive displays on the formation and evolution of the universe, the galaxy, stars and planets, including a mini-theatre where visitors can journey inside a black hole through computerized effects. There is even a display here entitled "The Search for Life", which examines the planetary systems on which life could exist – in case you hadn't questioned the meaning of existence enough by this point.

North on Broadway

Back on Broadway, at 72nd Street, tiny, triangular **Verdi Square** makes a fine place to take a break from the marvels of Lincoln Center. From the square, featuring a craggy statue in the likeness of the composer, you can fully appreciate the ornate balconies, round towers and cupolas of the **Ansonia Hotel** across the street at 2109 Broadway (at West 73rd St). Never actually a hotel (it was planned as upscale apartments), the *Ansonia* was completed in 1904 and the dramatic Beaux Arts building is still the *grande dame* of the Upper West Side. It's been home to luminaries like Enrico Caruso, Arturo Toscanini, Lily Pons, Florenz Ziegfeld, Theodore Dreiser, Igor Stravinsky and even Babe Ruth.

The enormous limestone **Apthorp Apartments**, at 2211 Broadway between 78th and 79th streets, occupy an entire block from Broadway to West End Avenue. Built in 1908 by William Waldorf Astor, the ornate iron gates of the former carriage entrance lead into a central courtyard with a large fountain visible from Broadway, though you won't be allowed to stroll in. The building's in a fair enough state now, though its fortunes have hiccuped over the years – it was used as the location for the crack factory in the 1991 movie *New Jack City*. The Upper West Side above 79th Street has seen a lot of changes in the last decade as the forces of gentrification have surged northward. One of the older establishments in the area is gourmet hub **Zabar's**, at 2245 Broadway on 80th Street, which has been selling baked goods, cheese, caviar, gourmet coffee and tea – as well as an exhaustive collection of cooking gadgets – since 1934. For more on the store, see p.299.

Nearby, the **Children's Museum of Manhattan, at** 212 West 83rd St near Broadway (Tues–Sun 10am–5pm, first Fri of the month until 8pm; $10, free Fri 5–8pm; ⓣ212/721-1234, ⓦwww.cmom.org), holds five storeys of interactive exhibits that stimulate learning, in a fun, relaxed environment for kids (and babies) of all ages. The storytelling room, filled with books kids can choose from, should keep everyone amused and quiet for at least an hour.

Riverside Park

At the western edge of 72nd Street begins the four-mile stretch of **Riverside Park** (ⓦwww.nycgovparks.org). The entrance is marked by Penelope Jencks' pensive *Eleanor Roosevelt Monument* on the corner of 72nd Street and Riverside Drive, dedicated in 1996 by then-First Lady Hillary Clinton. A less appealing local landmark is the new forest of skyscrapers overlooking the park from what used to be derelict shipping yards south of 72nd Street. This development, known as **Riverside South**, evolved – if that's the right word – from longtime plans to build something colloquially known as **Trump City** (who else but the billionaire developer?); at least the waterfront alongside has been preserved.

Riverside Park was conceived in the mid-nineteenth century as a way of attracting the middle class to the remote Upper West Side and covering the unappealing Hudson River Railway tracks that had been built along the Hudson in 1846. Though not as imposing or as spacious as Central Park, Riverside was designed by the same team: Frederick Law Olmsted and Calvert Vaux. Begun in 1873, the park took 25 years to finish; rock outcrops and informally arranged trees, shrubs and flowers surround its tree-lined main boulevards, and the overall effect is much the same today as it was then. The biggest changes to the park came in the 1960s, when Robert Moses widened it and added some of his usual concrete touches, including the rotunda at the 79th Street Boat Basin. The basin is a delightful place for a break, with paths leading down to it located on either side of 79th Street at Riverside Drive (you'll hit Moses' rotunda first – keep going until you see water). Not on many visitors' itineraries, this is a small harbour and one of the city's most peaceful locations; a few hundred Manhattanites live on the water in houseboats, while others just moor their motorboats and sailboats.

Riverside Drive

The main artery of this neighbourhood is **Riverside Drive**: starting at West 72nd Street, it winds north, flanked by palatial townhouses and multistorey apartment buildings, mostly thrown up in the early part of the twentieth century. In the 70s, especially, there is a concentration of lovely turn-of-the-twentieth-century townhouses, many with copper-trimmed mansard roofs and private terraces or roof gardens. Between 80th and 81st streets you will find a row of historic **landmark townhouses**: classic brownstones, they have bowed exteriors, bay windows and gabled roofs. You'll also find a number of other architectural surprises in this area, as many of the residences in the 80s between Riverside and West End have stained-glass windows as well as stone gargoyle faces leering from their facades.

Riverside Drive is also dotted with notable monuments: at West 89th Street, look for the **Soldiers and Sailors Monument** (1902), a marble memorial to the Civil War dead. Then there's the **Joan of Arc Monument** at West 93rd Street, which sits on top of a 1.6-acre cobblestone-and-grass park named Joan of Arc Island and is located in the middle of the Drive. Finally, you'll hit the **Firemen's Memorial** at West 100th Street, a stately frieze designed in 1913 with the statues of *Courage* and *Duty* on its ends.

There are more historic apartment buildings on Riverside Drive as you head north between 105th and 106th streets. What is now the Riverside Study Center (used by the shadowy Catholic sect Opus Dei) at 330 Riverside is a glorious five-story Beaux Arts house built in 1900 – note the copper mansard roof, stone balconies and delicate iron scrollwork. The current headquarters of the **New York Buddhist Church** is at 331 Riverside Drive, though it was formerly the home of Marion "Rosebud" Davies, a 1930s actress most famous for her role as William Randolph Hearst's mistress.

The odd little building next door to no. 331 is also part of the church; it showcases a larger-than-life bronze statue of Shinran Shonin (1173–1262), the Japanese founder of the Jodo-Shinsu sect of Buddhism. The statue originally stood in Hiroshima and somehow survived the atomic explosion of August 1945. In 1955 it was brought to New York as a symbol of "lasting hope for world peace" and has been in this spot ever since. When it arrived, local lore had it that the statue was still radioactive, so in the 1950s and 1960s children were told to hold their breath as they went by. The Beaux Arts **River Mansion**, as 337 Riverside Drive is called, was home to **Duke Ellington** – and the stretch of West 106th Street between here and Central Park has been tagged Duke Ellington Boulevard in his honour.

Nearby, in a manicured brownstone house at 319 West 107th St, is the overlooked but appealing **Roerich Museum** (Tues–Sun 2–5pm; suggested donation $5; Ⓣ212/864-7752, Ⓦwww.roerich.org). It contains a small, weird and virtually unknown collection of original paintings by Nicholas Roerich, a Russian artist who lived in India and was influenced by religious mysticism. Also on West 107th Street, at the terminus of West End Avenue – itself running more or less parallel to Riverside Drive – is the small, triangular **Strauss Park**. The statue by Augustus Lukeman of a reclining woman gazing over a water basin was dedicated by Macy's founder Nathan Strauss to his brother and business partner, Isidor, and Isidor's wife, Ida, both of whom went down with the *Titanic* in 1912.

Morningside Heights

North of the Upper West Side, **Morningside Heights** stretches from 110th Street to 123rd Street, west to the Hudson River and east to Morningside Park, a small and rather unspectacular green space. The neighbourhood has a somewhat funky, college-town aura, a diverse mix of academics, professionals and working-class families who have banded together in the name of community preservation. Excepting the massive **Cathedral of St John the Divine** and **Columbia University**, there are few sights here per se, but it's worth ambling up here to get a sense of a close-knit neighbourhood, a feeling that the Upper West Side lost some time ago.

The Cathedral Church of St John the Divine

The Cathedral Church of St John the Divine, at 1047 Amsterdam Ave on 112th Street (Mon–Sat 7am–6pm, Sun 7am–7pm except July & Aug 7am–6pm; free; Ⓣ212/316-7490, Ⓦwww.stjohndivine.org), rises out of its surroundings with a solid majesty – hardly surprising, since it is the largest Gothic-style cathedral in the world, a title it holds even though it remains incomplete.

This Episcopal church was conceived, in 1892, as a Romanesque monolith. When the architect in charge was replaced in 1911, the building's style shifted: it has ended up French neo-Gothic. Work progressed well until the outbreak of war in 1939, and it wasn't until the late 1970s it resumed. The church's problems aren't limited to timely construction, though: it declared bankruptcy in 1994, fraught with funding difficulties. Church members launched a massive international fundraising drive, which helped clear them from bankruptcy, but in 2001 church finances again became precarious following a fire that did significant damage to the cathedral. Even now it's unclear when the repairs will be completed. Don't let the building's raw state put you off visiting – the church is one of New York's most impressive sights.

Though the structure appears finished at first glance, take a look up into one of its huge, incomplete towers, and you'll see how much there is left to do. In reality, only two-thirds of the church is finished, and given the problems with funding, it's impossible to estimate when it'll be done. The one activity that continues is small-scale carving, much of it undertaken by locals who are trained by English stonemasons in the church's own sculpture/stone workshops. Regardless of when, or if, it is finished, its floor space – 600ft long by 320ft wide at the transepts – is big enough to swallow both the cathedrals of Notre Dame and Chartres whole.

The **Portal of Paradise** at the cathedral's main entrance was completed in 1997, and is dazzlingly carved from limestone and painted with metallic oxide. Keep an eye out for the 32 biblical figures depicted (both male and female) and such startling images as a mushroom cloud rising apocalyptically over Manhattan. The portal is evidence of just how slow progress here really is: the carving took ten years. Only after entering the church does its staggering size become clear; the space is awe-inspiring, and definitely adds to the building's spiritual power. The interior shows the melding of the two architectural styles, particularly in the choir, where a heavy arcade of Romanesque columns rises to a high, Gothic vaulting; it is hoped the temporary dome will someday be replaced by a tall, delicate Gothic spire.

Construction aside, St John's is very much a **community church**. It houses a soup kitchen and shelter for the homeless; sponsors AIDS awareness and health outreach initiatives; and has a gymnasium. The open-minded, progressive nature of the church is readily visible throughout the cathedral building: note the intricately carved wood **Altar for Peace**, the **Poets Corner** (with the names of American poets carved into its stone-block floor), and an altar honouring AIDS victims. The amazing stained-glass windows include scenes from both the Bible and American history. All kinds of art, both religious and secular, grace the interior, from teak Siamese prayer chests to seventeenth-century tapestries, to a rare religious work by the late graffiti artist Keith Haring – his final finished piece.

Outdoors, the cathedral's south side features the **Bestiary Gates**, their grilles adorned with animal imagery (celebrating the annual blessing of the animals ceremony held here on the Feast of St Francis), and a **Children's Sculpture Garden**, showcasing small bronze animal sculptures created by local schoolchildren. Afterwards, take a stroll through the cathedral yard and workshop where, if work has begun again, you can watch Harlem's apprentice masons tapping away at the stone blocks of the future cathedral.

Public **tours** are given Tuesday to Saturday at 11am, and Sunday at 1pm ($5) – meet at the Info Center, the blue booth right inside the main door. Access to the top of the cathedral was restricted for years due to the 2001 fire, but "vertical tours" have resumed. To clamber up spiral stone staircases to the roof, and be rewarded with a super view, call ⓣ212/932-7347 to make a reservation (Sat noon & 2pm; $15). Consider, too, visiting on a Monday around 1pm, for the free organ recital.

Columbia University and around

The Columbia University campus fills seven blocks between Broadway and Morningside Drive from 114th to 121st streets, with its main entrance at Broadway and 116th Street. It is one of the most prestigious academic institutions in the country and a member of the Ivy League. Established in 1754, Columbia has a long and venerable history – it is the country's fifth-oldest institution of higher learning, it awarded the first MD degree in America, and the university sponsored groundbreaking atomic research in the 1940s. The Morningside Heights campus, modelled after the Athenian *agora* (or town square), was laid out by McKim, Mead, and White after the university moved here from midtown in 1897.

Amid the campus's Italian Renaissance-style structures, the domed and colonnaded **Low Memorial Library**, at 116th Street on Broadway, is a real stunner. Built in 1902, the Neoclassical structure is on the New York City Register of Historic Places and is a commanding sight. Tours of the campus leave from the Visitor Center here (Mon–Fri 1pm; free; Ⓣ212/854-4900, Ⓦwww.columbia.edu). Across Broadway sits women's-only **Barnard College**, one of the Seven Sisters' institutions and a part of Columbia University.

Running alongside the campus, Broadway is characterized by a lively bustle, with numerous inexpensive restaurants, bars and cafés, and a few bookstores. The space at 2911 Broadway at 113th Street, the former West End tavern, was the hangout of Jack Kerouac, Allen Ginsberg and the Beats in the 1950s; it still serves a student crowd, although it's now a Cuban eatery.

Riverside Church and Grant's Tomb

Several blocks north and west of the university, **Riverside Church**, at 490 Riverside Drive on 120th Street (daily 7am–10pm, Sun service 10.45am; free; Ⓣ212/870-6700, Ⓦwww.theriversidechurchny.org), has a graceful French Gothic Revival tower, loosely modelled on the cathedral at Chartres. Like St John the Divine, it has become a community centre for the surrounding parish and puts on the odd musical and theatrical event. Twenty floors up, the **carillon** (the largest in the world, with 74 bells) has great views of Manhattan's skyline, New Jersey and beyond; however, tours up the tower have been suspended for a number of years – call on the off-chance they've started again. Make sure to root around inside the body of the church, too: its open interior stands in stark contrast to the mystery of St John the Divine.

Up the block from the church is **Grant's Tomb**, at Riverside Drive and 122nd Street (daily 9am–5pm; free; Ⓣ212/666-1640, Ⓦwww.nps.gov/gegr). This Greek-style memorial is the nation's largest mausoleum, home to the bodies of conquering Civil War hero (and blundering eighteenth US president) Ulysses S. Grant and his wife, in two black marble Napoleonic sarcophagi.

Harlem and north Manhattan

The most famous African-American community in America, **Harlem** languished as a low-rent, high-crime neighbourhood for much of the mid-twentieth century, justly earning a reputation as a place of racial tension and urban decay. Over the past couple of decades, though, things have begun to look up, and it's much safer than it once was. Indeed, despite being knocked back somewhat by the 2009 recession, the area is undergoing a second renaissance, making it one of New York's most enticing neighbourhoods. Many local observers worry, however, that the influx of investment may come at too high a price in the long run, diluting or wiping out the district's unique Afro-American spirit and history.

Further uptown is **Hamilton Heights**, a largely residential spot pepped up by an old Federal-style historic mansion and the campus of the City College of New York. Continuing north from there, you'll hit the Dominican stronghold of **Washington Heights**, while the northernmost tip of the island, known as **Inwood**, is home to **The Cloisters**, a museum-as-mock-medieval-monastery that holds the Met's superlative collection of medieval art. All the areas detailed below are generally safe for visitors, especially during the day when there are usually lots of people around – just take the usual precautions at night, and stick to the main thoroughfares.

Harlem

Practically speaking, **Harlem**'s sights are too spread apart to amble between: they stretch out over seventy blocks. You'll do best to make several trips if you want to see them all. It can also be helpful to take a **guided tour** (see p.35) to get acquainted with the area. Harlem is easily accessed by bus or subway (A, B, C, #1, #2 and #3), but it can be harder to find **taxis** up here; at night, your best bet is to grab one of the many gypsy cabs patrolling the main avenues (see p.27), and negotiate the fare in advance (around $20–25 to midtown). In summer, be sure to check out **Harlem Week** (Ⓦharlemweek.com), a series of concerts and special events held in July and August.

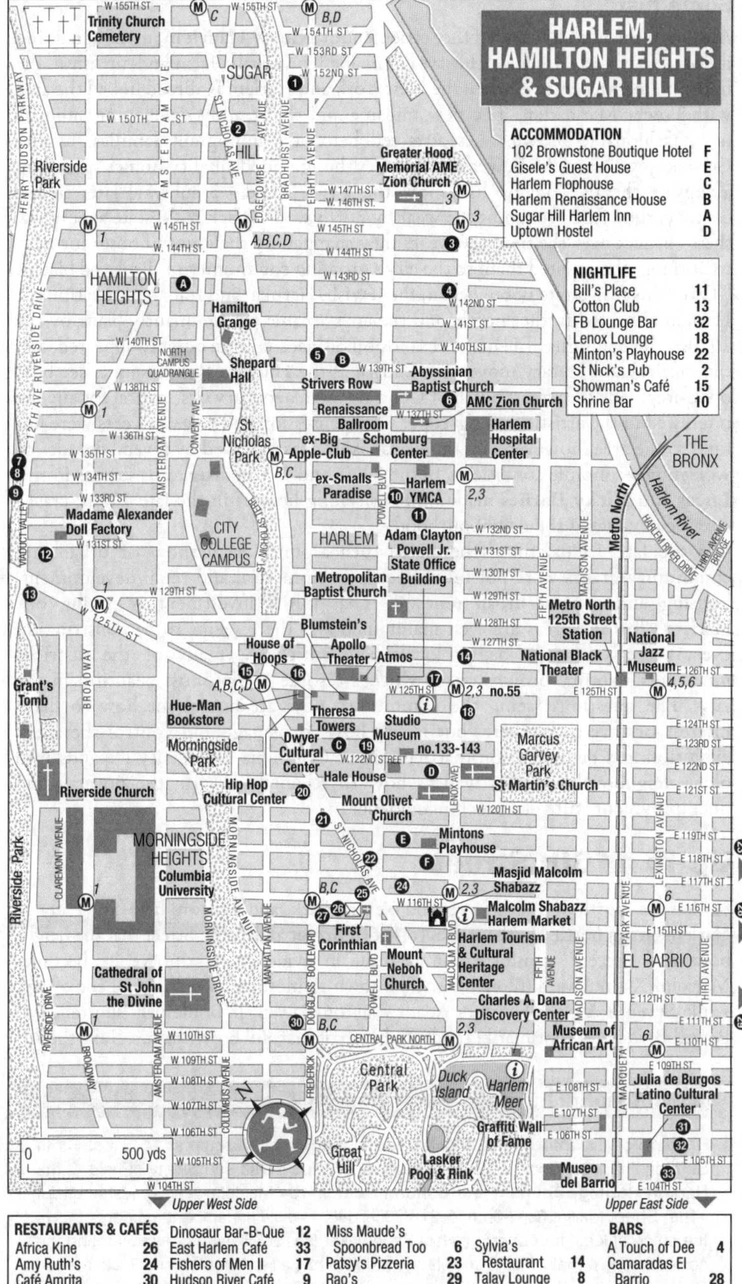

RESTAURANTS & CAFÉS

Africa Kine	26
Amy Ruth's	24
Café Amrita	30
Charles' Country Pan Fried	1
Covo Trattoria	7
Dinosaur Bar-B-Que	12
East Harlem Café	33
Fishers of Men II	17
Hudson River Café	9
La Fonda Boricua	31
Londel's Supper Club	5
Make My Cake	25
Miss Maude's Spoonbread Too	6
Patsy's Pizzeria	23
Rao's	29
Roti Plus	16
Salimata Restaurant	27
Strictly Roots	19
Sylvia's Restaurant	14
Talay Lounge	8

BARS

A Touch of Dee	4
Camaradas El Barrio	28
Moca Lounge	21
Nectar	20
Real's Lounge	3

Some history

Although the Dutch founded the settlement of **Nieuw Haarlem** in 1658, naming it for a town in Holland, the area remained primarily farmland up until the mid-nineteenth century, when the New York and Harlem Railroad linked the area with Lower Manhattan. The new rail line and the steadily developing suburb's new, fashionable brownstones attracted better-off immigrant families, mainly German Jews from the Lower East Side. Although good-quality homes sprang up alongside the IRT–Lenox line (now the #1, #2 and #3 subway) later in the century, they failed to tempt the wealthy northwards. Black real-estate agents saw their chance: over the next few years they snapped up the empty houses for next to nothing, then rented them to the city's growing community of displaced blacks.

Once this real-estate boom began, the Jewish, German and Italian populations of Harlem relocated farther north, and the area became predominantly black by the 1920s. The first signs of Harlem's explosion of black culture quickly appeared, and the musical and literary movement known as the **Harlem Renaissance** (see box, opposite) made the streets north of Central Park a necessary destination for anyone interested in the artistic cutting-edge. The Depression and postwar years were not kind to the area, however, and the Renaissance was followed by several decades of worsening economic conditions. In the 1960s and 1970s, drug lords such as **Frank Lucas** and **Nicky Barnes** made millions selling heroin; in the late 1980s, crack-cocaine devastated the neighbourhood.

In the late 1990s, things began to turn around. A plethora of urban and community grants were put into effect for commercial and retail development, housing and general urban renewal. That initial investment is paying off: Harlem's historic areas are well maintained and there seems to be construction everywhere you turn. Savvy locals have purchased many of the district's nineteenth-century brownstones, which are some of the most beautiful in the city. The questions facing the community now are not about how to drive interest or investment here, but rather how to manage and control the area's evolution and gentrification (particularly as Columbia University expands into older neighbourhoods), as well as how to reconcile it with the poverty and unemployment still very much in evidence.

Up to 116th Street

Harlem lies north of 110th Street and Central Park, and it's from here along any of Harlem's main north–south arteries to **116th Street** and 125th Street that the neighbourhood's recent transformation is most in evidence. Sixth Avenue becomes Malcolm X Boulevard (though it's still known to most by its old name Lenox Ave), while Seventh Avenue becomes Adam Clayton Powell, Jr Boulevard (shortened to Powell Blvd here), a primarily residential strip of graceful brownstones. Take the #B

Harlem information

Harlem's official **information kiosk** is inside the Studio Museum at 144 West 125th St (Mon–Fri noon–6pm, Sat & Sun 10am–6pm). You'll also find plenty of help at the **Harlem Heritage Tourism and Cultural Center**, 104 Malcolm X Blvd, just south of 116th Street (daily 10am–6pm; ⓣ212/280-7888, ⓦwww.harlemheritage.com); this is the office of local tour operator Neal Shoemaker (see p.35), who grew up around the corner and is a font of local knowledge (he also has a Harlem blog and Twitter feed). Of the websites that serve the neighbourhood, ⓦ**www.harlemonestop.com** has excellent listings and local information.

The Harlem Renaissance

The **Harlem Renaissance**, during which the talents of such icons as Billie Holiday, Paul Robeson and James Weldon Johnson took root and flowered, served as inspiration for generations of African-American musicians, writers and performers. In the 1920s, Manhattan's white residents began to notice Harlem's cultural offerings: after downtown went to bed, the sophisticated set drove north, where **jazz musicians** such as Duke Ellington, Count Basie and Cab Calloway played in packed nightspots like the Cotton Club, Savoy Ballroom, Apollo Theater and Smalls Paradise, and the liquor flowed freely, despite Prohibition. But the Harlem Renaissance wasn't just about music. It was also characterized by the rich body of **literature** produced by Johnson, Langston Hughes, Jean Toomer and Zora Neale Hurston, among many others – Hughes declared the movement to be over in 1931 after the death of noted Black socialite and patron **A'Lelia Walker**.

Yet even before the Great Depression, it was hard to scrape out a living here, and the economic downturn of the 1930s drove out the middle class. It may be because evening revellers never stayed longer than the last drink that neither they, nor many histories of the period, recall the rampant **poverty** that went hand-in-hand with Harlem's raunchy, anything-goes nightlife.

One of the lasting legacies of this period, however, has been the neighbourhood's sense of **racial consciousness**. First evidenced during the 1920s and 1930s in the writings and speeches of men like Marcus Garvey, W.E.B. DuBois and Charles S. Johnson, the same spirit is still alive today in such larger-than-life firebrands as reverends Al Sharpton (whose National Action Network is based in Harlem) and Calvin Butts (influential minister of Abyssinian Baptist Church).

or #C line to Cathedral Parkway and wander up **Frederick Douglass Boulevard** (Eighth Ave) between 110th and 125th streets to see the most obvious signs of change, with new cafés, stores and bars replacing vacant lots; the new condo buildings around here have been dubbed Harlem's "Gold Coast".

At 116th Street, turn right – the stretch between Frederick Douglass and Lenox avenues has become a hub for West African immigrants and is unofficially known as **Little Senegal** or Little West Africa. It's estimated that at least 40,000 Senegalese have settled in New York in the last few years, as well as smaller groups from Nigeria, Ivory Coast, Guinea and Mali. They've opened up shops, beauty parlours and restaurants here to create a thriving neighbourhood.

There are also some African-influenced buildings nearby, including the fanciful blue-and-white Moorish-style **First Corinthian Baptist Church** (usually locked; ⓣ212/864-5976), 1912 Powell Blvd at 116th Street. Originally built as the Regent Theater in 1912, this was one of America's earliest movie palaces before being transformed into a church in 1929.

Further east, it's the spirit of the late Malcolm X (see box, p.215) that is perhaps most palpable. Look for the green onion dome of the **Masjid Malcolm Shabazz**, 102 West 116th St at Lenox Avenue, once the Nation of Islam's Temple No.7 and Malcolm's base until his split with the Nation in 1964. After Malcolm's assassination in 1965, the mosque was firebombed then rebuilt with the dome you see today. The Nation of Islam later moved to 106 West 127th St, and the Shabazz mosque now serves an Orthodox Sunni community. At the time of writing, it was undergoing substantial restoration and should eventually feature a museum and cultural centre.

Just beyond Lenox at 52 West 116th St you'll see the bazaar-like **Malcolm Shabazz Harlem Market** (daily 10am–8pm; ⓣ212/987-8131), established in 1994 with help from the mosque, its entrance marked by colourful fake minarets.

▲ Harlem brownstones

The market's offerings include T-shirts, jewellery, clothing and more, all with a distinctly Afro-centric flavour – it's worth stopping by, mostly since what's on sale here differs so much from the usual flea-market staples (many stalls don't open till after lunch).

Mount Morris Park Historic District

The area around Lenox Avenue between West 118th and 124th streets is known as the **Mount Morris Park Historic District**. Initially inhabited by white commuters, the area then became home to the city's second-largest neighbourhood of Eastern European Jewish immigrants (after the Lower East Side), and finally shifted to a primarily black neighbourhood in the 1920s. This series of complex demographic shifts has created a profusion of diverse religious structures, and has helped place the neighbourhood on the National Register of Historic Places. Today, it's an eminently desirable place to live – Maya Angelou lives on 120th Street – and the district has an active community-improvement association that runs events and talks (ⓣ212/369-4241, ⓦwww.mmpcia.org).

One of the district's most interesting buildings is **Mount Olivet Baptist Church**, 201 Lenox Ave at 120th Street, a Greco-Roman–style temple that was built as a synagogue in 1907 (the Baptists bought it in 1925). Compare its design with the sombre, bulky Romanesque Revival **St Martin's Episcopal Church**, at the southeast corner of Lenox Avenue and 122nd Street; completed in 1889, it's noted for the 42-bell carillon installed in the tower (rung on Sundays). Both buildings open only for services.

Elsewhere, the Mount Morris district includes some lovely rowhouses that were constructed during the speculation boom of the 1890s: most outstanding of all are **133–143 West 122nd St**, a half block west of Lenox Avenue. Arguably the finest row of Queen Anne-style homes in the city, they were designed by leading architect Francis H. Kimball in 1885–87.

Heading east along 122nd Street from Lenox Avenue brings you to **Marcus Garvey Park**, formerly Mount Morris Park; it takes its new name from the black leader of the 1920s. The park is situated between East 120th and 124th streets, between Mount Morris Park West and Madison Avenue, its most notable feature being an octagonal **fire tower** built in 1857 on a peak in the centre, a unique example of the early-warning devices once found throughout the city.

125th Street and around

The stretch of **125th Street** between Broadway and Fifth Avenue is Harlem's main commercial drag. It's here that recent investment in the area is most obvious – note the presence of numerous chains, mobile-phone stores and fashion retailers like H&M. This was Malcolm X's beat in the 1950s and 1960s – he strolled and preached on 125th Street, and photos of him and his followers here have passed into legend.

Ex-President **Bill Clinton** – still much admired in Harlem – established his offices at 55 West 125th St just east of Lenox Avenue in 2001, a move that in large part accelerated the current renaissance of the area.

National Jazz Museum

Harlem – along with New Orleans – is one of the cradles of **jazz**. Duke Ellington, Thelonious Monk, Charlie Parker, Count Basie, John Coltrane and Billie Holiday all got their start here, yet there is surprisingly little to show for this musical heritage (see p.361 for current **jazz clubs** listings). The **National Jazz Museum** (Mon–Fri 10am–4pm; free; Ⓦwww.jazzmuseuminharlem.org) at 104 East 126th St, suite 2C, is a rare exception, though for now its more of an organizational body than a conventional museum; its main function is to arrange jazz-related programmes, classes and live events (check the website). Aficionados should still check out the visitors' centre, which is chock-full of books, CDs, DVDs and a first-class exhibit of photos of jazz legends and venues on the walls – the enthusiastic volunteers are a mine of information. The plan is to open a full-scale museum opposite the Apollo on 125th Street, but this is some years away. They also have a copy of the now legendary **"Great Day in Harlem"** photo, taken by Art Kane in 1958 and a one-time ensemble of all the era's top jazz musicians (Count Basie, Sonny Rollins and 55 others). Fans can visit the stoop where the shoot took place at 17 East 126th St.

Studio Museum in Harlem

The absorbing **Studio Museum in Harlem**, 144 West 125th St at Lenox Avenue (Wed–Fri & Sun noon–6pm, Sat 10am–6pm; $7, free Sun; Ⓣ212/864-4500, Ⓦwww.studiomuseum.org), has over 60,000 square feet of exhibition space dedicated to contemporary African-American painting, photography and sculpture. The permanent collection is displayed on a rotating basis and includes works by Harlem Renaissance-era photographer James Van Der Zee, as well as paintings and sculptures by postwar artists.

Adam Clayton Powell, Jr State Office Building and Theresa Towers

Looming over the middle of 125th Street, the Brutalist **Adam Clayton Powell, Jr State Office Building** was commissioned in 1972 and built on the corner of Powell Boulevard (it's still Harlem's tallest building). The building was named in honour of Harlem's first black congressman (see box, p.206), and his 12ft-high bronze **statue** was unveiled here in 2005. The surrounding plaza, dubbed African Square, is set for a major remodelling over the next few years.

Reverend Adam Clayton Powell, Jr

In the 1930s, the **Reverend Adam Clayton Powell, Jr** (1908–1972) was instrumental in forcing Harlem's stores, most of which were white-owned and retained a white workforce, to begin employing the blacks whose patronage ensured the stores' survival. Later, he became the first African-American on the city council, then New York's first black congressional representative, during which time he sponsored the country's first minimum-wage law. His distinguished career came to an embittered end in 1967, when amid strong rumours of the misuse of public funds, he was excluded from Congress by majority vote. This failed to diminish his standing in Harlem, where voters re-elected him: he sat until the year before his death, and there's a fitting memorial on the boulevard that today bears his name.

Across the way, the tall, narrow **Theresa Towers** office building, 2090 Powell Blvd at 125th Street, was until the 1960s the *Theresa Hotel*. Designed by George and Edward Blum in 1913, it still stands out from the rest of the street, thanks to its gleaming white terracotta patterns topped with sunbursts. Not desegregated until 1940, the hotel became known as the "Waldorf of Harlem". Fidel Castro was a guest here in 1960 while on a visit to the United Nations, when he shunned midtown luxury in a popular political gesture.

Apollo Theater and around

Walk a little further west along 125th Street from the Powell Building and you reach the legendary **Apollo Theater**, 253 West 125th St at Frederick Douglass Boulevard (Ⓣ212/531-5300, Ⓦwww.apollotheater.com). Although it's not much to look at from the outside, from the 1930s to the 1970s this venue was the centre of black entertainment in New York. Almost all the great figures of jazz and blues played here, along with singers, comedians and dancers; past winners of its famous **Amateur Night** (still running on Wed at 7.30pm; tickets from $17) have included Ella Fitzgerald, Billie Holiday, Luther Vandross, The Jackson Five, Sarah Vaughan and James Brown.

Yet the Apollo is not just a music venue; it's become the spiritual heart of black America, a place where locals and outsiders instinctively come together at important moments in history: when **James Brown**'s casket lay in state in the theatre in 2006, the lines to view it stretched for blocks, and when **Michael Jackson** died in 2009, fans gathered to celebrate his music outside – an official exhibit was arranged inside the theatre a few days later. It is possible to pre-arrange a one-hour **guided tour** of the Apollo (Mon, Tues, Thurs & Fri 11am, 1pm & 3pm; Wed 11am; Sat & Sun 11am & 1pm; $16 Mon–Fri, $18 Sat & Sun), but you'll need a group of twenty or more. Otherwise, call tour director Billy Mitchell at Ⓣ212/531-5337 and he'll try to add you to the next scheduled group.

On the other side of the street, look out for the old **Blumstein's** department store at 230 West 125th St, the Art Nouveau landmark completed in 1923 and scene of Adam Clayton Powell, Jr's biggest victory against the whites-only hiring policy in 1934 (see box above). Blumstein's itself is long gone, but the stores around here are well worth dipping into: **Atmos** (Ⓦwww.atmosnyc.com) at 203 West 125th St has a cult following for its ultra-hip sneakers, while **House of Hoops** at 268 West 125th St is dedicated to all things basketball. The **Hue-Man Bookstore & Café** (Mon–Sat 10am–8pm, Sun 11am–7pm; Ⓣ212/665-7400, Ⓦwww.huemanbookstore.com) at 2319 Frederick Douglass Blvd, just south of 125th Street, is the largest independent African-American bookstore in the country.

Hip-Hop Cultural Center and Dwyer Cultural Center

Hip-hop began in the South Bronx (see p.255), but Harlem has played a key role in its development; Kurtis Blow (who is now a church minister) and Doug E. Fresh still call the neighbourhood home. The **Hip-Hop Cultural Center**, on the second floor of the Magic Johnson Theatre (a cinema multiplex), at 2309 Frederick Douglass Blvd just south of 125th Street, makes a decent attempt to capture this legacy with a large warehouse-like space filled with panels, photos and a rare collection of hip-hop party flyers from the late 1970s on. For now, the centre primarily caters to school groups and you have to call ahead to schedule a visit – the aim is to eventually establish a public programme of hands-on displays (DJ booths, graffiti, dance), but call in advance to confirm.

The nearby **Dwyer Cultural Center** (Mon–Fri 10am–5pm, Sat 1–5pm; free; Ⓦwww.dwyercc.org) at 258 St Nicholas Ave (entrance on 123rd St between St Nicholas Ave and Frederick Douglass Blvd) is worth a look for the temporary art exhibitions and roster of events highlighting the culture, traditions and history of Harlem.

135th Street and around

The blocks north of 125th Street contain little of interest until you reach **135th Street**, the historic heart of Harlem; though the commercial pulse of the neighbourhood has drifted south over the years, back in the 1920s and 1930s this was where most of the action took place. The junction of Powell Boulevard and 135th Street was particularly important: legendary **jazz** clubs *Small's Paradise* and *Big Apple* faced each other on 135th Street, on the west side of Powell (see p.209). The streets nearby were also the haunt of ragtime composer **Scott Joplin**, who moved to Harlem around 1916, while Billie Holiday got her start on 133rd Street, known as "**Jungle Alley**" in the 1930s, when it was lined with speakeasies.

Equally storied is **136th Street**, a block of narrow faux brownstones (with plaster facades) between Powell and Douglass completed in 1896; no. 108–110 was the home of millionaire **A'Lelia Walker** (see p.203), where Harlem artists, writers and musicians gathered for all-night parties.

Continuing north on Powell, you'll see the forlorn looking **Renaissance Ballroom** (see box, p.209) on the right between 137th and 138th streets. Turn right on 138th for the Abyssinian Church – signs around here declaring "The Abyssinian Neighbourhood" usually mean the church owns property on that block.

Abyssinian Baptist Church

At 132 West 138th St, at Powell Boulevard, stands the **Abyssinian Baptist Church** (tourists are welcome at the Sun 11am service only; 1hr 30min; free; Ⓣ212/862-7474, Ⓦwww.abyssinian.org), first incorporated in 1808 in what is now Tribeca (making it the second oldest black church in the US). Its founders included a group of African-Americans living in New York, as well as some Ethiopian merchants, who were tired of segregated seating at Baptist churches (the church's name comes from the traditional name for Ethiopia). The Abyssinian started becoming the religious and political powerhouse that it is today in 1908, when the **Reverend Adam Clayton Powell, Sr** (1865–1953) was appointed pastor, moving the church to Harlem in 1920. Construction on the current Gothic and Tudor building was completed in 1923, and **Reverend Adam Clayton Powell, Jr** (see box opposite) took over in 1937. He remained pastor until 1971, and for a while this was the largest Protestant congregation in the US. It's worth a trip here just to see and hear the gut-busting **choir** – see box below for details – but remember that this is a religious service and not a show.

Sunday gospel and hip-hop church

Harlem's incredible **gospel music** has long enticed visitors and for good reason: both it and the entire revival-style Baptist experience can be amazing and invigorating. Gospel tours are big business; most are pricey, but they usually offer transportation uptown and brunch after the service. If you don't feel like shelling out the cash, or if you're looking for a more authentic experience, you can also easily go it alone. The choir at the **Abyssinian Baptist Church** (Sun 11am) is arguably the best in the city, but long lines of tourists (which can stretch around the block) make the experience, well, touristy (you'll need to get here at least 30min early). Another fairly popular option is the **Metropolitan Baptist Church**, 151 West 128th St at Powell Blvd (Sun 11am; ⓣ212/663-8990). **Mount Neboh Baptist Church**, 1883 Powell Boulevard at West 114th Street (Sun 8am & 11am; ⓣ212/866-7880), is much less of a circus; worship here is taken seriously and services are not designed as tourist attractions, but the congregation is very welcoming to non-members (you can catch the choir rehearsing at 6.30pm on Tues). Wherever you go, dress accordingly: jackets for men and skirts or dresses for women.

For a quite different experience, the **Hip-Hop Church** currently meets at the Greater Hood Memorial AME Zion Church, 160 West 146th St (Thurs 6.30pm; ⓣ212/281-3130); once again, this is a serious place of worship, but with rappers and DJs supplying the music. Hip-hop pioneer **Kurtis Blow** is one of the founders.

Strivers' Row

Just west of Powell Boulevard and the Abyssinian Church, along 138th and 139th streets, stands the three blocks known as **Strivers' Row**, some of the finest rowhouses in Manhattan. A dignified Renaissance-derived strip that's an amalgam of simplicity and elegance, it was conceived during the 1890s housing boom by McKim, Mead, and White among others. Note the unusual rear service alleys of the houses, reached via iron-gated cross streets (replete with the original "Walk your Horse" signs). At the turn of the nineteenth century, this came to be the desirable place for ambitious professionals within Harlem's burgeoning black community (starting with rail porters) to reside – hence its nickname.

Schomburg Center for Research in Black Culture

If you're interested in learning more about African-American history and culture, it's worth taking a walk across to Lenox Avenue and the **Schomburg Center for Research in Black Culture**, 515 Lenox Ave at 135th Street (exhibitions Mon–Sat 10am–6pm; general research and reference division Mon–Wed noon–8pm, Thurs & Fri noon–6pm, Sat 10am–5pm; moving image and recorded sound division Mon–Fri 10am–6pm, Sat 10am–5pm; free; ⓣ212/491-2200, ⓦwww.nypl.org/research/sc), a member of the New York Public Library system.

Primarily a **research library**, the main reason for a casual visit is to explore the superb temporary **exhibitions** here, held in three small galleries and covering a range of related African-American themes, such as the struggle to end segregation in US schools and President Obama. With more time you can peruse the **general research library**, containing a wonderful array of African, Caribbean and African-American literature, as well current periodicals, and the **movie archive**, a repository of black film, music and spoken-arts recordings. The centre is also the site of the ashes of renowned poet **Langston Hughes**, best known for penning *The Negro Speaks of Rivers*. That poem inspired Houston Conwill's terrazzo and brass "cosmogram" in the atrium beyond the main entrance; it's a mosaic built over

New York architecture

New York is a true architectural display-case – all of the significant and influential movements of the last two centuries are represented in the city's magnificent structural landmarks. For an up-close look, take a stroll around the concrete jungle – it will leave you with a crick in the neck, but also with a palpable sense of New York's remarkably dynamic and enduring urban landscape.

Haughwout Building ▲

Chrysler Building ▼

Federal to Beaux Arts

Around three hundred Federal–style rowhouses, built between 1790 and 1835, survive in Lower Manhattan, but it was the advent of cast-iron constructions, invented by James Bogardus in the 1840s, that really thrust New York into the forefront of architectural sophistication (see box, p.76). Notable examples include the 1859 **Haughwout Building** in Soho.

By the late nineteenth-century, the French Beaux Arts movement was influencing American architects such as Richard Morris Hunt (who worked on the Met) and the firm of McKim, Mead, and White (1880s–1920s) responsible for the **Metropolitan Club** (p.174), **Brooklyn Museum** (p.232) and **Morgan Library** (p.136), among many others. Beaux Arts also influenced the city's first wave of fanciful skyscrapers: the **Flatiron Building** on Madison Square (1902) is a fine example of Beaux-Arts styling, while the opulent **Woolworth Building** (1913), with its decorative spires and gargoyles, was designed by Cass Gilbert in Gothic Revival style. Warren and Wetmore's **Grand Central Terminal** (1919) is probably the crowning example of the Beaux Arts era.

Art Deco to Modernism

The boom years of the 1920s fuelled a golden age of architecture in New York, though the greatest Art Deco masterpieces – the **Chrysler Building** (1930) and the **Empire State Building** (1931) – went up just after the 1929 Wall Street Crash. Looming over the **Rockefeller Center**, which was worked on in the 1930s, the **GE Tower** marks the zenith of Art Deco style in New York.

The 1950s and 1960s saw the arrival of the Modernist (or "International") style based on European architectural movements like Bauhaus and Le Corbusier, whose mantra of form following function influenced the glass-curtain-wall buildings of Ludwig Mies van der Rohe: the **United Nations Complex** (1950) and the **Seagram Building** (1958), as well as Gordon Bunshaft's **Lever House** (1952), all in Midtown East. This style culminated, most famously, in the twin towers of the **World Trade Center**, destroyed in the 9/11 terrorist attacks.

New York architecture by neighbourhood

▸▸ **West Village** Still home to the city's best and oldest domestic architecture, with quiet mews and handsome Federal rowhouses from the 1830s.

▸▸ **Soho** The largest collection of cast-iron buildings in the world, built between the 1850s and 1880s with incredibly ornate, Neoclassical facades.

▸▸ **Park Slope** This tranquil, wealthy Brooklyn district is crammed with fabulous neo-Romanesque and neo-Gothic brownstones and mansions built in the 1880s and 1890s. See p.224 for more on outer borough architecture.

▸▸ **Harlem** Some of the most beautiful residential architecture in the city, exemplified by blocks of brownstones and other styles south of 125th Street, and developments farther north like Strivers' Row and Hamilton Heights.

▸▸ **Midtown Manhattan** A smorgasbord of twentieth-century architectural styles, including some of the city's greatest skyscrapers (the Empire State and GE buildings), Neoclassical beauties (the New York Public Library) and Modernist masterpieces (the Seagram Building and Lever House).

▲ Brownstone in Park Slope

▼ Gate in Strivers' Row, Harlem

Met Life Tower ▲

Empire State Building ▼

Postmodernism

Postmodernism afforded late twentieth-century architects a renewed playfulness – witness the Chippendale pediment on the 1983 Sony Building on Madison Avenue – though these kinds of conceits are toned down a bit on the **Citicorp Center** (1978). More recently, the twin towers of the **Time Warner Center** (2003) at Columbus Circle stand out mainly for their (gargantuan) size, while the **Condé Nast Building** (2000) on Times Square has been a major trendsetter in the move to "green" architecture. Frank Gehry's **IAC Building** (2007) in Chelsea and his **Beekman Tower** (2010) downtown are New York's most exuberant examples of contemporary architecture, while **One World Trade Center** should be the city's tallest building by 2012 (see p.56).

New York's tallest

New York is one of the best places in the world to see skyscrapers. Manhattan's iconic skyline traces over forty buildings higher than 650ft – there are more skyscrapers here than in any other urban centre, some of them over seventy years old. Yet until 1890, Trinity Church was the city's tallest building:

- **1846–1890 Trinity Church (284ft)**
- **1890–1899 World Building (348ft)**
- **1899–1908 Park Row Building (391ft)**
- **1908–1909 Singer Building (612ft)**
- **1909–1913 MetLife Tower (700ft)**
- **1913–1930 Woolworth Bldg (792ft)**
- **1930 Bank of Manhattan Trust (927ft)**
- **1930–1931 Chrysler Building (1046ft)**
- **1931–1972 Empire State Building (1250ft)**
- **1972–2001 World Trade Center – destroyed 2001 (1368ft)**
- **2001 onwards: Empire State Building**

a tributary of the Harlem River. Seven of Hughes' lines radiate out from a circle, and the last line, "My soul has grown deep like the rivers," located in a fish at the centre, marks where he is interred.

Originally a lending branch, the Division of Negro Literature, History and Prints was created in 1925 after the community began rallying for a library of its own. The collection grew dramatically, thanks to **Arthur Schomburg**, a black Puerto Rican nicknamed "The Sherlock Holmes of Black History" for his obsessive efforts to document black culture. Schomburg acquired over 10,000 manuscripts, photos and artefacts, and he sold them all to the NYPL for $10,000; he then worked as curator for the collection, sometimes using his own funds for upkeep, from 1932 until his death six years later. Since that time, the amassing of over ten million items has made the centre the world's top research facility for the study of black history and culture.

Harlem's historic jazz venues

Jazz remains a crucial part of Harlem's appeal, though most clubs today are small, intimate affairs – between the 1920s and 1960s, Harlem was home to some of the biggest nightspots in the city, many of which attracted hordes of white patrons from downtown as well as middle-class blacks.

The Abyssinian Development Corporation has acquired the **Renaissance Ballroom**, Powell Boulevard at 138th Street, as a likely future home for the Classical Theater of Harlem, though plans are moving ahead very slowly. This tile-trimmed, square-and-diamond-shaped dance club once hosted Duke Ellington and Chick Webb in the 1920s. Nicknamed the "Rennie," it was a haven for middle-class blacks but has been abandoned since the 1970s.

The same corporation, in partnership with the city, has transformed another former club, **Small's Paradise** on the southwest corner of Powell Boulevard and 135th Street. This finial-topped brick building was built in 1925 and hosted a mixed black and white crowd from the beginning, when the club was known as "The Hottest Spot in Harlem"; Malcolm X worked here in 1943. Today, it's occupied by an *International House of Pancakes* and topped by the state-of-the-art Thurgood Marshall Academy High School, opened in 2004. On the other side of 135th Street at 2300 Powell Blvd (now *Popeye's Chicken*), was the **Big Apple Restaurant and Jazz Club**, which is rumoured to be the birthplace of New York City's nickname. It's said that when jazzmen met on the road in the 1930s, they would call to each other, "See you at the Big Apple" as a sort of shorthand reference to the city. The term duly entered the vernacular after local journalists started using it and the city tourism authorities adopted it in the 1970s.

Opened in the 1930s, **Minton's Playhouse**, at 206–210 West 118th St between St Nicholas and Powell, became the birthplace of **bebop**. In the 1940s, after finishing their sets at Harlem's clubs, Dizzy Gillespie, Charlie Parker, John Coltrane and other greats would gather at Minton's for late-night jam sessions that gave rise to the improvised jazz style – innovator **Thelonius Monk** was actually house pianist here for three years. Miles Davis called Minton's "the black jazz capital of the world". Shuttered in the 1970s, Minton's reopened as a low-key jazz venue in 2006 (see p.362).

As for the **Cotton Club**, it was originally at 142nd Street and Lenox Avenue in the 1920s, and was a segregated establishment – though most of the performers here were black, as was the staff, only whites were allowed to attend as guests. That building was demolished in 1958, but a new version reopened in Harlem in 1978 at 666 West 125th St, where it continues to put on a good jazz show at night as well as a Sunday gospel brunch. For more on Harlem's nightlife today, see p.361.

El Barrio

East or **Spanish Harlem** extends from the affluence of the Upper East Side to East 132nd Street, and from the Harlem River as far west as Park Avenue. The neighbourhood has been a centre of New York's large **Puerto Rican** community since the 1950s, and is better known by locals as **El Barrio** – which simply means "the neighbourhood". Before World War II, this was actually **Italian Harlem**, a major Sicilian enclave: actor Al Pacino was born here in 1940, and *Rao's* restaurant (established in 1896) and *Patsy's Pizzeria* (which opened in 1933) still remain (see p.300 & p.337 for reviews).

Harlem's regeneration is gradually spilling over to El Barrio – optimistic realtors have dubbed it **"SpaHa"** – and the southern and western sections, particularly along Lexington Avenue, can be fun to explore (especially for the street art and the food). Yet most of the neighbourhood remains characterized by blocks of low-rise, low-income housing, shabby bodegas and gypsy-cab services that give the area an intimidating atmosphere. Until the 1970s, the hub of the area was **La Marqueta**, under the elevated Metro North railway tracks on Park Avenue between 111th and 116th streets; originally a five-block street market of Hispanic products, it's now largely vacant in spite of repeated attempts to revitalize it.

If you're looking for insight into New York's Latin culture, start at the **Museo del Barrio** (see below). To check out the contemporary art scene, stop by **Taller Boricua**, a gallery at 1680 Lexington Ave and 106th Street (Tues–Sat noon–6pm, Thurs 1–7pm; free; ⓣ212/831-4333, ⓦwww.tallerboricua.org), inside the red-brick **Julia de Burgos Latino Cultural Center**; they also run a popular **salsa** night on Wednesdays (5.30pm; $10, ladies $5 before 6.30pm). The centre is named for the lauded Puerto Rican poet who died poverty-stricken in Harlem in 1953, a striking mosaic **mural** (created by Manny Vega in 2006) of whom is on the opposite corner of 106th Street, part of the ongoing Hope Community project – you'll see *Nuyorican Poets Café* founder Pedro Pietri commemorated at 104th Street and Lexington, as well as the awe-inspiring **Spirit of East Harlem** mural (1978).

Nearby, the **Graffiti Wall of Fame** at Park Avenue and East 106th Street (on the west side of the railway viaduct) commemorates the street art that developed in New York in the 1970s. It's located in a school playground, so the gates are sometimes locked during term, when you'll have to ask at the school further along 106th Street for a closer look.

Museo del Barrio

Literally translated as "the neighbourhood museum", the **Museo del Barrio** (Wed–Sun 11am–6pm; suggested donation $6, free every 3rd Sat of month; ⓣ212/831-7272, ⓦwww.elmuseo.org), 1230 Fifth Ave at 104th Street, has two sections, both hosting temporary exhibits on various aspects of Puerto Rican and Latino culture. The permanent collection galleries display everything from the museum's rare **Taíno** artefacts, a pre-Colombian civilization that flourished in Puerto Rico and other Caribbean islands, to modern and conceptual art, while the other section hosts high-quality travelling exhibitions. In 2011, the "(S) Files bienal" will highlight contemporary cutting-edge Latino art, while "Caribbean: Crossroads of the World" will focus on the history and art of that region.

The galleries are relatively small, but there's also a decent **café** on site (selling duck, cheese and guava empanadas, tamales and rice pudding for around $3) and **El Teatro**, which shows Latin-influenced plays and movies (usually Wed 6.30pm; free). The museum also hosts concerts, poetry readings and other events, and is planning to offer local walking tours in the future – check the website for details.

Museum of African Art

The **Museum of African Art** (Ⓦwww.africanart.org) will be moving in late 2010 to 1280 Fifth Ave at East 110th Street, the first museum building built on Museum Mile since the completion of the Guggenheim in 1959. Exhibits will showcase a wide range of genres, from Congolese urban art and North African jewellery to modern photography and ancient Nigerian artefacts. Exhibitions slated for 2011 include a retrospective by Ghanaian-born El Anatsui, best known for his wall sculptures made from discarded bottle tops, and "Grass Roots: African Origins of an American Art".

Hamilton Heights and Sugar Hill

Much of West Harlem, between 125th and 155th streets, and from St Nicholas Avenue to the Hudson River, is taken up by the areas known as **Hamilton Heights**. Like Morningside Heights to the south, there's a blend of campus buildings (in this case, belonging to the City College of New York) and residences here, lightened by a sprinkle of slender parks on a bluff above Harlem. One stretch, the **Hamilton Heights Historic District**, bounded by Amsterdam and St Nicholas avenues from 140th to 145th streets, contains florid rowhouses in a variety of architectural styles, including Beaux Arts and Romanesque Revival. In the 1920s and 1930s, many affluent African-Americans began to migrate to the neighbourhood – as a result, the area between 145th and 155th streets and Edgecombe and Amsterdam avenues became known as **Sugar Hill**. Today, it's another area of gorgeous townhouses, well worth exploring.

City College

Visitors wandering up from the 125th Street and St Nicholas Avenue B or C subway station will be pleasantly surprised by **Convent Avenue** and the nearby grounds of **City College**. The rustic-feeling campus of Collegiate Gothic halls mantled with white terracotta fripperies occupies 35 acres along Convent Avenue, from 131st Street to 141st Street. The most impressive section is the **North Campus Quadrangle** just before 140th Street, designed by the noted architect George Browne Post and completed in 1908. Nearby **Shepard Hall** is the tallest and most striking building, soaring over the campus like a Gothic cathedral.

Founded downtown in 1847 (as the Free Academy of the City of New York), the college didn't charge tuition, and thus became the seat of higher learning for many of New York's poor, including polio-vaccine pioneer Jonas Salk, writer Mario Puzo and soldier-turned-statesman Colin Powell. The college has also produced an astounding ten Nobel laureates. Even though free education here came to an end in the 1970s, three-quarters of the students still come from minority backgrounds.

Hamilton Grange

Hamilton Heights' single historical lure – the house of founding father Alexander Hamilton – **Hamilton Grange National Memorial** (Ⓦwww.nps.gov/hagr), stands in the northwest corner of St Nicholas Park, next to City College at 141st Street. Completed in 1802, the Grange has bounced around the island a couple of times: it stood at its original site on 143rd Street until 1889, then was moved to

Alexander Hamilton

Alexander Hamilton's life is much more fascinating than his house. Born in the West Indies, he came to America as a young man. He was an early supporter of the Revolution, and his intelligence and enthusiasm quickly brought him to the attention of George Washington. Hamilton became the general's aide-de-camp, and rose quickly through military ranks. When Washington was elected President, he named Hamilton as the first Secretary of the Treasury. Hamilton, quick in both understanding and temper, tended to tackle problems head-on, a propensity that made him enemies as well as friends. He alienated both John Adams and Thomas Jefferson, and when Jefferson won the presidency in 1801, Hamilton was left out in the political cold. Temporarily abandoning politics, he moved away from the city to his grange (or farm) to tend his plantation and conduct a memorably sustained and vicious feud with **Aaron Burr**, who had beaten Hamilton's father-in-law in a Senate election.

Following a short tenure as Vice President under Jefferson, Burr ran for governor of New York; Hamilton strenuously opposed his candidacy and, after an exchange of extraordinarily bitter letters, the two men fought a duel in Weehawken, New Jersey (roughly where the Lincoln Tunnel now emerges), on July 11, 1804. When pistols were drawn, Hamilton honourably discharged his into the air, a happening possibly explained by the fact that his eldest son had been killed in a duel on the same field a few years earlier. Burr, evidently made of lesser stuff, aimed carefully and fatally wounded Hamilton. He remains one of two non-presidents to find his way onto US money (Benjamin Franklin's the other): you'll find his portrait on the $10 bill.

287 Convent Ave, in the shadow of the fiercely Romanesque St Luke's Church to which it was originally donated (Hamilton's statue remains here). In 2008, the 298-ton structure was lifted (in one piece, no less) up and over the church's entryway to begin the journey to its new home. The National Parks Service expects to complete a massive renovation project in late 2010 – check the website for the latest.

Washington Heights

The largely **Dominican** neighbourhood of **Washington Heights** encompasses most of the northern tip of Manhattan between 155th and Dyckman streets (200th St). From Sugar Hill, walk along St Nicolas Avenue, which eventually runs into Broadway some ten blocks north. This is the main drag of a once elegant, now mostly raggedy neighbourhood, though the gentrification of Harlem has also had an impact up here. It's worth coming for the food (see p.337) and for a couple of historic sights if you have time, though the area is probably best known as the stomping ground of New York's pioneer **graffiti** artists: **TAKI 183**, who started tagging in 1969 and lived on 183rd Street, is credited with sparking the craze after a *New York Times* article in 1971, while his inspiration was **Julio 204**, a Puerto Rican from 204th Street who had started a few years earlier.

Hispanic Society of America

One of the few sights worth at least a quick look in Washington Heights is **Audubon Terrace**, at 155th Street and Broadway (easily reached via the #1 train to 157th and Broadway). This Acropolis of folly is what's left of a weird, clumsy, nineteenth-century attempt to glorify 155th Street, when museums were dolled up as Beaux Arts temples.

There is only one museum left here (most of the complex is occupied by Boricua College), the **Hispanic Society of America** (Tues–Sat 10am–4.30pm, Sun 1–4pm, library closed Aug; free; ⓣ212/926-2234, ⓦwww.hispanicsociety.org), but it makes the trip worthwhile. The Hispanic Society owns one of the largest collections of Hispanic art outside Spain, including over 3000 paintings by masters

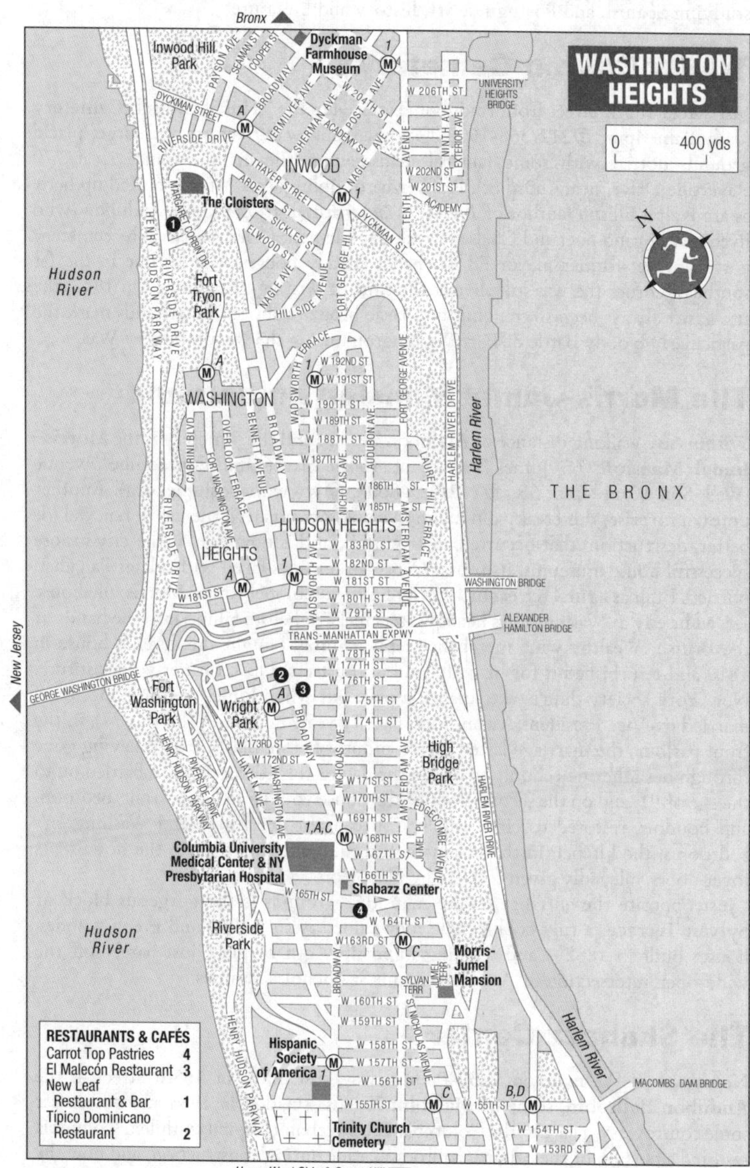

such as Goya, El Greco and Velázquez, as well as more than 6000 decorative works of art. The collection ranges from an intricately carved ivory box dating from 965 AD to fifteenth-century textiles to Joaquin Sorolla y Bastida's joyful mural series *Provinces of Spain* (commissioned specifically for the society in 1911). Displays of the permanent collection rarely change, so you can be fairly certain you'll see the highlights. The 200,000-book library, which includes over 16,000 works printed before the eighteenth century, is a major reference site for scholars studying Spanish and Portuguese art, history and literature.

Trinity Church Cemetery

Just across 155th Street from Audubon Terrace lies the **Trinity Church Cemetery** (daily 9am–4pm; ⓣ212/368-1600, ⓦwww.trinitywallstreet.org), its large, placid grounds dotted with some fanciful mausoleums (the main entrance is at 770 Riverside Drive, near 153rd St). Robber-baron John Jacob Astor is buried up here, as are Ralph Ellison (author of *Invisible Man*), naturalist John James Audubon (who lived nearby) and poet and Chelsea developer Clement Clark Moore. The cemetery is still in use: former mayor Ed Koch has already bought a headstone in the far southeast corner (he was still alive at the time of writing). Established in 1842, the site hasn't always been so tranquil: two large bronze slabs on the grounds mark the particularly bloody Battle of Fort Washington during the Revolutionary War.

The Morris–Jumel Mansion and around

Within easy walking distance of Audubon Terrace and the cemetery is the **Morris–Jumel Mansion**, 65 Jumel Terrace at 160th Street and Edgecombe Avenue (Wed–Sun 10am–4pm; $5; ⓣ212/923-8008, ⓦwww.morrisjumel.org). Another uptown surprise, this creaky old mansion somehow survived the urban renewal (or better, destruction) that occurred all around it, and is now one of the city's more successful house museums, its proud Georgian outlines faced with a later Palladian portico. Built as a rural retreat in 1765 by Loyalist Colonel Roger Morris, the house served briefly as Washington's headquarters in 1776 before falling into the hands of the British. Wealthy wine merchant Stephen Jumel bought the derelict house in 1810 and refurbished it for his wife (and ex-mistress) Eliza, formerly a prostitute. New York society didn't take to such a past, but when Jumel died in 1832, Eliza married ex-Vice President Aaron Burr, twenty years her senior (he was 77), in the front parlour: the marriage lasted for six months before old Burr left, having gone through her inheritance, only to die on the day of their divorce. Eliza battled on to the age of 91, and on the second floor of the house you'll find her portrait, bedroom and boudoir, restored to circa 1820s. You can also see Burr's and Washington's bedrooms, the kitchen in the basement and the gold wings above the downstairs foyer doors, allegedly given to Eliza by Napoleon.

Just opposite the entrance to the mansion's grounds is the gorgeous block of **Sylvan Terrace**, a tiny cobblestone mews lined with yellow and green wooden houses built in 1882 – and seeming impossibly out of place just barely off the wide-open intersection of Amsterdam and St Nicholas avenues.

The Shabazz Center

Northwest of the mansion at 3940 Broadway, just north of 165th Street, is the **Audubon Ballroom**, scene of **Malcolm X**'s assassination in 1965 and now, after some controversy, a part of the Columbia-Presbyterian Hospital complex. Columbia restored a portion of the original ballroom facade during construction, and now the

Malcolm X

Born Malcolm Little in 1925, in Omaha, Nebraska, influential African-American Muslim minister and political activist **Malcolm X** spent much of his later life in New York. He had a rough childhood and after moving to Harlem in 1943 became a small-time crook. In 1946, he ended up in jail; by the time he was released in 1952, he had become a committed follower of Elijah Muhammad's **Nation of Islam**. Despite the name, orthodox Muslims consider the Nation to be a separate religion, with many differences to Islam (members believe, for example, that Allah came to Earth in the person of one W. D. Fard, and that racial intermarriage is forbidden). Malcolm rose quickly within the Nation, setting up temples in Boston and becoming minister of Temple Number Seven in Harlem in 1954. Tall, handsome and an enigmatic speaker, he soon became the public face of the group, speaking out against the inequalities and racism of the time. Yet by 1964, Malcolm had fallen out with the Nation's leaders, who were finding it difficult to control their star speaker; Malcolm was becoming disillusioned with the Nation's unorthodox doctrine (not to mention Elijah Muhammad's alleged sex life). Malcolm converted to Sunni Islam (adopting the name **El-Hajj Malik El-Shabazz**), and took a life-changing pilgrimage to Mecca in 1964 – seeing Muslims of all races praying together was especially enlightening. Back in the US he started two new organizations – Muslim Mosque Inc, and the Organization of Afro-American Unity – but by now he was receiving regular death threats. He was finally gunned down on February 21, 1965, at a meeting in the Audubon Ballroom (see p.214). Three members of the Nation of Islam were eventually imprisoned for the murder (all three have since been released). Today, Malcolm X is considered one the greatest and most influential African Americans; his autobiography (co-written by Alex Haley) is still widely read, and he was portrayed by Denzel Washington in the lauded Spike Lee movie *Malcolm X* (1992).

Malcolm X and Dr. Betty Shabazz Memorial and Educational Center or just **Shabazz Center** (Mon–Fri 9am–6pm; free; ⓣ212/568-1341, ⓦtheshabazzcenter.net), commemorates the black leader, with murals, events and film screenings. The first floor also contains illuminating touch-screen panels that highlight important phases of Malcolm's life, including interviews and videos of the man himself.

The Cloisters Museum

The main reason visitors come this far uptown is to see **The Cloisters Museum** in Fort Tryon Park (Tues–Sun 9.30am–5.15pm, Nov–Feb until 4.45pm; suggested donation $20, includes same-day admission to the Metropolitan Museum of Art; ⓣ212/923-3700, ⓦwww.metmuseum.org). It stands above the Hudson like some misplaced Renaissance palazzo-cum-monastery, and is home to the Met's collection of medieval tapestries, metalwork, paintings and sculpture. The museum opened in 1938, largely thanks to donations from **George Grey Barnard** and **John D. Rockefeller, Jr**, and though it looks authentic, it was designed by modern architect Charles Collens (who also did Riverside Church; see p.199), with portions of five medieval cloisters (basically, covered walkways and their enclosed courtyards) cleverly incorporated into the structure. To get here, take the A train to 190th Street–Fort Washington Avenue, or the #M4 bus, which also passes the Met and terminates right outside the Cloisters (but can take 1hr 30min from midtown). A taxi from midtown will cost $25–30.

The collection

Once at the museum, start from the entrance hall and work counterclockwise: the collection is laid out in roughly chronological order. First off is the simplicity of the **Romanesque Hall** and the frescoed Spanish **Fuentidueña Chapel**, dominated by a huge, domed twelfth-century apse from Segovia that immediately induces a reverential hush. The hall and chapel form a corner on one of the prettiest of the cloisters, **St Guilhem**, which is ringed by Corinthian-style columns topped by carved capitals from late twelfth-century southern France. At the centre of the museum is the **Cuxa Cloister**, from the twelfth-century Benedictine monastery of Saint-Michel-de-Cuxa near Perpignan in the French Pyrenees; its Romanesque marble capitals are brilliantly carved, with monkeys, eagles and lions, whose open mouths reveal half-eaten human legs.

The nearby **Unicorn Tapestries** (c.1495–1505, Flanders) are even more spectacular – brilliantly alive with colour, observation and Christian symbolism. The most famous is the seventh and last, where the slain unicorn has miraculously returned to life and is trapped in a circular pen. It isn't just the creature's resurrection that's mystifying – the entire sequence is shrouded in mystery: aside from the fact that they were designed in France and probably made in Brussels, little else is known for certain, even who the intended original recipients were (the most plausible claim is Anne of Brittany, wife of King Louis XII). As for the tapestries' allegorical meaning, the unicorn is said to represent both a husband captured in marriage and Christ risen again.

Most of the Met's medieval paintings are to be found downtown, but one important exception is Dutch master **Robert Campin**'s *Merode Triptych*. This fifteenth-century oil painting depicts the Annunciation scene in a typical bourgeois Flemish home of the day, and is housed in its own antechamber next to the Boppard Room, outfitted with a chair, cupboard and other household articles from that period (though from different countries of origin). On the left of the altarpiece, the artist's patron and his wife gaze timidly on through an open door; to the right, St Joseph works in his carpenter's shop. St Joseph was mocked in the literature of the day, which might account for his rather ridiculous appearance – making a mousetrap, a symbol of the way the Devil traps souls.

The lower level

On the lower level, a large **Gothic chapel** boasts a high vaulted ceiling and mid- to late fourteenth-century Austrian stained-glass windows, along with the monumental **sarcophagus of Ermengol VII**, Count of Urgell (now in Catalunya, Spain), with its whole phalanx of (now sadly decapitated) family members and clerics carved in stone to send him off.

Also on the lower floor are two further cloisters to explore (one with a small café), along with the **Treasury** crammed with spellbinding objects. As you amble around this part of the collection, try not to miss the *Belles Heures de Jean, Duc de Berry*, perhaps the greatest of all medieval Books of Hours; it was executed by the Limburg Brothers with dazzling miniatures of seasonal life and extensive border-work in gold leaf. Other highlights include the twelfth-century walrus tusk **Cloisters Cross**, believed to be made by a craftsman known as Master Hugo for the now ruined great abbey at Bury St Edmunds in England. It contains a mass of 92 tiny expressive characters from biblical stories, as well as what seem to be disturbing anti-Semitic inscriptions. The cross is one of the most controversial pieces in the collection; experts still debate its provenance and meaning, and the story of how one of England's greatest pieces of medieval art ended up here is equally hazy – the Met outbid the British Museum for the piece in 1963 (paying $600,000), but how the shady Croatian seller acquired it is unknown.

18

Brooklyn

"The Great Mistake." So ran local newspaper headlines when **Brooklyn** became a borough of New York in 1898. Then the fourth-largest city in the US, it has since laboured in the shadow of its taller but smaller brother across the East River, drawing hordes to famous **Coney Island** beach – the closest white-sand beach to Manhattan – but generally not offering much in the way of high culture. Over the past decade, though, Brooklyn has come into its own, its signature brownstone townhouses and tree-lined streets complemented by top-rated restaurants, trendy bars, world-class museums, and galleries and performance spaces that present more daring work than you'll generally find in Manhattan.

The most accessible district in the borough is pretty, elite **Brooklyn Heights**, a clutch of old mansions and townhouses abutting the East River directly opposite Lower Manhattan. A little north of here, the once-derelict warehouses of the area known as **DUMBO** have been converted to expensive condos, art galleries and theatres overlooking a popular waterfront park space. Due south of the Heights lie **Boerum Hill**, **Cobble Hill** and **Carroll Gardens**, a trio of upscale neighbourhoods with no real attractions but block after block of historic brownstones and some of the borough's best restaurants and cafés. West of the Brooklyn–Queens Expressway, Carroll Gardens shades into **Red Hook**, whose half-exposed stone-block streets are lined with an oddball mix of hulking warehouses (some transformed into artists' studios), vacant lots, garden centres and detached three-storey houses, plus retail giants Ikea and Fairway.

A mile or so southeast of BoCoCa (as some, though not the locals, refer to the area), **Prospect Park**, designed by Central Park creators Frederick Law Olmsted and Calvert Vaux, contains the usual ballfields and trails, along with the first-rate Brooklyn Botanic Garden and Brooklyn Museum, while to the west is the leafy, cultured and kid-saturated neighbourhood of **Park Slope**. North of the park, increasingly trendy **Prospect Heights** leads into **Fort Greene**, where you'll find some of the most pristine residential blocks in the city along with the famous Brooklyn Academy of Music performance complex. Fort Greene adjoins **Bedford-Stuyvesant**, the largest African-American community in New York, which in turn links to **Crown Heights**, home to the newly expanded Brooklyn Children's Museum and a large Hasidic Jewish population.

Then there's coastal Brooklyn: start in polyglot **Bay Ridge** for a scenic bike ride along the water, then visit **Coney Island**, the venerable seaside amusement district known for its rattletrap roller coaster, the Cyclone, and the New York Aquarium. Grab some borscht at nearby **Brighton Beach**, where the Russian-born population tops 30,000.

Finally, anyone visiting New York for contemporary art should head to gallery-dotted **Williamsburg**, just one stop on the #L train from Manhattan's East Village and also a top choice for eating, drinking and live music among the young and trendy. **Greenpoint**, just north of Williamsburg on the border of Long Island City (see p.245), houses the artsy overflow from Williamsburg but maintains a quieter feel, thanks to the Polish old guard still prevalent.

Some history

In 1636, **Dutch colonists**, who had already settled New Amsterdam on Manhattan Island under the auspices of the Dutch West India Company, bought farmland from the **Lenape Indians** amid the flat marshes in the southwestern corner of Long Island. The **Village of Breuckelen** received a charter from the company in 1646. The town only began to take on its present form in 1814 when Robert Fulton's steamship service linked Long Island with Manhattan and Brooklyn Heights was established as a leafy retreat for wealthier Manhattanites.

Brooklyn's **incorporation** into the city of New York in 1898, ostensibly so that Manhattan's tax wealth would aid Brooklyn's poor, was a bitterly fought political battle. In the end it was decided by just 277 votes – a tiny percentage of the total 129,000 cast. By the early 1900s, Brooklyn had more than one million residents, many of them Jewish and Italian; in 1910, 35 percent of its population was foreign-born (the proportion is similar today).

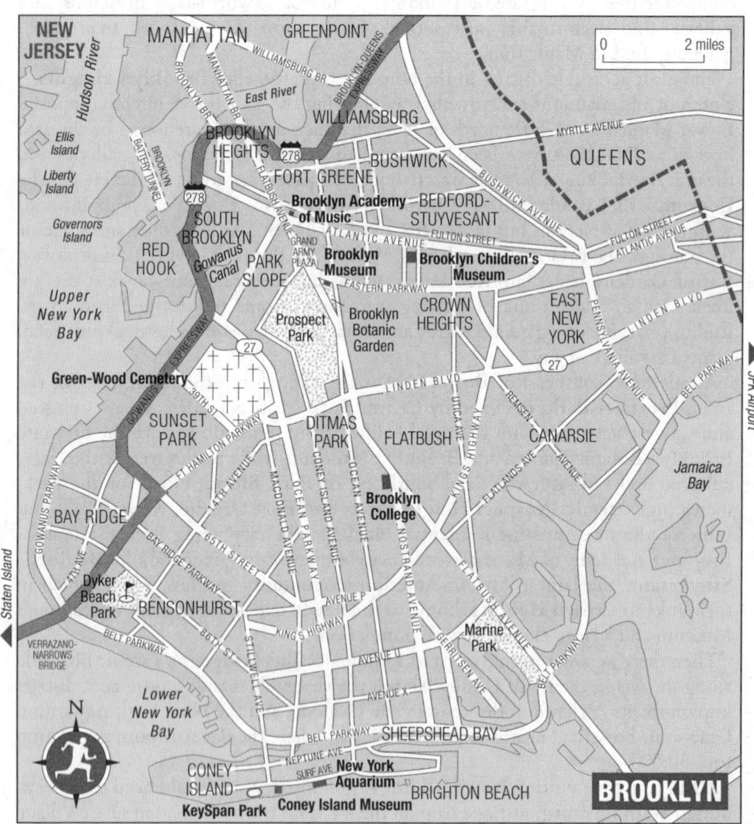

▲ *Juliette Bistro Café*, Williamsburg

Even with the population boom, Brooklyn suffered in the twentieth century: its strong manufacturing and shipping sectors dwindled, and unemployment climbed steadily. By the 1980s, "white flight", provoked first by racism, then by drug-related crime and violence, had left previously desirable residential neighbourhoods vacant and impoverished.

With a citywide drop in crime beginning in the mid-1990s, however, middle-class families began restoring townhouses in Park Slope, Cobble Hill, Prospect Heights and Fort Greene, and young artists and professionals flooded Williamsburg, offering Brooklyn a chance to rekindle its civic dignity, particularly in the realm of art and culture. This is, after all, the place that gave the world both "How ya doin'?" and "Fuhgeddaboudit," as well as countless artists, musicians, writers and film-makers. Now with 2.6 million residents, Brooklyn – independent or not – is still the fourth-largest urban centre in America, and it probably takes the prize for proudest.

Downtown Brooklyn and around

Spreading out from the foot of the Brooklyn and Manhattan bridges between Atlantic and Flatbush avenues, **Downtown Brooklyn** is a somewhat motley district of office buildings and commuter colleges. Aside from the Brooklyn Tourism and Visitors Center in Borough Hall (see p.224) and the underground New York Transit Museum, there's surprisingly little to see here. The neighbourhoods around downtown are a different story though.

To the east, **Fort Greene** has some of the city's most beautiful residential architecture. West of downtown is **Brooklyn Heights**, the borough's most prestigious neighbourhood. Northeast of the Heights is a historic sliver of land known as the Fulton Ferry District, which is adjacent to **DUMBO**, Brooklyn's answer to Tribeca, with its glossy mix of chichi design emporia, art galleries, waterfront parks, multimillion-dollar condos and trendy eateries. To start your

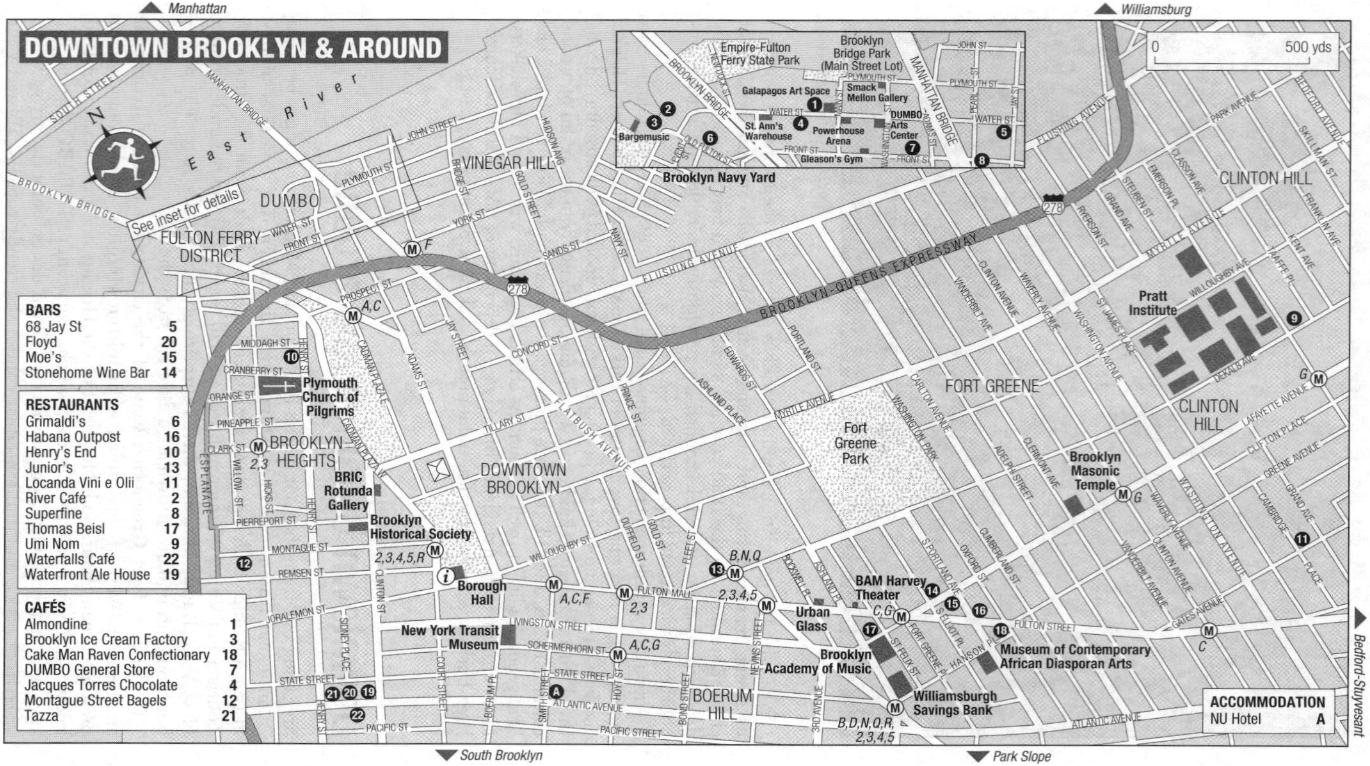

DOWNTOWN BROOKLYN & AROUND
Manhattan
Williamsburg
Bedford-Stuyvesant
South Brooklyn
Park Slope
0 500 yds
East River
See inset for details
DUMBO
FULTON FERRY DISTRICT
VINEGAR HILL
BROOKLYN HEIGHTS
DOWNTOWN BROOKLYN
FORT GREENE
CLINTON HILL
BOERUM HILL
Fort Greene Park
Brooklyn Navy Yard
Empire-Fulton Ferry State Park
Brooklyn Bridge Park (Main Street Lot)
Galapagos Art Space
Smack Mellon Gallery
DUMBO Arts Center
St. Ann's Warehouse
Powerhouse Arena
Gleason's Gym
Bargemusic
Plymouth Church of Pilgrims
BRIC Rotunda Gallery
Brooklyn Historical Society
Borough Hall
New York Transit Museum
Urban Glass
BAM Harvey Theater
Brooklyn Academy of Music
Williamsburgh Savings Bank
Museum of Contemporary African Diasporan Arts
Brooklyn Masonic Temple
Pratt Institute
BROOKLYN-QUEENS EXPRESSWAY
BROOKLYN BRIDGE
MANHATTAN BRIDGE
FLUSHING AVENUE
FLATBUSH AVENUE
MYRTLE AVENUE
FULTON STREET
ATLANTIC AVENUE
BARS
68 Jay St 5
Floyd 20
Moe's 15
Stonehome Wine Bar 14
RESTAURANTS
Grimaldi's 6
Habana Outpost 16
Henry's End 10
Junior's 13
Locanda Vini e Olii 11
River Café 2
Superfine 8
Thomas Beisl 17
Umi Nom 9
Waterfalls Café 22
Waterfront Ale House 19
CAFÉS
Almondine 1
Brooklyn Ice Cream Factory 3
Cake Man Raven Confectionary 18
DUMBO General Store 7
Jacques Torres Chocolate 4
Montague Street Bagels 12
Tazza 21
ACCOMMODATION
NU Hotel A

trip in grand style, walk or bicycle here from Lower Manhattan over the Brooklyn Bridge (see p.70), and try to be on the DUMBO waterfront or the Brooklyn Heights promenade at sunset – the light is magical.

Fulton Ferry District

Though you'd hardly guess it today, this small historic district, bounded by the East River, Old Fulton Street, Front Street and Main Street, was at one time the busiest spot on the Brooklyn waterfront. If you do arrive **on foot** from the Brooklyn Bridge, take the first set of stairs off the bridge and follow Cadman Plaza West down the hill to Old Fulton Street on the west edge of the district. The A and C trains to High Street will also let you off at Cadman Plaza West, and the **ferry** is a pleasant alternative in the summer months (see p.29).

Named for **Robert Fulton**, the area was the hub of steamship traffic until the 1883 opening of the Brooklyn Bridge precipitated an economic slump only recently remedied by the booming residential real estate market. Check out the imposing **Eagle Warehouse**, at 28 Old Fulton St; its penthouse, with the huge glass clock-window, is one of Brooklyn's most coveted apartments (though no match for the $25 million penthouse triplex in DUMBO's Clock Tower, at 1 Main St). The headquarters of *The Brooklyn Eagle*, the newspaper edited for a time by **Walt Whitman**, previously stood on this spot, and its old press room was integrated into the 1893 warehouse.

The landing is flanked by the area's two biggest tourist attractions, an old coffee barge that hosts classical music concerts – so-called **BargeMusic** (see p.370) – and the ritzy *River Café*, at 1 Water St, known as much for its views as for its fare. There are plenty of more authentic places to eat nearby, including *Grimaldi's*, at 19 Old Fulton St, which turn out some of the city's best pizza (see p.338).

DUMBO

Just east of the Fulton Ferry District, **DUMBO** is short for Down Under the Manhattan Bridge Overpass, a term coined in 1978 by residents of the neighbourhood – mostly artists – who thought the awkward moniker would deter developers. No such luck: many of DUMBO's handsome brick factories have been transformed into luxury condominiums, joined by glass towers housing more of the same. Still, the area has an undeniable allure, its cobblestone streets and jaw-dropping views of the Manhattan and Brooklyn bridges forming one of New York's most dramatic, Gotham-esque cityscapes. And in a canny move to maintain the district's cachet, DUMBO property owners have lured some top-notch galleries and performing-arts organizations with below-market-rate rents; cool restaurants and bars have followed.

DUMBO's core – which was landmarked by the city in 2007 – lies between the Brooklyn and Manhattan bridges, north of the Brooklyn–Queens Expressway. Water and Front streets are the main thoroughfares but any sidestreet is equally evocative, and the waterfront (see above) is the place to take your lunch or coffee and laze away a few hours. The centre of DUMBO's gallery scene, the **DUMBO Arts Center**, at 30 Washington St on Water Street, was the first nonprofit arts group in the neighbourhood. Its hosts five or six group shows a year in its space (Thurs–Mon 10am–6pm; Ⓣ718/694-0831, Ⓦwww.dumboartscenter.org) and also organizes the huge **Dumbo Arts Festival**, a three-day affair in late September showcasing work by emerging artists (see p.429). Most of DUMBO's other galleries are housed on the second floor of **111 Front St**, the ground floor of which is occupied by the excellent *Dumbo General Store* café (see p.300). Gallery hours vary, but you'll usually find seven or eight of them open on afternoons from

Wednesday to Saturday; on the first Thursday of each month, the neighbourhood pieces together a **Gallery Walk** (5.30–8.30pm), good for honing in on free receptions at participating art spaces.

To savour what's left of DUMBO's old-fashioned grit, head to **Gleason's Gym**, at 77 Front St, 2nd floor (Ⓣ718/797-2872, Ⓦwww.gleasonsgym.net), where tomorrow's prizefighters work out. Everyone from Jake LaMotta to Muhammad Ali has trained at Gleason's, first established in Manhattan in 1937; drop by to see people punch heavy bags or, if you're lucky, spar with each other ($10 entrance fee). Alternatively, call to see if they're hosting one of their Saturday night boxing events (usually monthly; $20).

Brooklyn Bridge Park and Empire–Fulton Ferry Park

The redeveloped waterfront along DUMBO and Brooklyn Heights goes by the umbrella name of **Brooklyn Bridge Park** (Ⓦwww.brooklynbridgepark.org), though the nomenclature can be confusing in parts. Just east of the Brooklyn Bridge, **Empire–Fulton Ferry State Park** has been closed for renovations to bring, among other things, a carousel to the green space, and should be reopening around the time of publication. Adjacent to that in the shadow of both bridges is a wonderful park, officially called Brooklyn Bridge Park (or sometimes "Main Street Lot"), with a playground, large lawn and giant steps for picnicking leading

Walt Whitman: Brooklyn Boy

Though he was only sporadically celebrated during his lifetime, poet **Walt Whitman** (1819–1892) has since been elevated to the pantheon of Great American Writers. And of all the places that he lived – and they were many – none was as influential as Brooklyn.

Born in Huntington, Long Island, Whitman moved to the borough at the age of 4, moving from place to place thanks to his family's precarious financial situation. His formal schooling ended at age 11, after which he began working as a typesetter's apprentice in what is now downtown Brooklyn. Whitman went on to found his own paper, the *Long-Islander*, which he sold after only nine months, but it was enough experience to get him hired as editor of the *Brooklyn Eagle*, a post he held for two years – a record for the peripatetic young writer.

During his tenure at the *Eagle* – still published in Brooklyn Heights – he argued for the establishment of Fort Greene Park and fought for recognition of local artists. But most important, he gathered ideas for his magnum opus, *Leaves of Grass*, which he would begin to write in 1850. Whitman himself paid for the publication of the first edition in 1855, even helping with the typesetting at a Scottish-owned press on Fulton Street to help keep costs down. Predictably, he couldn't even sell the first run of 795 copies, and when newspapers did get around to reviewing it, many denounced it as obscene.

Undeterred, Whitman revised *Leaves* for the rest of his life, expanding the original 12-poem booklet to a 400-page tome. These first lines of the penultimate poem, "Crossing Brooklyn Ferry", capture the theme that runs throughout the book – Whitman's wide embrace of all humanity – and display the repetitive cadences that would be so influential to later poets, from Gertrude Stein to Allen Ginsberg of the Beats:

Crowds of men and women attired in the usual costumes, how curious you are to me!
On the ferry-boats the hundreds and hundreds that cross, returning home, are more curious to me than you suppose,
And you that shall cross from shore to shore years hence are more to me, and more in my meditations, than you might suppose.

down to a rocky waterside. On the other side of the Brooklyn Bridge, the piers beneath the Brooklyn Heights Esplanade constitute what is considered the new Brooklyn Bridge Park. Pier One opened first, with a small play area and waterside promenade, but Pier Six is the more impressive space, with a fun water park, climbing area and a ferry link to Governors Island. In both areas, there's plenty of green for a picnic, and the views out to downtown Manhattan are perfect.

Brooklyn Heights

Brooklyn Heights is one of New York City's most beautiful and historical neighbourhoods, and still the borough's most coveted zip code. The best trains are the A or C to High Street, the #2 or #3 to Clark Street, or the #N or #R to Court Street. If you're already in the Fulton Ferry District, walk up the hill on Everit or Henry streets. The Brooklyn Historical Society (see below) provides a very useful walking-tour map, also available at the Brooklyn Tourism and Visitors Center (see p.224).

Downtown bankers and financiers began building brownstone townhouses here in the early nineteenth century, while writers flocked to the Heights after the subway opened in 1908; W.H. Auden, Carson McCullers, Truman Capote, Tennessee Williams, Norman Mailer and Paul and Jane Bowles (pre-Morocco) all lived in the neighbourhood. Although many single-family brownstones were divided into apartments during the 1960s and 1970s and the streets now feel fairly cosmopolitan – if a bit frumpier than you'd expect given what it costs to live here – Brooklyn Heights today is in many ways not much different from how it was a hundred years ago.

The north edge, along Henry Street and Columbia Heights, is the oldest part of the neighbourhood, where blocks are lined with Federal-style brick buildings. The unassuming, well-maintained wooden structure at **24 Middagh St** (at the corner of Willow), erected in 1824, is the area's longest-standing house, though other examples from around the era can be found along Middagh and Willow. Two streets south, its entrance on Orange Street, the simple **Plymouth Church of the Pilgrims**, at 75 Hicks St (Mon–Fri 9am–5pm, services Sun 11am; free; Ⓣ718/624-4743, Ⓦwww.plymouthchurch.org), went up in the mid-nineteenth century and became famous as the preaching base of **Henry Ward Beecher**, abolitionist and campaigner for women's rights. His fiery orations drew men like Horace Greeley and Abraham Lincoln, and Mark Twain based *Innocents Abroad* on travels with the church's social group. The building was also a stop on the Underground Railroad, where slaves were hidden on their way to freedom. Fitting then, that in 1963, Martin Luther King Jr delivered an early version of his "I Have a Dream" speech here. Tours of the church, focusing on the history and architecture, can be arranged with an advance call.

Continuing south on Henry, you soon reach **Pierrepont Street**, studded with fine brownstone townhouses. One block east of Henry, at the corner of Pierrepoint and Monroe Place, look in if you can on the **First Unitarian Church**, notable for its exquisite neo-Gothic interior, built in 1844. Across the street at no. 128, the **Brooklyn Historical Society** (Wed–Fri & Sun noon–5pm, Sat 10am–5pm; $6; Ⓣ718/222-4111, Ⓦwww.brooklynhistory.org) investigates the borough's neighbourhoods, architecture, ecology and subcultures with changing exhibits. The second-floor library with its local history collection is an evocative highlight, and the Society publishes detailed neighbourhood guides to a handful of Brooklyn districts, for sale at the front desk. Just down the street, **BRIC Rotunda Gallery**, at 33 Clinton St, presents multimedia work by Brooklyn-based artists (Tues–Sat noon–6pm; Ⓣ718/875-4047, Ⓦwww.bricartsmedia.org).

Walk back west on any street between Clark and Remsen to reach the **Promenade** (more formally known as the Esplanade), a pedestrian path with terrific views of the Statue of Liberty, downtown Manhattan's skyscrapers and the Brooklyn Bridge. Below is the still-developing Brooklyn Bridge Park (see opposite).

Downtown Brooklyn

The core of **downtown Brooklyn** – an area bordered by (clockwise from north) Sands and Middagh streets, Flatbush Avenue, Atlantic Avenue and Court Street – reflects the borough's split personality. While it still has touches of metropolitan grandeur and civic pride, for the most part it lacks Manhattan's sophistication, and in the past two decades much of the area has been transformed into an ill-planned assortment of ungainly office and academic buildings – the so-called **MetroTech Center** – linked by pedestrian streets devoid of life after the nine-to-five grind.

The situation is rapidly changing, though – since 2004 real-estate interests have invested billions here, with new hotels, condos and supermarkets going up; on the edge of the district bordering Prospect Heights, a huge shopping and entertainment complex seems, after much controversy and delay, inevitable (see "The new Battle of Brooklyn"box opposite).

The eastern edge of residential Brooklyn Heights is defined by **Cadman Plaza**, created after World War II when the city decided to move Brooklyn's elevated streetcars underground. Nowadays it hosts a farmers' market (Tues & Sat year-round, plus Thurs from April to mid-Dec). Just south of the plaza, at Court and Montague streets, stands the lovely, massive **State Supreme Court**, designed by the same architects who made the Empire State Building. Further south, the Greek-style **Borough Hall**, at 209 Joralemon St, looks tiny in comparison; it was erected in 1849, then topped with its odd cupolated belfry near the end of the century. Step inside to snag some local papers, maps and brochures from the **Brooklyn Tourism and Visitors Center** (Mon–Fri 10am–6pm; ⓣ718/802-3846, ⓦwww.visitbrooklyn.org).

New York Transit Museum

Two blocks south of Borough Hall, on the corner of Boerum Place and Schermerhorn Street, the **New York Transit Museum** (Tues–Fri 10am–4pm, Sat & Sun noon–5pm; $5, children 3–17 $3; ⓣ718/694-1600, ⓦwww.mta.info/mta/museum) is housed underground in the refurbished Court Street shuttle station from the 1930s. Exhibits include antique turnstiles, maps, models, photographs and some interactive displays of fuel technologies. The highlight for many is jumping on and off the varying models of restored subway and trolley cars in the lower level, though few parents will be able to resist the photo opportunity of placing their kids in the driver's seat of one of the buses on the main floor.

Fort Greene

Cross over chaotic Flatbush Avenue, and Fulton Street will bring you into the heart of **Fort Greene**, a historically African-American neighbourhood that

Outer boroughs architecture

Not all New York's most striking residential architecture is in Manhattan. The following streets/areas in the outer boroughs are worth the trek to see:

45th Avenue between 21st and 23rd streets, Long Island City, see p.246
Bed-Stuy historic district, see p.235
Grand Concourse, the Bronx, see p.256
Middagh Street, Brooklyn Heights, see p.223
South Portland Avenue, Fort Greene, see p.226

The new Battle of Brooklyn: Atlantic Yards

In a borough rampant with real-estate development, no single project is as huge or as controversial as the one known as **Atlantic Yards**. First proposed by Cleveland developer Forest City Ratner, a company headed by then-New Jersey Nets owner Bruce Ratner, in December 2003, the plan initially called for the building of sixteen skyscrapers and a Frank Gehry-designed arena for the Nets basketball team, all crammed onto a parcel only one and a half times the size of the World Trade Center site. Few disputed that the railyards that separated Fort Greene and Prospect Heights needed *some* sort of makeover, but Atlantic Yards was deemed way over the top – upon completion, it would form the most densely populated "subdivision" in America.

Residents of the surrounding neighbourhoods rebelled with an ongoing series of protests and lawsuits disputing, among other things, the environmental impact of the project (thousands more cars and people, but no additional schools or hospitals), but the slowing economy was what finally tripped up Ratner. In spring 2008 he was forced to admit that it was too risky to build anything but the stadium and three stubby glass towers around it on the eastern corner of the site (near the intersection of Flatbush and Atlantic aves) until market conditions improved. Two years later, a groundbreaking ceremony was held for the beginning of construction on **Barclays Center**, which when ready will bring the first professional team to Brooklyn since the Dodgers left town; to help with project financing, Ratner sold the Nets to Russian billionaire Mikhail Prokhorov. A month after the groundbreaking ceremony, the last of those who refused to move to make way for the project sold his condo to Ratner for $3 million – the state had already seized the property in an act of compulsory purchase.

withstood the dark days of the 1970s and 80s better than most places in Brooklyn and is now quite prosperous. The area is very easy to reach by subway: take any train to Atlantic Avenue or the C to Lafayette Avenue.

If you are arriving on foot from the Fulton Mall, the first place you'll reach is **UrbanGlass**, at 647 Fulton St (entrance at 57 Rockwell Place; Tues–Fri 10am–6pm, Sat & Sun 10am–5pm; ⓣ718/625-3685, ⓦwww.urbanglass.org), the East Coast's oldest and largest open glassworking studio. The studio hosts five open houses a year, during which you can tour the facility, watch glass-blowing demonstrations and try your hand at glassworking (call for schedule and reservations).

Right next door is the BAM Harvey Theater, where the **Brooklyn Academy of Music** stages most of its plays, many with top-tier actors. The interior has been preserved in a state of glamorous pseudo-decay. Turn south on Ashland Place to reach BAM's main building – the 1908 opera house, at 30 Lafayette Ave, with its colourful terracotta cornice and undulating glass canopy (ⓣ718/636-4100, ⓦwww.bam.org). Brooklyn's most acclaimed cultural centre, BAM also hosts opera, dance, classical music and film. The swanky, glittering *BAMcafé*, on the second floor of the opera house, offers free live music – jazz, blues, R&B – every Friday night from 9.30pm until around midnight.

Sharing the block with BAM is the **Williamsburgh Savings Bank Tower**, Brooklyn's second tallest building (for now; see box above) and its most iconic. Built in 1927 but only recently turned into luxury condos, it stands 512ft (34 storeys) tall and sports one of the biggest four-sided clocks in the world, each face measuring 27ft in diameter.

Walk east on Hanson Place to the intersection with South Portland Avenue, where the **Museum of Contemporary African Diasporan Arts**, at 80 Hanson Place, has made its home (Wed–Sun 11am–6pm; $4; ⓣ718/230-0492, ⓦwww.mocada.org). The gallery space is small, but the three multimedia exhibits mounted here every year are provocative, taking on issues like race, class and police violence. There's also a fine gift shop. Continue north on South Portland and you'll soon come to one of the prettiest blocks in all of New York City – South Portland Avenue between Lafayette and DeKalb avenues, which is lined with stately townhouses with high stoops under a lush canopy of trees. The annual Fort Greene House Tour in early May allows you to peek inside several residences, gardens and artists' studios (Ⓣ718/875-1855, Ⓦwww.historicfortgreene.org).

South Portland Avenue dead-ends at **Fort Greene Park**, designed by Frederick Law Olmsted and Calvert Vaux in 1867, and named after Revolutionary War general Nathaniel Greene. Seventy years later, Walt Whitman, as editor of the *Brooklyn Eagle*, urged that the space be turned into parkland, a "lung" for the growing borough. At the park's summit, the 148ft **Prison Ship Martyrs Monument** (1908) commemorates the estimated 11,500 Americans who died in the floating prison camps maintained by the British during the Revolutionary War. Sixteen squalid ships, rife with smallpox, were moored in old Wallabout Bay (just offshore from the Brooklyn Navy Yard). The bones of the dead, collected as they washed ashore for decades after, are housed in a small crypt at the base of the tower.

Continue east on Dekalb until you get to Clermont Street, then turn right and continue one block to Lafayette, where the 1909 **Brooklyn Masonic Temple**, at 317 Clermont St (Ⓣ718/638-1256, Ⓦwww.masonicboom.com) rises like a fortress. Masons no longer meet here, but hipsters do, with indie bands and DJs plying the renovated theatre. The schoolyard across the street hosts the **Brooklyn Flea** (Ⓦwww.brooklynflea.com) on Saturdays from 10am to 5pm, with about two hundred vendors selling all manner of vintage goods. A growing army of food carts serves *pupusas* (Salvadoran filled tortillas), Belgian waffles, lobster rolls and other treats. A Sunday market takes place indoors at 1 Hanson Place, also the current location for the winter Flea (see p.406).

South Brooklyn

The neighbourhoods of **Cobble Hill**, **Boerum Hill** and **Carroll Gardens**, along with the former industrial zone along the **Gowanus Canal** and the wharves of **Red Hook**, make up the area traditionally known as **South Brooklyn** – confusing, because geographically much of the borough is actually south of this area. Until 1894, however, this was the southern border of the city of Brooklyn, so the term has stuck. The most popular areas to visit here are Court and Smith streets, which run north–south through Cobble Hill and Carroll Gardens. They're lined with some of Brooklyn's best boutiques and – on Smith Street in particular – places to dine (see Chapter 24, Restaurants, for reviews). If industrial decay is more your style, don't miss the Gowanus Canal and Red Hook, both of which have active art scenes.

The F or G to Bergen Street deposits you on the border between Cobble Hill and Carroll Gardens; the Carroll Street stop on the same lines leaves you at the southern end of Carroll Gardens, closest to Gowanus and a bus ride (or long walk) to Red Hook. If you're walking here from Brooklyn Heights, simply continue on Court Street.

Cobble Hill and Boerum Hill

Just south of Atlantic Avenue, the main east–west streets through **Cobble Hill** – Amity, Congress and Warren – are a mix of brownstones and red-brick rowhouses built between the 1840s and the 1880s. **Court Street** is the neighbourhood's main commercial artery, though restaurants, bars and boutiques are probably slightly more abundant on **Smith Street**, which caters to a younger crowd.

Over on Clinton Street, which runs parallel to Court, sits the idyllic little **Cobble Hill Park**. Along the park's southern border is a cobblestone alleyway – **Verandah Place**, a renovated mews built in the 1850s. Writer Thomas Wolfe lived in the basement at no. 40 in the 1930s and described the apartment in his novel *You Can't Go Home Again*: "Here, in winter, the walls … sweat continuously with clammy drops of water. Here, in summer, it is he who does the sweating." Living conditions weren't nearly so dismal in the nearby **Home Buildings**, a tidy row of red-brick cottages lining a pedestrian mews, Warren Place. Built in 1878 as utopian workers' housing, the 44 homes are each only eleven feet wide.

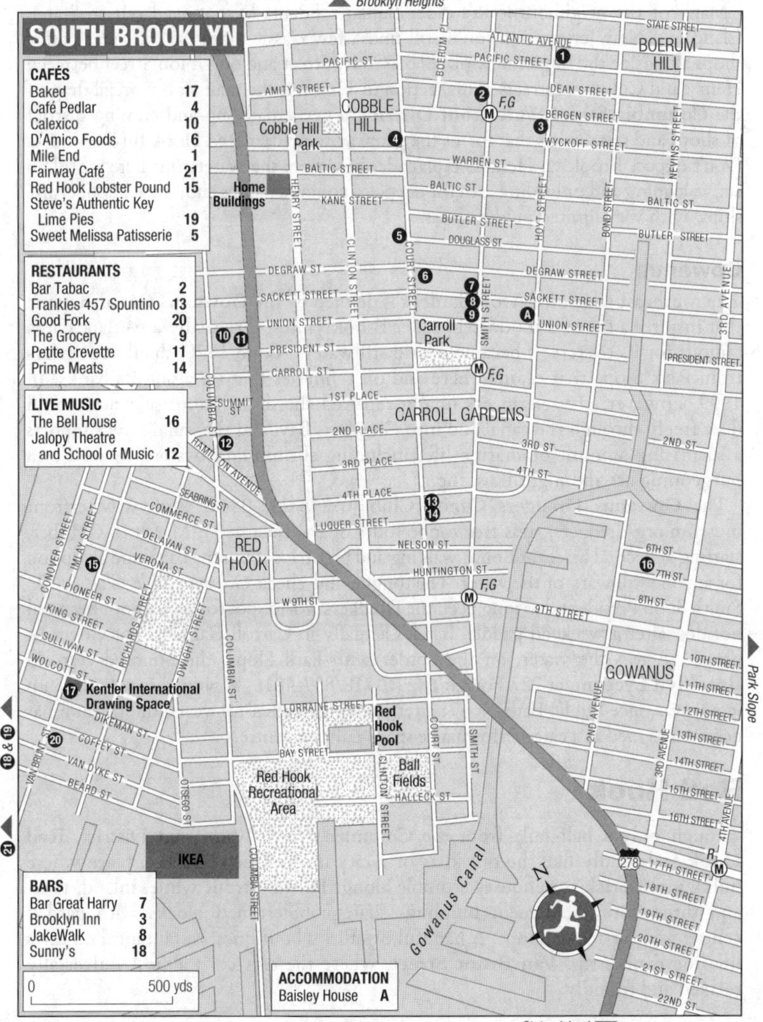

East of Cobble Hill, **Boerum Hill** is less architecturally impressive than its neighbour, though it has its share of sober Greek Revival and Italianate buildings, developed around the same period.

Carroll Gardens and Gowanus

As you walk south along Court Street, Cobble Hill blends into **Carroll Gardens** around Degraw Street. Built as a middle- and upper-class community between 1869 and 1884, this part of South Brooklyn has been an Italian enclave since dockworkers arrived here in the early 1900s; **Al Capone** is said to have been married in 1918 at the Saint Mary Star of the Sea Church on Court Street. The area was later named for Charles Carroll, the only Roman Catholic to sign the Declaration of Independence.

Many of the neighbourhood's older Italian residents have moved out to Staten Island and New Jersey, but you'll still find a few classic pizza parlours and pastry shops alongside the hipper new places on Court Street and on Union Street between Henry and Columbia streets. This section of Union is the main commercial drag of the **Columbia Street Waterfront District**, a perpetually up-and-coming district of shops and restaurants that forms the gateway to grittier Red Hook further south. Don't expect Brooklyn Heights esplanade, however; the waterfront here is still an active loading and unloading area for deep-sea container ships and, since 2006, cruise ships, with very limited public access.

Gowanus

The southeast edge of Carroll Gardens is defined by the **Gowanus Canal**, a name that inspires a bit of a shudder in older Brooklynites. Originally a wetlands area famous for its oysters, it became a fetid stillwater around 1870, thanks to sewers from Park Slope that drained here and oil refineries that sat along its banks. In 1999, however, city engineers finally repaired the drain pump so water could flow freely through the canal and into Gowanus Bay, and the canal now supports a surprising amount of marine life, including shrimp and oysters, as well as a burgeoning art and nightlife scene.

The **Gowanus Dredgers Canoe Club** (ⓣ718/243-0849, ⓦwww.waterfrontmuseum.org/dredgers) runs free canoe tours of the canal from March to October, starting at Second Street at Bond; walking and bike trips along the banks are an option for anyone still wary of the water. The tongue-and-cheek *Gowanus Yacht Club*, at 323 Smith St on President, has long been the Dredgers' go-to spot for an outdoor beer and hot dog after a weekend paddle, but it's actually in Carroll Gardens, not Gowanus proper. Across the water, on the border with Park Slope, the hundred-year-old **Brooklyn Lyceum**, at 227 Fourth Ave (ⓣ718/857-4816, ⓦwww.brooklynlyceum.com) was once Public Bath No. 7; after standing derelict for years, the Lyceum has been redesigned as a café-performance space-cultural centre.

Red Hook

Though only a half-mile from the Columbia Street Waterfront District, **Red Hook** feels oddly like the outskirts of a city in the Deep South, a place where hulking red-brick warehouses crumble along the waterfront while, inland, two- and three-storey apartment buildings share cobblestoned blocks with garden centres and car-repair shops. A handful of quirky boutiques, restaurants and cafés line the main strip, **Van Brunt Street**, where the service is almost universally relaxed and friendly.

No subway line goes out to Red Hook, but it's easy enough to reach by bus. Take the #B61 bus from Columbia Street in Cobble Hill or the #B77 bus from Smith and 9th streets in Carroll Gardens. **New York Water Taxi** (Ⓣ212/742-1969, Ⓦwww.nywatertaxi.com) also runs a free weekend ferry service from Pier 11 in Manhattan to **Ikea**, at the southern tip of Red Hook; boats leave and arrive every 40min.

Settled by the Dutch in 1636, Red Hook got its name from the colour of the soil and the shape of the land, which forms a corner, or *hoek*, where the Upper New York Bay meets the Gowanus Bay. It eventually became one of the busiest and toughest shipping centres in the US, inspiring Hubert Selby's book *Last Exit to Brooklyn* and Arthur Miller's play *A View from the Bridge*. Some say that urban planner **Robert Moses** deliberately severed the notoriously crime-ridden neighbourhood from the rest of Brooklyn when he routed the Brooklyn–Queens Expressway down Hicks Street in 1954. In any case, by the 1960s, the increasing automation of the docking industry left longshoremen out of work and sent most of the freighters from Red Hook to bigger ports in New Jersey.

The waterfront and piers

Red Hook's waterfront is now a curious assemblage of abandoned and repurposed warehouses and parkland. Head down Van Dyke Street to Pier 41, where at *Steve's Authentic Key Lime Pies*, at 204 Van Dyke St (Ⓦwww.stevesauthentic.com), you can pick up a four-inch tart made with freshly squeezed juice ($4) and eat it as you wander the area. From the end of the pier Governors Island appears almost within wading distance and Lady Liberty seems to raise her torch just for you. Nearby, the **Waterfront Museum and Showboat Barge** (Thurs 4–8pm, Sat 1–5pm; donation requested; Ⓣ718/624-4719, Ⓦwww.waterfrontmuseum.org), at Pier 44, presents historical exhibits and occasional children's shows in a restored railroad barge moored off a small park at the end of Conover Street.

Adjacent **Fairway**, at 480–500 Van Brunt St, is Brooklyn's best supermarket, with a staggering selection of produce and gourmet treats like olives, cheese and smoked fish. Thread your way to the back to the waterfront café (see review p.301). In the warehouse across the street from Fairway, the **Brooklyn Waterfront Artists Coalition (BWAC)**, at 499 Van Brunt St, holds three group shows per year, on weekends from mid-May to mid-June, from late July to mid-August, and from late September to late October (Ⓣ718/596-2507, Ⓦwww.bwac.org). The other gallery of note in the area is the **Kentler International Drawing Space**, at 353 Van Brunt St, which as its name suggests displays fine works on paper (Thurs–Sun noon–5pm; Ⓣ718/875-2098, Ⓦwww.kentlergallery.org).

Red Hook Ball Fields

There are a couple of good cafés and restaurants in the neighbourhood (see Listings), but if you're in Red Hook on a summer weekend it's a tradition to eat at the **Red Hook Recreational Area** (aka the **Red Hook Ball Fields**; Sat & Sun 11am–8pm), at Clinton and Bay streets, where Latinos gather for ultra-competitive soccer in the shadow of a long string of linked grain silos. Surrounding the pitch, a dozen or so food-stands dole out delicious tacos, ceviche, *tamales*, *pupusas*, *huaraches* and more. To reach the fields, head east on Van Dyke Street.

Prospect Park and around

Where Brooklyn really surpasses itself is on Flatbush Avenue in the vicinity of **Grand Army Plaza**, an elegant, if congested, traffic circle around a stately memorial arch. The plaza faces the **Brooklyn Public Library** and the entrance to **Prospect Park**, and immediately east of it on Eastern Parkway, the **Brooklyn Museum** houses, among other things, an excellent ancient Egyptian trove and the **Brooklyn Botanic Garden** teems with greenery. The plaza also acts as a border to several very different neighbourhoods, including up-and-coming **Prospect Heights** and the serene liberal bastion of **Park Slope**. The Grand Army Plaza stop on the #2 and #3 subway line is the most central for the arch, while the museum has its own stop just a few blocks further down the line. The B and Q trains to Prospect Park get you closest to the park's main attractions, while Park Slope's chief subway stops are the F to 7th Avenue/9th Street and the #R to 4th Avenue/Union Street.

Grand Army Plaza

Central Park architects Frederick Law Olmsted and Calvert Vaux designed **Grand Army Plaza** in the 1860s and 1870s as an approach to Prospect Park, but it didn't take on its current grandeur until the end of that century. The

80ft-tall triumphal **Soldiers' and Sailors' Memorial Arch**, modelled on Paris's Arc de Triomphe, a tribute to the Union victory in the Civil War, was unveiled in 1892.

Saturday is by far the best day to visit, when dozens of farmers from New York and New Jersey set up stalls here at the city's second-largest **Greenmarket** (year-round 8am–4pm). At the height of summer, expect to find bounteous produce, meats, flowers, jams and pickles, along with occasional cooking demonstrations. The wintertime selection can be thin, but you can always get a crunchy apple, donut and steaming cup of cider.

On the east side of the plaza, the immense **Brooklyn Public Library** (Ⓦwww.brooklynpubliclibrary.org), started in 1912 with the help of a $1.6 million donation from Andrew Carnegie and finally finished in 1941, is just as grand.

Prospect Park

Energized by their success with Central Park, Olmsted and Vaux landscaped **Prospect Park** (Ⓣ718/965-8951, Ⓦwww.prospectpark.org) in the early 1860s. Its 585 acres include a 60-acre lake on the east side, a 90-acre open meadow on the west, and a circular 3.35-mile park drive around the periphery, primarily reserved for runners, cyclists and rollerbladers (vehicular traffic is allowed during weekday rush hours only).

Despite attractions that have sprung up over the years – an Audubon Center, a tennis centre, an ice-skating rink (Nov–March) and the popular Celebrate Brooklyn outdoor music festival – Prospect Park remains for the most part remarkably bucolic. The **Audubon Center** (April–Dec Thurs–Sun noon–5pm; Ⓣ718/287-3400), in the Boathouse at mid-park on the east side, serves as the park's main visitor centre as well as the trailhead for the park's four nature trails; there's also a pleasant café here, some well-done ecology exhibits, free wi-fi and the dock for the *Independence*, an electric boat that spins around the lake on 25-minute tours from April to October ($8, children 3–12 $4).

Nearby, tour guides at the **Lefferts Historic House**, an eighteenth-century Dutch farmhouse, use the place as a prop to talk (mostly to children) about what Brooklyn was like in the 1820s (April–May & Oct–Nov Sat & Sun noon–5pm, June & Sept Thurs–Sat noon–5pm, July–Aug noon–6pm, Dec & Feb–March Sat–Sun noon–4pm; Ⓣ718/789-2822). Just south of the house stands a 1912 **carousel** (April, May, Sept & Oct Sat & Sun noon–5pm, July–Aug Thurs–Sun noon–6pm; $2) with 51 hand-carved horses and other animals; it was originally installed at Coney Island. The adjacent **Prospect Park Zoo**, run by the venerable Wildlife Conservation Society, showcases sea lions, kangaroos, red pandas, poisonous frogs, baboons and sundry other fauna in natural-looking habitats (April–Oct Mon–Fri 10am–5pm, Sat & Sun 10am–5.30pm; Nov–March daily 10am–4.30pm; $7, children 3–12 $3; Ⓣ718/399-7339, Ⓦwww.prospectparkzoo.org).

For less-structured fun, head to the **Drummers' Grove** near the Parkside and Ocean Avenue entrance on the southeast corner of the park; the crowd that gathers on Sunday afternoons is no amateur circle – some very accomplished musicians have been jamming here for decades. The **Celebrate Brooklyn** concert series likewise draws top-notch musical and dance talent to its summer series of outdoor concerts, held at the **Bandshell**, just off Prospect Park West at 10th Street ($3 donation requested; Ⓣ718/855-7882, Ⓦwww.celebratebrooklyn.org).

The Brooklyn Museum

East of Grand Army Plaza and the Public Library stands the imposing **Brooklyn Museum**, at 200 Eastern Parkway (Wed–Fri 10am–5pm, Sat & Sun 11am–6pm, first Sat of every month until 11pm; suggested donation $10; ⓣ718/638-5000, ⓦwww.brooklynmuseum.org). If you're coming by subway, take the #2 or #3 train to Eastern Parkway.

Designed by McKim, Mead, and White, it's second only to the Metropolitan Museum of Art in terms of exhibit space in New York City, with five floors of galleries. The museum is best known for its distinguished store of Egyptian relics but has recently won acclaim for adding a feminist art wing that includes Judy Chicago's groundbreaking 1970s installation, *The Dinner Party*. The museum's regular schedule of talks, arts-and-crafts demonstrations and performances are best experienced via the free **First Saturdays** programme, held on the first Saturday evening of each month. On these nights, the museum stays open until 11pm (admission is free after 5pm), transforming itself into a vast all-ages party with live music and often raucous dancing.

The collection

Just inside the front entrance stands a changing selection of a dozen bronze sculptures by Auguste Rodin. But the highlight of the first floor is the museum's collection of 5000 works of **African Art**, representing fifty cultures over a 2500-year span; particularly splendid is a sixteenth-century ivory gong from Benin.

The second floor is dedicated to the **Asian and Islamic galleries**, with pieces from China, Korea, India and Japan, as well as Ottoman Turkish and Qajar Persian textiles, mosaics, manuscripts and jewellery. Don't miss the ferocious *Head of a Guardian* from thirteenth-century Japan.

The delicately carved stone "Brooklyn Black Head" of the Ptolemaic period, arguably the museum's crown jewel, is one of 1200 objects in the authoritative **Ancient Egyptian Art** collection – one of the largest outside of Egypt – on the third floor. Sarcophagi and sculptures are nicely complemented by small galleries of Assyrian, Sumerian and other ancient Middle Eastern art; keep an eye out for the exquisite "Coffin for an Ibis", with its astonishing detail. On the same floor, **European Paintings** presents a non-chronological array of work from *The Adoration of the Magi* (c.1480) by Milanese artist Bernardo Butanone to Monet's *Houses of Parliament*; none is particularly essential.

One flight up, most of the **Decorative Arts collection** is in six evocative **period rooms**, including a nineteenth-century Moorish smoking room from John D. Rockefeller's estate. It shares the floor with the Elizabeth A. Sackler Center for Feminist Art, the centrepiece of which is **The Dinner Party**, a massive triangular dinner table with custom-made China place settings for 39 famous women. Constructed in 1974–79 by artist Judy Chicago and hundreds of volunteers, it's an impressive and moving display, even if the explanatory timeline – or "herstory" – in the adjoining gallery feels a bit dated.

On the fifth floor, Georgia O'Keeffe's sensual 1948 paean to the borough, *Brooklyn Bridge*, opens the somewhat uneven "American Identities" permanent exhibition, which draws thematic connections among works in the museum's extremely varied **Painting and Sculpture** collection. More interesting – in fact, one of the most diverting parts of the entire museum – is the **Visible Storage** exhibit, basically a bunch of museum holdings not part of the main museum. Besides paintings, hundreds of objects of Americana are packed behind glass, including chairs, lamps and bicycles.

The Brooklyn Botanic Garden

Located just behind the museum, the **Brooklyn Botanic Garden**, at 900 Washington Ave, is one of the most enticing park spaces in the city (March–Oct Tues–Fri 8am–6pm, Sat & Sun 10am–6pm; Nov–Feb Tues–Fri 8am–4.30pm & Sat 10am–4.30pm; $8, free Tues, Sat before noon, Nov–Feb weekdays; ⓣ718/623-7200, ⓦwww.bbg.org). Plants from around the world occupy 22 gardens and exhibits spread over 52 acres, all sumptuous but not overmanicured. What you'll see depends largely on the season. March brings colour to Daffodil Hill, while April sees the cherry trees bloom in the Japanese Garden, designed in 1914 and the oldest garden of its kind outside of Japan. The Rose Garden starts to flourish in the early summer, the elaborate water-lily ponds are at their best in late summer and early autumn, and the autumnal colours in the Rock Garden are striking. A winter visit lets you enjoy the warmth of the Steinhardt Conservatory, filled with orchids, tropical plants, palms, the largest collection of bonsai trees in the West and a lovely lower-level gallery for art inspired by nature. One part that's not season-determinant is the Celebrity Path, a stone walkway that honours Brooklyn's famous sons and daughters. A gift shop stocks a wide array of exotic plants, bulbs and seeds, and there is a pleasant outdoor café.

Park Slope

The western exits of Prospect Park leave you in **Park Slope**, a district of stately nineteenth-century brownstone townhouses inhabited since the 1970s by a notoriously liberal crew of urban pioneers; it's also in an eternal baby boom, and strollers jam the pavements, especially on weekends. The most central subway station is the Seventh Avenue stop on the #F line (the cross street is 9th St), but you can also walk down Fifth or Sixth avenues from the Bergen Street stop on the #2 and #3 trains.

The tree-lined blocks between Prospect Park West and Eighth Avenue from Union to 15th Street contain some of the finest Romanesque and Queen Anne residences in the US, helping this area earn the nickname "The Gold Coast of Brooklyn". Almost all the buildings were constructed in the 1880s and 1890s, but they're hardly uniform, displaying a fine array of building materials (brick, brownstone and granite in various combinations) and details, from original gaslights to turrets and bay windows. **Seventh Avenue** is the Slope's traditional main drag, lined with all the essentials, from florists and wine shops to cafés and boutiques, but it can feel a bit frumpy. These days you'll find a younger crowd, along with trendier shops, bars and restaurants, on **Fifth Avenue**.

Though they are far outnumbered by straight couples, lesbians have flocked to Park Slope since the 1970s, and there are a couple of lesbian bars in the neighbourhood (see Chapter 28, Gay and lesbian New York, for hangouts). The **Brooklyn Pride Festival & Parade**, a community-oriented, relatively noncommercial event, takes place every June. Older festival-goers say it resembles New York Pride in its early days.

You can learn about the Slope's history at the **Old Stone House** in J.J. Byrne Park, at Fifth Avenue on 3rd Street (Sat & Sun 11am–4pm; $3; ⓣ718/768-3195, ⓦwww.theoldstonehouse.org), famous as the site of one of the most dramatic skirmishes of the Battle of Brooklyn and the first headquarters of the Brooklyn Dodgers baseball team. The reconstructed building contains changing exhibits and a diorama of the house as it looked in its early days.

Prospect Heights

Just north of Grand Army Plaza, **Prospect Heights** has handsome and varied late nineteenth-century residences that rival those of nearby Park Slope. You could spend a pleasant hour or so walking up and down its lovely sidestreets, but its main appeal will likely be its **food and drink** options, which are within easy walking distance of the Brooklyn Museum and the Brooklyn Botanic Garden; **Vanderbilt Avenue** is your best bet.

Green-Wood Cemetery

Southwest of Prospect Park is the famed **Green-Wood Cemetery** (daily: May–Aug 7am–7pm, March–April & Sept–Oct 7.45am–6pm, Nov–Feb 8am–5pm; Ⓦwww.green-wood.com). You can walk here from Park Slope or take the #R train to 25th Street; the cemetery's main entrance is about a block away from the subway stop at Fifth Avenue.

Founded in 1838 and almost as large as Prospect Park at 478 acres, Green-Wood was very much the place to be buried in the nineteenth century. Interred here are politician and crusading newspaper editor Horace Greeley; famed preacher Henry Ward Beecher; William Marcy "Boss" Tweed, Democratic chief and scoundrel; and the entire Steinway clan of piano fame, at peace in a 119-room mausoleum. If you happen to be around during October's **Open House New York**, this is a must-stop for "Angels and Accordions": a walk among the tombstones and catacombs with live dance-and-accordion accompaniment.

Central Brooklyn

The neighbourhoods within **Central Brooklyn** – most notably **Bedford-Stuyvesant** and **Crown Heights**, to the northeast and east of Prospect Park – are far rougher than those in South Brooklyn, but they are worth a look for their architecture and street culture. Predominantly African-American, Bed-Stuy, as it's called, is experiencing a real-estate rush on its brownstone houses, and Crown Heights, with its Hasidic Jewish and West Indian populations, may not be far behind. Keep in mind that while the area is generally safe during the daytime, there's still some street crime, so remain alert.

Bedford-Stuyvesant

Immediately east of Clinton Hill, **Bedford-Stuyvesant** is the nation's largest black community after Chicago's South Side, with more than 400,000 residents. It stretches north–south from Flushing to Atlantic avenues, and east as far as Saratoga; its main arteries include Bedford and Nostrand avenues and Fulton Street. The **Nostrand Avenue** stop on the C train lies closest to the centre of the neighbourhood.

Originally two separate areas, the adjacent districts of Bedford and Stuyvesant were populated by both blacks and whites in the nineteenth century. During the Great Migration between 1910 and 1920, large numbers of southern African Americans moved north and settled in this area. In the 1940s the white population began to leave, taking funding for many important community services with it. Economic decline continued for several decades, reaching an all-time low in the 1980s.

Weeksville

In the shadow of a housing project on the eastern reaches of Bed-Stuy stands one of the most fascinating historical sights in Brooklyn – the remnants of the once-thriving town of **Weeksville**. Founded by African-American James Weeks in 1838 just eleven years after New York abolished slavery, Weeksville soon became a refuge for both escaped slaves from the South and free blacks fleeing racial violence in the North. By the 1860s it had its own schools and businesses, and had begun turning out some of the city's first black professionals. Weeksville existed until the 1930s, but an influx of Eastern European immigrants and a flurry of construction brought it to its end, and by the 1950s all but four wood-frame cottages from the town had been destroyed. Fortunately, in the 1960s local activists petitioned the city to preserve these, the so-called **Hunterfly Road Houses**, at 1698 Bergen St between Buffalo and Rochester, and eventually open three of them to the public. Tour guides do an admirable job filling in atmosphere with stories about Weeksville, gleaned from ongoing research, oral histories and archeological digs (Tues–Fri at 1, 2 & 3pm; $5; ⓣ718/756-5250, ⓦwww.weeksvillesociety.org). To get to Weeksville, take the A or C train to Utica Avenue, walk four blocks south on Utica to Bergen, and turn left.

The poverty and neglect had an unintended upside: because few of its brownstones were razed in the name of economic development, the neighbourhood has the densest collection of pre-1900 homes in New York, attracting a fervent crowd of young fixer-uppers – both white and black – over the past decade.

Gothic, Victorian and other classic brownstones abound, especially inside the **Stuyvesant Heights Historic District**, which includes parts of MacDonough, Macon, Decatur, Bainbridge and Chauncey streets primarily between Tompkins and Stuyvesant avenues; an annual five-hour house tour is conducted in October ($15–20; ⓦwww.brownstonersofbedstuy.org). Outside the main historic section, make sure to swing by the landmark **Boys' High School**, at 832 Marcy Ave, on any wanderings; the Romanesque Revival pile is an astonishing sight and saw the likes of Norman Mailer pass through its halls. The couple of blocks of Jefferson and Hancock streets between Nostrand and Tompkins are as dignified and radiant as any in the city.

Crown Heights

South of Bedford-Stuyvesant and east of Prospect Heights is thrumming **Crown Heights**, bounded by Atlantic Avenue and Empire Boulevard to the north and south, and Ralph and Washington avenues to the east and west. This community is home to the largest **West Indian** community in New York as well as an active, established population of about ten thousand **Hasidic Jews**, most of them belonging to the Russian Lubavitcher sect.

Eastern Parkway, the large throughway that runs past the Brooklyn Museum, is the main traffic artery of Crown Heights, and landscaped walkways on either side of the path provide much-needed green space. North of Eastern Parkway, the **Brooklyn Children's Museum**, at 145 Brooklyn Ave on St Mark's Avenue (Wed–Fri 11am–5pm, Sat & Sun 10am–5pm; $7.50; ⓣ718/735-4400, ⓦwww.brooklynkids.org), was the first museum of its kind, founded way back in 1899; a recent "green" renovation and expansion by Uruguayan architect Rafael Viñoly added solar panels and other energy-saving devices, doubled the space and gave the museum the chance to modernize its collection. Galleries hold hands-on exhibits concentrating on science, the environment, local neighbourhood life and much more; the "Waterworks" play area and the live animals on display downstairs should especially thrill the younger set. The closest subway is the #3 to Kingston Avenue.

Over Labor Day weekend, Crown Heights hosts the annual **West Indian–American Day Parade and Carnival**, during which almost two million revellers dance, eat and applaud colourful floats and steel-drum outfits. The parade, which organizers claim is the biggest in the nation, runs west along Eastern Parkway from Rochester Avenue in Crown Heights to Grand Army Plaza (see Chapter 32, "Parades and festivals", for more information). To get a taste of West Indian culture and cuisine year-round, take the #3 train to Nostrand Avenue, where there's a string of dirt-cheap Caribbean snack joints. Of these, *Imhotep Health and Vegan*, at 734 Nostrand Ave on Park Place, and *Gloria's*, at 764 Nostrand Ave on Sterling Place, are both reliably good.

Ditmas Park and Midwood

South of Prospect Park, a few undervisited areas provide some fun exploration, assuming you have the time and aren't set on just seeing major parks and museums. **Ditmas Park** has the city's most attractive collection of stand-alone Victorian mansions, on the lot bordered by Stratford, Cortelyou, Marlborough and Albemarle; it feels as far removed from the city as you can get. After wandering up and down, hit Cortelyou Road for its burgeoning collection of cool restaurants and cafés.

A bit further south, **Brooklyn College** is the most attractive part of **Midwood**, and you're free to walk around the manicured green of the small campus. The area's other claim to fame is as the home to *Di Fara's* (see review, p.302), which many consider to be the best pizzeria in the whole of New York.

Coney Island and around

It's possible, in theory, to walk, rollerblade or bike almost the entire southern **coast** of Brooklyn. On occasion paths disappear, and you must share the service road off the highway with cars, but you'll never be on the highway itself. Even those of less sturdy stock will find this area – which stretches east from **Bay Ridge** through **Coney Island**, **Brighton Beach** and several smaller neighbourhoods all the way to maritime Sheepshead Bay – worth visiting for the breathtaking views, carnival amusements and varied cuisine. If you're not on a bike or similarly speedy transport, though, you'll do best to focus on Brighton Beach and adjacent Coney Island, which make an easy afternoon trip by subway.

Bay Ridge

The last few stops of the R train are in Bay Ridge, in the farthest corner of southwest Brooklyn. This large, quiet neighbourhood is known for its ethnic mix (Chinese, Irish, Italians, Scandinavians and Lebanese) and good schools; senior citizens, many of them longtime residents, make up a large chunk of the population.

The main reason to visit Bay Ridge is to ride the **Shore Road Bike Path**, which offers a glorious ride along the bay, including views of the shimmering **Verrazano Narrows Bridge** (built in 1964), which flashes its minimalist message across the entrance to New York Bay. At 4260ft, this slender, beautiful span was, until Britain's Humber Bridge opened in 1981, the world's longest. The bridge, which connects Brooklyn to Staten Island (p.264), is named for the first European explorer of New York Harbour, Giovanni da Verrazano. You can't pedal across it, unfortunately: urban planner Robert Moses vetoed the pedestrian/bicycle pathways that flanked the roadway in the original design for fear they'd lead to a rash of suicides.

To reach the bike path, get off the #R train at Bay Ridge Avenue (locals know it as 69th St) and ride west toward the water (if you are on foot, the B1 and B9 buses can take you this way). At the pier, a path leads south right along the water's edge, but to see some of Bay Ridge's nicest homes, turn left before the water on Shore Road. Wind through Shore, Narrows and River roads between 75th and 83rd streets, where you'll see some Greek and Gothic Revival houses. Most distinctive is the **Gingerbread House**, at 8220 Narrows Ave on 83rd Street; the 1916 structure, done in a rare style known as Black Forest Art Nouveau, looks like a witch's backwoods lair, all piled-up stones and drooping eaves.

A bit less pastoral but still worth a visit, the **US Army Garrison Fort Hamilton** is a historic military base at 101st Street and Fort Hamilton Parkway. The **Harbor Defense Museum** of Fort Hamilton (Mon–Fri 10am–4pm, Sat 10am–2pm; free; Ⓣ718/630-4349, Ⓦwww.harbordefensemuseum.com) is in an 1840 stone structure once used to protect the fort from any possible rear attack. Artefacts and weapons – guns, mines, missiles, cannon – tell the official history of the defence of New York Harbor.

Coney Island

Accessible to anyone for the price of a subway ride (take the D, F, N or Q train to the last stop at Stillwell Ave), beachfront **Coney Island** has given working-class New Yorkers a holiday ever since a kerosene-lit carousel opened here in 1867. A series of fabulous amusement parks drew huge crowds on hot summer days over the years until the 1960s, when the area fell into slow decline, only to be adopted and re-popularized by a hip crowd of historians and artists drawn to its retro charm in the 1990s.

While Coney's down-at-the-heel days may be numbered (see box below), it remains an enjoyable place to spend an afternoon or evening, despite its seediness. Most rides and attractions are open daily only from late May to early September, with weekend hours in the spring and autumn. If you can, visit Coney Island on a Friday night during the season, when the beach is lit up by an impressive **fireworks** display. The raucous annual **Mermaid Parade** (Ⓦwww.coneyisland.com) in mid- to late June ranks as one of the oddest, glitziest small-town festivals in the country, where participants dress (barely) as mermaids, King Neptunes and other sea-dwellers.

Upon arrival, head straight for **Nathan's**, on the corner of Surf and Stillwell avenues. This is the home of the "famous Coney Island hot dog", a must for all

A corporate Coney Island?

Since the cleanup in Times Square in the 1990s, Coney Island has stood as the city's last great outpost of borderline-seedy, honky-tonk commercialism. But in recent years, all sorts of rumours have swirled over what direction it will take and whether or not its ramshackle charm will withstand new developments. A local developer, Thor Equities, bought up big swathes of the district in 2006 with the idea of building a billion-dollar **Vegas-style resort** on the boardwalk, complete with luxury condos and "entertainment retail". As well as not passing zoning muster, the plans angered community leaders, who argued that a national treasure would be lost in the corporate makeover. The city and the Municipal Arts Society, an important preservation advocacy group, each have their own competing ideas of what should be done; the only thing that seems certain is that the most iconic features – its wooden boardwalk, roller coaster, Ferris wheel, hot dog stand, baseball park and museum – will remain intact.

visitors (bar vegetarians). *Nathan's* holds a well-attended annual **Hot Dog Eating Contest** on July 4; the record is held by repeat-champion Joey Chestnut, who downed 68 hot dogs in ten minutes. One block from *Nathan's* is the famous **boardwalk**, where hip-hop blares from boom boxes and loudspeakers, and the language of choice is Spanish or Russian as often as English.

The amusement park area, inland of the boardwalk, has at its centre the newly constructed **Luna Park** ($26–30 for unlimited rides; Ⓦ www.lunaparknyc.com), which is flanked by the two best, most thrilling attractions – **the Wonder Wheel** and **the Cyclone** (each has its own attendant park and is operated independently). The **Wonder Wheel** ($6; Ⓣ 718/372-2592, Ⓦ www.wonderwheel.com) is good fun: an official New York City landmark, the 1920 ride is the world's tallest Ferris wheel aside from the London Eye. From the top you get panoramic views of Coney Island and the ocean. Far scarier, the **Cyclone** roller coaster ($8;

▲ The Cyclone, Coney Island

Ⓣ718/265-2100, Ⓦwww.coneyislandcyclone.com), a creaky wooden contraption more than 80 years old, is not for the faint of heart – as you wait in the snaking line, you can actually see the cars lose contact with the metal rails at one point. Sit in front for the most terrifying view, in back for an extra-strong sense of vertigo.

Another great summer attraction is **KeySpan Park**, on Surf Avenue between West 17th and 19th streets, the scenic oceanside baseball stadium that has helped lend a more prosperous air to the neighbourhood. The park is home to the **Brooklyn Cyclones** (see p.413), a New York Mets-affiliated minor-league team that draws a dedicated crowd. Seating is intimate, beer flows freely and tickets start at just $8.

Coney Island Museum and New York Aquarium

East of Stillwell Avenue, the nonprofit **Coney Island Museum**, at 1208 Surf Ave (Fri & Sat noon–5pm; 99¢; Ⓣ718/372-5159, Ⓦwww.coneyisland.com/museum.shtml), is one indoor destination you don't want to miss. You can tour relics of Coney Island past, hear a lecture on the beach's history or catch a night-time burlesque performance or film screening. **Sideshows by the Seashore**, on West 12th St at Surf Ave, is a 45-minute show featuring sword-swallowers, contortionists, fire-eaters, glass walkers and other skilful masochists (late May to early Sept Fri 2–8pm, Sat–Sun & holidays 1–9pm; weekends only from Easter to Memorial Day and Sept; $7.50 adults, $5 children under 12; no reservations).

Continue east on the boardwalk, halfway to Brighton Beach, to reach the seashell-shaped **New York Aquarium**, at Surf Ave and West 8th St (June–Aug Mon–Fri 10am–6pm, weekends until 7pm; Sept–Oct & April–May daily 10am–5.30pm, Nov–March daily 10am–4.30pm; $13, children 3–12 $9; Ⓣ718/265-FISH, Ⓦwww.nyaquarium.com), a top-of-the-line operation run by the Wildlife Conservation Society, which also administers New York's four excellent zoos. More than eight thousand eye-grabbing creatures from all over the world live here in an array of indoor and outdoor tanks and pools. Especially worth seeing are the otherworldly jellies, corals and anemones in the Alien Stingers Exhibit.

Brighton Beach

East along the boardwalk from Coney Island, at Brooklyn's southernmost end, **Brighton Beach** was once an affluent seaside resort of its own. Often called Little Odessa, it is now home to the country's largest community of immigrants from Russia and the former Soviet states, who started relocating here in the 1970s. The eldest of them pack the boardwalk benches to soak up the sun and gossip. Reach the neighbourhood by riding the B or Q train to the Brighton Beach stop, or just walk down the boardwalk from Coney Island.

Brighton Beach Avenue runs parallel to the boardwalk; the street is a bustling mixture of Russian souvenir shops and **food emporiums**. Pick up picnic fixings at **M & I International**, at 249 Brighton Beach Ave (Ⓣ718/615-1011), which has a staggering selection of smoked fish, sausages, cheeses, pickles (many soaked in vodka rather than vinegar) and breads. Sit-down food is also readily available at restaurants on the boardwalk, though you might want to wait until evening, when the **supper clubs** open up. These cavernous places offer a near-parody of a rowdy Russian night out, complete with lots of food, loud music, surreal floor shows and plenty of vodka (see "Restaurant" listings, p.340, for reviews).

Northern Brooklyn

Northeast of downtown and past Fort Greene are the neighbourhoods of **Williamsburg**, which is divided among artsy refugees from Manhattan and sections that are strongly Hasidic Jew or Latino, and **Greenpoint**, a Polish stronghold that's in turn being inundated by artsy refugees from Williamsburg. While short on typical tourist attractions, these districts are long on atmosphere, whether you want to ogle tattooed twenty-somethings or immerse yourself in the sounds of Spanish, Yiddish or Polish.

Williamsburg

Get off the L train at the **Bedford Avenue** stop and you'll be in the hipster heart of Williamsburg, where the streets teem with a particular breed of self-consciously downmarket bohemian, decked out in vintage clothes and hopping from coffee shop to record store to nifty boutique. Some would argue that the real hipsters have decamped to the far east of the area or Bushwick or some other

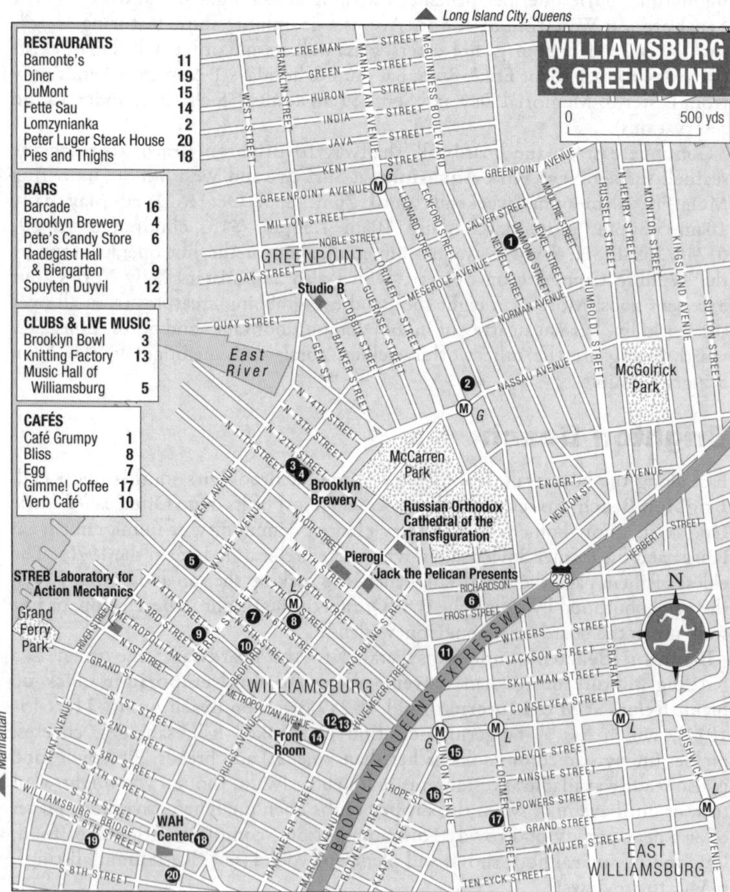

on-the-verge neighbourhood, but there's still enough of an alternative pulse to keep things interesting.

The densest concentration of activity is on Bedford itself, but many of the more interesting spots are found elsewhere, having gravitated towards cheaper rents. **Grand Street**, for one, is lined with some fine galleries and shops, and some of the formerly industrial spaces on **North Sixth Street** between Bedford and Wythe avenues are now filled with bars and design stores. **Metropolitan Avenue** also has some good bars and restaurants.

The forty or so galleries in the neighbourhood include the pioneering **Pierogi**, at 177 North 9th St between Bedford and Driggs, though its heyday is past; some of the city's best secondhand clothing shops are close by (see Chapter 30, Shopping). On the other end of the neighbourhood, next to the Williamsburg Bridge, the **Williamsburg Art and Historical Center**, at 135 Broadway on Bedford (Sat & Sun noon–6pm or by appointment; ⓣ718/486-7372, ⓦwww.wahcenter.net), displays local painting and sculpture in a vast gallery on the second floor of the imposing Kings County Savings Bank.

If you're interested in doing serious gallery-hopping in the neighbourhood, pick up the free monthly booklet *Wagmag* (ⓦwww.wagmag.org), which includes a Williamsburg gallery map and a list of special events, at any bookstore or gallery (Pierogi always has a good supply), or visit on the second Friday night of the month for **Williamsburg Every Second**, when many galleries stay open until 9 or 10pm and host performances and parties.

As befits a place with vast warehouses to be used and culture-hungry twenty-somethings to be fed, Williamsburg hosts a thriving music and performance scene, with venues like the **Music Hall of Williamsburg**, at 66 North 6th St on Wythe (see p.360 for review), sponsoring some of the best indie-rock shows in the city. Nearby at the **STREB Laboratory for Action Mechanics**, at 51 North 1st St on Kent (ⓣ718/384-6491, ⓦwww.streb.org), a troupe of gymnastic athletes puts on a stripped-down version of Cirque du Soleil – flying through the air in harnesses, dodging spinning iron beams, springing off trampolines, and doing flips off the wall – during its fall and spring SLAM shows.

But the cutting-edge feel of Williamsburg is already changing: ultra-sleek waterfront high-rises have sprouted up, capitalizing on views like the one from tiny **Grand Ferry Park**, where Grand Street dead-ends between a power station and another industrial complex; just south the Williamsburg Bridge soars over the river and the massive Domino's Sugar Factory is itself being converted into housing. Many artists have been forced further down the L line to find affordable space.

Brooklyn beer

In 1900 nearly fifty breweries operated in Brooklyn, but the last of these, Schaefer and Rheingold, closed in 1976. For years after its founding in 1987, the **Brooklyn Brewery**, at 79 North 11th St (ⓣ718/486-7422, ⓦwww.brooklynbrewery.com), was "Brooklyn" in name only – the founders had their beer produced upstate. But in 1996 the operation moved into its Williamsburg headquarters, reviving Brooklyn's brewing tradition and making Brooklyn Lager a very popular beverage citywide.

The community-oriented Brooklyn Brewery hosts events throughout the year; hang out in its cafeteria-style beer hall 6–11pm Fridays or take a free tour on Saturdays (1, 2, 3, 4 and 5pm, no reservations necessary). Tours are perfunctory – they're just a hurdle on the way to the free beer at the end, when you can sample a half-glass each of the two best drafts (Brooklynator Dobbelbock and Brooklyn Extra Brune) or the special seasonal brews.

South-side Williamsburg, by contrast, seems frozen in time, especially in the vicinity of **Lee Avenue** or Bedford Avenue, which run parallel between Division Avenue and the Brooklyn–Queens Expressway. Here, kosher delicatessens line the streets and signs are written in Yiddish and Hebrew thanks to the large population of **Hasidic Jews** in the area. The community has been here since 1903, when the Williamsburg Bridge brought over many Jews from the cramped Lower East Side. At the end of World War II a further settlement of Yiddish-speaking Hasidic Jews, mainly from Romania, became the majority.

Greenpoint

Quiet **Greenpoint**, which hugs the northern border of the borough, has the distinction of being the childhood home of Mae West, the birthplace of the oft-ridiculed Brooklynese accent, and home to the largest Polish community in New York City; there's also a substantial Puerto Rican contingent. Reachable by the #G train to Greenpoint Avenue, the homely, low-rise area has absorbed some of the artsy feel of Williamsburg to the south, but the younger residents haven't diluted the Polish character of the businesses along its tidy main strip, **Manhattan Avenue** (partly because they're establishing their own strip on **Franklin St**).

While Greenpoint and neighbouring areas were originally known as Boswijck (later Bushwick), meaning "wooded district", the Industrial Revolution took the "green" out of Greenpoint, as the area became home to the "Black Arts" – printing, pottery, gas, glass and iron. In 1950, refineries caused a 17- to 30-million-gallon underground oil spill, larger than the *Exxon Valdez* disaster in Alaska, which spilled "only" 11 million gallons. It's not immediately visible except as an occasional slick on the surface of Newtown Creek, which separates Greenpoint from Queens, but it's very much on the minds of residents who fear the toxic effects of the residue. Cleanup is ongoing, but still has years to finish – if that's even possible at this point.

These things aside, Greenpoint merits a quick visit for its blend of Polish and hipster cultures and their respective cuisines. If you're coming from Williamsburg, take Driggs Avenue north past the **Russian Orthodox Cathedral of the Transfiguration**, at North 12th St on Driggs, a New York City landmark whose five green-copper onion domes hover above the trees of **McCarren Park**. The park itself forms the unofficial line between Greenpoint and Williamsburg, and is undergoing a major renovation until 2012 – when the pool will be restored and reopened, ending its status as a summer rock venue (concerts have moved over to East River State Park, on Williamsburg's waterfront).

Turn left on Manhattan Avenue and continue straight to get to the heart of Greenpoint. Along the way you'll find an assortment of Polish delis and bakeries, which spill over onto Nassau, where **Steve's Meat Market**, at 104 Nassau Ave between Leonard and Eckford (Ⓣ718/383-1780), claims to make the best *kielbasa* (spicy Polish sausage) in the US. Wander down the narrow sidestreets and you'll get a feel for the tightknit local community – and how it is changing. *Café Grumpy*, at 193 Meserole Ave on Diamond, is a magnet for newcomers, with top-of-the-line espresso and a consistently cool soundtrack, while further toward the water, an assortment of bars and restaurants has sprouted up along Franklin Street and around Greenpoint Avenue.

19

Queens

Of New York City's four outer boroughs, **Queens** was for many years probably the least visited – not counting when outsiders passed through Queens' airports, JFK and LaGuardia. If Brooklyn, with its strong neighbourhood identities and elegant architecture, represents the old, historic city, then Queens, with its ever-shifting ethnic composition and frankly utilitarian housing stock, represents the "new" New York – the city as an international crossroads, the melting pot on full boil.

Queens is, in fact, the most diverse county in the US, with nearly half of the borough's 2.3 million residents foreign-born, and these hailing from 150 different countries. Not surprisingly, the borough is something of a culinary hotspot. Take the elevated #7 train to **Woodside**, **Jackson Heights** and **Flushing** and you can eat Thai drunken noodles, Indian vindaloo and Colombian *arepas*, respectively. In **Astoria** (N & R trains) you'll find Bosnian *burek* and Greek *spanikopita*, Brazilian *feijoada* (black bean stew) and Egyptian braised lamb cheeks.

Culturally, the richest spot in Queens is **Long Island City**, where a cluster of galleries has cropped up around the contemporary art centre MoMA PS 1, an affiliate of midtown's Museum of Modern Art. Farther out, **Flushing Meadows–Corona Park** draws sports fans and families – the former to the **New York Mets**' new stadium, Citi Field, and the USTA Billie Jean King National Tennis Center, home of the **US Open Tennis Championships** each autumn, and the latter to the Queens Museum, Queens Zoo and New York Hall of Science. At the southeast end of the borough (accessible via the #A train), in **Jamaica Bay** and the **Rockaways**, lie pristine parks and beaches that feel miles from the city.

For information on the borough and discounts at local merchants, contact Discover Queens (ⓣ718/263-0546, ⓦwww.discoverqueens.info).

Navigating Queens

One reason many New Yorkers have no love for Queens is the deeply unsettling street-number system, which can leave you baffled on the corner of 30th Road and 30th Street. But the so-called "Philadelphia method" of addressing, applied borough-wide in the 1920s, does have an underlying logic. Basically, **streets** run north–south, while **avenues, roads and drives** run east–west. Avenue numbers get higher as you head south, while street numbers get higher as you head east (First Street is on the East River, and 180th is in Jamaica). And in Queens, addresses let you know right where you are: the digits before the hyphen indicate the cross street: 20-78 33rd Street, for instance, is between 20th and 21st avenues.

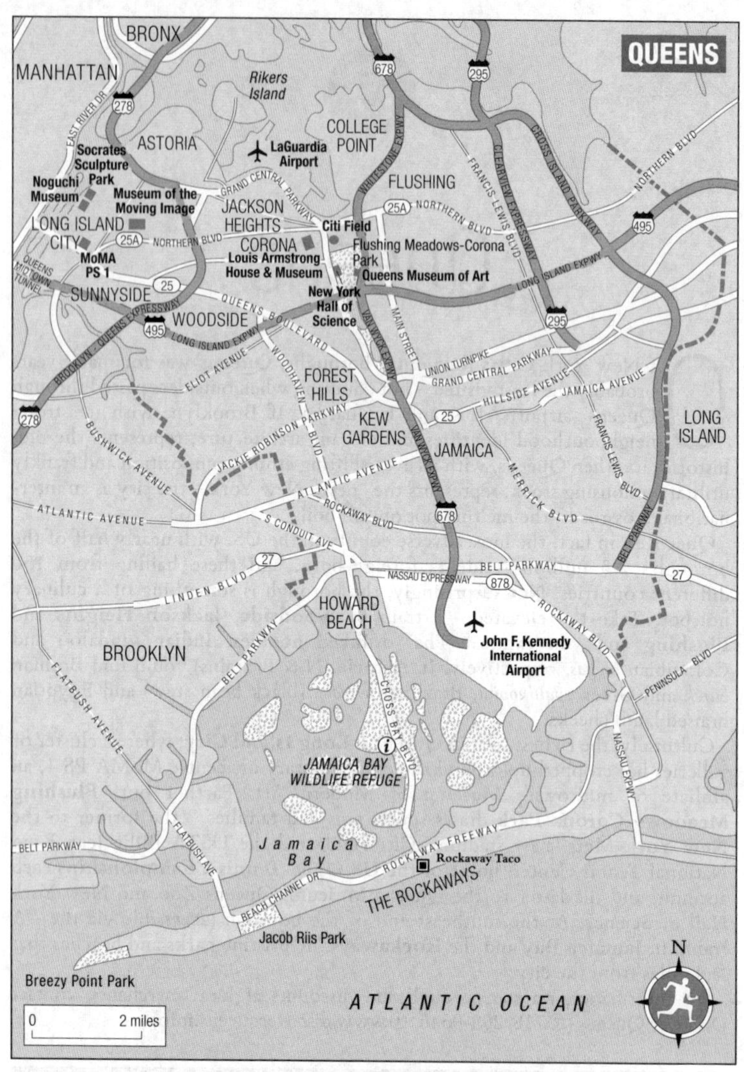

Long Island City and Astoria

Long Island City and **Astoria**, only a few minutes by subway from midtown Manhattan, rank as the hippest neighbourhoods in Queens. It can be a little unclear which is which given that the whole area is technically Long Island City, with Astoria a self-designated neighbourhood within it. Practically speaking, though, most people think of Astoria as the part of Long Island City north of 36th Avenue, and Long Island City as the area south of the Queensboro Bridge and north of the Long Island Expressway. Astoria is far more residential and has more destination-type sights, like museums focusing on movie history and the sculptor Isamu Noguchi, though Long Island City does have some charming pockets among its largely industrial streets as well as cultural draws of its own.

Long Island City

Edging the East River right across from the United Nations, **Long Island City** is but a five-minute ride on the #7 train from Grand Central Terminal, well worth the trip if you're interested in cutting-edge art. If you've been to MoMA, your ticket stub from that institution gets you free entrance into the main attraction, **MoMA PS 1**, while **SculptureCenter** and the **Fisher Landau Center for Art** also put on first-rate shows, as do a number of small galleries. The other cultural claim to local fame is as home to **Silvercup Studios**, the largest film and television production studio on the East Coast, which stretches out along 21st Street next to the Queensboro Bridge. *Sex and the City* (both movies included) and *The Sopranos* were shot here; *30 Rock* still is.

Despite the recent construction of some massive high-rise condo buildings on the waterfront, there's a keen sense of community, which you can feel in the eating and drinking establishments in the **Hunters Point** neighbourhood along **Vernon Boulevard** between 46th and 51st avenues. Stroll two blocks west to get some eye-grabbing views of the United Nations and the east side of Manhattan from sylvan **Gantry Plaza State Park** or **Water Taxi Beach**, a swatch of white sand with an outdoor bar and grill, picnic tables, volleyball courts and live bands in the summer.

In the warmer months, the **New York Water Taxi** (Ⓦwww.nywatertaxi.com) docks at the beach, providing a scenic alternative to the subway; you can catch it from East 34th Street in Manhattan, four minutes away, or at a handful of other docks (see the website for schedule and map). The #Q103 bus, which runs along Vernon Boulevard, connects Long Island City with the Noguchi Museum and Socrates Sculpture Park in Astoria.

PS 1 Contemporary Art Center and around

Just steps from the 45th Road–Court Square stop on the #7 (as well as the E, and G trains at 23rd St–Ely Ave) or a ten-minute walk from Hunters Point, the

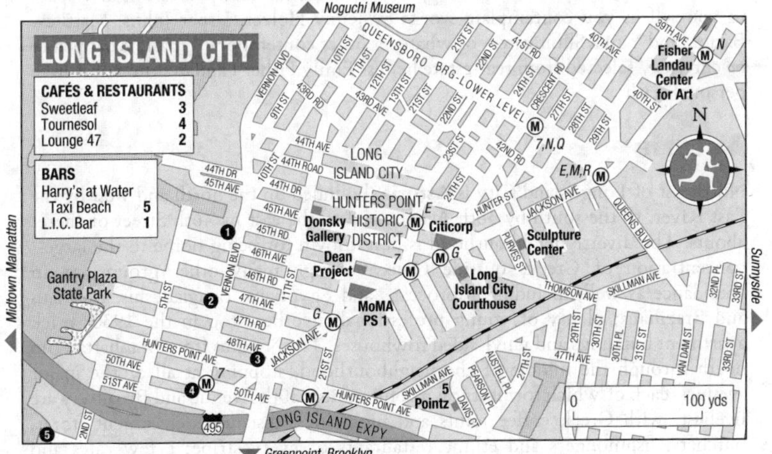

renowned **MoMA PS 1 Contemporary Art Center**, at 22–25 Jackson Ave on 46th Avenue (Mon & Thurs–Sun noon–6pm; $5 suggested donation, free with MoMA ticket; ⓣ718/784-2084, ⓦwww.ps1.org), occupies a hundred-room nineteenth-century brick schoolhouse. Founded in 1971, PS 1 became affiliated with the **Museum of Modern Art** in 2000. Aside from a few long-term installations, it has no permanent collection of its own, instead using its substantial space to mount sprawling thematic shows and retrospectives. *Le Rosier Café* on the ground floor (museum admission not required) is a pleasant, airy spot to rest your feet while grabbing a bite (soups, salads, sandwiches, sorbets), glass of wine or coffee.

There are a few art galleries in the vicinity of PS 1 that are worth popping into if you have the time, including **Dean Project**, at 45-43 21st St, and **Dorsky Gallery**, at 11-03 45th Ave. Across Jackson Avenue from PS 1, the block-long warehouse complex known as **5 Pointz**, at 45–46 Davis St, is covered with graffiti art contributed by hundreds of artists over the course of a decade; it faces an uncertain future, but for the moment you can only stand in awe at the kaleidoscopic work.

Nearby, the **Hunters Point Historic District** centres on 45th Avenue between 21st and 23rd streets, with an immaculate string of late nineteenth-century rowhouses in the shadow of the Citigroup Building, which is the tallest building in the city outside of Manhattan. Past that tower and the Neoclassical **Long Island City Courthouse**, at SculptureCenter, 44-19 Purves St (Mon & Thurs–Sun 11am–6pm; $5 suggested donation; ⓣ718/361-1750, ⓦwww.sculpture-center.org), displays innovative work in a former trolley-repair shop that was cleverly renovated by architect Maya Lin.

Fisher Landau Center for Art

Continuing along Jackson Avenue, you'll soon reach dank, chaotic Queens Plaza, where a spider's web of elevated trains tops an even more elaborate web of congested roads, including those to and from the Queensboro Bridge. On the north side of the plaza, Jackson turns into 31st Street, over which the #N trains rumble into Astoria. Follow the path of the train to 39th Avenue and turn left, then right on 30th Street (or take the N train to 39th Ave), to get to the **Fisher Landau Center for Art**, at 38-27 30th St (Mon & Thurs–Sun noon–5pm; free; ⓣ718/937-0727, ⓦwww.flcart.org). You'll almost certainly have this airy space to yourself as you contemplate works by Jenny Holzer, Jasper Johns, Matthew Barney and Yinka Shonibare – or whatever other contemporary masters happen to be currently selected from real-estate heiress Emily Fisher Landau's thousand-item personal stash.

Astoria

Northeast of Long Island City is **Astoria**, bounded on the north and west by the East River, to the south by 36th Avenue and to the east by 46th Street or thereabouts. The diverse neighbourhood is best known for being home to the largest concentration of Greeks outside Greece though many other groups are in abundance as well, including Moroccans and Egyptians, Bangladeshis, Bosnians and Brazilians; plenty of young professionals live here too in the 1930s brick apartment buildings and vinyl-sided rowhouses. The N trains from Manhattan run north through the middle of the neighbourhood, stopping at all of the major avenues, each of which forms its own community: 30th Avenue and Broadway are liveliest, with Greek coffee joints and nightclubs, discount department stores, butchers, fishmongers and ethnic restaurants of every stripe; a few cafés and

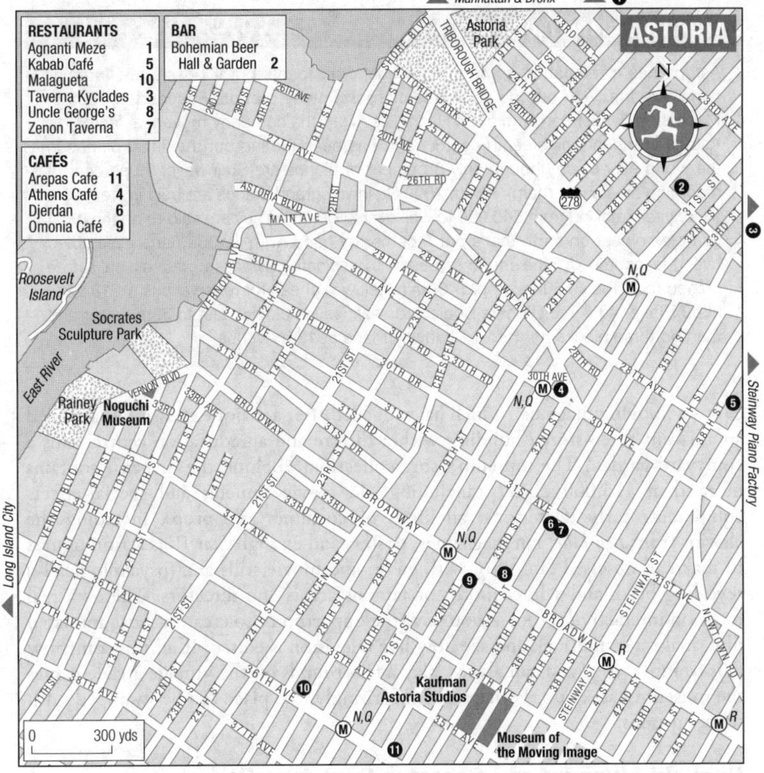

restaurants on 34th and 35th avenues cater to **Kaufman Astoria Studios**' workers and visitors. The **Astoria Boulevard** stop will get you closest to New York's biggest and best beer garden, *Bohemian Hall* (see p.356). Quieter Ditmars Boulevard is home to some of Astoria's oldest residents – the Italians predate the Greeks – and is near **Astoria Park**, which has beautiful views of Manhattan and a mammoth public pool.

Alternatively, you can take the #R to Steinway Street, which accesses the east side of the neighbourhood; between 28th Avenue and Astoria Boulevard, Steinway is a strip of Egyptian- and Moroccan-run businesses, including a glut of **hookah cafés** where you can watch Arabic TV, sip tea and savour sweet apple tobacco.

Museum of the Moving Image

Between 1920 and 1928, Astoria was the capital of America's **silent film industry**, and Paramount Pictures got its start at the present site of Kaufman Astoria Studios, at 35th Avenue on 36th Street, drawing stars such as Rudolph Valentino and the Marx Brothers. Business dried up in the 1930s, when movie-makers were lured to Los Angeles by more reliable weather, but was rekindled in the 1977 with the shooting of Sidney Lumet's **The Wiz**, and the studios are now extremely busy with everything from commercials to blockbusters.

Part of the Kaufman Astoria complex is dedicated to the **Museum of the Moving Image** (call or check website for new hours; ⓣ718/784-0077,

Steinway piano factory

Astoria has a reputation as an international crossroads, but it boasts few international exports, with one notable exception: **Steinway pianos**. Founded in 1853 in Manhattan by German immigrant Henry Steinway, the company moved its factory to Astoria in the late nineteenth century and has been turning out the finest pianos in the world ever since (though only 3 percent of pianos are Steinways, 98 percent of recording artists use them). About 2000 Steinway grand pianos are built in New York every year, retailing from $40,000 to well over $100,000. They are said to be the most complex object on earth that's put together by hand, with 12,000 parts assembled over the course of nine months. See this fascinating process yourself on a free guided tour (Tues 9.30am, approx 90min; call well ahead for reservations ⓣ718/721-2600). Take the #N to Ditmars Boulevard, walk seven blocks east to 38th Street and then go three blocks north to 1 Steinway Place at 19th Avenue.

ⓦwww.movingimage.us), which has reopened after a major expansion that added an adjacent three-storey building with a theatre and an education centre, plus a courtyard garden. The museum's core collection, "Behind the Screen", contains more than 125,000 objects, including old movie cameras and special-effects equipment; early televisions; all kinds of costumes and props, including the chariot from *Ben Hur*; fan magazines, posters and enough *Star Wars* action figures to make an obsessed fan drool with envy; and movie stills and (psychologically) revealing black-and-white photos of famous actors and directors. There's a real focus on interactivity, too, as you have the opportunity to create a short animated film, make a soundtrack and see how live television is edited. If all this somehow fails to move you, you can always play a few rounds on the vintage arcade games the museum has set up. Perhaps not surprisingly, the place can be swamped with school groups.

Noguchi Museum and Socrates Sculpture Park

Off the beaten track but definitely worth the detour, the **Isamu Noguchi Garden Museum**, at 9-01 33rd Rd (Wed–Fri 10am–5pm, Sat & Sun 11am–6pm; $10; ⓣ718/204-7088, ⓦwww.noguchi.org), is devoted to the works of Japanese-American abstract sculptor Isamu Noguchi (1904–88), who worked in Long Island City for many years and designed this museum at his studio site shortly before his death. At its centre is a garden filled with his stone sculptures, while the surrounding galleries include a special section on his design work. It's a place for quiet contemplation of the artist's sublime exercises in simplicity. To get to the museum, take the #N train to the Broadway (Queens) station; head west to Vernon Boulevard, then south two blocks to 33rd Road – about a fifteen-minute walk or a five-minute ride on the #Q104 bus. You can also take the #Q103 bus from Hunters Point or, on Sundays, take a shuttle bus from the Asia Society (p.177); departures are at 12.30pm, 1.30pm, 2.30pm and 3.30pm, with return trips on the hour between 1 and 5pm. The cost is $5 each way.

While you're out this way, stop in at **Socrates Sculpture Park**, one block north of the Noguchi Museum, on Broadway at Vernon Boulevard (daily 10am–sunset; ⓣ718/956-1819, ⓦwww.socratessculpturepark.org). The park was an abandoned landfill until 1986, when sculptor Mark di Suvero transformed it into an outdoor studio, with space for artists to build on a massive scale. The resulting works range from ingenious kinetic installations to bizarre structures that appear to be growing out of the lawn.

Sunnyside, Woodside and Jackson Heights

After Astoria, the E and R trains run north of **Sunnyside** and **Woodside**, historically Irish enclaves now also home to many Asian and Latino immigrants. You're not missing too much if you skip these neighbourhoods on your way to the more interesting **Jackson Heights**, though planning enthusiasts may want to see the **Sunnyside Gardens** development, a utopian working-class "garden city" built in 1924 with encouragement from Eleanor Roosevelt and Lewis Mumford; take the #7 train (which runs straight through Sunnyside and Woodside) to the 46th Street stop and walk north on 46th (the opposite direction from the Art Deco "Sunnyside" sign on Queens Boulevard).

Jackson Heights

East of Sunnyside, the #7 train swings away from Queens Boulevard and heads up narrower Roosevelt Avenue. Get off at 74th Street or 82nd Street (or take the E, F or R to Roosevelt Ave), and you'll find yourself in central **Jackson Heights**, where English is rarely the language of choice.

Developed just after the construction of the elevated train in 1917, the area was laid out as a unified district of tidy brick homes and apartment blocks with attractive garden courtyards (the term "**garden apartment**" was coined here), lending the area a cohesiveness that's rare in Queens. Walking tours of the **historic district** – including its private gardens – are offered during Historic Jackson Heights Weekend each June (ⓦwww.jhbg.org). If you're not on a tour, take a stroll down 35th and 37th avenues between 78th and 88th streets to get a feel for the architecture.

The neighbourhood is the most diverse in the city, with especially large concentrations of Latin American immigrants. Amble up **Roosevelt Avenue** and you'll find Argentine steakhouses, Colombian street vendors selling treats such as *arepas* (savoury corn cakes) and Mexican bakeries displaying stacks of bread and pastries.

Little India, along 74th Street between Roosevelt and 37th Avenue, is something of a contrast. This is the largest Indian community in New York, and South Asians from all over come here to find colourful saris, elaborate gold jewellery for weddings, groceries and music, and perhaps a pungent betel leaf from a street cart. The restaurants here far surpass the more quotidian fare on better-known East 6th Street in Manhattan: *Jackson Diner*, at 37-47 74th St, is one of the best – see p.343 for a review.

Corona and Flushing Meadows

East of Jackson Heights is gritty **Corona**, immortalized in Queens native Paul Simon's song *Me and Julio Down by the Schoolyard*. Once entirely Italian (*corona* is Italian for "crown"), the neighbourhood is now mostly first-generation immigrants from the Dominican Republic, Mexico, Ecuador and Colombia, and about a fifth of households live below the poverty line. It's also home to **Louis Armstrong House** and **Flushing Meadows–Corona Park**, home to the Mets' Citi Field and the USTA National Tennis Center.

To get to the **Louis Armstrong House**, at 34-56 107th St, between 34th and 37th avenues (Tues–Fri 10am–5pm, Sat & Sun noon–5pm; $8; ⓣ718/478-8274, ⓦwww.satchmo.net), take the #7 train to 103rd Street–Corona Plaza, walk north on 104th Street, turn right on 37th Avenue and then left on 107th Street. Opened as a museum in 2003, the great jazz artist's home has been preserved just as he and his wife, Lucille, left it. Armstrong, who lived here from 1943 until his death in 1971, made audio recordings of the day-to-day goings-on in the house, and these play inside, creating a ghostly atmosphere. Guided tours, which show off Armstrong's trumpets and various other artefacts, start every hour on the hour (last one begins at 4pm). If you'd like to learn more about Queens' substantial jazz history, you can also see the house as part of the **Queens Jazz Trail Tour**, which runs from Flushing Town Hall (see p.252) on the first Saturday of every month and visits the neighbourhoods where Ella Fitzgerald, Count Basie and others lived.

Flushing Meadows–Corona Park

About seven blocks east of the Armstrong House, **Flushing Meadows–Corona Park** is an enormous (1200-acre) swathe of green first laid out in the 1930s, and its few key attractions – a couple of interesting museums, a zoo, and some relics of the two World's Fairs held here (see box below) – make for a good afternoon out, especially if you have children who need space to run around. Take the #7 train to the Mets-Willets Point stop and walk south past the tennis complex to the park; or head directly to the museums by getting off at the 111th Street station and walking south on 111th Street until you hit the park's northwest corner.

Citi Field replaced decrepit Shea Stadium as the home field of the **New York Mets** baseball team in April 2009. The new stadium seats 45,000 (10,000 fewer than Shea) and has an old-fashioned facade of brick, granite and cast-stone, mimicking that of old Ebbets Field in Brooklyn, former home of the Brooklyn Dodgers, New York's previous National League franchise. The Mets have a loyal fan base, if for no other reason than that many Queens and Brooklyn residents can't stand the Yankees, though the team's recent woes have alienated many. Due south of the stadium stands the US Tennis Association's **Billie Jean King National Tennis Center**, the largest public tennis facility in the world, with more than twenty indoor and outdoor courts. The main event, the US Open Tennis Championships, takes place at the end of each summer. Tickets to the early matches are easy enough to come by; closer to the finals, you may have to buy from touts. For more details on seeing the Mets and the US Open, see p.413 and p.418; for other sports activities in the park, including one of the few miniature golf courses in the city, see p.421.

The world comes to Queens

In late April 1939, as the US emerged from the Great Depression and war loomed, 1200 acres of the new Flushing Meadows–Corona Park became the stage for America's love affair with modernity. Drawing visitors from across the nation (and delegates from 62 others), the **1939–40 World's Fair** featured displays of technologies yet to be realized, including robotics and fluorescent lights. General Motors sponsored a "Futurama" ride through a utopian modern city, and New Yorkers saw broadcast television for the first time. The fair was a great success, and brought attention to this little-known borough. In part due to the reputation established by the expo, the United Nations briefly operated from here following World War II.

The **1964–65 World's Fair**, held in the same location, in many ways book-ended the era of jubilant optimism that the 1939 fair had opened. While technological and engineering advances such as lasers and computers thrilled 52 million fair-goers, the fair's tone – in the wake of President Kennedy's assassination – was markedly different. Many of the temporary structures stand around the park, either appropriated for other uses or left to decay.

▲ Street scene, Queens

A concrete and stained-glass structure retained from the 1964 World's Fair, the **New York Hall of Science**, 47-01 111th St at 46th Avenue, dazzles imaginative kids with interactive science exhibits (July & Aug Mon–Fri 9.30am–5pm, Sat & Sun 10am–6pm; April–June Mon–Thurs 9.30am–2pm, Fri 9.30am–5pm, Sat & Sun 10am–6pm, Sept–March same hours but closed Mon; $11, children 2–17 $8, free Sept–June Fri 2–5pm & Sun 10–11am; ⓣ718/699-0005, ⓦwww.nysci.org). Parking ($10, but $14 during a Mets home game) is not available during the US Open.

The adjacent **Queens Zoo**, at 53-51 111th St (April–Oct Mon–Fri 10am–5pm, Sat & Sun 10am–5.30pm; Nov–March daily 10am–4.30pm; $7, ages 3–12 $3; ⓣ718/271-1500, ⓦwww.queenszoo.com), is not nearly as spectacular as those in Central Park and the Bronx, although it has transformed Buckminster Fuller's 1964 geodesic dome into a dizzying aviary, and some beautiful big animals – including bison, Shetland cattle and elk – roam the grounds.

East of the zoo, the **Unisphere** is a 140ft-high, stainless-steel globe that weighs 380 tons – probably the main reason why it was never moved after the 1964 fair. Robert Moses intended this park to be the "Versailles of America", but the severe, perfectly symmetrical pathways radiating out from the sphere, the anachronistic and often bizarrely ugly architecture, and the roaring Grand Central Parkway all feel more Eastern Bloc than French – particularly when you look south and see the rusting towers of Philip Johnson's 1964 **New York Pavilion**, now home to Queens Theatre in the Park (Ⓣ718/760-0064, Ⓦwww.queenstheatre.org). Fortunately, the whole picture is softened a bit on sunny days, when the park swarms with kids on bikes and skateboards.

The park's finest attraction is the **Queens Museum of Art**, housed right next to the Unisphere in a building from the 1939 fair that served briefly as the first home of the United Nations (Wed–Sun noon–6pm, Fri until 8pm in July & Aug; suggested donation $5; Ⓣ718/592-9700, Ⓦwww.queensmuseum.org). Plans are afoot to double the size of the museum by incorporating half of the adjacent building currently occupied by the World's Fair Skating Rink by 2012. The one must-see item in the museum – which should be open throughout the renovation – is the **Panorama of the City of New York**, a product of the 1964 fair. With a scale of one inch to one hundred feet, the 9300-square-foot panorama is the world's largest architectural model, incorporating 895,000 buildings, each hand-carved out of wood, as well as rivers, harbours, bridges and even tiny planes drifting in and out of the airports. Guided tours are held on Sundays at 2, 3 & 4pm. The two other permanent exhibits of note in the museum are the collection of glassworks by **Louis Comfort Tiffany**, who established his design studios in Corona in the 1890s, and the relief map of New York's water supply system, a wood-and-plaster model that dates back to the time of the 1939 World's Fair.

For refreshment after seeing the park, visit the *Lemon Ice King of Corona*, at 52-08 108th St, which has been dishing out refreshing handmade fruit ices for some seventy years.

Flushing

Beyond the eastern edge of the park, at the end of the #7 line, lies **Flushing**, originally an early Quaker community but now most notable as New York's second Chinatown: 55 percent of its population claims Asian ancestry. While it's not as architecturally quaint as Manhattan's Chinatown, it feels more authentic, its bustling **restaurants** and shops catering almost exclusively to locals rather than tourists. Chowhounds say they can taste the difference. (See p.343 for recommendations.)

Head north on **Main Street** from the subway station and you'll pass a couple of old Quaker landmarks, as well as a few other historical buildings. On the west side of Main Street between 39th and 38th avenues is **St George's Church**, an elegant 1854 Gothic landmark with a tall central tower. Just around the corner from Main Street a few blocks north, Romanesque Revival **Flushing Town Hall**, at 137-35 Northern Blvd (daily noon–5pm; Ⓣ718/463-7700, Ⓦwww.flushingtownhall.com), is now a cultural centre with a sophisticated calendar of musical performances; there's also an art gallery inside. Just across the street is a shingle cottage, the **Friends Meeting House**, which dates from 1694, making it the oldest surviving house of worship in the city and the second-oldest Quaker institution in the country. It is open Sundays at 11am for services and noon for tours (free), on which you can also see the centuries-old cemetery (without headstones, as per Quaker tradition).

Flesh out the Quaker story with a quick visit to the **Kingsland Homestead**, at 145-35 37th Ave (Tues, Sat & Sun 2.30–4.30pm; $3; Ⓣ718/939-0647, Ⓦwww.queenshistoricalsociety.org), a small wooden farmhouse maintained by the Queens Historical Society. You can see the house from Bowne Street (which runs south from Northern Boulevard), where it is set back in **Weeping Beech Park**. South of the park on Bowne Street, the 1661 Quaker-style **Bowne House** was the home of John Bowne, who helped Flushing acquire the tag "birthplace of religious freedom in America" by resisting discrimination at a time when the Dutch persecuted anyone who wasn't Calvinist; the house is currently being restored.

Alternatively, you might head south from the Main Street subway station; at the first intersection, with 40th Road, a pavement counter, *Corner 28 Restaurant and Caterers* (full restaurant inside), serves succulent Peking duck to go, either on the bone or in a bun. More treats can be had at the nearby **Golden Mall**, at 41-28 Main St, such as hand-pulled noodles, dumplings and cumin-flavoured lamb. Veer off on Kissena Boulevard and you'll pass the stately **Free Synagogue of Flushing**, no. 41-60 (Ⓣ718/961-0030, Ⓦwww.freesynagogue.org), on your right. The oldest surviving Reform Jewish synagogue in the US, it looks like a small-town courthouse, but with brick additions and blue stained-glass windows.

The #Q65 bus runs south from the synagogue into an Indian community, passing the impressive **Sri Mahã Vallabha Ganapati Devasthãnam**, at 45–57 Bowne St (Mon–Fri 8am–9pm, Sat & Sun 7.30am–9pm; Ⓣ718/460-8484, Ⓦwww.nyganeshtemple.org). Also known as the **Ganesh Temple**, this building honours the elephant-headed Hindu god. *Dosa Hutt*, next door on Bowne Street, provides tasty South Indian snacks while you're down this way.

Jamaica Bay and the Rockaways

The southern edge of Queens is the place to take a break from urban life. **Jamaica Bay Wildlife Refuge** (daily: trails sunrise to sunset, visitor centre 8.30am–5pm; Ⓣ718/318-4340, Ⓦwww.nps.gov/gate) is named for the Jameco Indians, whose territory this once was. Near Broad Channel on the largest of these islands (take the A train to Broad Channel and walk a half-mile north; the #Q53 bus from Rockaway Park or Jackson Heights and the #Q21 from Rockaway Park or Woodhaven also stop here), you can hike trails through the diverse habitats of more than 325 varieties of migrating **birds**; the main loop encircles the West Pond, home to flocks of ducks and geese. A unit of the 26,607-acre Gateway National Recreation Area, which extends through coastal areas of Queens, Brooklyn, Staten Island and New Jersey, this is one of the most important urban wildlife areas in the United States.

Partly enclosing the bay, the spit of **Rockaway** stretches for ten miles southwest of Brooklyn, and is the only place to surf in New York City – take the #A or the #S Rockaway Shuttle, depending on the time of day, to Rockaway Park–Beach 116th Street. *Rockaway Taco*, a couple of stops away at 95-19 Rockaway Beach Blvd (closed Oct–April), makes great snacks for summer beach days. The lovely sands of **Jacob Riis Park** (Ⓣ718/318-4300, Ⓦnyharborparks.org) on the western end of the spit are quieter and more pristine, because it's part of the Gateway NRA. The subway doesn't go there – instead, take the #Q22 bus from Beach 116th or the #Q35 from Flatbush Avenue in Brooklyn; the latter is by far the faster option from Manhattan. This is widely considered to be New York City's best beach, and it features a brick bathhouse and an outdoor clock that have been New York City landmarks since the 1930s. At the westernmost tip of the peninsula, beyond the reach of public transit but an easy bicycle ride from the end of the train line, the heavily Irish cooperative community of **Breezy Point** feels like a beach town imported from another state – come here to truly escape New York.

20

The Bronx

"The **Bronx**?" wrote poet Ogden Nash in 1931. "No thonx!" Nash eventually recanted his two-line barb, but most New Yorkers harbour similar feelings due to the borough's reputation for being tough and crime-ridden. Still, what is true in the **South Bronx** – one of the city's poorest areas – hardly applies to the whole of the Bronx, which harbours beautiful parks, posh neighbourhoods, a world-class botanic garden and zoo, and, of course, **Yankee Stadium**.

With a unique landscape that ranges from greenery to high-rises, the Bronx is New York's only mainland borough. As might be expected, its hilly geography is more like neighbouring Westchester County than Long Island and Manhattan.

First settled in the seventeenth century by a Swedish landowner named **Jonas Bronck**, it became part of New York City in the late nineteenth century. For half a century, it was solidly working class and middle class, only taking a turn into serious poverty in the 1950s, when urban planner Robert Moses sliced the borough in half with the **Cross Bronx Expressway**, severing the South Bronx from its wealthier neighbours to the north. The South Bronx was literally left to burn in the 1970s, taking the reputation of the whole borough down with it, but it has been making a slow recovery in the years since, with substantial residential development over the past decade.

With a few exceptions, such as the **Little Italy** section of Belmont, which is within walking distance of the **Bronx Zoo** and the **New York Botanical Garden,** the Bronx doesn't lend itself to extensive wandering, mainly because sights are spread so far apart. Smart use of public transport, though, can make getting around pretty painless, especially if you use the **bus** and **commuter train** in addition to the subway. The #Bx12 bus winds a useful west–east route, connecting many of the Central Bronx sights and linking the north–south subway lines. (Pick up a Bronx bus map in any subway station.) Special **express buses** run up Madison Avenue (#BxM11), heading straight to the zoo and botanical garden. And the Metro North train will get you to the spectacular **Wave Hill** estate from Grand Central Terminal in less than half an hour.

Find out more about the borough from the **Bronx Tourism Council** (Ⓦwww.ilovethebronx.com) or the **Bronx Council on the Arts** (Ⓣ718/931-9500, Ⓦwww.bronxarts.org). BCA sponsors the free **Bronx Cultural Card**, which provides ten- to fifty-percent discounts on 25 or so of the Bronx's best attractions, shops and restaurants. Pick up a card at any public library in the Bronx or at the BCA office, at 1738 Hone Ave.

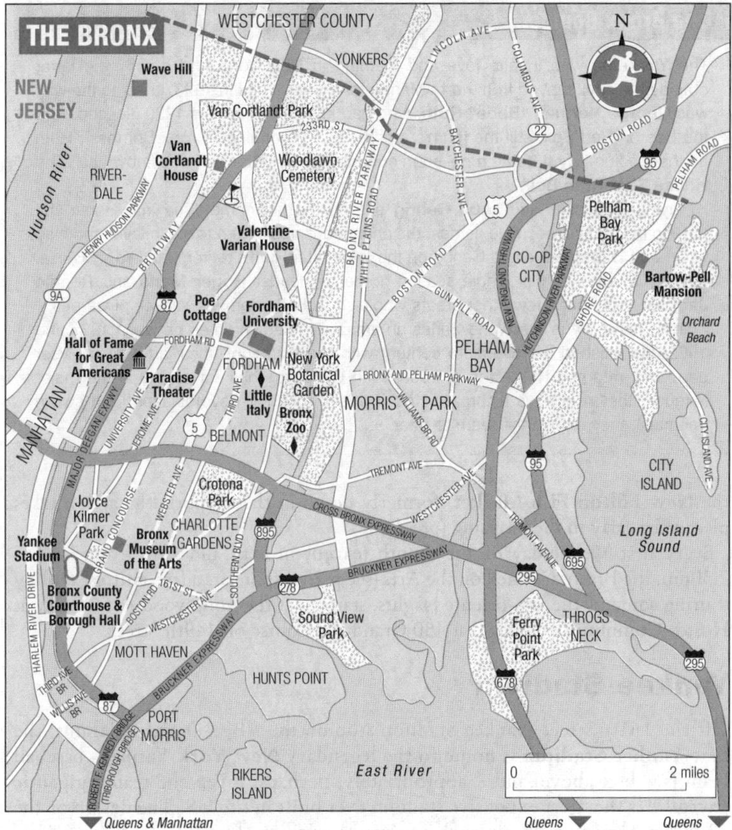

The South Bronx

When most people hear the words "the Bronx", they think of the **South Bronx**, the mostly residential, mostly impoverished area south of the Cross-Bronx Expressway. It was here, on the streets of Hunts Point and other tough neighbourhoods of "the Boogie Down" – hip-hop's name for the borough – that rap, break-dancing and graffiti art were born in the late 1970s. Anyone interested in street culture should do a lot of random strolling, preferably by day, or take a **Birthplace of Hip-Hop Bus Tour** (Ⓣ212/209-3370, Ⓦwww.hushtours.com; $68), led by well-known scene insiders.

The main reason most people visit the South Bronx, though, is to see the New York **Yankees** play on their home field, the new **Yankee Stadium**, which replaced the storeyed "House That Ruth Built" in 2009.

The area southeast of the stadium – mostly in the neighbourhoods of **Hunts Point** and **Mott Haven** – is also a locus of culture for the Bronx, with a handful of community-oriented art galleries and boutiques, and some small performance spaces. Mott Haven, especially, has interesting corners to poke around, with a couple of designated historic districts full of elegant brownstone townhouses, fanciful churches and apartment houses. Hunts Point, meanwhile, is the home of

The Bronx Bombers

The **Yankees**, who inspire love and loathing in New York (and mostly the latter outside the city), moved from north Manhattan to the Bronx in 1923. Leading the way was **George Herman "Babe" Ruth**, who had joined the team in 1920 (fleeced from the Boston Red Sox, still the team's archrivals). The original "Bronx Bomber", Ruth hit the stadium's first home run – soon enough, Yankee Stadium was known as **"The House That Ruth Built"**.

Playing alongside Ruth, **Lou Gehrig** earned the nickname "The Iron Horse" by playing in 2130 consecutive games; the championships began to roll in, even more so when **Joe DiMaggio** joined Gehrig on the team after Ruth's retirement. **"Yogi" Berra**, **Mickey Mantle**, former single season home run leader **Roger Maris** and **Reggie Jackson** were but a few other greats who also wore the famous Yankee pinstripes.

The Yankees won the World Series an amazing nineteen times between 1927 and 1962 and finished the twentieth century with three straight titles; after a nine-year gap, they returned to the top in 2009. With by far the highest payroll in the major leagues, they're always a threat to do it again; for their devoted fans (and sworn enemies), they remain the team to beat.

the **New Fulton Fish Market**, formerly down in the Seaport; the action takes place very early in the morning (pre 7am).

Every first Wednesday of the month (except in Sept and Jan), from 5.30 to 7.30pm, the Bronx Council on the Arts (see p.254) sponsors a free **culture trolley** touring some of the arts-oriented sights, starting at the Longwood Art Gallery at Hostos Community College, at 450 Grand Concourse on 149th Street.

Yankee Stadium

Off the 161st Street–Yankee Stadium stop on the #B, #D and #4 trains, the new **Yankee Stadium** is home to the legendary **New York Yankees** baseball team (see box above) and – appropriately, perhaps, given the team's gigantic payroll – is the most expensive stadium ever built in the US. The design of the 53,000-capacity, open-air park revives aspects of the 1923 stadium – "the house that (Babe) Ruth built" – that were lost in subsequent renovations, such as the limestone and granite exterior facade, and includes a spot for Monument Park, where fans can find retired jersey numbers and plaques honouring famous Yankees.

The best way to see the stadium is, of course, to catch a game (see p.419 for ticket information), though diehards may want to take an hour-long guided tour, which offers access to Monument Park, the field, the dugouts, the press box and clubhouse when available (schedules vary; $20 adults, under 14 and seniors $15; Ⓣ718/579-4531, Ⓦwww.yankees.com). If you do snag tickets to a game, consider taking the **ferry** (Ⓣ1-800/533-3779, Ⓦwww.nywaterway.com) or **Metro North Railroad** (Ⓦwww.mta.info) instead of the jam-packed subway.

The Grand Concourse

From the stadium, walk east up to the aptly named **Grand Concourse**, which is a rather low-income area, though you wouldn't guess it from the street's architecture. In its southern reaches, the concourse is a magnificent wide boulevard marked by tree-lined medians and opulent Art Deco buildings that now house apartments, social-service organizations and retirement homes. Across from Yankee Stadium at 161st Street is the massive **Bronx County Courthouse and Borough Hall**, a 1933 construction that combines Neoclassical columns with Art Deco friezes and statuary. North of here stretches **Joyce Kilmer Park**, named for the man who penned the lines "I think that I shall never see / A poem lovely as a tree…" A monument to Louis J. Heintz, who first proposed the Grand Concourse, and the white Lorelei Fountain form a gracious backdrop for residents, who come here to take in the sun on benches and stroll at sunset.

At Grand Concourse and East 165th Street, the **Bronx Museum of the Arts** (Thurs, Sat, & Sun 11am–6pm, Fri 11am–8pm; suggested donation $5; ⓣ718/681-6000, ⓦwww.bronxmuseum.org) occupies a converted synagogue that was expanded and modernized by the renowned firm Arquitectonica in 2006; look for the jagged glass facade. Exhibits of contemporary art by Asian, Latino and African-American artists lie within, and eclectic performances are held on the **first Friday** evening of each month, when admission is free.

Further north along the Grand Concourse, the landmark 1929 **Paradise Theatre**, at no. 2403 (ⓦwww.paradisetheater.com), is an elaborate confection, at least on the inside – though you can only enter if you're here to see a show.

The Central Bronx

The **Central Bronx**, north of the Cross-Bronx Expressway and south of Gun Hill Road, has neither the intense grit of the South Bronx nor the quiet ritz of the borough's extreme north. As in much of the Bronx, its inhabitants are working-class African-Americans, Puerto Ricans and Dominicans, though its historical centre is prestigious (and predominantly white) **Fordham University**, founded by Jesuits in 1841 and set on lush green lawns. Other points of interest include **Belmont**, better known as the Bronx's Little Italy, and verdant **Bronx Park**, home to the city's prized **Bronx Zoo** and **New York Botanical Garden**. Serious sightseers can seek out the **Poe Cottage** and the **Hall of Fame for Great Americans**.

Belmont

Smack in the middle of the Bronx, and within easy walking distance of the Fordham University campus, the New York Botanical Garden, and the Bronx Zoo, **Belmont** is home to one of New York's largest Italian-American communities, with its main thoroughfare, **Arthur Avenue**, offering a more authentic and low-key alternative to Little Italy in Manhattan. To get here, take the #4 or D train to Fordham Road, then transfer to the eastbound #Bx12 for the short ride to Arthur Avenue, or take the #2 train to Pelham and transfer to the #Bx12 bus headed west. Almost everything you'll want to see (and taste) lies on Arthur between Crescent Avenue and East 187th Street.

The neighbourhood dates to the late nineteenth century, when Italian craftsmen building the Bronx Zoo settled here, and although Haitians, Mexicans and Albanians also operate businesses on Arthur Avenue, the Italian community dominates, with daily mass at **Our Lady of Mount Carmel Church**, at East 187th Street on Belmont Avenue, still held in Italian (a few days in Spanish as well). Try to come during the Ferragosto di Belmont, on the second Sunday in

September, when residents turn out in their festive best to dance, eat, perform commedia dell'arte and compete in the annual cheese-carving contest.

There is no better part of the Bronx to visit if you want to **eat**. For a snack, opt for clams or oysters on the half-shell from *Cosenza's Fish Market*, at 2354 Arthur Ave, which runs a pavement stand outside the shop in warm weather, or step in to the **Arthur Avenue Retail Market**, no. 2344, a small maze of hanging salami and mozzarella; try *Mike's Deli* near the back for an enormous focaccia sandwich. If you'd rather build your own sandwich, pick up some cheese, meat and antipasto in the market, then head down the block to what is arguably the best Italian bakery in the city, *Madonia Brothers Bakery*, at no. 2348 – the olive bread, thick and chewy and studded with whole salty olives, is a knockout. For pastries and Italian ice cream, drop by 85-year-old *DeLillo Bakery*, at 606 East 187th St on Arthur, once owned by author and native son Don DeLillo's parents. *Roberto*, at 603 Crescent Ave on Arthur, is your best bet for dinner in the area, with elegantly prepared fresh pasta served family style. See p.343 for full reviews.

Bronx Zoo

One of the Bronx's main attractions, the **Bronx Zoo** is the largest urban wildlife park in the country (April–Oct Mon–Fri 10am–5pm, Sat, Sun & holidays 10am–5.30pm; Nov–March daily 10am–4.30pm; $15, seniors $13, kids ages 3–12 $11; Wed by donation, parking $10, additional charges for some rides and exhibits; ⓣ718/367-1010, ⓦwww.bronxzoo.org). If you're walking from Arthur Avenue, follow 187th Street seven blocks east to reach the main entrance, at Southern Boulevard. The closest subway stop is West Farms Square–East Tremont Avenue on the #2 or #5, three blocks south of the Asia Gate at the southeast corner of the zoo. Another option is the #BxM11 express bus ($5, exact change), which runs from Madison Avenue in midtown Manhattan, dropping

▲ Bronx Zoo

visitors near the Bronx River Gate, on the northeast corner. Plan ahead and bring a picnic lunch; there are tables throughout the park where you can spread your feast. Also check the website for daily feeding times, animal exercise times and educational events, and try to come on a weekday to avoid large crowds.

Opened in 1899, the zoo has significantly expanded from its small cluster of original buildings to reach 265 wooded acres harbouring nearly 18,000 creatures in natural-looking habitats. The forty-acre **Wild Asia** exhibit (May–Oct; $4), where tigers, elephants and gaur (big cows) roam relatively freely, is one of the zoo's highlights, though don't expect to linger; the only way to see it is on a narrated twenty-minute, all-inclusive ride on the Bengali Express Monorail train. Also open only in warm weather is the **Children's Zoo** (April–Oct; $3), which allows kids to climb with lemurs, learn camouflage skills from tortoises and feed farm animals.

The innovative **Congo Gorilla Forest** ($3) houses more than 400 African animals representing 55 species, including tiny colobus monkeys, mandrill baboons and the largest population of western gorillas in the country. **Madagascar!**, one of the newer exhibit areas, showcases lemurs, crocodiles, parrots and the plump, reddish-orange tomato frog, among other rare species. Look also at the **Sea Bird Colony**, **World of Reptiles** and the **Himalayan Highlands**, home to endangered species like the red panda and the snow leopard.

In winter, many animals are kept in indoor enclosures without viewing areas, but the endangered Siberian tigers love a snowy day; if you visit the three-acre **Tiger Mountain** habitat at that time, it may just be you and these enormous cats, separated by a thin plate of glass.

New York Botanical Garden

Adjacent to the zoo, just north of Fordham Road, is a quieter but equally worthwhile attraction: the lush, 250-acre **New York Botanical Garden** (Tues–Sun 10am–6pm; $20, under 12 $7, parking $12; ⓣ718/817-8700, ⓦwww.nybg.org). Prices listed above are for all-access tickets, including the conservatory, children's garden, rock and native plant garden, and tram tour; for a short visit, grounds-only tickets ($6, under 12 $1) offer a lot of bang for the buck, especially in warm weather. The main entrance, on Kazimiroff Boulevard opposite Fordham University, is a short walk north from the zoo along Southern Boulevard, which changes to Kazimiroff Boulevard; the gates will be on your left. The nearest subway stop is Bedford Park on the B or D lines (about a twenty-minute walk), but the quickest way to get here from Manhattan is on the Metro North Railroad's Harlem Line, a twenty-minute ride from Grand Central. Get off at the Botanical Garden station and walk across Kazimiroff Boulevard to the Mosholu Gate.

The glittering glass **Enid A. Haupt Conservatory**, built when the park opened in 1891, acts as a dramatic entrance, magnificently showcasing rainforest, aquatic and desert ecosystems. It also houses a palm court with towering old trees and a fern forest, and hosts special exhibits like the popular orchid show in March and the **Holiday Train Show**, a twinkling winter wonderland of miniature structures and model trains, which opens the day after Thanksgiving and runs until mid-January. Elsewhere in the garden, cherry, lilac, maple, conifer, crab apple and rock gardens edge a 50-acre core of native **forest**, and nearly four thousand plants make up the **Peggy Rockefeller Rose Garden**, in bloom in late May/June and early September.

Kids can head to the **Everett Children's Adventure Garden**, twelve acres of plant and science exhibits and some nifty mazes. Programmes let kids cook, taste and draw popular plants such as peppermint, chocolate and vanilla.

Poe Cottage and the Valentine-Varian House

West of Fordham University, just off the Kingsbridge Road stop on the B and D trains, is the **Edgar Allan Poe Cottage**, at Grand Concourse and East Kingsbridge Road (Sat 10am–4pm, Sun 1–5pm; $5; ⓣ718/881-8900, ⓦwww.bronxhistoricalsociety.org), built in 1812. This white-clapboard anachronism on a twenty-first-century working-class Latino block was Edgar Allan Poe's rural home from 1846 to 1849, just before he died in Baltimore. It originally sat on East Kingsbridge Road near East 192nd Street, but was moved here when threatened with demolition. Never a particularly stable character and dogged by financial problems, Poe also had to contend with the death of his wife, Virginia, shortly after they moved in. In his gloom, he did manage to write the short, touching poem *Annabel Lee* (in homage to his wife) and other famous works, including *The Bells*, during his stay. The cottage displays several rooms as they were in Poe's time, as well as a small gallery of 1840s artwork; first stop before the actual house, though, is the new visitor centre, with its sharply angled roof meant to conjure the image of a raven.

The Bronx Historical Society also runs the **Valentine-Varian House**, at 3266 Bainbridge Ave (Sat 10am–4pm, Sun 1–5pm; $5; ⓣ718/881-8900, ⓦwww.bronxhistoricalsociety.org), an eighteenth-century Georgian stone farmhouse that was occupied by the British during the American Revolution. Only recommended for serious history buffs (it requires an extra jaunt north two stops on the D to Norwood–205th St), the museum stands in a small park and contains numerous old photographs that show just how rapidly the Bronx shifted from an agrarian landscape to an urban one.

Hall of Fame for Great Americans

On the picturesque campus of the Bronx Community College – formerly New York University's Bronx campus – stands the **Hall of Fame for Great Americans** (daily 10am–5pm; free; tours ⓣ718/289-5161 or 5877, ⓦwww.bcc.cuny.edu/halloffame), a 630ft-long open-air hilltop colonnade designed by the renowned architect Stanford White in 1900 and studded with bronze busts of the 98 honourees. Together they form a peculiar cast of characters, with world-famous figures like George Washington and Henry David Thoreau rubbing shoulders with virtual unknowns like steamboat builder James Buchanan Eads and dentist William Thomas Green Morton. To get here, take the #4 to Burnside Avenue and walk four blocks west to University Avenue, two blocks north to Hall of Fame Terrace, then west again two blocks to the entrance.

The North Bronx

The **North Bronx**, shorthand for the area above 225th Street in the west and Gun Hill Road in the east, is the northernmost area of the city; anyone who makes it up here usually wants to see the stately **Riverdale** neighbourhood and its incredible riverfront estate **Wave Hill**, the rolling hills of **Woodlawn Cemetery** and **Van Cortlandt Park**, or the ocean views of **City Island** and **Orchard Beach**. Getting up this way by public transport is not impossible – the Metro North Railroad is particularly useful in getting to Riverdale – but if you have access to a car, this is a good time to use it.

Woodlawn Cemetery

With entrances at Jerome Avenue at Bainbridge (last stop, Woodlawn, on the #4) and at Webster Avenue and East 233rd Street (#2 or #5 to 233rd St or Metro North Harlem Line railroad to Woodlawn), venerable **Woodlawn Cemetery** (daily 8.30am–5pm; ⓣ718/920-0500, ⓦwww.thewoodlawncemetery.org) is a huge place and a bucolic joy to walk around. Like Green-Wood in Brooklyn, it boasts a number of tombs and mausoleums that are memorable mainly for their gaudiness, although a few monuments stand out: Oliver Belmont, financier and horse dealer, rests in a Gothic fantasy modelled on the resting place of Leonardo da Vinci in Amboise, France; F.W. Woolworth built himself an Egyptian palace guarded by sphinxes; John H. Harbeck is interred in a (not-so) mini-cathedral with heavy bronze doors; and sculptor Patricia Cronin's 2002 marble *Memorial to a Marriage* depicts the artist and her partner, Deborah Kass, locked in a sleepy embrace. Walking tours run on Sundays at 2pm ($10, $5 students and seniors; call for availability and reservations ⓣ718/920-1470), or you can pick up a self-guided walking tour map at the main gates and security booths to locate the many famous individuals buried here, including Herman Melville, Irving Berlin, Elizabeth Cady Stanton, Joseph Pulitzer, Fiorello LaGuardia, Robert Moses, Celia Cruz, Miles Davis and Duke Ellington.

Van Cortlandt Park

Immediately west of the cemetery across Jerome Avenue (you can also take the #1 train to the end of the line at 242nd St and Broadway) lies vast **Van Cortlandt Park**, a forested and hilly all-purpose recreation space. Apart from the pleasure of hiking and running through its woods or watching a cricket game on the parade ground, the best thing here is the **Van Cortlandt House Museum** (Tues–Fri 10am–3pm, Sat & Sun 11am–4pm; $5, Wed free; ⓣ718/543-3344, ⓦwww.vancortlandthouse.org), nestled in the park's southwestern corner not far from the #1 subway station. This is the Bronx's oldest building, an authentically restored Georgian structure built in 1748, complete with a historically accurate herb garden. New York City's archives were buried for safekeeping on the hills above, and it was in this house that George Washington slept before marching to victory in Manhattan in 1783. The park also holds the country's oldest public golf course (see p.421).

Riverdale and Wave Hill

The lovely, moneyed heights of **Riverdale** – one of the most desirable neighbourhoods in the city – rise above Van Cortlandt Park. The simplest way to get here is to take the Metro North Hudson Line train to Riverdale, a twenty-minute ride from Grand Central; the spectacular country estate of **Wave Hill**, at 249th Street on Independence Avenue, is only a short walk from the station and offers one of the city's best escapes from the urban grind, with lush exotic gardens, greenhouses, an art gallery, several easy but varied nature trails and rolling lawns dotted with Adirondack chairs overlooking the Hudson River and dramatic Palisades (mid-April to mid-Oct Tues–Sun 9am–5.30pm; mid-Oct to mid-April Tues–Sun 9am–4.30pm; $8, Sat 9am–noon & all day Tues free, except May, June, Sept & Oct when Tues is free 9am–noon; ⓣ718/549-3200, ⓦwww.wavehill.org). From the Metro North Station, walk up 254th Street three steep blocks, turn right on Independence Avenue, and proceed two blocks to Wave Hill gate.

At various times home to Teddy Roosevelt (as a child), Arturo Toscanini and Mark Twain, the Wave Hill house was built in 1843 by jurist William Lewis Morris, but credit for the site's astounding beauty goes to George W. Perkins, a partner at J.P. Morgan, who linked the house's property with that of the adjacent villa (now called the Glyndor House) in the early twentieth century and landscaped the grounds with an artistry rivalling that of Central Park creator Frederick Law Olmsted. The Perkins family donated the estate to the city in 1960. Free garden and greenhouse tours begin at the Perkins Visitor Center every Sunday at 2pm; they offer free gallery tours too (Wed & Thurs noon, Sat 2pm). The busy events calendar includes everything from classical music concerts to family art classes to beekeeping workshops. Check the website for details.

City Island

On the east side of the Bronx, 230-acre **City Island** juts into Long Island Sound and has the feel of a seaside New England town (the population is around 5000), albeit one with a bit of urban grit. To get here, take the #6 train to the end of the line (Pelham Bay Park) and transfer to the #Bx29 bus, which runs over a short causeway to and from the mainland, or visit on the first Friday of the month, from 5.30 to 9.30pm, when a **free trolley** runs from the subway station to the Bartow-Pell Mansion Museum, around the island, and back (Ⓣ718/885-9100, Ⓦwww.cityislandchamber.org).

There are a few quirky shops here, like Exotiqa International Arts, at 280 City Island Ave, as well as a small museum, the **City Island Nautical Museum**, at 190 Fordham St (Sat & Sun 1–5pm or by appointment; donation; Ⓣ718/885-0008, Ⓦwww.cityislandmuseum.org), which touts all of the island's claims to fame – the yachts that won the America's Cup from 1958 to 1987 were built here, for instance – and often hosts interesting lectures by local historians.

Most people come for the waterfront **restaurants** though: the food may not be particularly creative, but waterfront dining is a treat. To avoid crowds, come on a weekday, when the fish is also fresher. Try the venerable *Lobster Box*, at 34 City Island Ave (see review, p.344), for old-school seafood, or romantic *Le Refuge Inn*, at 586 City Island Ave (see review, p.344), for French country fare; a few of the fishing piers sell fried clams and beer – *Johnny's* at the end of the road is a good bet.

The Bronx's phantom theme-park

Pelham Bay Park looks to the west over **Co-op City**, a seemingly endless tract of middle-class housing that is one of the Bronx's bleaker icons. Few residents know that their homes stand on New York's great, lost amusement park: **Freedomland**.

Built in the shape of the United States, the 205-acre park opened in 1960 with entertainments based on American history: the great fire of 1871 raged in Chicago, gunfights blazed in the Old Southwest, and earthquakes rocked San Francisco. Reporters loved Freedomland because it inspired such headlines as "Stagecoach Wreck Injures 10 in the Bronx". But the public was not so enthralled. Park developers blamed competition from the 1964 World's Fair in Flushing, though the expo had barely begun when Freedomland declared bankruptcy late in the year. By 1965, Co-op City was in progress: Freedomland had vanished without a trace.

If you'd like to catch your own dinner, rent a boat and pick up some bait at Jack's Bait and Tackle, at 551 City Island Ave (4-person boats $49.99 day Mon–Fri, $59.99 Sat & Sun, including gear; ⓣ718/885-2042, ⓦwww.jacksbaitandtackle.com), or charter a boat with a captain who knows the waters (inquire at Jack's for rates and availability).

Pelham Bay Park and Orchard Beach

From City Island, it's an easy walk to **Orchard Beach**, the easternmost part of expansive **Pelham Bay Park** and one of the few really pleasant additions the "master builder" Robert Moses made to the city. Just make a right after the causeway, then follow the path along the water. Beach and boardwalk pulse constantly with a salsa beat, and **free concerts** are common in summer.

At the northern end of the boardwalk, a sign for the **Kazimiroff Nature Trail** points the way into a wildlife preserve named for Theodore Kazimiroff, co-founder of the Bronx County Historical Society and an amateur naturalist who helped stop these wetlands from being turned into a landfill. The network of trails, which winds through 189 acres of meadow, forest and marsh, is serene and peaceful – a stark contrast with the rest of Pelham Bay Park, now criss-crossed by highways.

The Greek Revival **Bartow-Pell Mansion Museum** (Wed, Sat & Sun noon–4pm; $5; ⓣ718/885-1461, ⓦwww.bartowpellmansionmuseum.org) is a national landmark worth seeing for its beautifully furnished interior, which gives a glimpse of how the other half lived in the 1800s (Mayor LaGuardia wisely commandeered the place for his summer office in 1936); the lavish gardens overlook Long Island Sound. To get there, go back to the Pelham Bay Park subway #6 station and take Westchester Bee-Line bus #45.

21 Staten Island

The free ride across the harbour to **Staten Island** is one of the highlights of New York, but is there any point in getting off the ferry? Primarily a collection of 65 sleepy suburban communities, culturally Staten Island has more in common with New Jersey than with the other four boroughs – most tourists promptly hop on the next boat back to the big city. Yet it would be a mistake to dismiss the "forgotten borough" so readily; its leafy streets harbour some real gems, not least a fabulous Chinese garden, a Tibetan gallery and an authentic colonial village, as well as some excellent Sri Lankan restaurants and plenty of parks and beaches that seem a million miles away from the hectic streets of Manhattan.

Roughly triangular, Staten Island is almost 14 miles long and 7.5 miles wide, making it more than twice the size of Manhattan, and **to get around** you'll need to take a bus or the single-line Staten Island Railway (SIR; 24hr); you can use your MetroCard on both modes of transport, but the railway fare ($2.25) is only payable at St George, Tompkinsville and Ballpark (free otherwise). Bus maps are available at the ferry terminals. For more information on Staten Island events and attractions, or to download free maps, visit Ⓦwww.statenislandarts.org or www.statenislandusa.com.

Some history

Like the rest of New York City, "Staaten Eylandt" was first settled by the Dutch in the 1630s, though their initial villages were destroyed in wars with the local Lenape Indians. The Lenape "sold" the island to the British in 1670, and by the mid-1700s had been driven out of the region. The island remained a sleepy rural backwater well into the nineteenth century, when the north shore started to develop as a Manhattan suburb. The island was known as Richmond County until 1898, when a referendum saw 73 percent of islanders approving absorption into New York City. It wasn't until 1964, when the **Verrazano Narrows Bridge** connected the island with Brooklyn, that development really took off; the resulting influx of land-hungry New Yorkers promptly turned the island's rural landscape into a fully fledged suburbia. Today, the island has one of the largest Italian-American populations in the country, though there are also sizeable Sri Lankan communities and the largest Liberian community outside Africa.

St George

Passengers disembark the ferry on the northeast corner of the island, in the town of **St George**, Staten Island's "Downtown" district, home to most of the borough government offices and law courts. While it's no waterfront paradise, with views blocked by high-rises and the town cut off from the harbour by large roads, it does boast a handful of mildly appealing attractions. The 1906 French Renaissance

Borough Hall (Mon–Fri 9am–5pm; ⓣ718-816-2000), straight ahead as you walk out of the ferry terminal at 10 Richmond Terrace, has a marble lobby adorned with vivid WPA murals illustrating the island's history (enter at the back on Stuyvesant Place). Local artist Frederick Charles Stahr completed the thirteen murals in the late 1930s, beginning with Verrazano's "discovery" of Staten Island in 1524 and ending with the construction of the Bayonne Bridge (1928–1931). Further west, the **Staten Island Museum**, 75 Stuyvesant Place (Mon–Fri & Sun noon–5pm, Sat 10am–5pm; $2, free noon–2pm; ⓣ718/727-1135, ⓦwww.statenislandmuseum.org), has exhibits on the history of the ferry, the island's geology and some rare **Lenape Indian** artefacts, though the most intriguing object on display is a large chunk of the **Canyon Diablo Meteorite**, which crashed into Arizona 50,000 years ago. If touching something from outer space doesn't give you a kick, try lifting it – it's 92 percent iron.

Snug Harbor Cultural Center

In contrast to the more urban area around the ferry terminal, the atmosphere of the **Snug Harbor Cultural Center**, 1000 Richmond Terrace (ⓣ718/448-2500, ⓦwww.snug-harbor.org), in nearby New Brighton, is one of bucolic calm, with museums, gardens, performance spaces, artists' studios and galleries spread over

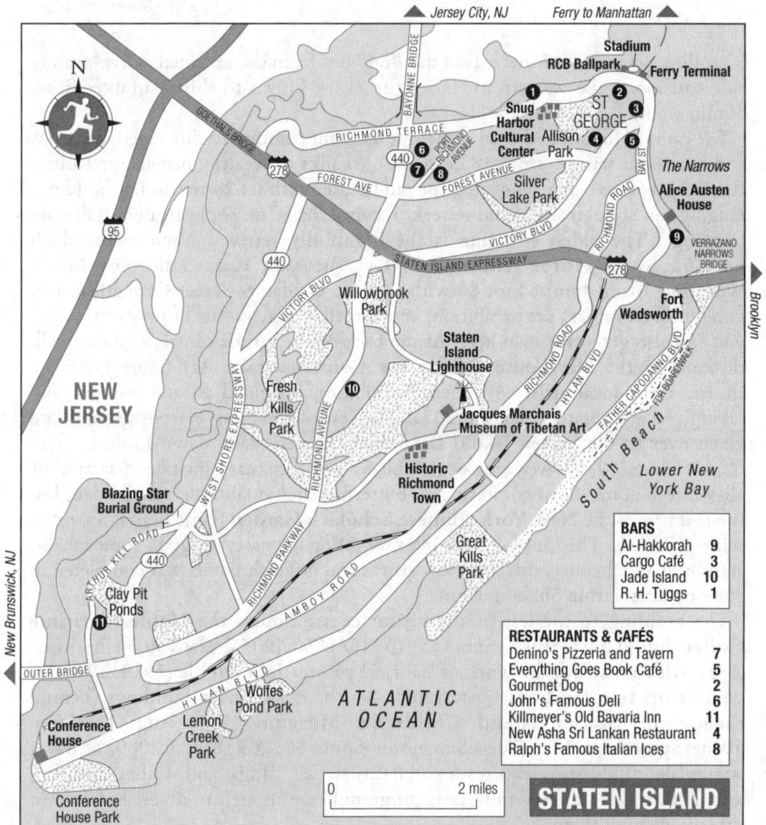

▲ The Staten Island Ferry

83 rolling acres. To get there, take the #S40 bus from the terminal, a five-minute ride east along the waterfront; buses run every fifteen to thirty minutes (it's a 30min walk).

The campus functioned as an affluent retirement community for "aged, decrepit, and worn-out sailors" from 1833 to 1976 (thanks to wealthy benefactor Robert Randall), before being renovated for public use, with its 28 remaining buildings ranging in style from grand Greek Revival halls to sophisticated Italianate buildings. The oldest structure is the beautifully restored Main Hall, which functions as the **visitor centre** (April–Oct Tues–Sun 10am–5pm; Nov–March Wed–Sun 10am–4pm; $3, or $6 with Chinese Garden & Secret Garden). Inside, you'll find temporary art exhibitions and a small display on the history of the site; you can also get a free map here. At the back of the visitor centre, you can walk through to the **Newhouse Center for Contemporary Art** (same hours), a showcase for local artists – a recent exhibition imagined an archeological dig taking place on Staten Island in 2074. The rest of the Snug Harbor grounds are given over to the **Staten Island Botanical Garden** (daily dawn to dusk; free; Ⓣ718/273-8200, Ⓦwww.sibg.org). This 53-acre sanctuary includes a section of all-white blooms, flowers catering to butterflies and an antique rose garden, but the real gem is the **New York Chinese Scholar's Garden** (same hours; $5, or $6 with galleries). This one-acre complex of Ming Dynasty, pagoda-roofed halls, artfully planted courtyards, bamboo groves and goldfish ponds was completed in 1999 by artists from Suzhou, China.

The building to the left of the visitor centre houses the **Noble Maritime Collection** (Thurs–Sun 1–5pm; $5; Ⓣ718/447-6490, Ⓦwww.noblemaritime.org), which displays the work of nautical painter John Noble (1913–1983), as well as his restored houseboat studio. South of the main buildings (behind them), the **Staten Island Children's Museum** (June–Aug Tues–Sun 10am–5pm; Sept–May Tues–Sun noon–5pm; $6; Ⓣ718/273-2060, Ⓦwww.statenislandkids.org) features exhibits such as "Bugs and Other Insects", animal feedings and arts-and-crafts programmes – enough to divert kids, if not utterly enthrall them.

The Alice Austen House

Southeast of St George, the **Alice Austen House**, 2 Hylan Blvd (March–Dec Thurs–Sun noon–5pm; suggested donation $2; ⓣ718/816-4506, Ⓦwww.aliceausten.org), is a tiny clapboard cottage facing the Verrazano Narrows. Reach the house by taking the #S51 bus from the ferry dock to Hylan Boulevard, then walking one block east down the hill toward the waterfront.

Austen (1866–1952) was a pioneering amateur photographer whose work comprises one of the finest records of American daily life in the early twentieth century. Her work was rediscovered only shortly before her death in 1952 (bankrupt, in 1950 she'd been admitted to the borough poorhouse). The house exhibits only a small selection of her photos, but they're fascinating, and the home's beautiful location is a sight in itself; built in 1690, the house was bought and modified by Austen's grandfather in the nineteenth century.

Fort Wadsworth and South Beach

At the base of the Verrazano Narrows Bridge, a critical position for the defence of the New York Harbour, sits **Fort Wadsworth** (Wed–Sun 10am–5pm; free; ⓣ718/354-4500, Ⓦwww.nps.gov/gate); take the #S51 bus, or walk fifteen to twenty minutes from the Alice Austen House.

Start at the **visitor centre**, where you can watch a ten-minute video and peruse an exhibition that provides the historical context, as well as pick up ranger-led tours (Wed–Sun 2.30pm; free). The site itself comprises three main parts: **Fort Tompkins**, behind the visitor centre (which was built between 1859 and 1876), with imposing 30ft-high granite walls; the adjacent and ruined **Battery Duane** (1896); and far below, **Battery Weed**, built between 1847 and 1862 – this was the site of the original fort, which dates back to the colonial period and was originally known as Fort Richmond. You can't go inside any of these fortifications, and the real star is the view from the **overlook** above Battery Weed – the panorama of the harbour, Manhattan and the Verrazano Bridge is mesmerizing.

South of here is the more upscale neighbourhood of **South Beach** (bus #S51), known for its two-and-a-half-mile **FDR Boardwalk**, a great place to jog or rollerblade.

The Jacques Marchais Museum of Tibetan Art

In the centre of Staten Island's residential heartland, the **Jacques Marchais Museum of Tibetan Art**, 338 Lighthouse Ave (Wed–Sun 1–5pm; closed Jan; $5; ⓣ718/987-3500, Ⓦwww.tibetanmuseum.org), is an unlikely find. Take the #S74 bus and ask to be let off at Lighthouse Avenue (the bus driver may not know of the museum), then hike about ten minutes up the steep hill. A cab from the ferry terminal will cost around $15.

Despite being christened Jacques, Marchais (1887–1948) was actually female. Starting in the 1920s, she became a successful art dealer, and used her income to indulge a passion for Tibetan art (though she never visited Tibet). Eventually, she assembled about 3000 pieces, and between 1943 and 1947 built this small field-stone complex, which clutches onto the steep hillside much as monasteries in Tibet do. One building houses the museum gift shop and a small gallery, and the other, designed to resemble a *gompa*, or temple, displays changing exhibits and a small fraction of the collection, including religious sculptures, *thangka* paintings, a rare Bhutanese sand *mandala* and a 250-year-old carved-wood *stupa*. In October, monks in maroon robes perform ritual ceremonies, and food and crafts are sold, at the annual Tibetan Festival.

Historic Richmond Town

Spread out along the main Richmond Road at Arthur Kill Road, a short walk west and south from the Tibetan museum (or a ride on the #S74 bus from the ferry terminal) lies **Historic Richmond Town**, 441 Clarke Ave (July & Aug Wed–Sat 10am–5pm, Sun 1–5pm; Sept–June Wed–Sun 1–5pm; $5; ⓣ718/351-1611, ⓦwww.historicrichmondtown.org). Home to the Staten Island Historical Society, it's an open-air museum of around 27 historic buildings; at its core is the old village of Richmond, centre of the island's government until 1898 (when St George started to take over), as well as clapboard houses transported from other parts of the island.

The **visitor centre**, housed in the stately courthouse, built in 1837, is home to a gift shop, maps and small exhibitions in the site. Opposite lies the **Historical Museum**, which contains exhibits about the history of Staten Island, while in the streets nearby there are around fifteen restored buildings you can go inside (including the 1696 Dutch-style **Voorlezer's House**, the nation's oldest existing school building) – at weekends and during peak months, these are often staffed by costumed volunteers who use traditional techniques to make wooden water buckets and weld tin, all carried off to surprisingly picturesque and un-gimmicky effect. Free guided tours run weekdays at 2.30pm and on weekends at 2 and 3.30pm. From here, the #S74 bus continues on to Tottenville, near Conference House.

Conference House

At the far southern end of the island, in the quiet seaside neighbourhood known as **Tottenville**, the **Conference House**, 7455 Hylan Blvd (SIR to Tottenville; 1hr tours April to mid-Dec Fri–Sun 1–4pm; $3; ⓣ718/984-6046, ⓦwww.conferencehouse.org), is a fine rubble stone manor built by English Captain Christopher Billopp around 1680. Other than its age (ancient by American standards), its claim to fame is acting as host to the failed **peace conference** in 1776 during the American Revolution, the Americans led by Benjamin Franklin and John Adams, the British by Admiral Richard Howe. The nearby **visitor centre** lays out the history of the site, while guided tours (every 20min or so) take you inside the house for a peek at period furnishings and the original kitchen, which has been restored to working order. The surrounding grounds are occupied by the lovely 267-acre **Conference House Park**.

Listings

Listings

22 Accommodation

Accommodation in New York eats up the lion's share of most travellers' budgets. Many **hotels** in the city charge more than $200 a night; $400–500 in high season can be common (these are **pre-tax rates** – see p.272). It is certainly possible to get a safe, clean room for less than that, but it's almost always easier to find a place to splurge on than it is to find a bargain.

Anywhere you're going to want to stay is going to require **reservations**; make them as far in advance as you can. At certain times of the year (May, Sept & Oct as well as the weeks leading up to Christmas and New Year) – you're likely to find everything chock-full if you wait until the last minute. Most hotels in New York only hold reservations until 5 or 6pm unless you've warned them that you'll be arriving late.

There are three ways to book a room: directly through the hotel (either by phone or through its website), on a travel website or through a travel agent. If you're going to do it yourself, try to use the local phone number, as it can be much more expedient than going through the national service at the "800" (or 866, 877 or 888) number. In either case, enquire about discounts: business hotels downtown reduce prices on weekends; special offers may be available; and months like January, February, July and August tend to give better deals. Travel websites list all-inclusive flight and hotel package vacations and occasionally offer special deals.

There are plenty of **hostels** with dormitory accommodation for the young or budget-minded. Other moderately priced options include **bed and breakfasts**, which basically entail staying in somebody's spare room with all the amenities of a private apartment. These rooms go for approximately $120 and up for a double and can be booked through an agency listed in the appropriate section below.

Depending on how you book the place, you'll either have to **pay in advance** (a requirement of some hotel booking sites) or, at the least, have your credit card swiped when you arrive (but not charged until you leave).

Keep in mind that even though there are thousands of guest rooms, there still aren't enough to go around. Most properties have a steady parade of occupants and as a result show some wear and tear. Unless you're checking into a new or luxury hotel – and sometimes even then – don't be surprised to occasionally see chipped furniture and scuffs on the wall. That said, there is a difference between continuous use and unsanitary conditions; if you feel your room is dirty or unsafe, don't hesitate to talk to the management.

Hotels

Most of New York's **hotels** are in midtown Manhattan, in close proximity to many of the main tourist sights, though there are a growing number of options downtown. The Upper West or Upper East sides should do if your taste runs more

▲ *Mansfield Hotel*

to Central Park and the high culture of museums and Lincoln Center, though you won't have as many options.

A full **breakfast** is rarely included as part of the deal, though you may be offered some sort of complimentary continental breakfast. Tipping is expected at upmarket hotels: unless you firmly refuse, a bellhop will grab your bags when you check in and expect a few dollars to carry them to your room. The cleaning staff will really appreciate your tip when you leave (figure $2 minimum per day for cheaper hotels, $5 a day for the nicer establishments). Minibars, stocked with booze and chocolate goodies at astronomical prices, are formulated to appeal to your sense of laziness; these and the hotel shops that sell basic necessities at three times the street price should be avoided.

Taxes are added to your hotel bill, and hotels will nearly always quote you the price of a room before tax. Taxes will add 14.75 percent to your bill, plus $3.50 per night in "occupancy tax" and room fees.

The following selection of hotels runs the gamut from the city's cheapest to most luxurious and/or hippest. Unless noted, the prices quoted at the end of each listing represent the expected price of the hotel's cheapest double room, excluding all taxes, during the high season when rates are at a premium; note, though, that there's hardly such a thing as a fixed room price, and figures quoted to you can change on a daily basis. You could easily get a quote much better or worse.

Financial District

Ritz-Carlton 2 West St, Battery Park City ⓣ212/344-0800, ⓦwww.ritzcarlton.com. Subway #1 to Rector St; #4, #5 to Bowling Green. The views of New York Harbor and the Statue of Liberty don't get much better than from this elegant high-rise hotel. It features 425-square-foot rooms with soothing muted tones – all with dazzling vistas and "bath butlers" to draw baths and warm towels (the harbour rooms even come with telescopes). $475

Soho and Tribeca

Cosmopolitan 95 W Broadway, at Chambers St ⓣ1-888/895-9400 or 212/566-1900, ⓦwww.cosmohotel.com. Subway A, C, #1, #2, #3 to Chambers St. A great Tribeca location, smart, well-maintained rooms, and incredibly low prices make the *Cosmopolitan* a steal. $195

Crosby Street Hotel 79 Crosby St, between Spring and Prince sts ⓣ212/226-6400, ⓦwww.firmdale.com. Subway N, R to Prince St, #6 to Spring St. It's very expensive, but you get bright and spacious rooms set around a courtyard on the edge of trendy Soho, with fluffy towels, luxurious bathrooms, floor-to-ceiling windows and contemporary sculpture and art splashed all over the hotel. Get a room on the higher floors for spectacular views. English afternoon tea ($34) is served all day in the tranquil drawing room. $495.

Holiday Inn SoHo 138 Lafayette St, at Howard St ⓣ1-800/HOLIDAY or 212/966-8898, ⓦwww.hidowntown-nyc.com. Subway A, C, E, J, M, N, Q, R, Z, #1, #6 to Canal St. Just north of busy Canal St, this member of the well-known chain is also a stone's throw from Soho and Tribeca. Though the rooms are small for the price, the rates fluctuate so booking early should get you a better deal. $331

Mercer 147 Mercer St, at Prince St ⓣ212/966-6060, ⓦwww.mercerhotel.com. Subway N, R to Prince St. Housed in a Romanesque Revival building in Soho, the *Mercer* has been one of the top accommodation choices of visiting celebs such as Leonardo DiCaprio since it opened in 1998. Some loft-like guest rooms also have massive baths with 90 square feet for splashing around, and the *Mercer Kitchen* garners rave reviews. It's all worth it for the amenities, though: the concierge can arrange private training or massage virtually around the clock, and there's free access to local gyms. $450

Smyth Tribeca 85 West Broadway, between Warren and Chambers sts ⓣ212/587-7000, ⓦwww.thompsonhotels.com. Subway A, C, #1, #2, #3 to Chambers St. One of the newest boutiques in this part of town, with plush, contemporary design and furnishings with Classical and Art Deco touches; iPod docking station, plasma TV and large bathroom (with Kiehl products) included. $445

SoHo Grand 310 W Broadway, between Canal and Grand sts ⓣ212/965-3000, ⓦwww.sohogrand.com. Subway A, C, E to Canal St. In a great location at the edge of Soho, this place draws guests of the model/actor variety. The stylish, chocolate-hued rooms have personality to match, while cast-iron staircases with vault lights, a glass elevator shaft and 20ft ceilings lend the common areas an industrial yet inviting feel. There's also a sharp-looking bar, restaurant and hidden outdoor terrace. $401

Tribeca Grand 2 Sixth Ave, between White and Walker sts ⓣ212/519-6600, ⓦwww.tribecagrand.com. Subway #1 to Franklin St. Craving anonymity, the *Tribeca Grand* is unlabelled and tucked behind a brick facade. Inside, the striking *Church Lounge* beckons with a warm glow (it's a great space in which to hang out). Rooms are fashionably understated, though bathrooms boast phones and TVs, and the staff is extra attentive. Off-season weekends can be several hundred dollars cheaper. $425

Lower East Side and East Village

Blue Moon 100 Orchard St, between Delancey and Broome sts ⓣ212/533-9080, ⓦwww.bluemoon-nyc.com. Subway F to Delancey St; J, M, Z to Essex St. Lower East Side tenement transformed into a luxurious boutique, with rooms named after 1930s and 1940s celebrities and decked out with period iron-frame beds and the odd antique – rooms on the 6th, 7th and 8th floors also come with fabulous views across the city. Continental breakfast and wi-fi included. $295.

Bowery Hotel 335 Bowery at E 3rd St. ⓣ212/505-9100, ⓦwww.theboweryhotel.com. Subway #6 to Bleecker St. This fabulous boutique property oozes sophistication and tempts guests with countless amenities, including iPod docks, DVD players, floor-to-ceiling windows, marble tubs with a view and a hip lounge bar. All this luxury comes at a price though. $425

Hotel 91 91 E Broadway ⓣ646/438-6600, ⓦwww.thehotel91.com. Subway F to East Broadway. Funky Lower East Side boutique, with a slight Asian theme – orchids grace every room, and a statue of Buddha sits in the lobby. Rooms are compact but well equipped, with LCD TVs and plush marble bathrooms – this is a real bargain, but ask for a room away from the Manhattan Bridge if you're a light sleeper. Free wi-fi. $139.

West Village

Larchmont 27 W 11th St, between Fifth and Sixth aves ⓣ212/989-9333, ⓦwww.larchmonthotel.com. Subway F, L to 14th St. A budget hotel, in a terrific location on a tree-lined street in Greenwich Village. Rooms are small but homey and clean. A robe and slippers are thoughtfully provided so you can

Rooms with a view

Hilton Times Square Midtown West; p.279
Gansevoort Meatpacking District, p.274
Jumeirah Essex House Midtown West, p.279
Mandarin Oriental New York Upper West Side, p.281
Ritz-Carlton Financial District, p.272

traipse down the hall to the shared bath. Includes continental breakfast. $119

Washington Square 103 Waverly Place, at Washington Square Park ⓣ212/777-9515, ⓦwww.washingtonsquarehotel.com. Subway A, B, C, D, E, F, M to W 4th St. In the heart of Greenwich Village, this hotel is quite close to the area's many nightlife options. Don't be deceived by the posh-looking lobby – the rooms are surprisingly plain for the price (though the Art Deco "Deluxe" rooms have a bit more character). Continental breakfast is included. $222

Chelsea and the Meatpacking District

Chelsea Lodge 318 W 20th St, between Eighth and Ninth aves ⓣ1-800/373-1116 or 212/243-4499, ⓦwww.chelsealodge.com. Subway C, E to 23rd St. The *Lodge* is a gem of a place: a converted boarding house with Early American/Sportsman decor, down a nice block. Normal rooms, which offer in-room showers and sinks (there's a shared toilet down the hall) are a little snug for two, but the few deluxe rooms are great value and have full bathrooms. A three-day cancellation policy applies. $129

Chelsea Savoy Hotel 204 W 23rd St, at Seventh Ave ⓣ212/929-9353, ⓦwww.chelseasavoynyc.com. Subway #1 to 23rd St. A few doors away from the *Chelsea Hotel*, the *Savoy* has none of its neighbour's funky charm. The rooms, decent-sized, are clean and nicely decorated and the staff is reasonably helpful. Try to avoid rooms facing the main drags outside though; they can be noisy. $250

Gansevoort 18 Ninth Ave, at W 13th St ⓣ1-877/426-7368 or 212/206-6700, ⓦwww.hotelgansevoort.com. Subway A, C, E to 14th St. When cobblestone streets in the Meatpacking District were torn up to make room for this sleek hotel, preservationists were horrified, but the neighbourhood seems to have benefited. Rooms, in muted tones, are spiffy, with top-notch electronics, but you're really paying for the 360-degree views, the full spa, the heated rooftop pool (one of very few in the city) and the scene. $525

Hotel Chelsea 222 W 23rd St, between Seventh and Eighth aves ⓣ212/243-3700, ⓦwww.hotelchelsea.com. Subway C, E to 23rd St. One of New York's most notorious landmarks, this ageing neo-Gothic building boasts a fabulously seedy and artistic past (see p.117). Most of the spacious rooms and suites have been renovated, but not so that they've given up their history: they still come with wood floors, log-burning fireplaces and kitchenettes. $199

Union Square, Gramercy and the Flatiron District

Ace 20 W 29th St at Broadway ⓣ212/679-2222, ⓦwww.acehotel.com. Subway N, R to 28th St. Capturing the spirit of old New York yet fully modern, the *Ace Hotel* sets a new standard for bohemian chic. A whole host of different room styles are on offer (including bunks), with retro-style fridges, guitars, muted tones and artwork that can make it feel more expensive than it is. $300.

Carlton 88 Madison Ave ⓣ1-800/601-8500 or 212/532-4100, ⓦwww.carltonhotelny.com. Subway #6 to 28th St. A smartly located, Beaux Arts building entered by a stylish if unflashy portal, the *Carlton* offers roomy quarters outfitted in cream-and-tan-striped wallpaper and mahogany furnishings. Beds are all fluffiness and the restaurant offers superb service. $369

Comfort Inn Chelsea 18 W 25th St, between Sixth Ave and Broadway ⓣ212/645-3990, ⓦwww.comfortinn.com. Subway F, M to 23rd St. The *Comfort Inn Chelsea* is a solid hotel with very good prices and clean, albeit smallish, rooms. Near Madison Square Park, it's equidistant from downtown and midtown. Off-season rates drop significantly. $259

Giraffe 365 Park Ave S, at 26th St ⓣ1-877/296-0009 or 212/685-7700, ⓦwww.hotelgiraffe.com. Subway #6 to 28th St. The tall and slender *Giraffe* is similar in tone and amenities to sister hotels *Library* (see p.277) and *Casablanca* (see p.278), but these rooms invoke the sleek Art Moderne style of the 1920s and 1930s. Prices include complimentary breakfast, afternoon wine and cheese, and a 24hr espresso bar. $489

Gramercy Park 2 Lexington Ave, at E 21st St ⓣ1-866/784-1300 or 212/920-3300, ⓦwww.gramercyparkhotel.com. Subway #6 to 23rd St. The Ian Schrager Group (enlisting the help of artist Julian Schnabel) renovated the once-bohemian *Gramercy Park* into a very different property: the grand entrance got a red carpet and a chandelier, but also

Best luxury hotels

The Mark Upper East Side, p.280
Morgans Midtown East, p.277
The Plaza Midtown East, p.277
Sherry Netherland Midtown East, p.277
Waldorf-Astoria Midtown East, p.278

reclaimed lumber, modern artworks, strange light fixtures and a toreador's jacket. Rooms are similarly eclectic, bold and luxurious. It's also in a lovely location – guests get a key to the adjacent private park. $495

Herald Square 19 W 31st St, between Fifth Ave and Broadway ⓣ1-800/727-1888 or 212/279-4017, ⓦwww.heraldsquarehotel.com. Subway N, R to 28th St. The original home of *Life* magazine, *Herald Square* still features Philip Martiny's sculpted cherub *Winged Life* over its Beaux Arts doorway. The inside is clean but somewhat soulless and without much in the way of extras. $239

Hotel 17 225 E 17th St, between Second and Third aves ⓣ212/475-2845, ⓦwww.hotel17ny.com. Subway L, N, Q, R, #4, #5, #6 to 14th St–Union Square. *Seventeen*'s rooms come with basic amenities; many share baths. The hotel itself is neat and nicely situated on a pleasant tree-lined street just minutes from Union Square and the East Village. $150

Hotel 31 120 E 31st St, between Park and Lexington aves ⓣ1-800/804-4480 or 212/685-3060, ⓦwww.hotel31.com. Subway #6 to 33rd St. An affordable Murray Hill option run by the folks who own *Hotel 17*. The sixty rooms are clean (some share a bath) and the location is quiet. $145

Murray Hill Inn 143 E 30th St, between Lexington and Third aves ⓣ212/683-6900, ⓦwww.murrayhillinn.com. Subway #6 to 28th St. It's easy to see why young travellers and backpackers line the *Inn*'s narrow halls. Although the inexpensive rooms can be tiny, they all have a telephone, a/c and cable TV; some also have private bathrooms. $139

Roger Williams 131 Madison Ave, at E 31st St ⓣ1-888/448-7788 or 212/448-7000, ⓦwww.hotelrogerwilliams.com. Subway #6 to 33rd St. The first thing you'll notice at the *Roger* is the use of colour; the Scandinavian/Japanese fusion rooms utilize both mellow and vibrant tones (even the business card dons bright stripes). Some come with views of the Empire State from their small terraces. $400

Thirty Thirty 30 E 30th St, between Park and Madison aves ⓣ1-800/804-4480 or 212/689-1900, ⓦwww.thirtythirty-nyc.com. Subway #6 to 28th St. Small, welcoming hotel, with a few minor but welcome design touches, including CD players, dataports and framed black-and-white scenes of old New York in all the rooms. $329

W Union Square 201 Park Ave S at E 17th St ⓣ212/253-9119, ⓦwww.starwoodhotels.com. Subway L, N, Q, R, #4, #5, #6 to 14th St–Union Square. This stylish chain of luxury hotels – there are four other locations in Manhattan – offers top-to-bottom comfort; rooms (Wonderful, Spectacular and Mega) are outfitted with all the amenities a traveller could ever need. Also houses a branch of celebrity chef Todd English's *Olives* restaurant. $399

Midtown East: 30th to 59th streets

Affinia Shelburne 303 Lexington Ave, between E 37th and 38th sts ⓣ212/689-5200, ⓦwww.affinia.com. Subway #6 to 33rd St. Luxurious, newly renovated hotel in the most elegant part of Murray Hill. All the rooms have kitchenettes, and there's a separate restaurant downstairs, *Rare*, that specializes in gourmet burgers (and provides room service). There's also a buzzing bar scene on the roof terrace in season. $369

Alex Hotel 205 E 45th St, off Third Ave ⓣ212/867-5100, ⓦwww.thealexhotel.com. Subway #4, #5, #6, #7 to 42nd St–Grand Central. This sleek, beige-toned spot is a serene midtown oasis. Rooms are bright and airy, with modern Scandinavian touches and a handful of fun eccentricities (a tiny TV in the bathroom, hideaway cabinets and compartments). The restaurant-bar *Riingo* provides 24hr room service. $469

Algonquin **59 W 44th St, between Fifth and Sixth aves ⓣ1-888/304-2047 or 212/840-6800, ⓦwww.algonquinhotel.com. Subway B, D, F, M to 42nd St.** New York's oldest continuously operated hotel and one of the city's famed literary hangouts (see p.129) has retained its old-club atmosphere and decor from the days of the Round Table, though the rooms have been refurbished to handsome effect (large flat-screens, refreshed carpets and bedding). Ask about summer and weekend specials. $549

▲ Algonquin Hotel

Beekman Tower **3 Mitchell Place, at E 49th St and First Ave ⓣ1-866/298-4606 or 212/355-7300, ⓦwww.thebeekmanhotel.com. Subway #6 to 51st St; E, M to Lexington Ave–53rd St.** Populated with 174 traditional-looking rooms (actually, suites with fully equipped kitchens) on 26 floors, the hotel is one of the more stylish in the area, with great views from the *Top of the Tower* bar/lounge. It's also quiet, if a bit out of the way. $349

Bryant Park Hotel **40 W 40th St, between Fifth and Sixth aves ⓣ1-877/640-9300 or 212/869-0100, ⓦwww.bryantparkhotel.com. Subway B, D, F, M to 42nd St.** This hotel shows off its edgy attitude in its stylish contemporary rooms, luxurious 70-seat film-screening room, and funky *Cellar Bar*, which is always filled with media types. $425

Chambers Hotel **15 W 56th St, between Fifth and Sixth aves ⓣ1-866/204-5656 or 212/974-5656, ⓦwww.chambershotel.com. Subway F to 57th St.** Designed by architect David Rockwell, *Chambers* is well-placed for Central Park and MoMA visits, though you can just sit and admire the 500 original works of art in its gallery-sized hallways. The modern, tasteful rooms approximate a New York apartment, as do the mezzanine-level lounge spaces. The latest *Momofuku* offspring, *Má Peche*, is the on-site restaurant. $425

Comfort Inn Manhattan **42 W 35th St, between Fifth and Sixth aves ⓣ212/947-0200, ⓦwww.comfortinnmanhattan.com. Subway B, D, F, M to 34th St–Herald Square.** The best things about this hotel are the free, deluxe continental breakfast and cheery, good-value rooms. The management, though, can be less than helpful; it's not always possible to see a room before you decide to bunk down. $249

Dylan **52 E 41st St, between Park and Madison aves ⓣ1-866/55-DYLAN or 212/338-0500, ⓦwww.dylanhotel.com. Subway #4, #5, #6, #7 to Grand Central–42nd St.** Classy and clever, *Dylan*'s rooms have been attentively designed (the 11ft ceilings make them look quite large) and bathrooms are clad in Italian marble. If you're looking to splurge, book the Alchemy Suite, a one-of-a-kind Gothic bedchamber with a vaulted ceiling and stained-glass windows. $459

Fitzpatrick Manhattan **687 Lexington Ave, between E 56th and 57th sts ⓣ212/355-0100 or 1-800/367-7701, ⓦwww.fitzpatrickhotels.com. Subway #4, #5, #6, N, R to 59th St–Lexington Ave.** This handsome Irish-themed hotel is perfectly situated for visits to midtown stores, Upper East Side museums and Central Park. A hearty Irish breakfast ($19) is served all day. $359

Iroquois **49 W 44th St, between Fifth and Sixth aves ⓣ1-800/332-7220 or 212/840-3080, ⓦwww.iroquoisny.com. Subway B, D, F, M to 42nd St.** Once a haven for rock bands, this elegant, reinvented boutique hotel has comfortable, tasteful rooms with Italian-marble baths and mahogany and suede headboards. The lounge is named for actor James Dean, one of the hotel's residents from 1951 to 1953 (room #803). $499

Jolly Madison Towers **22 E 38th St, at Madison Ave ⓣ212/802-0600, ⓦwww.jollymadison.com. Subway #4, #5, #6, #7 to Grand Central–42nd St.**

This NYC outpost of the leading Italian chain offers restful, fairly spacious rooms outfitted with handcrafted furnishings and Venetian glass. Check the website for specials. $309

Library 299 Madison Ave (entry on E 41st St) ⓣ1-877/793-READ or 212/983-4500, ⓦwww.libraryhotel.com. Subway #4, #5, #6, #7 to Grand Central–42nd St. The *Library*'s concept, one of New York hostelry's quirkier, has each floor devoted to one of the ten major categories of the Dewey Decimal System. Coloured in shades of brown and cream, the rooms are average in size but nicely appointed with big bathrooms. There's a wine-and-cheese get-together every weekday evening. $469

Mansfield 12 W 44th St, between Fifth and Sixth aves ⓣ1-800/255-5167 or 212/277-8700, ⓦwww.mansfieldhotel.com. Subway B, D, F, M to 42nd St. One of the nicest little hotels in the city, the *Mansfield* manages to be both grand and intimate. A clubby library lounge and live jazz during the week (not to mention free wi-fi and a gym), lends the place an affable air, conducive to simply wandering around. Complimentary continental breakfast and all-day cappuccino. $399

The Metro 45 W 35th St, between Fifth and Sixth aves ⓣ212/947-2500, ⓦwww.hotelmetronyc.com. Subway B, D, F, M to 34th St–Herald Square. A very stylish hotel, with some minimal Hollywood theming, a delightful seasonal rooftop, clean, understated rooms and free continental breakfast. There's also free wi-fi, a fitness room and a nice restaurant, the *Metro Grill*. $375

Morgans 237 Madison Ave, between E 37th and E 38th sts ⓣ1-800/334-3408 or 212/686-0300, ⓦwww.morganshotel.com. Subway #6 to 33rd St. Still one of the chicest flophouses in town. Rooms, with maple panelling and neutral tones are soothing, with specially commissioned black-and-white photos by the late Robert Mapplethorpe. $509

The Plaza Fifth Ave at Central Park South ⓣ212/759-3000, ⓦwww.theplaza.com. Subway N, R to Fifth Ave–59th St. Silencing the naysayers, *The Plaza* has come back from its hiatus looking better than ever. The grand tradition of the hotel is still there in the Baccarat chandeliers (in the rooms, too) and 24-carat-gold fixtures, but now there's also a huge screen for your viewing pleasure, and a wireless flat-panel gadget that can turn on the DVD, dim the lights and summon the floor butler. Needless to say, service is impeccable. $895

Pod 230 E 51st St, between Second and Third aves ⓣ212/355-0300, ⓦwww.thepodhotel.com. Subway #6 to 51st St. This pleasant hotel (the former *Pickwick Arms*) is one of the best deals in Midtown. All 370 pods (solo, double, bunk or queen, all reminiscent of a colourful ship's quarters) come with a/c, iPod docks, free wi-fi and LCD TVs, although some are shared bath. The open-air roof-deck bar is a bonus, with stunning views. $249

Radisson 511 Lexington Ave, at E 48th St ⓣ1-800/448-4471 or 212/755-4400, ⓦwww.lexingtonhotelnyc.com. Subway #6 to 51st St. Nicer than one would expect, with airy rooms, fully furnished fitness centre and capable concierge. $309

Roger Smith 501 Lexington Ave, at E 47th St ⓣ1/800/445-0277 or 212/755-1400, ⓦwww.rogersmith.com. Subway #6 to 51st St. Stylish and helpful, with inviting rooms individually decorated in contemporary, whimsical American style, and bold, colourful artwork on display in the public spaces. In sum, lots of personality. Breakfast is included. $349

Sherry Netherland 781 Fifth Ave, between E 59th and 60th sts ⓣ212/355-2800, ⓦwww.sherrynetherland.com. Subway N, R to 59th St. If a large sum of money ever comes your way, rent a whole floor here and live-in permanently (many of the guests do) – the stunning views of Central Park are worth it. The service is excellent; the room service is by renowned restaurateur Harry Cipriani. $674

Shoreham 33 W 55th St, between Fifth and Sixth aves. ⓣ212/247-6700, ⓦwww.shorehamhotel.com. Subway F to 57th St. The *Shoreham* is done up, or rather, down, in minimalist chic: a cool white marble lobby, polished steel columns and clean room designs emphasize the fact. There's a lively bar scene downstairs. $439

Stanford 43 W 32nd St, between Broadway and Fifth Ave ⓣ1-800/365-1114 or 212/563-1500, ⓦwww.hotelstanford.com. Subway B, D, F, M, N, Q, R to 34th St–Herald Square. A clean, moderately priced hotel on the block known as Little Korea. The rooms are a tad small, but attractive and very quiet. Free continental breakfast, jazz Sat nights in the *Maxim* lounge, and an efficient, friendly staff. $299

The Strand 33 W 37th St, between Fifth and Sixth aves ⓣ212/448-1024, ⓦwww.thestrandnyc.com. Subway B, D, F, M, N, Q, R to

34th St–Herald Square. The rooms, some of which have views of the Empire State Building, are fresh and comfortable, but it's the soothing lobby and lovely roof-deck bar that help the hotel stand out. $355

Waldorf-Astoria 301 Park Ave, at E 50th St ⓣ1-800/WALDORF or 212/355-3000, ⓦwww.waldorfnewyork.com. Subway #6 to 51st St. One of the city's first grand hotels (see p.138), the *Waldorf* has been restored to its 1930s glory and is a wonderful place to stay, if you can afford it (or someone else is paying). It's no wonder this is a favourite pick for presidents and visiting heads of state – the spacious accommodations feature the latest electronic gadgets, triple sheeting and marble baths. At least drop by for a drink at the legendary mahogany bar downstairs, a peek at one of the opulent banquet halls or a treatment at the full-service spa. $499

Warwick 65 W 54th St, at Sixth Ave ⓣ1-800/223-4099 or 212/247-2700, ⓦwww.warwickhotelny.com. Subway F to 57th St. Legendary newspaperman William Randolph Hearst commissioned the hotel in 1926, and stars of the 1950s and 1960s – including Cary Grant, Rock Hudson, the Beatles, Elvis Presley and JFK – stayed here as a matter of course. Although the hotel has lost its showbiz cachet, the elegant lobby, restaurant and cocktail lounge still make it a pleasant place to stay. The staff are helpful and quite friendly. $399

Midtown West: 30th to 59th streets

414 414 W 46th St, between Ninth and Tenth aves ⓣ1-866/414-HOTEL or 212/399-0006, ⓦwww.414hotel.com. Subway C, E to 50th St. Popular with Europeans but welcoming to all, this guesthouse, which has larger-than-ordinary rooms across two townhouses, makes a nice camp a bit removed from Times Square's bustle. The backyard garden is a wonderful place to enjoy your morning coffee. $210

Affinia Manhattan 371 Seventh Ave, at W 31st St ⓣ1-866/233-4642 or 212/563-1800, ⓦwww.affinia.com. Subway #1, #2, #3 to 34th St–Penn Station. This (almost) all-suite hotel is housed in a 1929 building opposite Penn Station and Madison Square Garden. Though it's a bustling address, the elegant lobby, in-room spa service and pillow menu all help foster relaxation. Some rooms come with terraces ($50 extra); you'll need to request it. $329

Ameritania Hotel 54 230 W 54th St, at Broadway ⓣ1-800/555-7555 or 212/247-5000, ⓦwww.ameritaniahotelnewyork.com. Subway B, D, E to Seventh Ave. With sleek, angular furnishings, soaring columns and a bold colour palette, this retro-inspired hotel is one of the cooler-looking options in the city. All rooms have cable and CD players, and deluxe rooms (only a little pricier than the standard ones) feature marble baths. $319

Casablanca 147 W 43rd St, between Sixth Ave and Broadway ⓣ1-888/922-7225 or 212/869-1212, ⓦwww.casablancahotel.com. Subway B, D, F, M, #1, #2, #3 to 42nd St. Geometric Moorish tiles, inlaid wood and *Rick's Café* are all here in this theme hotel along with a daily wine-and-cheese reception and complimentary gym passes. While the decor is 1940s Morocco, the rooms all have up-to-date amenities. Two-night minimum on weekends. $349

Distrikt 342 W 40th St, between Eighth and Ninth aves ⓣ1-888/444-5610 or 212/706-6100, ⓦwww.distrikthotel.com. Subway A, C, E to 42nd St–Port Authority. With a city neighbourhood theme – subtle in the decor, more obvious in having floors named after "Chelsea", "the Village", etc – the welcoming *Distrikt* has nice-sized rooms done in classy muted browns and beiges; choose one of the upper floors ("Harlem") for the best views. The street is on the unsalubrious side. $269

Edison 228 W 47th St, between Broadway and Eighth Ave. ⓣ212/840-5000, ⓦwww.edisonhotelnyc.com. Subway C, E, #1 to 50th St. The most striking thing about the 1000-room *Edison* is its beautifully restored Art Deco lobby, built in the same style as Radio City Music Hall. The rooms, while not fancy, are clean, and prices are reasonable for midtown. $259

Flatotel 135 W 52nd St, between Sixth and Seventh aves ⓣ1-800/352-8683 or 212/887-9400, ⓦwww.flatotel.com. Subway B, D, E to Seventh Ave. A comfortable, stylish hotel in the heart of Midtown highlighting clean lines and motifs inspired by architect Frank Lloyd Wright. Though some might find it a dizzying place for a workout, check out the Sky Gym fitness centre on the 46th floor. $359

Grace 125 W 45th St, between Sixth and Seventh aves ⓣ212/354-2323, ⓦwww.room-matehotels.com. Subway B, D, F, M to 42nd St. You won't find many hotels like this one, with a lobby that more closely resembles a concession stand; a tiny glassed-in pool overlooked by a louche loungey bar; different, funky retro wallpaper on each floor; and ultra-modern (and pet-friendly) rooms, with platform beds. $399

Hampton Inn Times Square 851 Eighth Ave, between W 51st and 52nd sts ⓣ212/581-4100, ⓦwww.hamptoninn.com. Subway C, E to 50th St. While the facade has absolutely zero character, the hotel warms up slightly inside. Rooms, if not exactly trendy, are decorated in maroon, brown and gold, with free in-room internet access, coffee makers and movie channels. $359

Hilton Times Square 234 W 42nd St, between Seventh and Eighth aves ⓣ1-800/HILTONS or 212/840-8222, ⓦwww.hilton.com. Subway A, C, E, N, Q, R, #1, #2, #3, #7 to 42nd St–Times Square. This gorgeous property is housed in a 44-storey tower, which yields awesome views in all directions. The neutral-toned rooms are good-sized, with attractive furnishings in blonde wood. Ask about packages or specials. $379

Hotel 41 at Times Square 206 W 41st St ⓣ212/703-8600, ⓦwww.hotel41nyc.com. Subway A, C, E, N, Q, R, #1, #2, #3, #7 to 42nd St–Times Square. With just 47 rooms, this boutique hotel blends classic and contemporary styles to pleasing effect. Rooms come with high-speed internet access, Aveda bath products, free internet and satellite TV. $279

Hudson 356 W 58th St, between Eighth and Ninth aves ⓣ1-800/444-4786 or 212/554-6000, ⓦwww.hudsonhotel.com. Subway A, B, D, C, #1 to 59th St–Columbus Circle. Once you get past the *Hudson*'s chartreuse-lit escalators and space-shuttle-esque bar, the rooms are surprisingly tasteful (though minuscule), and there's the added cache of a library and sky terrace. Rates are lower during the week than on weekends. $479

Jumeirah Essex House 160 Central Park S, between Sixth and Seventh aves ⓣ1-888/645-5697 or 212/247-0300, ⓦwww.jumeirahessexhouse.com. Subway F, N, Q, R to 57th St. Formerly known as simply *Essex House*, this beautiful hotel has been restored to its original Art Deco splendour with a $90 million renovation. The best rooms have spectacular Central Park views, and despite the attentive service and marble lobby, the atmosphere is quite relaxed. $549

Le Parker Meridien 118 W 57th St, between Sixth and Seventh aves ⓣ212/245-5000, ⓦwww.parkermeridien.com. Subway F to 57th St. This hotel maintains a shiny, clean veneer, with comfortably modern rooms, a huge fitness centre, rooftop swimming pool, and 24hr room service. The *Burger Joint*, tucked away in a corner of the lobby, is a fun place for a bite to eat. $519

Marriott Marquis 1535 Broadway, at W 45th St ⓣ1-800/843-4898 or 212/398-1900, ⓦwww.marriott.com. Subway N, Q, R, #1, #2, #3 to Times Square–42nd St. It's worth dropping by here even if only to gawk at the split-level atrium and ride the glass elevators to New York's only revolving bar and restaurant. The hotel is well designed for conference or convention guests, though the rooms themselves are modest for the high price. $429

Mayfair 242 W 49th St, between Broadway and Eighth Ave ⓣ1-800/556-2932 or 212/586-0300, ⓦwww.mayfairnewyork.com. Subway C, E, #1 to 50th St. This boutique-style hotel, across the street from the St Malachy Actors' Chapel, has toile-wallpapered rooms and a charming, old-fashioned feel. A nice touch is the preponderance of historic photographs on loan from the Museum of the City of New York. $225

Michelangelo 152 W 51st St, between Sixth and Seventh aves ⓣ1-800/237-0990 or 212/765-0505, ⓦwww.michelangelohotel.com. Subway N, R to 49th St; #1 to 50th St; B, D, E to Seventh Ave. A veritable palazzo on Broadway, this hotel, part of an Italian chain, features acres of marble. While no expense is spared in the luxurious "standard" rooms, suites come in Art Deco, Empire or Country French – take your pick. Make sure to check out the special internet rates. $445

Millennium Broadway 145 W 44th St, between Broadway and Sixth Ave ⓣ1-866/866-8086 or 212/768-4400, ⓦwww.millenniumhotels.com. Subway N, Q, R, #1, #2, #3, #7 to Times Square–42nd St. Black marble and modern Italian wall-to-ceiling artwork dominate the *Millennium Broadway* lobby; the sleek lines continue in the beautiful off-white bedrooms. $409

Muse 130 W 46th St, between Sixth and Seventh aves ⓣ1-877/NYC-MUSE or 212/485-2400, ⓦwww.themusehotel.com. Subway B, D, F, M to 47–50th sts–Rockefeller Center. A small hotel in the centre of the Times Square area, *Muse* is popular with Europeans. The slightly dark and off-putting lobby contrasts with the airy rooms, done in bold black-and-white patterns. $429

Best boutique hotels

Ace Flatiron District, p.274
Alex Midtown East, p.275
Blue Moon Lower East Side, p.273
Mansfield Midtown East, p.277
Smyth Tribeca Tribeca; p.273

Novotel 226 W 52nd St, at Broadway ⓣ212/315-0100 or 1-800/NOVOTEL, ⓦwww.novotel.com. Subway #1 to 50th St; B, D, E to Seventh Ave. This international chain hotel is large enough to offer a decent range of facilities while small enough (though not approaching true boutique size) to cultivate some character. The look is casual but sleek, featuring uncluttered wood with blue accents. $289

Paramount 235 W 46th St, between Broadway and Eighth Ave ⓣ212/764-5500, ⓦwww.nycparamount.com. Subway A, C, E, N, Q, R, #1, #2, #3, #7 to 42nd St–Times Square. A former budget hotel renovated into a boutique bolt hole by Ian Schrager (he's moved on and it's since been updated again), the *Paramount* offers chic, closet-sized rooms with splashes of red to liven things up. $329

Park Savoy 158 W 58th St, between Sixth and Seventh aves ⓣ212/245-5755, ⓦwww.parksavoyhotel.com. Subway F, N, Q, R to 57th St. Despite a somewhat chilly desk staff, the cosy rooms of the *Park Savoy*, just a block from Central Park, represent great value for the area. $185

Salisbury 123 W 57th St, between Sixth and Seventh aves ⓣ212/246-1300, ⓦwww.nycsalisbury.com. Subway F to 57th St. Good service, large (somewhat old-fashioned) rooms with kitchenettes, and proximity to Central Park and Carnegie Hall are the attractions here. $319

The Time 224 W 49th St, between Broadway and Eighth Ave ⓣ1-877/TIME NYC or 212/246-5252, ⓦwww.thetimeny.com. Subway C, E, #1 to 50th St. *Tempus fugit* – and everything here reminds you of this fact, from the waist-level clock in the lobby to the hallways bedecked with Roman numerals. Smallish rooms are tricked out with Bose sound systems, ergonomic workstations and LCD screens. $309

Wellington 871 Seventh Ave, at W 55th St ⓣ1-800/652-1212 or 212/247-3900, ⓦwww.wellingtonhotel.com. Subway B, D, E to Seventh Ave; N, Q, R to 57 St–Seventh Ave. Close to Carnegie Hall and Lincoln Center, the old standby *Wellington* is reasonably priced for this neck of town. $299

Westin New York at Times Square 270 W 43rd St at Eighth Ave ⓣ1-866/837-4183 or 212/201-2700, ⓦwww.westinnewyork.com. Subway A, C, E to 42nd St–Port Authority. The copper-and-blue-glass high-rise seems a little out of place – it was designed by Miami architects – but it's nonetheless been a welcome addition to the Times Square scene. The high-tech rooms have comfortable beds and sweeping views, while baths come with 5-speed double shower heads. $449

Upper East Side

Franklin 164 E 87th St, between Lexington and Third aves ⓣ212/369-1000, ⓦwww.franklinhotel.com. Subway #4, #5, #6 to 86th St. An apparent contradiction: how can one establishment win kudos as both "sexiest hotel" and "best bed and breakfast"? In any case, the quiet residential location makes up for its distance to the heart of the city, and the cheery rooms and baths fitted with Bulgari bath products prove very relaxing. $349

Mark 25 E 77th St, at Madison Ave ⓣ212/744-4300, ⓦwww.themarkhotel.com. Subway #6 to 77th St. This hotel really lives up to its claims of sophistication and elegance. The lobby is decked out in Biedermeier furniture and sleek Italian lighting, and there's a pervasive sense of refinement in the plush guest rooms, restaurant and invitingly dark bar. $670

Pierre 2 E 61st, at Fifth Ave ⓣ1-800/743-7734 or 212/940-8101, ⓦwww.tajhotels.com. Subway N, R to 59th St. The *Pierre* is consistently named one of New York's top hotels. It was Salvador Dalí's favourite in the city, though the only surreal aspects today are the prices. If these prohibit a stay, afternoon tea in the glorious frescoed *Rotunda* is highly recommended. $580

Wales 1295 Madison Ave, at E 92nd St ⓣ212/876-6000, ⓦwww.waleshotel.com. Subway #6 to 96th St. Just steps from "Museum Mile", this Carnegie Hill hotel has hosted guests for over a century. Rooms are attractive with antique details, thoughtful in-room amenities, and some views of Central Park. Complimentary bottled spring water and continental breakfast. $215

Upper West Side

Amsterdam Inn 340 Amsterdam Ave, at W 76th St ⓣ212/579-7500, ⓦwww.amsterdaminn.com. Subway #1 to 79th St; B, C to 81st St. From the owners of the *Murray Hill Inn* (see p.275), the rooms here are fairly spare but clean, and the staff are friendly and helpful. $139

Beacon 2130 Broadway, at W 75th St ⓣ212/787-1100, ⓦwww.beaconhotel.com. Subway #1, #2, #3 to 72nd St. The *Beacon* is perfectly situated for strolling the gourmet markets and museums of the Upper West Side. While the rooms are comfortable and reasonably sized (with kitchenettes), they probably won't win any style awards. $285

Lucerne 201 W 79th St, at Amsterdam Ave ⓣ1-800/492-8122 or 212/875-1000, ⓦwww.thelucernehotel.com. Subway #1 to 79th St; B, C to 81st St. This beautifully restored 1904 brownstone, with its extravagant Baroque terracotta entrance, charming rooms and accommodating staff, is just a block from the Museum of Natural History (see p.193) and close to the liveliest stretches of Broadway and Columbus Avenue. $310

Mandarin Oriental New York 80 Columbus Circle, W 60th St between Broadway and Columbus Ave ⓣ212/805-8800, ⓦwww.mandarinoriental.com. Subway A, B, C, D, #1 to 59th St–Columbus Circle. The pampering is on a par with the astronomical rates at this entertainment-industry favourite. A plush palace of spacious, handsome rooms complete with Frette linens and floor-to-ceiling windows, the hotel offers both guests and diners spectacular views from the 35th floor *Lobby Lounge*. $955

Milburn 242 W 76th St, between Broadway and West End ⓣ1-800/833-9622 or 212/362-1006, ⓦwww.milburnhotel.com. Subway #1 to 79th St. Once past the classic-feel lobby, the rooms (all with kitchenettes) and suites are a little less showy but are on the large side for the neighbourhood. And the presence of a library of children's books and videogame players make this welcoming and well-situated hotel great for families. $259

On the Ave 222 W 77th St, between Amsterdam and Broadway ⓣ1-800/509-7598 or 212/362-1100, ⓦwww.ontheave-nyc.com. Subway #1 to 79th St. With its stainless-steel sinks, minimalist baths and dark-wood bed platforms, *On the Ave* feels forward-looking yet somehow out of step. It's clean, comfortable and discounts are sometimes available. $295

Harlem and north Manhattan

102 Brownstone Boutique Hotel 102 W 118th St, between Lenox and Powell aves ⓣ212/662-4223, ⓦwww.102brownstone.com. Subway #2, #3 to 116th St. Choice of elegant studio apartments (with kitchens) or suites, all with a romantic Victorian theme but equipped with wi-fi, free local phone and cable TV – it's a real bargain and only a short subway ride from Times Square. $175.

Brooklyn

NU Hotel 85 Smith St, at Atlantic Ave ⓣ718/852-8585, ⓦwww.nuhotelbrooklyn.com. Subway F, G to Bergen St; A, C, G to Hoyt–Schermerhorn sts. Cool, bright rooms, some with hammocks, in one of the few convenient Brooklyn hotels that's not a depressing chain. Though on a high-traffic thoroughfare, it's close to some of the nicest walking neighbourhoods around. $279

Apartment swapping

If you're coming to New York for more than a few nights and you happen to own a place in your home city/country, the least expensive and most authentic accommodation option by far is **apartment swapping**. You'd be amazed at the number of New Yorkers who would like to get out of the city for a few days or weeks; what's more, your humble Dublin or Seattle flat may seem spacious and exotic to a Manhattanite. Don't be afraid to play up your dwelling's positive features – the mountain view or medieval church that you take for granted may be just what your swap-partner's doctor ordered – and to ask for pictures and references of the potential swap in return. One of the most reputable exchange organizations is **Home Exchange** (ⓣ310/798-3864 or 1-800/877-8723, ⓦwww.homeexchange.com).

Hostels

Hostels are just about the only option for backpackers in New York. While they can vary greatly in quality, most are fine as long as you don't mind sleeping in a bunk bed and sharing a room with strangers (though if you're travelling in a group of four or six you can often book a room for yourselves).

Some hostels are affiliated with organizations that require you to be a member in order to stay, so be sure to ask when calling for a reservation. Although not all hostels require memberships, it's a good rule of thumb that the ones which do are generally cleaner, safer and more affordable. For hostels that do not participate in the larger budget-travel community, always ask about safety, security and locker availability before checking in and bunking down.

Hostels in New York are especially busy – and fairly rowdy – when the legions of summer backpackers descend on the city. The following is a small selection of the best hostels and YMCAs in the city, all of which have dorms for $50 or under and rooms usually around $100 or so.

Big Apple Hostel 119 W 45th St, between Sixth and Seventh aves ⓣ212/302-2603, ⓦwww.bigapplehostel.com. Subway B, D, F, M to 42nd St. You can't beat this hostel's Times Square location – it's easily one of the city's best budget picks. There's a secure luggage room, communal refrigerator and even an outdoor deck with barbeque. All rooms have a/c and shared baths. Dorms $45, private double rooms $125–160, including tax.

Central Park Hostel 19 W 103rd St, at Central Park ⓣ212/678-0491, ⓦwww.centralparkhostel.com. Subway B, C to 103rd St W. Upper West Side hostel in a renovated five-storey walk-up, with dorm beds for 4, 6, 8, or 10 people, as well as private rooms. All rooms share clean bathrooms, and lockers are available (bring a padlock). Sheets and blankets are included, payment in cash or travellers' cheques only; you must have a passport, or an international student or non–New York State ID. Dorms $34–55, private rooms $89–135, includes tax.

Chelsea Center Hostel 313 W 29th St, at Eighth Ave ⓣ212/643-0214, ⓦwww.chelseacenterhostel.com. Subway A, C, E to 34th St. This small, clean, safe, private hostel has beds for $35 (including tax), including sheets, blankets and a light breakfast. Private rooms $100–140. Reservations are essential in high season. Cash only.

Chelsea International Hostel 251 W 20th St, between Seventh and Eighth aves ⓣ212/647-0010, ⓦwww.chelseahostel.com. Subway C, E to 23rd St. A smart choice located in the heart of Chelsea. Share the clean, rudimentary rooms with 3 or 5 other people, or book a private double room. All guests must leave a $10 key deposit. No curfew; passport required. Dorms $40, private rooms $115, including tax.

▲ *Gershwin*

Gershwin 7 E 27th St, between Fifth and Madison aves ⓣ212/545-8000, ⓦwww.gershwinhotel.com. Subway N, R to 28th St. This hostel/hotel is geared toward younger travellers, with Pop Art decor, a bar/cocktail lounge and bunk-bed dorms with shared bath. Reservations highly recommended. Dorm beds $39–59, private rooms from $150.

Hostelling International-New York 891 Amsterdam Ave, at W 103rd St ⓣ212/932-2300, ⓦwww.hinewyork.org. Subway B, C, #1 to 103rd St. Dorm beds start at $29 (in 10-bed rooms); members pay a few dollars less per night. The massive facilities – 624 beds in all – include a restaurant, garden, games room (with a PlayStation 2), self-catering kitchen, TV room and laundry. Reserve well in advance – this hostel is very popular, partly due to the range of scheduled activities and tours offered.

Jazz on the Park 36 W 106th St, at Central Park ⓣ212/932-1600, ⓦwww.jazzhostels.com. Subway B, C to 103rd St W. This groovy bunkhouse boasts a TV/games room, a café and lots of activities, including live jazz on weekends. Rooms sleep between 2 and 14 people, and are clean, bright and have a/c. Reserve at least one week in advance. Dorms from $26, private double rooms with bath from $135.

Uptown Hostel 239 Lenox Ave, at W 122nd St ⓣ212/666-0559, ⓦwww.uptownhostel.com. Subway #2, #3 to 125th St. Clean, comfortable beds in the heart of Harlem. Bunk rooms sleeping 4–6 people, singles, and doubles are available. Enquire about weekly rates at the kindly owner's annexed property. Dorms $20, singles $35, doubles $55.

Vanderbilt YMCA 224 E 47th St, between Second and Third aves ⓣ212/912-2500, ⓦwww.ymcanyc.org. Subway E to 51st St. Smaller and quieter than most of the hostels listed here, and neatly placed in midtown Manhattan, only five minutes' walk from Grand Central. Swimming pool, gym and laundromat on the premises. All rooms have a/c and shared baths. Singles $105, bunk-bed doubles $115.

Wanderers Inn Hostel West 257 W 113th St, between Frederick Douglass and Adam Clayton Powell blvds ⓣ212/222-5602, ⓦwww.wanderersinn.com. Subway #1 to 110th St. Located close to Columbia and the Cathedral Church of St John the Divine, this renovated space features a backyard (with deck), kitchen and internet access. Dorm rooms have their own bathroom, but private rooms must share. Reception open 24hr. Passport required, no smoking and no curfew. Dorms $27, bunk and double rooms $97–106.

West Side YMCA 5 W 63rd St, at Central Park W ⓣ212/875-4100, ⓦwww.ymcanyc.org. Subway A, B, C, D, #1 to 59th St–Columbus Circle. This "Y" is steps from Central Park and housed in a landmark building that boasts pool tiles gifted from the King of Spain. It has two floors of rooms, an inexpensive restaurant, swimming pool, gym and laundry. All rooms have a/c and semi-private or shared bathroom. Singles and bunk-bed doubles around $102–112.

Whitehouse Hotel of New York 340 Bowery, at Bond St ⓣ212/477-5623, ⓦwww.whitehousehotelofny.com. Subway #6 to Bleecker St. This is the only hostel in the city that offers private single and double rooms at dorm rates. Unbeatable prices combined with an ideal downtown location, and amenities such as a/c, ATMs, cable TV and linens, make this hostel great value. Singles $29.57, doubles $56.50.

Bed and breakfasts and apartments

Staying at a **bed and breakfast** can be a good way of visiting New York at an affordable price. But don't go looking for B&Bs on the streets: most rooms – except for a few which we've found off the beaten track (listed below) – are let out via the following official agencies, which all recommend making your reservations as far in advance as possible, especially for the cheapest rooms. Rates tend to run to about $120 for a double, or $160 and up a night for a studio apartment. Don't expect to socialize with your temporary landlord/lady, either. In the case of a "hosted" room, chances are your space will be self-contained, and you'll hardly see them. Renting an "unhosted" apartment means that the owner won't be there at all. B&Bs are also your best bet in the outer boroughs, and especially in Brooklyn, where hotels are few and far between. There are quite a few to choose from, many of which are housed in Brooklyn townhouses and provide a welcome change to the corporate high-rise accommodations typically available in Manhattan.

You might also want to consider looking on ⓦnewyork.craigslist.org or a nationwide site like ⓦwww.vrbo.com for deals on vacation **apartments** that homeowners let for short or long-term stays.

B&B agencies

Affordable New York City ⓣ**212/533-4001,** ⓦ**www.affordablenyc.com.** Detailed descriptions are provided by this established network of 120 properties (B&Bs and apartments) around the city. B&B accommodation from $95 (shared bath) and $125 (private bath), unhosted studios $150–250, and one-bedrooms $175–300. Cash or travellers' cheques only; four- and five-night minimums. Very customer-oriented and personable staff.

Bed and Breakfast Network of New York ⓣ**1-800/900-8134 or 212/645-8134,** ⓦ**www.bedandbreakfastnetny.com.** Call at least one month in advance, and ask about weekly and monthly specials. Lists hosted doubles for $120–200, but has apartments as well.

City Lights Bed & Breakfast ⓣ**212/737-7049,** ⓦ**www.citylightsbandb.com.** There are more than 400 carefully screened B&Bs (and short-term apartment rentals) on this agency's books, with many of the hosts involved in theatre and the arts. Hosted doubles are $80–175; unhosted apartments cost $135–300 and up per night depending on size. Two- or three-night minimum stay.

CitySonnet ⓣ**212/614-3034,** ⓦ**www.citysonnet.com.** This small, personalized, artist-run B&B/short-term apartment agency offers accommodation all over the city, but specializes in Greenwich Village. Singles start at $120, doubles are $125–175 and unhosted studio flats start at $215.

Colby International 21 Park Ave, Eccleston Park, Prescot L34 2QY, UK ⓣ**0151/292-2910,** ⓦ**www.colbyinternational.com.** Guaranteed accommodation can be arranged from the UK. Book at least a fortnight ahead in high season for these excellent-value apartments (studios to 3 bedrooms $200–450) and B&B singles ($90) and doubles ($110–120).

Manhattan B&Bs and guesthouses

East Village Bed and Coffee 110 Ave C, between E 7th and E 8th sts ⓣ**12/533-4175,** ⓦ**www.bedandcoffee.com. Subway L to First Ave; F to Lower East Side–Second Ave.** Unusual location in the East Village/Alphabet City, in one of the most cutting-edge neighbourhoods in the city, with cheap, cosy rooms (shared bath), friendly owners, kitchens, free wi-fi and computers, and a tranquil garden. On the downside, it's a long walk to the subway (and there's no breakfast). $130

Gisele's Guest House 134 W 119th St, between Powell Blvd and Lenox Ave ⓣ**212/666-0559,** ⓦ**nygiselebnb.com. Subway #2, #3 to 116th St.** Set in a lovely old brownstone in central Harlem, this B&B features comfortable double rooms (shared bathrooms), dressed in a simple nineteenth-century style. $110

Harlem Flophouse 242 W 123rd St between Powell and Frederick Douglass blvds ⓣ**212/662-0678,** ⓦ**www.harlemflophouse.com. Subway A, B, C, #2, #3 to 125th St** This hip, beautiful, artist-owned 1890s brownstone has just four rooms each with sinks, and two shared bathrooms with antique clawfoot tubs. Charming, but it's an old building and dimly lit throughout; not to everyone's taste. $100 for one person, plus $25–35 for second person.

Harlem Renaissance House 237 W 139th St between Powell and Frederick Douglass blvds ⓣ**212/226-1590,** ⓦ**harlemrenaissancehouse.com. Subway B, C, #2, #3 to 135th St.** Located on historic Strivers' Row, this friendly B&B occupies a Renaissance Revival townhouse with just two rooms equipped with bath, wi-fi, cable TV and iPod docks – continental breakfast included. Gay-friendly. $220

Inn at Irving Place 56 Irving Place, at E 17th St ⓣ**1-800/685-1447 or 212/533-4600,** ⓦ**www.innatirving.com. Subway L, N, Q, R, #4, #5, #6 to 14th St–Union Square.** Frequented by celebrities, this handsome pair of 1834 brownstones ranks as one of the most exclusive guesthouses in the city. Rooms are usually around $325–645 a night to stay in one of the twelve rooms (or "residences") – each named for a famous architect, designer or actor. The *Inn* also offers five-course high teas ($35 per person).

Inn on 23rd St 131 W 23rd St, between Sixth and Seventh aves ⓣ**1-877/387-2323 or 212/463-0330,** ⓦ**www.innon23rd.com. Subway F, M, #1 to 23rd St.** This family-run B&B is adorned with heirlooms and comfortable furniture in a series of theme quarters. Options like the 1940s Room, Maritime Room and Bamboo Room feature pillow-top mattresses and white-noise machines to block out any extraneous din. $299.

Jones Street Guesthouse 31 Jones St, between Bleecker and West 4th sts ⓦ**www.jonesstreetguesthouse.com. Subway A, B, C, D, E, F, M to West 4th St; #1 to Christopher St.** Rare B&B in the heart of the West Village, just off Bleecker; two nicely renovated en-suite rooms, spotlessly clean, with friendly owners in the apartments above – closest you'll get to "living like a local". Breakfast is courtesy of a $5 per person voucher at nearby *Doma*. Free wi-fi. $175

Room in Soho Loft 153 Lafayette St at Grand St ⓣ212/965-3000, listing at ⓦwww.bedandbreakfast.com. Subway N, R, #6 to Canal St. In a great location at the edge of vibrant Soho, these unique, quirky (and cheap) loft apartments above a gallery managed by the owners, are a great way to experience the neighbourhood; two en-suite 7th-floor rooms (walk-up only!) and two fifth-floor rooms with shared bathroom. Kitchen included. $157

Sugar Hill Harlem Inn 460 W 141st St, between Amsterdam and Convent aves ⓣ917/464-3528, ⓦwww.sugarhillharleminn.com. Subway A, B, C, D to 145th St, #1 to 137th St. If you fancy escaping the carnival in Midtown, opt for this gracious B&B, set in a 1906 townhouse tucked away on a quiet street in Hamilton Heights. Rooms with bath have all been renovated but maintain a Victorian feel; rugs, fireplaces, antiques and huge beds. Cable TV, DVD players and breakfast included. $125

Brooklyn B&Bs and guesthouses

Akwaaba Mansion 347 MacDonough St, at Stuyvesant Ave, Bedford-Stuyvesant ⓣ718/455-5958, ⓦwww.akwaaba.com. Subway A, C to Utica Ave. A New York landmark, this Victorian mansion is one of a kind, featuring Afrocentric details like Daffodil rag dolls and Adrinkra fabrics. A tearoom, sunny porch and Southern-style breakfast will make anyone feel right at home. In case you were wondering, the Ghanaian name translates as "welcome". $175

Baisley House 294 Hoyt St, between Union and Sackett sts, Carroll Gardens ⓣ718/935-1959. Subway F, G to Carroll St. Another charming Victorian brownstone, this one dates from 1865. Single $125, doubles $150–175, all with shared bath. There's a two-night minimum stay.

Bed & Breakfast on the Park 113 Prospect Park W, between 6th and 7th sts, Park Slope ⓣ718/499-6115, ⓦwww.bbnyc.com. Subway F, G to Seventh Ave. A handsome 1892 limestone townhouse with views over Prospect Park. There are five double rooms with private baths ranging from $175–325 a night.

23

Cafés, bakeries and snacks

Eateries geared toward people on the go are omnipresent in New York. Travellers will be hard-pressed to find an area that doesn't offer something in the way of a small meal: breads, pastries, pizzas, sandwiches, bagels, meats, cheeses, juices, ice creams and vegetarian goodies are among the myriad options available. Every neighbourhood has several favourite haunts; this chapter details establishments good for breakfast, lunch, snacks and coffee pit-stops. See Chapter 24, "Restaurants", if you're in the mood for a larger, sit-down affair.

New York's **cafés** and **bakeries** have been greatly influenced by the city's diverse ethnic populations; American, French and Italian establishments are the most visible. Many of the more long-established cafés are in downtown Manhattan, and are perfect for lingering or just resting up between sights. One of the newest trends is the arrival of innovative mobile food trucks, a cut above your average kebab van – we've included our favourites on p.295.

New York also has a number of **coffeehouses** and **tearooms** that provide fresh coffee, tea and juices, pastries and light snacks. There are **coffee shops** or **diners** on just about every block that serve cheap, decent breakfast specials. The more upscale midtown hotels are good places to stop for formal tea, too, if you can afford the prices they charge for the English country-house atmosphere they often try to contrive. And plenty of attention has been devoted in recent years to perfecting **sandwich**, **pizza slice**, **burger**, **hot dog** and **taco** variations – if you can think of it, no matter how unusual, it's probably already been done here.

Financial District and City Hall Park

Bakeries and cafés

Financier Patisserie 62 Stone St ⓣ212/344-5600. Subway #2, #3 to Wall St. High-quality French pastry shop known for its cakes (from $3.50), macaroons ($1.75) and "financier" almond cakes ($1.35). Coffee, made-to-order salads, paninis and soups (from $.7.50) accompany the assorted vienoisserie, all made daily on the premises. Also located in World Financial Center and at 35 Cedar St. Mon–Fri 7am–8pm, Sat 8.30am–6.30pm.

Sandwiches and snacks

BonChon Chicken 104 John St at Cliff St ⓣ646/682-7747. Subway #2, #3 to Fulton St. This Korean fast-food franchise has a cult

Rough Guide favourites

We've highlighted particular types of snacks and drink options and listed them in boxes on the following pages.

Bagels p.290
Coffee (and tea) p.301
Pizza by the slice p.296
Street food p.295

following for its fried chicken wings and drumsticks, basted in two sauces (soy-garlic and hot and spicy). Sets $9–22. Daily 11am–11pm.

Burger Burger 44 Stone St ⓣ212/269-9100. Subway R to Whitehall St. One of the few downtown snack stops open on Sundays, this small takeaway joint knocks out some of the best burgers in town; the classic Angus beef burger is $7.95, but the Chili Cheese ($9.50) and New Yorker ($10.95) are a real treat (they also sell *Nathan's* hot dogs). Mon–Fri 11am–10pm, Sat & Sun noon–9pm.

Leo's Bagels 3 Hanover Square at Stone St ⓣ212/785-7828. Subway #2, #3 to Wall St. Get your bagel fix at this popular local joint, with the hand-rolled, chewy main event going for $1 or $2.50–3.50 with huge dollops of cream cheese and various *schmears*. Also does salads, soups and sandwiches. Daily 6am–5pm.

Tribeca and Soho

Bakeries and cafés

Balthazar Bakery 80 Spring St, between Crosby St and Broadway ⓣ212/965-1785. Subway #6 to Spring St. This bakery has wonderful breads (including a dark chocolate loaf) and pastries of all sorts (from $2 for the madeleines). They also serve great home-made fizzy lemonade ($3.25). Mon–Fri 7.30am–8pm, Sat & Sun 8am–8pm.

Duane Park Patisserie 179 Duane St at Greenwich St ⓣ212/274-8447. Subway #1, #2, #3 to Chambers St. This small café is classic Tribeca; excellent coffee, great food, stylish space and pricey pastries. Top picks include the zesty lemon tart ($4) and the creamy éclair ($3.50); the cookies are pretty good, too ($1.50). Mon–Sat 8am–6.30pm, Sun 9am–5pm.

Grandaisy Bakery 250 West Broadway at Beach St ⓣ212/334-9435. Subway #1 to Franklin St. Also 73 Sullivan St near Spring St. The best coffee in Tribeca comes with some fabulous extras; tasty vegetarian pizza slices featuring cauliflower, potato, tomato and zucchini, as well as superb pastries. Try the flourless chocolate cake ($4.50) or the Nutella cookies ($2). Mon–Sat 7am–7pm, Sun 9am–5pm.

Once Upon a Tart 135 Sullivan St, between Houston and Prince sts ⓣ212/387-8869. Subway C, E to Spring St. A good place to come for a light lunch (sandwiches $6.95) or to satisfy a sugar craving. The interior is a bit cramped but intimate and oh-so-quaint. Also plenty of options for vegetarians (vegetable tarts from $5.95). Mon–Fri 8am–7pm, Sat 9am–7pm, Sun 9am–6pm.

Sandwiches and snacks

Hampton Chutney 68 Prince St, at Crosby St ⓣ212/226-9996. Subway R to Prince St. Don't let the name deceive you: this place is all about *dosas* and *uttapas* (from $7.95), traditional South Indian fare, albeit with plenty of American ingredients. Orders are spiced up with a choice of fresh, home-made chutneys: cilantro, curry, mango, tomato or peanut. Daily 11am–9pm.

Pepe Rosso To Go 149 Sullivan St, between Houston and Prince sts ⓣ212/677-4555. Subway C, E to Spring St. Deservedly popular Italian takeaway, offering cheap but imaginative pasta dishes (such as penne vodka with pancetta) and panini (both from $6.95). Everything on the menu is under $12. Daily 11am–11pm.

Chinatown

Unless stated otherwise, all the below can be accessed from J, N, Q, R, Z and #6 lines to Canal Street.

Bakeries and cafés

Fay Da Bakery 83 Mott St, at Canal St ☎212/791-3884. Chinatown is littered with Hong Kong–style bakeries, but this is one of the best. Try the hot dog-like sausage or pork floss buns ($1.25), egg custard tarts (*dan tat* in Cantonese) and the fresh mango or green-tea *mochi* rice balls ($0.95). Daily 7am–8pm.

New Golden Fun Wong 41 Mott St between Bayard and Pell sts. Top place for Chinese cakes, from thick mooncakes ($2.75) and *hopia* (Filipino-style bean-filled cakes; $2.50) to tasty taro cakes and custard tarts (both $0.75). Daily 8am–8pm.

Sandwiches and snacks

Chinatown Ice Cream Factory 65 Bayard St, between Mott and Elizabeth sts ☎212/608-4170. An essential after-dinner stop, though the wondrously unusual flavours are good any time. Specialties include black sesame, taro, green tea, ginger, almond cookie and lychee (from $3.75). Daily 11am–11pm.

Fong Inn Too 46 Mott St, between Bayard and Pell sts. This basic shop sells two delicious main dishes, primarily to the line of eager takeaway customers: fried radish (or "turnip") cake ($1.50) and silky soft soy-bean pudding, served piping hot with sweet syrup ($1–2.25). Daily 7am–9pm.

Laoshan Shandong Guotie 106 Mosco St, between Mulberry and Mott sts ☎212/693-1060. Identified simply by a "Fried Dumpling" sign in English, this hole-in-the-wall specializes in pan-fried pork dumplings characteristic of northern China, with the absolute bargain price of $1 for five. Squeeze onto a bench inside or takeaway. Daily 8am–9pm.

Xi'an Famous Foods 88 East Broadway (entrance at 106 Forsyth St, under Manhattan Bridge). Subway F to East Broadway. Tiny takeaway counter serving delicious specialties from northwest China: hand-pulled noodles with chilli oil and cumin-spiked lamb ($5), and savoury cumin lamb burger ($2.50), chunks of succulent lamb stuffed into pitta bread. Daily 11am–8pm.

Little Italy and Nolita

Bakeries and cafés

Bread 20 Spring St, between Mott and Elizabeth sts ☎212-334-1015. Subway #6 to Spring St. Stylish café specializing in creative baguette and panini sandwiches (from $10) packed with high-quality meats and cheeses; highlights include the fresh sardines and tuna, and aged Italian salami. Daily 10.30am–midnight, Thurs–Sat till 12.30pm.

Café Gitane 242 Mott St, between Prince and Houston sts ☎212/334-9552. Subway R to Prince St. Come here for a bowl of delicious café crème ($3.50). For those looking for a bite to eat, zesty Moroccan-influenced food is also on offer (couscous is $11.50). Chock-full of posers, but still one of the best cafés around. Daily 9am–midnight, Fri & Sat till 12.30pm.

Ceci-Cela 55 Spring St, between Mulberry and Lafayette sts ☎212/274-9179. Subway #6 to Spring St. Tiny Cute French patisserie with tables in the back, as well as a stand-up counter and bench out front. The croissants ($2) and *palmiers* (elephant-ear-shaped, sugar-coated pastries) are divine, as are the cocoa-dusted truffles (from $3.75). Mon–Thurs 6.30am–8pm, Fri & Sat 6.30am–8.30pm, Sun 7.30am–8pm.

Ciao Bella Gelato 285 Mott St, between Houston and Prince sts ☎212/431-3591. Subway B, D, F to Broadway-Lafayette St. Heavenly take-away gelato and sorbet, some of the best in the city; the blood-orange sorbet is to die for and the coffee gelato equally delicious (scoops from $3.25). Daily noon–7pm.

Ferrara Café 195 Grand St, between Mott and Mulberry sts ☎212/226-6150. Subway #6 to Spring St. The best known and most traditional of Little Italy's coffeehouses, this neighbourhood landmark has been around since 1892. Try the New York cheesecake, hand-dipped chocolate cannoli ($3.50–5), or, in summer, *granite* (Italian ices). Outdoor seating is available in warmer weather. Daily 8.30am–11.30pm, Fri & Sat till midnight.

Sandwiches and snacks

Ray's 27 Prince St, between Mott and Elizabeth sts ⓣ212/966-1960. Subway R to Prince St. While countless pizzerias in the city claim to be the "original *Ray's*", this Little Italy mainstay is perhaps the first (1959) and the most distinctive of the bunch. Grab a quintessential New York slice for $2.65, or a whole pizza for $16. Daily 11am–midnight.

Rice to Riches 37 Spring St, between Mott and Mulberry sts ⓣ212/274-0008. Subway #6 to Spring St. Rice pudding made hip and utterly irresistible, served up in this funky space in a variety of sweet flavours, from peanut butter and choc chip to mango and cinnamon. Bowls start at $6.75. There are a few tables inside. Daily 11am–11pm, Fri & Sat till 1am.

Saigon Vietnamese Sandwich 369 Broome St, between Mott and Elizabeth sts ⓣ212/219-8341. Subway #6 to Spring St. One of the best makers of Vietnamese sandwiches (known as *bánh mì*) in the city. The classic is made with a large chunk of French bread, and stuffed with grilled pork, sausage and thinly sliced pickled vegetables, all for less than $5. Daily 8am–8pm.

Lower East Side

Bakeries and cafés

DessertTruck Works 6 Clinton St, between Houston and Stanton sts, ⓦdt-works.net. Subway F, J, M, Z to Delancey St–Essex St. Tiny café run by ex-*Le Cirque* pastry chefs serving a small, crafted menu of $6 desserts; think warm chocolate bread pudding, brioche donuts with Nutella, and buttermilk panna cotta tarts. Daily 11am–11pm.

Kossar's 367 Grand St, at Essex St ⓣ212/473-4810. Subway F, J, M, Z to Delancey St–Essex St. This generations-old kosher treasure serves, bar none, the city's best *bialys* ($0.90), a flattened savoury dough traditionally topped with onion or garlic; the bagels aren't far behind. Sun–Thurs 6am–8pm, Fri 6am–3pm.

Sugar Sweet Sunshine 126 Rivington St, between Essex and Norfolk sts ⓣ212/995-1960. Subway F, J, M, Z to Delancey St–Essex St. Pudding lovers will be in serious danger at this fabulous bakery, established by two ex-employees of *Magnolia* (see p.292). Choose 12oz ($4) or 16oz ($6) cups of banana, choc chip or pumpkin puddings, as well as delectable cupcakes ($1.50) and other treats. Mon–Thurs 8am–10pm, Fri 8am–11pm, Sat 10am–11pm, Sun 10am–7pm.

Yonah Schimmel Knish Bakery 137 E Houston St, between Forsyth and Eldridge sts ⓣ212/477-2858. Subway F to Lower East Side–Second Ave. The fine *knishes* ($5) at this 1910 store, rounds of vegetable, cheese or potato and meat-stuffed dough, are baked fresh on the premises, as are the wonderful bagels ($0.85). Daily 9am–7pm, Fri & Sat till 10pm.

Sandwiches and snacks

Doughnut Plant 379 Grand St, between Essex and Clinton sts ⓣ212/505-3700. Subway F, J, M, Z to Delancey–Essex St. Serious (and seriously delicious) donuts ($2–3); be sure to sample the seasonal flavours and glazes, including chestnut cake, pumpkin and passion fruit. Tues–Sun 6.30am–till the donuts run out (5–7pm).

Il Laboratorio del Gelato 95 Orchard St, between Broome and Delancey sts ⓣ212/343-9922. Subway F, J, M, Z to Delancey–Essex St. This shrine to cream and sugar serves up over 75 flavours (20 offered daily), including fig, lavender and malt (scoops from $3.50). Expected to open second spot at 188 Ludlow St and East Houston in late 2010. Daily 10am–6pm.

Mikey's Burger 134 Ludlow St, between Rivington and Stanton sts ⓣ212/979-9211. Subway F, J, M, Z to Delancey–Essex St. Michael Huynh's burger bar offers four types of 6oz burgers on potato rolls, including a beef burger with mustard seeds and corned beef hash ($5.50) and Asian-accented BLT and lamb burgers ($6). Cheese fries ($4) and shakes (try sesame; $5) make a fitting accompaniment. Daily noon–2am.

Bagels

Theories abound as to the **origin of the modern bagel**. Most likely, it is a derivative of the pretzel, with the word "bagel" coming from the German *biegen*, "to bend." Whatever their birthplace, it is certain that bagels have become a **New York institution**. Until the 1950s, bagels were still handmade by Eastern European Jewish immigrants in cellars scattered around New York's Lower East Side.

Modern-day bagels are softer and have a smaller hole than their ancestors – the hole made them easy to carry on a long stick to hawk on street corners. Their curiously chewy texture is a result of being boiled before they are baked. They are most traditionally (and famously) served with cream cheese and lox (smoked salmon). The last decade has witnessed the invention of such flavours as blueberry and cheese, which purists decry as reducing their revered bagel to a low-class muffin alternative.

Though bagels are now an American dietary staple, New Yorkers would say only a few places serve **the real thing**. Here is a list of some of the city's better bagelsmiths.

Absolute Bagels Upper West Side p.298
Ess-A-Bagel Midtown East p.294
H & H Bagels Upper West Side p.299
Kossar's Lower East Side p.289
Russ & Daughters Lower East Side p.290

Russ & Daughters 179 E Houston St, between Allen and Orchard sts ⓣ212/475-4880. Subway F to Lower East Side–Second Ave. The original Manhattan gourmet shop, it was set up in 1914 to sate the appetites of homesick immigrant Jews with smoked fish, and now sells caviar, halvah, pickled vegetables, fine cheese and amazing hand-rolled bagels with smoky lox (from $8.45); try the "Super Heebster", whitefish and baked salmon salad with wasabi roe on a bagel ($10.45). Regular bagels with cream cheese start at $2.45. Mon–Fri 8am–8pm, Sat 9am–7pm, Sun 8am–5.30pm.

Vanessa's Dumpling House 118A Eldridge St, between Grand and Broome sts ⓣ212/625-8008. Subway B, D to Grand St. This always-busy Chinese eatery knocks out various combinations of steamed or fried pork, shrimp and vegetable dumplings at the bargain price of $1 for 4. Daily 7.30am–10.30pm, Sun till 10pm.

East Village

Bakeries and cafés

De Robertis 176 First Ave, between E 10th and E 11th sts ⓣ212/674-7137. Subway L to First Ave. Traditional Italian bakery/café that's been around since 1904. The old-New York vibe is so good that the establishment has been featured in multiple Woody Allen flicks. Try the cheesecake-on-a-stick ($3.50), ices and gelato ($3.25). Daily 9am–11am, Fri & Sat till midnight, Sun till 10pm.

Momofuku Milk Bar 207 Second Ave (entrance on E 13th St) ⓣ212/254-3500. Subway L to Third Ave. David Chang's bakery (around the corner from his *Ssäm Bar*) sells his famous pork buns ($9 for two) as well as a host of sweet treats: thick shakes ($6), crack pie (oat crust and buttery filling; $5.25) and compost cookies (pretzels, coffee and choc chips; $1.85). Mon–Fri 8am–midnight, Sat & Sun 9am–midnight.

Spot Dessert Bar 13 St Mark's Place, between Second and Third aves ⓣ212/677-5670. Subway #6 to Astor Place. Celebrated chef Pichet Ong has concocted some irresistible treats for this basement café, decked out in a vaguely East Asian rustic style: "tapas" puddings might come with coconut, persimmon or chocolate banana ($7–8), while cupcakes ($2.75) and cookies ($1.75) are equally inventive. Daily 11am–11pm, Thurs–Sat till 1am.

▲ *Veniero's Pasticceria & Café*

Veniero's Pasticceria & Café 342 E 11th St, between First and Second aves ☎212/674-7070. Subway L to First Ave; #6 to Astor Place. An East Village bakery and neighbourhood institution since 1894, *Veniero's* desserts and decor are fabulously over the top. The ricotta cheesecake ($4.25) and home-made gelato ($3) are great in the summer. Daily 8am–midnight, Fri & Sat till 1am.

Sandwiches and snacks

Artichoke 328 E 14th St between First and Second aves ☎212/228-2004. Subway L to First Ave. Fabulous late-night pizza slices to take away, with just four choices: sumptuous cheese-laden Sicilian ($3.50), Margarita ($3.50), crab ($4) or the trademark artichoke-spinach, topped with a super-creamy sauce ($4). Daily noon–3am, Fri & Sat until 5am.

Crif Dogs 113 St Mark's Place, between First Ave and Ave A ☎212/614-2728. Subway #6 to Astor Place. Hot-dog aficionados swear by these deep-fried, shiny wieners bursting with flavour ($2.75), enjoyed Philly-steak style, smothered in cheese ($4), or topped with avocado and bacon ($4.50). Daily noon–2am, Fri & Sat till 4am.

Dos Toros Taqueria 137 Fourth Ave, between 13th and 14th sts ☎212/677-7300. Subway #4. #5, #6 to Union Square. This authentic, reasonably priced Tex-Mex takeaway (with a few benches inside) attracts plenty of students and long lines at lunchtime. Opt for burritos ($7.35), tacos ($3.67) or quesadillas ($5.97) stuffed with *carne asada* (steak), *carnitas* (pork) or *pollo asado* (grilled chicken). Mon–Sat 11.30am–11pm, Sun noon–10pm.

Liquiteria 170 Second Ave, at E 11th St ☎212/358-0300. Subway #6 to Astor Place. The smoothies here are by far the best in Manhattan (try the "Orangasm" or the "Reggae Rumba"; $6.45). There are over 30 combos, and loads of supplement shots. You can also get delicious, healthy lunches such as oatmeal with fresh fruit ($5.50) or organic PBJs ($4.60). Mon–Fri 7am–8pm, Sat & Sun 8am–8pm.

Mamoun's Falafel 22 St Mark's Place, between Second and Third aves. Subway #6 to Astor Place. This tiny takeaway (with a few seats inside) is the best place for cheap, wholesome falafel and *baba ganoush* in the city, with filling plates for $5 (sandwiches $2.50), kebabs from $10 and convenient late-night hours. Daily 11am–5am.

Otafuku 236 E 9th St, between Second and Third aves ☎212/353-8503. Subway #6 to Astor Place. Excellent Japanese hole-in-the-wall, serving generous octopus *takoyaki* balls ($5), various types of scrumptious *okonomiyaki* (savoury pancake; $8) and pan-fried noodles ($7). Mon–Thurs 1–10pm, Fri & Sat noon–11pm, Sun noon–10pm.

Pommes Frites 123 Second Ave, between E 7th St and St Mark's Place ☎212/674-1234. Subway #6 to Astor Place. Not the best fries in the city, but the gooey, Belgian-style toppings ($1 extra) make all the difference; try the rosemary garlic mayo or curry ketchup. Fries portions range from $4.50 to $7.75. Daily 11.30am–1am, Fri & Sat till 3.30am.

Porchetta 110 E 7th St, between First Ave and Ave A ☎212/777-2151. Subway #6 to Astor Place. This tiny takeaway shop (with a few stools and counter inside) has developed a loyal following for its luscious Tuscan *porchetta* sandwiches ($10), thick slabs of roasted, seasoned pork in ciabatta roll. Daily 11.30am–10pm, Fri & Sat till 11pm.

This Little Piggy Had Roast Beef 149 First Ave at 9th St ☎212/253-1500. Subway #6 to Astor Place. This takeaway place does just three things: glorious roast beef sandwiches on a roll, au jus with Cheez Whiz ($4.50), or on a hero loaf with fresh mozzarella and gravy ($7.50); and pastrami on rye ($6.50). Add hand-cut fries for $2.50. Daily 11am–11pm.

West Village

Bakeries and cafés

Caffè Dante 79 MacDougal St, between Bleecker and Houston sts ⓣ212/982-5275. Subway A, B, C, D, E, F, M to W 4th St. A morning stopoff for many locals since 1915. It's often jammed with NYU students and professors sipping cappuccinos, espressos and caffè alfredo with ice cream (drinks from $2.50). Daily 10am–2am, Fri & Sat till 3am.

Caffè Reggio 119 MacDougal St, between Bleecker and W 3rd sts ⓣ212/475-9557. Subway A, B, C, D, E, F, M to W 4th St. Another historic Village coffeehouse, this time dating back to 1927, embellished with all sorts of Italian antiques, paintings and sculpture. Tennessee Williams sipped espresso here (now $2.75) and scenes from *Godfather II* were filmed inside. Daily 10am–2am.

Di Fiore Marquet 15 E 12th St, between Fifth Ave and University Place ⓣ212/229-9313. Subway N, Q, R, L, #4, #5, #6 to Union Square. Thanks to its convenient location, ample tables and low-key atmosphere, this French café is the perfect place to warm up or cool down and rest your feet. There's an emphasis on café fare (coffee $2.50, wine $8), but they serve more substantial if a bit pricey meals, too: quiche, salads and sandwiches ($13–16). Daily 7.30am–10pm. Mon till 6pm.

▲ *Magnolia Bakery*

Doma 17 Perry St, at Seventh Ave ⓣ212/929-4339. Subway #1 to Christopher St. A corner window, good brews (from $1.75), and a linger-all-day vibe make this a neighbourhood favourite; it's the anti-*Starbucks*. Daily 7.45am–midnight.

Grey Dog's Coffee 33 Carmine St, between Bleecker and Bedford sts ⓣ212/462-0041. Subway A, B, C, D, E, F, M to W 4th St. Casual café specializing in warm muffins and huge "Michigan-style" sandwiches ($9). Try the awesome Philly cheese steak ($9.25) or cobb salad ($13.95). Mon–Thurs 6.30am–11.30pm, Fri 6.30am–12.30am, Sat 7.30am–12.30am, Sun 7.30am–11.30pm.

Magnolia Bakery 401 Bleecker St, at W 11th St ⓣ212/462-2572. Subway #1 to Christopher St. There are lots of baked goods on offer here, but everyone comes for the heavenly and deservedly famous multicoloured cupcakes (celebrated in both *Sex and the City* and *Saturday Night Live*), $2.75 each. Lines can stretch around the block. Mon noon–11.30pm, Tues–Thurs 9am–11.30pm, Fri 9am–12.30am, Sat 10am–12.30am, Sun 10am–11.30pm.

Tea & Sympathy 108 Greenwich Ave, between W 12th and 13th sts ⓣ212/807-8329. Subway A, C, E, L to 14th St. Self-consciously cutesy British tearoom, serving an afternoon high tea ($35) replete with finger sandwiches, scones and clotted cream, as well as traditional staples like Sunday roast ($28), bangers and mash ($15.50) and shepherd's pie ($14.95). Mon–Fri 11.30am–10.30pm, Sat & Sun 9.30am–10.30pm.

Thé Adoré 17 E 13th St, between Fifth Ave and University Place ⓣ212/243-8742. Subway N, Q, R, L, #4, #5, #6 to Union Square. A charming Japanese-run tearoom, with a downstairs takeaway counter and a small, cosy café upstairs. Serves selection of Chinese, Japanese and black teas (from $4.50), with excellent pastries; also does baguette sandwiches ($6.50–8) and tasty bowls of soup (add $1.50). Mon–Fri 8am–6pm, Sat 9am–5pm.

Sandwiches and snacks

Cones 272 Bleecker St, between Seventh Ave and Morton St ⓣ212/414-1795. Subway #1 to

Christopher St. Wonderful gelatos by two Argentine brothers. Flavours like tiramisu and rich chocolate attract long lines, especially on warm summer nights (scoops from $4.25). Daily 1pm–11pm, Fri & Sat till 1am.

Faicco's Pork Store 260 Bleecker St, between Morton and Leroy sts ☎212/243-1974. Subway A, B, C, D, E, F, M to W 4th St. This old-school Italian butcher serves some of the best-value sandwiches in the city, huge rolls of ham, sausage, and chicken cutlet with aged provolone from $6. Add a tangy *prosciutto* ball for $1. Tues–Fri 8.30am–6pm, Sat 8am–6pm, Sun 9am–2pm.

Gray's Papaya 402 Sixth Ave at 8th St ☎212/260-3532. Subway A, B, C, D, E, F, M to W 4th St. For a real New York experience, grab a crispy hot dog ($1.50) at this standing-room-only chain, the more established rival of *Papaya Dog* down the road. The "papaya" refers to the fresh tropical fruit drinks ($1.25) also sold here (gimmicky, but delicious). Open 24hr.

Joe's Pizza 7 Carmine St at Sixth Ave ☎212/366-1182. Subway A, B, C, D, E, F, M to W 4th St. Classic New York pizza to go ($2.50); nothing fancy, just thin-crusted slices, with cheese that tastes like cheese and a rich tomato base – add pepperoni for some bite ($3.50). Daily 9am–5am.

Num Pang 21 E 12th St at University Place ☎212/255-3271. Subway N, Q, R, L, #4, #5, #6 to Union Square. Superb Cambodian-style sandwiches served on freshly toasted semolina flour baguettes with chilli mayo and house-made pickles; try the pulled duroc pork or peppercorn catfish (both $7.50). Mon–Sat 11am–10pm, Sun noon–9pm.

Peanut Butter & Company 240 Sullivan St, between Bleecker and W 3rd Sts ☎212/677-3995. Subway A, B, C, D, E, F, M to W 4th St. Peanut butter in ways you never imagined. Try the "Elvis" – a grilled peanut butter and honey sandwich with bananas ($7.50), or the slightly more adventurous "Pregnant Lady", made with pickles ($6.25). Sandwiches are $5–8. Daily 11am–9pm, Fri & Sat till 10pm.

Two Boots to Go West 201 W 11th St at Seventh Ave ☎212/633-9096. Subway #1, #2, #3 to 14th St. Great thin-crust pizzas with a cornmeal dusting and Cajun flavour. Try a small "Newman" (sopressata, sweet sausage and ricotta; $9.95) or the "Earth Mother" (vegetable Sicilian; $9.95). Mon–Wed 11am–midnight, Thurs 11am–1am, Fri & Sat 11am–2am, Sun noon–midnight.

Chelsea

Bakeries and cafés

Billy's Bakery 184 Ninth Ave, between 21st and 22nd sts; second location in Tribeca. Subway C, E to 23rd St. Opened by a former employee of *Magnolia Bakery*, though the rustic farmhouse interior is far less crowded and the cupcakes cheaper and just as scrumptious. Other highlights include a tangy Key Lime Pie. Mon–Thurs 8.30am–11pm, Fri & Sat 8.30am–midnight, Sun 9am–10pm.

Rafaella on Ninth 178 Ninth Ave, at 21st St. Subway C, E to 23rd St. The main attraction at this local café is the gracious, antique ambience, enhanced by Victorian-style chairs, shabby sofas and gilded antiques. Stick with coffee, as the food is just average. Daily 10am–midnight.

Sandwiches and snacks

Amy's Bread 75 Ninth Ave, between W 15th and 16th sts. Subway A, C, E, L to 14th St. Other locations in Hell's Kitchen and West Village. You can find *Amy's* breads in fine stores citywide, but it's freshest here in the Chelsea Market. Their grilled-cheese sandwiches ($6.50), made with chipotle peppers, are some of the best in the city. Mon–Fri 7.30am–9pm, Sat 8am–8pm, Sun 9am–7pm.

Eleni's Cookies 75 Ninth Ave, between 15th and 16th sts. Subway A, C, E, L to 14th St. This bright, pink-hued store in Chelsea Market is super-moist cupcake and cookie heaven; the Everything Cookie (combining cranberries, walnuts and coconut) is virtually a meal in itself. It's also a great place for gifts. Mon–Fri 9am–8pm, Sat 9am–7pm, Sun 10am–7pm.

Union Square, Gramercy Park and the Flatiron District

Bakeries and cafés

The City Bakery 3 W 18th St, between Fifth and Sixth aves. Subway F, M to 14th St. A good place to come for a filling lunch. Try the tortilla pie, the idiosyncratic pretzel croissant, or – for sweet tooths – the beer hot chocolate with home-made marshmallow, so thick you'll need a fork. Mon–Fri 7.30am–7pm, Sat 7.30am–6.30pm, Sun 9am–6pm.

Lady Mendl's 56 Irving Place, at E 17th St, in the Inn at Irving Place (see p.284). Subway L, N, Q, R, #4, #5, #6 to 14th St–Union Square. Classic English high teas are the stock-in-trade of this small inn set in a handsome pair of brownstones. As per tradition, their five-course menus are served in the afternoon, complete with silver service and a tower of sandwiches ($35/person). Mon–Fri 3pm & 5pm, Sat & Sun noon, 2.30pm & 5pm.

Stumptown Coffee Roasters 20 W 29th St between Broadway and 5th Ave, in the *Ace Hotel* (see p.274). Subway N, R, #6 to 28th St. One of the country's most celebrated coffee roasters brings its brews to a hip new hotel; you'll have your latte methodically made by baristas dressed as 1920s dandies and can drink it in the cool lobby. Daily 6am–8pm.

Sandwiches and snacks

Defonte's of Brooklyn 261 Third Ave, at E 21st St. Subway #6 to 23rd St. Main location 379 Columbia St, Red Hook. The Brooklyn original is a weathered classic on an obscure corner by the BQE; easier to hit this new outpost near Gramercy, where the huge roast pork or roast beef sandwiches (add fried eggplant, fresh mozzarella and the special "hot salad") are just as toothsome ($8.50–10). Mon–Sat 9.30am–8pm.

Dogmatic 26 E 17th St between Broadway and Fifth Ave. Subway L, N, Q, R, #4, #5, #6 to 14th St–Union Square. A bright, hypermodern storefront with innovative seating for innovative snack food – baguettes are hollowed and cooked on prongs, then stuffed with your choice of designer sausage and sauce (such as truffle Gruyére); dogs are $4.50, sides are $3. Mon–Thurs 11am–8pm, Fri & Sat 11am–9pm, Sun noon–7pm.

Eisenberg's Sandwich Shop 174 Fifth Ave, at 22nd St. Subway N, R to 23rd St. A colourful luncheonette, this shop has been serving cheesy Reubens ($8.50), great tuna sandwiches ($7.25), matzoh-ball soup and old-fashioned fountain sodas at a well-worn counter since 1930. Daily 6.30am–8pm, Sat till 6pm, Sun till 4pm.

Roomali 97 Lexington Ave at 27th St. Subway #6 to 28th St. Quick, inexpensive ($5) and tasty Indian *roti* wraps – vegetarian and chicken mainly – with just the right amount of spice. Mon–Sat noon–11pm, Sun 1–11pm.

Shake Shack Madison Square Park, multiple other locations. Subway N, R to 23rd St. Danny Meyer's leafy food kiosk in the centre of Madison Square Park has proved wildly popular since opening in 2004 (there are now offshoots on the Upper East and West sides, in the Theater District and at Citi Field), with assorted office workers, tourists and foodies forming long lines for the perfectly grilled burgers and frozen-custard shakes. You can also buy beer and wine to sip outside, with everything around $7 or less. Daily 11am–11pm.

Wichcraft 11 E 20th St, at Broadway, multiple other locations. Subway N, R to 23rd St. This gourmet sandwichery is a fine wallet-friendly lunch option, though the Flatiron outpost is the only one also serving dinner (meatballs, shrimp and grits). Tuck into a moist Sicilian tuna sandwich ($8.50) paired with one of their excellent veggie sides ($2). Mon–Fri 8am–10pm, Sat & Sun 10am–6pm.

Midtown East

Bakeries and cafés

Buttercup Bake Shop 973 Second Ave, between 51st and 52nd sts. Subway #6 to 51st St. Also on Upper West Side. This *Magnolia Bakery* offshoot is similarly known for its 1950s-style comfort sweets, especially the moist cupcakes and banana pudding. Mon–Wed 8am–9pm, Thurs & Fri 8am–1pm, Sat 10am–10pm, Sun 10am–7pm.

Ess-a-Bagel 831 Third Ave, at 51st St. Subway #6 to 51st St. Several other locations.

Neighbourhood residents swear by this shop, filled with all the lox, whitefish salad and cream cheese you can possibly want. Go early, as the tables fill up quickly. Daily 6am–9pm, Sat & Sun till 5pm.

La Maison du Chocolat 30 Rockefeller Concourse, 49th St between Fifth and Sixth aves. Subway B, D, F, M to 47–50th St–Rockefeller Center. Several other locations. The French vibe here is palpable: the original *Maison* is in Paris. The two hot chocolates on the menu (and two iced in summer; all $8–10) are so thick you'll need a spoon to eat them, but they're not as sweet as you might expect.

Food trucks of New York

In the last ten years, the **food truck** has become a key fixture on New York streets, with some 4000 licensed by the city, ranging from tiny carts to full-size RVs. While most of them follow the standard kebab/falafel/halal-chicken-with-rice format and cater to hungry office workers, a growing number of thoughtful, creative options have emerged; convenient, relatively cheap and very tasty. Most have websites, and many also use Twitter – the best way to keep track of their varying locations and opening times.

Biryani Cart 46th St and Sixth Ave Ⓦwww.biryani.cart. This is actually one of those doling up grilled meat over rice ($6), but it's fresh and flavourful, plus there are unusual options like shrimp or salmon and kati rolls.

Calexico Carne Asada Wooster and Prince sts, Soho Ⓦwww.calexicocart.com. Simple cart managed by three Californian brothers, specializing in delicious *carne asada* tacos ($4) and burritos ($8) – luscious chopped steak stuffed into maize tacos with zesty salsa. See p.301 for their Brooklyn restaurant. Mon–Fri 11.30am–3.30pm.

El Rey Del Sabor Several Midtown locations (60th St and Third Ave; 49th St and Park Ave; 43rd St and Sixth Ave). Burritos and tamales, plus some of the best *al pastor* tacos around, for just $2.

The Jamaican Dutchy W 51st St and Seventh Ave Ⓦthejamaicandutchy.net. Changing daily specials, including breakfast options. The jerk chicken is pleasantly spicy; you can get a "mini", though still substantial portion, for $6.50. Mon–Thurs 7am–4pm, Fri 7am–7pm.

NY Dosa Washington Square South at Sullivan St, West Village ⓣ917/710-2092. Thiru Kumar is one of New York's best-loved street vendors, cooking up spicy South Indian vegan food and filling *dosas* at his tiny cart; basic *sadha dosas* are $4, while the tasty *masala dosa* is $5. Mon–Sat 11am–4pm.

NYC Cravings Truck Midtown and Financial District Ⓦwww.nyccravings.com or twitter.com/nyccravings. Go for the Taiwanese-style fried chicken over rice with special pork sauce ($7) and expect to have leftovers; handmade steamed pork dumplings ($3) are pretty tasty, too.

Patty's Tacos E 86th St at Lexington Ave, Upper East Side ⓣ347/216-9362. Get stuck into the pork, steak or tongue (*lengua*) tacos ($3), cow's-foot tostadas ($4) and the chipotle-stuffed sandwiches ($8) at this popular truck. Mon–Sat 2–11pm.

Schnitzel and Things Chelsea, Dumbo, Financial District and Midtown ⓣ347/772-7341, Ⓦwww.schnitzelandthings.com. Austrian-themed truck serving decent chicken, pork and cod schnitzel (breaded cutlets; $8) and various sides (like sauerkraut) for $3.

Treats Truck Mainly Midtown ⓣ212/691-5226, Ⓦwww.treatstruck.com. If you're in the mood for a delicious fresh cookie ($1–2) or brownie ($2.50–3) to top off your street-food tour, track down the Treats Truck – location changes daily.

Wafels and Dinges Various locations ⓣ1-866/429-7329, Ⓦwww.wafelsanddinges.com or twitter.com/waffletruck. Belgian-themed waffle truck, offering crispy waffles (from $5) and *dinges* (toppings) like Belgian chocolate fudge for $1. Open most days from 8am till 10pm (1am Fri & Sat).

Sandwiches and snacks

Algonquin Hotel lobby 59 W 44th St, between Fifth and Sixth aves. Subway B, D, F, M to 42nd St. The archetypal American interpretation of the English drawing room, located in the airy, attractive lobby of the hotel of the same name (see p.276), and reeking of faux nineteenth-century robber-baron splendour. A light menu is served in the afternoon, and cocktails are available as well. Daily 11am–12.15am.

Fresco by Scotto on the Go 40 E 52nd St, between Madison and Park aves. Subway #6 to 51st St. This welcoming Italian takeaway serves up fresh pastas, home-made pizzas and toothsome sandwiches; everything is under $10. Mon–Fri 6.30am–6pm.

Oms/b 156 E 45th St between Lexington and Third aves. Subway #4, #5, #6, #7 to 42nd St. Omusubi is the perfect food for a light lunch: plump rice balls wrapped with seaweed, stuffed with seafood, meat or vegetables. The Kalbi beef and the eel are good bets; lots of combination specials with soup for around $8. Mon–Fri 8am–7.30pm, Sat 11am–5.30pm.

Prime Burger 5 E 51st St between Madison and Fifth aves. Subway E, M to Fifth Ave–53rd St. This classic coffee shop makes a nice stopoff before or after a MoMA visit. Squeeze into one of the retro swivel tables, order one or two of the juicy namesakes ($5.25 and up) and try to save room for a piece of home-made pie. Mon–Fri 6am–7pm, Sat 6am–5pm.

Midtown West

Bakeries and cafés

Cupcake Café 545 Ninth Ave between 40th and 41st sts. Subway A, C, E to 42nd St. The coffee and cupcakes are impeccable at this shabby-chic café; there's another location within Books of Wonder (see p.395). Mon–Fri 7am–7pm, Sat 8am–7pm, Sun 9am–7pm.

Little Pie Company 424 W 43rd St, between Ninth and Tenth aves; also downtown location. Subway A, C, E to 42nd St. True to its name, the *Little Pie Company* serves pies to die for. The peach–raspberry, available only in summer, has earned quite a passionate following. Mon–Fri 8am–8pm, Sat 10am–8pm, Sun 10am–6pm.

Poseidon Bakery 629 Ninth Ave, between W 44th and 45th sts. Subway A, C, E to 42nd St. Known best for the phyllo dough hand-rolled on the premises and supplied to many of the city's restaurants, *Poseidon* also sells decadent *baklava*, strudel, cookies, spinach-and-meat pies and assorted other sweet Greek pastries. Tues–Sat 9am–7pm.

Pizza by the slice

New Yorkers are passionate about their pizza, but that's where agreement on the topic largely ends. There are many strongly held opinions when it comes to **defining a good slice**, and one man's mozzarella epiphany is often his neighbour's tasteless cardboard triangle. **New York-style pizza** was pioneered by Italian immigrants in the early 1900s: Gennaro Lombardi's pizzeria opened in 1905 and three of his staff went on to found *Totonno's* in 1924, *John's Pizzeria* in 1929 and *Patsy's* in 1933. Characterized by its wide, thin slices (often eaten folded in half) and thin hand-tossed crust, aficionados claim that the flavour of New York pizza crust is due to the purity of the city tap water used to make the dough.

Here are some places to sample New York's myriad pizza possibilities – for sit-down pizzerias, see p.329.

Artichoke East Village, see p.291

Di Fara Pizza Midwood, Brooklyn, see p.302

Joe's Pizza West Village, see p.293

Patsy's Pizza East Harlem, see p.300

Two Boots to Go West West Village, see p.293

Sandwiches and snacks

Brasserie Maison 1700 Broadway, at W 53rd St. Subway B, D, E to Seventh Ave. This is a good place to linger over a coffee or a meal – a rarity in midtown. The menu offers a range of burgers, soups, salads, pastas and average French-tinged brasserie standards (stick with the simpler items on the menu), running $9–18. Large outdoor seating area. Open 24hr.

Café Edison 228 W 47th St between Broadway and Eighth Ave. Subway C, E, #1 to 50th St. Once you find this old-style coffee shop, tucked inside the Art Deco *Hotel Edison* (see p.278), you might get a little attitude with the service, but that's just part of the gruff charm. It manages to be a favourite with theatre-types in any case – and the tasty matzoh-ball soup and brisket sandwiches more than make up for it. Daily 6am–9.30pm, Sun till 7.30pm.

Café Forant 449 W 51st St between Ninth and Tenth aves. Subway C, E to 50th St. Cafés don't come friendlier than this quiet neighbourhood spot, hidden down an infrequently trafficked street in Hell's Kitchen. The brunch food is stellar, sandwiches and salads are fresh, the coffee is strong and the price is right; you can eat well for around $10 or so. Mon–Fri 7am–7pm, Sat & Sun 10am–7pm.

Cosmic Diner 888 Eighth Ave, at W 52nd St. Subway C, E to 50th St. The perfect stop pre- or post-theatre. All the usual suspects are here: burgers (from pizza to Texas to bison; $6–10), hearty lumberjack pancakes ($6.50–9), stuffed sandwiches ($5–11) and yummy salads ($9.50–15.50). Open 24hr.

Upper East Side

Bakeries and cafés

Café Sabarsky in the Neue Galerie 1048 Fifth Ave, at E 86th St ☎212/288-0665. Subway #4, #5, #6 to 86th St. Sumptuous decor that harkens back to Old Vienna fills the handsome parlour of the former Vanderbilt mansion. The menu reads like that of an upscale Central European *Kaffeehaus*; it includes superb pastries, like Linzertorte and strudels ($8), and small sandwiches ($12), many made with cured meats. Mon & Wed 9am–6pm, Thurs–Sun 9am–9pm.

FC Chocolate Bar 4/F, 714 Madison Ave, between 63rd and 64th sts ☎212/759-1600. Subway F to 63rd St. This is real French chocolate and real pastry – buttery, creamy and over the top. The macaroons ($2.25), mousse ($6.50) and hot chocolate ($5.50) are made to the exacting standards of the very finest Parisian patisseries, and while it's a bit pricey it's worth every dime. You have to walk through Mauboussin jewellery store and then take the elevator up to the fourth floor. Mon–Sat 11am–6.30pm, Sun noon–5pm.

Neil's Coffee Shop 961 Lexington Ave at 70th St ☎212/628-7474. Subway #6 to 68th St. Classic neighbourhood diner, with gruff service, hearty breakfasts, beer ($5) and cheap coffee ($1.40). You won't spend more than $10. Popular with Hunter College staff and students. Daily 6am–9pm.

▲ *Café Sabarsky*

M. Rohrs' 310 E 86th St, between First and Second aves ☎212/608-6473. Subway #4, #5, #6 to 86th St. Coffee connoisseurs can choose from a wide range of brews here ($3–$7.95), though it's a little past its prime – it still just about pips *Starbucks*. The company has been around since 1896, but their current digs are fairly new. Daily 6am–midnight.

Serendipity 3 225 E 60th St, between Second and Third aves ☎212/838-3531. Subway N, R, #4, #5, #6 to 59th St. Adorned with Tiffany lamps, this long-established café and ice-cream parlour has been a favourite spot for sweet-sixteen parties and first dates for years. The frozen hot chocolate is out of this world ($8.95), and the wealth of ice-cream sundae offerings ($9.50) are a real treat, too. Mon–Thurs & Sun 11am–midnight, Fri 11.30am–1pm, Sat 11.30am–2am.

Sandwiches and snacks

Alice's Tea Cup 156 E 64th St, at Lexington Ave ☎212/486-9200. Subway F to 63rd St. *Alice's* offers afternoon tea "all day, every day" ($10). The place also does a brisk business with its menu of crêpes, egg dishes and light and tasty sandwiches ($8–12). Cupcakes are great, too, and there are (naturally) over 95 tea varieties on sale for you to take home. Other branches at 102 W 73rd St and 220 E 81st St. Daily 8am–8pm.

Mitchel London Foods 22A E 65th St, between Fifth and Madison aves ☎212/737-2850. Subway F to 63rd St. The goods from caterer/restaurateur Mr London are justifiably praised. Try the salmon Niçoise salad ($8.95) or turkey and manchego sandwiches ($7.95), with one of their unbelievably rich brownies ($3.75) for dessert. Mon–Fri 8.30am–8pm, Sat 10am–7pm, Sun noon–7pm.

Tal Bagels 333 E 86th St, between First and Second aves ☎212/427-6811. Subway #4, #5, #6 to 86th St. The bagels (with *schmears* from $1.75) may be a little too chewy, but the spread selection at this family institution is to die for, especially the smoked fish (from $6). Don't let the lines scare you; they move fast. Daily 5.30am–10pm, Sun till 8pm.

Viand 673 Madison Ave, at E 61st St; other locations on Upper East and West sides. Subway N, R to Fifth Ave–59th St. Affordable little chain coffee shop near Barney's, serving rich brews, awesome turkey sandwiches and all-around delicious snacks. Service is speedy and the prices sweet. Daily 6am–10pm.

Upper West Side and Morningside Heights

Bakeries and cafés

Bouchon Bakery Ten Columbus Circle, Third Floor, Time Warner Center. Subway A, B, C, D, #1 to 59th St–Columbus Circle. At this Thomas Keller café, you can get something to go from the counter or sit at a table and stare through the windows onto the corner of Central Park, grazing on a ham-and-cheese sandwich, croissant or decadent pastry. Daily 11.30am–9pm, Sun till 7pm.

Café Lalo 201 W 83rd St, between Amsterdam and Broadway. Subway #1 to 86th St. Reminiscent of Paris, down to the cramped tables and inconsistent service. Try the "shirred" eggs (made fluffy with a cappuccino machine) with all sorts of herbs and other add-ins ($5.50–14), or the wonderful Belgian waffles ($12). Great desserts, too. Mon–Thurs 8am–2am, Fri 8am–4am, Sat 9am–4am, Sun 9am–2am.

Hungarian Pastry Shop 1030 Amsterdam Ave, between W 110th and 111th sts. Subway #1 to 110th St. This simple, no-frills coffeehouse is a favourite with Columbia University affiliates. You can sip your espresso and read Proust all day if you like (madeleines, anyone?); the only problem is choosing among the pastries, cookies and cakes, all made on the premises. Mon–Fri 7am–11.30pm, Sat 8.30am–11.30pm, Sun 8.30am–10.30pm.

Sandwiches and snacks

Absolute Bagels 2788 Broadway between 107th and 108th sts. Subway #1 to 110th St–Cathedral Parkway. There's more to bagels on the Upper West Side than *H&H*. This tiny shop, rather unusually (for the product) Thai-owned, bakes hot, fresh, chewy bagels that some claim as the best in the city. After trying one with cream cheese and lox, you might find it hard to disagree. Daily 6am–9pm.

Barney Greengrass 541 Amsterdam Ave, between 86th and 87th sts. Subway #1 to 86th St. The "sturgeon king" is an Upper West Side fixture; the deli (and restaurant) have been around since time began. The smoked-salmon section is a particular treat. Deli Tues–Sun 8am–6pm, restaurant Tues–Fri 8.30am–4pm, Sat & Sun 8.30am–5pm.

EJ's Luncheonette 447 Amsterdam Ave, between W 81st and 82nd sts. Subway #1 to 79th St. This retro, family-friendly diner serves huge club sandwiches ($8.45–9.45), excellent inexpensive chilli ($5.95–7.45) and the best cobb salads in the city ($12.50). Daily 8.30am–10pm, Fri–Sun till 10.30pm.

Gray's Papaya 2090 Broadway, at W 72nd St; other locations. Subway #1, #2, #3 to 72nd St. This insanely popular hot-dog joint is an NYC institution, famous for their long-running "Recession Special": 2 dogs and a drink for $4.50. Open 24hr.

Grom 2185 Broadway, at W 76th St. Subway #1 to 79th St. Another location downtown. You can cheer *Grom* for bringing authentic, bold-flavoured *gelati* to the Big Apple (this was their first outpost outside Italy) or curse them for being the first frozen purveyor to break the $5 mark for one scoop. Daily noon–11pm, Thurs–Sat till midnight.

H&H 2239 Broadway at W 80th St. Subway #1 to 79th St. Another location in Hell's Kitchen. The most famous of the contenders for top New York bagel, *H&H* is said to bake more than 50,000 a day, many of them shipped worldwide. Purely a place to stock up on bagels or have a DIY snack – no sandwiches made or seating available. Open 24hr.

P&W Sandwich Shop 1030 Amsterdam Ave, between W 110th and 111th sts. Subway #1 to 110th St. A luncher connected with the *Hungarian Pastry Shop* next door (see opposite), serving a few good Eastern European specialties. Mon–Fri 7am–7pm, Sat & Sun 9am–7pm.

Popover Café 551 Amsterdam Ave, at 87th St. Subway B, C, #1 to 86th St. Charming, casual eatery (decorated with stuffed bears) where the dishes come with the home-made touch. Best to go for breakfast, lunch or brunch rather than dinner. Mon–Fri 8am–10pm, Sat & Sun 9am–10pm.

▲ *H&H*

Tom's Restaurant 2880 Broadway, at 112th St. Subway #1 to 110th St. The greasy-spoon diner – whose exterior doubled for *Monk's* in *Seinfeld* – is no great shakes food-wise, but the prices almost make up for the quality. Often filled with Columbia University students who come for the great breakfast deals (under $6) on weekday mornings. Mon–Wed & Sun 6am–1.30am, Thurs–Sat 24hr.

Zabar's Café 2245 Broadway, at W 80th St. Subway #1 to 79th St. Adjacent to the Upper West Side institution (where you can pick up all manner of comestibles; see p.195), this small spot is always crowded with locals and tourists. Best for the cheap, freshly prepared bagel-and-lox sandwiches, but everything's tasty: scones, panini sandwiches, soups, coffee drinks, frozen yogurt and smoothies. Mon–Fri 7am–7pm, Sat 7.30am–7pm, Sun 8am–6pm.

Harlem and north Manhattan

Bakeries and cafés

Café Amrita 301 W 110th St, between Manhattan Ave and Frederick Douglass Blvd ☎212/222-0683. Subway B, C to Cathedral Parkway. If your ramble through Central Park leaves you at its northwest corner, sink into a leather chair at this friendly half bar, half café for an excellent coffee ($1.55), beer ($5) or Martini ($8). Mon–Fri 7am–9pm, Sat & Sun 8am–9pm.

Carrot Top Pastries 3931 Broadway, between 164th and 165th sts ☎212/927-4800. Subway A, C, #1 to 168th St. See

"Washington Heights" map p.212. It's worth making the trip up here for the freshly baked tins of carrot, blueberry and chocolate-chip muffins ($1.40), cakes ($2.75 per slice) and sweet-potato cheesecake ($3.25). Mon–Sat 6am–9pm, Sun 7am–6pm.

East Harlem Café 1651 Lexington Ave, at 104th St ⓣ212/996-2080. Subway #6 to 103rd St. Chilled-out coffee shop epitomizing the area's "SpaHa" pretensions, full of comfy sofas, Latino art and engrossed laptop users enjoying the superb hot drinks ($1.25) and pastries ($1.25). Mon–Fri 7.30am–7pm, Sat & Sun 9.30am–5pm.

Make My Cake 121 St Nicholas Ave at 116th St. Subway #2, #3 to 116th St ⓣ212/932-0833. Generously sized chocolate and red velvet cupcakes ($3–4) lead the offerings at this smart new bakery. The shop opened in 1996, but its baking secrets date back to 1940s Mississippi. Mon–Thurs 8am–8pm, Fri 8am–9pm, Sat 9am–9pm, Sun 9am–7pm.

Sandwiches and snacks

Patsy's Pizzeria 2287 First Ave, between 117th and 118th sts ⓣ212/534-9783. Subway #6 to 116th St. Opened by Pasquale "Patsy" Lancieri in 1933, this is one of the last vestiges of Italian Harlem, churning out paper-thin slices ($1.75) from its coal-burning brick oven; Patsy learnt his trade at *Lombardi's*, but it was here that he "invented" the pizza slice concept. Daily 11am–11pm.

Brooklyn

Fulton Ferry District and DUMBO

The places below are marked on the "Downtown Brooklyn" map on p.220.

Almondine 85 Water St, near Main St. Subway A, C to High St or F to York St. Excellent patisserie, run by a former *Le Bernadin* pastry chef with chocolatier Jacques Torres (below), that churns out all kinds of buttery, flaky treats, as well as sandwiches on crusty baguettes ($7–8), soups and quiches. Mon–Sat 7am–7pm, Sun 10am–6pm.

Brooklyn Ice Cream Factory 1 Water St, at the Fulton Ferry pier. Subway A, C to High St. An old fireboat house contains the perfect reward for the walk across the Brooklyn Bridge: super-rich ice cream with toppings created by the pastry chef at the neighbouring *River Café*. Daily noon–10pm, Thurs–Sun till 11pm; closed Mon Oct–April.

DUMBO General Store 111 Front St, at Washington and Adams sts. Subway F to York St. This café, in an airy former art-supply store, has long rustic tables ideal for reading or conversation, and delicious panini and salads. Live music Fri & Sat. Daily 8am–6pm, Thurs–Sun till midnight.

Jacques Torres Chocolate 66 Water St; other locations in Soho and Upper East Side. Subway A, C to High St or F to York St. Warm up in winter with the super-thick hot chocolate, enjoy a flaky *pain au chocolat*, or just pig out on truffles. Mon–Sat 9am–8pm, Sun 10am–6pm.

Brooklyn Heights

The places below are marked on the "Downtown Brooklyn" map on p.220.

Montague Street Bagels 108 Montague St, at Hicks St. Subway #2, #3 to Clark St or M, R, #2, #3, #4, #5 to Borough Hall. Brisk service and fantastic, doughy bagels make this the perfect place to grab a snack before heading down to the Esplanade and parking yourself on a bench. Open 24hr.

Tazza 311 Henry St, at Atlantic. Subway #4, #5 to Borough Hall. Right on the border with Cobble Hill, this likable *enoteca* serves Italian wines by the glass, espresso, sweets culled from the city's best bakeries and particularly fine panini – try the fig and ricotta ($4.95). Ample pavement seating in warm weather. Mon–Fri 7am–10pm, Sat & Sun 8am–10pm.

Fort Greene

The places below are marked on the "Downtown Brooklyn" map on p.220.

Cake Man Raven Confectionery 708A Fulton St, at Hanson Place. Subway G to Fulton St. The Cake Man is best known for his stunning red velvet cake, which he has baked for everyone from Harry Belafonte to Spike Lee. You can also pick up a delicious coconut-cream pie and other sweets (cake slices $6). Daily 9am–10pm.

Habana Outpost 757 Fulton St, at S Portland. Subway C, G to Lafayette Ave–Fulton St. The seasonal Brooklyn branch of the ever-popular Nolita institution *Café Habana* wears its green credentials on its sleeve: the place is solar-powered and holds a weekend market on its outdoor dining patio with an emphasis on recycled products. Opt for a burrito or quesadilla (both around $7) with a side of sweet plantains and an ear of corn slathered with mayo, cheese and lime. Mid-April to Oct daily noon–midnight.

Cobble Hill and Carroll Gardens

The places below are marked on the "South Brooklyn" map on p.227.

Café Pedlar 210 Court St, between Warren and Wyckoff sts. Subway F, G to Bergen St. Simply but elegantly adorned hangout for excellent coffee and baked goods, including an unusual olive-oil cake ($3.50). Daily 7am–7pm.

Calexico 122 Union St, between Hicks and Columbia sts. Subway F, G to Carroll St. A small Mexican joint that started off as a Soho street cart (still around; see p.295); the *carne asada* is super tasty, whether in a taco or one of the miraculous rolled quesadillas. Tues–Sat 11.30am–10pm, Sun 11am–4pm.

D'Amico Foods 309 Court St, between Sackett and Degraw. Subway F, G to Carroll St. All sorts of Italian provisions, but best known for its espresso, served since 1948. Mon–Sat 10am–5pm.

Mile End 97A Hoyt St, between Pacific and Atlantic. Subway F, G to Bergen St or A, C, G to Hoyt–Schermerhorn St. They serve breakfast, but most come for the smoked-meat sandwich at lunch: piled on rye bread with a smear of mustard, this peppery morsel is the Montréal version of a Jewish classic ($8/13, depending on size). Mon–Fri 8am–3/4pm, Sat & Sun 10am–3/4pm or until the meat is gone.

Sweet Melissa Patisserie 276 Court St, at Douglass St. F, G to Bergen or Carroll St. For a snack to go, the home-made fruit tarts, cakes, cookies and muffins crowding the narrow front counter here are hard to beat, but the creamy quiches and fancy sandwiches, like filet mignon on a baguette, hold their own, especially when enjoyed in the idyllic backyard garden. There's a larger branch (also with a garden) at 175 Seventh Ave, at 1st St, in Park Slope.

Red Hook

The places below are marked on the "South Brooklyn" map on p.227. The closest subway is the F, G to Smith–9th Street; you can then take bus #77 (bus #61 also goes to Red Hook).

Baked 359 Van Brunt St, at Dikeman St. Relaxed neighbourhood café that's justly celebrated for its cookies, cakes, muffins, Rice Krispy treats, granola and marshmallows, all made on the premises but found in cafés and shops throughout the northeast. Mon–Fri 7am–7pm, Sat & Sun 8am–7pm.

Fairway Café 480–500 Van Brunt St, at Reed St. You'll have to thread your way through the mammoth gourmet supermarket to get here, but it's well worth it for the wallet-friendly sandwiches (eg $10 lobster roll), salads and hot entrees, which you can eat on the back deck overlooking the water. Daily 8am–8pm.

Red Hook Lobster Pound 284 Van Brunt St, at Verona St. More of a place to purchase live lobsters, but the *Pound* also does

Coffee (and tea)

Coffee is big business in New York, and there are tons of places to find *baristas* elegantly swirling a leaf on the top of a latte or touting the latest micro-produced, Fair Trade bean. The following pour the best cups in the city (and we've included an option for tea-lovers, too):

Café Grumpy Greenpoint and Park Slope, Brooklyn, see p.303

Gimme! Coffee Williamsburg, Brooklyn, see p.303

Gorilla Coffee Park Slope, Brooklyn, see p.302

Stumptown Coffee Roasters Flatiron District, see p.294

Thé Adoré West Village, see p.292

delectable lobster rolls ($15), filled with fresh, plump chunks of lobster meat – the perfect snack on a warm spring or summer day. Fri–Sun noon–7pm.

Steve's Authentic Key Lime Pies 204 Van Dyke St, between Conover and Ferris sts. Tucked away on the Red Hook waterfront, this tiny shop dishes up some of the tastiest Key Lime pies in the northeast ($4.50 for individual pies). Typically Mon–Fri 9am–5pm, Sat & Sun 10am–6pm.

Park Slope and Prospect Heights

The places below are marked on the "Prospect Park" map on p.230.

Bark Hot Dogs 474 Bergen St, between Fifth Ave and Flatbush. Subway #2, #3 to Bergen St. If you want to feel good about your hot-dog consumption, this is the place: an artisanal wiener shack where most everything is home-made or locally sourced, recyclable and, most important, tasty (dogs are $4.25–7); good local draft beers, too ($5). Mon–Thurs noon–midnight, Fri noon–2am, Sat 10am–2am, Sun 10am–10pm.

Café Regular 318 11th St, at Fifth Ave. Subway F, G, R to Fourth Ave–9th St. Excellent coffee and pastries in a tiny, Eurocentric café that feels a little hidden off the main drag. Mon–Fri 7am–7pm, Sat & Sun 8am–7pm.

Chip Shop 383 Fifth Ave, at 6th St; another location in Brooklyn Heights, 129 Atlantic Ave, between Clinton and Henry sts. Subway F, G, R to Fourth Ave–9th St. Upscale chippie beloved by UK expats as well as non-carb-conscious New Yorkers. Kid-friendly atmosphere.

Cocoa Bar 228 Seventh Ave, between 3rd and 4th sts; another location on Lower East Side. Subway F, G to Seventh Ave. Slim neighbourhood café right in the heart of the Seventh Ave scene, with a mix of twenty-somethings tapping on laptops and moms with kids. Good, strong coffee with chocolatey pastries, spacious back garden, fine wine and beer selection, and free wi-fi. Daily 8am–midnight, Thurs–Sat till 2am.

Gorilla Coffee 97 Fifth Ave, at Park Place. Subway #2, #3 to Bergen St. Punk-rock outpost serves the best (Fair Trade) java in the neighbourhood, with strong, fresh drip coffee and expert espresso drinks topped off with perfect crema. Mon–Sat 7am–9pm, Sun 8am–9pm.

Joyce Bakeshop 646 Vanderbilt Ave, at Park Place. Subway B, Q to Seventh Ave or #2, #3 to Grand Army Plaza. Friendly spot on Prospect Heights' burgeoning main strip with fresh-baked sweet and savoury scones, muffins, tarts and croissants, with high tea served Tues–Fri noon–5pm. Mon–Fri 7.30am–7.30pm, Sat & Sun 9am–6pm.

Press 195 195 Fifth Ave, between Sackett and Union. Subway R to Union St. Thirty varieties of hot pressed sandwiches on home-made ciabatta, including several good vegetarian options, plus tasty salads, with a pretty backyard garden to boot. Daily 11am–10pm, Thurs–Sat till 11pm.

Tom's 782 Washington Ave, at Sterling Place. Subway #2, #3 to Grand Army Plaza or Eastern Parkway. Brooklyn institution that's handily located just a few blocks from the Brooklyn Museum, with standard-issue diner fare and old-fashioned fountain drinks like lime rickeys and egg creams. Best, though, is the amiable vibe, with garrulous Tom and his whole family making you feel like a long-lost friend. Mon–Sat 6am–4pm, Sun 8am–4pm.

Bay Ridge and Midwood

Di Fara Pizza 1424 Ave J. Subway Q to Ave J – walk one block west on Ave J. It might be hard to fathom a piece of pizza worth $5 (whole pizzas are a much better deal at $25) plus an hour's wait, yet neither deters people making the pilgrimage to the consensus best slice in the city. Go early. Wed–Sun noon–4.30pm & 6–9pm.

Hinsch's Confectionery 8515 Fifth Ave, between 85th and 86th sts. Subway R to 86th St – walk one block east on 86th St, then left on Fifth Ave. A Bay Ridge icon, as famous for its ice cream (try the fresh strawberry syrup topping) and old-fashioned diner food as for its beautiful, unchanged luncheonette setting. Mon–Sat 8am–7.30pm, Sun 10am–5pm.

Coney Island

Nathan's 1310 Surf Ave, at Stillwell Ave, Coney Island. Subway D, F, N, Q to Coney Island–Stillwell Ave. Right there when you get off the subway, this is the home of the "famous Coney Island hot dog". Serving since 1916, *Nathan's* holds a nationally televised annual Hot Dog Eating Contest on July 4. Daily 8am–1pm.

▲ Nathan's

Williamsburg and Greenpoint

The places below are marked on the "Williamsburg and Greenpoint" map on p.240.

Bliss 191 Bedford Ave, between North 6th and North 7th sts. Subway L to Bedford Ave. Vegans can get their fix at this crunchy, no-meat, no-dairy spot. They even serve a full vegan breakfast. Others might find the fare a little bland. Mon–Fri 9am–11pm, Sat & Sun 10am–11pm.

Café Grumpy 193 Meserole Ave, at Diamond St; other locations in Chelsea and Park Slope. Subway G to Greenpoint Ave. Spacious Greenpoint outpost for the artsy set, with exposed brick walls, lots of light, expertly made espresso, regular coffee made to order, granola, pastries and pre-made vegetarian sandwiches. Mon–Thurs 7am–7pm, Fri 7am–8pm, Sat 8am–9pm, Sun 8am–7pm.

Egg 135 North 5th St, between Bedford Ave and Berry St. Subway L to Bedford Ave. Delicious Southern-style breakfasts, including biscuits and gravy, served through lunchtime, though the sandwiches (ham and pimento cheese, duck and duck-liver pâté) are good choices, too. The dinner menu (Wed–Sun only) showcases belt-breaking comfort food like fried chicken, Brunswick stew and toasted pound cake topped with lemon custard and vanilla ice cream. Mon & Tues 7am–3pm, Wed & Thurs 7am–10pm, Fri–Sun 9am–10pm.

Gimme! Coffee 495 Lorimer St, between Grand and Powers sts; another location at 228 Mott St in Nolita. Subway L to Lorimer St; G to Metropolitan Ave. This coffee haven is not your typical lounge-about-all-day Williamsburg café, but a bright, narrow spot to pick up a shot of espresso or cup of the house roast and kick-start your next few hours. Daily 7am–8pm.

Verb Café 218 Bedford Ave, at 5th St. Subway L to Bedford Ave. Wedged between a bookstore and a record shop, *Verb* was one of the first bohemian spots on Bedford, and still anchors the scene with an appropriately lackadaisical vibe, strong coffee, pastries, peanut-butter-and-banana sandwiches and a reliably kickin' alt-rock soundtrack. Mon–Fri 7am–11.30pm, Sat & Sun 7.30am–11.30pm.

Queens

Astoria and Long Island City

Unless otherwise stated, the places below are marked on the "Astoria" map on p.247.

Arepas Cafe 33-07 36th Ave, at 33rd St, Astoria. Subway N, Q to 36th Ave. A casual, friendly spot for *arepas* – a kind of thick cornmeal pocket that's like a pitta, stuffed with everything from shredded beef with plaintain and cheese to saucy shrimp. Tues–Thurs 11am–10pm, Fri & Sat 11am–11pm, Sun noon–9pm.

Athens Café 32-07 30th Ave, at 32nd St, Astoria. Subway N, Q to 30th Ave. The place to see and be seen on 30th Ave. On warm days, the prime pavement tables are packed full of young Greeks all nursing frappés – foamy, Greek-style iced coffees. It's also great for spinach pies and desserts. Daily 8am–1am.

Djerdan 34-04 31st Ave, at 34th St, Astoria. Subway N, Q to Broadway or 30th Ave. Cheap and filling, *burek* – savoury meat, spinach or cheese pies, which go for $4 a slice – is the specialty of this simple Balkan eatery, and a tasty alternative to pizza. Try the "special" version, drizzled with garlicky yogurt. Daily 8am–11pm.

Omonia Café 32–20 Broadway, at 33rd St, Astoria. Subway N, Q to Broadway. Broadway's liveliest café is still a stronghold for Greek men poring over Hellenic newspapers during the day, but after dinner the international crowd is younger and more upbeat. Make sure to order a thick wedge of flaky, buttery, sticky-sweet *baklava*, the best of the desserts here. Daily 7am–3am.

Sweetleaf 10–93 Jackson Ave, at 49th Ave and 11th St, LIC. Subway #7 to Vernon Blvd/Jackson Ave. **See "Long island City" map on p.245.** A small spot with a dedicated following for its caffeinated beverages. Mon–Fri 7.30am–7pm, Sat 8am–7pm, Sun 10am–6pm.

Jackson Heights and Corona

Empanadas del Parque Café 56–27 Van Doren St, at 108th St, Corona. Subway #7 to 111th St – take a left at 108th St, then walk fifteen blocks. The traditional Latin American meat pie is given a gourmet spin at this celebrated place, with a veggie version stuffed with guava and cheese and a sweet one that comes with Nutella and sliced bananas. Nothing costs more than $2. Daily 7am–10pm.

Shaheen Sweets 72–09 Broadway, Jackson Heights. Subway E, F, R, #7 to Roosevelt Ave–74th St – walk northwest along Broadway. Stashed inside *Dera Restaurant* is this tidy sweets counter offering Pakistani treats like *gulabjam*, sweet dough balls soaked in syrup, and *kheer*, Pakistani-style rice pudding. Daily 9am–7pm.

Flushing

Tai Pan Bakery 37–25 Main St, between 37th and 38th sts; other locations. Subway #7 to Main St–Flushing; walk two blocks north on Main St. Snag a tray and a pair of tongs and get to work assembling your own Chinese carb feast from among the vast assortment of sweet (pineapple) and savoury (roasted pork) buns, sugary donuts and custard tarts in this chaotic and popular spot. There are a few hard-won tables. Daily 7.30am–8pm.

The Bronx

The Feeding Tree 892 Gerard Ave, at 161st St. Subway B, D, #4 to 161st St–Yankee Stadium. Spicy jerk shrimp and chicken, curry goat stew and other Jamaican specialties come with rice and beans, mixed vegetables and sweet plantains at this friendly, no-frills fixture near Yankee Stadium (lunch specials start at $4.99, most dishes $6.50–13). Mon–Sat 8.30am–10pm, Sun 10am–8pm.

Staten Island

Everything Goes Book Café 208 Bay St ☎718/273-3675. Alternative café and bookstore, a short walk from the ferry along Bay Street (with internet); has organic muffins and a huge selection of teas. Tues–Thurs 10.30am–6.30pm, Fri & Sat 10.30am–10pm, Sun noon–5pm.

John's Famous Deli 15 Innis St and Nicholas Ave, Port Richmond ☎718/815-9100. Take #S46 bus. Justly lauded as producing the best hot roast-beef sandwiches in the state ($6 or $19.99 per foot), huge plates dripping with onions, mozzarella and gravy. Mon–Sat 6am–6pm.

Ralph's Famous Italian Ices 501 Port Richmond Ave, at Catherine St ☎718/273-3675. Take #S44 bus. In business since 1928, this beloved place has spawned numerous franchises. Its unusual and wide selection of water ices (honeydew, root beer and blueberry) and sherbets (spumoni, cremalata and cannoli) have won many a heart and taste bud. Tends to open during the summer months only – call ahead.

24

Restaurants

A large part of visiting New York City is experiencing not just the food but the **culture of dining**. As a port city, New York has long received the best foodstuffs from around the globe and, as a major immigration gateway, it continues to attract chefs who know how to cook all the world's cuisines properly, even exceptionally, as well as populations who know the real thing. Then there are the "foodies", locals who make it their business to seek out the best, most unique and newest dining establishments in the city, and aren't shy about sharing the fruits of their labours. Travellers will soon find that restaurant-hopping is one of the city's most popular pastimes.

This chapter includes eateries that offer everything from fried chicken to foie gras (and sometimes both), though you should keep in mind that New York's culinary scene is extremely dynamic – even the most food-obsessed locals have a hard time keeping up. Restaurants are always opening and closing, trends change quickly and the establishment *du jour* can change in the blink of an eye; gastronomes and those on the prowl for something new turn to magazines like *Time Out New York* or *New York*, or the *New York Times*' Wednesday *Dining Out* section for reviews on the latest hotspots. More serious foodies look to sites like Ⓦwww.chowhound.com, www.eater.com, www.seriouseats.com and www.grubstreet.com or more localized neighbourhood blogs (say, www.midtownlunch.com, though that's more for places in the "Cafes and snacks" chapter) for opinions and leads on sizzling new chefs and gourmet hotspots. For travellers, the most important aspect of exploring the city's diverse culinary landscape, though, is having a sense of adventure – eating is one of the great joys of being in New York, and it would be a shame to waste time on the familiar.

Cuisines

American cooking is an umbrella term for a vast array of dishes. It includes such standards as steaks, burgers, fried chicken and macaroni and cheese, but it also refers to menus that highlight local and seasonal ingredients, and recipes that draw on years of tradition as well as new culinary concepts. The **locavore** movement – an emphasis on the farm-to-table process and local food sourcing – has found favour not just in haute cuisine but in plenty of casual neighbourhood joints putting their own spin on the usual suspects. Many American restaurants offer a rich array of regional specialties: everything from New England clam chowder and Cajun jambalaya to Southern grits and Texas barbecue ribs. **Continental** cuisine is generally a hybrid of American, Italian and French influences, featuring pastas, meats, poultry and fish or seafood in light sauces.

Specialty eating

We've highlighted particular types of restaurants and listed them in boxes in the text. We've also picked out a few favourites in the city, which is very hard to do; most of the places recommended in this chapter are exactly that – recommended – though this might give you an easy guide:

Burgers p.317
Haute cuisine p.327
Pizza p.329
Quintessential New York p.312
Vegetarian (and vegetarian-friendly) p.326

You'll encounter an astonishing range of **ethnic cuisines**. **Chinese** food, at its best in Chinatown but available all over the city, is comprised of familiar Cantonese dishes as well as spicier Sichuan and Hunan ones – most restaurants specialize in one of the three. **Japanese** food runs the price gamut from super cheap to extremely expensive; there are a plethora of sushi establishments in the city. Other Asian cuisines are also in abundance, including **Indian** (best in Jackson Heights, Queens), **Korean** (increasingly prominent due to David Chang's *Momofuku* mini-empire), **Thai** and **Vietnamese**.

Italian cooking is widespread and not terribly expensive, especially if you stick to pizza or pasta. Further down the Mediterranean, **Greek** food is probably best in Astoria, Queens, where you'll find fresh, simply prepared fish and seafood dishes. **French** restaurants tend to be pricier, although there are plenty of bistros and brasseries turning out less costly but authentic and reliable French dishes.

There is also a whole range of **Eastern European** restaurants – Russian, Ukrainian, Polish and Hungarian – that serve well-priced, filling fare (emphasis on the filling), including *pierogi* (meat-, potato-, or cheese-stuffed dumplings) and *borscht*. The historical legacy of **Jewish food**, meanwhile, is most obvious in the ubiquitous bagel, of which New York can be justly proud (see box, p.290); relatively few full-scale dinner restaurants serving the cuisine still exist.

Central and South American and **Caribbean** restaurants have a strong presence in New York, especially in north Manhattan and the outer boroughs. The large, satisfying, frequently spicy meals on offer are often good deals. For years it was hard to find good **Mexican** in the city, but that, fortunately, has changed of late. In a way, these ethnic places only represent the tip of the iceberg: you could also seek out **Bukharan**, **Persian**, **Tibetan**, **Serbian** or anything else under the sun. Numerous **vegetarian** and **wholefood** eateries cater to any taste or health trend.

Financial District

Although the neighbourhood is slowly becoming more residential, eating options in the Financial District remain geared to the great daily tide of commuters coming in and out of the city, a strange mix of takeaway feeding troughs, kebab stalls (even on Wall Street) and overpriced power-lunch spots. New Yorkers tend to deem this part of town a culinary wasteland; we've included places that prove the exception to that rule. Many restaurants close early and either have reduced hours or are closed on weekends.

American and Continental

Bridge Café 279 Water St, at Dover St ⓣ212/227-3344, ⓦwww.bridgecafenyc.com. Subway #4, #5, #6 to Brooklyn Bridge. You wouldn't guess from this café-restaurant's up-to-the-minute interior that it is the city's oldest surviving tavern, opening in 1847 (the building is 50 years older). The crab cakes are excellent, as is the list of microbrew beers. Entrees $23–34. Sun & Mon 11.45am–10pm, Tues–Thurs 11.45am–11pm, Fri 11.45am–midnight, Sat 5pm–midnight.

Delmonico's 56 Beaver St, at William St ⓣ212/509-1144, ⓦwww.delmonicosny.com. Subway #2, #3 to Wall St. Patrons tend to come to this 1837 landmark steakhouse for its historic charms, murals and classic dishes; the Delmonico Steak (boneless ribeye; $44), Lobster Newburg (created in 1876; now $49), and baked Alaska ($12), created here in 1867. Cheaper fare is available in the bar. Mon–Fri 11.30am–10pm, Sat 5–10pm.

Harry's 1 Hanover Square, at Pearl St ⓣ212/785-9200, ⓦwww.harrysnyc.com. Subway #2, #3 to Wall St. Housed in the basement of historic India House and traditionally the haunt of Wall Street deal-makers, the relaxed café serves pastas (from $16.50) and sandwiches (from $13.50), while the posher, pricier steakhouse gets rave reviews for its porterhouses ($45) and "Gilded Age" atmosphere. Come for the Saturday brunch, with cheaper dishes (think corned beef hash; $16) and free champagne. Mon–Fri 11.30am–midnight, Sat noon–midnight.

Izzy & Nat's 311 South End Ave ⓣ212/619-5100, ⓦwww.izzyandnats.com. Subway R, #1 to Rector St. Best place for breakfast or lunch on this side of FiDi, with a long takeaway counter and a cosy diner-like seating area; the hand-rolled bagels (from $1.20) and lox are excellent (try the sweet French toast bagel), and they also do salads ($9.95) and sandwiches (from $7.95). Mon – Fri 7am–3pm, Sat & Sun 8am–4pm.

The Paris Café 119 South St ⓣ212/240-9797, ⓦtheparistavern.com. Subway A, C, J, Z, #2, #3, #4, #5 to Fulton St. Established in 1873, this old-fashioned restaurant (more Irish pub than French bistro) has played host to a panoply of luminaries, but these days the elegant square bar, decent draught Guinness ($7.50), pub-food menu and sports on TV pull in a lively crowd; try the shepherd's pie ($14), fish and chips ($14) or mussels ($12). Daily 11.30am–4am.

SHO Shaun Hergatt 40 Broad St ⓣ212/809-3993, ⓦwww.shoshaunhergatt.com. Subway #2, #3 to Wall St; J, Z to Broad St. Australian native Shaun Hergatt's hot new restaurant offers exceptional service, quality and value for money; the three-course prix-fixe lunch ($30) and dinner ($69) include exquisite Aussie-influenced dishes like roasted pork loin, ocean trout tartare and fabulous shellfish. Mon–Fri 7am–9am, noon–2pm, 5–10pm; Sat 5–10pm.

French

Brasserie Les Halles 15 John St, between Broadway and Nassau St ⓣ212/285-8585, ⓦleshalles.net/brasserie. Subway A, C, J, M, Z, #2, #3, #4, #5 to Fulton St. One of two *Les Halles* in New York (the other in the Flatiron District), this French bistro serves "French Beef, American Style". The Rive Gauche fantasy of celebrity chef Anthony Bourdain, the meat-heavy menu also includes dishes like escargots in garlic butter and duck confit shepherd's pie. Most entrees $20–30; the steak frites, at the low end of that scale, is a great deal. Mon–Fri 7.30am–midnight, Sat & Sun 11.30am–midnight.

Italian

Acqua at Peck Slip 21 Peck Slip at Water St ⓣ212/349-4433, ⓦwww.acquarestaurantnyc.com. Subway A, C, J, Z, #2, #3, #4, #5 to Fulton St. Most authentic Italian food downtown, served in a bright, exposed brick dining room; home-made, local and Italian ingredients make excellent pastas and pizzas (around $20 entrée). Close to South St Seaport, but not touristy. Daily noon–midnight.

Adrienne's Pizzabar 54 Stone St ⓣ212/248-3838, ⓦwww.adriennespizzabar.com. Subway #2, #3 to Wall St. One of the better restaurants downtown, with seating in Stone St in summer. The food is fantastic; *nonna*-style square pizzas ("old-fashioned" pizza; $16.50) with crispy crust come in innovative combinations, but the crumbled sausage topping is especially tasty, and all the cheeses are extremely high quality. Mon–Sat 11am–midnight, Sun 11am–10pm.

Scandinavian

Smorgas Chef Downtown 53 Stone St ⓣ212/422-3500, ⓦwww.smorgaschef.com. Subway #2, #3 to Wall St. Established by Norwegian masterchef Morten Sohlberg, this smart restaurant dishes out traditional dishes such as Swedish meatballs with lingonberry preserve ($16) and Norwegian-style North Sea cod ($26). The outdoor tables (summer only) and old-world feel enhance the European ambience. Mon–Fri 10.30am–11.30pm, Sat & Sun 11am–11.30pm.

Tribeca

Tribeca's enclave of very fine restaurants has long attracted Manhattan's "beautiful people", but dining in this part of town can leave a serious hole in your wallet.

American and Continental

Bubby's 120 Hudson St, between Franklin and N Moore sts ⓣ212/219-0666, ⓦwww.bubbys.com. Subway #1 to Franklin St. A relaxed place serving American comfort food, like matzoh-ball soup ($9) and pulled pork ($20). It's the pies, though, that really pull in the crowds – try a slice of the Key Lime ($7). The weekend brunch menu is very popular. Open 24hr (closed Mon midnight–Tues 8am).

City Hall 131 Duane St, between Church St and W Broadway ⓣ212/227-7777, ⓦwww.cityhallnewyork.com. Subway A, C, #1, #2, #3 to Chambers St. With a nod toward old-time New York City, *City Hall* is all class, serving amazing steaks (from $26) and always-fresh oysters ($2.75 each). Mon noon–10pm, Tues–Thurs 7.30am–10.30am & noon–10pm, Fri 7.30am–10.30am & noon–11pm, Sat 10am–3pm & 5–11pm.

▲ *Blaue Gans*

Harrison 355 Greenwich St, at Harrison St ⓣ212/274-9310, ⓦwww.theharrison.com. Subway #1 to Franklin St. Upscale version of an upstate country inn, with a smart cherry-wood dining room and a contemporary American menu that includes Arctic char with peanut potatoes, and skate wing with cauliflower and curry; don't skip the duck fat fries ($9). The desserts are also must-try: ice-cream brownie sandwich ($8). Entrees from $20–34. Mon–Thurs 5.30–10.30pm, Fri & Sat 5.30–11pm, Sun 5–10pm.

Tribeca Grill 375 Greenwich St, at Franklin St ⓣ212/941-3900. Subway #1 to Franklin St. The *Grill* is owned by Robert De Niro, but it's really the food – fine American cooking with Asian and Italian accents – that takes centre stage. The setting is nice, too: an airy, brick-walled eating area around a central Tiffany bar. Entrees average $20–30. Mon–Thurs 11.30am–11pm, Fri 11.30am–11.30pm, Sat 5.30–11.30pm, Sun 11.30am–3pm & 5.30–10pm.

Austrian/German

Blaue Gans 139 Duane St between Church St and W Broadway ⓣ212/571-8880, ⓦwww.wallse.com. Subway A, C, #1, #2, #3 to Chambers St. Poster-filled walls and a long bar made of zinc add personality to this bright Austro-German restaurant, with tasty schnitzels, goulash and fresh fish (entrees $22–29) the highlights of Chef Kurt Gutenbruner's menu. The beer selection includes some unusual – and unusually tasty – German draughts. Daily 11am–midnight (bar open until 2am).

French and Belgian

Bouley **163 Duane St ⓣ212/964-2525, ⓦwww.davidbouley.com. Subway #1, #2, #3 to Chambers St.** Contemporary French food made from the freshest ingredients by celebrated chef David Bouley. Popular with celebs, the prices are fairly steep (entrees $35–43); soften costs by opting for one of the prix-fixe options (from $48). Daily 11.30am–3pm & 5–11.30pm.

Corton **239 West Broadway, between Walker and White sts ⓣ212/219-2777, ⓦwww.cortonnyc.com. Subway #1 to Franklin St.** Mesmerizing modern French cuisine prepared by Paul Liebrandt, one of America's up-and-coming chefs. He serves a three-course prix fixe ($85) or tasting menu ($145), featuring delicacies such as foie gras with apple, scallop and truffles, and wild duckling in honey and turnip gelée. Mon–Thurs 5.30–10.30pm, Fri & Sat 5.30–11pm.

Petite Abeille **134 W Broadway, between Duane and Thomas sts ⓣ212/791-1360, ⓦwww.petiteabeille.com. Subway #1, #2, #3 to Chambers St.** *Tintin* comic books cover the walls at this nice little Belgian chain restaurant. It's notable for its 2lb pots of mussels (from $18), *pommes frites* ($4) and Belgian beer ($7); on Wed the mussels are all-you-can-eat ($23.95). Sun & Mon 9am–10pm, Tues–Fri 9am–11pm, Sat 8am–11pm.

Italian

Locanda Verde **377 Greenwich St at N Moore St ⓣ212/925-3797, ⓦlocandaverdenyc.com. Subway #1 to Franklin St.** This casual Italian taverna is a showcase for star chief Andrew Carmellini's exceptional creations; try the porchetta sandwich ($17), stuffed mountain trout ($26) or his fabulous pastas ($17–19). Daily 8am–3pm & 5.30–11pm.

Japanese

Megu **62 Thomas St between West Broadway and Church St ⓣ212/964-7777, ⓦwww.megurestaurants.com. Subway #1, #2, #3 to Chambers St.** Modern Japanese cuisine in what seems like a private club – enter at the hip bar area, before going down to the restaurant with its giant bronze bell, ice sculptures of Buddha, fine sushi and Kobe beef that cuts like butter; count on $300 for two. Sun–Thurs 5.30–10.15pm, Fri–Sat 5.30–11.15pm.

Nobu **105 Hudson St, at Franklin St ⓣ212/219-0500, ⓦwww.noburestaurants.com. Subway #1 to Franklin St.** *Nobu*'s lavish woodland decor complements its superlative Japanese cuisine. Try the black cod with miso ($26) and chilled sake served in hollow bamboo trunks. Prices are high (entrees from $28) and reservations hard to get; if you can't get in, try the adjacent *Next Door Nobu*. Mon–Fri 11.45am–2.15pm & 5.45–10.15pm, Sat & Sun 5.45–10.15pm.

South Asian

Pakistan Tea House **176 Church St, at Reade St ⓣ212/240-9800. Subway A, C to Chambers St.** Great, cheap Pakistani tandooris, baltis and curries. The staff will also create made-to-order flatbreads. Main dishes average $7. Mon–Sat 9am–4am.

Turkish

Turks & Frogs **458 Greenwich St, at Desbrosses St ⓣ212/966-4774, ⓦwww.turksandfrogs.com. Subway #1 to Canal St.** This authentic, red-walled Turkish restaurant has become a local favourite thanks to the excellent service, exotic, antique-laden interior, and exquisite food such as stuffed baby eggplants, creamy caviar, and feta cheese and lamb dumplings. Entrees average $20. Daily 11am–11pm.

Soho

Though best known for its posh boutiques and upscale galleries, a number of the city's top restaurants still make their home here – expect to pay top dollar for the more venerable hotspots.

American and Continental

Aquagrill 210 Spring St, at Sixth Ave ⓣ212/274-0505, ⓦwww.aguagrill.com. Subway C, E to Spring St. The moderately expensive seafood at this cosy Soho spot is so fresh it's practically still flopping. Russian Osetra Caviar chimes in at $155 per ounce, or try the grilled yellowfin tuna for $26. The excellent raw bar and Sunday brunch dishes are cheaper, between $12 and $23. Mon–Thurs noon–3pm & 6–10.45pm, Fri noon–3pm & 6–11.45pm, Sat noon–3.45pm & 6–11.45pm, Sun noon–3.45pm & 6–10.30pm.

Cupping Room Café 359 W Broadway, between Broome and Grand sts ⓣ212/925-2898, ⓦwww.cuppingroomcafe.com. Subway A, C, E to Canal St. Snuggle in at this affordable American bistro for comfort food, but avoid visiting on weekends – the brunch line can stretch around the block. Good bets are the vast choice of salads ($12.95) or the juicy burgers ($11.95). Live music on Wed and Fri nights. Mon–Thurs 7.30am–midnight, Fri 7.30am–2am, Sat 8am–2am, Sun 8am–midnight.

Lure Fishbar 142 Mercer St at Prince St T212/431-7676, Wwww.lurefishbar.com. Subway N, R to Prince St. Stylish basement seafood restaurant and sushi bar, with everything from steamed red snapper ($29) and calamari ($14), to lobster rolls ($29) and clam chowder ($12) on the menu. Mon–Thurs 11.30am–11pm, Fri & Sat 11.30am–midnight, Sun 11.30am–10pm.

Mercer Kitchen Mercer Hotel, 99 Prince St, at Mercer St ⓣ2122/966-5454, ⓦwww.jean-georges.com. Subway N, R to Prince St. This café and dimly-lit cellar restaurant entices hotel guests and scenesters alike with its casual modern American creations and wood-burning oven; think raw tuna and wasabi pizza, fine steaks, burgers and slow-cooked salmon. With entrees ranging from $10 to $28, this is one of the cheaper members of the Jean-Georges stable, and a good choice for Sunday brunch. Mon–Thurs 7am–midnight, Fri & Sat 7am–1am, Sun 7am–11pm.

Spring Street Natural Restaurant 62 Spring St, at Lafayette St ⓣ212/966-0290, ⓦwww.springstreetnatural.com. Subway #6 to Spring St. Though not wholly vegetarian, this restaurant serves up freshly prepared health-food in a large, airy space. Try the "Mayan" eggs ($11), served with tortillas, black beans and guacamole, for brunch. Mon–Thurs 9am–11.30pm, Fri 9am–12.30am, Sat 10.30am–12.30am, Sun 10.30am–11.30pm.

Asian

Blue Ribbon Sushi 119 Sullivan St, between Prince and Spring sts ⓣ212/343-0404, ⓦwww.blueribbonrestaurants.com. Subway C, E to Spring St. Widely considered one of the best sushi restaurants in New York, with fish flown in daily from Japan. Have some cold sake and feast on the outstanding oysters at the raw bar. Special rolls around $10, platters from $15. Daily noon–2am.

Kelley and Ping 127 Greene St, between Prince and Houston sts. ⓣ212/228-1212, ⓦwww.kelleyandping.com. Subway N, R to Prince St. Sleek pan-Asian tearoom and restaurant that serves tasty bowls of Thai and Malaysian curry ($14) and other dishes at moderate prices ($11–18). Dark wood cases filled with Thai herbs and cooking ingredients add to the informal, streetmarket-esque ambience. Daily 11.30am–5pm & 5.30pm–11pm.

Omen 113 Thompson St, between Prince and Spring sts ⓣ212/925-8923. Subway C, E to Spring St. Traditional Kyoto eatery with beautiful crockery and menus made from rice paper. Though named for its famous Udon noodle soup ($18), it also serves some of the best sushi in the area (mixed sashimi platter; $33), with a rotating seasonal menu and an extensive sake list. Daily 6pm–midnight.

French

Balthazar 80 Spring St, between Crosby St and Broadway ⓣ212/965-1414, ⓦwww.balthazarny.com. Subway #6 to Spring St. Keith McNally's bistro is still one of the hottest restaurants in town. The tastefully ornate Parisian décor keeps your eyes busy until the food arrives; then all you can do is savour the fresh oysters and mussels ($21), the exquisite pastries, and everything in between. Entrees $20–30. Mon–Fri 7.30am–midnight, Sat & Sun 8am–1am.

L'Ecole 462 Broadway, at Grand St ⓣ212/219-3300, ⓦwww.frenchculinary.com/lecole.htm. Subway N, Q, R to Canal St. Students of the French Culinary Institute serve up affordable French delights – even the bread basket deserves reverence. The superb prix-fixe dinner menu is $42 per person for four-courses (Mon–Sat 5.30–7pm) or five courses (Mon–Sat 7–8pm); it's $28 for lunch (three courses, Mon–Fri 12.30–2pm); and $19.50 for weekend brunch (Sat & Sun 11.30am–2.30pm). Book in advance.

Raoul's 180 Prince St, between Sullivan and Thompson sts ⓣ212/966-3518, ⓦraouls.com. Subway C, E to Spring St. Sexy French bistro seemingly lifted from Paris. The food, especially the steak frites ($37), is wonderful – a fact your wallet won't let you forget. The service is great too. Reservations recommended. Daily 5pm–1am.

Italian

Mezzogiorno 195 Spring St, at Sullivan St ⓣ212/334-2112, ⓦwww.mezzogiorno.com. Subway C, E to Spring St. This bright Soho restaurant is as much a place to people-watch as it is a place to eat. The inventive menu, including excellent pizzas ($10–16), great salads ($10–14), and *prosciutto* with caramelized pears ($15) makes up for the slightly higher prices. Mon–Fri noon–4pm & 6–11pm, Sat & Sun noon–midnight.

Mexican

Dos Caminos 475 W Broadway at Houston St ⓣ212/277-4300, ⓦwww.brguestrestaurants.com. Subway #1 to Houston St. Thoughtful, real-deal Mexican served with style – try the table-side guacamole. Brunch should set you back $12–15 per person, while dinner entrees range between $18 and $28. Mon & Tues noon–10.30pm, Wed & Thurs noon–11pm, Fri noon–midnight, Sat 11.30am–midnight, Sun 11.30am–10.30pm.

Chinatown

If you're after authentic (not to mention cheap) Chinese or Southeast Asian food, head for the bustling streets of **Chinatown**, where the streets are lined with dumpling houses and roast-duck window displays. Weekends are especially busy, as New Yorkers come to this neighbourhood for *dim sum*. Walk down Eldridge Street and you'll see **Fujianese** fish-ball shops, while **Vietnamese** food dominates Baxter Street. All the restaurants listed below can be accessed via lines J, N, Q, R, Z and #6 to Canal Street.

Chinese

Big Wong 67 Mott St, between Bayard and Canal sts ⓣ212/964-0540. This cheap, cafeteria-style Cantonese BBQ joint serves some of Chinatown's tastiest *char siu* (roast pork) for just $4.50 and congee (savoury rice stew) from $3.75; try the pork and 1000-year-old egg version. Daily 7am–10pm.

Excellent Dumpling House 111 Lafayette St, between Canal and Walker sts ⓣ212/219-0212. The thing to order is obviously the most excellent dumplings, lots of them, any way you like them. Their scallion pancakes are also delicious (everything is under $5). Daily 11am–9pm.

Hop Kee 21 Mott St, at Mosco St ⓣ212/267-2729. Not much to look at (really a diner) but this ageing Cantonese place has some of the best seafood in Chinatown, including sizzling stir-fried calamari and hard-shell crab for $15–20. Also serves excellent pork and onion dumplings ($7.50). Sun–Thurs 11am–1am, Fri & Sat 11am–4am.

Hsin Wong Restaurant 72 Bayard St, between Mott and Elizabeth sts ⓣ212/925-6526. Best place to try mouth-watering *char siu* (seasoned barbecue pork; $4.25) and congee ($1.50–4.50). Usually full of Hong Kong regulars – a good sign.

Great N.Y. Noodletown 28 1/2 Bowery, at Bayard St ⓣ212/349-0923. *Noodletown* is best during soft-shell crab season (May–Aug), when the crustaceans are crispy, salty and delicious ($16). The roast meats, *lo mein* (noodles) and soups are good year-round (try the baby pig on rice for $7.95). Daily 9am–4am.

Peking Duck House 28 Mott St, between Chatham Square and Pell St ⓣ212/227-1810, ⓦwww.pekingduckhousenyc.com. This chic and shiny-clean eatery dishes up – you guessed it – duck; the crispy fried birds are carved tableside ($43; or served as part of a special dinner for $27.50 per person, minimum of 4 people). Slightly pricier than the competition, but worth it. Sun–Thurs 11.30am–10.30pm, Fri & Sat 11.45am–11pm.

Ping's Seafood 22 Mott St, between Chatham Square and Pell St ☎212/602-9988. While this Hong Kong-style seafood restaurant is good any time, it's most enjoyable on weekends for *dim sum*, when carts of tasty, bite-sized delicacies whir by every thirty seconds. Offers superb bang for your buck (most plates well under $10). Daily 10.30am–midnight.

Tasty Hand-Pulled Noodles 1 Doyers St at the Bowery ☎212/791-1817. Freshly made, hand-pulled noodles made to order – choose from seven different types, then opt for pan-fried ($5–6) or boiled noodles ($4.50) with pork, fish, beef, chicken, shrimp and several other combos. They also do excellent dumplings (from $3). Daily 10.30am–10.30pm.

Southeast Asian

Bo Ky 80 Bayard St, at Mott St ☎212/406-2292. The inexpensive noodle soups ($4–5) are good value at this cramped Chinese–Vietnamese eatery. The house specialty is a big bowl of rice noodles with shrimp, fish or duck. Daily 8am–10pm.

New Malaysia Chinatown Arcade, 46-48 Bowery between Bayard and Canal sts ☎212/964-0284. Tucked away in a dingy arcade, this is one of the best Malaysian restaurants in town, with perfect *roti canai*, *laksas* and crunchy satay sauce (dishes $5–8). Daily 11am–10.30pm.

Sanur 18 Doyers St at Pell St ☎212/349-3132. Don't be put off by the shabby exterior; this Indonesian hole-in-the-wall serves knockout meals from just $4, and crispy curry puffs for $0.80. Tues–Sun 8am–10pm.

Little Italy and Nolita

Mulberry Street is **Little Italy**'s main drag, and though often crowded with weekend tourists, the mostly Southern Italian eateries and carnival-like atmosphere can make for an entertaining dinner or dessert excursion. It's best not to have high culinary hopes for the neighbourhood, however: Little Italy's many red-sauce restaurants are fair, but not great. In contrast, **Nolita** is notable for its popular budget restaurants, which are often packed to the gills with aspiring fashionistas and film-industry hipsters.

American

Mac Bar 54 Prince St, between Lafayette and Mulberry sts ☎212/226-0211, Ⓦwww.macbar.net. Subway N, R to Prince St; #6 to Spring St. Celebration of macaroni and cheese, with offerings starting at the classic ($5.99), moving on to the mac stroganoff ($7.25), mac lobsta' ($8.99) and the mac quack ($7.99). Sun–Thurs 11am–11pm, Fri & Sat 11am–2am.

Quintessential New York

Amy Ruth's Harlem, p.336
Katz's Deli Lower East Side, p.314
Lombardi's Little Italy, p.313
Oyster Bar Midtown East, p.326
Peter Luger Steak House Williamsburg, Brooklyn p.341

Brazilian

Bar Bossa 232 Elizabeth St, between Prince and Houston sts ☎212/625-2340. Subway #6 to Spring St. The great ambience at this Brazilian café complements the extremely yummy food, including ginger-tomato soup ($6), outstanding seafood stew ($15) and a very rich Guinness chocolate cake ($7). Daily 10am–11.30pm.

Cuban

Café Habana 17 Prince St, at Elizabeth St ☎212/625-2001, Ⓦwww.cafehabana.com. Subway N, R to Prince St. Small and always crowded, this Cuban–South American eatery features some of the best skirt steak ($11.25) and fried plantains ($3) this side of Havana. They also have a takeaway window next door that serves great *café con leche*. Daily 9am–midnight.

Italian

Angelo's 146 Mulberry St between Hester and Grand sts. ⓣ212/966-1277, ⓦangelomulberry .com. Subway N, R, #6 to Canal St. Little Italy's red-sauce restaurants cater firmly to tourists these days, but this 1902 classic is the best place to get a sense of the area's original style, flavours and home-made pastas ($16–24). *Secondis* are more like $30. Tues–Thurs & Sun noon–11.30pm, Fri noon–12.30am, Sat noon–1am.

Emilio's Ballato 55 E Houston, between Mulberry and Mott sts ⓣ212/274-8881. Subway B, D, F, M to Broadway–Lafayette St. Serving by far the best Italian cuisine in the area, *Ballato* has a great low-key atmosphere, a spicy penne *arrabiata*, tasty spaghetti *vongole* and veal chops so tender they melt in your mouth. Dishes average $15–25. Mon–Fri noon–11pm, Sat 4pm–midnight, Sun 4–11pm.

Lombardi's 32 Spring St, at Mott St ⓣ212/941-7994, ⓦwww.firstpizza.com. Subway #6 to Spring St. The oldest pizzeria in Manhattan (since 1905), *Lombardi's* serves some of the best pizzas in town (large from $19.50), with extra toppings from $3; no slices though. There's open-air dining upstairs. Sun–Thurs 11.30am–11pm, Fri & Sat 11.30am–midnight.

Peasant 194 Elizabeth St, between Prince and Spring sts ⓣ212/965-9511, ⓦwww .peasantnyc.com. Subway N, R to Prince St; J, M, Z to Bowery; #6 to Spring St. A bit of a hangout after hours for city chefs, here you'll pay around $22–30 for Frank De Carlo's beautifully crafted Italian food such as *porchetta arrosto* (roasted suckling pig) and sumptuous pastas, or $12 for brick-oven-fired pizzas. Tues–Sun 6pm–2am.

Umberto's Clam House 178 Mulberry St, at Broome St. ⓣ212/431-7545, ⓦwww .umbertosclamhouse.com. Subway J, M, Z to Bowery. Specializing in rich, Italian seafood for almost forty years, though the best dish is the simplest – linguine in white clam sauce ($21.95). Daily 11am–4am.

▲ *Lombardi's*

Southeast Asian

Nyonya 199 Grand St, between Mott and Mulberry sts ⓣ212/334-3669, ⓦwww .penangusa.com. Subway B, D to Grand St. The grub at this Malaysian restaurant is superb, and comes at wallet-friendly prices. Try the chicken curry, spicy squid or clay-pot noodles ($6–7). If you're in the mood for something sweeter, order some coconut milk ($4.25) – it's served chilled in the shell. Sun–Thurs 11am–11.30pm, Fri & Sat 11am–midnight.

Pho Bang 157 Mott St, between Grand and Broome sts ⓣ212/966-3797. Subway B, D to Grand St, J, Z, #6 to Canal St. One of the most popular Vietnamese restaurants in the city, often packed with diners at weekends. The main event is *pho*, Vietnamese beef noodle soup ($5.50), which comes in several varieties, but the crispy spring rolls ($3.95) and chicken curry ($4.95) are also excellent. Daily 10am–10pm.

Lower East Side

The trendy **Lower East Side**, once dominated by immigrant tenements and sweatshops, has turned into something of a culinary destination, with Stanton, Rivington and Clinton streets as the main thoroughfares. You'll find some inviting gastronomic highlights here, such as *WD-50*, that have garnered dedicated fans for their sophisticated and unusual menus. There are also some terrific little Latin *comedores*, along with some stalwart old-time joints selling Jewish and Eastern European delicacies.

American and Continental

Schiller's Liquor Bar 131 Rivington St, at Norfolk St ⓣ212/260-4555, ⓦwww.schillersny.com. Subway F, J, M, Z to Essex St. Fairly high-end restaurant made up to look like a Prohibition-era speakeasy. Menu offerings ($16–29) are eclectic and self-consciously "American", including pan-fried trout and pork chops smothered in sautéed onions. Mon–Wed 11am–1am, Thurs 11am–2am, Fri 11am–3am, Sat 10am–3am, Sun 10am–1am.

Shopsin's Stall 16, Essex St Market, 120 Essex St (no phone), ⓦwww.shopsins.com. Subway F to Delancey St; J, M, Z to Essex St. Something of a New York institution, Kenny Shopsin ran his famously idiosyncratic diner in the West Village for years (no cell phones or parties larger than four), but was forced into this tiny space (two tables and counter top) by high rents. His addictive (and numerous) creations – like peanut-butter-filled pancakes – have a loyal following (filling plates average $12–14). Tues–Sat 9.30am–2pm.

Stanton Social 99 Stanton St, between Ludlow and Orchard sts ⓣ212/995-0099, ⓦwww.thestantonsocial.com. Subway F to Lower East Side–Second Ave. Chandeliers, lizard-skin banquettes and retro booths draw a young, hip crowd to this 1940s-inspired restaurant-cum-lounge bar. Tapas-style food here is designed for sharing: try the zesty snapper tacos with mango salsa ($10) or lobster pizzetta ($18). Mon–Wed 5pm–2am, Thurs & Fri 5pm–3am, Sat 11.30am–3am, Sun 11.30am–2am.

WD-50 50 Clinton St, between Rivington and Stanton sts ⓣ212/477-2900, ⓦwww.wd-50.com. Subway F, J, M, Z to Essex St. Though the buzz has died somewhat, celebrated chef Wylie DuFresne still pulls in the crowds with his experimental haute cuisine; think cuttlefish with cashew, rootbeer and watercress ($19) and parsnip tart with hazelnuts ($25). Wed–Sat 6–11pm, Sun 6–10pm.

Chinese

Congee Village 100 Allen St, between Delancey and Broome sts ⓣ212/941-1818, ⓦwww.congeevillagerestaurants.com. Subway F, J, M, Z to Delancey St–Essex St. You'll see this Cantonese restaurant as you exit the rear of the tenement museum, a shrine to the eponymous fragrant, soupy rice dish served in numerous varieties ($2–4.95) and a wide range of other Hong Kong favourites for less than $10. Daily 10.30am–2am.

Dominican

Cibao Restaurant 72 Clinton St, at Rivington St ⓣ212/228-0873. Subway F, J, M, Z to Delancey St–Essex St. *El Cibao* is the best of a slew of Dominican restaurants on the Lower East Side. The fare is hearty and inexpensive; the rice and beans ($6) and huge sandwiches, particularly the Cubano ($4.50), are bargains. Daily 6am–2am.

French/African

Les Enfants Terribles 37 Canal St, at Ludlow St ⓣ212/260-4555, ⓦwww.lesenfantsterriblesnyc.com. Subway F to East Broadway. French colonial-themed place with an exotic menu featuring French, West African, Moroccan and Brazilian dishes. Highlights include *koroghofefemugu*, a spicy dish from the Ivory Coast ($24) and the Brazilian seafood stew ($22). Daily 8am–4am.

Jewish

Katz's Deli 205 E Houston St, at Ludlow St ⓣ212/254-2246, ⓦwww.katzdeli.com. Subway F to Lower East Side–Second Ave. 1888 Jewish stalwart *Katz's* overstuffed pastrami or corned beef sandwiches should keep you going for about a week (sandwiches $14.95). The egg creams are also delicious. Famous faux-gasm scene from *When Harry Met Sally* was shot here. Sun, Wed, Thurs 8am–10.45pm, Mon & Tues 8am–9.45pm, Fri & Sat 8am–2.45am.

Sammy's Roumanian Steakhouse 157 Chrystie St, at Delancey St ⓣ212/673-0330. Subway B, D to Grand St; Z to Bowery; F to Lower East Side–Second Ave. This basement Jewish steakhouse offers much more than many customers are prepared for, including schmaltzy songs, delicious-but-heartburn-inducing food (complete with home-made *rugelach* and egg creams for dessert), and vodka chilled in blocks of ice. Entrees range $14–36. Mon–Thurs 4–10pm, Fri & Sat 4–11pm, Sun 3–9.30pm.

East Village

Over time, the **East Village**'s mix of radicals, professionals and immigrants has produced one of the most potent dining scenes in the city. The range of culinary options makes dining in this neighbourhood a real pleasure: you can peruse menus on Indian Row; sample dishes at the handful of Ukrainian eateries; or hit one of the numerous Japanese ramen bars around East 9th Street. The American and Continental dining scene here is not as exotic, but is certainly as equally enticing.

American and Continental

DBGB Kitchen & Bar 299 Bowery, at E Houston St ⓣ212/933-5300, ⓦwww.danielnyc.com/dbgb.html. Subway #6 to Bleecker St. Popular outpost of the Daniel Boulud empire, blending huge mirrors, rustic tables and modern styling – it's US diner meets French brasserie, where sausages are a speciality (14 types, from Tunisian spicy lamb to Vermont cheese; $8–14), though the burgers ($11) and foie gras ($21) are equally good. Daily noon–midnight.

Five Points 31 Great Jones St, between Bowery and Lafayette St ⓣ212/253-5700, ⓦwww.fivepointsrestaurant.com. Subway #6 to Bleecker St. Upscale New American/Med cuisine by Marc Meyer, including some of the best brunch below 14th St. Try the beer-battered fish tacos ($14) or the lemon-ricotta pancakes ($12). Mon–Fri noon–3pm & 5–11.30pm, Sat 11am–3pm & 5–11.30pm, Sun 11am–3pm and 5–10pm.

Graffiti Food & Wine Bar 244 E 10th St, between First and Second aves ⓣ212/677-0695, ⓦwww.graffitiny.com. Subway #6 to Astor Place. Pastry chef Jehangir Mehta cooks up a fusion of Chinese, American and Indian flavours in this artsy space, with just four tables and courses ranging $7–15: chickpea-crusted skate and cumin eggplant buns grace the menu. Tues & Sun 5.30–10.30pm, Wed–Sat 5.30–11.45pm.

Jack's Luxury Oyster Bar 101 Second Ave at 6th St. ⓣ212/979-1012. Subway #6 to Astor Place. Deconstructed small plates, such as potato-fried octopus ($14) and roasted oysters ($7), and a 24-seat dining room make this eatery an intimate and full-on romantic experience. Mon–Thurs 6–11pm, Fri & Sat 6pm–midnight.

Luke's Lobster 93 E 7th St, between First and A aves ⓣ212/387-8487, ⓦwww.lukeslobster.com. Subway #6 to Astor Place. Maine lobsters come to the East Village; this small place offers classic lobster rolls ($8–14), crab rolls ($5–9), shrimp rolls ($4–7) and various seafood plates ($9–38). Sun–Thurs 11am–10pm, Fri & Sat 11am–midnight.

Mama's Food Shop 200 E 3rd St, between aves A and B ⓣ212/777-4425, ⓦwww.mamasfoodshop.com. Subway F to Lower East Side–Second Ave. Enjoy whopping portions of tasty and cheap homestyle dishes like meatloaf and fried chicken from $11, with sides including macaroni and cheese and a good selection of roasted vegetables. Mon–Fri 5–11pm, Sat & Sun 4–11pm.

Prune 54 E 1st St, between First and Second aves. ⓣ212/677-6221, ⓦwww.prunerestaurant.com. Subway F to Lower East Side–Second Ave. This Mediterranean-influenced American bistro still delivers one of the city's most exciting dining experiences, serving dishes like sweetbreads wrapped in bacon, wild striped bass with cockles, and ricotta ice cream with salted caramel chunks (entrees average $20). Mon–Thurs 11.30am–11pm, Fri 11.30am–midnight, Sat 10am–midnight, Sun 10am–11pm.

Sarita's Mac & Cheese 345 E 12th St, between Second and First aves ⓣ212/358-7912, ⓦwww.smacnyc.com. Subway L to First Ave. Indulge your macaroni and cheese cravings at this homey joint, with ten creative varieties on offer, blending cheddar, Gruyère, brie and goat's cheese with herbs and meats. Pick your portion sizes: nosh, major munch or mongo ($4.75–13.50). Sun–Thurs 11am–11pm, Fri & Sat 11am–1am.

East Asian

Dok Suni 119 First Ave, between E 7th and St Mark's Place ⓣ212/477-9506. Subway #6 to Astor Place. Hip around the edges with great prices to boot, this is a fine bet (and longtime local favourite) for Korean home cooking, including *bibimbop* and *kim chee* rice. The only real drawbacks here are the metal chopsticks, which can retain heat and can be frustratingly slippery. Entrees $12–17. Mon 4.30–11pm, Tues–Fri 4.30pm–midnight, Sat noon–midnight, Sun noon–11pm.

Momofuku Noodle Bar 171 First Ave, between E 10th and E 11th sts ⓣ212/387-8487, ⓦwww.momofuku.com. Subway #6 to Astor Place. Celebrated chef David Chang's first restaurant, where his simplest creations are still the best: silky steamed pork buns, laced with hoisin sauce and pickled cucumbers ($9), or steaming bowls of chicken and pork ramen noodles ($10). Sun–Thurs noon–11pm, Fri & Sat noon–2am.

Rhong-Tiam 87 Second Ave, at 5th St ⓣ212/260-8018, ⓦwww.rhong-tiam.com. Subway #6 to Astor Place. This acclaimed Thai restaurant moved from the West to East Village in 2010, but it still serves top-notch cuisine: noodles, curries and aromatic fish for around $10. Lunch specials from $7. Sun–Thurs noon–3.30pm & 5pm–2am, Fri–Sun noon–3.30pm & 5pm–4am.

Tsampa 212 E 9th St, between Third and Second aves ⓣ212/614-3226. Subway #6 to Astor Place. Absorb the Buddhist vibes at this Tibetan restaurant, adorned with prayer flags and giant images of the Dalai Lama. Vegetarians have plenty to choose from, with lots of fresh greens, barley soup, various noodles and *momo* (Tibetan dumplings), though there are also several meat dishes (entrees average $10). Daily 5–11.30pm.

Indian

Brick Lane Curry House 343 E 6th St, between First and Second aves ⓣ212/979-2900, ⓦwww.bricklanecurryhouse.com. Subway #6 to Astor Place. Smack in the heart of curry row, and hands down the best Indian in the East Village, thanks to its wide selection of Brit-Indian favourites, including a tasty *bhaji* ($7), baltis (from $15) and some fiery *phaal* curries ($14–20). Sun–Thurs 1–11pm, Fri & Sat 1pm–1am.

Haveli 100 Second Ave, between E 5th and 6th sts ⓣ212/982-0533. Subway #6 to Astor Place. Far superior to most of its neighbours on E 6th St (with the notable exception of *Brick Lane*), this roomy Indian restaurant serves creative and well-executed classics (curries $11–14). Daily noon–midnight.

Italian

Frank 88 Second Ave, between E 5th and 6th sts ⓣ212/420-0202, ⓦwww.frankrestaurant.com. Subway F to Lower East Side–Second Ave; #6 to Astor Place. A tiny neighbourhood favourite, where basic, traditional American–Italian dishes like seared salmon ($15.95) and roasted rosemary chicken ($14.95) are served at communal tables. Cash only. Mon–Thurs 10.30am–1am, Fri & Sat 10.30am–2am, Sun 10.30am–midnight.

Il Buco 47 Bond St, between Lafayette St and Bowery ⓣ212/533-1932, ⓦilbuco.com. Subway #6 to Bleecker St. This antiques-filled Mediterranean eatery delivers authentic dishes from southern Europe with creative flair (entrees $20–30). The wine cellar is alleged to have inspired Edgar Allan Poe's *The Cask of Amontillado*. Mon–Thurs noon–11pm, Fri & Sat noon–midnight, Sun 5–10.30pm.

Il Posto Accanto 190 E 2nd Street between aves A and B. ⓣ212/228-0977, ⓦilbagattonyc.com/index_ilposto.html. Subway F to Lower East Side–Second Ave. Nab a spot at a high wooden table at this small, intimate wine bar serving a vast array of Italian reds by the glass. You can easily make a meal from the excellent small plates of pasta ($12–15), panini ($8) and the like. Can get crowded, like its popular parent restaurant next door (*Il Bagatto*). Mon 5pm–3am, Tues–Thurs noon–3am, Fri–Sun noon–3.30pm & 5pm–3am.

Lavagna 545 E 5th St, between aves A and B ⓣ212/979-1005, ⓦwww.lavagnanyc.com. Subway F to Lower East Side–Second Ave. This red-hued hideaway seduces East Villagers with potato-cheese gratin, pasta with sausage and succulent pork dishes. It's been described by local regulars as perfect from beginning to end, including the bill (pastas $12–16, *secondis* $17–24). Mon–Thurs 6–11pm, Fri 6pm–midnight, Sat noon–3pm & 6pm–midnight, Sun noon–3pm & 5–11pm.

Japanese

BondSt 6 Bond St, between Broadway and Lafayette St ⓣ212/777-2500, ⓦbondst restaurant.com. Subway #6 to Bleecker St. Very hip, super-suave Japanese restaurant on multiple storeys (there's a happening lounge on the ground floor). The sushi is amazing, the miso-glazed sea bass exquisite, and the steak a treat. Entrees $22–32, sushi sets from $26. Sun–Wed 6pm–midnight, Thurs–Sat 6pm–1.30am.

Curry-Ya 214 E 10th St, between First and Second aves ⓣ866/602-8779. Subway #6 to Astor Place. Grab a stool at the marble-top bar at this narrow, slick Japanese curry house for its nine types of freshly made mouthwatering curry, from slightly sweet classic Japanese, to organic chicken and seasonal vegetable (from $8). Daily noon–11pm.

Hasaki 210 E 9th St, at Stuyvesant St ⓣ212/473-3327, ⓦwww.hasakinyc.com. Subway #6 to Astor Place. Some of the best sushi in the city is served at this popular but mellow downstairs cubbyhole. Sit at the bar and the chefs will try to tempt you with a variety of improvised dishes not found on the menu (five pieces from $22). No reservations. Mon & Tues 5.30–11pm, Wed & Thurs noon–3pm & 5.30–11pm, Fri noon–3pm & 5.30–11.30pm, Sat 1–4pm & 5.30–11.30pm, Sun 1–4pm & 5.30–11pm.

Ippudo 65 Fourth Ave, between 9th and 10th sts. ⓣ212/388-0088, ⓦwww.ippudo.com/ny. Subway #6 to Astor Place. The first overseas outpost of Fukuoka-based "ramen king" Shigemi Kawahara, this popular Japanese ramen shop offers steaming bowls of classic *tonkotsu*-style noodles for $8–14 in booths and communal wooden tables, as well as tasty pork buns and roast chicken appetizers. Be prepared for a long wait at weekends (no reservations). Mon–Thurs 11am–3.30pm & 5–11.30pm, Fri & Sat 11am–3.30pm & 5pm–12.30am, Sun 11am–10.30pm.

Robataya NY 231 E 9th St, between Second and Third aves ⓣ212/979-9674. Subway #6 to Astor Place. Place to experience *Robatayaki*-style cuisine; choose your fresh ingredients first, then watch as the chef cooks them on a hearth in front of you, before delivering it to your table via a long paddle. Order vegetables ($5) and meats from $3–11. Sun & Tues–Thurs 6–10.45pm, Fri & Sat 6–11.45pm.

Latin American

Boca Chica 13 First Ave, at E 1st St ⓣ212/473-0108. Subway F to Lower East Side–Second Ave. Authentic South American food, piled high and served with black beer or tropical drinks. Everything is good, but the coco shrimp ($7.50) is exceptional, and the green plantain balls are a simple but tasty snack ($6.50). Entrees $12–15. Mon–Thurs 5.30–11pm, Fri & Sat 5.30–11.30pm, Sun noon–11pm.

Caracas Arepa Bar 91 E 7th, at 1st Ave ⓣ212/529-2314, ⓦwww.caracasarepabar.com. Subway #6 to Astor Place. Delicious Venezuelan home-made *arepas* ($4.75–7) and *empanadas* ($4.25–5) served in a tiny cafeteria – there's a small takeaway place next door (both tend to get swamped at the weekend). Choose from various cheeses to shredded beef and chorizo fillings. Daily noon–11pm.

Hecho en Dumbo 354 Bowery between Great Jones and E 4th sts ⓣ212/937-4245, ⓦwww.hechoendumbo.com. Subway #6 to Astor Place. This authentic Mexican diner migrated across the East River in 2010, but it still knocks out wonderful small plates and Mexico City contemporary cuisine such as house-cured beef, lamb shank confit and an innovative selection of tacos, *sopes* and burritos. Sun–Wed noon–4pm & 5.30pm–midnight, Thurs–Sat noon–4pm & 5.30pm–2am.

Ukrainian

Veselka 144 Second Ave, corner of E 9th St ⓣ212/228-9682, ⓦwww.veselka.com. Subway #6 to Astor Place. This always crowded Ukrainian diner has been an East Village institution since the 1960s, offering fine home-made hot borscht (and cold in summer) from $4.50, *kielbasa* sausage ($14.95), veal goulash ($14.95), *pierogi* ($4.75) and great burgers and fries (from $7.50). Daily 24hr.

Vegetarian

Angelica Kitchen 300 E 12th St, between First and Second aves ⓣ212/228-2909, ⓦwww.angelicakitchen.com. Subway L to First Ave. Vegetarian macrobiotic restaurant with various daily specials for a decent price. Patronized by a colourful downtown crowd and serving some of the best veggie food in Manhattan. Entrees $10–16.75. Cash only. Daily 11.30am–10.30pm.

B & H Dairy 127 Second Ave, between E 7th St and St Mark's Place ⓣ212/505-8065. Subway #6 to Astor Place. A tiny kosher vegetarian luncheonette since the 1950s, serving home-made soup (try the split pea; $4.50), blintzes ($6.75) and absolutely divine challah French toast ($5). You can also create your own juice combinations (carrot–beet, for example). Daily 7.30am–11pm.

Burgers

Txikito Chelsea, p.322
Corner Bistro West Village, p.318
Diner Williamsburg, Brooklyn, p.341
Minetta Tavern West Village, p.318
Shake Shack Flatiron District, p.294

West Village

Restaurants in the **West Village** cater to the neighbourhood's many and varied residents – everyone from students to celebrities – so the culinary scene is fairly diverse. You'll find loads of takeaway spots and places with prix-fixe meals around New York University. Farther west, dining rooms get snazzier, menus more interesting and prices higher, particularly beyond Seventh Avenue, where there's a preponderance of French and Italian bistros.

American and Continental

Blue Hill 75 Washington Place, between MacDougal and 6th sts ⓣ212/539-1776, ⓦwww.bluehillfarm.com. Subway A, B, C, D, E, F, M to W 4th St. One of the better restaurants in the West Village, lauded for the rustic American and New England fare, including squash soup ($15) and Berkshire pig ($35), using seasonal upstate ingredients. Don't miss the rich chocolate bread pudding ($12). Mon–Sat 5.30–11pm, Sun 5.30–10pm.

Corner Bistro 331 W 4th St, at Jane St ⓣ212/242-9502, ⓦcornerbistrony.com. Subway A, C, E, L to 14th St. A down-home pub with cavernous cubicles, paper plates and maybe the best burger in town ($6.75). It's a long-standing haunt for West Village literary and artsy types, with a mix of locals and die-hard fans queuing up nightly for excellent and inexpensive grub. Mon–Sat 11.30am–4am, Sun noon–4am.

Gotham Bar & Grill 12 E 12th St, between Fifth Ave and University Place ⓣ212/620-4020, ⓦwww.gothambarandgrill.com. Subway L, N, Q, R, #4, #5, #6 to Union Square. Generally reckoned to be one of the city's best New American restaurants; if you don't want to splurge on a full meal, at least go for a drink at the bar, where you can watch the beautiful patrons drift in. Seasonal menu features Niman Ranch pork, miso cod, Maine lobster and more (average $25–30). Mon–Thurs noon–2.15pm & 5.30–10pm, Fri noon–2.15pm & 5.30–11pm, Sat 5–11pm, Sun 5–10pm.

Home 20 Cornelia St, between Bleecker and W 4th sts ⓣ212/243-9579, ⓦwww.homerestaurantnyc.com. Subway A, B, C, D, E, F, M to W 4th St; #1 to Christopher St. One of those rare restaurants that manages to pull off cosy with flair. The creative and reasonably priced American food is always fresh and tasty, though it may be a better deal at lunch (around $20/person) than dinner ($30–40/person). Mon–Fri 11.30am–11pm, Sat 10.30am–11pm, Sun 10.30am–10pm.

Mary's Fish Camp 64 Charles St, at W 4th St ⓣ646/486-2185, ⓦwww.marysfishcamp.com. Subway #1 to Christopher St. Lobster rolls, bouillabaisse and grilled whole fish adorn the menu at this small, noisy West Village spot. Go early, as they don't accept reservations and the line lasts into the night. Definitely one of the best seafood spots in the whole city – you can almost smell the salty air. Entrees $17–25. Mon–Sat 11am–3pm & 6–11pm.

Minetta Tavern 113 MacDougal St at Minetta Lane ⓣ212/475-3850, ⓦwww.minettatavernny.com. Subway A, B, C, D, E, F, M to W 4th St. This classic restaurant from 1937 is loaded with atmosphere, with old photos on the walls and mural-clad dining room beyond the bar. It was revamped in 2008 by the *Balthazar* folks, and now serves upscale French and New American cuisine; the Black Label Burger ($26) is one of the city's best, while weekend brunch involves delicacies such as slow-baked ham in hay ($22) and salt cod ($19). Excellent service. Mon–Fri 5.30pm–2am, Sat & Sun 10am–2am.

Pearl Oyster Bar 18 Cornelia St, between Bleecker and W 4th sts ⓣ212/691-8211,

▲ *Pearl Oyster Bar*

Ⓦ www.pearloysterbar.com. **Subway A, B, C, D, E, F, M to W 4th St; #1 to Christopher St.** This upmarket version of a New England fish shack is best known for its pricey (around $27) lemony-fresh lobster roll (which featured in *The Sopranos*). You may have to fight for a table here, but the thoughtfully executed seafood dishes are well worth it. Small plates around $10, large plates $16. Mon–Fri noon–2.30pm & 6–11pm, Sat 6–11pm.

The Spotted Pig **314 W 11th St, at Greenwich St Ⓣ212/620-0393, Ⓦ www.thespottedpig.com. Subway #1 to Christopher St.** New York's best gastropub, courtesy of Mario Batali and English chef April Bloomfield. The menu is several steps above ordinary bar food – think grilled beef tongue with duck fat potatoes and pickled beets ($28) – and the wine list is excellent. Mon–Fri noon–2am, Sat & Sun 11am–2am.

Asian

Baoguette **120 Christopher St, between Bleecker and Bedford sts Ⓣ212/929-0877, Ⓦ www.baoguette.com. Subway #1 to Christopher St.** Tiny modern diner specializing in richly flavoured Vietnamese *banh mi* sandwiches for $5 – they also do a great spicy catfish version ($7), noodles and rice plates (from $8). Mon–Sat 11.30am–11pm, Sun noon–10pm.

Fatty Crab **643 Hudson St, between Gansevoort and Horatio sts Ⓣ212/352-3590, Ⓦ www.fattycrab.com. Subway A, C, E, L to 14th St.** This laidback but stylish Malaysian diner serves high-quality, authentic fare: the *kang kong* comes with perfect shrimp paste, the oyster omelette is Penang-style, and the bowls of glorious, finger-licking chili crab are worth the effort (and the mess). Expect to pay $14–21 per dish. Mon–Wed noon–midnight, Thurs–Fri noon–2am, Sat 11am–2am, Sun 11am–midnight.

Tomoe Sushi **172 Thompson St, between Bleecker and Houston sts Ⓣ212/777-9346. Subway #1 to Houston St.** The nightly queues may look daunting, but there's a good reason to join them: this is some of the best, freshest sushi in Manhattan, and it's affordable, to boot (sushi lunch set $17.75; fish entrees less than $10). There are some seasonal dishes (like a soft-shell crab roll) on the menu, but the fresh fish on offer is what draws the crowds. Mon 5–11pm, Tues–Sat 1–3pm & 5–11pm, Sun 5–10pm.

Austrian

Wallsé **344 W 11th St, at Washington St Ⓣ212/352-2300, Ⓦ www.wallserestaurant.com. Subway #1 to Christopher St.** The Austrian fare offered here has been updated for the 21st century, and the dining room is adorned with Julian Schnabel canvases. The uniquely crafted menu features light-as-air schnitzel, frothy Riesling sauces and fantastic strudels, and the wine list includes some rare vintages. Entrees $25–36. Mon–Fri 5.30–11pm, Sat & Sun 11am–2.15pm & 5.30–11pm.

French

Cornelia Street Café **29 Cornelia St, between Bleecker and W 4th sts Ⓣ212/989-9319, Ⓦ www.corneliastreetcafe.com. Subway #1 to Christopher St.** As much American diner as French café, there is no more comfortable restaurant in NYC. The pastas, salads and weekend brunch offerings are great, and the prices aren't bad either (dinner entrees $14–24). Downstairs is a cabaret featuring occasional jazz, poetry and performance art. Sun–Thurs 10am–midnight, Fri & Sat 10am–1am.

Tartine **253 W 11th St at W 4th St Ⓣ212/229-2611. Subway #1 to Christopher St.** The French creations are worth lining up for at this tiny bistro; try the *quiche du jour* ($8.95), *bouchée à la reine* (chicken pot pie; $16) and the custard-filled tarts ($5). Cash only but you can bring your own bottle. Mon–Sat 9am–10.30pm, Sun 9am–10pm.

Italian

Babbo **110 Waverly Place, between MacDougal St and Sixth Ave Ⓣ212/777-0303, Ⓦ www.babbonyc.com. Subway A, B, C, D, E, F, M to W 4th St; #1 to Christopher St.** Originally a coach house, this Mario Batali establishment is deservedly touted as one of the best Italian restaurants in the city. Try the mint love-letters or goose-liver ravioli, or go for one of the expensive tasting menus ($69–75). Reservations are hard to get (you can book up to one month in advance), so just show up early and either eat at the bar or try for an open table along the window – they don't take reservations for those. Mon–Sat 5.30–11.30pm, Sun 5–11pm.

'ino **21 Bedford St, between Downing sts and W Houston sts ⓣ212/989-5769, ⓦwww.cafeino.com. Subway #1 to Houston St.** Duck in here for a satisfying and nicely priced meal; choose from a list of *bruschette* ($3), *tramezzine* (a hearty cousin of the tea sandwich; $7) and Italian wines. The sweet *coppa* ham sandwich ($11) with fiery hot peppers and *rucola* (rocket) is one of the best in the city, served with sugary roasted garlic cloves on the side. Daily 9am–2am.

John's Pizzeria **278 Bleecker St, between Sixth and Seventh aves ⓣ212/243-1680, ⓦwww.johnsbrickovenpizza.com. Subway A, B, C, D, E, F, M to W 4th St; #1 to Christopher St.** This full-service restaurant serves some of the city's most popular pizzas, thin with a coal-charred crust ($12–18). Be prepared to wait in line for a table; they don't do slices, and there is no takeaway. Mon–Thurs 11.30am–11.30pm, Fri 11.30am–midnight, Sat 11.30am–12.30pm, Sun noon–11.30pm.

Kesté Pizza & Vino **271 Bleecker St, between Jones and Cornelia sts ⓣ212/243-1500, ⓦkestepizzeria.com. Subway A, B, C, D, E, F, M to W 4th St; #1 to Christopher St.** Newest pizzeria on the block, stirring things up with its Neapolitan-designed wood-fire oven and its perfect pizzas; try the original Mast'nicola (lardo, pecorino romano and basil; $9) or lip-smacking Pizza del Papa (butternut squash cream, smoked mozzarella and artichoke; $16). Mon–Sat noon–3.30pm & 5–11pm, Sun noon–3.30pm & 5–10pm.

Lupa **170 Thompson St, between Bleecker and Houston sts ⓣ212/982-5089, ⓦwww.luparestaurant.com. Subway #1 to Houston St.** This second Batali outpost serves hearty, rustic Italian specialties such as crispy duck *Agrodolce* ($22) and *gnocchi* with fennel sausage ($16). Hint: go for lunch or before 6.30pm and you'll have no problem getting a table. Daily noon–midnight.

Mexican

Tortilla Flats **767 Washington St, at W 12th St ⓣ212/243-1053, ⓦwww.tortillaflatsnyc.com. Subway A, C, E to 14th St.** This Mexican dive has great margaritas, a loud sound system and plenty of kitsch, including hula-hoop contests. Be careful, it gets really crowded. Most dishes $12–16. Sun–Thurs noon–2am, Fri & Sat noon–4am.

Middle Eastern

Moustache **90 Bedford St, between Grove and Barrow sts ⓣ212/229-2220, ⓦmoustachepitza.com. Subway #1 to Christopher St.** A small, cheap spot specializing in "pitzas" (pizzas of pitta bread and eclectic toppings) $8–11; also offers great hummus, chickpea and spinach salad, and bargain lamb ribs ($14). Daily noon–midnight.

Spanish

Sevilla **62 Charles St, at W 4th St ⓣ212/929-3189, ⓦwww.sevillarestaurantandbar.com. Subway #1 to Christopher St.** A Village favourite since 1941, *Sevilla* is dark, fragrant (from garlic), and serves good, moderately priced food ($15–30). Try the garlic soup, the fried calamari, and the large pitchers of strong *sangría*. Mon–Thurs noon–midnight, Fri–Sat noon–1am, Sun 1pm–midnight.

Vegetarian

Souen **28 E 13th St, between University Place and Fifth Ave ⓣ212/627-7150, ⓦsouen.net. Subway N, Q, R, W, #4, #5, #6 to Union Square.** This Japanese vegetarian and macrobiotic restaurant uses only organic produce, fish, shrimp and grains (mains $8.50–19). The food is likewise tasty enough to whet the appetites of meat-eaters. Mon–Sat 10am–11pm, Sun 10am–10pm.

Chelsea

Once characterized by retro diners and places to people-watch rather than eat, **Chelsea** has sprouted some respectable eating establishments that manage to please the palate as well as the wallet. There's a mosaic of cuisines – Thai, Spanish, Mexican, Italian and traditional American, among others – and atmospheres available, with something for everyone.

American and Continental

Cafeteria 119 Seventh Ave, at W 17th St ☎212/414-1717, Ⓦwww.cafeteriagroup.com. Subway #1, #2, #3 to 14th St. Don't let the name fool you: *Cafeteria* may be open 24 hours and serve great chicken-fried steak, meatloaf, and macaroni and cheese, but it's nothing like a truckstop. Expect a smart all-white interior, gold-rimmed mirrors and a fashionable clientele. Daily 24hr.

Cookshop 156 Tenth Ave, at 20th St ☎212/924-4440, Ⓦwww.cookshopny.com. Subway C, E to 23rd St. Part of the Marc Meyer stable, with ever-busy street-side tables and a menu of seasonal, contemporary American fare – dishes change frequently, but might include pheasant pasta, grilled rabbit from the Hudson Valley and Vermont suckling pig (most $25–28); interesting brunch options, too ($12–16). Mon–Fri 8am–3pm & 5.30–11.30pm, Sat 11am–3pm & 5.30–11.30pm, Sun 11am–3pm & 5.30–10pm.

Moran's 146 Tenth Ave, at W 19th St ☎212/627-3030, Ⓦwww.moranschelsea.com. Subway C, E to 23rd St; #1 to 18th St. You can get good swordfish and lobster (priced per pound) here, but it's the steaks and chops ($25–37) that are most impressive. The plush, stained-wood seating area is tasteful; try and get a table in the cosy back room, especially in winter, when the fireplace is roaring. Sun & Mon 11am–10pm, Tues–Sat 11am–11pm; bar stays open an hour or two later.

The Old Homestead 56 Ninth Ave, between W 14th and 15th sts ☎212/242-9040, Ⓦwww.theoldhomesteadsteakhouse.com. Subway A, C, E, L to 14th St. Steak. Period. But really gorgeous steak, served in an almost comically old-fashioned walnut dining room by waiters in black vests. Expensive (most cuts are $40–50; a handful of entrees $25–35), but portions are huge. Mon–Fri noon–10.30pm, Sat 1–11.30pm, Sun 1–9.30pm.

The Park 118 Tenth Ave, between W 17th and 18th sts ☎212/352-3313, Ⓦwww.theparknyc.com. Subway A, C, E, L to 14th St; #1 to 18th St. It's easy to get lost in *Park*'s vast warren of rooms filled with fireplaces, geodes and even a Canadian redwood in the middle of the floor. The garden is a treat. Pizza, pasta, catfish and burgers ($12–18) fill the New American menu. Mon–Thurs & Sun 10am–1am, Fri & Sat 11am–2am.

Red Cat 227 Tenth Ave, between W 23rd and 24th sts ☎212/242-1122, Ⓦwww.theredcat.com. Subway C, E to 23rd St. Superb service, a fine American–Mediterranean kitchen and a warm atmosphere all make for a memorable dining experience at *Red Cat*. It's a big local favourite and popular for dates – book ahead. Mains $21–36. Mon 5–11pm, Tues–Thurs noon–2.30pm & 5–11pm, Fri & Sat noon–2.30pm & 5pm–midnight, Sun 5–10pm.

French

Gascogne 158 Eighth Ave between 17th and 18th sts ☎212/675-6566, Ⓦwww.gascognenyc.com. Subway A, C, E, L to Eighth Ave–14th St. The beautiful backyard garden is the perfect setting for hearty dishes from southwest France like cassoulet and foie gras (around $25). Various prix fixes are available at lunch and dinner, with an especially good four-course Monday night deal ($29). Mon 5.30–11pm, Tues–Fri noon–3pm & 5.30–11pm, Sat & Sun noon–11pm.

La Lunchonette 130 Tenth Ave, at W 18th St ☎212/675-0342. Subway A, C, E, L to 14th St. Even though it's tucked away in a remote corner of Chelsea, this understated little restaurant is always packed with loyal patrons. The good-value menu features the best of French country cooking, including lamb sausage with sautéed apples ($15.50), skate wing ($16.50), steak *au poivre* ($24), though the specialty is slow-cooked cassoulet (not always available). Mon–Thurs & Sun 11am–11pm, Fri & Sat 11am–11.30pm.

Paradou 8 Little W 12th St, between Greenwich and Washington sts ☎212/463-8345, Ⓦwww.paradounyc.com. Subway A, C, E, L to 14th St. This underrated Provençal-style French bistro is a far better (and more authentic) option than some of the more touristy places in the area. Great wines by the glass (actually glass-and-a-half; $12–17) and relatively digestible prices for the food ($21–29 for mains; prix-fixe menus available, too). Mon–Thurs 6–11pm, Fri 6pm–midnight, Sat & Sun 11am–4pm & 6pm–midnight.

Italian

Bottino 246 Tenth Ave, between W 24th and 25th sts ☎212/206-6766, Ⓦwww.bottinonyc.com. Subway C, E to 23rd St. One of Chelsea's most popular restaurants, *Bottino* attracts the in-crowd looking for authentic Italian food served in a slick, downtown atmosphere. The home-made leek tortellini (winter months only) is truly tantalizing. Pastas range $15–20, meaty entrees $20–30. Mon 6–11pm, Tues–Sat noon–3.30pm & 6–11pm Sun 6–10pm.

Co. **230 Ninth Ave, at W 24th St ⓣ212/243-1105. Subway C, E to 23rd St.** Fashionable spot, one of the new wave of pizzerias in town. Start with some *crostini* ($4) and an escarole salad ($8), then share a few of the oddly shaped pizzas, like fennel & sausage ($18). Mon 5–11pm, Tues–Sat 11.30am–11pm, Sun 11am–10pm.

Latin American

La Taza de Oro **96 Eighth Ave, between W 14th and 15th sts ⓣ212/243-9946. Subway A, C, E, L to 14th St.** Come here for a tasty, filling Puerto Rican meal. Specials change daily, but are always served with a heap of rice and beans (and most under $10). Don't miss the delicious *café con leche*. Mon–Sat 6am–10.30pm.

Rocking Horse **182 Eighth Ave, between W 19th and 20th sts ⓣ212/463-9511, ⓦwww.rockinghorsecafe.com. Subway C, E to 23rd St or #1 to 18th St.** Wash down inventive Mexican cuisine (like *mixiote*, a chilli pork stew; $19.95) with deliciously potent mojitos and margaritas ($10–13) from the bar. Try to keep track of the tab, if you can; drinks make the bill go up quickly. Mon–Fri noon–11pm, Sat 11am–midnight, Sun 11am–11pm.

Spanish

El Quijote **226 W 23rd St, between Seventh and Eighth aves ⓣ212/929-1855. Subway C, E, #1 to 23rd St.** *El Quijote* has changed very little over the years (it needed only a minimal makeover when it appeared in the 1996 film *I Shot Andy Warhol*, though the movie was set in 1968). It still serves decent *mariscos* and fried meats ($15.95–35.95), but the bland paella should be avoided. Mon–Thurs & Sun noon–midnight, Fri & Sat noon–1am.

La Nacional **239 W 14th St, between Seventh and Eighth aves ⓣ212/243-9308. Subway A, C, E, L, #1, #2, #3 to 14th St.** Home of the Spanish Benevolent Society, *La Nacional* retains the feel of a club while being open to all comers. Try croquetas ($8), shrimp with garlic sauce ($9) and top-notch paella ($18). Mon–Wed noon–10pm, Thurs–Sat noon–11pm.

Txikito **240 Ninth Ave, between W 24th and 25th sts ⓣ212/242-4730, ⓦwww.txikitonyc.com. Subway C, E to 23rd St.** The rough-hewn interior of this Basque tapas bar-cum-restaurant feels a little like the inside of a wooden ship – albeit one that serves its passengers crispy beef tongue ($16), octopus carpaccio ($15), an occasional special of suckling pig ($30) and, at lunch, one of the more original burgers in town ($11), a smoky treat. The crisp fries with spicy cod roe mayonnaise ($7) should accompany any order. Tues–Thurs noon–3pm & 5pm–midnight, Fri & Sat noon–3pm & 5pm–1am, Sun 5–11pm.

Union Square, Gramercy Park and the Flatiron District

The neighbourhoods of **Union Square**, **Gramercy Park** and the **Flatiron District** are heavily trafficked, and are therefore prime spots for restaurants. Some of the city's best (and most upscale) dining establishments are in this part of town, the finest of which have come to help define New American cuisine. There are also plenty of places to grab a cheap meal.

American and Continental

Blue Water Grill **31 Union Square W, at 16th St ⓣ212/675-9500. Subway L, N, Q, R, #4, #5, #6 to 14th St–Union Square.** All-round high-quality seafood restaurant. It's hard to go wrong here, whether you choose the grilled fish, caviar or delicacies from the raw bar. Prices are commensurately high (entrees $26–30). Mon 11.30am–10pm, Tues–Thurs 11.30am–11pm, Fri 11.30am–midnight, Sat 10.30am–midnight, Sun 10.30am–10pm.

City Crab **235 Park Ave S, at E 19th St ⓣ212/529-3800, ⓦwww.citycrabnyc.com. Subway #6, N, Q, R to 23rd St.** This large and very popular eatery prides itself on its large selection of fresh East Coast oysters and clams ($14/$9, respectively, for a half-dozen). Most people come to consume great piles of these bivalves (and pints of ale). Roughly $20–30 per person for mains, though you can spend much more. Mon–Thurs noon–11pm, Fri noon–midnight, Sat noon–4pm & 5pm–midnight, Sun noon–4pm & 5–11pm.

Craft 43 E 19th St, between Broadway and Park Ave S ⓣ212/780-0880, ⓦwww.craftrestaurant.com. Subway #6, N, Q, R to 23rd St. The buzz has come and gone at Tom Colicchio's signature restaurant, making this a relatively relaxed place for some of New York's most inventive food. Popular dishes include roast sweetbreads ($18), diver scallops ($30) and tasty, sautéed wild mushroom sides ($12–15). Everything is a la carte, so expect to spend $100 or more per person. Mon–Thurs 5.30–10pm, Fri & Sat 5.30–11pm, Sun 5.30–10pm.

Gramercy Tavern 42 E 20th St, between Broadway and Park Ave S ⓣ212/477-0777, ⓦwww.gramercytavern.com. Subway #6 to 23rd St. The neo-colonial decor, exquisite New American cuisine and perfect service make for a memorable meal. The seasonal tasting menus are well worth the steep prices ($112 for five courses; otherwise $86 for starter and main), but if you don't want to splurge, you can also drop in for a drink or more casual meal in the lively front room (three courses for $35). Main room Mon–Thurs noon–2pm & 5.30–10pm, Fri noon–2pm 5.30–11pm, Sat 5.30–11pm, Sun 5.30–10pm; Tavern Mon–Thurs & Sun noon–11pm, Fri & Sat noon–midnight.

Hill Country 30 W 26th St, between Broadway and Sixth Ave ⓣ212/255-4544, ⓦwww.hillcountryny.com. Subway R to 28th St or F to 23rd St. Most authentic Texas barbecue joint in the city, with huge servings of moist, fatty brisket, roast pork, and peppery sausage brought in from Kreuz Market near Austin. Grab a table then order your meats (priced by the pound) and sides (such as macaroni and cheese) from the counters. Daily noon–2am, though kitchen closes 10pm Sun–Wed, 11pm Thurs–Sat.

The House 121 E 17th St, between Union Square and Irving Place ⓣ212/353-2121, ⓦwww.thehousenyc.com. Subway L, N, Q, R, #4, #5, #6 to 14th St–Union Square. One of the more romantic restaurants in the city, set in a gorgeous three-storey carriage house built in 1854, with a fabulous menu based around seasonal ingredients – oysters with green apples and *yuzu* ($15), macaroni and cheese with summer truffles ($25) and so on. The wine cellar is also top-notch. Mon–Fri noon–3.30pm & 5pm–1am, Sat & Sun 11am–3.30pm & 5pm–1am.

Pure Food & Wine 54 Irving Place, between E 17th and 18th sts ⓣ212/477-1010, ⓦwww.oneluckyduck.com. Subway L, N, Q, R, #4, #5, #6 to 14th St/Union Square. Upscale, raw-food restaurant, where food is never heated to more than 118 degrees Fahrenheit. Prepare for goat-cheese-stuffed squash blossoms and chilli lime tortilla wraps, though the desserts are the real standouts; first courses $14–20, mains $24–34. Daily noon–4pm & 5.30–11pm.

Union Square Café 21 E 16th St, between Fifth Ave and Union Square W ⓣ212/243-4020, ⓦwww.unionsquarecafe.com. Subway L, N, Q, R, #4, #5, #6 to 14th St–Union Square. Choice California-style dining (with an Italian bent) in a classy but comfortable atmosphere. The creative menu changes regularly, but the Italian-leaning dishes tend to stand out. Meals aren't cheap (mains $28–35). Mon–Thurs & Sun noon–2.15pm & 5.30–9.45pm, Fri & Sat noon–2.15pm & 5.30–10.45pm.

Asian

15 East 15 E 15th St between Fifth Ave and Broadway. ⓣ212/647-0015, ⓦwww.15eastrestaurant.com. Subway L, N, Q, R, #4, #5, #6 to 14th St–Union Square. The attention given to both cooked dishes like slow-poached octopus ($12) and sea urchin risotto ($24), and the fresh sushi and sashimi (chef's selection of either $55) help elevate this stylish Japanese restaurant to among the best in the city. Mon–Fri 11.45am–2pm & 6–10.30pm, Sat 6–10.30pm.

Choshi 77 Irving Place, at E 19th St ⓣ212/420-1419. Subway #6 to 23rd St. Don't worry about wearing a T-shirt and jeans to this casual Japanese establishment. The fresh sushi ($17–20 dinner) is first-rate. Mon–Thurs noon–3.15pm & 5–10.15pm, Fri noon–3.15pm & 5–10pm, Sat 1–10.30pm, Sun 1–10pm.

Jaiya Thai 396 Third Ave, between E 28th and 29th sts ⓣ212/889-1330, ⓦwww.jaiya.com. Subway #6 to 28th St. The food at this affordable restaurant is red hot and delicious. Don't let the bland decor deceive you – when the menu says "medium spicy", expect to get your head blown off. Spice-averse palates can aim for tamer but decent *pad thai* ($9.95–12.95). Mon–Thurs & Sun 11am–11pm, Fri & Sat 11.30am–midnight.

L'Annam 393 Third Ave, at E 28th St ☎212/686-5168. Subway #6 to 28th St. Solid Vietnamese in a hip dining room. Good for a quick meal, especially lunch ($6.95 specials available) as the service is quite fast. Mon–Thurs & Sun 11.30am–11.30pm, Fri & Sat 11.30am–midnight.

Indian

Curry in a Hurry 119 Lexington Ave, at E 28th St ☎212/683-0900. Subway #6 to 28th St. A local favourite, offering inexpensive and delicious buffet-style Indian food. Most entrees are priced around $12.99, but you can get combination plates for less than that. Mon & Wed–Sun noon–11pm.

Madras Mahal 104 Lexington Ave, between E 27th and 28th sts ☎212/684-4010, Ⓦwww.madrasmahal.com. Subway #6 to 28th St. A kosher vegetarian's dream, but everyone else will like it too. Curries are around $10 though the South Indian specialities, like dosai ($7.95–8.95) and idli ($4.95–5.95) are the better bets. Mon–Thurs noon–10pm, Fri & Sat noon–10.30pm.

Tabla Metropolitan Life Building, 11 Madison Ave, at E 25th St ☎212/889-0667, Ⓦwww.tablany.com. Subway R, W, #6 to 23rd St. This restaurant's spicy nouveau-Indian fare is served across two floors: the top is the more elegant choice, the bottom, which used to be a casual offshoot but has been incorporated into the main restaurant, remains less formal. Prices are reasonable for the high-level execution (entrees $22–33); the family-style tasting menu ($54/person) makes ordering easy for those who can't choose. Mon–Thurs noon–10pm, Fri & Sat noon–11pm, Sun 5–9pm.

Italian

I Trulli Enoteca and Ristorante 122 E 27th St, between Lexington and Park aves ☎212/481-7372, Ⓦwww.itrulli.com. Subway #6 to 28th St. Choose between the lovely restaurant, which features robust entrees like *orecchiette* (ear-shaped pasta) with rabbit *ragù* ($24) and roasted rack of lamb with potato pie ($36), and the wine bar, with cheeses, cured meats and a handful of fresh pasta dishes. Mon–Thurs noon–10.30pm, Fri & Sat noon–11pm, Sun noon–10pm (wine bar 3pm onward).

Maialino Gramercy Park Hotel, 2 Lexington Ave ☎212/777-2410, Ⓦwww.maialinonyc.com. Subway #6 to 23rd St. If a place can be both rustic and refined, Danny Meier's attractive Roman trattoria is it. Much of the focus is on the hog (which gives the place its name) – there's excellent cured *salumi* ($7–16), pasta with *guanciale* ($15) or suckling pig *ragù* ($19) and, as a special, roast suckling pig – but everything's well prepared, and desserts are exceptional. Reservations essential. Mon–Thurs 7.30–10am, noon–2pm & 5.30–10.30pm, Fri 7.30–10am, noon–2pm & 5.30–11pm, Sat 10am–2pm & 5.30–11pm, Sun 10am–2pm & 5.30–10.30pm.

Spanish and Portuguese

Aldea 31 W 17th St between Fifth and Sixth aves ☎212/675-7223, Ⓦwww.aldearestaurant.com. Subway F, M to 14th St. In a cool, relaxed dining room, Portuguese-accented dishes come exquisitely prepared and full of flavour. For this kind of refined cooking – say, duck confit with crisped duck skin and chorizo, or cod with braised chickpeas – prices are eminently reasonable (entrees $24–29) and a $24 lunch prix-fixe seals the deal. Mon–Thurs 11.30am–2pm & 5.30–11pm, Fri 11.30am–2pm & 5.30pm–midnight, Sat 5.30pm–midnight.

Casa Mono 52 Irving Place, at E 17th St ☎212/253-2773, Ⓦwww.casamononyc.com. Subway L, N, Q, R, #4, #5, #6 to 14th St–Union Square. This eclectic tapas bar both challenges and enchants the palate with such dishes as pumpkin and goat cheese croquetas ($9) and mussels with cava and chorizo sausage ($15). The adjacent and sherry-heavy *Bar Jamón* (125 E 17th St; see p.351) is open until 2am daily. Daily noon–midnight.

Turkish

Turkish Kitchen 386 Third Ave, between 27th and 28th sts ☎212/679-6633, Ⓦwww.turkishkitchen.com. Subway #6 to 28th St. Ruby-red walls and balconies lend a suitably exotic backdrop to this excellent Turkish restaurant, with dishes such as tender lamb kebabs and *tavuk pirzola* (chicken stuffed with green peppers and creamy cheese) starting at around $18. Mon–Fri noon–3pm & 5.30–11pm, Fri noon–3pm & 5.30–11.30pm Sat 5–11.30pm, Sun 11am–3pm & 5–10.30pm.

Midtown East

Catering mostly to weekday office crowds, **Midtown East** overflows with restaurants, some nondescript and overpriced, but some excellent too: timeworn favourites such as the *Oyster Bar* in Grand Central Terminal or the classy and refined *Aquavit* and *Four Seasons*.

American and Continental

'21' Club 21 W 52nd St, between Fifth and Sixth aves ⓣ212/582-7200, ⓦwww.21club.com. Subway E, M to Fifth Ave–53rd St. This is simply one of New York's most enduring institutions – the city's Old Boys come here to meet and eat. There's a dress code, so wear a jacket and tie. Three-course early dinner prix-fixe menus are $35 per person in the *Bar Room*, which is a pretty good deal, considering some entrees (such as the boar chop and loin, and leg of Vermont lamb with crushed purple potatoes) go for $45 on their own. Mon 5.30–10pm, Tues–Fri noon–2.30pm & 5.30–10pm, Sat 5.30–11pm.

Aquavit 65 E 55th St, between Madison and Park aves ⓣ212/307-7311, ⓦwww.aquavit.org. Subway E, M to Fifth Ave–53rd St. Go for a blowout in the main dining room or a more casual, and much less expensive, meal in the bistro of this renowned Scandinavian restaurant. Exquisite fish dishes abound at both – silky gravlax, herring every which way, smoked Arctic char and the like – alongside a few more exotic dishes, like wild boar. The Sunday smorgasbord ($48) is a good time to stuff yourself silly. Reserve well ahead. Mon–Fri & Sun noon–2.30pm & 5.30–10.30pm, Sat 5.30–10.30pm.

db Bistro Moderne *City Club Hotel*, 55 W 44th St, between Fifth and Sixth aves ⓣ212/391-2400, ⓦwww.danielnyc.com/dbbistro.html. Subway B, D, F, M, #7 to 42nd St. Famous chef-owner Daniel Boulud made things decidedly more affordable here than his other culinary shrines (except the new, casual *DBGB*, p.315), though you'll still spend a pretty penny, especially for the sublime $32 burger, layered with foie gras, black truffle and short-rib meat. Hours vary slightly by weekday but roughly Mon–Fri 7–10am, noon–2.30pm & 5–11pm, Sat 8am–2.30pm & 5–11pm, Sun 8am–2.30pm & 5–10pm.

El Rio Grande 160 E 38th St, between Lexington and Third aves ⓣ212/867-0922. Subway #4, #5, #6, #7 to Grand Central–42nd St. Long-established Murray Hill Tex-Mex place with a gimmick: you can eat Mexican, or if you prefer, Texan, by simply crossing the "border" and walking through the kitchen. Personable and fun, if nothing special (except, perhaps, the margaritas). Daily noon–10pm.

Emporium Brasil 15 W 46th St, between Fifth and Sixth aves ⓣ212/764-4646. Subway B, D, F, M to 47th–50th St–Rockefeller Center. *The* place to go on Little Brazil St for *feijoada* (a stew of black beans with hunks of dried pork, pig parts and more) on Saturdays. Fairly casual during the day, it becomes a little classier for dinner. Mon–Wed 8am–10pm, Thurs & Fri 8am–11pm, Sat 11am–11pm.

Four Seasons 99 E 52nd St, between Lexington and Park aves ⓣ212/754-9494, ⓦwww.fourseasonsrestaurant. Subway E, M to Lexington Ave–53rd St or #6 to 51st St. The face of New York's fine dining for decades, this timeless Philip Johnson-designed restaurant delivers on every front. If you can't swing the grotesque prices of the dishes on the French-influenced American

▲ *Aquavit*

menu (entrees $38–56, though a somewhat reasonable prix-fixe is available), go for a cocktail and peek at the famous pool room. Housed in the Seagram Building, it is much stuffier than other top restaurants in the city. Mon–Fri noon–2.30pm & 5–9.30pm, Sat 5–9.30pm.

The Modern 9 W 53rd St, inside the Museum of Modern Art ⓣ212/333-1220, ⓦwww.themodernyyc.com. Subway E, M to Fifth Ave–53rd St. The highly praised *Modern* seems elegant without trying too hard and without adding any unnecessary stuffiness. Fresh, seasonal ingredients are artfully combined to yield unexpected but wholly delicious dishes. Chorizo-crusted codfish with white cocoa-bean purée, and sausage, apple and lobster risotto are just two of the unlikely options. Set meals start at $88; the bar room has less expensive dining. Mon–Thurs noon–2pm & 5.30–10.30pm, Fri noon–2pm & 5.30–11pm, Sat 5.30–11pm, bar room only on Sun 11.30am–9.30pm.

Oyster Bar Lower level, Grand Central Terminal, at E 42nd St and Park Ave ⓣ212/490-6650, ⓦwww.oysterbarny.com. Subway #4, #5, #6, #7 to 42nd St–Grand Central. This wonderfully distinctive place is down in the vaulted dungeons of Grand Central. Midtown office-workers who pour in for lunch come to choose from a staggering menu – she-crab bisque ($6.95), steamed Maine lobster (priced by pound) and sweet Kumamoto oysters ($2.95 each) top the list. Prices are moderate to expensive; you can eat more cheaply at the bar or just enjoy a chowder and beer while taking in the atmosphere. Mon–Fri 11.30am–9.30pm, Sat noon–9.30pm.

Quality Meats 57 W 58th St, between Fifth and Sixth aves ⓣ212/371-7777, ⓦwww.qualitymeatsnyc.com. Subway F to 57th St or N, R, Q to Fifth Ave. The front doors give the impression you're stepping into a meat locker – and you are, in a sense. Top-notch beef (rib steak $46 for one; $110 for two); in contrast to many steakhouses, the appetizers and sides are well done, too. Mon–Wed 11.30am–3pm & 5–10.30pm, Thurs & Fri 11.30am–3pm & 5–11.30pm, Sat 5–11.30pm, Sun 5–10pm.

Smith & Wollensky 797 Third Ave, at E 49th St ⓣ212/753-1530, ⓦwww.smithandwollensky.com. Subway #6 to 51st St. A grand, if clubby, steakhouse, where waiters – many of whom have worked here for twenty years or more – serve you the primest cuts of beef imaginable. Quite pricey (you'll pay $40–50/steak; NY sirloin or porterhouse are the best options) but it's worth the splurge. Go basic with the sides (hashed browns and creamed spinach) and wines. Daily 11.45am–midnight.

Asian

Cho Dang Gol 55 W 35th St, between Fifth and Sixth aves ⓣ212/695-8222, ⓦwww.chodanggolny.com. Subway B, D, F, M, N, Q, R to 34th St. Korean restaurants proliferate on 32nd Street between Fifth and Sixth; this one, a little off the beaten path, specializes in home-made tofu. There's more, though, like simmered pork belly served as part of a spicy lettuce wrap ($33.95). Daily 11.30am–10.30pm.

Hatsuhana 17 E 48th St, between Fifth and Madison aves ⓣ212/355-3345, ⓦwww.hatsuhana.com. Subway #6 to 51st St. *Hatsuhana* was one of the first restaurants to introduce sushi to New York many moons ago, and it's still going strong. Despite the spartan decor, this place is not cheap. Mon–Fri 11.45am–2.45pm & 5.30–10pm, Sat 5–10pm.

Menchanko Tei 131 E 45th St between Lexington and Third aves, another branch on 55th St ⓣ212/986-6805, ⓦwww.menchankotei.com. Subway #4, #5, #6, #7 to 42nd St. A solid entry from the recent ramen craze that swept the city, and one of the better outside the East Village. Slurp up a steaming cauldron of soy or miso-flavoured broth,

Vegetarian (or vegetarian-friendly) restaurants

Angelica Kitchen East Village p.317
Cho Dang Gol Koreatown/Midtown East p.326
Madras Mahal Gramercy Park p.324
Pure Food and Wine Union Square p.323
Spring Street Natural Restaurant Soho p.310

Haute cuisine

Aquavit Midtown East, p.325
Corton Tribeca, p.309
Daniel Upper East Side, p.331
Le Bernardin Midtown West, p.329
Per Se Upper West Side, p.333
SHO Shaun Hergatt Financial District, p.307

chewy noodles, simmered pork and whole shrimp (around $10); there are non-soup options too. Mon–Thurs 11.30am–11.30pm, Fri 11.30am–midnight, Sat 11.30am–11pm, Sun 11.30am–10.30pm.

New York Kom Tang 32 W 32nd St, between Broadway and Fifth Ave ⓣ212/947-8482. Subway B, D, F, M to 34th St–Herald Square. There's fresh sushi or sashimi ($22.95/$39.95) and excellent grill-it-yourself barbecue (*kalbi* $24.99), but the rich, bountiful soups are the stars – everything from oxtail ($13.95) to young chicken with ginseng ($19.95). Good lunch deals. Mon–Sat 24hr.

Szechuan Gourmet 21 W 39th St, between Fifth and Sixth aves ⓣ212/921-0233, ⓦwww.szechuangourmetnyc.com; another location 242 W 56th St. Subway B, D, F, M to 42nd St. Szechuan cuisine done right, in dishes like spicy dan dan noodles ($4.50), braised lamb with chilli ($15.95) and double-cooked sliced pork belly with leeks ($13.95). The lunch specials are a steal. Daily 11.30am–10pm.

French

La Bonne Soupe 48 W 55th St between Fifth and Sixth aves ⓣ212/586-7650, ⓦwww.labonnesoupe.com. Subway F, N, R to 57th St. This friendly bistro, spread over two levels, makes a good post-museum or pre-Carnegie Hall stop; tasty burgers ($13.95) and soups ($18.25 as a meal with bread, salad, dessert and a drink) highlight an extensive menu. Mon–Thurs 11.30am–11pm, Fri & Sat 11.30am–11.30pm, Sun 11.30am–10.30pm.

La Grenouille 3 E 52nd St, between Fifth and Madison aves ⓣ212/752-1495, ⓦwww.la-grenouille.com. Subway E to Fifth Ave–53rd St. The *haute* French cuisine here has melted hearts and tantalized palates since 1962. All the classics are done to perfection, and the service is beyond gracious. Its prix-fixe lunch is $38–52, and dinner is $78–95 per person without wine. Mon & Sat 5–11pm, Tues–Fri noon–3pm & 5–11pm.

Italian

Caffe Linda 149 E 49th St between Lexington and Third aves ⓣ212/308-8882. Subway #6 to 51st St. One of the better casual Italian restaurants in a neighbourhood awash in mediocre eateries. It's straightforward and unpretentious, with well-prepared pastas ($15–21), a handful of meat and seafood dishes ($19–29) and good panini at lunchtime. Mon–Fri 11am–10.30pm, Sat & Sun 5–10.30pm.

Naples 45 Met Life Building (p.138), 200 Park Ave, at E 45th St ⓣ212/972-7001. Subway #4, #5, #6, #7 to Grand Central–42nd St. The Neapolitan pizzas at this place are flavourful (with toppings like roasted vegetables, fennel and *prosciutto di Parma*) and come with just the right amount of wood-burning-oven char (individual pizzas $16.95–17.95). Also fish, chicken, steak and pasta specialties ($18–31). Mon–Fri 7.30am–10pm.

Jewish

2nd Avenue Deli 162 E 33rd St, between Lexington and Third aves ⓣ212/689-9000, ⓦwww.2ndavedeli.com. Subway #6 to 33rd St. This reincarnation of a downtown family-run Jewish institution may no longer be on Second Ave, but the stuffed cabbage ($24.95), pastrami sandwich ($14.95) and matzoh-ball soup ($6.95) are all as tasty as ever. It may seem expensive, but the sandwiches (around $20) are filling enough for two. Mon–Thurs & Sun 6am–midnight, Fri & Sat 6am–4am.

Mexican

Zarela 953 Second Ave, between E 50th and 51st sts ⓣ212/644-6740, ⓦwww.zarela.com. Subway #6 to 51st St. If you've ever wondered what home-cooked Mexican food really tastes like, this festive restaurant is the place to go. It's more expensive than most Mexican places (eg slow-cooked lamb $20; fajitas $22), but worth every cent. Mon–Fri noon–3pm & 5–11pm, Fri noon–3pm & 5–11.30pm, Sat 5–11.30pm, Sun 5–10pm.

Midtown West

While many of Manhattan's best dining establishments are located downtown, manifold good meals await you in **Midtown West**. Restaurant Row (West 46th Street between Eighth and Ninth avenues) is a frequent stopover for theatre-goers seeking a late-night meal, though cheaper (and better) alternatives can be found along Ninth Avenue and farther west into Hell's Kitchen. Be advised that many restaurants in the Times Square area (not the ones we have included here) are overpriced and not of the highest quality.

Afghan

Ariana Afghan Kebab 787 Ninth Ave, between West 52nd and 53rd sts ⓣ212/262-2323, ⓦwww.ariananyc.com. Subway C, E to 50th St. A casual neighbourhood restaurant serving inexpensive kebabs (chicken, lamb, and beef; $14) and vegetarian meals like eggplant curry ($12). Daily 11.30am–10.30pm.

American and Continental

Thalia 828 Eighth Ave, at W 50th St ⓣ212/399-4444, ⓦwww.restaurantthalia.com. Subway C, E to 50th St. *Thalia* is a decent choice for imaginative, New American cuisine in the Theater District. The 5000-square-foot eating area is full of colour and the prices aren't bad either. Try the "Thaliatelle" (pasta with rock shrimp, mussels, mushrooms, fava beans, tomatoes, pecorino, mint and white wine; $19) or the skate with fine herb butter ($21). Mon noon–2.30pm & 5–11.30pm, Tues, Thurs & Fri noon–2.30pm & 5pm–midnight, Wed 11.45am–2.30pm & 5pm–midnight, Sat 11am–3pm & 5pm–midnight, Sun 11am–3pm & 4.30–11.30pm.

Virgil's Real BBQ 152 W 44th St, between Sixth and Seventh aves ⓣ212/921-9494, ⓦwww.virgilsbbq.com. Subway B, D, F, M, N, R, #1, #2, #3, #7 to 42nd St. *Virgil's*, one of New York's earliest entries in the BBQ game, is one of the few Times Square eateries that's not just for tourists. All the food groups – Memphis ribs ($24.95), Carolina pulled pork ($20.50), Texas brisket ($22.50), Maryland ham ($18.50) – are well represented, and to get the most out of it you'd be advised to skip breakfast in the morning. Mon 11am–11pm, Tues–Fri 11.30am–midnight, Sat 9am–midnight, Sun 9am–11pm.

West Bank Café 407 W 42nd St, at Ninth Ave ⓣ212/695-6909. Subway A, C, E, N, Q, R, #1, #2, #3, #7 to 42nd St–Times Square. The menu here features mostly straightforward American dishes (grilled salmon $19, skirt steak $23), with a few Italian pastas thrown in for good measure ($17–18.50), all of which are delicious and won't break the bank. It's very popular with theatre people, especially after performances. Mon–Thurs & Sun 11.30am–midnight, Fri & Sat 11.30am–12.30am.

Asian

Pam Real Thai 404 W 49th St, between Ninth and Tenth aves ⓣ212/333-7500. Subway C, E to 50th St. Of the number of Thai restaurants in this part of Hell's Kitchen, *Pam* has won a following for its spicy (but not overwhelmingly so) food, good prices and some slightly unusual dishes (eg fermented fish kidneys). Better to stick with a *larb* (salad with minced meat) and one of the curries. Daily 11.30am–11pm.

Ruby Foo's 1626 Broadway, at W 49th St ⓣ212/489-5600. Subway C, E, #1 to 50th St. *Ruby Foo's* has a wide-ranging Asian menu that includes everything from sushi platters to *dim sum* to Thai noodle dishes, all done surprisingly well. Mon–Thurs 11.30am–11pm, Fri 11.30am–11.30pm, Sat 11.30am–midnight, Sun 11.30am–11pm.

Sugiyama 251 W 55th St, between Broadway and Eighth Ave ⓣ212/956-0670, ⓦwww.sugiyama-nyc.com. Subway A, B, C, D, #1 to 59th St–Columbus Circle; N, Q, R to 57th St or B, D, E to 7th Ave. Though you may want to take out a loan before dining at this superb Japanese restaurant, you're guaranteed an exquisite experience, from the enchanting *kaiseki* (chef's choice) dinners (from $96, though three-and five-course dinners can go for $32 or $58) to the regal service. Tues–Sat 5.30–11.45pm.

Yakitori Totto 251 W 55th St (second floor), between Broadway and Eighth Ave ⓣ212/245-4555, ⓦtottonyc.com. Subway A, B, C, D, #1 to 59th St–Columbus Circle; N, Q, R to 57th St or B, D, E to Seventh Ave. This popular hideaway is perfect for late-night snacking – though by that time you may miss out on some of the more esoteric grilled skewers (soft knee bone served rare, anyone?). Chicken heart, skirt steak and chicken thigh with spring onions all burst with flavour; a fistful of skewers along with some sides and a cold Sapporo draft make a nice meal. Mon–Thurs 5.30pm–1am, Fri & Sat 5.30pm–2am, Sun 5.30pm–midnight.

French

Aureole One Bryant Park, Sixth Ave between 42nd and 43rd sts ⓣ212/319-1660. Subway B, D, F, M to 42nd St. *Aureole*'s French-accented American food is unbelievably tasty and inventive. It's also quite expensive: the prix-fixe options start at $84 per head, or $108 for the five-course tasting menu. Stop by just for the show-stopping desserts (like the berry *millefeuille* with lavender *crème fraîche* and pistachio filo crisps), a pre-theatre dinner ($55 at 5–6pm) or the somewhat-affordable lunch special ($34). Mon–Thurs noon–2.30pm & 5–10.30pm, Fri & Sat noon–2.30pm & 5–11pm, Sun 5–10.30pm.

Chez Napoleon 365 W 50th St, between Eighth and Ninth aves ⓣ212/265-6980, ⓦwww.cheznapoleon.com. Subway C, E to 50th St. One of several authentic Gallic eateries that sprang up in this area during World War II, when it was a hangout for French soldiers. A friendly, family-run bistro, it's stuck in a time warp in a good way. There's a $30 three-course dinner or you can go for classics like *boeuf bourguignon* ($20) or *sole meunière* ($24); the wines are solid and well priced. Mon–Thurs noon–2.30pm & 5–10pm, Fri noon–2.30pm & 5–11pm, Sat 5–11pm.

Le Bernardin 155 W 51st St, between Sixth and Seventh aves ⓣ212/554-1515, ⓦwww.le-bernardin.com. Subway B, D, F, M to 47–50th St–Rockefeller Center; #1 to 50th St. The most storeyed seafood restaurant in the United States, serving incomparable new angles on traditional Brittany fish dishes in elegant surroundings. This is one dinner you'll never forget – marinated hamachi, seared langoustine, crispy bass in a ham and peppercorn sauce – though you may cry when the bill arrives ($112 prix fixe). Mon–Thurs noon–2.30pm & 5.30–10.30pm, Fri noon–2.30pm & 5.30–11pm, Sat 5.30–11pm.

German

Hallo Berlin 626 10th Ave, between W 44th and W 45th sts ⓣ212/977-1944. Subway A, C, E, #7 to 42nd St–Port Authority. Come to *Berlin* to enjoy all manner of German sausages and unusual ales in a pleasant bench-and-table beer-garden setting. At $15–20 for mains, the prices aren't bad. Mon–Thurs noon–11pm, Fri & Sat noon–1am, Sun 4–11pm.

Italian

Becco 355 W 46th St, between Eighth and Ninth aves ⓣ212/397-7597, ⓦwww.becco-nyc.com. Subway A, C, E, #7 to 42nd St–Port Authority. Catering to the pre-theatre crowd, *Becco* is most notable for its $23 *Sinfonia di Pasta*: the all-you-can-eat dinner with a choice of three pasta-and-sauce combinations. Mon & Thurs noon–3pm & 5pm–midnight, Tues noon–3pm & 4.30pm–midnight, Wed & Sat 11.30am–2.30pm & 4pm–midnight, Fri 11.30am–3pm & 5pm–midnight, Sun noon–midnight.

Trattoria dell'Arte 900 Seventh Ave, at W 57th st ⓣ212/245-9800, ⓦwww.trattoriadellarte.com. Subway N, R, Q to 57th St. Unusually nice restaurant for this stretch of midtown, with an airy interior, excellent service and good food. Great, wafer-thin crispy pizzas (around $30 for a large one), decent and imaginative pasta dishes from around $24, upscale items like the veal chop ($47) and snapper *livornese* ($31), and a mouthwatering antipasto bar – all eagerly patronized by an elegant, out-to-be-seen crowd. Mon–Sat 11.45am–11.30pm, Sun 11am–10.30pm.

Jewish and Russian

Carnegie Deli 854 Seventh Ave, between W 54th and 55th sts ⓣ212/757-2245, ⓦwww.carnegiedeli.com/home.php. Subway B, D, E to Seventh Ave. The most generously stuffed sandwiches in the city are served by the rudest of waiters at this famous Jewish deli. It trades mainly on its reputation as a must-do experience, like the *Stage* (see p.330); you're probably better off going to

Pizza

Grimaldi's DUMBO, Brooklyn, p.338
Kesté West Village, p.320
John's Pizzeria West Village, p.320
Lombardi's Little Italy, p.313
Totonno's Coney Island, Brooklyn, p.340

Katz's (see p.314) or *Second Avenue Deli* (p.327). Daily 6.30am–4am.

Petrossian 182 W 58th St, at Seventh Ave ⓣ212/245-2214. Subway A, B, C, D, #1 to 59th St–Columbus Circle; N, R, Q to 57th St. Pink granite and etched mirrors set the mood at this decadent Art Deco establishment, where champagne and caviar are the norm. If you want to head down a more affordable route, go with the $35 prix-fixe dinner and just pretend. Mon–Sat 11.30am–3pm & 5.30–11.30pm, Sun 11.30am–3pm & 5.30–10.30pm.

Russian Tea Room 150 W 57th St, between Sixth and Seventh aves ⓣ212/581-7100, ⓦwww.russiantearoomnyc.com. Subway B, D, F, N, R, Q to 57th St. In its third incarnation, the restaurant has nowhere near the cachet of the original, but is nonetheless recommended (the stroganoff and the chicken Kiev are faves). With appetizers from $15–20 and mains $30–40, you'll need plenty of dough. Mon–Fri 11.30am–3pm & 4.45–11pm, Sat 11am–3pm & 4.45–11pm, Sun 11am–3pm.

Stage Deli 834 Seventh Ave, between W 53rd and 54th sts ⓣ212/245-7850, ⓦwww.stagedeli.com. Subway B, D, E to Seventh Ave. New York attitude and gigantic, overstuffed sandwiches are what's on the menu at this open-all-night rival to the better-known *Carnegie Deli*. The food (and the prices) are a bit better here. 24hr.

Uncle Vanya Café 315 W 54th St, between Eighth and Ninth aves ⓣ212/262-0542. Subway C, E to 50th St. Moderately priced Russian delicacies, comprising more than the obligatory borscht and caviar; entrees around $15. Mon–Sat noon–11pm, Sun 1–10pm.

Latin American

Churrascaria Plataforma 316 W 49th St, between Eighth and Ninth aves ⓣ212/245-0505, ⓦwww.churrascariaplataforma.com. Subway C, E to 50th St. Meat (the fare of choice) is served in this huge, open Brazilian dining room by waiters carrying swords stabbed with succulent slabs of grilled pork, chicken and lots of beef. The $57 prix fixe (your only option) covers all of these various grilled meats and more. Don't miss the addictive *caipirinhas* (Brazil's national drink). Daily noon–midnight.

Hell's Kitchen 679 Ninth Ave, between W 46th and 47th sts ⓣ212/977-1588, ⓦwww.hellskitchen-nyc.com. Subway C, E to 50th St. Lively atmosphere aided and abetted by six different kinds of frozen margarita and nouveau renderings of Mexican cuisine. Favourites include tuna tostadas ($10) to start and caramelized banana *empanadas* to finish off with. Sun & Mon 5–11pm, Tues & Wed 11.30am–3pm & 5–11pm, Thurs & Fri 11.30am–3pm & 5pm–midnight, Sat 5pm–midnight.

Upper East Side

Upper East Side restaurants mostly exist to serve a discriminating mixture of Park Avenue matrons and young professionals, and the cuisine here is much like that of the rest of Manhattan: a middling mixture of Asian, standard American, Italian and especially posh French restaurants. New Yorkers and visitors alike rarely come up here solely for the food, but since they are so many museums and sights in the neighbourhood you're likely to need a place to eat, at least for lunch.

American and Continental

Barking Dog Luncheonette 1678 Third Ave, at E 94th St ⓣ212/831-1800. Subway #6 to 96th St. This diner-like place offers outstanding, cheap American food (like mashed potatoes and gravy) – hot plates $13–17. Kids will feel at home, especially with the puppy motif. Adults will appreciate the excellent and huge Cobb salad ($11.95). Daily 8am–11pm.

E.A.T. 1064 Madison Ave, between E 80th and 81st sts ⓣ212/772-0022, ⓦwww.elizabar.com. Subway #6 to 77th St. Owned by restaurateur and gourmet grocer Eli Zabar, *E.A.T.* is expensive and crowded (main dishes $24–28) but the food is excellent, notably the soups, breads, salads ($12), and sandwiches ($14.50); the mozzarella, basil and tomato fillings are fresh and heavenly. The takeaway counter and bakery is a bit cheaper. Daily 7am–10pm.

Flex Mussels 174 E 82nd St, between Third and Lexington aves ⓣ212/717-7772, ⓦwww.flexmusselsny.com. Subway #4, #5, #6 to

86th St. Mussels fresh from Prince Edward Island (Canada) take centre stage here, with plates with various sauces ranging $17.50–20. Make a point of trying the special hand-cut fries ($6). Mon–Thurs 5.30–11pm, Fri & Sat 5.30–11.30pm, Sun 5.30–10pm.

JG Melon Restaurant 1291 Third Ave at 74th St ⓣ212/650-1310. Subway #6 to 77th St. One of the few old-school bars on the Upper East Side, but best known for its juicy burgers ($8.50) and crispy waffle-cut fries. Daily 11.30am–2.30am.

Kings' Carriage House 251 E 82nd St, between Second and Third aves ⓣ212/734-5490, ⓦwww.kingscarriagehouse.com. Subway #4, #5, #6 to 86th St. You'll feel as if you've been transported to the country at this romantic, converted carriage-house. With rustic American/French cuisine (such as foie gras flan and pheasant pot pie), it's a fine place for a meal or afternoon tea (daily 3–5pm; $24.95); prix fixe meals only: $18 for lunch to $49 for dinner. Daily noon–10pm.

Pastrami Queen 1125 Lexington Ave at 78th St ⓣ212/734-1500, ⓦwww.pastramiqueen.com. Subway #6 to 77th St. This friendly diner has been knocking out giant hot pastrami sandwiches ($13.95) since 1956, as well as corned beef and a host of Jewish kosher classics (matzoh-ball soups from $1.75 per ball). Daily 10am–11pm.

Asian

Donguri 309 E 83rd St, between First and Second aves ⓣ212/737-5656. Subway #4, #5, #6 to 86th St. Sushi lovers won't want to miss this little five-table, family-run spot featuring some of the best sashimi sets in town (from $35), as well as superb Kumamoto oysters, mushroom tempura ($12) and soba noodles ($12). There are only two seatings per night (7 & 9pm) and they tend to hustle out the early shift ASAP, so don't plan on lingering. Tues–Sun 5.30–9.30pm.

Naruto Ramen 1596 Third Ave, between E 89th and 90th sts ⓣ212/289-7803. Subway #4, #5, #6 to 86th St. Tiny Japanese noodle shop, cooking up excellent bowls of ramen ($8.50) with pork, miso or curry, fried rice ($7.50) and Japanese curry ($8.75). Daily noon–11pm.

Pig Heaven 1540 Second Ave, between E 80th and 81st sts ⓣ212/744-4333. Subway #6 to 77th St. Good-value Chinese–American restaurant, with Taiwanese, Cantonese and Sichuan influences. The accent, not surprisingly, is on pork; dumplings ($5.95), spare ribs ($12.50), BBQ suckling pig ($13.50) and so on, but everything else is good too (dishes average $12). Sun–Thurs noon–11.15pm, Fri & Sat noon–12.15am.

French

Café Boulud 20 E 76th St, between Madison and Fifth aves ⓣ212/772-2600, ⓦwww.danielnyc.com. Subway #6 to 77th St. The muted but elegant interior of chef Daniel Boulud's second Manhattan eatery is an exceedingly pleasant place to savour his sublime concoctions (case in point: Moroccan spiced duck). Entrees $31–42. Mon 5.45–11pm, Tues–Sat noon–2.30pm & 5.45–11pm, Sun, 11.30am–2.30am & 5:45–10pm.

Daniel 60 E 65th St, between Madison and Park aves ⓣ212/288-0033, ⓦwww.danielnyc.com. Subway #6 to 68th St. Upscale and expensive fare from chef Boulud (again) – think black sea bass in Syrah sauce and "quartet of pig *provençale*". Prix-fixe dinners only from $105; there's even an elaborate, seasonal, vegetarian version. One of the best French restaurants in New York City. Mon–Thurs 5.30–11pm, Fri & Sat 5.30–11pm.

Jojo 160 E 64th St, between Lexington and Third aves ⓣ212/223-5656, ⓦwww.jean-georges.com. Subway F to Lexington Ave–63rd St. Lavish townhouse restaurant created by feted chef Jean-Georges Vongerichten, serving excellent French fusion cuisine with the freshest ingredients – one of the few top French places open for lunch. Entrees $19–40. Mon–Thurs noon–2.30pm & 5.30–10.30pm, Fri & Sat noon–2.30pm & 5.30–11pm, Sun noon–2.30pm & 5.30–10pm.

Le Refuge 166 E 82nd St, between Lexington and Third aves ⓣ212/861-4505. Subway #4, #5, #6 to 86th St. Quiet, intimate and deliberately romantic old-style French restaurant in an old city brownstone. The bouillabaisse and other seafood dishes are delectable. Expensive, but worth it (most entrees $19.50–26.50). Mon–Sat 5–10pm, Sun 5–9.30pm.

German

Heidelberg 1648 Second Ave, between E 85th and 86th sts ⓣ212/628-2332, ⓦwww.heidelbergrestaurant.com. Subway #4, #5, #6 to 86th St. The atmosphere here is *mittel*-European kitsch, with gingerbread trim and waitresses in Alpine goatherd costumes. The food is the real deal, featuring excellent liver-dumpling soup, *Bauernfrühstück* omelettes, and pancakes, both sweet and potato (most entrees $16.95–24.95). And they serve *Weissbier* the right way, too – in giant, boot-shaped glasses. Mon–Thurs 11.30am–11pm, Fri & Sat 11.30am–midnight, Sun noon–11pm.

Greek

Persephone 115 E 60th St, between Park and Lexington aves ☎212/339-8363, ⓦwww.persephoneny.com. Subway #4, #5, #6 to 86th St. The best Greek taverna in Manhattan, with salty fried sheep's-milk cheese, rabbit stew, moussaka and grilled lamb ranging $17–26; the $24.95 prix-fixe three-course lunch is a great deal. Mon–Thurs noon–3pm & 5.30–11pm, Fri noon–3pm & 5.30–11.30pm, Sat 5.30–11.30pm, Sun 5–10.30pm.

Italian

Caffè Buon Gusto 236 E 77th St, between Second and Third aves ☎212/535-6884, ⓦwww.caffebuongusto.com. Subway #6 to 77th St. The Upper East Side has no shortage of middling Italian restaurants, but the food at *Buon Gusto* is a notch better than its peers (and a notch lower in price – pastas are $10.95). The penne alla vodka is excellent. Daily noon–11.30pm.

Paola's 1295 Madison Ave at 92nd St ☎212/794-1890, ⓦwww.paolasrestaurant.com. Subway #6 at 96th St. One of the neighbourhood's best upscale Italian restaurants, with fresh and tasty pastas ($20) – the bolognese is especially full of flavour. Sun–Mon 5–10pm, Tues–Sat 5–11pm.

Mexican

Cascabel Taqueria 1542 Second Ave, between 80th and 81st sts ☎212/717-7800, ⓦwww.nyctacos.com. Subway #6 to 77th St. Funky taco shop offering two fresh corn tacos for $8.50, with fillings like chorizo, fish, shrimp and *carnitas* (plus veggie choices). Also does bigger chicken plates ($12.50), a decent flan ($4) and delicious *churros* ($1). Great salsas and Spanish wines ($6). Daily 11.30am–midnight (Fri & Sat until 1am).

Maya 1191 First Ave, between E 64th and 65th sts ☎212/585-1818, ⓦwww.richardsandoval.com/mayany. Subway #6 to 68th St; F to 63rd St. Excellent, high-end Mexican entrees are served in a large, colourful and noisy dining room. The rock shrimp *ceviche*, chicken *mole* and grilled dorado fillet make this one of the best restaurants on the Upper East Side – and among the best Mexican spots in the whole city. Mains from $19–28. Sun–Thurs 5–10pm, Fri & Sat 5–11pm.

Taco Taco 1726 Second Ave, at E 90th St ☎212/289-8226. Subway #4, #5, #6 to 86th St. High-quality, super-cheap taco ($7.50 for two) depot with some unconventional fillings (pork with smoked jalapeños) in addition to the standards. The fish tacos ($16) are especially good. Cash only. Mon–Thurs 11.30am–11pm, Fri 11.30am–midnight, Sat 11am–midnight, Sun 11am–11pm.

Persian and Middle Eastern

Persepolis 1407 Second Ave, between E 73th and 74th sts ☎212/535-1100, ⓦwww.persepolisnyc.com. Subway #6 to 77th St. One of the few places in New York for Persian food, this is also one of the best. Smells of rose, cherry and cardamom fill the dining room. It's affordable, too, with entrees ranging $14–25. Daily noon–11.30pm.

Rectangles 1431 First Ave, between E 74th and 75th sts ☎212/744-7470, ⓦwww.rectanglesrestaurant.com. Subway #6 to 77th St. Probably the best Middle Eastern food in the city, this Yemeni–Israeli restaurant features tasty standards like hummus, *baba ghanoush* and a spicy chicken soup that can instantly cure the common cold. Most entrees range $17.95–22.95. Daily 11.30am–11pm.

Turkish

Beyoglu 1431 Third Ave, at 81st St ☎212/650-0850. Subway #4, #5, #6 to 86th St. Place to go for mouthwatering mezes (the Turkish version of appetizers) for $5.50–6.50; the doner kebabs and fish specials are super as well. Loud (the second floor is quieter), reasonably priced, and definitely filling. Daily noon–11.30pm.

Vegetarian

Candle Café 1307 Third Ave, at 75th St ☎212/472-0970, ⓦwww.candlecafe.com. Subway #6 to 77th St. This vegan favourite does its best to dress up all that tofu and seitan, often with surprising results. Salads are a standout, as are the soups and juices from the "farmacy". Moderately priced (entrees around $15). Mon–Sat 10.30am–11.30pm, Sun 11.30am–9.30pm.

Upper West Side and Morningside Heights

The **Upper West Side** is yuppie-residential, with the cuisine on offer tailored to local tastes: generous burger joints, coffee shops and Latin American-influenced lounges, but also an increasing number of modestly ambitious restaurants, especially around Lincoln Center, the Museum of Natural History and Columbia University.

African

Awash 947 Amsterdam Ave, between 106th and 107th sts ⓣ212/961-1416, ⓦwww.awashnyc.com. Subway #1 to 103rd St. Ethiopian expats flock to this brightly coloured restaurant offering sumptuous vegetarian and meat combo platters ($12–17). Dig in with your hands, but lay off the too-sweet honey wine. Daily noon–11pm.

American and Continental

Big Nick's 2175 Broadway at 77th St ⓣ212/362-9238, ⓦwww.bignicksny.com. Subway #1 to 79th St. Burgers, pizzas, sandwiches, chops and much more at this old school coffee shop. The food is more than serviceable, but you'll go for the atmosphere, convenience and wide selection as much as anything. Daily 24hr.

Boat Basin Café W 79th St, at the Hudson River with access through Riverside Park ⓣ212/496-5542, ⓦwww.boatbasincafe.com. Subway #1 to 79th St. An outdoor restaurant, the *Boat Basin* is only open seasonally. The informal tables are covered in red-and-white-checked cloths, and the food is standard – burgers with fries, sandwiches ($8–11) and some more serious entrees like grilled salmon ($18.95) – but inexpensive considering the prime location. On weekend afternoons a violin trio adds to the pleasant ambience. June–Aug Mon–Wed noon–11pm, Thurs & Fri noon–11.30pm, Sat 11am–11.30pm, Sun 11am–10pm; April, May, Sept & Oct daily noon until dusk, all weather permitting.

Boathouse Café Central Park Lake, at W 72nd St entrance ⓣ212/517-2233, ⓦwww.thecentralparkboathouse.com. Subway B, C to 72nd St. A peaceful retreat after a hard day's trudging around the Fifth Ave museums. You get great views of the famous Central Park skyline and decent American/Continental cuisine, but at very steep prices. April–Nov Mon–Fri noon–4pm & 5.30–9.30pm, Sat & Sun 9.30am–4pm & 6–9.30pm.

Miss Mamie's Spoonbread Too 336 W 110th St between Columbus and Manhattan aves ⓣ212/865-6744, ⓦwww.spoonbreadinc.com/miss_mamies.htm. Subway B, C to Cathedral Parkway–110th St. Excellent soul-food restaurant with a 1950s-themed interior, addictive North Carolina ribs ($15.95) and some of the best fried chicken ($13.95) in the city (allegedly the favourite of ex-President Clinton). Mon–Thurs noon–10pm, Fri & Sat noon–11pm.

Per Se 1 Central Park W, 10 Columbus Circle, Time Warner Center ⓣ212/823-9335, ⓦwww.perseny.com. Subway A, B, C, D, #1 to 59th St–Columbus Circle. The $275 nine-course prix fixe is a series of small plates that seek to transcend the standard dining experience; whimsical ideas like "Pearls and oysters", which pairs oysters with tapioca and caviar, should give you some idea – and it all works. Menu changes regularly; reservations accepted only by phone two months prior to the day, and jackets are required for men. Mon–Thurs 5.30–10pm, Fri–Sun 11.30am–1.30pm & 5.30–10pm.

Ouest 2315 Broadway, between W 83rd and 84th sts ⓣ212/580-8700, ⓦwww.ouestny.com. Subway #1 to 86th St. This New American restaurant has earned a loyal following for its exceptional gourmet comfort-food, such as braised beef short rib ragout with gnocchi ($29) or squab with duck liver risotto ($33); there's also a $34 three-course pre-theatre menu (weekdays only). Mon & Tues 5–9.30pm, Wed & Thurs 5–10.30pm, Fri & Sat 5–11pm, Sun 11am–2pm & 5–9.30pm.

Recipe 425 Amsterdam Ave between 81st and 82nd sts ⓣ212/501-7755, ⓦwww.recipenyc.com. Subway #1 to 79th St. The focus is squarely on local farm-fresh ingredients in this slip of a restaurant, with industrial-meets-country decor. The prices are reasonable (entrees $17–24; great lunch prix fixe of $11.95) and the dishes, from the foie gras terrine ($10) to the crisp and tender duck ($22) hit the mark with frequency. Mon–Fri noon–3pm & 5.30–10.30pm, Sat 11am–3.30pm & 5.30–10.30pm, Sun 11am–3.30pm & 5.30–10pm.

Rosa Mexicano 61 Columbus Ave, between W 62nd and 63rd sts ⓣ212/977-7700, ⓦwww.rosamexicano.com. Subway A, B, C, D, #1 to 59th St–Columbus Circle. Right across from Lincoln Center, it's the perfect location for a post-opera meal. Try the guacamole ($14 per order), which is mashed at your table, and their signature pomegranate margaritas ($11). Mon 11.30am–10.30pm, Tues–Fri 11.30am–11.30pm, Sat 11.30am–2.30pm & 4–11.30pm, Sun 11.30am–2.30pm & 4–10.30pm.

Santa Fe 73 W 71st St, between Columbus Ave and Central Park W ⓣ212/724-0822. Subway B, C to 72nd St. Southwestern cuisine in lovely surroundings. It's a neighbourhood favourite; entrees like chipotle shrimp and skirt steak fajitas run $17–24, and there's a very large tequila menu. Mon–Thurs & Sun 11.30am–11pm, Fri & Sat 11.30am–midnight.

Sarabeth's 423 Amsterdam Ave, between W 80th and 81st sts ⓣ212/496-6280. Subway #1 to 79th St. Best for brunch, this country-style restaurant serves delectable baked goods ($12) and impressive omelettes ($9–12). Expect to wait in line for a table, especially for weekend brunch. Mon–Sat 8am–10.30pm, Sun 8am–10pm.

Asian and Indian

Sapphire 1845 Broadway, between W 60th and 61st sts ⓣ212/245-4444, ⓦwww.sapphireny.com. Subway A, B, C, D, #1 to 59th St/Columbus Circle. Capable Indian eatery conveniently located near the Time Warner Center; curries and tandoori meals run $14–27. Mon–Thurs 11.45am–2.45pm & 5–10.30pm, Fri & Sat 11.45am–2.45pm & 5–11pm, Sun 5–10.30pm.

Shun Lee 43 W 65th St, at Columbus Ave ⓣ212/595-8895, ⓦwww.shunleewest.com. Subway #1 to 66th St. This venerable local institution – conveniently across the street from Lincoln Center – has top-notch Chinese food. The service and table settings are strictly formal (though there's a café with *dim sum* attached) but you should feel free to dress casually. Steer yourself toward the menu's many seafood delicacies ($28–32). Mon–Fri noon–midnight, Sat 11.30am–midnight, Sun 11.30am–10.30pm.

French

Café Luxembourg 200 W 70th St, between Amsterdam and West End aves ⓣ212/873-7411, ⓦwww.cafeluxembourg.com. Subway #1, #2, #3 to 72nd St. Popular Lincoln Center-area bistro that packs in a slightly sniffy crowd to enjoy first-rate, contemporary French food. Entrees in the high $20s, but the brasserie menu is a bit cheaper. Mon & Tues 8am–11pm, Wed–Fri 8am–midnight, Sat 9am–midnight, Sun 9am–11pm.

Jean Georges *Trump International Hotel*, 1 Central Park W, between W 60th and 61st sts ⓣ212/299-3900, ⓦwww.jean-georges.com. French fare at its finest, crafted by star chef Jean-Georges Vongerichten. The gracious service is a throwback to another, more genteel, era. With meals starting at $98 (tasting menus from $148), it's definitely the place for a special occasion; for the more price-conscious, the front-room *Nougatine* offers reasonable and more casual meals (about $40 for two courses). The wine list includes bottles ranging from $30 all the way to $12,000. Mon–Thurs noon–2.30pm & 5.30–11pm, Fri & Sat noon–2.30pm & 5.15–11pm.

Picholine 35 W 64th St, between Broadway and Central Park W ⓣ212/724-8585, ⓦwww.picholinenyc.com. Subway #1 to 66th St. Right near Lincoln Center, this pricey French favourite executes Gallic fare with flair. The Scottish game, when available, is a treat (menus are seasonal; $92 for 3 courses) and the cheese plate is to die for ($20). A terrific spot for a celebratory dinner. Tues–Thurs 5–10pm, Fri & Sat 5–11.45pm.

Italian

Carmine's 2450 Broadway, between W 90th and 91st sts ⓣ212/362-2200, ⓦwww.carminesnyc.com. Subway #1, #2, #3 to 96th St. A family-style Southern Italian joint with big portions, big flavours and a big personality. Though often packed to the rafters, it's a bit more civilized than the outpost in Times Square (200 W 44th St ⓣ212/221-3800). Mon–Thurs & Sun 11.30am–11pm, Fri & Sat 11.30am–midnight.

Gennaro 665 Amsterdam Ave, between W 92nd and 93rd sts ⓣ212/665-5348. Subway #1, #2, #3 to 96th St. A bustling source of very good Italian food. The excellent menu includes such moderately priced favourites as a warm potato, mushroom

▲ *Gennaro*

and goat cheese tart ($10), and braised lamb shank in red wine ($16.95). Don't forget to save room for dessert. No credit cards. Mon–Thurs 5–10.30pm, Fri & Sat 5–11pm.

V&T Pizzeria 1024 Amsterdam Ave, between W 110th and 111th sts ⓣ212/663-1708, ⓦwww.vtpizzeriarestaurant.com. Subway #1 to 110th St. Checked tablecloths and a low-key feel are the hallmarks of this pizzeria near Columbia University, with predictably college-aged patrons. There's plenty more than just pizza ($18 for large with one topping), like pastas and classic Italian dishes with veal, chicken and shrimp. Good and inexpensive. Sun & Mon 11.30am–11pm, Tues–Sat 11.30am–midnight.

Jewish and Eastern European

Artie's Delicatessen 2290 Broadway, between W 82nd and 83rd sts ⓣ212/579-5959, ⓦwww.arties.com. Subway #1 to 79th St. All the wise-cracking attitude of an old-timer, but the place is only a little over a decade old. Best choices: knish dogs ($4.95), corned beef and pastrami ($11.95), potato pancakes ($4.25) and black-and-white cookies ($2.50). Don't forget the pickles! Mon–Thurs 9am–11.30pm, Fri & Sat 9am–1am.

Fine & Schapiro 138 W 72nd St, between Broadway and Columbus ⓣ212/877-2721, ⓦwww.fineandschapiro. Subway #1, #2, #3 to 72nd St. Long-standing Jewish deli that's open for lunch and dinner, serving delicious old-fashioned kosher fare. Great chicken soup ($9.50 for large). Daily 10am–10pm.

Latin American

Café con Leche 424 Amsterdam Ave, at W 80th St ⓣ212/595 7000. Subway #1 79th St. This great neighbourhood Dominican restaurant serves roast pork ($11.95), rice and beans, and some of the hottest chilli sauce you've ever tasted. Cheap and very cheerful. Also at 726 Amsterdam Ave, between 95th and 96th sts. Mon–Fri 10am–9pm, Sat & Sun 9.30am–9pm.

Calle Ocho 446 Columbus Ave, between W 81st and 82nd sts ⓣ212/873-5025, ⓦwww.calleochonyc.com. Subway B, C to 81st St. Very tasty Latino fare, including *ceviche* (there's a wide selection priced $11–16) and *chimichurri* steak ($25) with yucca fries, served in an immaculately designed restaurant with a hopping lounge. The mojitos ($9–12) are as tasty and potent as any in the city. Mon–Thurs 6–11pm, Fri 6pm–midnight, Sat noon–midnight, Sun noon–10pm.

Middle Eastern

Turkuaz 2637 Broadway, at W 100th St ⓣ212/665-9541, ⓦwww.turkuaz.com. Subway #1, #2, #3 to 96th St. Sip a glass of *raki* in *Turkuaz*'s cavernous dining room and linger over such Turkish delicacies as vine leaves stuffed with grilled salmon cubes ($16.95). There are some vegetarian options. Mon–Thurs noon–11pm, Fri & Sat noon–midnight, Sun 11am–11pm.

Vegetarian

Josie's 300 Amsterdam Ave, at 74th St ⓣ212/769-1212, ⓦwww.josiesnyc.com. Subway #1, #2, #3 to 72nd St. Fresh, tasty, meatless dishes with an Asian twist, as well as organic chicken and wild seafood. Mon–Thurs noon–10.30pm, Fri noon–11.30pm, Sat 1am–11.30pm, Sun 10.30am–10.30pm.

Harlem

While visitors to **Harlem** will find plenty of cheap **Caribbean** and **West African** restaurants, it would be unthinkable not to try the **soul food** for which the area is justifiably famous. Whether it's ribs or fried chicken and waffles you're craving, you simply can't go wrong. Fast-food and Beastie Boys fans note that there is a 24 hour *White Castle* at Douglass Avenue and 125th Street.

African

Africa Kine 256 W 116th St between Douglass and Powell blvds ⓣ212/666-9400, ⓦwww.africakine.com. Subway B, C to 116th St. Best place on the emerging Little Senegal strip to try authentic West African and Senegalese dishes, such as lamb curry, lamb and peanut butter stew and spicy fish with okra, served with heaps of rice, all for around $10 at lunch (dinner $11–15). There's also a small takeaway counter on the first floor. Daily noon–2am.

Salimata Restaurant 2132 Frederick Douglass Blvd, between 115th and 116th sts ⓣ212/280-6980. Subway B, C to 116th St. Basic Guinean dining room catering primarily to expats, with rich, meaty soups and aromatic stews from around $10–15. Daily 7am–4pm, but tends to vary, so call ahead.

Cajun, Soul Food and Barbeque

Amy Ruth's 113 W 116th St, between Lenox Ave and Powell Blvd ⓣ212/280-8779, ⓦwww.amyruthsharlem.com. Subway #2, #3 to 116th St. The barbecue chicken ($13.25), named in honour of President Obama, is more than enough reason to visit this small, casual family restaurant, but the waffle breakfasts (from $6.50) and desserts (think peach cobbler and banana pudding) are equally enticing. Mon 11.30am–11pm, Tues–Thurs 8.30am–11pm, Fri 8.30am–5.30am, Sat 7.30am–5.30am, Sun 7.30am–11pm.

Charles' Country Pan Fried 2841 Frederick Douglass Blvd, between 151st and 152nd sts ⓣ212/281-1800. Subway B, D to 155th St. Fried chicken, barbecue chicken breast and smothered chicken leg are the specialities at this tiny Harlem spot, but the filling macaroni and cheese, collard greens and candied yams are equally good. Two pieces with two sides costs just $9.21, but there's an open lunch buffet for $11.91 ($15.16 for dinner and Sat/Sun all day). Mon–Thurs 11am–11pm, Fri & Sat 11am–1pm, Sun 11am–8pm.

Londel's Supper Club 2620 Frederick Douglass Blvd, between W 139th and 140th sts ⓣ212/234-6114, ⓦwww.londelsrestaurant.com. Subway B, C to 135th St. A little soul

Viaduct Valley (ViVa)

Way out on Twelfth Avenue, underneath the Henry Hudson Parkway, some of the warehouses and factories along the Hudson River have been transformed into smart restaurants in recent years, dubbed **Viaduct Valley** or "ViVa". Thanks in part to the 2009 recession, the area hasn't quite taken off the way its investors would have hoped, but if you're in Harlem it's worth a look, especially at the weekends – take the #1 subway to 137th Street or a taxi to avoid a long walk.

Covo Trattoria 701 West 135th St, at Twelfth Ave ⓣ212/234-9573, ⓦwww.covony.com. Rustic Italian taverna, with amazing wood-fire pizzas. Daily 11am–midnight.

Dinosaur Bar-B-Que 646 West 131 St, at Twelfth Ave ⓣ212/694-1777, ⓦwww.dinosaurbarbque.com. This convivial joint, an outpost of the original (in Syracuse, NY, of all places) is especially known for its pit-smoked chicken wings. Live blues every Sat from 10pm onwards. Mon–Thurs 11.30am–11pm, Fri & Sat 11.30am–midnight, Sun noon–10pm.

Hudson River Café 697 W 133rd St at Twelfth Ave ⓣ212/491-9111, ⓦwww.hudsonrivercafe.com. Modern American and continental cuisine served in an elegant upstairs dining room or outdoor patio complete with terrace. Mon–Tues 5–11pm, Wed–Sat 5pm–midnight, Sun 11am–3pm & 5–10pm.

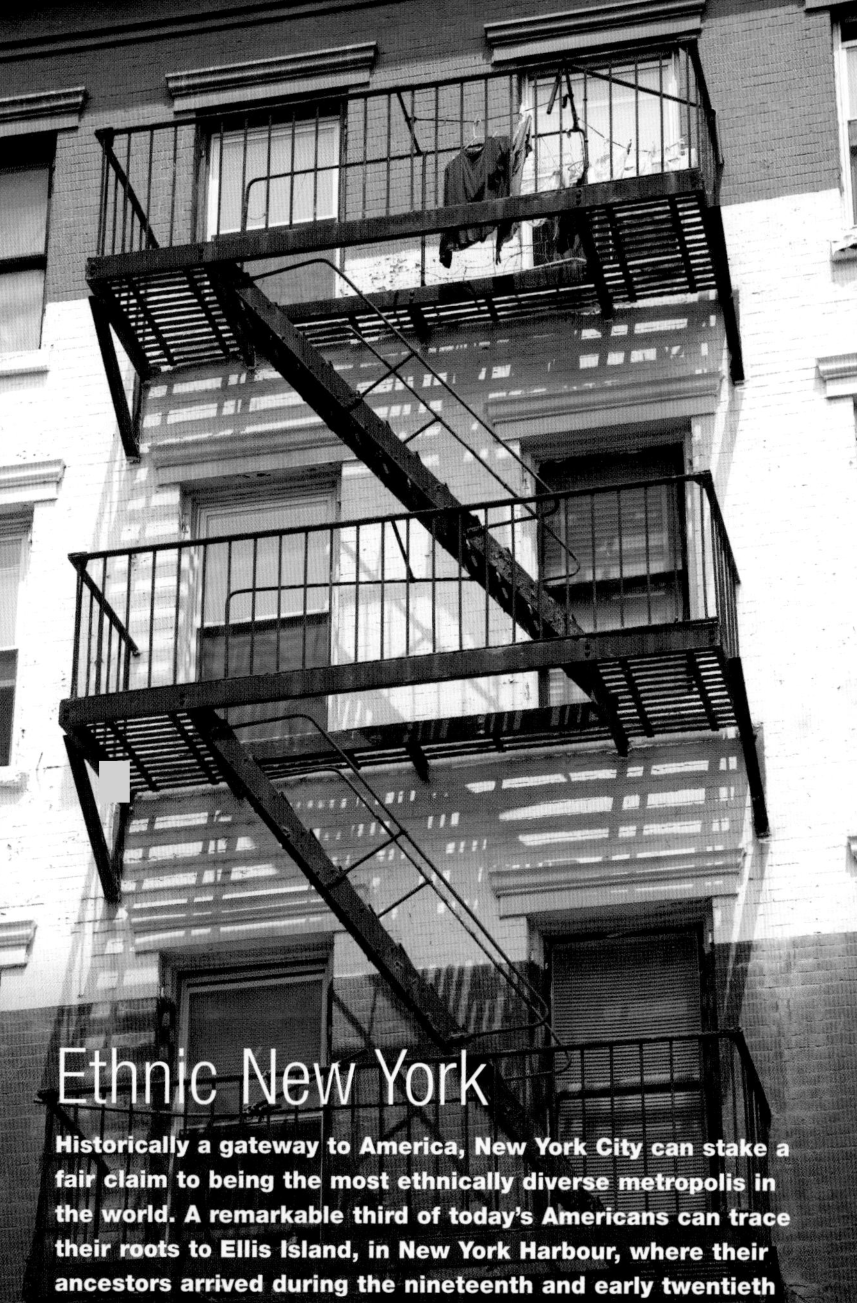

Ethnic New York

Historically a gateway to America, New York City can stake a fair claim to being the most ethnically diverse metropolis in the world. A remarkable third of today's Americans can trace their roots to Ellis Island, in New York Harbour, where their ancestors arrived during the nineteenth and early twentieth centuries. Many immigrants stayed in New York and built a life in the city, with the result that just about every ethnic community in the United States is now present here.

Bagels for sale ▲

Sign for sale in Little Italy, part 1 ▼

Russian restaurant at Brighton Beach ▼

People

New York City is in some ways a giant processing machine – it assimilates its newcomers, who then move on to other parts of the city or country. **Irish and Italians** were among the first to come in large waves and settled areas like Hell's Kitchen and Little Italy, neither of which retain much of a sense of their ethnic past. **Eastern European Jews** dominated late nineteenth- and early twentieth-century immigration, colonizing the Lower East Side, though this era was also the beginning for burgeoning **Chinese and Greek** populations in the city.

Today, many of New York's ethnic communities – both the above groups and newer arrivals – flourish in the outer boroughs. **Queens** is the most ethnically varied place of all: nearly half its residents are foreign-born. Large communities of South Americans and South Asians live in **Jackson Heights**, while **Flushing** is known as the city's second Chinatown, though Koreans, Malaysians and Vietnamese also make up a sizeable percentage of the population.

Food

New York's food is defined by its signature ethnic cuisines and dishes: **Jewish** (bagels, pastrami sandwiches), **Chinese** (everything from roast duck to soup dumplings) and **Italian** (pizza most of all) are probably the most notable. All these and more are covered in more detail in the introduction (see box, p.8) and in the Cafes and Restaurants chapters (see p.286 & p.305). The key to getting the most authentic food is generally to head to the **outer boroughs**; Manhattan's restaurants may be among the best in the world, but real-estate prices mean that most mom-and-pop style places have set up shop elsewhere. It's not just the non-touristy eateries that make a trip out worthwhile; giant food shops like Titan Foods (for Greek groceries in Astoria) and M & I International (for Russian goods in Brighton Beach) offer opportunities to taste delicacies on the cheap or take some home with you.

A guide to ethnic neighbourhoods

▸▸ **Astoria, Queens** All sorts of groups have settled here, but its most famous for its Greek population and the Hellenic shops and tavernas; the greatest concentration is along Broadway.

▸▸ **Belmont, the Bronx** Home to far more Italians than touristy Little Italy; the main drag, Arthur Avenue, bustles with salumerias and bakeries.

▸▸ **Brighton Beach, Brooklyn** Since the 1970s, Brighton Beach has been a strong Russian enclave; a walk down Brighton Beach Avenue takes you by food emporia and cheap electronic stores, all just a block from the ocean.

▸▸ **Chinatown, multiple boroughs** Which one? Busy restaurants pepper Mott Street in Manhattan's original Chinatown; Main Street in Flushing has plenty of street food stalls; and Eighth Avenue in Brooklyn's Sunset Park might boast the cheapest groceries anywhere.

▸▸ **SE Williamsburg and Crown Heights, Brooklyn** These areas are where much of today's Orthodox Jews live (along with Borough Park in Brooklyn); Lee Avenue in Williamsburg is a real centre of commerce.

▸▸ **Jackson Heights, Queens** Best-known for its Indian population, focused on 74th Street between Roosevelt and 37th Street, but Roosevelt Avenue east of there is like a Latin American bazaar.

▲ Pizza being flipped at *Lombardi's*

▼ Sign for sale in Little Italy, part 2

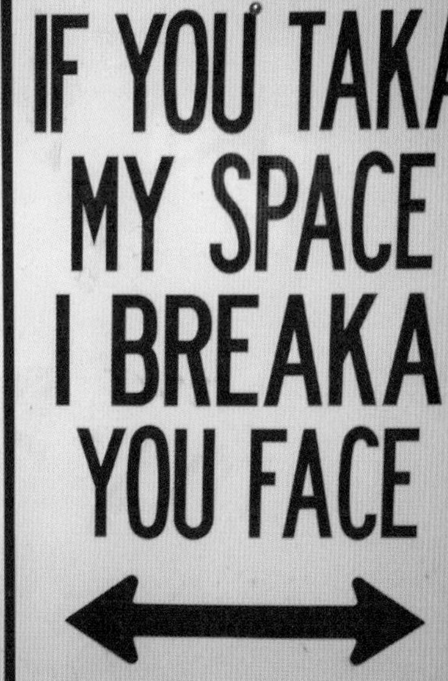

▼ Snacks for sale in Chinatown

Gospel choir of the Abyssinian Church ▲

Greek Indepence Day parade ▼

Chinese New Year ▼

Culture

Certain city neighbourhoods are practically synonymous with a group's culture. North of Central Park, **Harlem** is the most famous African-American community in the United States; besides the hallowed Apollo Theater and numerous jazz clubs, it holds museums showcasing African-American art and history, renowned soul food restaurants and Baptist churches with gospel choirs. In truth, architecturally rich **Bedford-Stuyvesant** in Brooklyn has a larger African-American community and is just as much of a cultural centre, even if it doesn't have as many sights for visitors.

If you want to seek out particular sights focusing on ethnicity, you've got plenty of choice: for a start, there's the Museum of Chinese in America (see p.85), the Museo del Barrio (see p.210), Museum of Jewish Heritage (see p.60) and, of course, the Museum of Immigration at Ellis Island (see p.48).

Parades and festivals

New York's ethnic communities celebrate their heritage in parades and festivals held throughout the year. Most last a day but some go for a week – or even a month. Visitors to New York will be hard-pressed to miss the events, as they often take over whole neighbourhoods. Some of the best are:

▸▸ **Lunar (Chinese) New Year** The first full moon between January 21 and February 19 (see p.424).

▸▸ **Greek Independence Day Parade** Late March (see p.425)

▸▸ **Ukrainian Festival** Mid-May (see p.426)

▸▸ **National Puerto Rican Day Parade** Second Sunday in June (see p.427)

▸▸ **West Indian-American Day Parade and Carnival** Labor Day (see p.428) food, a little Cajun, a little Southern-fried food. This is an attractive, down-home place where you can eat upscale items like sautéed prawns ($22.95) or more common treats such as fried chicken and waffles ($13.95); either way, follow it up with some sweet-potato pie. Jazz and R&B on Fri and Sat evenings at 8pm and 10pm. Tues–Sat 11.30am–midnight, Sun 11am–5pm.

Miss Maude's Spoonbread Too 547 Lenox Ave, between W 137th and 138th sts ⓣ212/996-0660, ⓦwww.spoonbreadinc.com/miss_maudes.htm. Subway #2, #3 to 135th St. Some of the best soul-food in Harlem – Norma Jean Darden's generations-old family recipes include succulent ribs ($14.95), Louisiana catfish ($15.95) and fried chicken ($12.95). Mon–Sat 11.30am–9.30pm, Sun 11am–7pm.

Sylvia's Restaurant 328 Lenox Ave, between W 126th and 127th sts ⓣ212/996-0660, ⓦwww.sylviassoulfood.com. Subway #2, #3 to 125th St. Established in 1962, this is the most well-known Southern soul-food restaurant in Harlem – so famous that Sylvia Woods has her own food line. While the BBQ ribs ($14.95) are exceptional and the candied yams are justly celebrated, *Sylvia's* has become a bit of a tourist trap – try to avoid Sundays when tour groups arrive for the Gospel brunch. Mon–Sat 8am–10.30pm, Sun 11am–5pm.

Caribbean

Fishers of Men II 12 W 125th St, between Lenox and Powell blvds ⓣ212/678-4268. Subway #2, #3 to 125th St. Fast-food Harlem style, specializing in fried fish sandwiches (meals $6–8). Mon–Thurs 10am–9pm, Fri & Sat 10am–10pm.

Strictly Roots 2058 Powell Blvd between 122nd and 123rd sts ⓣ212/864-8699. Subway #2, #3 to 125th St. Rasta-inspired vegan diner, with plates of healthful tofu, soy and spicy vegetable dishes ranging $5–10. Mon–Fri 8am–10pm, Sat 11am–10pm, Sun noon–8pm.

El Barrio (East Harlem)

El Barrio sees far fewer visitors than Harlem, but its restaurants are definitely worth a try; Puerto Rican and Latino cuisines dominate, though the strip along Lexington Avenue around 106th Street is developing a more varied scene.

El Paso Taqueria 1642 Lexington Ave at 104th St ⓣ212/831-9831, ⓦwww.elpasotaqueria.com. Subway #6 to 103rd St. One of three authentic Mexican restaurants managed by a couple of chefs from Puebla – this is the newest and smartest venue, with fabulous tacos from $2.25, larger dinner burritos ($9.50) and a range of regional Mexican dishes (11.95–16.95) like *Carnitas Estilo Michoacan* (pork in tequila). Daily 11am–11pm.

La Fonda Boricua 169 E 106th St, between Lexington and Third aves. Subway #6 to 103rd St ⓣ212/410-7292, ⓦwww.fondaboricua.com. Subway #6 to 103rd St. Authentic Puerto Rican diner, where huge plates of rich meat stews, roast pork, rice and beans rarely top $8. Daily 11am–10pm.

Rao's 455 E 114th St, between First and Pleasant aves ⓣ212/722-6709, ⓦwww.raos.com. Subway #6 at 116th St. You must reserve waaaay in advance (it's only got 10 tables, and one seating a night), but if the stars are aligned, you can be part of the most authentic Italian (Neapolitan) dining experience in the city. (If not, there's always their mail order operation.) Cash only. Mon–Fri 7–11pm.

Washington Heights

Northern Manhattan is the best place on the island to try authentic **Dominican** food, and you can often eat like a king for just a few dollars.

El Malecón Restaurant 4141 Broadway, between 175th & 176th sts ⓣ212/927-3812, ⓦwww.maleconrestaurants.com. Subway A to 175th St. This old-school Cuban joint is best known for its glistening spit-roasted chicken, but aromatic *asopaos* (soupy rice), plantains and puddings are just as good – all for less than $15. Daily 7am–midnight.

New Leaf Restaurant & Bar 1 Margaret Corbin Drive, Fort Tyron Park ⓣ212/568-5323, ⓦnewleafrestaurant.com. Subway A to 190th St. An airy, renovated 1930s building with views of Fort Tyron Park, offering fresh, American cuisine like ricotta ravioli ($12) and sirloin burger and fries ($16), mostly to visitors coming from the nearby Cloisters. Tues–Fri noon–3.30pm & 6–10pm, Sat 11am–3.30pm & 6–10pm, Sun 11am–3.30pm & 5.30–9.30pm.

Típico Dominicano Restaurant 4172 Broadway at 177th St ⓣ212/781-3900. Subway #1 to 181st St, A to 175th St. Smart, lively Dominican restaurant serving all the favourites: the huge *paella típica Dominicana* ($18.95) *mofongo* (mashed plantains with pork) and plenty of stews, beans and rice – most dishes are under $10. Open 24hr.

Brooklyn

Over the past several years **Brooklyn** has turned into a seriously food-centric borough, with dozens of ambitious restaurants cropping up everywhere in gentrified or rapidly gentrifying neighbourhoods like Park Slope, Carroll Gardens, Fort Greene, Williamsburg, even out in Bushwick and Ditmas Park. Eateries here tend to be more relaxed and cheaper than comparable spots in Manhattan, though there are plenty of places where you can splurge if you want to. As elsewhere, local and organic foods dominate the most progressive menus. Ethnic restaurants flourish in other parts of the borough, from long-established Polish spots in Greenpoint to Russian supperclubs in Brighton Beach.

Fulton Ferry District and DUMBO

Grimaldi's 19 Old Fulton St, between Water and Front sts ⓣ718/858-4300, ⓦwww.grimaldis.com. Subway A, C to Brooklyn Bridge–High St. People queue down the pavement for the delicious, thin and crispy pizzas, legendary throughout the city. Lunchtime is a better bet for avoiding crowds. Cash only. Mon–Thurs & Sun 11.30am–11pm, Fri & Sat 11am–midnight.

River Café 1 Water St, between Furman and Old Fulton sts ⓣ718/522-5200, ⓦwww.rivercafe.com. You can get better food for the price (or even cheaper) in New York, but *River Café* is more about the romantic atmosphere and spectacular views of the Brooklyn Bridge. The prix-fixe dinner, with dishes like foie gras and rock lobster, costs $98 per person for three courses, $125 for six, excluding wine. There's also a prix-fixe Sunday brunch ($55). Lunch (Mon–Sat) is à la carte but still pricey. Mon–Fri 11.30am–3pm & 5.30–11pm, Sat & Sun 11.30am–2.30pm & 5.30–11pm.

Superfine 126 Front St, between Jay and Pearl sts ⓣ718/243-9005. *Superfine*'s ever-changing menu has a fresh, Mediterranean bent, with big salads (shrimp, calamari), pork chops and pasta ($12–22), while Sunday brunch skews Southwestern: *huevos rancheros* with New Mexican green chillis ($8.50) is a nod to the chef's roots. The bar is a cool hangout; there's a free pool table, too. Tues–Fri 11am–3pm & 6–11pm, Sat 6–11pm, Sun 11am–3pm & 6–10pm; bar remains open until 2am weekdays, 4am weekends.

Brooklyn Heights

Henry's End 44 Henry St, at Cranberry St ⓣ718/834-1776, ⓦwww.henrysend.com. Subway #2, #3 to Clark St. Neighbourhood bistro with a loyal following for its hearty if somewhat old-fashioned fare and laidback atmosphere. Mains run from $18.95 for chicken breast with goat cheese and fig jam to $25.95 for steak *au poivre*. Not a good choice for vegetarians at any time of year, it's known for its wild-game festival, which runs from Oct to Feb. Mon–Thurs 5.30–10pm, Fri & Sat 5.30–11pm, Sun 5–10pm.

Waterfalls Café 144 Atlantic Ave, at Henry St ⓣ718/488-8886. Subway R to Court St; #2, #3, #4, #5 to Borough Hall; F, G to Bergen St. Middle Eastern specialties with a Syrian touch, touted by many as the best in the city, and certainly the finest on Atlantic Ave. The rotisserie chicken isn't bad, but the vegetarian salads, with everything from thick home-made yogurt to roasted cauliflower to spicy roasted eggplant, are the way to go. Daily noon–10pm.

Waterfront Ale House **155 Atlantic Ave, between Clinton and Henry sts ⓣ718/522-3794, ⓦwww.waterfrontalehouse.com. Subway R to Court St; #2, #3, #4, #5 to Borough Hall; F, G to Bergen St.** This inexpensive, friendly pub serves good spicy chicken wings ($7.95), chilli (including a venison version, $9.95), burgers ($8.95) and killer Key Lime Pie. Sun–Thurs noon–11pm, Fri & Sat noon–midnight.

Downtown Brooklyn

Junior's **386 Flatbush Ave, at DeKalb Ave ⓣ718/852-5257. Subway B, Q, R to Dekalb Ave.** Open 24hr and with enough lights to make it worthy of Vegas, *Junior's* offers everything from chopped-liver sandwiches to ribs to a full cocktail bar. Most of it is just so-so – the real draw is the cheesecake, for which the place is justly famous. The servings are mammoth. Mon–Thurs 6.30am–midnight, Fri & Sat 6.30am–2am.

Fort Greene

Locanda Vini e Olii **129 Gates Ave, at Cambridge Place ⓣ718/622-9202, ⓦwww.locandavinieolii.com. Subway C, G to Clinton–Washington aves.** Gorgeous, inventive Italian fare served in a restored pharmacy, all gleaming dark wood and glass. Duck *papardelle*, fluffy *gnocchi*, even beef tongue in parsley sauce may show up on the menu. Very affordable (pasta $12–16, grilled meat and fish $18–27) and worth the walk to the far reaches of Fort Greene (aka Clinton Hill). Reservations recommended. Tues–Thurs 6–10.30pm, Fri & Sat 6–11.30pm, Sun 6–10pm.

Thomas Beisl **25 Lafayette Ave, between Ashland Place and St Felix St ⓣ718/222-5800. Subway B, Q, #2, #3, #4, #5, B, Q to Atlantic Ave; G to Fulton St.** Directly across the street from BAM (see p.225), this recreated Viennese café is just elegant enough to set the tone for a pre-show dinner. Rich beef-cheek goulash ($18), sauerkraut-and-trout crêpes ($9), fantastic desserts and a year-round patio are all highlights. Mon 3.30pm–midnight, Tues–Fri noon–midnight, Sat & Sun 10.30am–midnight.

Umi Nom **433 Dekalb Ave at Classon Ave ⓣ718/789-8806, ⓦwww.uminom.com. Subway G to Classon Ave.** Southeast Asian small plates from a classically trained chef, who has settled in a bit of a removed location near Pratt. The room is warm and lively; go with friends and order to share. The roasted clams ($11), sautéed sausage ($11.50), pork belly (a frequent special) and greens should provide a nice starting point. Mon–Sat 11.30am–3.30pm & 6–11pm.

Boerum Hill and Carroll Gardens

Bar Tabac **128 Smith St, at Dean St ⓣ718/923-0918, ⓦwww.bartabacnyc.com. Subway F, G to Bergen St.** High-spirited French bistro with an all-French wine list and well-turned-out, generously portioned staples like onion soup ($6.50), *moules frites* ($15.95) and steak frites ($19.95). Live music on weekends, pavement tables in warm weather and great brunch to boot. Cash and AMEX only. Mon & Tues 11am–1am, Wed & Thurs 11am–2am, Fri 11am–3am, Sat 10am–3am, Sun 10am–1am.

Frankies 457 Spuntino **457 Court St, at Luquer St; another location on Lower East Side ⓣ718/403-0033, ⓦwww.frankiesspuntino.com. Subway F, G to Carroll St.** Co-chefs Frank and Frank revive and refine Italian–American favourites on the south side of Carroll Gardens. Home-made pastas ($13–17) are the way to go, coupled with a fresh salad of seasonal greens and a few crostini. Enjoy your meal on the breezy garden patio out back. Cash only. Mon–Thurs & Sun 11am–11pm, Fri & Sat 11am–midnight.

The Grocery **288 Smith St, between Sackett and Union sts ⓣ718/596-3335, ⓦwww.thegroceryrestaurant.com. Subway F, G to Carroll St.** Among the first serious restaurants that kick-started the area's gourmet aspirations, *Grocery* still chugs away with its emphasis on seasonal ingredients combined in simple but satisfying ways (guinea hen with spring peas and creminis, for instance). Reservations recommended, though the garden is unreserved; entrees $24–29. Tues & Wed 5.30–10pm, Thurs noon–2pm & 5.30–10pm, Fri noon–2pm & 5.30–11pm, Sat noon–2pm & 5–11pm.

Petite Crevette **144 Union St, at Hicks St ⓣ718/855-2632. Subway F, G to Carroll St.** The cosy, casual *Petite Crevette* employs a rather straightforward approach to fish and seafood: you pick it, they grill or sauté or do whatever to it, you eat every bite. Corn-crab chowder and soft-shell crabs (when in season) are standouts; alcohol is BYO. Mon–Sat noon–3pm & 5–11pm, Sun 5–11pm.

Prime Meats **465 Court St, at Luquer St ⓣ718/254-0327, ⓦwww.frankspm.com.**

Subway F, G to Carroll St. Frequently packed, this sibling of *Frankie's* (see p.339) serves up excellent steaks ($24 for a NY strip), burgers ($15) and a few select specialities in a room that feels decades old; earlier in the day, content yourself with a breakfast sandwich or eggs with wild mushrooms and bratwurst ($14). Cash only, no reservations. Mon–Wed & Sun 7am–1am, Thurs–Sat 7am–2am.

Red Hook

Good Fork 391 Van Brunt St, between Coffey and Van Dyke sts ⓣ718/643-6636, ⓦwww.goodfork.com. Though it feels very much a neighbourhood restaurant, this sliver of a place with exposed brick and thrift-store decor turns out terrific fare with a focus on local ingredients that's worth travelling for. The changing menu is New American with Asian flourishes, as per the delectable dumplings ($9) and Korean-style grilled skirt-steak with *kim chee* rice and a fried egg ($21). Tues–Sat 5.30–10.30pm, Sun 5.30–10pm.

Park Slope and Prospect Heights

Al Di Là 248 Fifth Ave, at Carroll St ⓣ718/783-4565. Subway R to Union St–Fourth Ave. Venetian country cooking at its finest at this husband-and-wife-run trattoria. Standouts include beet and ricotta ravioli, a delicate *malfatti* (spinach gnocchi), *saltimbocca* and the daily risotto. Early or late, expect at least a 45min wait (they don't take reservations); they've opened up a wine bar around the corner, where you can wait if you like. Mon 6–10.30pm, Wed & Thurs noon–3pm & 6–10.30pm, Fri noon–3pm & 6–11pm, Sat noon–3.30pm & 5.30–10.30pm, Sun noon–3.30pm & 5–10pm.

Bonnie's 278 5th Ave ⓣ718/369-9527. Subway R to Union St–Fourth Ave. Casual, fun-loving diner that's great for its juicy, Cajun-spiced burgers ($11) and impressive beer list. As the owners are natives of western New York, *Bonnie's* also serves up big plates of sticky Buffalo chicken wings ($7.95 small order). Mon–Thurs & Sun noon–10pm, Fri & Sat noon–11pm.

Rose Water 787 Union St, at Sixth Ave ⓣ718/783-3800, ⓦwww.rosewaterrestaurant.com. Subway M, R to Union St–Fourth Ave. Intimate Mediterranean-American bistro, serving excellent seasonal dishes with flavourful accents, including a three-course market-menu dinner Mon–Thurs for $26. Excellent brunch too. Mon–Fri 5.30–11pm, Sat & Sun 10am–3pm & 5.30–11pm.

Ditmas Park

Purple Yam 1314 Cortelyou Rd, ⓣ718/940-8188, ⓦwww.purpleyamnyc.com. Subway Q to Cortelyou Rd. After years running a restaurant down in Soho, the husband-and-wife owners (head chef and host, too) have decamped to up-and-coming Ditmas Park, which has received the homestyle Filipino cooking and friendly prices as if a piece to a missing puzzle. The *porky sisig* ($12) and *lechon* ($18) are musts, and the *adobo* ($16) and daily *kimchi* ($3) are not far behind. Finish it off with coconut buko pie ($6). Mon–Fri 5.30–10.30pm, Sat noon–3.30pm & 5.30–11pm, Sun noon–3.30pm & 5.30–10pm.

Coney Island

Gargiulo's 2911 W 15th St, between Surf and Mermaid aves ⓣ718/266-4891, ⓦwww.gargiulos.com. Subway D, F, N, Q to Coney Island–Stillwell Ave. A gigantic, noisy, century-old family-run Coney Island restaurant famed for its large portions of hearty Neapolitan food. Most pasta dishes are $10–20, most meat and seafood dishes $16–25. Mon, Wed & Thurs noon–10.30pm, Fri & Sat noon–11.30pm, Sun noon–9.30pm.

Totonno's Pizzeria Napolitano 1524 Neptune Ave, between 15th and 16th sts ⓣ718/372-8606, ⓦwww.totonnos.com. Subway D, F, N, Q to Coney Island–Stillwell Ave. The coal-oven-fired pizzas at this ancient (circa 1924), no-frills spot inspire devotion among pizza lovers for their sweet, fresh mozzarella and crispy crust. Try the half-bianca, half-margherita ($21.95). No slices; cash only. Wed–Sun noon–8pm.

Brighton Beach

Café Glechik 3159 Coney Island Ave, between Brighton Beach Ave and 10th St ⓣ718/616-0494, ⓦwww.glechik.com. Subway B, Q to Brighton Beach. A refreshing break from the flashier places in the neighbourhood, this *tchotchke*-laden Ukrainian restaurant is known for its dumplings – *pelmeni* and *vareniki* ($5–8) – as well as its borscht ($5), stews ($9–15) and stuffed cabbage ($9). Cash only. Daily 10am–10pm.

Primorski 282 Brighton Beach Ave, between 2nd and 3rd sts ⓣ718/891-3111, ⓦprimorski.net. Subway B, Q to Brighton Beach. One of the best of Brighton Beach's Russian hangouts, with a huge menu of authentic Russian dishes, including *blintzes*, stuffed cabbage and chicken Kiev. All sorts of banquet and couples deals are on offer; you could drop by for the $5.99 prix-fixe lunch, but then you'd miss the live dance music every evening. Mon–Thurs 11am–10pm, Fri–Sun 1pm–midnight.

Rasputin 2670 Coney Island Ave, at Ave X ⓣ718/332-8111, ⓦwww.rasputinny.com. Subway Q to Neck Rd. Though most people come for the way-over-the-top, Vegas-style entertainment, including scantily clad dancers doing cheesy floor routines, the food here is actually quite good, with banquet fare starting at $75 a person. A real "only in New York" experience. Fri–Sun 9pm–3am.

Williamsburg

Bamonte's 32 Withers St, at Union Ave ⓣ718/384-8831. Subway L to Lorimer St; G to Metropolitan Ave. Red-sauce restaurants abound in NYC, but this is one of the legends, serving traditional Italian-American dishes like handmade giant cheese ravioli ($14.95) since 1900. Mon, Wed & Thurs noon–10.30pm, Fri noon–11pm, Sat 1–11pm, Sun 1–10pm.

Diner 85 Broadway, at Berry St ⓣ718/486-3077, ⓦwww.dinernyc.com. Subway L to Bedford Ave; J, M, Z to Marcy Ave. This groovy eatery in a Pullman diner-car has a tiny menu of upscale American grub (burgers, roasted chicken, fantastic fries), along with a dozen varieties of Champagne. Next door they've opened up *Marlow and Sons*, which does fresh oysters, chicken-under-a-brick and elegant cocktails. Daily 11am–2am, kitchen open until midnight most nights, 1am on weekends.

DuMont 432 Union Ave, at Devoe St ⓣ718/486-7717, ⓦwww.dumontrestaurant.com. Subway L to Lorimer St; G to Metropolitan Ave. This bistro's sensitive restoration of the old-timey space is matched by the well-edited menu. Try the signature salad of *haricots verts*, pecans, Danish blue cheese and bacon ($11) followed by a burger ($12.50). The tiny offshoot *DuMont Burger*, at 314 Bedford Ave (between First and Second), offers the obvious, along with a few simple salads and fries. Mon–Thurs & Sun 11am–11pm, Fri & Sat 11am–midnight.

Fette Sau 345 Metropolitan Ave, at Havemeyer St ⓣ718/963-3404, ⓦwww.fettesaubbq.com. Subway L to Bedford Ave; G to Metropolitan Ave. The industrial-chic vibe (it's in an old auto repair shop) of this barbecue specialist seems fitting for the neighbourhood. Order your meat by the pound (beef brisket or pork shoulder $16), tack on a couple of sides, (burnt end baked beans $5.25) and wash it all down with a microbrew ($6 pints). Mon–Fri 5pm–2am, Sat & Sun 2pm–2am.

Peter Luger Steak House 178 Broadway, at Driggs Ave ⓣ718/387-7400, ⓦwww.peterluger.com. Subway J, M, Z to Marcy Ave. Catering to carnivores since 1887, *Peter Luger* may just be the city's finest steak-house. The service is surly and the decor plain, but the porterhouse steak – the only cut served – is divine (roughly $42.50/person). Old-school sides like creamed spinach are just a distraction, though don't pass on the bacon starter ($3/slice); the lunchtime burger is a great deal if you can't get there for dinner. Cash only; reservations required. Mon–Thurs 11.45am–9.45pm, Fri & Sat 11.45am–10.45pm.

Pies and Thighs 166 S 4th St, at Driggs Ave ⓣ347/529-6090, ⓦwww.piesnthighs.com Subway J, M, Z to Marcy Ave. This one-time underground institution has found a bright corner location in which to serve its southern-style food: great chicken biscuits (a scone with a fried chicken filling; $5), expertly fried chicken ($11 with a side) and a changing rotation of pies (slice $4.50; Key Lime and rhubarb are a few favourites). Mon–Fri 8am–4am & 5pm–midnight, Sat & Sun 10am–4pm & 5pm–midnight.

Greenpoint

Lomzynianka 646 Manhattan Ave ⓣ718/389/9439. Subway G to Nassau Ave. The service isn't the quickest, but the prices are astonishingly low (dinner plates $5 and up) at this homey Polish restaurant. Both kinds of borscht – white and red – are must-trys; if you want to play it safe with your entree, the hearty *kielbasa* is quite good. Daily noon–9pm.

Queens

The most ethnically diverse of all the boroughs, **Queens** offers some of the city's best opportunities to sample a wealth of authentic foreign flavours, from Bosnian and Greek to Brazilian and Colombian to Szechuan and Thai. Most places listed here are easily accessible by subway.

Long Island City and Astoria

Agnanti Meze 19-06 Ditmars Blvd, Astoria ⓣ718/545-4554, ⓦwww.agnantimeze.com. Subway N, Q to Astoria–Ditmars Blvd. Specializing in Greek meze – small plates for snacking – this restaurant overlooks Astoria Park. Don't miss the "specialties from Constantinople" section of the menu, with goodies like *bekri-meze*, wine-soaked cubes of tender meat. There's a second location in Bay Ridge, Brooklyn. Daily noon–11pm.

Kabab Café 25-12 Steinway St, Astoria ⓣ718/728-9858. Subway N, Q to Astoria Blvd. The culinary highlight of Steinway Sts "Little Egypt", this tiny, velvet-swathed den is the domain of Chef Ali, who lavishes patrons with traditional Middle Eastern goodies (smoky *baba ganoush*, lighter-than-air falafel) as well as his own creations – don't miss the honey-glazed duck. Ask the prices of off-the-menu specials if you're on a budget – they can be quite high. Tues–Sun 1–5pm & 6–10pm.

Lounge 47 47-10 Vernon Blvd, Long Island City ⓣ718/937-2044. Subway #7 to Vernon Blvd. This funky restaurant and bar with a gorgeous back patio offers spruced-up American basics like macaroni and cheese with rosemary crumb topping ($10) and juicy hamburgers ($9–13), as well as more international morsels like Indian samosas ($5) and a lamb sandwich with spicy chipotle mayo spread ($10). Mon–Thurs & Sun noon–1am, Fri & Sat 11am–2am.

Malagueta 25-35 36th Ave, Astoria ⓣ718/937-4821, ⓦwww.malaguetany.com. Subway N, Q to 36th Ave. Refined (but reasonably priced) Brazilian cuisine served in a simple, white-washed corner space. If you want to spice up the *moqueca de camarão* (shrimp in coconut milk; $14), ask for a side of hot *molho* sauce. Come on Saturday for *feijoada* ($15), Brazil's national dish, a black-bean clay-pot stew served with collard greens and rice. Tues–Fri 11.30am–10pm, Sat 1–11pm, Sun 1–10pm.

Taverna Kyclades 33-07 Ditmars Blvd, Astoria ⓣ718/545-8666, ⓦwww.tavernakyclades.com. Subway N, Q to Astoria–Ditmars Blvd. Friendly, popular Greek *taverna* specializing in seafood. Start with a selection of dips, including the garlic-yogurt-cucumber *tzatziki* ($5.50 on own, $9.95 as part of a trio), then move on to grilled calamari ($12.95) or grilled scallops ($22.95). Dessert, a traditional Greek custard, is on the house. Mon–Thurs noon–11pm, Fri & Sat noon–11.30pm, Sun noon–10.30pm.

Tournesol 50-12 Vernon Blvd, Long Island City ⓣ718/472-4355, ⓦwww.tournesolnyc.com. Subway #7 to Vernon Blvd. Warm French bistro in Hunters Point, steps from the Vernon Blvd #7 stop and an easy walk from MoMA PS 1. Staples like steak frites ($18) and tarragon *escargots* ($9.50) are reliably good, the wine list is small but well chosen, and brunch is very tasty. Mon 5.30–11pm, Tues–Thurs 11.30am–3pm & 5.30–11pm, Fri 11.30am–3pm & 5.30–11.30pm, Sat 11am–3.30pm & 5.30–11.30pm, Sun 11am–3.30pm & 5.30–10pm.

Uncle George's 33-19 Broadway, Astoria ⓣ718/626-0593. Subway N, W to Broadway. This 24hr joint serves simple, ultra-cheap Greek food on red-checked tablecloths. Go for the roasted half-chicken with lemon potatoes or the *spanakopita* (spinach pie), with a carafe of *retsina*. Most entrees are around $10. Daily 24hr.

Zenon Taverna 34-10 31st Ave, between 34 and 35th sts, Astoria ⓣ718/956-0133, ⓦwww.zenontaverna.com. Subway N to 30th Ave; R to Steinway St. Charred octopus ($13.95), grilled meatballs ($8.50) and taramasalata ($5.95) get your meal off on the right foot at this super-friendly Greek-Cypriot tavern; grilled bass ($21.95) or one of the lamb specials ($19.95) keeps it heading in the right direction. Daily 11am–11pm.

Sunnyside and Woodside

Spicy Mina 64-23 Broadway, Woodside ⓣ718/205-2340. Subway G, R to 65th St. Absolutely the best Indian and Bangladeshi food in all five boroughs – the samosa *chaat* appetizer ($4.95), the Bengali-style mustard fish ($14.95) and the *daal* fry (split peas; $8.95) are exceptionally good. Be prepared for a wait, as the eponymous Mina cooks entirely from scratch. Daily noon–11pm.

Sripraphai 64-13 39th Ave, Woodside–61st St ⓣ718/899-9599. Subway #7 to 69th St. Truly authentic Thai food that puts anything in Manhattan to shame – sweet, sour, (very) spicy and cheap. Try the "drunken" noodles with beef and basil ($8.50) or a whole steamed striped bass with ginger, chilli and lime ($20), along with staples like papaya salad and hot-and-sour lemongrass soup. An outdoor patio is open in the summer. Mon, Tues & Thurs–Sun 11.30am–9.30pm.

Jackson Heights

Jackson Diner 37-47 74th St, between 37th and Roosevelt aves ⓣ718/672-1232, ⓦwww.jacksondiner.com. Subway E, F, G, R to Roosevelt Ave; #7 to 74th St–Broadway. The best-known Jackson Heights Indian restaurant, with outstanding versions of classics like tandoori chicken ($9.95) and goat curry ($11.95). Cash only. Mon–Thurs & Sun 11.30am–10pm, Fri & Sat 11.30am–10.30pm.

La Pequeña Colombia 83-27 Roosevelt Ave, at 84th St ⓣ718/478-8700, ⓦwww.pequenacolombia.com. Subway #7 to 82nd St. Literally "Little Colombia", this simple spot doles out inexpensive but filling *empanadas* (meat pies) and *arepas* (corn cakes) along with a gut-busting "Mountain Platter" – ground beef and rice with fried egg, rice, pork rind and plantains ($11) – and other specialties. Try the fruit drinks, such as *maracuya* (passion fruit) or *guanabana* (soursop). Mon–Fri 11am–11pm, Sat 8am–midnight, Sun 8am–11pm.

Flushing

66 Lu's Seafood 38-18 Prince St ⓣ718/321-0904. Subway #7 to Main St–Flushing. Bright Taiwanese spot that attracts a local crowd. The special menus hold some real treats – try the clams with basil ($10.95) and sea bass with dried bean curd sauce ($19.95) – though many also swear by the pork chop over rice ($7); feel free to ask for help with recommendations. The ice-cold beer on tap pairs well with the food. Daily 11am–4am.

Spicy and Tasty 39-07 Prince St ⓣ718/359-1601. Subway #7 to Main St–Flushing. Tea-smoked duck ($11.95) is the signature dish at this Sichuan specialist, regarded by many as the finest in NYC; prepare yourself for plenty of spicy noodle dishes as well. Daily 11am–11pm.

The Bronx

In the **Bronx**, and the whole of the city, Belmont is *the* place to taste old-school Italian–American "red sauce" cuisine, while City Island's family establishments specialize in fresh-caught seafood, best enjoyed on warm summer evenings when the waterside dining is at its most scenic.

South Bronx

Sam's 596–598 Grand Concourse, at 150th St ⓣ718/665-5341. Subway #2, #4, #5 to 149th St–Grand Concourse. About a ten-minute walk from Yankee Stadium, *Sam's* makes for a tasty, cheap pre-game meal, whether you want American soul food or Caribbean standards. Tues–Sun 11am–10pm.

Bedford Park and Belmont

Com Tam Ninh Kieu 2641 Jerome Ave ⓣ718/365-2680. Subway B, D, #4 to Kingsbridge Rd. A convenient stop if you're close to the Poe Cottage, Fordham or the Botanical Garden (though Belmont's Little Italy isn't far away either), this small, casual Vietnamese joint has excellent renditions of *pho*, *bun*, *banh mi* and other inexpensive specialities. Daily 8.30am–8.30pm.

Dominick's 2335 Arthur Ave, at 187th St ⓣ718/733-2807. Subway B, D to 182nd–183rd sts. All you would expect from a Belmont neighbourhood Italian: communal family-style seating, hearty food, and (usually) low prices – sometimes hard to gauge, as there's no printed menu or written bill. Just tell your server what you're in the mood for and listen closely. Cash only. Mon–Sat noon–9.30pm, Sun 1–9pm.

Roberto Restaurant 603 Crescent Ave, between Arthur Ave and Hughes St ⓣ718/733-9503, ⓦwww.roberto089.com. Subway B, D to

182nd–183rd sts. Not quite so stuck in a time warp as other Belmont favourites, *Roberto* is renowned for its rich pastas, served with style on giant platters or, sometimes, baked in foil. Chef's specials are usually the way to go; entrees ($18–36) are big enough to share. Mon–Thurs noon–2.30pm & 5–10pm, Fri noon–2.30pm & 5–11pm, Sat 4–11pm.

City Island

Le Refuge Inn 586 City Island Ave, at Cross St ⓣ718/885-2478. Bus #BxM78. A romantic getaway at a historic B&B, this place might be a little frilly for some, but the French-inflected menu, with dishes like duck *à l' orange*, is a nice change from standard City Island fare. Prix-fixe brunch, lunch and dinner are $25, $45 and $50 respectively. Cash only. Tues–Sun 6–10pm.

Lobster Box 34 City Island Ave, at Rochelle St ⓣ718/885-1952, ⓦwww.lobsterbox restaurant.com. Bus #BxM78. Don't mess around with appetizers or sides at this City Island old-timer at the south end of the island – lobster fried, grilled or steamed is the choice (market price). Mon–Thurs & Sun 11.30am–midnight, Fri & Sat 11.30am–2am.

Staten Island

Staten Island is a bit of a hike, but nice break from the city; food here is not a major attraction, though it does do Sri Lankan cuisine particularly well, and has its own pizza legend in *Denino's*.

Denino's Pizzeria & Tavern 524 Port Richmond Ave, at Hooker Place ⓣ718/442-9401. Take bus #S44. A Staten Island favourite since 1937, serving pizza with a slightly thicker, chewier crust than most brick-oven joints in the city (from $16). *Ralph's Famous Italian Ices* (p.304) is right across the street, making dessert a no-brainer. Cash only. Sun–Thurs 11.30am–11pm, Sat & Sun 11.30am–midnight.

Gourmet Dog 40 Richmond Terrace ⓣ718/727-1234. Even if you're heading straight back to Manhattan, try the hot dogs here: perfectly grilled beef hot dogs start at $1.50, but try the Reuben (dog wrapped in pastrami, sauerkraut and cheese) for $2.50, or the "crunchy dog", encrusted with potato chips. Daily 6am–10pm.

Killmeyer's Old Bavaria Inn 4254 Arthur Kill Rd, at Sharrotts Rd ⓣ718/984-1202, ⓦwww.killmeyers.com. Take bus #S74. A full-tilt German beer garden near the south end of the island, complete with schnitzel, *sauerbraten* and giant steins of beer, and live oompah music outside on the weekends. Entrees ($15–29) are large enough to feed two. Mon–Thurs 11.30am–10pm, Fri & Sat 11.30am–midnight, Sun noon–9pm.

New Asha Sri Lankan Restaurant 322 Victory Blvd, at Cebra Ave ⓣ718/420-0649. Take bus #S48, #S61 or #S66. Head here for no-frills paper plates heaped with veggie roti, spicy chicken, curries and idlis, all for less than $10. Mon–Fri 10am–10pm.

25

Drinking

The **bar scene** in New York City is quite eclectic, with a broader range of places to drink than in most American cities and prices to suit most pockets. Bars generally open their doors at noon and close them in the early hours of the morning – 4am at the latest, when they have to close by law (clubs can open later). In a basic bar, you'll pay around $6–7 for a pint of beer "on tap" (also referred to as "on draft"). At the other end of the spectrum are the city's plush hotel and rooftop bars, where **prices** tend to start at around $15 per drink. Keep an eye out for "happy hour" bargains and two-for-one drink deals. Wherever you go, you'll be expected to tip a buck per drink.

The most obvious drink choice is typically **beer**. You'll see the usual American standards – Budweiser, Sam Adams, etc – alongside such European staples as Stella Artois and Heineken pretty much everywhere. Bars with bigger selections often feature real ales on tap and **microbrews** from across the country. Try some of the **local brews**: the *Brooklyn Brewery* does a fine range of beers in all styles (lager, pilsner, wheat and so on; see p.356) and the excellent Sixpoint Craft Ales brand can be found around town more and more (especially in Brooklyn, where it's based).

Wine demands a better-filled wallet than beer does. When in a restaurant or bar, expect a one-hundred-percent mark-up (at least) on the cost of a bottle. There are a couple of points of potential confusion for overseas visitors when it comes to **liquor**. Bear in mind that whether you ask for a drink "on the rocks" or not, you'll most likely get it poured into a glass filled with ice; if you don't want it like this ask for it "straight up". Also, American shots are approximately double the size of British and European shots, meaning you get more bang for your buck.

When **buying your own liquor or wine**, you'll need to find a liquor store – supermarkets only sell beer. You must be over age 21 to buy or consume alcohol in a bar or restaurant, and it's against the law to drink alcohol on the street. Note that some bars insist **you show photo ID** to get in (even if you look well over 21), so make sure you carry some. Also by law, all NYC bars must serve **non-alcoholic drinks**, though you shouldn't expect to pay less for them; sodas, juices and sparkling waters often sell for the same price as beer.

The bar scene

New York's watering holes are much more interesting below 14th Street than above. Some of the best establishments are located in the **East Village**, the **West Village**, **Nolita**, **Soho** and the western reaches of the **Lower East Side**. There's a decent mix of **Midtown** drinking spots, though bars here tend to be geared to tourists and an after-hours office crowd and, consequently, can be pricey and

Top 5 historic pubs

Pete's Tavern Gramercy Park, see p.352
Ear Inn Tribeca, see p.347
Fanelli Café Soho, See p.347
Subway Inn Upper East Side, see p.354
McSorley's Old Ale House East Village, see p.350

rather dull (there are a few notable exceptions). The **Upper East Side** is home to quite a few raucous sports and Irish bars, while the **Upper West Side** has a serviceable array of bars, although most tend to cater to Columbia University students and more of a clean-cut yuppie crowd. Farther uptown, the bars of **Harlem**, while not numerous, offer some of the city's most affordable jazz in a relaxed environment (see p.361 for more jazz clubs).

Check out the scene in the outer boroughs if you can, where bars range in feel from neighbourly to über hip. **Williamsburg** is an easy ride from Manhattan on the L train and the best place if you're short of time. Other areas to try are **Park Slope** and the collective of **Boerum Hill**, **Cobble Hill** and **Carroll Gardens** (known as Bococa), especially along Smith Street; head out to **Fort Greene** or **Prospect Heights** if this still feels too tame.

The listings that follow are grouped, approximately, according to the chapter divisions outlined in the Guide. Bear in mind that many places double as bar and restaurant, and you may therefore find them listed not here but in the previous chapter. For ease of reference, however, all specifically **gay and lesbian bars** are gathered together in Chapter 28 "Gay New York".

The Financial District and City Hall Park area

The Beekman 15 Beekman St, between Nassau and William sts ☎212/732-7333. Subway #4, #5, #6 to Brooklyn Bridge–City Hall. This Wall St landmark's great selection of more than twenty draught beers is complemented by frequent live music. One of numerous Irish pubs downtown. Mon–Sat 11am–1am.

Jeremy's Alehouse 228 Front St, at Peck Slip ☎212/964-3537. Subway #2, #3, #4, #5, A, C, J, Z to Fulton St. Unpretentious neighbourhood bar, with bras and ties hanging from the rafters (donated by happy patrons), serving well-priced pints of beer from $3.75 (served in styrofoam cups) and excellent burgers ($4) – happy hour Mon–Fri 4–6pm. The fried clams ($7.95) also get rave reviews. Mon–Fri 8am–midnight, Sat 10am–midnight, Sun noon–midnight.

Ulysees 95 Pearl St–58 Stone St ☎212/482/0400. Subway #2, #3 to Wall St. This Irish pub anchors the burgeoning Stone St scene, though it still primarily caters to an after-work Wall St crowd. Does decent Guinness and pub food, including plenty of roasts, and one of the few pubs open down here on Sundays. Daily 11am–4am.

Tribeca and Soho

Bar 89 89 Mercer St between Spring and Broome sts. Subway R to Prince St; #6 to Spring St. Slick, modern lounge with soft blue light spilling down over the bar, giving the place a trippy, pre-dawn feel. Check out the clear liquid crystal bathroom doors that go opaque when shut ($10,000 each, reportedly) and the strong, pricey drinks that pay for them. Daily noon–1am, Fri & Sat till 2am.

Bubble Lounge 228 W Broadway, between Franklin and White sts ⓣ212/431-3433. Subway #1 to Franklin St. Swanky place to pop a cork or two. There's a long list of Champagnes and sparklers, but beware the skyrocketing tabs. Mon–Wed 5pm–1am, Thurs 5pm–2am, Fri & Sat 5pm–4am.

Church Lounge *Tribeca Grand Hotel*, 2 Ave of the Americas, at White St ⓣ212/519-6600. Subway A, C, E to Canal St; #1 to Franklin St. Fabulous hotel bar, set at the bottom of the *Grand*'s spacious atrium – being surrounded by twinkling lights and beautiful people (it's much more atmospheric at night) eases the pain when it's time to pay. Daily 7am–1am.

Ear Inn 326 Spring St, between Washington and Greenwich sts ⓣ212/226-9060. Subway C, E to Spring St; #1 to Houston St. "Ear" as in "Bar" with half the neon "B" chipped off. This historic pub, a stone's throw from the Hudson River, opened in 1890 (the building dates from 1817). Its creaky (and some claim, haunted) interior is as cosy as a Cornish inn, with a good mix of beers on tap and basic, reasonably priced American food. Daily noon–4am.

Fanelli Café 94 Prince St, at Mercer St ⓣ212/226-9412. Subway R to Prince St. Established in 1922 (the building dates from 1853), *Fanelli* is one of the city's oldest bars. Relaxed and informal, it's a favourite destination of the not-too-hip after-work crowd, with a small dining room at the back. Daily 10am–2am, Thurs–Sat till 4am.

Greenwich Street Tavern 399 Greenwich St, at Beach St ⓣ212/334-7827. Subway #1 to Franklin St. Friendly neighbourhood bar, refreshingly unpretentious for this part of town, with a solid menu of snack food, easy-going (generally male) clientele, and beers for $3 in happy hour (Wed & Thurs 5–7pm). Mon–Fri 11am–11pm, Sat 4–11pm, Sun noon–8pm.

Kenn's Broome Street Bar 363 W Broadway at Broome St ⓣ212/925-2086. Subway A, C, E to Canal St. Open since 1972 but set in an ageing 1825 Federal-style house, this comfortable bar offers fifteen real ales (eight drafts), from Harpoon Winter Warm to Flying Dog Pale Ale (they also have Stella on tap), and decent burgers from $8. Daily 11am–4am.

M1-5 Lounge 52 Walker St, between Church St and Broadway. Subway N, Q, R to Canal St. Ultra-hip lounge bar, with a decent range of beers, wines and cocktails to accompany the sleek design and good food. Live music and DJs set the scene. Mon–Fri 4pm–4am, Sat 7pm–4am.

Puffy's Tavern 81 Hudson St, between Harrison and Jay sts ⓣ212/766-9159. Subway #1 to Franklin St. Far from being P. Diddy's hangout, this small dive serves cheap booze without a single ounce of attitude, rare in this area. The cool jukebox specializes in old 45s. Daily 11.30am–4am.

The Room 144 Sullivan St, between Houston and Prince sts ⓣ212/477-2102. Subway C, E to Spring St. Dark, homey two-room bar with exposed brick walls and comfortable couches. No spirits, but an impressive array of domestic and international beers. Daily 5pm–4am.

Toad Hall 57 Grand St, between W Broadway and Wooster St ⓣ212/431-8145. Subway A, C, E to Canal St. With a pool table, good service and excellent bar snacks, this stylish alehouse is a little less hip and a little more of a local hangout than some of its neighbours. Daily noon–4am.

Chinatown, Little Italy and Nolita

Mulberry Street Bar 176-1/2 Mulberry St, between Broome and Grand sts. ⓣ212/226-9345. Subway J, Z to Bowery; #6 to Canal St. Though it looks like a back-room hangout from *The Sopranos*, this is actually a friendly local dive-bar open to all. Formerly known as *Mare Chiaro*, the wooden bar, tile floor and pressed tin roof have barely changed since it opened in 1908. Daily 11.30am–2am.

Pravda 281 Lafayette St, between Prince and Houston sts ⓣ212/226-4944. Subway R to Prince St. This chic Soviet Russian caviar bar serves over seventy stiff vodka drinks (like "Leninade"), cocktails and hard-boiled eggs ($4) for snacking. Now that its heyday has passed, there are fewer crowds, and hence a more relaxed vibe, but it's still a great place. Try the coconut vodka. Mon–Wed 5pm–1am, Thurs 5pm–2am, Fri & Sat 5pm–3am, Sun 6pm–1am.

Room 18 18 Spring St, at Elizabeth St ⓣ212/219-2592. Subway J, Z to Bowery. Somehow, this inexpensive, romantic, Asian tapas bar has remained under the radar for years. Sound choice for a date – the exotic cocktails (think pomegranate mojitos and grape Martinis) are always fabulous. Daily noon–1am, Fri–Sun till 4am.

Sweet & Vicious 5 Spring St, between Bowery and Elizabeth St ⓣ212/334-7915. Subway J, Z to Bowery. *Sweet & Vicious* is the epitome of rustic chic, with exposed brick, lots of wood, and antique chandeliers. The back garden is just as cosy as the inside bar. Daily 4pm–4am.

Lower East Side

Back Room 102 Norfolk St, between Delancey and Rivington sts ⓣ212/677-9489. Subway F, J, M, Z to Delancey St–Essex St. With a hidden, back-alley entrance, this former speakeasy was reputedly once a haunt of gangster Meyer Lansky. To find it, walk down the metal steps and through to the back of the building. Tues–Sat 7.30am–4am.

Barramundi 67 Clinton St, between Stanton and Rivington sts ⓣ212/529-6900. Subway F, J, M, Z to Delancey St–Essex St. The infused vodka, decent beers, red-leather booths, tree-trunk tables and mounted deer's head attracts an early-thirtys crowd to this affable bar (there's no Australian connection, despite the name). Daily 6pm–4am.

Barrio Chino 253 Broome St, at Orchard St ⓣ212/228-6710. Subway B, D to Canal St. Don't be confused by the Chinese lanterns or drink umbrellas here – the owner's specialty is tequila, and there are a dozen brands to choose from. Shots are served with a traditional *sangría* chaser, made from a blend of tomato, orange and lime juices. Mon 5.30pm–1am, Tues–Thurs & Sun 11.30am–1am, Fri & Sat 11.30am–2am.

The Delancey 168 Delancey St, at Clinton St ⓣ212/254-9920. Subway F, J, M, Z to Delancey St–Essex St. Williamsburg hipsters meet Lower East Side chic at this bar and rock club, with a rooftop lounge in summer. Things can get frisky in the basement, which pulsates with live music. Daily 5pm–4am.

Happy Ending Lounge 302 Broome St, between Eldridge and Forsyth sts ⓣ212/334-9676. Subway J, Z to Bowery; B, D to Grand St. This former erotic massage parlour has been reborn as an exceptionally cool bar and club, with the original tiled sauna rooms downstairs converted to cosy booths. Drinks $8–12. Tues 10pm–4am, Wed–Sat 7pm–4am.

Kush 191 Chrystie St, between Stanton and Rivington sts ⓣ212/677-7328. Subway J, Z to Bowery. Beguiling Moroccan bar with live music, excellent salty bar snacks and even belly dancing. Exempt from the smoking ban, *Kush* offers hookah pipes. Wed–Thurs 6pm–4am, Fri & Sat 7pm–4am.

Libation 137 Ludlow St, between Stanton and Rivington sts ⓣ866/216-1263. Subway F, J, M, Z to Delancey St–Essex St. A sexy lounge spanning two floors. It's a bit eclectic, with $12 cocktails, an American tapas menu and DJs spinning '80s, hip-hop and everything in between. Wed–Sun 5pm–4am.

Magician 118 Rivington St, between Essex and Norfolk sts ⓣ212/673-7881. Subway F, J, M, Z to Delancey St–Essex St. Dark and sedate, couples come here as much for the intimate atmosphere as for the drinks, which are all of average price. Daily 5pm–4am.

Max Fish 178 Ludlow St, between Houston and Stanton sts ⓣ212/529-3959. Subway F to Lower East Side–Second Ave. Local hipsters head here in droves, lured by the arty but unpretentious vibe, the pinball machine, pool table and jukebox – bit of a pick-up joint at the weekends. Cheap beers, too. Daily 5.30pm–4am.

East Village

7B 108 Ave B, at E 7th St ⓣ212/473-8840. Subway L to First Ave. Aka the Horseshoe Bar, this quintessential East Village hangout has often been used as the sleazy set in films and commercials. It features deliberately mental bartenders, cheap pitchers of beer and one of the best punk and rock 'n' roll jukeboxes in the East Village. Daily noon–4am.

Angel's Share 8 Stuyvesant St, between E 9th St and Third Ave ⓣ212/777-5415. Subway #6 to Astor Place. This serene, candlelit haven is a great date spot, kept deliberately romantic by the entry rules – parties larger than four will not be admitted. The cocktails are reputed to be some of the best in the city. Can be hard to find: walk into the *Village Yokocho* complex, up the stairs to the *Gyu-ya* restaurant and look for the door on the left. Daily 6pm–2.30am, Thurs till 2am.

Bar Veloce 175 Second Ave, between E 11th and 12th sts ⓣ212/260-3200. Subway L to Third Ave. Narrow, slick Italian wine bar fit for the Mod Squad, with excellent hors d'oeuvres and a fine wine list. Daily 5pm–3am.

Bourgeois Pig 111 E 7th St, between First Ave and Ave A ⓣ212/475-2246. Subway L to First Ave; #6 to Astor Place. The decadent Versailles theme at this funky wine bar, replete with wall-sized mirrors, chandeliers and crimson satin couches, is backed by an extensive cocktail menu (using just wines, beers and Champagne), including bubbly served in silver punch bowls (from $12). Daily 5pm–2am, Fri & Sat till 3am.

Burp Castle 41 E 7th St, between Second and Third aves ⓣ212/982-4756. Subway #6 to Astor Place. Delightfully weird place: the bartenders wear monks' habits, choral music is piped in and you are encouraged to speak in tones below a whisper. Oh, and there are over 550 different types of beer. Mon–Fri 5pm–4am, Sat & Sun 4pm–4am.

Cozy Café Hookah Lounge 43 E 1st St, between First and Second aves ⓣ212/475-0177. Subway F to Lower East Side–Second Ave. Comfortable sofas and soft pillows make this subterranean Middle Eastern hookah bar all the more relaxing. Belly dancers Fri & Sat nights. Cash only. Mon–Thurs & Sun 2.30pm–2.30am, Fri & Sat 3pm–4am.

Croxley Ales 28 Ave B, between E 2nd and 3rd sts ⓣ212/253-6140. Subway F to Lower East Side–Second Ave. This top-notch sports bar smells strongly of BBQ wings and has a great selection of 30 draft and 75 bottled brews, all reasonably priced. Countless TVs are tuned into all the night's big games. Mon–Fri 5pm–4am, Sat & Sun noon–4am.

d.b.a. 41 First Ave, between E 2nd and 3rd sts ⓣ212/475-5097. Subway F to Lower East Side–Second Ave. A beer-lover's paradise, *d.b.a.* has at least sixty bottled beers, fifteen brews on tap and an authentic hand-pump. Garden seating (with a small smoking section) is available in summer. Daily 1pm–4am.

Decibel 240 E 9th St, between Second and Third aves ⓣ212/979-2733. Subway #6 to Astor Place. A rocking atmosphere (with good tunes) pervades this beautifully decorated underground sake bar. The inevitable wait for a wooden table will be worth it, guaranteed. Daily 6pm–3am, Sun till 1am.

Grassroots Tavern 20 St Mark's Place, between Second and Third aves ⓣ212/475-9443. Subway #6 to Astor Place. This wonderful, roomy underground den has cheap pitchers, baskets of popcorn for a buck, an extended happy hour and at least three of the manager's pets roaming around at all hours of the day or night. Daily 4pm–4am.

Hi Fi 169 Ave A, between E 10th and 11th sts ⓣ212/420-8392. Subway L to Third Ave. Formerly a live music venue, this spot has been stripped of its stage, but is still great for music, featuring an mp3 jukebox with over 19,000 albums. Great-looking hipster boys and girls pack this place, drinking hard pretty much every night of the week. Mon–Thurs 4pm–4am, Fri–Sun 3pm–4am.

Holiday Cocktail Lounge 75 St Mark's Place, between Second and First aves ⓣ212/777-9637. Subway #6 to Astor Place. Unabashed dive with a mixed bag of customers, from old-world grandfathers to young professionals. Auden and Sinatra both drank here, and urban legend claims (dubiously) that it inspired Madonna's first big hit (she was a regular in the 1980s). Mon & Sun 6pm–2am, Tues–Sat 5pm–3am.

KGB Bar 85 E 4th St, at Second Ave ⓣ212/505-3360. Subway F to Lower East Side–Second Ave; #6 to Astor Place. On the second floor, this dark bar is set in what was the HQ of the Ukrainian Communist Party in the 1930s. Better known now for its marquee literary readings and the Kraine Theater in the basement (see p.368). Daily 7pm–4am.

Lakeside Lounge 162 Ave B, between E 10th and 11th sts ⓣ212/529-8463. Subway L to First Ave. The owners, a local DJ and a record producer, have stocked the *Lakeside* jukebox with old rock, country and R&B records. Live performers frequently pack into one small corner. Daily 4pm–4am.

The Lobby Bar *Bowery Hotel*, 335 Bowery at 3rd St ⓣ212/505-9100. Subway #6 to Bleecker St. Perhaps the most lavish hotel bar in the city, adorned with thick Persian rugs, velvet sofas and wood panelling – a bit like one of those decadent clubs on the Upper

East Side, but open to the public. Daily 5pm–2am, Thurs–Sat till 4am.

Manitoba's 99 Ave B, between E 6th and 7th sts ⓣ212/982-2511. Subway L to First Ave; #6 to Astor Place. Run by Dick Manitoba, lead singer of the punk group The Dictators, the kickin' jukebox and rough-and-tumble vibe at this spot make it a favourite among East Villagers who really just like to drink. Daily 2pm–4am.

McSorley's Old Ale House 15 E 7th St, between Second and Third aves ⓣ212/473-9148. Subway #6 to Astor Place. Yes, it's often full of tourists and NYU students, but you'll be drinking in history at this landmark bar that opened in 1854 – it's the oldest pub in NYC. Today, it only pours its own ale – light or dark. Try the turkey sandwich with hot mustard; it's one of the best bar snacks in the city. Mon–Sat 11am–1am, Sun 1pm–1am.

The Sunburnt Cow 137 Ave C, between E 8th and 9th sts ⓣ212/529-0005. Subway #6 to Astor Place. This popular Aussie bar and BBQ joint uses wooden stumps for stools and has lighting designed to resemble sunsets. Cocktails are decidedly strong and the grilled shrimp almost as good as back home. Mon–Wed 4pm–2am, Thurs & Fri 4pm–4am, Sat 11am–4am, Sun 11am–midnight.

Temple Bar 332 Lafayette St, between Bleecker and Houston sts ⓣ212/925-4242. Subway #6 to Bleecker St. One of the most discreet and romantic spots for a drink downtown, this sumptuous, dark lounge evokes the glamour of the early 1940s. They take their Martinis very seriously; the guacamole appetizer is the best dish on the short snack menu. Daily 5pm–1am, Fri & Sat till 2am.

Von 3 Bleecker St, between Bowery and Lafayette St ⓣ212/473-3039. Subway #6 to Bleecker St. Like an old pair of jeans, this wine-and-beer-only bar is comfortable (and welcoming) through and through. The prices are pretty nice, too. Mon 5pm–2am, Tues–Thurs & Sun 2pm–2am, Fri & Sat 2pm–4am.

Zum Schneider 107–109 Ave C, at E 7th St ⓣ212/598-1098. Subway #6 to Astor Place. A German beer-hall (and indoor garden) with a mega-list of brews and *wursts* from the Fatherland. It can be a bit packed with frat-boy types; in the early evening, though, the old-world vibe is sublime. Mon–Thurs 5pm–2am, Fri 4pm–4am, Sat 1pm–4am, Sun 1pm–2am.

West Village

55 Bar 55 Christopher St, between Sixth and Seventh aves ⓣ212/929-9883. Subway #1 to Christopher St. A gem of an underground dive-bar that's been around since the days of Prohibition, with a great jukebox, congenial clientele and live jazz music seven nights a week. Daily 3pm–3am.

8th St Winecellar 28 W 8th St, between Fifth Ave and MacDougal St ⓣ212/260-9463. Subway A, B, C, D, E, F, M to W 4th St. Simple, clean space with wooden tables and knowledgeable bartenders; fabulous wine selection, with most bottles in the $30–40 range (and twenty by the glass from $8). Daily 5pm–2am, Sat & Sun from 3pm.

Blind Tiger Ale House 281 Bleecker St, at Jones St. Subway A, B, C, D, E, F, M to W 4th St; #1 to Christopher St. This wood-panelled pub is the home of serious ale connoisseurs, with 28 rotating drafts (primarily US microbrews such as Sixpoint and Smuttynose for around $6.50), a couple of casks and loads of bottled beers – they also serve cheese plates from *Murray's* (see p.407). The prime location means it tends to get packed. Daily 11.30am–4am.

The Dove Parlour 288 Thompson St, between Bleecker and W 3rd sts ⓣ212/254-1435. Subway A, B, C, D, E, F, M to W 4th St. Filled with the post-college crowd, this subterranean Victorian-looking bar is always chilled. Jazzy happy hours evolve into upbeat late nights. Daily 4pm–4am.

Fat Black Pussycat 130 W 3rd St, between Sixth Ave and MacDougal St ⓣ212/533-4790. Subway A, B, C, D, E, F, M to W 4th St. This lively pub is an NYU favourite, with popular happy hours (weekdays 4–8pm), plenty of cosy wooden booths, darts and billiards. The pub's original location on MacDougal St is where Bob Dylan allegedly wrote *Blowin' in the Wind*. Daily 1pm–4am.

Jane Ballroom *Jane Hotel*, 113 Jane St, between Washington and West sts. ⓣ212/924-6700 Subway A, C, E to 14th St. Gorgeous hotel bar, with opulent furnishings that make it look like a stately home (with a disco ball). Head up to the balcony for the best people-watching.

Wine $10 by the glass. Mon, Tues & Sun 5pm–2am, Wed–Sat 5pm–4am.

Kettle of Fish 59 Christopher St, at Seventh Ave ☎212/414-2278. Subway #1 to Christopher St. This basement bar is a great escape from the scene on Seventh Ave, with plenty of real ales (including Sixpoint), no-nonsense staff and a mix of sports fans, tourists and students. The original *Kettle* on MacDougal St was a legendary Beat hangout. Mon–Fri 3pm–4am, Sat & Sun 2pm–4am.

White Horse Tavern 567 Hudson St, at W 11th St ☎212/243-9260. Subway #1 to Christopher St. A Greenwich Village institution, opening in 1880: Dylan Thomas supped his last here before being carted off to the hospital with alcohol poisoning, while Norman Mailer and Hunter S. Thompson were also regulars. The beer and food are cheap and palatable, and outside seating is available in summer. Daily 11am–3am.

Chelsea and the Meatpacking District

El Quinto Pino 401 W 24th St at Ninth Ave ☎212/206-6900. Subway C, E to 23rd St. There are relatively few seats in this elegant tapas bar, so come early to nibble on pork cracklings ($6) and an uncanny sea urchin sandwich ($15), paired with a good selection of Spanish wines. Mon–Thurs 8am–2pm & 5pm–midnight, Fri 8am–2pm & 5pm–1am, Sat 5pm–1am, Sun 5–11pm.

Half King 505 W 23rd St, between Tenth and Eleventh aves ☎212/462-4300. Subway C, E to 23rd St. This popular Irish pub is owned by a small group of writers/artists and features good food (burgers $12, fish and chips $16) and regular literary events; they've been known to book some heavy hitters (see p.377). Mon–Fri 11am–4am, Sat & Sun 9am–4am.

Hiro Ballroom *Maritime Hotel*, 371 W 16th St, at Ninth Ave ☎212/242-4300. Subway A, C, E, L to 14th St-Eighth Ave. Chic, spacious indoor/outdoor lounge in one of the city's latest (and most successful) architectural conversions, decked out like a Hong Kong nightclub in the 1940s. Live bands and guest DJs provide entertainment Thurs–Sun; cover charge applies. Hours change, but usually daily 10pm–4am.

Hogs & Heifers 859 Washington St, at W 13th St ☎212/929-0655. Subway A, C, E, L to 14th St–Eighth Ave. "Hogs" as in the burly motorcycles parked outside; "heifers" as in, well, ladies. Though officially there's no more bar dancing, those bold enough to venture into this rough-and-tumble Meatpacking District joint can still drink to excess. Avoid on weekend nights. Mon–Fri 11am–4am, Sat 1pm–4am, Sun 2pm–4am.

Peter McManus Café 152 Seventh Ave at 19th St ☎212/929-9691. Subway #1 to 18th St. Unlike many Irish pubs in the city, this is the real deal, moving to this location in 1936 and since appearing in episodes of *Seinfeld* and *Law & Order*. The worn oak bar adds character, along with the tasty in-house McManus Ale and two old-style telephone booths inside. Mon–Sat 11am–4am, Sun noon–4am.

Union Square, Gramercy Park and the Flatiron District

Except where noted, all the bars below can be reached by subway L, N, Q, R, #4, #5, #6 to 14th Street–Union Square.

119 Bar 119 E 15th St between Park Ave and Irving Place. A nicely tatty dive, with well-priced pints and a rocking soundtrack – perfect for a warm-up or post-show drink if you're hitting the Irving Plaza (see p.360). Mon–Fri 4pm–4am, Sat & Sun 6pm–4am.

Bar Jamón 125 E 17th St, at Irving Place ☎212/253-2773. A superb place to sip on sherry and nosh on Spanish tapas. Be forewarned though: there are only fourteen stools. Mon–Fri 5pm–2am, Sat & Sun noon–2am.

Belmont Lounge 117 E 15th St, between Union Square and Irving Place ☎212/533-0009. Oversized couches, dark, cavernous rooms and an outdoor garden reel in a continuous stream of twenty-something singles. The strong drinks help liven things up. Daily 4pm–4am.

Cibar 56 Irving Place, between E 17th and 18th sts ⓣ212/460-5656. The strong, innovative cocktails, elegant decor and pretty, well-tended herb garden make this cosy hotel bar the place of choice for a tryst. Mon–Thurs 5pm–1am, Fri 5pm–2am, Sat 6pm–2am.

Molly's 287 Third Ave between E 22nd and E 23rd sts. Subway #6 to 23rd St. While the city trends to gastropubs and handcrafted cocktails, the friendly bartenders at *Molly's* are content to pour some of the best pints of Guinness around. Daily 11am–4am.

Old Town Bar & Grill 45 E 18th St, between Broadway and Park Ave S ⓣ212/529-6732. This atmospheric Flatiron District bar is popular with publishing types and photographers. Opened in 1892, much of the creaking interior is original, including the rickety dumbwaiter and fine mahogany bar. Mon–Sat 11.30am–1am, Sun 1pm–1am, opens later on Sun in summer.

Pete's Tavern 129 E 18th St, at Irving Place ⓣ212/473-7676. Open since 1864, this former speakeasy now trades unashamedly on its history, which has included such illustrious patrons as O. Henry. Mon & Tues 11.30am–11.45pm, Wed–Fri 11.30am–12.45am, Sat 10.30am–12.45am, Sun 10.30am–11.45pm.

Revival 129 E 15th St, between Irving Place and Third Ave ⓣ212/253-8061. Walk down the stairs and into this friendly narrow bar with great outdoor seating in the backyard. Popular with fans waiting for concerts at Irving Plaza around the block.

Midtown East

Campbell Apartment Southwest balcony in Grand Central Terminal ⓣ212/953-0409. Subway #4, #5, #6, #7 to 42nd St–Grand Central. Once home to businessman John W. Campbell, who oversaw the construction of Grand Central, this majestic space – built to look like a Florentine palace – was sealed up for years. Now, after a snappy refit by designer Nina Campbell (no relation), it's one of New York's most distinctive cocktail bars. Go early and don't wear sneakers. Mon–Thurs noon–1am, Fri noon–2am, Sat 3pm–2am, Sun 3–11pm.

Casa Lever 390 Park Ave, at E 53rd St ⓣ212/888-2700. Subway #6 to 51st St; E, M to Lexington Ave–53rd St. Inside this landmark building is a very modern (with the art to match) restaurant, but you can just duck into the bar for a glass of wine and a look around. Daily 11.30am–11pm.

Le Colonial 149 E 57th St, between Lexington and Third aves ⓣ212/752-0808. Subway N, Q, R, #6 to 59th St–Lexington Ave. The upstairs bar of this Vietnamese restaurant is decked out in opulent Asian style, with red velvet chairs, teak tables and ageing photos of Saigon. Try the specialty cocktails; Le Colonial is a mix of gin, cassis and raspberry (average drinks $16). Daily 4.30pm–1am, Mon & Sun till midnight.

King Cole Bar 2 E 55th St, between Fifth and Madison aves, in the *St Regis* hotel. Subway E, M to Fifth Ave–53rd St. You might want to dress smart and be ready to spend at the reputed home of the Bloody Mary, but sipping a cocktail at a table or under the Maxfield Parrish mural at the bar, you'll surely feel like a million bucks. Mon–Thurs 11.30am–1am, Fri & Sat 11.30am–2am, Sun noon–midnight.

P.J. Clarke's 915 Third Ave, at E 55th St ⓣ212/317-1616; other locations Upper West Side and Battery Park. Subway #6 to 51st St; E, M to Lexington Ave–53rd St. Friendly bartenders serve thirty varieties of wine (twelve by the glass) and a moderate selection of beers at *P.J. Clarke's*, one of the city's most famous watering holes. The bar is casual, though there is a pricey restaurant out back. Daily 11.30am–4am.

Midtown West

Ardesia 510 W 52nd St between Tenth and Eleventh aves. Subway C, E to 50th St. A sleek but comfortable Hell's Kitchen wine bar with a bold snack menu (home-made pretzels, quail-egg toast) and diverse selection of vintages, about thirty of which are available by the glass (most $7–13). Mon & Tues 5pm–midnight, Wed–Fri 5pm–2am, Sat noon–2am, Sun noon–midnight.

Jimmy's Corner 140 W 44th St, between Broadway and Sixth Ave ☎212/221-9510. Subway B, D, F, M, N, Q, R, #1, #2, #3 to 42nd St. The walls of this long, narrow corridor of a bar, owned by ex-fighter/trainer Jimmy Glenn, are a virtual boxing hall of fame. You'd be hard-pressed to find a more characterful dive anywhere in the city – or a better jazz/R&B jukebox. Mon–Sat 11am–4am, Sun 1pm–4am.

Kashkaval 856 Ninth Ave between 55th and 56th sts. Subway A, B, D, #1 to 59th St–Columbus Circle. Tucked in the back of a cheese shop, this cosy wine bar serves up tasty bites, including excellent cheese and meat plates, cold meze (beetroot *skordalia* is a must) and an array of fondues. Mon–Sat 9am–11pm, Sun 10am–10pm.

Landmark Tavern 626 Eleventh Ave, at W 46th St ☎212/757-8595. Subway A, C, E to 42nd St. Off-the-beaten-path but long-established Irish tavern (open since 1868), with great Guinness and a tasty menu of pub food such as shepherd's pie and fish and chips – the Irish soda bread is baked fresh every day. Daily 11.30am–3am.

P.J. Carney's 906 Seventh Ave, between 57th and 58th sts ☎212/664-0056. Subway N, Q, R to Seventh Ave–57th St. Despite the historic pedigree (this tiny bar was established in 1927) and a straggle of loyal locals, *Carney's* is crammed most nights with tourists and sports fans. The beer and pub food isn't bad, though; consider for an afternoon pit stop between Midtown and the park. Mon–Sat 10.30am–4am, Sun noon–4am.

Rudy's 627 Ninth Ave, between W 44th and 45th sts ☎212/974-9169. Subway A, C, E to 42nd St. One of New York's cheapest, friendliest and liveliest bars, a favourite with local actors and musicians. *Rudy's* offers free hot dogs, a backyard that's great in summer and some of the cheapest pitchers of beer in the city ($9). Daily 8am–4am.

Russian Vodka Room 265 W 52nd St, between Broadway and Eighth Ave ☎212/307-5835. Subway C, E, #1 to 50th St. They serve more than fifty different types of vodka here, as well as their own fruit-flavoured and sublime garlic-infused concoctions; there's also caviar and plenty of small plate choices. Under the dim lighting, office workers mingle with Russian and Eastern European expats; don't ask for a mixer with your shot, unless you want to attract a stare or laugh. Daily 4pm–midnight, Fri–Sun till 4am.

Stout 133 W 33rd St, between Sixth and Seventh aves ☎212/629-6191. Subway A, B, C, D, E, F, M, #1, #2, #3 to 34th St. With around twenty excellent beers on tap, another 125 by the bottle (including thirty varieties of the bar's namesake) and an equally expansive menu, this Irish-theme pub is a great after-work, pre-MSG option. Daily 11.30am–4am.

Upper West Side

Dead Poet 450 Amsterdam Ave, between W 81st and 82nd sts ☎212/595-5670. Subway #1 to 79th St. You'll be waxing poetic and then dropping dead if you stay for the duration of this sweet little bar's happy hour – usually involving $4 pints and running most open hours. The back room has armchairs, books and a pool table. Mon–Sat 9am–4am, Sun noon–4am.

Ding Dong Lounge 929 Columbus Ave, between 105th and 106th sts ☎212/663-2600. Subway B, C to 103rd St. This punk bar with a DJ and occasional live bands attracts a vibrant mix of graduate students, neighbourhood Latinos and stragglers from the nearby youth hostel. Happy hour 4–8pm, with $3 draft beer and $5 cocktails. Daily 4pm–4am.

Dublin House Tap Room 225 W 79th St, between Broadway and Amsterdam Ave ☎212/874-9528. Subway #1 to 79th St. Beneath the cool neon sign, this lively, sometimes-overcrowded Upper West Side Irish pub is the place to go before or after a gig at the Beacon Theatre. Mon–Sat 8am–4am, Sun noon–4am.

MObar *Mandarin Oriental*, 80 Columbus Circle, at W 60th St between Ninth Ave and Broadway ☎212/805-8876. Subway A, B, C, D, #1 to 59th St–Columbus Circle. On the 35th floor of the *Mandarin Oriental*, this *boîte* is a cozy alternative to the hotel's main lobby lounge, with a shiny nickel bar and leather seating; choose from more than twenty wines by the glass and a host of exotic cocktails that will surely put a dent in your wallet. Tues–Sat 4pm–12.30am.

Prohibition 503 Columbus Ave, at W 84th St ☎212/579-3100. Subway B, C, #1 to 86th St. Stylish bar and lounge with funky decor (check out the lamps suspended in wine bottles) and free live music every night (usually funk or jazz). The back room is always much quieter, the beer selection is good if unsurprising and the house-made Martinis are spectacular. Mon–Fri 5pm until an hour after the last band ends (usually 3am), Sat 3pm until the same.

Upper East Side

American Trash 1471 First Ave, between E 76th and 77th sts ☎212/988-9008. Subway #6 to 77th St. Don't let the name put you off: this self-styled "professional drinking establishment" has a friendly bar staff, a pool table, a sing-along jukebox, a photo booth and a happy hour (Mon–Fri 5–8pm) dedicated to getting you pleasantly intoxicated. Daily noon–4am.

Auction House 300 E 89th St at Second Ave ☎212/427-4458. Subway #4, #5, #6 to 86th St. This is a cosier, smarter alternative to the frat-boy pubs that dominate this part of town, with two quiet candlelit rooms decked out like Victorian parlours. Perfect for couples. Daily 7.30pm–2am, Thurs till 3am, Fri & Sat till 4am.

Bar Pléiades *The Surrey*, 20 E 76th St, between Fifth and Madison aves ☎212/772-2600. Subway #6 to 77th St. This stylish Art Deco hotel bar is a homage to Chanel, with black-and-white lacquered surfaces, quilted walls and leather banquettes; cocktails (from $19) and pricey canapés from *Café Boulud* ($28). Daily noon–midnight.

Bemelmans Bar *Carlyle Hotel*, 35 E 76th St, at Madison Ave ☎212/744-1600. Subway #6 to 77th St. This hotel bar oozes old-school New York class, with Ludwig Bemelman's exuberant murals plastered all around, live piano, white-jacket waiters and an opulent gold-leaf ceiling. Daily noon–1am, Sat & Sun till 1.30am.

Metropolitan Museum of Art 1000 Fifth Ave, at E 82nd St ☎212/535-7710. Subway #4, #5, #6 to 86th St. It's hard to imagine a more romantic spot to sip a glass of wine and kick off the evening (bars close at 8.30pm Fri & Sat), whether on the *Roof Garden Café* (May–Oct Tues–Thurs & Sun 10am–4.30pm, Fri & Sat 10am–8pm), which has some of the best views in the city, or in the *Balcony Bar* overlooking the Great Hall (Fri & Sat 4–8.30pm).

Stir 1363 First Ave, at E 73rd St ☎212/744-7190. Subway #6 to 77th St. Funky lounge bar and popular date venue, with comfy sofas and seductive pillows making another stark contrast to the mainly sports-bar territory around here. It becomes more club-like later on, with plenty of dancing, and the bar food and cocktails (especially the margaritas) are excellent. Mon–Wed 5pm–1am, Thurs 5pm–2am, Fri 5pm–3am, Sat 6pm–4am, Sun 6pm–1am.

Subway Inn 143 E 60th St, at Lexington Ave ☎212/223-8929. Subway N, R, #4, #5, #6 to Lexington Ave–59th St. This neighbourhood dive-bar, across from Bloomingdale's, has been serving customers since 1937 and is great for a late-afternoon beer. Mon–Sat 11am–4am, Sun noon–2am.

Harlem

Most Harlem bars double as jazz and live music venues – see p.361.

A Touch of Dee 657 Malcolm X Blvd, at 143rd St ☎ 212/283-945. Subway #3 to 145th St. Classic local bar that seems stuck in the 1970s (or earlier), serving bottled beers (cash only) and featuring a Motown-heavy jukebox. Mon, Tues & Sun noon–midnight, Wed & Thurs 2pm–2am, Fri & Sat 10am–4am.

Camaradas El Barrio 2241 First Ave, at 115th St ☎212/348-2703. Subway #6 to 116th St. No-frills local bar in the heart of Spanish Harlem, with great Puerto Rican food and bottled beers from all over Latin America; expect the salsa to get louder as the night progresses. Daily 4pm–midnight, Thurs–Sat till 4am.

Moca Lounge **2210 Frederick Douglass Blvd, at 119th St ☎212/862-1511. Subway B, C, #2, #3 to 116th St.** Funky cocktail bar (try the Harlem Shuffle or the Booty Call Martini), with plenty of comfy sofas and bar snacks to go around – morphs into club mode at the weekends. Mon & Tues 5pm–2am, Wed, Thurs & Sun 11am–2am, Fri & Sat 11am–4am.

Nectar **2235 Frederick Douglass Blvd, at 121st St ☎212/961-9622. Subway A, B, C, D to 125th St.** Harlem's first wine bar is a smart, bright space offering a decent spread of vintages and varieties ($6–19) by the glass (happy hour 5–7pm). Daily 4pm–1am.

Real's Lounge **695 Lenox Ave, at 145th St ☎917/346-2706. Subway #3 to 145th St.** Casual bar with plenty of action each night, from karaoke (Tues), open-mike comedy (Thurs), jazz (Sun) and DJs spinning dance tunes at the weekend. Daily 4pm–4am.

Brooklyn

Fulton Ferry District and DUMBO

68 Jay St **68 Jay St, at Water St. Subway F to York St.** A friendly neighbourhood bar with good happy-hour deals (daily 4–7pm), a rock soundtrack and a relaxed, vaguely arty vibe. Mon–Fri 2pm–2am, Sat 3pm–2am, Sun 4pm–midnight.

Brooklyn Heights

Floyd **131 Atlantic Ave, between Clinton and Henry sts ☎718/858-5810. Subway F, G to Bergen St; #2, #3, #4, #5 to Borough Hall.** Tricked out with antique couches and comfy leather chairs, the main draws here are the cheap draft beers (includes Brooklyn Lager), popular indoor bocce court and live English Premier League games. Mon–Thurs 5pm–4am, Fri 4pm–4am, Sat 10am–4am, Sun 11am–4am.

Fort Greene

Moe's **80 Lafayette Ave, at S Portland Ave ☎718/797-9536. Subway C to Lafayette Ave; G to Fulton St.** Vintage furniture and candles set the tone at this two-level bar, with a young, eclectic clientele, frequent DJ sets and two-for-one happy hour (3–7.30pm, from noon on weekends). Perfect for pre- or post-BAM drinks (p.225). Mon–Thurs & Sun 3pm–2am, Fri & Sat noon–4am.

Stonehome Wine Bar **87 Lafayette Ave, between S Portland Ave and S Elliot Place ☎718/624-9443. Subway C to Lafayette Ave; G to Fulton St.** Stylish wine bar with the added bonus of backyard patio, perfect for spring and summer evenings (and smokers). The bar itself is a gorgeous, curving cherry-wood masterpiece, and the carefully crafted wine list is impressively long (including thirty available by the glass). Daily 5pm–midnight.

Boerum Hill and Carroll Gardens

Bar Great Harry **280 Smith St, at Sackett St, Carroll Gardens ☎718/222-1103. Subway F, G to Carroll St.** Essential stop on any Carroll Gardens pub crawl, with a vast list of micro-brews and select imports (twenty on tap, seventy in bottles). Prices range from $5 to $8. Daily 2pm–4am.

Brooklyn Inn **148 Hoyt St, at Bergen St, Boerum Hill ☎718/522-2525. Subway F, G to Bergen St.** Locals – and their dogs – gather at this convivial favourite with high ceilings, a solid wood bar imported from Germany in the 1870s and friendly staff. Great place for a daytime buzz or shooting pool in the back room. Mon–Thurs 4pm–4am, Fri–Sun 3pm–4am.

Jakewalk **282 Smith St, at Sackett St, Carroll Gardens ☎347/599-0294. Subway F, G to Carroll St.** Neighbourhood wine bar decked out in orange and gold, with around fifteen wines by the glass (from $5) to sample (along with plenty of whiskeys and specialty cocktails). Be sure to order one of the 25 cheeses ($5 each) to go with your drink, sourced from the gourmet cheese shop a block down. Mon–Fri 5pm–2am, Sat & Sun 2pm–2am.

Red Hook

Sunny's **253 Conover St, between Beard and Reed sts ☎718/625-8211. Subway F, G to Smith–9th St, then #B77 bus.** Red Hook is off the subway grid, but it's a great place to explore and make an evening of it; if you do, make sure to grab at least one drink at this pub by the river. Open, on-and-off, since 1890, it's an old-school dive with $4 bottle beers and loyal regulars. Expect erratic opening hours, swing bands and impromptu jam sessions. Wed, Fri & Sat 8pm–4am.

Park Slope

O'Connor's 39 Fifth Ave, at Bergen St ⓣ718/783-9721. Subway #2, #3 to Bergen St. A dive-bar in a bunker-like setting, with cheap bottled beers and a good jukebox. It's been here more than seventy years, having bravely withstood the nearby gentrification. Mon–Sat 10.30am–4am, Sun noon–4am.

Union Hall 702 Union St, between Fifth and Sixth aves ⓣ718/638-4400, ⓦunionhallny.com. Subway M, R to Union St. Vast bar, restaurant and live music venue, with a library-like interior of bookshelves, fireplaces and sofas near the bar, and two wildly popular bocce courts (arrive early to get a game). The basement hosts bands three or four times a week – check out the website for the schedule. Mon–Fri 4pm–4am, Sat & Sun noon–4am.

Williamsburg

Barcade 388 Union St, between Powers and Ainslie sts ⓣ718/302-6464. Subway L to Lorimer St; G to Metropolitan Ave. This former metalwork shop is crammed with old-fashioned arcade games (think Donkey Kong), each of which take the original 25 cents per game. The beers are good, too, with an excellent choice of 25 brews on tap. Mon–Fri 5pm–4am, Sat & Sun 2pm–4am.

Brooklyn Brewery 1 Brewers Row, 79 N 11th St ⓣ718/486-7422. Subway L to Bedford Ave. New York's best-known micro-brewery, open Friday nights for "happy hour" (beers $4). See box, p.241, for more on brewery tours. Fri 6–11pm (happy hour), Sat & Sun noon–6pm (tours only).

Pete's Candy Store 709 Lorimer St, between Frost and Richardson sts ⓣ718/302-3770. Subway L to Lorimer St. This terrific little spot was once a real candy store. There's free live music every night, a reading series, Scrabble and Bingo nights, pub quizzes and some well-poured cocktails. Daily 5pm–2am, Thurs till 3am, Fri & Sat till 4am.

Radegast Hall and Biergarten 113 N 3rd St, at Berry St ⓣ718/963-3973. Subway L to Bedford St. This Austro-Hungarian *biergarten* is fairly authentic, a spacious wooden beer hall serving steins of foamy German brews. The dining room does great food and is popular with families, while the beer garden attracts serious boozers. Mon–Fri 4pm–4am, Sat & Sun noon–4am.

Spuyten Duyvil 359 Metropolitan Ave at Havemeyer St ⓣ718/963-4140. Subway L to Lorimer St. Beer lovers should make for this popular pub, stocking over a hundred bottled brands (mostly potent Belgian brews), six on tap, and a rotating selection of cask-pulled ales. Mon–Fri 5pm–2am, Sat & Sun 1pm–4am.

Queens

Astoria

Bohemian Hall and Beer Garden 29-19 24th Ave, between 29th and 30th sts ⓣ718/274-4925. Subway N to Astoria Blvd. This old Czech bar is the real deal, catering to old-timers and serving a good selection of pilsners, as well as other hard-to-find brews. In back, there's a very large beer garden, complete with picnic tables, trees, burgers and sausages, and a bandstand for polka groups. Great fun in good weather, and worth the trip from Manhattan. Daily noon–2am, Thurs–Sat till 3am.

▲ *Bohemian Hall and Beer Garden*

Long Island City

Harry's at Water Taxi Beach 2 Borden Ave, at 2nd St ⓦwww.watertaxibeach.com. Subway #7 to Vernon Blvd; E to 23rd St–Ely Ave. The sand may be imported from Jersey, but the festive spirit is real at this summertime phenomenon with smashing views across the East River to the UN. Cheap beers and grilled food are served up from a tiki hut, with a small cover charge for dance parties on weekend nights. Summer Mon–Thurs 4–10pm, Fri 4pm–3am, Sat noon–3am, Sun 1–10pm.

L.I.C. Bar 45–58 Vernon Blvd, at 46th Ave ⓣ718/786-5400. Subway #7 to Vernon Blvd–Jackson Ave or 45th Rd–Courthouse Square; G to 21st St. A friendly, atmospheric place for a beer, burger and some free live music (Mon & Wed); hunker down at the old wooden bar or in the pleasant outdoor garden. Mon–Thurs & Sun 4pm–2am, Fri & Sat 2pm–4am.

The Bronx

Yankee Tavern 72 E 161st St, at Gerard Ave ⓣ718/292-6130. Subway B, D, #4 to 161st St–Yankee Stadium. Since 1923, this has been the "original sports bar". Everyone wears their pinstripes on their sleeves in this dive, and Yankees employees come to blow off steam (or celebrate). Hours vary depending on if there's a home game, but generally daily 10am–2am (or later).

Staten Island

Al-Hakkorah 1271 Bay St, at Scarboro Ave ⓣ718/981-2222. Authentic hookah bar and Arabian restaurant, not far from the Alice Austen Museum; smoke up while enjoying live music and belly dancing. Daily 2pm–midnight, Thurs–Sat till 4am.

Cargo Café 120 Bay St, at Slosson Terrace, St George ⓣ718/876-0539. Inside this electric-blue building (marked by a scary toddler statue) you'll find a welcoming local dive with plenty of drink specials, all within stumbling distance of the ferry. Mon–Fri 11am–2am, Sat & Sun noon–2am.

Jade Island 2845 Richmond Ave, between Platinum and Yukon aves ⓣ718/761-8080. Staten Island's tiki bar (cum Chinese restaurant) offers bamboo booths, blowfish lamps, rum cocktails in coconuts and girls in hula skirts. And you wanted to head straight back to Manhattan. Mon–Thurs 11.30am–11.30pm, Fri & Sat 11.30pm–12.30am, Sun noon–11.30pm.

R.H. Tugs 1115 Richmond Terrace, between Bard Ave and Snug Harbor Rd ⓣ718/447-6369. Just across from Snug Harbor, on the Kill Van Kull shore, the views of Jersey oil refineries are a bit grim, but beers are $2 in happy hour (Mon–Fri 3–6pm). Daily 11.30am–10pm, Fri & Sat till midnight.

26 Nightlife

As the city that never sleeps, New York is undeniably a **nightlife** hotspot. Bars don't start to fill up until 11pm, if not later, and clubs look like empty rooms until midnight or 1am. Even confirmed early birds should try to stay out late at least a few times during their stay, as the city's legendary energy is most obvious when most other cities have bedded down for the night.

Since the early 2000s, New York's **live music** scene has been undergoing a post-punk and garage-rock revival, fuelled by bands from the East Village, the Lower East Side and Williamsburg in Brooklyn. The city also continues to set the standard in **jazz**, with a number of venues where you can hear the most popular contemporary performers, as well as local stars, especially in Harlem. **Hip-hop** remains a vital part of the musical scene in New York – Mos Def, 50 Cent and Jay-Z are all based here, among many others – though clubs and larger venues are the best place to catch live sets.

Whatever you're planning to do after dark, remember to **carry ID** at all times to prove you're over 21 – you'll likely be asked by every doorman. Note that some venues do not even allow under-21s to enter, let alone drink – call to check if you're concerned. Note also that although **smoking is illegal** at most clubs, you'll soon realize that in practice, this is rarely enforced (despite recent police crackdowns).

The sections that follow provide accounts of the pick of the city's venues, but it's a good idea to get up-to-date info once you hit the ground. *Time Out New York* is pretty reliable ($4.99). Otherwise, grab a freesheet like *The Village Voice* (Ⓦwww.villagevoice.com) or *The Onion* (whose cultural listings are excellent; Ⓦwww.theonion.com). These can be found on street corners in self-serve newspaper boxes, as well as in many music stores; all of them contain detailed **listings** for most scenes.

Live music

New York has a vibrant **live music** scene, though like the city, most places are eclectic when it comes to genres; the same place can feature rock, hip-hop, folk and Latin music on different nights, and though rock/indie often dominates, only jazz has a truly separate club culture (see p.361).

> For most of the large venues listed below, tickets are sold through **Ticketmaster** (Ⓦwww.ticketmaster.com). For many mid-sized and small venues, tickets are sold through **Ticketweb** (Ⓦwww.ticketweb.com).

New York's **rock scene** currently leans heavily toward garage- and indie rock, with bands like Vampire Weekend, MGMT, Interpol, The Bravery, The Strokes, The Rapture and the Yeah Yeah Yeahs leading the charge.

As for **venues**, rising rents have forced many smaller and medium-sized places to close or decamp to Brooklyn (especially Williamsburg) and New Jersey. Most of the best performance spaces are still in Manhattan, though; there's a large cluster of exceptionally good venues in the East Village and Lower East Side.

Large venues

Hammerstein Ballroom 311 W 34th St, between Eighth and Ninth aves ⓣ212/564-4882, ⓦwww.mcstudios.com. Subway A, C, E to 34th St. This grand 1906 building has seen many incarnations: it's been an opera house, a vaudeville hall and a Masonic temple, and it now hosts indie and rock bands. Capacity is 3600, but the sound system and acoustics are of high enough quality that most seats are pretty good. Tickets $50 and up.

Madison Square Garden Seventh Ave, at W 32nd St ⓣ212/465-6741, ⓦwww.thegarden.com. Subway A, C, E, #1, #2, #3 to 34th St. New York's principal big stage, the *Garden* hosts not only hockey and basketball games but also a good portion of the stadium rock and pop acts that visit the city. Seating capacity is 20,000-plus, so the arena's not exactly the most soulful place to see a band – but for big names, it's the handiest option.

Radio City Music Hall 1260 Sixth Ave, at 50th St ⓣ212/247-4777, ⓦwww.radiocity.com. Subway B, D, F, M to 47–50th St. Not the prime venue it once was; it occasionally hosts a terrific concert, but for the most part its schedule is clogged with cutesy tribute shows, schlocky musicals and, of course, the "Christmas Spectacular". The acoustics are flawless and the building itself does have a great sense of occasion (see p.131) – it seems to inspire the artists who play here to put on a memorable show.

Mid-sized and small venues

Arlene's Grocery 95 Stanton St, between Ludlow and Orchard sts ⓣ212/473-9831, ⓦwww.arlenesgrocery.net. Subway F to Lower East Side–Second Ave. An intimate, erstwhile *bodega* (hence the name) that hosts nightly gigs by local, reliably good indie bands. Regularly patronized by musicians, talent scouts and open-minded rock fans. Go on Mon nights (free) after 10pm for punk and heavy-metal karaoke, when you can sing along with a live band. Tues–Sun cover $8–10. Daily 5pm–2am.

The Bell House 149 7th St, between Second and Third Aves, Brooklyn ⓣ718/643-6510, ⓦwww.thebellhouseny.com. Subway F, M, G, R to Fourth Ave–9th St. A converted printing house on a bleak stretch in Gowanus provides the setting for indie band performances and wacky events – cook-offs, Burt Reynolds' film celebrations and so on. The front-room bar is a pleasantly spacious place to drink, with happy-hour specials. Shows usually $12–30. Daily 5pm–4am.

The Bitter End 147 Bleecker St, between LaGuardia Place and Thompson St ⓣ212/673-7030, ⓦwww.bitterend.com. Subway A, B, C, D, E, F, M to W 4th St. Young MOR bands in an intimate club setting, mostly folky rockers in the Dylan mould since 1961, though Lady Gaga got started here in 2007. A catalogue of the famous people who've played the club is posted by the door – it's a pretty long list. Cover is usually $8–12, but some gigs are free, and there is a two-drink minimum. Daily 7pm–1am, Mon, Fri & Sat till 4am.

Bowery Ballroom 6 Delancey St, at Bowery ⓣ212/533-2111, ⓦwww.boweryballroom.com. Subway J, Z to Bowery; B, D to Grand St. No attitude, great acoustics and even better views have earned this site praise from both fans and bands. Major labels test their up-and-comers here, so it's a great place to catch the Next Big Thing of any genre. Shows cost $15–55. Pay in cash at the *Mercury Lounge* box office (see below), at the door or by credit card through Ticketweb. Daily from 7pm.

Brooklyn Bowl 61 Wythe Ave, between 11th and 12th sts, Williamsburg, Brooklyn ⓣ718/963-3369, ⓦwww.brooklynbowl.com. Subway L to Bedford Ave. A converted warehouse with live concerts, DJ sets, karaoke, food by the Blue Ribbon group (of Blue Ribbon Sushi and Blue Ribbon Bakery) and … oh yeah, the purported main attraction: bowling (see p.420). Shows usually $5–15, with the odd big name a lot more. Mon–Thurs 6pm–2am,

Fri 6pm–4am, Sat noon–4am, Sun noon–2am.

Cake Shop 152 Ludlow St, between Rivington and Stanton sts ⓣ212/253-0036, ⓦwww.cake-shop.com. Subway F, J, M, Z to Delancey St–Essex St. This unassuming coffee shop and record store becomes one of the city's most cutting-edge venues for indie rock most nights – cover ranges $7–10. Daily 9am–2am, Fri & Sat till 4am.

City Winery 155 Varick St, between Spring and Vandam sts ⓣ212/608-0555, ⓦwww.citywinery.com. Subway #1 to Houston St; C, E to Spring St. Since opening in a converted club space a few years ago, *City Winery* has put a nice roster of rock, folk and roots music performers on its stage; it has full dinner service (food is OK, nothing special) and wine is actually made on the premises. Tickets $12–50.

High Line Ballroom 431 W 16th St, between Ninth and Tenth aves ⓣ212/414-5994, ⓦwww.highlineballroom.com. Subway A, C, E to 14th St. One of the newer venues in town, with table seating available (full dinner if you like) for shows– acts run from indie rock to hip-hop, reggae and big band. DJ sets, too. $10 minimum for table seating during shows.

Irving Plaza 17 Irving Place, at E 15th St ⓣ212/777-6800, ⓦwww.irvingplaza.com. Subway L, N, Q, R, #4, #5, #6 to Union Square. Once home to Off-Broadway musicals (hence the dangling chandeliers and blood-red interior), *Irving Plaza* now features an impressive array of rock, electronic and techno acts. The main room has wildly divergent acoustics; stand toward the back on the ground floor for the truest mix of sound. Tickets usually range $20–50.

Jalopy Theatre and School of Music 315 Columbia St, at Woodhull St ⓣ718/395-3214, ⓦwww.jalopy.biz. Subway F, G to Carroll St. If you want to hear bluegrass, folk or the occasional hard-to-classify musician in a relaxed setting, this tiny instrument shop-cum-venue will be just your speed. Lessons and workshops as well. Most shows $5–15. Mon & Wed–Fri 2pm–2am, Sat & Sun noon–2am.

Knitting Factory 361 Metropolitan Ave, at Havemeyer St, Wiliamsburg ⓣ347/529-6696, ⓦbk.knittingfactory.com. Subway L to Bedford Ave; G, L to Metropolitan Ave. This intimate showcase for indie rock and underground hip-hop moved to Brooklyn in 2009, but has maintained a loyal following and quality acts. Most tickets $5–15.

The Living Room 154 Ludlow St, between Stanton and Rivington sts ⓣ212/533-7235, ⓦwww.livingroomny.com. Subway F, J, M, Z to Delancey St–Essex St. Comfortable couches (hence the name) and a friendly bar make for a relaxed setting in which to hear local, low-key folk and acoustic rock – Nora Jones got her start in music here. Shows usually free (with $5 donation). Daily 6pm–2am, Fri & Sat till 4am.

Mercury Lounge 217 E Houston St, at Essex St ⓣ212/260-7400, ⓦwww.mercuryloungenyc.com. Subway F to Lower East Side–Second Ave. Dark, Lower East Side mainstay featuring a mix of local, national and international rock and pop acts. It's owned by the same crew as the *Bowery Ballroom*, and is similarly used as a trial venue by major labels for up-and-coming artists. Tickets usually $8–15. Daily shows from 7pm.

Music Hall of Williamsburg 66 N 6th St, between Wythe and Kent aves, Williamsburg ⓣ718/486-5400, ⓦwww.musichallofwilliamsburg.com. Subway L to Bedford Ave. A large performance space with excellent acoustics, set in an old factory. One of Brooklyn's really great venues and another in the *Bowery Ballroom* stable – expect the same kind of acts. From 6pm until the opening band starts, all drinks and draft beer are $3. Tickets $10–20.

Pianos 158 Ludlow St, between Stanton and Rivington sts ⓣ212/505-3733, ⓦwww.pianosnyc.com. Subway F, J, M, Z to Delancey St–Essex St. There's no cover to get in the door at this converted piano factory (hence the name), but to get into the tiny back room – where the music is – you'll need to fork out extra ($5–10). The sound system's a standout, and the endless roster of mostly rock bands (expect four choices nightly) means the place is usually packed. Drink prices are somewhat high, and the line to get in habitually long. Daily 3pm–4am.

(Le) Poisson Rouge 158 Bleecker St, at Thompson St ⓣ212/505-3474 ⓦlepoissonrouge.com. Subway A, B, C, D, E, F, M to W 4th St. Mix of live rock, folk, pop and electronica Thurs at 7pm ($10–15), with dance parties most Fri and Sat (often free). Daily 5pm–2am, Fri & Sat till 4am.

Postcrypt Coffeehouse Broadway and 116th St, in the basement of St Paul's Chapel ⓦwww.postcrypt.org. Subway #1 to 116th St. Venerable Columbia student-run folk venue, with hardly any seating but free music and cheap drinks. Fri & Sat 9pm–midnight when school's in session.

Rockwood Music Hall 196 Allen St, between Houston and Stanton sts ⓣ212/477-4155, ⓦwww.rockwoodmusichall.com. Subway F to Lower East Side–Second Ave. Seven nights of live music draw hordes of locals to this tiny space. Though there are no bad seats, it's a good idea to come early – it's often packed. Mon–Thurs 6pm–4am, Fri–Sun 5.30pm–4am.

SOB's (Sounds of Brazil) 204 Varick St, at W Houston ⓣ212/243-4940, ⓦwww.sobs.com. Subway #1 to Houston St. Premier place to hear hip-hop, Brazilian, West Indian, Caribbean and World Music acts within the confines of Manhattan. Vibrant and danceable, with a high quality of music. Shows most nights; ticket prices vary according to the performer. Mon–Thurs hours vary depending on shows, Fri 5pm–4am, Sat 6.30pm–4am, Sun noon–4pm.

Southpaw 125 Fifth Ave, between Sterling Place and St John's Place, Park Slope ⓣ718/230-0236, ⓦwww.spsounds.com. Subway #2, #3 to Bergen St; D, R to Union St. Brooklyn's premier live venue, with 5000 square feet of space and a wide range of acts and DJs from almost every genre. Admission varies but is rarely more than $10–12, while a cab from lower Manhattan costs around $15. Daily 8pm–2am, Fri & Sat till 4am.

Village Underground 130 W 3rd St, at Sixth Ave ⓣ212/777-7745, ⓦwww.thevillageunderground.com. Subway A, B, C, D, E, F, M to W 4th St. Tiny basement performance space that is one of the most intimate and innovative clubs around. Mon is jam-session night, the house band (playing vintage rock and R&B, funk and reggae) holds court Wed–Fri, and Tues & Sat are club nights (all from 8.30pm). Cover $7–15.

Jazz

Jazz in New York has seen a major resurgence since the 1990s. You'll find the best clubs in the **West Village** and particularly **Harlem**, where a host of small, intimate venues showcase a variety of local talent, from Hammond-organ players to Afro-beat performers. Midtown venues have also steadily been improving in quality and there are a few decent places in **Chelsea** and the **East Village**.

To find out **who's playing**, check the usual sources, notably the *Village Voice* (ⓦwww.villagevoice.com) and *Time Out New York* (ⓦwww.timeoutny.com); other good jazz rags are the monthlies *Hothouse* (ⓦwww.hothousejazz.com), a free magazine available at venues and hotels, and *Down Beat* (ⓦwww.downbeat.com).

Price policies vary from club to club; the major places that attract famous performers charge a hefty cover ($20–50) and a minimum for food and drinks. Smaller venues (especially in Harlem) come cheaper; some have neither admission fee nor minimum drink charge.

Harlem jazz venues

Bill's Place 148 West 133rd St, between Malcolm X and Powell Blvds ⓣ212/281-0777, ⓦwww.billsaxton.com. Subway #2, #3 to 135th St. Showcase for local star saxophonist Bill Saxton, hosted in an old speakeasy on what was Jungle Alley; he performs Fri only, at 10pm and midnight ($15, BYOB).

Cotton Club 656 W 125th St, at Twelfth Ave ⓣ212/663-7980, ⓦwww.cottonclub-newyork.com. Subway #1 to 125th St. No relation to the famous original (this version opened in 1977), it packs in the tourists nonetheless with the Cotton Club All Stars knocking out swing, blues and jazz classics Thurs–Sat from 8pm ($48, including buffet dinner). Sat & Sun afternoon shows (with buffet) are $35, and Mon is swing dance night ($20).

FB Lounge Bar 172 E 106th St, between Lexington and Third aves ⓣ212/410-7292. Subway #6 to 103rd St. Spanish Harlem hangout (across the street from *Fonda Boricua*) best known for its sizzling Latin Jazz performances. Thurs–Sat 5pm–2am.

Lenox Lounge **288 Malcolm X Blvd, at 124th St ⓣ212/427-0253, ⓦwww.lenoxlounge.com. Subway #2, #3 to 125th St.** Entertaining Harlem since 1939, this renovated, historic jazz lounge has an over-the-top Art Deco interior (check out the Zebra Room) and features three sets nightly. Cover $25, with a $16 drink minimum at weekends; you're paying for the historic atmosphere as much as the music. Daily noon–4am.

Minton's Playhouse **206–210 W 118th St, between St Nicholas Ave and Powell Blvd ⓣ212/864-8346, ⓦmintonsuptown.com. Subway B, C, #2, #3 to 116th St.** The birthplace of bebop reopened in 2006, and though it's not the same without Dizzy, Bird and Thelonius Monk, the atmosphere remains (look for the famous mural behind the bandstand), and Tues nights often feature Omar Edwards, the famous tap dancer from the Apollo. Mon–Sat 5.30pm–4am (cover Mon–Fri $5, Sat $10).

Showman's Café **375 W 125th St, at Morningside Ave ⓣ212-864-8941. Subway A, B, C, D at 125th St.** This small, long-established blues, jazz and gospel-music haunt (since 1942) is often packed with Harlemites and, increasingly, tourists – one of only two joints featuring a real Hammond organ. Jazz shows Tues–Thurs 8.30pm, Fri and Sat 10.30pm; $5 cover Fri & Sat. Mon–Sat 1pm–4am.

Shrine Bar **2271 Powell Blvd, between 133rd and 134th sts ⓣ212/690-7807, ⓦwww.shrinenyc.com. Subway B, #2, #3 to 135th St.** Named for Fela Kuti's legendary joint in Lagos, this cosy bar and performance space features African decor and walls lined with album sleeves. The focus here is on World Music (note the United World Music sign at the front), but the jazz open-mic sessions on Sun (1pm) are a great time. Shows start at 6pm most nights, and there's flavoursome Israeli and West African food from the owners. Daily 4pm–4am.

St Nick's Pub **773 St. Nicholas Ave, at 149th St ⓣ212/690-7807, ⓦwww.stnicksjazzpub.net. Subway A, B, C, D to 145th St.** This small basement is one of Harlem's top jazz venues, dating back to 1930, with jumpin' live shows six nights a week from 10pm (7pm weekends) – no cover ($3 for a table seat); recent regular performers have included multi-instrumentalist and vocalist Atiba Kwabena-Wilson. Mon–Thurs 1pm–3am, Fri & Sat 4pm–4am.

West Village jazz venues

Bar Next Door **129 MacDougal St, between 3rd and 4th sts ⓣ212/529-5945, ⓦlalanternacaffe.com. Subway A, B, C, D, E, F, M to W 4th St.** Great underground venue, with live sets Mon–Thurs & Sun 6pm–2am, Fri & Sat 6pm–3am. Cover $12 and one drink.

Blue Note **131 W 3rd St, between Sixth Ave and MacDougal St ⓣ212/475-8592, ⓦwww.bluenotejazz.com. Subway A, B, C, D, E, F, M to W 4th St; #1 to Christopher St.** Open since 1981 (and unrelated to the record label), this jazz institution regularly hosts top international performers, with the likes of Sarah Vaughan, Dizzy Gillespie and Oscar Peterson making lauded appearances over the years. Tickets usually range $15–25. Daily 6pm–1am, Fri & Sat till 3am.

Village Vanguard **178 Seventh Ave, between Perry and 11th sts ⓣ212/255-4037, ⓦwww.villagevanguard.com. Subway #1, #2, #3 to 14th St.** An NYC jazz landmark, the *Village Vanguard* celebrated its seventieth anniversary in 2005. There's a regular diet of big names. Cover is $35, including a $10 drink minimum (Mon $30). Cash only. Daily 8pm–1am.

Zinc Bar **82 W 3rd St, between Thompson and Sullivan sts ⓣ212/477-8337, ⓦwww.zincbar.com. Subway A, B, C, D, E, F, M to W 4th St.** Great jazz venue with strong drinks and a loyal bunch of regulars. The blackboard above the entrance announces the evening's featured band. Cover is $10 with a one-drink minimum (two at the tables). Hosts both new talent and established greats, with an emphasis on Latin American rhythms. Daily 6pm–2.30am, Sat & Sun till 3am.

Other jazz venues

Birdland **315 W 44th St, at Ninth Ave ⓣ212/581-3080, ⓦwww.birdlandjazz.com. Subway A, C, E to 42nd St.** Not the original place where Charlie Parker played, but nonetheless an established supper club that hosts some big names. Sets nightly at 9pm and 11pm. Music charge of $20–50; at a table, you'll need to spend a minimum of $10 or more on food or drink, while at the bar, the cover includes your first drink. Daily 5pm–1am.

Café Carlyle ***Carlyle Hotel*****, 35 E 76th St, at Madison Ave ⓣ212/744-1600, ⓦwww.thecarlyle.com. Subway #6 to 77th St.** This intimate, dressy spot was home to legendary crooner Bobby Short, and Woody Allen still plays clarinet here most Mon nights in spring, fall and winter; it's a chic, Upper East Side scene, and well worth the ticket price – $30–60 cover, no minimum. Mon–Sat 6.30pm–midnight.

Iridium Jazz Club 1650 Broadway, at W 51st St ☎212/582-2121, ⓦwww.iridiumjazzclub.com. Subway #1 to 50th St. Contemporary jazz performed seven nights a week amid Surrealist decor described as "Dolly meets Disney". The late godfather of electric guitar, Les Paul, once played weekly, and the current weekly tribute honours him. Cover $25–50, $10 food and drink minimum; Sun jazz brunch. Daily 8pm–midnight.

Jazz at Lincoln Center 33 W 60th St, at Columbus Circle ☎212/258-9800, ⓦwww.jalc.org. Subway #1, A, B, C, D to 59th St. There are three different spaces at this venue, but the 140-seater *Dizzy's Club Coca-Cola* has the best shows, panoramic views and a speakeasy-style atmosphere – the food is great also. Wynton Marsalis performed during the 2009–2010 season. Cover varies, usually $20–35. Daily 6pm–1am, Fri & Sat till 2.30am.

Louis 649 649 E 9th St, between aves B and C ☎212/673-1190. Subway L to First Ave; #6 to Astor Place. With no cover and live performances seven nights a week, *Louis 649* is a must if you love jazz. Mon and Thurs are lively, and weekends get downright hectic. They serve gourmet bottled beer and a number of excellent vintages but no cocktails. Daily 6pm–4am.

Smoke 2751 Broadway, at 106th St ☎212/864-6662, ⓦwww.smokejazz.com. Subway #1 to 103rd St. This Upper West Side joint is a real neighbourhood treat, with plush couches, lavish chandeliers and a retro, upscale feel. Sets start at 9pm, 11pm and 12.30am. Cover varies. Mon–Fri 2pm–3am, Sat & Sun 10am–3am.

Nightclubs

New York's **nightclubs** have had a hard time over the last decade, with a series of crackdowns limiting the dance scene and a small group of over-priced bottle-service establishments catering to the rich and famous. You'll find the action spread out across the city, with the Lower East Side, Tribeca, the East and West Village and even Brooklyn offering as many venues as the Meatpacking District, now the city's premier, if slightly overrated, nightlife hub. The really cutting-edge stuff is hard to find out about for casual visitors: Brooklyn's impromptu **warehouse party** scene has really taken off in the past few years, while some of the best nights are organized by outfits such as **Blackmarket Membership** (ⓦblkmarketmembership.com; $15–20; you have to RSVP to find the location), ReSolute (ⓦwww.resolutenyc.com) and Wolf and Lamb (see below).

In terms of what you can expect to find at a club, New York's DJs rely on a varied diet of **house music, electro-house and techno**, though there's a growing cadre of inventive hip-hop, retro soul, indie rock and Latin-jazz venues. Regarding **dress codes**, New York is a casual kind of town where clubs are concerned – unless noted in our reviews, you can usually turn up in smart-casual dress and be fine.

Below is a list of the current hot venues. It's important to check up-to-date info with one of the free magazine/newspapers like the *Village Voice*, or pick up a copy of *Time Out New York*. Fliers are always the best way to hear about the latest night-spots: see the list of record stores on p.408 for places to pick them up.

Apt 419 W 13th St, at Ninth Ave ☎212/414-4245, ⓦwww.aptwebsite.com. Subway L to Eighth Ave; A, C, E to 14th St. Hidden behind an unmarked doorway, this bar/club is known for its inventive, eclectic DJ roster (including iPod-powered DIY nights). There are two spaces: a lounge-like upstairs room and a sleek, wood-panelled downstairs bar. Cover $10. Mon & Sun 9pm–4am, Tues–Sat 7pm–4am.

bOb Bar 233 Eldridge St, between Houston and Stanton St. Subway F to Lower East Side–Second Ave. This cosy bar turns into one of the best dance parties in town after midnight, with DJs spinning a mix of hip-hop, reggae and R&B. Daily 7pm–4am.

Cielo 18 Little W 12th St, at Ninth Ave ⓣ212/645-5700, ⓦwww.cieloclub.com. Subway L to Eighth Ave; A, C, E to 14th St. Expect velvet rope-burn at this super-exclusive see-and-be-seen place: there's only room for 250 people. Though run by Nicolas Matar, a former DJ at Ibiza's legendary *Pacha* club, it's the Mon-night reggae and dub party Deep Space from François K that most people talk about. Best sound system in the city. Cover $20. Mon & Wed–Sat 10pm–4am.

Don Hill's 511 Greenwich St, at Spring St ⓣ212/219-2850, ⓦwww.donhills.com. Subway #1 to Houston St. Some of the most diverse parties in the city happen here, where live bands (mostly indie and punk) warm up the crowd before the real stars – the DJs – take to the stage. Cover $5–15. Daily 7pm–2am, Thurs–Sat till 4am.

Love 40 W 8th St, at MacDougal St ⓣ212/477-5683, ⓦwww.musicislove.net. Subway A, B, C, D, E, F, M to W 4th St. This West Village club hosts some of the hottest nights in the city, from drum and bass to house and hip-hop, with an awesome sound system and a regular line-up of top international DJs – check the website first, though, to see what's on. Cover is usually $15. Wed–Sun 10pm–4am.

The Lounge at the Marcy Hotel 108 Marcy Ave at S 2nd St, Williamsburg ⓣ212/477-5683, ⓦwww.wolflambmusic.com. Subway J, M, Z to Marcy Ave. Happening DJ duo Wolf & Lamb run club nights at this hip hangout for Brooklyn cool kids. Cover is usually $10–20 (check website for upcoming events).

Pacha 618 W 46th St ⓣ212/209-7500, ⓦwww.pachanyc.com. Subway A, C, E to 42nd St. The New York outpost of the chain of Ibiza superclubs. Sprawling over 30,000 square feet, and featuring a spine-tingling high-tech sound system, three floors, palm trees and mosaic mirrors, this is the place for a big, corporate club experience, and a generally non-local clientele – expect large, sweaty crowds. Cover $30–40. Fri & Sat 10pm–6am.

Pyramid Club 101 Ave A, between E 6th and 7th sts ⓣ212/228-4888, ⓦthepyramidclub.com. Subway L to First Ave; #6 to Astor Place. This small club has been an East Village standby for years. Mon is drum and bass ($5–10), Tues is an open-mike music competition ($5–10), but it's the insanely popular 1980s Dance Party on Thurs that is not to be missed ($6). Mon 11pm–4am, Tues & Sun 9pm–1am, Thurs & Sat 9pm–4am, Fri 10pm–4am.

Santos Party House 96 Lafayette St, at Walker St ⓣ212/584-5492 ⓦsantospartyhouse.com. Subway, J, N, Q, R, Z, #6 to Canal St. Current trend-setter, with wild hip-hop, Latin and house parties most nights; hosts lauded Danny Krivits 718 sessions (check the website). Cover usually $15. Daily 7pm–4am.

Sapphire Lounge 249 Eldridge St, at Houston St ⓣ212/777-5153, ⓦwww.sapphirenyc.com. Subway F to Lower East Side–Second Ave. DJ bar and lounge, with an arty, sleazy, sexy vibe, created by the dark lights and enhanced by the moody Lower East Side regulars. The programming is inventive, offering music of almost every genre on different nights, from reggae to hip-hop to breakbeat – as a plus, it's open every night of the week, and the cover is usually minimal ($5). Daily 7pm–4am.

Stanton Public 17 Stanton St, between Bowery and Chrystie St, ⓦwww.stantonpublic.com. Subway F to Lower East Side–Second Ave. Another bar doubling as indie dance club, with DJs spinning Brit Pop Sat nights, 1980s, punk, electro and indie on Fri, with two floors and over seventeen beers on tap. Happy hour 4–8pm, and entry is normally free. Mon–Fri 4pm–4am, Sat 2pm–4am, Sun 3pm–4am.

Sullivan Room 218 Sullivan St, between W 3rd St and Bleecker St ⓣ212/252-2151, ⓦwww.sullivanroom.com. Subway A, B, C, D, E, F, M to W 4th St. Hidden basement club for serious dancing, popular with students from nearby NYU. The only downside: two bathrooms for the whole place. Cover $10–25. Thurs–Sat 10pm–5am.

27

Performing arts and film

"**Performing arts**" is really an all-encompassing title for New York's legion of cultural offerings. While many travellers tend automatically to think of the glittery Broadway productions housed in and around Times Square, locals will inform you that such a heading also includes more experimental Off-Broadway theatre companies, as well as comedy clubs, cabarets, dance troupes and the opera, to name but a few of the city's options.

Prices for live performances vary wildly: expect to shell out $150 for a night at the opera, while Shakespeare is performed for free in Central Park every summer. The high prices of many shows can be off-putting; see the box on p.366 for some tips on how to see Broadway blockbusters on a budget.

The silver screen is just as important a part of New York's arts scene as its live performances are. New York gets the first run of most American **films** as well as many foreign ones, often long before they open in Europe (or the rest of America). There's also a very healthy arthouse and revival scene.

Listings for the arts can be found in a number of places. The most useful sources are the clear and comprehensive listings in *Time Out New York* magazine, the free *New York Press* and the "Voice Choices" section of the free *Village Voice*. Fancier events are usually touted in *New York* magazine's "Agenda" section, "Goings On About Town" in the *New Yorker*, and both Friday's "Weekend" and Sunday's "Arts and Leisure" sections of the *New York Times*. You'll find specific Broadway listings in the free *Official Broadway Theater Guide*, available at theatre and hotel lobbies.

If you want to plan your itinerary before you leave home, websites such as Ⓦwww.newyork.citysearch.com and www.timeoutny.com have information on arts events in New York. You can also check the useful sites Ⓦwww.nytheatre.com, www.broadway.com, and www.offbroadway.com for up-to-date info on both major Broadway shows and local theatre listings. The best sites from which to purchase tickets are Ⓦwww.telecharge.com and www.ticketmaster.com.

Theatre

Theatre venues in the city are referred to as being "**Broadway**," "**Off-Broadway**" or "**Off-Off-Broadway**". These groupings don't necessarily mean a theatre's address is physically on or off Broadway; instead they represent a descending order of ticket prices, production polish, elegance and comfort. In theory at least, the

Buying your tickets

Tickets for Broadway shows can cost as much as $125 for orchestra seats at the hottest shows, and as little as $25 for day-of-performance rush tickets (often standing room only) for some of the long-runners; check listings magazines for availability. Off-Broadway's best seats are cheaper than those on Broadway, averaging $30–70. Off-Off-Broadway tickets should rarely set you back more than $25.

The best places to go for bargains are the **TKTS booths** (ⓦwww.tdf.org), which offer cut-rate, day-of-performance tickets for many Broadway and Off-Broadway shows. Expect to pay half the face value, plus a $2.50 service charge (cash or travellers' cheques only). The booth at Duffy Square, located at Broadway between 45th and 47th streets is open Mon, Thurs & Fri 3–8pm, Tues 2–8pm, Wed & Sat 10am–2pm (for matinees) & 3–8pm, Sun 11am–7pm; there's another outlet near the South Street Seaport at the corner of Front and Water streets (near the rear of 199 Water St) and one in Downtown Brooklyn at 1 Metro Tech Center, open Tues–Sat 11am–6pm.

If you're prepared to pay full price for tickets, you can, of course, go directly to the theatre (or the theatre website) or call one of the following **ticket sales agencies**. **Telecharge** (ⓣ1-800/432-7250 or 212/239-6200, ⓦwww.telecharge.com) and **Ticketmaster** (ⓣ1-800/755-4000 or 212/307-4100, ⓦwww.ticketmaster.com) sell Broadway tickets over the phone; note that no show is represented by both these agencies. **Ticket Central at Playwrights Horizon Theater**, 416 W 42nd St, between Ninth and Tenth avenues (ⓣ212/279-4200, ⓦwww.playwrighthorizons.org; daily noon–8pm) sells tickets to many Off-Broadway theatres. Expect a $5–7 surcharge per ticket. When buying tickets, always ask where your seats are located, as once you get to the theatre and find yourself in the last row of the balcony, it's too late (for most seating plans, check ⓦwww.playbill.com).

further off-Broadway and down the price scale you go, the more innovative productions are.

Although **Broadway** shows have diversified somewhat of late, they remain predominantly grandiose tourist-magnet musicals, packing in the biggest crowds and boasting the biggest-name stars. Musical adaptations of movies and revivals of well-known oldies tend to be the flavours of the month. The majority of Broadway theatres are located in the blocks just east or west of Broadway (the avenue) between 41st and 53rd streets, conveniently near the larger Times Square tourist hotels.

A bit less glitzy is **Off-Broadway**, the best place to discover new talent and adventurous new American drama and musicals. Off-Broadway theatres are home to lower-budget social and political dramas, satire, ethnic plays and repertory – in other words, anything that can make money without having to fill a huge hall each night (most of these seat between 100 and 500). Lower operating costs also mean that Off-Broadway often serves as a forum to try out what sometimes ends up as a big Broadway production.

Off-Off-Broadway is the fringe of New York's theatre world. Off-Off venues (often with fewer than 100 seats) aren't bound by union regulations to use professional actors, and shows range from shoestring productions of the classics to outrageous and experimental performance art. Prices range from free to cheap, and the quality can vary from execrable to electrifying. Frankly, there's a lot more of the former than the latter, so it's best to use weekly reviews as your guide.

We've picked out a smattering of reliable Off- and Off-Off venues (the Broadway theatres generally book whatever shows they can, and therefore don't offer a consistent type of production).

Off-Broadway

Astor Place Theater 434 Lafayette St, at Astor Place ⓣ212/254-4370, ⓦwww.blueman.com. Subway #6 to Astor Place; N, R to 8th St–NYU. Showcase for exciting work since the 1960s, when Sam Shepard's *The Unseen Hand* and *Forensic and the Navigators* had the playwright himself playing drums in the lobby. For the last fifteen years, however, the theatre has been the home of the comically absurd but very popular performance artists Blue Man Group.

Atlantic Theater Company 336 W 20th St, at Eighth Ave ⓣ212/645-8015, ⓦwww.atlantictheater.org. Subway C, E to 23rd St; #1 to 18th St. As you'd expect from a theatre founded by David Mamet and William H. Macy, this place is known for accessible, intelligent productions of modern dramatic classics, works by everyone from Harold Pinter to Martin McDonagh. The ATC also runs an acting school nearby on 16th St, and you can sometimes catch student performances here too.

Barrow Street Theatre 27 Barrow St, at Seventh Ave S ⓣ212/243-6262, ⓦwww.barrowstreettheatre.com. Subway A, B, C, D, E, F, M to W 4th St; #1 to Christopher St. This small theatre inside a landmark West Village building was once the long-term home of Off-Broadway favourite the Drama Dept. That company has been replaced by a more profit-minded organization, which is generating artistically excellent but more commercially viable productions.

Brooklyn Academy of Music 30 Lafayette Ave, Brooklyn ⓣ718/636-4100, ⓦwww.bam.org. Subway B, D, N, Q, R, #2, #3, #4, #5 to Atlantic Ave–Pacific St. Despite its name, Brooklyn Academy of Music (usually referred to as BAM) regularly presents theatrical productions on its three stages, often touring shows from Europe and Asia. Every autumn BAM puts on the Next Wave festival of large-scale performance art (see p.225). Not so much Off-Broadway as Off-Manhattan, but well worth the trip.

New World Stages 340 W 50th St, between Eighth and Ninth aves ⓣ212/239-6200, ⓦwww.newworldstages.com. Subway C, E to 50th St. Five stages, actually, with good sightlines, ranging in size from 200 to 500 seats. Several productions that debuted here have grown into small-scale hits.

New York City Center 131 W 55th St, at Seventh Ave ⓣ212/581-1212, ⓦwww.citycenter.org. Subway B, D, E to Seventh Ave; F to 57th St. This large, midtown venue is best known for its Encores! series. These readings and studio performances usually run for one weekend only, and are designed to revive long-forgotten or overlooked musicals, from Gilbert & Sullivan to modern dance. It's also home to the Manhattan Theatre Club (ⓦwww.mtc-nyc.org), which deals in serious new theatre featuring major American actors. Many productions eventually transfer to Broadway; see them here first, though prices aren't that much cheaper.

Orpheum Theater 126 Second Ave, between 7th St and St Mark's Place ⓣ212/477-2477. Subway #6 to Astor Place. One of the East Village's biggest theatres, once known for hosting David Mamet and other influential new American shows, but more recently the home of the percussion group Stomp. Wheelchair-accessible.

Playwrights Horizons 416 W 42nd St, at Ninth Ave ⓣ212/564-1235, ⓦwww.playwrightshorizons.org. Subway A, C, E, N, Q, R, S, #1, #2, #3 to 42nd St. This well-respected drama-centric space is located smack in the centre of Times Square, though its mission remains the same as it was when it was founded in a YMCA in 1971 – championing works by undiscovered playwrights. They also get top-line actors.

▲ Brooklyn Academy of Music

The Public Theater 425 Lafayette St ⓣ212/539-8500, ⓦwww.publictheater.org. Subway #6 to Astor Place. Founded by Broadway legend Joe Papp as the Shakespeare Workshop, The Public Theater is the city's primary presenter of the Bard's plays. In the summer, the Public produces the free Shakespeare in the Park series at the open-air Delacorte Theater in Central Park (see p.159). For most of the year, though, this major Off-Broadway institution delivers thought-provoking and challenging productions from new, mostly American, writers.

Vivian Beaumont Theater and the Mitzi E. Newhouse Theater Lincoln Center, Broadway, at W 65th St ⓣ212/362-7600, ⓦwww.lct.org. Subway #1 to 66th St. Technically Broadway theatres, these stages are far enough away from Times Square in distance and, usually, quality, to qualify as Off. A great place to see stimulating new work by playwrights like Tom Stoppard and John Guare.

Westside Theatre 407 W 43rd St, between Ninth and Tenth aves ⓣ212/315-2244, ⓦwww.westsidetheatre.com. Subway A, C, E to 42nd St. Two small theatres, known for productions of Shaw, Wilde and Pirandello. The downstairs one has wheelchair access.

Off-Off-Broadway and performance-art spaces

Dixon Place 161A Chrystie St, between Rivington and Delancey sts ⓣ212/219-0736, ⓦwww.dixonplace.org. Subway B, D to Grand St; F to Second Ave; J to Bowery. Very popular small venue dedicated to experimental theatre, dance and literary readings.

The Drilling Company 107 W 82nd St ⓣ212/877-0099, ⓦwww.drillingcompany.org. Subway B, C to 81st St. Third home of Lower East Side performance group, formerly known as Ludlow Ten, that's best known for producing the summer-long Shakespeare in the Park(ing Lot) series of free performances at the Municipal Parking Lot at Broome and Ludlow.

The Flea 41 White St, at Church St ⓣ212/226-2407, ⓦwww.theflea.org. Subway #1 to Franklin St; N, Q, R to Canal St. Cutting-edge drama space run by Jim Simpson, Sigourney Weaver's husband. The programme stretches from performance art and drama to acrobatics. Though many of the actors here are not professionals, the quality remains impressively high.

Franklin Furnace Archive 80 Hanson Place #301, at Portland Ave, Brooklyn ⓣ718/398-7255, ⓦwww.franklinfurnace.org. An archive dedicated to installation work and performance art, the Franklin Furnace has launched the careers of performers as celebrated and notorious as Karen Finley and Eric Bogosian. Performances take place at various downtown locations – check the website or call for updated schedules.

Here 145 Sixth Ave, at Spring St ⓣ212/647-0202, ⓦwww.here.org. Subway C, E to Spring St. A very open-minded, intriguing space supporting experimental fare from both new artists and established performers like Suzanne Vega. Puppetry and performance art are special strengths.

Kraine 85 E 4th St, between Second and Third aves ⓣ212/777-6088, ⓦwww.horsetrade.info. Subway F to Second Ave. This 99-seat East Village theatre is home to twelve different residential companies and is mostly known for presenting unusual comedies. Another plus for this budget space is the raked seating, which makes for good sightlines. It's in the basement of the same building as artsy *KGB*, a bar known for its author readings (see p.349).

La Mama E.T.C. (Experimental Theater Club) 74A E 4th St, at Second Ave ⓣ212/475-7710, ⓦwww.lamama.org. Subway F to Second Ave. The mother of all Off-Off venues, founded fifty years ago. A real gem with four different auditoria, La Mama is known for politically and sexually charged material as well as visiting dance troupes from overseas. For raw amateur performances, check out The Galleria space a few blocks away.

New York Theater Workshop 79 E 4th St, at Second Ave ⓣ212/460-5475, ⓦwww.nytw.org. Subway F to Second Ave. An eminent experimental workshop that often chooses cult hit shows and has presented plays by Tony Kushner, Susan Sontag and Paul Rudnick; best known these days as the place the global musical mega-hit *Rent* was first shown to the public.

Performing Garage 33 Wooster St, at Grand St ⓣ212/966-3651, ⓦwww.thewoostergroup.org. Subway A, C, E to Canal St. The famous Wooster Group (which includes Willem Dafoe) performs regularly in this Soho space. Tickets are like gold dust (very hard to come by), but the effort to find them is worth it.

P.S. 122 150 First Ave, at 9th St ⓣ212/477-5829, ⓦwww.ps122.org. Subway #6 to Astor Place; L to First Ave; F to Second Ave. A converted school in the East Village that is perennially popular for its jam-packed schedule of revolutionary performance art, dance and one-person shows in its two theatres.

St Ann's Warehouse 38 Water St, Brooklyn ⓣ718/254-8779, ⓦwww.stannswarehouse.org. Subway A, C to High St; F to York St. Housed in a hulking industrial space down in DUMBO, St Ann's is consistently impressive for both drama and music – there are Broadway tryouts here and musicians like Lou Reed often play private sets. There's also a café and gallery space in the entrance.

Theater for the New City 155 First Ave, at 10th St ⓣ212/254-1109, ⓦwww.theaterforthenewcity.net. Subway #6 to Astor Place; L to First Ave; F to Second Ave. This major performance venue is best known as the site where Sam Shepard's Pulitzer Prize-winning *Buried Child* premiered in 1978. It's still churning out fine drama through its emerging-playwrights programme. TNC also performs outdoors for free at a variety of venues throughout the summer and hosts the Lower East Side Festival of the Arts at the end of May.

Tribeca Performing Arts Center 199 Chambers St, at Greenwich St ⓣ212/220-1460, ⓦwww.tribecapac.org. Subway #1, #2, #3 to Chambers St. TriPac, as it's known, is owned by Manhattan Community College, a fact reflected in its programming: mostly high-end local theatre and dance groups, plus kids' workshops and multicultural events. It's also known for fine jazz performances.

Classical music and opera

New Yorkers take their **classical music and opera** seriously. Long queues form for anything popular, many concerts sell out, and summer evenings can see a quarter of a million people turning up in Central Park for free performances by the New York Philharmonic. Tickets can be somewhat easier to come by for performances by the city's top-notch chamber-music ensembles (most of the patrons are members of the city's geriatric crowd).

Opera venues

David H Koch Theater Lincoln Center, 65th St, at Columbus Ave ⓣ212/870-5570, ⓦwww.nycopera.com. Subway #1 to 66th St. This is where the New York City Opera plays David to the Met's Goliath. Its wide and adventurous programme varies wildly in quality depending on the production (check out a *NY Times* review before purchasing) – some quite creative, others boringly mediocre – but seats go for less than half the Met's prices.

Dicapo Opera Theatre 184 E 76th St, between Lexington and Third aves ⓣ212/288-9438, ⓦwww.dicapo.com. Subway #6 to 77th St. A full season of performances (Sept–April/May; $50) with a programme of child-friendly opera recitals as well ($10 for kids, $20 for adults).

Juilliard School 60 Lincoln Center Plaza, at 65th St ⓣ212/799-5000, ⓦwww.juilliard.edu. Subway #1 to 66th St. Located right next door to the Met (see opposite), Juilliard students often perform under the direction of a famous conductor, usually for low ticket prices.

Metropolitan Opera House Lincoln Center, Columbus Ave, at 64th St ⓣ212/362-6000, ⓦwww.metoperafamily.org. Subway #1 to 66th St. More popularly known as the Met, New York's premier opera venue is home to the world-renowned Metropolitan Opera Company from September to late April. Tickets are expensive (up to $295) and can be well-nigh impossible to snag, though 175 ($20) standing-room tickets go on sale 10am on day of performance and "rush-tickets" for orchestra seats ($20) go on sale at 6pm. The limit is one ticket per person, and the queue has been known to form at dawn.

Concert halls

92nd Street Y Kaufman Concert Hall 1395 Lexington Ave, at 92nd St ⓣ212/996-1100, ⓦwww.92y.org. Subway #4, #5, #6 to 86th St; #6 to 96th St. This wood-panelled space is especially welcoming since performers are usually available to chat or mingle with the audience after shows. Great line-up of chamber music and solo events.

Alice Tully Hall Lincoln Center, Broadway and W 65th St ⓣ212/671-4050, ⓦnewlincolncenter.org. Subway #1 to 66th St. A smaller Lincoln Center hall for the top chamber orchestras, string quartets and instrumentalists. The weekend chamber series are deservedly popular, though the crowd is composed almost exclusively of the 65-and-over set. Tickets for performances vary greatly ($15–100).

Avery Fisher Hall Lincoln Center, Broadway and W 65th St ⓣ212/875-5030, ⓦnewlincolncenter.org or ⓦnyphil.org. Subway #1 to 66th St. The permanent home of the New York Philharmonic. Ticket prices for the Philharmonic range $29–109. The open rehearsals (9.45am on concert days) are a great bargain; tickets are $16. Avery Fisher also hosts the very popular annual Mostly Mozart Festival in August.

Bargemusic Fulton Ferry Landing, Brooklyn ⓣ718/624-4061 or 2083, ⓦwww.bargemusic.org. Subway A, C to High St; F to York St. Chamber music in a wonderful river setting on a moving barge below the Brooklyn Bridge. Wed–Sat 8pm, Sun 3pm. Tickets are $35–40, $15–20 for full-time students.

Brooklyn Academy of Music 30 Lafayette Ave, Brooklyn ⓣ718/636-4100, ⓦwww.bam.org. Subway #2, #3, #4, #5, N, R to Atlantic Ave. The BAM Opera House is the perennial home of Philip Glass operatic premieres and Laurie Anderson performances. It also hosts a number of contemporary imports from European and Chinese companies, often with a large modern-dance component.

Carnegie Hall 154 W 57th St, at Seventh Ave ⓣ212/247-7800, ⓦwww.carnegiehall.org. Subway N, Q, R to 57th St–Seventh Ave. The greatest names from all schools of music have performed here, from Tchaikovsky (who conducted the hall's inaugural concert) to Toscanini to Gershwin to Billie Holiday. The tradition continues, and the stunning acoustics – said to be the best in the world – lure big-time performers at sky-high prices. Check the website for up-to-date admission rates and schedules. To learn more about the building itself, head to the Rose Museum on the 2nd floor or take a tour (see p.151).

Cathedral of St John the Divine 1047 Amsterdam Ave, at 112th St ⓣ212/316-7490, ⓦwww.stjohndivine.org. Subway B, C, #1 to 110th St. A magnificent Morningside Heights setting that hosts occasional classical and New Age performances. Also home to the Early Music Foundation (ⓦwww.earlymusicny.org), which performs scores from the eleventh to the eighteenth centuries.

Lehman Center for the Performing Arts 250 Bedford Park Blvd, Bronx ⓣ718/960-8833, ⓦwww.lehmancenter.org. Subway D, #4 to Bedford Park. First-class concert hall that puts on an array of performances: modern ballet, gospel, funk, oldies and major international names.

Merkin Concert Hall 129 W 67th St, at Broadway ⓣ212/501-3330, ⓦwww.merkinconcerthall.org. Subway #1 to 66th St. This intimate and adventurous venue in the Elaine Kaufman Cultural Center is a great place to hear music of any kind. Plays host to the New York Guitar Festival in January.

Symphony Space 2537 Broadway, at 95th St ⓣ212/864-5400, ⓦwww.symphonyspace.org. Subway #1, #2, #3 to 96th St. The Symphony Space has a varied performance schedule, from "ground-breaking, style-crashing" new classical to jazz and even the odd rock event.

Town Hall 123 W 43rd St, at Sixth Ave ⓣ212/840-2824, ⓦwww.the-townhall-nyc.org.

▲ Carnegie Hall

Subway B, D, F, M to 42nd St. This midtown hall has an unusual history: it was designed by Stanford White (the mastermind of the original Madison Square Garden) and commissioned by suffragettes as a protest-friendly space. One of the egalitarian innovations in the design was the omission of any box seats in order to provide better acoustics and sightlines from every seat in the house. As for programming, it's got an eclectic policy – from Broadway celebrations and folk singers to Cole Porter tributes and klezmer music.

Dance

Dance – especially experimental or avant-garde performance – is quite popular in New York. The city has five major ballet companies, dozens of modern troupes and untold thousands of soloists; all performances are listed in broadly the same periodicals and websites as music and theatre, though you might also want to pick up *Dance Magazine* (Ⓦwww.dancemagazine.com) for extra specifics. The official dance season runs from September to January and April to June.

The following is a list of some of the major dance venues in the city, though a lot of the smaller, more esoteric companies and solo dancers also perform at spaces like Dixon Place and P.S.122, listed on p.369 under Off-Off Broadway. Dance fans should also note that the annual week-long Dance on Camera Festival (Ⓣ212/727-0764, Ⓦwww.dancefilmsassn.org) of dance films takes place at the Walter Reade Theater at Lincoln Center in January.

92nd Street Y Harkness Dance Center 1395 Lexington Ave, at 92nd St Ⓣ212/415-5500, Ⓦwww.92y.org. Subway #4, #5, #6 to 86th St; #6 to 96th St. Hosts performances and discussions, often for free.

Brooklyn Academy of Music 30 Lafayette St, Brooklyn Ⓣ718/636-4100, Ⓦwww.bam.org. Subway #2, #3, #4, #5, N, R to Atlantic Ave. America's oldest performing-arts academy is still one of the busiest and most daring dance producers in New York. In the autumn, BAM's Next Wave festival features the hottest international attractions in avant-garde dance and music, and each spring since 1977 BAM has hosted the annual Dance Africa Festival, America's largest showcase for African and African-American dance and culture.

Cunningham Studio 55 Bethune St, at Washington St Ⓣ212/255-8240, Ⓦwww.merce.org. Subway A, C, E to 14th St. The home of the Merce Cunningham Dance Company stages performances by emerging modern choreographers, usually on weekend nights.

Dance Theater Workshop 219 W 19th St, at Seventh Ave Ⓣ212/924-0077, Ⓦwww.dancetheaterworkshop.org. Subway #1 to 18th St. Founded in 1965 as a choreographers' collective to support emerging artists in alternative dance, DTW is now housed in a multimillion-dollar building. There's a mid-sized main stage, an art gallery and smaller workshop spaces, all of which boast more than 175 performances from nearly 70 artists and companies each season. The relaxed, friendly vibe and reasonable ticket prices (from $15–25) haven't changed.

Danspace Project St Mark's-Church-in-the-Bowery, 131 E 10th St, at Second Ave Ⓣ212/674-8194, Ⓦwww.danspaceproject.org. Subway #6 to Astor Place. Experimental contemporary dance, with a season running from September to June, in one of the more beautiful performance spaces around.

David H Koch Theater Lincoln Center, 65th St at Columbus Ave Ⓣ212/870-5570, Ⓦnew.lincolncenter.org. Subway #1 to 66th St. Lincoln Center's other major ballet venue (see Met, p.369) is home to the revered New York City Ballet (Ⓦwww.nycballet.com), which performs for an eight-week season each spring.

The Joyce Theater 175 Eighth Ave, at 19th St Ⓣ212/242-0800, Ⓦwww.joyce.org. Subway #1 to 18th St; C, E to 23rd St. The Joyce is one of the best-known downtown dance venues. It hosts short seasons by a wide variety of acclaimed dance troupes such as Pilobolus, the Parsons Dance Company and Momix. The Joyce also gives performances at their Soho space, a former fire station (155 Mercer St, at Prince St Ⓣ212/431-9233).

Juilliard Dance Workshop 155 W 65th St, at Broadway Ⓣ212/799-5000, Ⓦwww.juilliard.edu. Subway #1 to 66th St. The dance

Free summer concerts

Concert prices just keep getting higher, but in summer there are often budget-priced or free alternatives.

Bryant Park (☎212/768-4242, Ⓦwww.bryantpark.org) is home to free Broadway and Off-Broadway musical performances during the summer (one weekday lunchtime; check schedules), as well as a Fall Festival with music and dance.

Lincoln Center Out-of-Doors (☎212/875-5108, Ⓦnew.lincolncenter.org) hosts a varied selection of daily free performances of music and dance events on the plaza in July and August.

SummerStage Festival (☎212/360-2756 or 2777, Ⓦwww.summerstage.org) in Central Park puts on an impressive range of free concerts of all kinds of music throughout the summer; performances take place at the Rumsey Playfield (near the 72nd St and Fifth Ave entrance). A highlight is the occasional Wednesday night performance of Verdi by the **New York Grand Opera**, at the nearby Naumburg Bandshell. Also at Rumsey Playfield is a Friday morning summer concert series put on by the television show *Good Morning America*.

New York Philharmonic's Concerts in the Park (☎212/875-5709, Ⓦwww.nyphil.org) is a series of concerts and fireworks displays that turns up all over the city and the outer boroughs in July. Similarly, there's the **Met in the Parks** series (☎212/362-6000, Ⓦwww.metopera.org) in June and July.

For other free classical music and jazz performances, try the **Washington Square Music Festival** (☎212/252-3621, Ⓦwww.washingtonsquaremusicfestival.org) on Tuesdays at 8pm throughout July, or the **Celebrate Brooklyn Festival** (☎718/855-7882, Ⓦwww.bricartsmedia.org) at Prospect Park Bandshell in Brooklyn, June to early Aug usually Thurs–Sat but other days as well.

division of the Juilliard School often holds free workshop performances and each spring six students work with six composers to present a Composers and Choreographers concert.

Lincoln Center's Fountain Plaza 65th St at Columbus Ave ☎212/875-5766, Ⓦwww.new.lincolncenter.org. Subway #1 to 66th St. Open-air venue for the enormously popular Midsummer Night Swing, where each night you can learn a different dance style en masse (everything from polka to rockabilly) and watch a performance – all for $17. Tickets go on sale at 5.45pm the night of the show; the season runs June–July. Lessons begin at 6.30pm, music and dance at 7.30pm.

Metropolitan Opera House Lincoln Center, 65th St at Columbus Ave ☎212/362-6000, Ⓦwww.metoperafamily.org. Subway #1 to 66th St. Home of the renowned American Ballet Theater (Ⓦwww.abt.org), which performs at the Opera House from early May into July. Prices for ballet at the Met range from as little as $20 up to $375 for the best seats at special performances (usually more like $175 tops); $20 standing-room tickets go on sale the morning of the performance.

New York City Center 131 W 55th St, at Seventh Ave ☎212/581-1212, Ⓦwww.nycitycenter.org. Subway B, D, E to Seventh Ave; N, Q, R to 57th St–Seventh Ave; F to 57th St–Sixth Ave. This large, midtown venue, finishing a renovation for autumn 2011, hosts some of the most important troupes in modern dance, including the Paul Taylor Dance Company, the Alvin Ailey American Dance Theater and the American Ballet Theater; there's September Fall for Dance Festival as well.

Cabaret and comedy

New York is one of America's **comedy** capitals, and there are several major clubs that feature professional performers, some of whom you'll recognize from television and film. There are also a good number of alternative comedy venues in downtown Manhattan that eschew the standard "comedy routine" fare for zanier "conceptual" comedy. Most mainstream clubs have shows every night, with two or more on weekends; it's usual to be charged a cover plus a two-drink minimum fee.

Cabaret has cooled off a bit of late, but there are still a couple of top venues where you can see some truly amazing stuff from the likes of Woody Allen and KT Sullivan.

The list below represents the best-known comedy and cabaret venues in town, but performances can also be found at a multitude of bars, clubs and art spaces all over the city. Check *Time Out New York* magazine and the *Village Voice* for the fullest and most up-to-date listings.

Comedy clubs

Carolines on Broadway 1626 Broadway, at 49th St ⓣ212/757-4100, ⓦwww.carolines.com. Subway #1 to 50th St; N, R to 49th St. *Carolines* books some of the best stand-up acts in town; this is where most of the biggest names perform. Cover $15–40. Two-drink minimum. Also has a "supper lounge", *Comedy Nation*, downstairs.

Chicago City Limits Theater 318 W 53rd St, at Eighth Ave ⓣ212/888-5233, ⓦwww.chicagocitylimits.com. Subway C, E to 50th St. The oldest improvisation theatre in New York. $10–15 admission with a two-drink minimum.

Comedy Cellar 117 MacDougal St, at Bleecker St ⓣ212/254-3480, ⓦwww.comedycellar.com. Subway A, B, C, D, E, F, M to W 4th St. Popular Greenwich Village comedy club now in its third decade. It's a good late-night hangout. $10–15 cover plus two-drink minimum.

Comic Strip Live 1568 Second Ave, between 81st and 82nd sts ⓣ212/861-9386, ⓦwww.comicstriplive.com. Subway #4, #5, #6 to 86th St. Famed showcase for stand-up comics and young singers going for the big time. Cover $15–25 plus two-drink minimum.

Dangerfield's 1118 First Ave, at 61st St ⓣ212/593-1650, ⓦwww.dangerfields.com. Subway #4, #5, #6, N, R to 59th St. Vegas-style new-talent showcase founded by Rodney Dangerfield. $20 cover with, unusually, no minimum drink charge.

Gotham Comedy Club 208 W 23rd St, between Seventh and Eighth aves ⓣ212/367-9000, ⓦwww.gothamcomedyclub.com. Subway C, E, #1 to 23rd St. A swanky comedy venue in Chelsea, highly respected by New York media types and those who scout up-and-coming comics. Cover $20–30 plus two-drink minimum.

Stand-Up New York 236 W 78th St, at Broadway ⓣ212/595-0850, ⓦwww.standupny.com. Subway #1 to 79th St. Upper West Side all-ages forum for established comics, many of whom have appeared on *Leno* and *Letterman*. Hosts the Toyota Comedy Festival in June. Cover $12–16 plus two-drink minimum – you're required to arrive a half-hour before showtime, so call or check the website for the night's schedule before arriving.

Upright Citizens Brigade Theatre 307 W 26th St, between Eighth and Ninth aves ⓣ212/366-9176, ⓦwww.ucbtheatre.com. Subway C, E to 23rd St; #1 to 28th St. Consistently hilarious sketch-based and improv comedy, seven nights a week. You can sometimes catch *Saturday Night Live* cast members in the ensemble. Cover $5–15.

Cabarets

Café Carlyle inside *Carlyle Hotel*, 35 E 76th St, at Madison Ave ⓣ212/744-1600, ⓦwww.thecarlyle.com. Subway #1 to 77th St. This regal room is where Woody Allen plays clarinet every Monday, and divas like the ageless Elaine Stritch drop by for a week's residency. If you don't want to eat (the food's expensive and unexciting), standing at the bar is just as fun – though it's still a pricey night out. Cover $60–100, jacket required.

Don't Tell Mama 343 W 46th St, at Ninth Ave ⓣ212/757-0788, ⓦwww.donttellmamanyc.com. Subway A, C, E, N, Q, R, #1, #2, #3 to 42nd St. Lively and convivial Midtown West piano bar and cabaret featuring rising stars and singing waitresses. Cover free to $20, two-drink minimum.

Duplex 61 Christopher St, at Seventh Ave ⓣ212/255-5438, ⓦwww.theduplex.com. Subway #1 to Christopher St. West Village cabaret popular with a boisterous gay and tourist crowd. Barbra Streisand and Lea Delaria have performed here (though not together), and Off-Off-Broadway shows like *Nunsense* played here in their infancy. Has a rowdy piano bar downstairs and a cabaret room upstairs. Open 4pm–4am. Cover free to $20 plus two-drink minimum.

Joe's Pub 425 Lafayette St, between Astor Place and 4th St ⓣ212/539-8778, ⓦwww.publictheater.org. Subway #6 to Astor Place; N, R to 8th St. The hipper, late-night arm of the Joseph Papp Public Theater, this is one of the sharpest and most popular music venues in the city, with a wide range of cabaret acts nightly.

The Oak Room at the *Algonquin Hotel*, 59 W 44th St, between Fifth and Sixth aves ⓣ212/419-9331, ⓦwww.algonquinhotel.com. Subway B, D, F, M to 42nd St. A site with some history (it has introduced luminaries like Diana Krall and Michael Feinstein) and perhaps the best place for cabaret, though it's also an expensive ticket. Cover $50 (less for late Fri & Sat shows), with mandatory seating for dinner ($60).

Film

Despite rising costs that put a normal ticket at $12–13, New York is a movie-lover's dream. There are plenty of state-of-the-art **cinemas** all over the city; most are charmless multiscreen complexes, and have all the charm of large airports, but they also have the advantages of superb sound, luxurious seating and perfect sightlines.

For listings, your best bets are *Time Out New York* magazine or freebies like the *Village Voice*; otherwise, check the local papers on Fridays, when the papers publish new reviews and schedules for the following week. For accurate showtimes, and to book a ticket in advance, call ⓣ212/777-FILM or check ⓦwww.fandango.com and www.moviefone.com. Despite the per-ticket surcharge of around $1.50 or so, it's often worth booking ahead: hot new releases usually sell out on opening weekend among the cut-throat New York cinema crowd.

New York used to be one of the best cities in the world to see **old movies**, but the cinema landscape has changed considerably in recent years. Many of the old repertory houses that showed a regular menu of scratchy prints of old chestnuts and recent favourites have gone. In their place is an impressive selection of museums and revival houses that show retrospectives of particular directors and actors, series from different countries, and programmes of specific genres. We've highlighted our pick of New York's best cinemas below, divided into those showing first-run mainstream and indie fare, and the venues that specialize in revivals and more obscure and experimental flicks, though the list is by no means exhaustive.

First-run movies

AMC Empire 25 234 W 42nd St, at Eighth Ave ⓣ212/398-2597. Subway A, C, E, N, Q, R, #1, #2, #3, #7 to 42nd St. One of the few skyscraper multiplexes: 25 screens, all with stadium seating, soaring upward. Though it's usually crowded on weekends, it offers a decent mix of mainstream and arthouse films, and even has its own restaurant.

AMC Loews Lincoln Square 13 & IMAX 1998 Broadway, at 68th St ⓣ1-888/262-4386. Subway #1 to 66th St. More and more mainstream films are being converted to IMAX technology and are being re-released on the huge screens here in high resolution just months after their original theatrical debuts. Worth checking out for sci-fi spectaculars, if nothing else. Oh, and the venue has 12 other first-run theatres besides, though it's often bedlam.

BAM Rose Cinemas 30 Lafayette Ave, at Ashland Place, Brooklyn ⓣ718/636-4100, ⓦwww.bam.org. Subway C, G to Lafayette Ave; B, D, M, N, Q, R, #2, #3, #4, #5 to Atlantic Ave. There are four screens at BAM's film site. The programming is mostly one or two current films mixed with a couple of classics or rarities; the year-round BAMcinématek series usually offers the most interesting choices.

Clearview's Ziegfeld 141 W 54th St, between Sixth and Seventh aves ⓣ212/307-1862. Subway B, D, E to Seventh Ave; F to 57th St. Sitting on the site of the old Ziegfeld Follies (hence the name), this midtown movie palace with its massive screen (one of the biggest in the country) is the place locals come to for an old-fashioned cinema

TV-show tapings

If you want to experience American TV up close, there are **free tickets** for various shows. For most shows you must be 16, sometimes 17 or 18 to be in the audience; if you're underage or travelling with children, call ahead.

Morning shows

Good Morning America ⓣ**212/580-5176,** ⓦ**abcnews.com/GMA.** Show up at the Broadway entrance (at 44th St) around 6.45am or earlier for a shot at a standby ticket; you can also try ahead of time through the website.

Today There's no way to get advance tickets, just show up at 49th Street, between Fifth and Sixth avenues, as early as possible. Unlike the rest of the morning shows, which run until 9am, *Today* ends at 10am.

Daytime shows

Live with Regis and Kelly ⓣ**212/456-1000.** Request online at ⓦbventertainment.go.com/tv/buenavista/regisandkelly/get_tickets.html or send a postcard with your name, address and telephone number to Live Tickets, PO Box 230777 Ansonia Station, New York, NY 10023-0777. Include your preferred date(s) and number of tickets (limit 4). For standby, go to ABC at 67th Street and Columbus Avenue as early as 7am Monday to Friday.

Late-night shows

The Colbert Report ⓦ**www.colbertnation.com.** In theory you can book tickets on the website, but it's almost always sold out. For standby tickets arrive by 4pm at the studio at 513 W 54th St, between Fifth and Sixth avenues.

The Daily Show with Jon Stewart ⓣ**212/586-2477,** ⓦ**www.thedailyshow.com/tickets.** Again, a very hard ticket to secure. There's no point in showing up for standby tickets; as a last resort call ⓣ212/586-2477 to find out if there are any cancellations.

David Letterman ⓦwww.cbs.com/latenight/lateshow/tickets has all the info; you can, if you like, request tickets in person at 1697 Broadway, between W 53rd and W 54th streets (Mon–Fri 9.30am–noon, Sat & Sun 10am–6pm). Standby tickets are available by calling ⓣ212/247-6497 from 11am on the day you wish to attend. Shoots Monday to Thursday at 5.30pm, with an additional show Thursday at 8pm.

Late Night with Jimmy Fallon ⓣ**212/664-3056,** ⓦ**www.latenightwithjimmyfallon.com/about/tickets.** Get advance tickets around a month ahead; standby tickets can be had the morning of the show on the 49th Street side of 30 Rockefeller Plaza (get there no later than 9am). Taping is at 5.30pm.

Saturday Night Live ⓣ**212/664-4000.** It's tough to get tickets in advance; for each upcoming season (usually Oct–May), you must send an email, in August only, to ⓔsnltickets@nbcuni.com – include all contact information. If selected, you'll get two tickets assigned randomly (you cannot fix the date). Alternatively, standby tickets are distributed at 7am on the 49th Street side of 30 Rockefeller Plaza on Saturday morning (some weeks are reruns; call ahead). You can opt for either the 8pm dress rehearsal or the 11.30pm live taping.

experience. Numerous film premieres also take place here.

Regal Battery Park 11 102 North End Ave ⓣ212/945-3418. Subway #1, #2, #3 to Chambers St. One great reason to visit: its out-of-the-way siting means it's possibly the quietest multiplex around.

Regal Union Square 14 850 Broadway, at 13th St ⓣ212/253-6266. Subway L, N, Q, R, #4, #5, #6 to 14th St–Union Square. Stadium seating venue in a central location.

Indies and foreign

Angelika Film Center 18 W Houston St, at Mercer St ⓣ212/995-2000, ⓦwww.angelikafilmcenter.com. Subway B, D, F, M to Broadway–Lafayette. Six-screen arthouse venue, with a rather overhyped reputation – screens are tiny, floors are hardly sloped and the subway tends to rumble by at inopportune moments, rattling the subterranean rooms. Still, it's one of the few surviving venues for smaller films in the city.

Cinema Village 22 E 12th St, between University and Fifth aves ⓣ212/924-3363, ⓦwww.cinemavillage.com. Subway L, N, Q, R, #4, #5, #6 to 14th St/Union Square. A 50-year-old cinema with three screens (and limited seating) showing indie flicks and numerous documentaries.

IFC Center 323 Sixth Ave, at W 3rd St ⓣ212/924-7771, ⓦwww.ifccenter.com. Subway A, B, C, D, E, F, M to W 4th St. An independent with three screens, new indies, foreign and documentaries, and popular midnight shows. Features a much larger screen and a better sound system than you'll find at most other arthouses.

Landmark Sunshine Cinema 143 E Houston St, at First Ave ⓣ212/330-8182, ⓦwww.landmarktheatres.com. Subway F to Second Ave. When this former Yiddish vaudeville house opened as a cinema a decade ago, it quickly seized the Angelika's crown as the best place to see indie films, thanks to larger screens, better seating and a less threadbare building.

Lincoln Plaza 1886 Broadway, at 62nd St ⓣ212/757-2280, ⓦwww.lincolnplazacinema.com. Subway A, B, C, D, #1 to 59th St/Columbus Circle. This six-screen cinema is as close as the Upper West Side gets to an arthouse venue. While it plays an occasional smaller mainstream Hollywood picture, it's known for acclaimed foreign and independent films.

Paris Theatre 4 W 58th St, at Fifth Ave ⓣ212/688-3800, ⓦwww.theparistheatre.com. Subway F to 57th St; N, Q, R to 59th St/Fifth Ave. An old-fashioned cinema (there's even a balcony) that specializes in foreign films as well as well-reviewed mainstream fare.

The Quad 34 W 13th St, between Fifth and Sixth aves ⓣ212/255-8800, ⓦwww.quadcinema.com. Subway F, M to 14th St. Shows a selection of indie movies quite hard to find anywhere else.

Film festivals and seasonal screenings

There always seems to be some **film festival** or other running in New York. The granddaddy of them all, the **New York Film Festival**, starts at the end of September and runs for two weeks at the Lincoln Center. It's well worth catching if you're in town, though tickets for the most popular films can sell out very quickly. If you're determined to see something, watch the reviews in the *New York Times* each morning – when movies are panned, there's usually a cluster of people trying to sell off their tickets outside the theatre that night. More info: ⓦwww.filmlinc.com.

See Chapter 32, "Parades, festivals and events" for info on the larger filmfests; here's a list of some of the smaller, but still worthwhile, festivals and seasonal screenings:

Asian American Film Festival ⓦwww.asiancinevision.org; July

Bryant Park Summer Film Festival (free; outdoor screenings of old Hollywood favourites on Mon nights at sunset) ⓦwww.bryantpark.org; June–August

GenArt Film Festival ⓦwww.genart.org; April

Human Rights Watch International Film Festival ⓦwww.hrw.org; June

Margaret Mead Film & Video Festival (anthropological films at the Museum of Natural History) ⓦwww.amnh.org; October or November

NewFest: The New York LGBT Film Festival ⓦwww.newfestival.org; June

New York International Children's Film Festival ⓦwww.gkids.com; March, though screenings on weekend mornings year-round

New York Jewish Film Festival at Lincoln Center ⓦwww.thejewishmuseum.org; January

River Flicks at Hudson River Park (free screenings of box-office hits and cult crowd-pleasers) ⓦwww.hudsonriverpark.org; July–August Wed for adults, Fri for kids

Socrates Sculpture Garden Film Festival (free screenings of classics every Wed starting at sunset in Long Island City, Queens) ⓦwww.socratessculpturepark.org; July–August

Revivals

Anthology Film Archives **32 Second Ave, at 2nd St ☎212/505-5181, Ⓦwww.anthologyfilmarchives.org. Subway F to Second Ave.** A bastion of experimental film-making. Programmes of mind-bending abstraction, East Village grunge flicks and auteur retrospectives all rub shoulders here. Tickets $9.

Chelsea Classics **at the Clearview Chelsea, 260 W 23rd St, between Seventh and Eighth aves ☎212/691-5519. Subway C, E, #1 to 23rd St.** Thursday nights belong to campy classics (more often than not starring Joan Crawford and/or Bette Davis). Introduced by the blonde "lady" with green streaks, Hedda Lettuce. Tickets $7.50.

Film Forum **209 W Houston St, between Sixth and Seventh aves ☎212/727-8110, Ⓦwww.filmforum.org. Subway #1 to Houston St; A, B, C, D, E, F, M to W 4th St.** The cosy three-screen Film Forum has an eccentric but famously popular programme of new independent movies, documentaries and foreign films, as well as a repertory programme specializing in silent comedy, camp classics and cult directors. All in all, one of the best alternative spaces in town.

The Museum of Modern Art **11 W 53rd St, at Fifth Ave ☎212/708-9480, Ⓦwww.moma.org. Subway E, M to Fifth Ave/53rd St.** MoMA is famous among local cinephiles for its vast collection of films, its exquisite programming and its regular audience of cantankerous senior citizens. The movies themselves range from Hollywood screwball comedies to hand-painted Super 8. Tickets $10.

Museum of the Moving Image **35th Ave, at 36th St, Astoria, Queens ☎718/784-0077, Ⓦwww.movingimage.us. Subway N to 36th Ave; G, R to 36th St.** The AMMI is usually well worth a trip out to Queens, either for the pictures – which are often serious director retrospectives and silent films, with a strong emphasis on cinematographers – or for the cinema museum itself (see p.247 for review).

Symphony Space **2537 Broadway, at 95th St ☎212/864-5400, Ⓦwww.symphonyspace.org. Subway #1, #2, #3 to 96th St.** A varied and often surprising programme of festivals (including one for shorts), special director's series and weekend double features.

Walter Reade Theater **Lincoln Center, 165 W 65th St, at Broadway ☎212/875-5600, Ⓦwww.filmlinc.com. Subway #1 to 66th St.** Programmed by the Film Society of Lincoln Center, the Walter Reade is simply the best place in town to see great films. This beautiful, modern theatre has perfect sightlines, a huge screen and impeccable acoustics. The emphasis is on foreign films and the great auteurs; it's also home to many of the city's festivals (see box opposite). Tickets $12.

Literary events and readings

New York has long been viewed as a **literary hotspot**. The city's proliferation of competitive bookstores means that you can see someone performing wordy wonders any night of the week. (For recommendations on specific stores, see Chapter 30, "Shopping", and Chapter 32, "Parades, festivals and events" for book festivals.)

92nd Street Y Unterberg Poetry Center **1395 Lexington Ave ☎212/415-5760, Ⓦwww.92y.org. Subway #4, #5, #6 to 86th St.** Quite simply, the definitive place to hear all your Booker, Pulitzer and Nobel prize-winning favourites, as well as many other exciting new talents. Name almost any American literary great – from Tennessee Williams to Langston Hughes – and they've probably appeared here; expect the current line-up to have big headliners too. Additional programmes are held at 92Y Tribeca (200 Hudson St, at Canal St).

Barnes & Noble The city's numerous B&Ns host a surprisingly diverse range of readings almost every night of the week. The Union Square branch generally gets the highest-profile authors and events.

Half King **505 W 23rd St, at Tenth Ave ☎212/462-4300, Ⓦwww.thehalfking.com. Subway C, E to 23rd St.** Large, casual bar owned by macho author Sebastian Junger (writer of *The Perfect Storm*): it's not surprising, then, that most Monday nights are devoted to free readings by a big-name contemporary author. On other occasions

Poetry slams and readings

Poetry and story slamming is a literary version of freestyle rapping, in which performers take turns presenting stories and poems (often mostly or entirely improvised) on stage. At their best, slams can be thrilling, raw and very funny (not to mention competitive – many feature a judges' panel). We've pulled out the three best places to sample New York slams, including the eatery where it all began, the *Nuyorican Poets Café*.

Bowery Poetry Club 308 Bowery, at Houston St ⓣ212/614-0505, ⓦwww.bowerypoetry.com. Subway F to Second Ave; #6 to Bleecker St. A combination café/bar/bookstore with a small stage at the back, this community-focused space is owned by Bob Holman, who used to run *Nuyorican* (see below). There are occasional big names on stage, but it's mostly impressively enthusiastic amateurs. The space is quite busy, with several different events (even the nonliterary: drag king/queen bingo? BadAss Burlesque?) in the course of an evening.

The Moth (at Storyville Center for the Spoken Word) 330 W 38th St, between Ninth and Tenth aves ⓣ212/742-0551, ⓦwww.themoth.org. Subway A, C, E to 34th or 42nd St. Offbeat literary company that's known for its story slams – open-mic nights where amateurs vie for a five-minute on-stage storytelling spot. There's also the yearly Moth Ball (November) that sends the funds raised from ticket sales to local charities. Though most events take place at the Moth's home base here, there are also sporadic offshoots round town – check the website for schedules.

Nuyorican Poets Café 236 E 3rd St, between aves B and C ⓣ212/780-9386, ⓦwww.nuyorican.org. Subway F to Second Ave. Alphabet City's *Nuyorican* remains one of the most talked-about performance spaces in town. Its poetry slams are what made it famous, but there are also theatre and film-script readings, occasionally with well-known downtown stars.

there's an intriguing programme centred on great magazine writing read by a group of journalists. Check the calendar on the site for schedules.

KGB 85 E 4th St at Second Ave ⓣ212/505-3360, ⓦwww.kgbbar.com. Subway F to Second Ave; #6 to Astor Place. Grubby but welcoming little bar that hosts free readings every Sunday and Tuesday, though there are readings (everything from poetry to nonfiction to items like "Kinky Jews' Evening of Jewish Lit-Erotica") most other nights as well. To read here is a prestigious honour; expect to see top names, like Michael Cunningham. Call or check the website for up-to-date schedules. The building also houses the Kraine Theater (p.368).

Symphony Space 2537 Broadway, at 95th St ⓣ212/864-5400, ⓦwww.symphonyspace.org. Subway #1, #2, #3 to 96th St. The highly acclaimed Selected Shorts series, in which actors read the short fiction of a variety of authors (everyone from James Joyce to David Sedaris), usually packs the Symphony Space theatre; Bloomsday on Broadway, a one-day celebration of James Joyce's *Ulysses*, has been going on since 1981.

28

Gay New York

There are few places in America – indeed in the world – where **gay culture** thrives as it does in New York City. Open gays and lesbians are considered mainstream here – so much so that the city is one of the few places where Republican administrations avidly court gay voters. By some estimates, about twenty percent of New Yorkers identify themselves as gay or lesbian; when you add in bisexual and transgender individuals, the figure climbs even higher – as it does when you take into account the number of gay visitors who come to New York each day.

The largely liberal orientation of city politics has been generally beneficial to the gay community since the 1969 riots at the *Stonewall Bar* marked the onset of the gay-rights movement (see box, p.112). Nonetheless, significant issues still remain disputed, **marriage equality** most of all. The New York State Supreme Court ruled gay marriage illegal in 2006; former governor Eliot Spitzer's promises of equality were derailed upon his resignation, and Spitzer's replacement, David Patterson, issued a directive that required state agencies to recognize same-sex marriages officiated elsewhere as valid in New York. He followed that with legislation to legalize such marriage in the city, which the State Assembly passed but the Senate voted down in late 2009.

Socially, gay men and lesbians are fairly visible in the city, and there are a few **neighbourhoods** where the gay community makes up the majority of the population. **Chelsea** (especially Eighth Ave between 14th and 23rd sts), the **East Village/Lower East Side** and Brooklyn's **Park Slope** are the largest of these, and have all but replaced the West Village as gay New York's hub. A strong gay presence still lingers in the vicinity of **Christopher Street** in the West Village, but it's in Chelsea that gay male socializing is most ubiquitous and open. Lesbians will find large communities in laidback Park Slope and around East Houston Street. Other neighbourhoods with a strong gay and lesbian presence are Hell's Kitchen, Morningside Heights (Columbia University's college town), Queens' Astoria and Brooklyn's Prospect Heights (mainly residential), DUMBO and Williamsburg. All of the city's alternative communities come together in major events like **Pride Week** in late June (Pride Month), which includes a rally, Dyke March, Dyke Ball, Brooklyn Pride, Black Pride, innumerable parties and the infamous (if commercialized and sweltering) **Lesbian & Gay Pride Parade** (see p.427).

Several free weekly **newspapers and magazines** serve New York's gay community: *Gay City News* (Ⓦwww.gaycitynews.com), *Next* (for men; Ⓦwww.nextmagazine.com) and *GO* (for women; trans-friendly; Ⓦwww.gomag.com). You'll find these at the LGBT Community Services Center (see p.380), at street-corner boxes, bars, cafés, lesbian and gay bookstores, and occasionally at newsstands, where glossy national mags such as *Out*, *POZ*, *Girlfriends*, *DIVA*, *Metrosource* and others are also available. The listings in *Time Out New York* magazine are helpful as well. If you're looking for a date, some action or just people to party with while you're here, post a personal (or respond to someone else's) on craigslist (free; Ⓦnewyork.craigslist.org), the popular online message-board. Other useful resources are listed throughout this chapter.

Resources

The Audre Lorde Project 85 S Oxford St, Brooklyn Ⓣ718/596-0342, Ⓦwww.alp.org. Centre for LGBT people of non-Caucasian ethnicity, focused on the New York City area.

Gay Men's Health Crisis (GMHC) 119 W 24th St, between Sixth and Seventh aves Ⓣ212/367-1000, Ⓦwww.gmhc.org. Despite the name, this incredible organization – the oldest and largest not-for-profit AIDS organization in the world – provides testing, information and referrals to everyone: gay, straight and transgender.

The Lesbian, Gay, Bisexual & Transgender Community Services Center 208 W 13th St, west of Seventh Ave Ⓣ212/620-7310, Ⓦwww.gaycenter.org. The Center houses well over a hundred groups and organizations, sponsors workshops, parties, movie nights, guest speakers, youth services, programmes for parents and lots more. Even the bulletin boards are fascinating.

SAGE: Senior Action in a Gay Environment 305 Seventh Ave, at 27th St, 6th floor Ⓣ212/741-2247, Ⓦwww.sageusa.org. Support and activities for gay seniors. Most activities take place at the Center, at 208 W 13th St (see above), where the group maintains another small office.

Accommodation

The following places to stay are particularly friendly to gays and lesbians and convenient for the scene. The prices at the end of each listing represent the lowest price for a double in high season, excluding taxes.

Chelsea Pines Inn 317 W 14th St, between Eighth and Ninth aves Ⓣ1-888/546-2700 or 212/929-1023, Ⓦwww.chelseapinesinn.com. Subway A, C, E to 14th St. Housed in an old brownstone on the Greenwich Village/Chelsea border, this hotel offers clean, comfortable, "shabby chic" rooms. Best to book in advance. $269

Colonial House Inn 318 W 22nd St, between Eighth and Ninth aves Ⓣ212/243-9669, Ⓦwww.colonialhouseinn.com. Subway C, E to 23rd St. You won't mind that this B&B is a little worn around the edges – its attractive design and contributions to the GMHC (see above) make for a feel-good experience. Only deluxe rooms include en-suite bathrooms, while some rooms have refrigerators and fireplaces. Continental breakfast included. $130

Incentra Village House 32 Eighth Ave, between 12th and Jane sts Ⓣ212/206-0007, Ⓦwww.incentravillage.com. Subway A, C, E to 14th St. Some of the dozen Early American-look studios in this residential neighbourhood townhouse come with kitchenettes and one has access to a private garden; there's a suite, too. Three-night cancellation policy and three-night minimum stay at weekends. $219

Hotel 17 255 E 17th St, between Second and Third aves Ⓣ212/475-2845, Ⓦwww.hotel17ny.com. See review p.275.

Arts and culture

There's always a good amount of gay and gay-friendly performance and visual art on in New York, much of it in mixed venues: check the listings in the *Village Voice*, *Time Out New York* magazine and the free papers noted in the introduction to this chapter. You'll only be able to scratch the surface of New York's gay scene on a brief visit. If you're here for a longer trip, and are so inclined, check out "out" sports teams and women's self-defence organizations, which provide a terrific opportunity to meet people. Contact the LGBT Community Services Center for more information (see p.380).

Center for Lesbian and Gay Studies CUNY Graduate Center, 365 Fifth Ave, between 34th and 35th sts ⓣ212/817-1955, ⓦwww.clags.org. Fascinating talks and seminars featuring academic luminaries. Particular attention is paid to international, transgender and disability studies.

Lesbian Herstory Archives 484 14th St, Park Slope, Brooklyn ⓣ718/768-DYKE, ⓦwww.lesbianherstoryarchives.org. Original materials on dyke life, mostly throughout the past century. Old-school and inspiring. Open a few hours a day on a variable schedule, so call ahead or visit the website for times.

Leslie-Lohman Gay Art Foundation 26 Wooster St, between Grand and Canal sts ⓣ212/431-2609, ⓦwww.leslielohman.org. The Foundation maintains an archive and permanent collection of lesbian and gay art, with galleries open to the public during shows. Tues–Sat noon–6pm.

MIX (New York Lesbian and Gay Experimental Film/Video Festival) ⓣ212/742-8880, ⓦwww.mixnyc.org. This celebrated annual festival, which takes place in November, offers politically radical and technically avant-garde films.

National Archive of LGBT History/The Pat Parker-Vito Russo Center Library LGBT Community Services Center (see p.380) ⓣ212/620-7310. Terrific, interesting archive of gay life in America, and a lending library with 12,000 titles. The archive is open Thurs 6–8pm, and also by appointment Sun (afternoons) and Mon–Wed (evenings).

NewFest ⓣ646/290-8136, ⓦwww.newfest.org. This not-to-be-missed annual film festival is held the first week of June, kicking off Pride Month. Expect celebrities, outrageous parties and an interesting array of flicks.

New York City Gay Men's Chorus ⓣ212/344-1777, ⓦwww.nycgmc.org. Wildly popular 250-member gay men's choral group that has sung with Cyndi Lauper and other famous names at major venues like Carnegie Hall. Call or check website for concert schedule and membership information.

Cafés and restaurants

The spaces listed below are perennial favourites; it's not an exhaustive list by any means (and any of the cafés and restaurants recommended in chapters 23 and 24 should be more than welcoming).

Bluestockings 172 Allen St, between Stanton and Rivington sts ⓣ212/777-6028, ⓦbluestockings.com. Subway F to Second Ave or Delancey St. Fair Trade café and lefty bookstore that functions as an informal centre of the lesbian and bi community. Hosts Dyke Knitting Circle, as well as readings, performances, meetings and screenings. Daily 11am–11pm.

Cafeteria 119 Seventh Ave, at W 17th St ⓣ212/414-1717. Subway #1 to 18th St. Don't let the name fool you: *Cafeteria* may be open all night and serve great meatloaf ($15) and macaroni and cheese ($8), but it's no truckstop. It's more like a transplanted Miami Beach café: the modern, plastic-accented interior is always packed with beautiful diners and sexy waiters. Daily 24hr.

Cowgirl 519 Hudson St, at W 10th St ⓣ212/633-1133, ⓦwww.cowgirlnyc.com. Subway #1 to Christopher St. Genial eatery with a Texas/Western theme. It's big on burger-and-bbq offerings ($11.25–19.25), and hosts a sometimes lively bar scene among the kitschy decor. Mon–Thurs 11am–11pm, Fri 11am–midnight, Sat 10am–midnight, Sun 10am–11pm.

East of Eighth 254 W 23rd St, between Seventh and Eighth aves ⓣ212/352-0075, ⓦwww.eastofeighthny.com. Excellent dishes with a variety of influences; crabcakes ($11), southern-style pork chops ($18), pizzas and pastas ($12–18) sit alongside matzoh-ball soup ($7), Southeast Asian pot stickers ($9) and Oaxacan guacamole ($8). Mon–Fri noon–midnight, Sat 11am–12.30am, Sun 11am–10.30pm.

Manatus 340 Bleecker St, between Christopher and W 10th sts ⓣ212/989-7042, ⓦwww.manatusnyc.com. Subway #1 to

Christopher St–Sheridan Square. Laidback and comfortable diner, with a comprehensive menu, on one of the Village's more active streets. Daily 24hr.

Petite Abeille 466 Hudson St, between Barrow and Grove sts ⓣ212/741-6479, ⓦwww.petiteabeille.com; three other downtown locations. Subway #1 to Christopher St–Sheridan Square. Charming, tiny spot specializing in omelettes, grilled sandwiches and French and Belgian favourites. Locals enjoy the *moules marinières* ($18) and the *croque madame* ($12); all-you-can-eat mussels nights ($23 including one beer) take place Wednesdays. Mon–Sat 8am–11pm, Sun 8am–10pm.

Bars

Gay men's bars cover the spectrum from relaxed pubs to hard-hitting clubs full of glamour and attitude. Most of the more-established places are in Greenwich Village and Chelsea, and along Avenue A in the East Village. Park Slope in Brooklyn and the East Village are the centres of the **lesbian** scene, while dyke bars and club nights can be found in Chelsea and along Hudson Street in the West Village as well. Williamsburg has become a major hotspot for young, hip, mixed LGBT club nights. Check local weeklies for current listings.

Mainly for men

Barracuda 275 W 22nd St, between Seventh and Eighth aves ⓣ212/645-8613. Subway C, E, #1 to 23rd St. A favourite spot in New York's gay scene, and pretty laidback for Chelsea. Two-for-one happy hour 4–9pm during the week, crazy drag shows, and a look that changes several times a year. Daily 4pm–4am.

The Boiler Room 86 E 4th St, between First and Second aves ⓣ212/254-7536. Subway F to Second Ave. Used to be one of the hottest bars in the city but now it's really just a local bar with a pool table. While still a good hangout (mostly gay but with some lesbian presence) don't expect any atmosphere; it's always got the look of a retiree's garage during the summer. Daily 4pm–4am.

Boxer's NYC 37 W 20th St, between Fifth and Sixth aves ⓣ212/255-5082, ⓦwww.boxersnyc.com. Subway F, M, R to 23rd St. This hot new sports bar is spread across two levels, with pool tables, TVs all over the place and brick-oven pizzas to soak up some of the beer. Mon–Fri noon–2am, Sat & Sun 1pm–2am.

Brandy's Piano Bar 235 E 84th St, between Second and Third aves ⓣ212/744-4949. Subway #4, #5, #6 to 86th St. Handsome uptown cabaret/piano bar with a crazy, mixed and generally mature clientele. Definitely worth a visit; note there's a two-drink minimum during the nightly sets (which start at 9.30pm). Daily 4pm–3am.

The Cock 29 Second Ave, between E 1st and 2nd sts ⓣ212/777-6254. Subway F to Second Ave. A litte on the trashy side but – entirely depending on your way of thinking – fun.

The Eagle 554 W 28th St, between Tenth and Eleventh aves ⓣ646/473-1866, ⓦwww.eaglenyc.com. Subway C, E to 23rd St; #1 to 28th St. The place for leather-bar fans, with a super-cool industrial feel and bi-level, multi-room layout, plus an open roof terrace that's inevitably the most packed part of the bar. Dress code some nights. Tues–Sat 10pm–4am, Sun 5pm–4am.

Eastern Bloc 505 E 6th St, between aves A and B ⓣ212/777-2555, ⓦwww.easternblocnyc.com. Subway F to Second Ave. Think high-class dive bar with a vaguely Russian motif. Drink specials every night, go-go boys on the weekends. Go early for a chilled-out neighbourhood crowd, and later for the East Village mob scene. Daily 7pm–4am.

Excelsior 390 Fifth Ave, between 6th and 7th sts, Park Slope, Brooklyn ⓣ718/832-1599. Subway F, M, R to Fourth Ave–9th St. The amusingly versatile jukebox, friendly rather than overtly cruisey clientele and two outside spaces make this Brooklyn's best bar for gay men. Mon–Fri 6pm–4am, Sat & Sun 2pm–4am.

g 223 W 19th St, between Seventh and Eighth aves ⓣ212/929-1085. Nearly as stylish as its "guppie" clientele, this deservedly popular lounge features a different DJ every night of the week. Daily 4pm–4am.

GYM 167 Eighth Ave, between 18th and 19th sts ⓣ212/337-2439, ⓦwww.gymsportsbar.com.

Subway A, C, E, L to 14th St–Eighth Ave; #1 to 18th St. Casual, friendly, non-scene hangout that features large-screen TVs, video games, pool table and smokers' patio. Rare sports bar where you can actually watch a game. Mon–Thurs 4pm–2am, Fri 4pm–4am, Sat 1pm–4am, Sun 1pm–2am.

Marie's Crisis 59 Grove St, between Seventh Ave S and Bleecker St. Subway #1 to Christopher St–Sheridan Square. Well-known cabaret/piano bar popular with tourists and locals alike. Features old-time singing sessions nightly. Often packed, always fun. Daily 4pm–4am.

Metropolitan 559 Lorimer Ave, at Metropolitan Ave, Brooklyn ⓣ718/599-4444. Subway L to Lorimer St; G to Metropolitan Ave. Hipster hangout without (much) attitude. Hosts 80s night every other Saturday. Daily 3pm–4am.

Phoenix 447 E 13th St, between Ave A and First Ave ⓣ212/477-9979. Subway L to First Ave. This relaxed East Village pub is much loved by the so-not-scene boys who live there, and other guys who just want reasonably priced drinks and a fun crowd. Daily 4pm–4am.

Stonewall Inn 53 Christopher St, between Waverly Place and Seventh Ave S ⓣ212/488-2705, ⓦwww.thestonewallinnnyc.com. Subway #1 to Christopher St–Sheridan Square. Yes, that *Stonewall*, site of the seminal 1969 riot, mostly refurbished and flying the pride flag like they own it – which, one could say, they do. Bingo, DJs, drag variety shows, male dancers and lesbian nights; call ahead to see what's on.

Therapy 348 W 52nd St, between Eighth and Ninth aves ⓣ212/397-1700, ⓦwww.therapy-nyc.com. Subway C, E to 50th St. Sleek bar/lounge geared to Midtowners and the post-work drinking crowd. DJ sets (Thurs–Sat) and drag shows, comedy sets and the like (rest of week), washed down with signature cocktails that keep up the psychological theme like the Gender Bender (citron vodka, lemonade and watermelon juice) and the Anorexic (rum and diet Red Bull in a Splenda-rimmed glass). Mon–Thurs & Sun 5pm–2am, Fri & Sat 5pm–4am.

Vlada 331 W 51st St, between Eighth and Ninth aves ⓣ212/974-8030, ⓦwww.vladabar.com. Subway C, E to 50th St. Another Russian-leaning gay bar? This one couldn't be more different from *Eastern Bloc* (see opposite): it's in Midtown West, with a decidedly posh and trendy feel. Infused vodka is the house specialty: the seventeen options range from cherry to horseradish. Daily 4pm–4am.

XES 157 W 24th St, between Sixth and Seventh aves ⓣ212/604-0212, ⓦwww.xesnyc.com. Subway F, M, #1 to 23rd St. A comfortable neighbourhood spot with karaoke nights, long happy hours and an outdoor patio. Mon & Tues 4pm–2am, Wed–Sun 4pm–4am.

Mainly for women

Cubbyhole 281 W 12th St, at W 4th St ⓣ212-243-9041, ⓦwww.cubbyholebar.com. Subway A, C, E, L to 14th St–Eighth Ave. This welcoming, kitschy, small but famous West Village dyke bar is something of a required stopover, since it's been here for what seems like forever. Mon–Fri 4pm–4am, Sat & Sun 2pm–4am.

Ginger's 363 Fifth Ave, between 5th and 6th sts, Park Slope, Brooklyn ⓣ718/788-0924. Subway F, R to Fourth Ave–9th St. The best dyke bar in New York is this dark, laidback Park Slope joint with a pool table, outdoor space and plenty of convivial company. Mon–Fri 5pm–4am though sometimes earlier, Sat & Sun 2pm–4am.

Henrietta Hudson 438 Hudson St, at Morton St ⓣ212/924-3347, ⓦwww.henriettahudson.com. Subway #1 to Houston St or Christopher St–Sheridan Square. Laidback in the afternoon but brimming by night, especially on weekends, this is the top lesbian place in Manhattan. Weekly theme nights – karaoke, game night, DJs, etc. Mon–Fri 4pm–4am, Sat & Sun 2pm–4am.

Clubs

Gay and lesbian **club nights** in New York can be some of the most outrageous in the world. Check *Time Out New York* magazine, *Next Magazine* (ⓦwww.nextmagazine.com), and *GO NYC* (ⓦwww.gomag.com) for up-to-date info. The clubs and nightclubs listed below have stood the test of time; all have their coveted cabaret licence, so go forth and dance.

Don Hill's 511 Greenwich St, at Spring St ⓣ212/219-2850, ⓦwww.donhills.com. Subway C, E to Spring St. An open-to-all-up-for-anything place, where you will find Britpop drag queens, mod rock dominatrixes and mohawked Johnny Rotten wannabes. Pole dancers and porn complete the vibe. Lots of live music and dance parties; weekend covers (or advance tickets) can be $10–20.

Escuelita 301 W 39th St, at Eighth Ave ⓣ212/631-0588, ⓦwww.escuelita.com. Subway A, C, E, #7 to 42nd St–Port Authority. This is one of the city's very best gay clubs, and also popular with the crowd from New Jersey. The Latino-flavoured party is all about kitsch, dress-up, salsa, cruising and drag.

The Monster 80 Grove St, at Sheridan Square ⓣ212/924-3558, ⓦwww.manhattan-monster.com. Subway #1 to Christopher St. Large, campy bar with drag cabaret, piano and downstairs dancefloor. Very popular, especially with tourists, yet has a strong "neighbourhood" feel. Every night brings something else, from amateur and professional go-go boys to Latin grooves and a Sunday tea dance (5.30pm). Usually no cover; $5–7 when there is one. Mon–Fri 4pm–4am, Sat & Sun 2pm–4am.

Splash 50 W 17th St, between Fifth and Sixth aves ⓣ212/691-0073, ⓦwww.splashbar.com. Subway F, M to 14th St. Large (10,000 sq ft), loud club with all the trimmings: smoke, lights and go-go boys on pedestals; there's also a basement lounge. Cover can be free to $20; it's cheaper the earlier you go. Daily 4pm–4am.

The Web 40 E 58th St, between Park and Madison aves ⓣ212/308-1546, ⓦwww.thewebnewyork.com. Subway N, R, #4, #5, #6 to Lexington Ave–59th St. Spacious dance club for the city's gay Asian population. Occasional cover of $8–10.

Shops

Babeland 94 Rivington St, between Orchard and Ludlow sts ⓣ212/375-1701; also 43 Mercer St, between Grand and Broome sts ⓣ212/966-2120, ⓦwww.babeland.com. Subway F to Delancey St. Superlative, sophisticated feminist (and queer) sex-toy store, perhaps the best in the nation. Sex workshops fill up quickly. Mon–Wed & Sun noon–10pm, Thurs–Sat noon–11pm.

Bent Pages Used Books and Ephemera 391 Van Duzer St, Staten Island. #S52 or 78 to Beach and Van Duzer sts. With the closing of the long-running Oscar Wilde Bookshop in 2009, this newish, lesbian-run spot is the only dedicated gay bookstore in the city. Thurs & Fri 5–8pm, Sat noon–8pm.

The Leather Man 111 Christopher St ⓣ212/243-5339. Subway #1 to Christopher St–Sheridan Square. Leather accessories, clothes and the like. Mon–Sat noon–9pm, Sun noon–8pm.

Nasty Pig 265A W 19th St, between Seventh and Eighth aves ⓣ212/691-6067, ⓦwww.nastypig.com. Subway #1 to 18th St. Home-grown clothing and fetish store with a friendly attitude. Mon–Sat noon–8pm, Sun 1–6pm.

Nickel 77 Eighth Ave, at 14th St ⓣ212/242-3203. Subway A, C, E, L to 14th St–Eighth Ave. Housed in an old bank building, this men-only spa also sells hair-and skincare products from various companies. Mon–Fri 11am–9.30pm, Sat & Sun 10am–9pm.

Rainbows and Triangles 192 Eighth Ave, between 19th and 20th sts ⓣ212/627-2166, ⓦwww.rainbowsandtriangles.com. Subway C, E to 23rd St. A good source for fiction and nonfiction as well as coffee-table pictorial books. The store carries T-shirts, "adult" gear and videos, candles, CDs, cards and seasonal gifts.

Universal Gear 140 Eighth Ave, between 16th and 17th sts ⓣ212/206-9119, ⓦwww.universalgear.com. Subway A, C, E, L to 14th St–Eighth Ave. Stylish garb for gays, and a huge underwear selection. Mon–Thurs & Sun 11am–10pm, Fri & Sat 11am–midnight.

29

Commercial galleries

Art, especially **contemporary art**, is huge in New York. The city remains at the centre of the global art market, with hundreds of dealers and over six hundred **galleries**, major auction houses such as Sotheby's, a highly successful public art programme and numerous high-profile art schools and colleges: the Pratt Institute, Parsons School of Design and NYU's Tisch School of the Arts among them. Though several other cities claim to have more innovative scenes – the 1950s and 1960s were really New York's creative heyday – plenty of artists continue to live here, from classical realist Jacob Collins and "relational" artists Maurizio Cattelan and Liam Gillick, to well-known figures such as Maya Lin. New York is also the home of modern **graffiti** (see p.212), with street artists such as Ellis Gallagher and Swoon leading the current scene.

Even if you have no intention of buying, many of the high-profile galleries are well worth a visit, as are some of the alternative spaces, run on a nonprofit basis and less commercial than mainstream galleries. Broadly speaking, Manhattan galleries fall into five main areas: the **Upper East Side**, **57th Street** between Sixth and Park avenues; **Soho** for established artists; **Chelsea** for most of the galleries (300) and up-and-coming artists; and **Tribeca** and the **Lower East Side** for more experimental displays. Some of the most vibrant gallery scenes in the city are to be found outside Manhattan, however, in **DUMBO** and **Williamsburg** (in Brooklyn) and the neighbourhood of **Long Island City** (Queens).

Several of the city's more exclusive galleries are invitation-only, but most accept walk-ins (although sometimes with a bit of attitude). Check Ⓦ oneartworld.com, www.artdealers.org or the weekly *Time Out New York* for openings and listings of the major commercial galleries. Admission is almost always free; the galleries that do charge a fee are considered a bit tacky.

Listed below are some of the more interesting exhibition spaces in Manhattan and elsewhere. The best time to gallery-hop is on weekday afternoons; the absolute

Art tours

A great way to see the top galleries in the city is through an art tour. Here are a couple of your best bets:

Art Entrée 48–18 Purves St, Queens Ⓣ718/391-0011, Ⓦwww.artentree.com. This excellent Long Island City-based company provides studio, gallery, museum, architecture and public art tours throughout NYC. Note that they're personalized, and therefore, expensive.

New York Gallery Tours 526 W 26th St, Manhattan Ⓣ212/946-1548, Ⓦwww.nygallerytours.com. First-rate tours of Chelsea and Soho galleries ($25), including $20 Saturday visits to the neighbourhood's "eight most fascinating shows".

worst time is on Saturday, when out-of-towners flood into the city's trendier areas to do just that. Openings – usually free and easily identified by crowds of people drinking wine from plastic cups – are excellent times to view work, eavesdrop on art-world gossip and even eat free food.

New York Gallery Week started in May 2010 and promises to be an annual celebration of art, with special events held at galleries throughout the spring – see Ⓦ www.newyorkgalleryweek.com for details.

Tribeca and Soho

Arts Projects International 429 Greenwich St, Suite 5B, between Vestry and Laight sts. Subway #1 to Canal St. Highly respected for showing leading contemporary artists from Asia, this gallery's engaging exhibits are mostly in print and have featured artists like Zheng Xuewu, Gwenn Thomas and Richard Tsao. No sign – just buzz in. Tues–Fri 11am–5pm.

The Drawing Center 35 Wooster St Ⓣ 212/219-2166, Ⓦ www.drawingcenter.org. Subway A, C, E, N, R, Q to Canal St. Presents shows of contemporary and historical works on paper, from emerging artists to the sketches of the Great Masters. Wed–Sun noon–6pm, Thurs till 8pm.

Louis K. Meisel Gallery 141 Prince St Ⓣ 212/677-1340, Ⓦ www.meiselgallery.com. Subway R to Prince St. Specializes in Photorealism – past shows have included Richard Estes and Chuck Close – as well as Abstract Illusionism (owner Meisel claims to have invented both terms). Also exhibits saucy American pin-ups. July Tues–Fri 10am–5pm; Aug by appointment only; Sept–June Tues–Sat 10am–6pm.

O K Harris 383 W Broadway Ⓣ 212/431-3600, Ⓦ www.okharris.com. Subway C, E to Spring St. Named for a mythical travelling gambler, O K is the gallery of Ivan Karp, a cigar-munching champion of Super-Realism. One of the first Soho galleries and, although not as influential as it once was, still worth a look. July Tues–Fri 10am–5pm; Sept–June Tues–Sat 10am–6pm.

Team Gallery 83 Grand St, at Greene St Ⓣ 212/279-9219, Ⓦ www.teamgal.com. Subway A, C, E, N, R, Q to Canal St. Beautiful, voyeuristic and cutting-edge work by artists such as Tracey Emin and Genesis P-Orridge is shown here. Tues–Sat 10am–6pm.

East Village and Lower East Side

Feature 131 Allen St, between Delancey and Rivington sts, Lower East Side Ⓣ 212/675-7772, Ⓦ www.featureinc.com. Subway F, J, M, Z to Delancey St–Essex St. This former Chicago gallery tends toward briefly exhibiting fairly cerebral modern artists (such as the controversial Richard Kern of "New York Girls" fame) rather than extensively highlighting a select few. Wed–Sat noon–6pm, Sun 1–6pm.

Fuse Gallery 93 Second Ave, between E 6th and 5th sts, East Village Ⓣ 212/777-7988, Ⓦ www.fusegallerynyc.com. Subway #6 to Astor Place. Funky, contemporary art at the back of the *Lit Lounge*; up-and-coming artists such as Rick Froberg and Ellen Stagg. Wed–Sat 3–8pm.

West Village

Gavin Brown's Enterprise 620 Greenwich St, at Leroy St Ⓣ 212/627-5258, Ⓦ www.gavinbrown.biz. Subway #1 to Houston St. An ultra-hip space featuring the young, cool and fearless of the mixed-media art world; look out for the white building marked "The Whole World". Tues–Sat 10am–6pm.

Chelsea

The galleries listed below are housed in independent spaces, but there are also several large **warehouses** in this neighbourhood that hold multiple galleries and are worth exploring as a group, if you have time. Unless otherwise stated, the closest subway is C, E to 23rd Street, and the galleries are located between Tenth and Eleventh avenues.

303 Gallery 547 W 21st St ⓣ212/255-1121, ⓦwww.303gallery.com. 303 Gallery shows works in a comprehensive range of media by fairly well-established contemporary artists. Tues–Sat 10am–6pm.

Allen Sheppard Gallery 530 W 25th St ⓣ212/989-9919, ⓦwww.allensheppardgallery.com. One of the most interesting painter galleries in the district, this space exhibits great stuff from the likes of David Konigberg, Willy Lenski and Sonya Sklaroff. Tues–Sat noon–6pm.

Barbara Gladstone Gallery 515 W 24th St ⓣ212/206-7606, ⓦwww.gladstonegallery.com. Paintings, sculpture and photography by hot contemporary artists like Matthew Barney and Rosemarie Trockel. Tues–Sat 10am–6pm.

Edward Thorp 210 Eleventh Ave, 6th floor, between W 24th and 25th sts ⓣ212/691-6565, ⓦwww.edwardthorpgallery.com. Mainstream contemporary American, South American and European painting and sculpture. Highlights of their roster include painter Matthew Blackwell and sculptor Deborah Butterfield. July Tues–Fri 11am–5pm; Aug by appointment only; Sept–June Tues–Sat 11am–6pm.

Gagosian Gallery 555 W 24th St ⓣ212/741-1111, ⓦwww.gagosian.com. A stalwart fixture on the New York scene, the Gagosian features both modern and contemporary works, including pieces by artists such as Damien Hirst, David Salle, Eric Fischl and Richard Serra, and photographer Alec Soth. There's also a branch uptown, at 980 Madison Ave. Tues–Sat 10am–6pm.

Greene Naftali 508 W 26th St, 8th floor ⓣ212/463-7770, ⓦwww.greenenaftaligallery.com. A wide-open, airy gallery noted for its top-notch large group shows and conceptual installations. Very cool stuff. Tues–Sat 10am–6pm.

Lehmann Maupin 540 W 26th St ⓣ212/255-2923, ⓦwww.lehmannmaupin.com. Shows a range of established international and American contemporary artists working in a variety of media, among them Tracey Emin, Juergen Teller and Gilbert & George. Also showcases diverse new talent. Tues–Sat 10am–6pm.

Mary Boone Gallery 541 W 24th St ⓣ212/752-2929, ⓦwww.maryboonegallery.com. An extension of Boone's uptown gallery (745 Fifth Ave; see p.388), this Chelsea space has facilities for large-scale works and installations by the up-and-coming darlings of the art world. At least a couple of the artists nurtured by Boone – David Salle and Julian Schnabel – have achieved superstar status. Tues–Sat 10am–6pm.

Matthew Marks Gallery 522 W 22nd St ⓣ212/243-0200, ⓦwww.matthewmarks.com. The centerpiece of Chelsea's art scene, Matthew Marks shows pieces by such well-known minimalist and abstract artists as Cy Twombly and Ellsworth Kelly. They also have nearby branches at 523 W 24th St and 521 W 21st St. Tues–Sat 11am–6pm.

Paula Cooper 521 W 21st St; 534 W 21st St; and 465 W 23rd St ⓣ212/255-1105, ⓦwww.paulacoopergallery.com. An influential gallery that shows a wide range of contemporary painting, sculpture, drawings, prints and photographs, particularly minimalist and conceptual works, and even has a recording label, Dog w/a Bone. Tues–Sat 10am–6pm.

Robert Miller 524 W 26th St ⓣ212/366-4774, ⓦwww.robertmillergallery.com. Exceptional shows of twentieth-century artists (Lee Krasner, Joan Nelson and Bernar Venet, to name but a few) – this is one of New York's true big-gun galleries. Tues–Sat 10am–6pm.

Sikkema Jenkins & Co 530 W 22nd St ⓣ212/929-2262, ⓦwww.sikkemajenkinsco.com. This somewhat controversial space often features exhibits with a definite political slant. Recently, they've been focusing on illustration. Tues–Sat 10am–6pm.

▲ Sonnabend

Sonnabend 536 W 22nd St ⓣ212/627-1018. A top gallery featuring painting, photography and video from contemporary American and European artists. Regular exhibitions from the likes of Robert Morris and Gilbert & George. Tues–Sat 10am–6pm.

Sperone Westwater 415 W 13th St, between Washington St and Ninth Ave ⓣ212/999-7337, ⓦwww.speronewestwater.com. Subway A, C, E to 14th St. High-quality European and American painting and works on paper. Artists have included Francesco Clemente, Frank Moore and Susan Rothenberg. Tues–Sat 10am–6pm.

Zach Feuer 530 W 24th St ⓣ212/989-7700, ⓦwww.zachfeuer.com. A relatively new and young power broker in the Chelsea scene, Zach Feuer shows works by bold young artists in the mould of Dana Schutz. Tues–Sat 10am–6pm.

Upper East Side

Gemini G.E.L. at Joni Moisant Weyl 980 Madison Ave, 5th floor, between E 76th and E 77th sts ⓣ212/249-3324, ⓦwww.joniweyl.com. Subway #6 to 77th St. Etchings and contemporary graphics, with some vintage prints; has shown works by Roy Lichtenstein and Robert Rauschenberg. Tues–Sat 10am–6pm.

Knoedler & Co 19 E 70th St, at Madison Ave ⓣ212/794-0550, ⓦwww.knoedlergallery.com. Subway #6 to 68th St. Renowned, nearly ancient gallery specializing in postwar and contemporary art, particularly the New York School. Shows some of the best-known names in twentieth-century art, such as Stella, Rauschenberg and Fonseca. Tues–Fri 9.30am–5.30pm, Sat 10am–5.30pm.

Leo Castelli 18 E 77th St, between Madison and Fifth aves ⓣ212/249-4470, ⓦwww.castelligallery.com. Subway #6 to 77th St. One of the original dealer-collectors, Castelli was instrumental in aiding the careers of Rauschenberg and Warhol, and this gallery offers big contemporary names at high prices. Tues–Sat 10am–6pm.

West 57th Street and around

Marlborough Gallery 40 W 57th St, between Fifth and Sixth aves ⓣ212/541-4900, ⓦwww.marlboroughgallery.com. Subway F to 57th St; N, R to Fifth Ave–59th St. Specialising in famous American and European names, with sister galleries in Chelsea, London, Monaco and Madrid. The original London gallery was founded in 1947 to help foster artistic talents such as Henry Moore and Phillip Guston. Mon–Sat 10am–5.30pm.

Mary Boone 745 Fifth Ave, between 58th and 57th sts, 4th floor ⓣ212/752-2929, ⓦwww.maryboonegallery.com. Subway F to 57th St; N, R to Fifth Ave–59th St. Mary Boone was Leo Castelli's protégée, and her gallery specializes in installations, paintings and works by up-and-coming European and American artists, as well as established artists already involved with the gallery. There's now also an interesting branch in Chelsea (see p.387). Tues–Fri 10am–6pm, Sat 10am–5pm.

Pace Wildenstein 32 E 57th St, 2nd floor, between Madison and Park aves ⓣ212/421-3292, ⓦwww.pacewildenstein.com. Subway #5, #4, #6 to 59th St. This celebrated gallery exhibits works by most of the great modern American and European artists, from Picasso to Calder to Noguchi and Rothko. Recent shows have included Diane

Arbus and Agnes Martin. Also has a good collection of prints and African art. Two Chelsea satellites located at 534 W 25th St (ⓣ212/929-7000) and 545 W 22nd St (ⓣ212/989-4258) specialize in edgier works and large installations. Tues–Fri 9.30am–5.30pm, Sat 10am–6pm; Chelsea galleries Tues–Sat 10am–6pm.

DUMBO and Brooklyn Heights

BRIC Rotunda Gallery 33 Clinton St, Brooklyn Heights ⓣ718/875-4047, ⓦwww.bricartsmedia.org. Subway R, #2, #3 to Court St–Borough Hall. This mixed-media, not-for-profit exhibition space features work by Brooklyn-based contemporary artists. Tues–Sat noon–6pm (exhibitions only).

DUMBO Arts Center 30 Washington St, at Water St, DUMBO ⓣ718/694-0831, ⓦwww.dumboartscenter.org. Subway F to York St, A, C to High St. A huge warehouse space dedicated to showing innovative new group work in five to six shows yearly. The self-proclaimed origin and centre of DUMBO's art scene. Wed–Sun noon–6pm ($2 donation suggested).

Smack Mellon Gallery 92 Plymouth St, at Washington St, DUMBO ⓣ718/834-8761, ⓦwww.smackmellon.org. Subway F to York St, A, C to High St. An interesting space that displays multidisciplinary, high-tech work by artists who have for the most part flown under the radar of art critics and spectators. Wed–Sun noon–6pm.

UrbanGlass 647 Fulton St, 3rd floor (entrance at 57 Rockwell Place around the corner), DUMBO ⓣ718/625-3685, ⓦwww.urbanglass.org. Subway B, Q, R to DeKalb Ave. Small but amazing glass gallery attached to the studio of the same name. Tues–Fri 10am–6pm, Sat & Sun 10am–5pm.

Williamsburg

Front Room 147 Roebling St, between Metropolitan Ave and Hope St ⓣ718/782-2556, ⓦwww.frontroom.org. Subway L to Bedford Ave. One of the neighbourhood's best galleries and also a popular performance-art space. Best place to get a good first sense of the local scene. Fri–Sun 1–6pm.

Pierogi 177 N 9th St, between Bedford Ave and Driggs Ave ⓣ718/599-2144, ⓦwww.pierogi2000.com. Subway L to Bedford Ave. This former workshop mounts fascinating installations of various kinds. It is noted in the art world for its travelling "flatfiles", a collection of folders containing the work of six hundred or so artists, stored clinically and provocatively in metal, sliding cabinets. Tues–Sun 11am–6pm.

WAH (Williamsburg Art and Historical Center) 135 Broadway, at Bedford Ave ⓣ718/486-6012, ⓦwww.wahcenter.net. Subway J, M, Z to Marcy Ave. Beautiful, fascinating multimedia arts centre, with a focus on painting and sculpture. Sat & Sun noon–6pm. See p.241.

Alternative spaces

The galleries listed above (at least those in Manhattan) are part of a system designed to channel artists' work through the gallery spaces and, eventually, into the hands of collectors. While initial acceptance by a major gallery is an important rite of passage for an up-and-coming artist, it shouldn't be forgotten that this system's philosophy is based on making money for gallery owners, who normally receive fifty percent of the sale price. For an artist's work to be non-commercial in these spaces is perhaps an even greater sin than being socially or politically unacceptable.

The galleries included below, often referred to as **alternative spaces**, provide a forum for the kind of risky and non-commercially viable art that many other galleries may not be able to afford to show. Those mentioned here are at the cutting edge of new art in the city.

Apex Art 291 Church St, between White and Walker sts ⓣ212/431-5270, ⓦwww.apexart.org. Subway N, Q, R to Canal St; #1 to Franklin St. A nonprofit exhibition space that invites dealers, artists, writers, critics and international art-world bodies to act as curators and mount idea-based shows, along with lectures and associated events. Tues–Sat 11am–6pm.

Art in General 79 Walker St, between Broadway and Lafayette St ⓣ212/219-0473, ⓦwww.artingeneral.org. Subway N, Q, R to Canal St. Founded in 1981, this exhibition space is devoted to the unconventional art of emerging artists. Recent exhibits have featured Croatian video artists and a parody of roadside signage. Tues–Sat noon–6pm.

Artists Space 38 Greene St, at Grand St, 3rd floor ⓣ212/226-3970, ⓦwww.artistsspace.org. Subway A, C, E, N, R, Q to Canal St. One of the most respected alternative spaces, with frequently changing theme-based exhibits, film screenings, videos, installations and events. In over thirty years of existence, Artists Space has presented the work of thousands of emerging artists. Tues–Sat noon–6pm.

Exit Art 475 Tenth Ave, at 36th St ⓣ212/966-7745, ⓦwww.exitart.org. Subway A, C, E to 34th St. A hip crowd frequents this huge alternative gallery. It favours big installations, up-and-coming, multimedia and edgy cultural and political subjects. Tues–Thurs 10am–6pm, Fri 10am–8pm, Sat noon–8pm.

PS122 Gallery 150 First Ave, entrance on E 9th St, between First Ave and Ave A ⓣ212/228-4249, ⓦwww.ps122gallery.org. Subway L to First Ave. Nonprofit gallery, affiliated with a high-profile experimental performance space that highlights emerging artists. Thurs–Sun noon–6pm.

White Columns 320 W 13th St, entrance on Horatio St, between Hudson St and W 4th St ⓣ212/924-4212, ⓦwww.whitecolumns.org. Subway A, C, E to 14th St. White Columns focuses on emerging artists, and is considered very influential. Check out the fascinating, ever-changing group shows. Tues–Sat noon–6pm.

30

Shopping

Retail junkies beware: **shops** are one of New York's killer attractions. The city is the undisputed commercial capital of America, especially in fashion. There are flagship stores for every major brand, both ubiquitous (H&M) and exclusive (Vera Wang), so you can stock up just as easily on a designer leather clutch as you can a pair of tennis socks. In between all the big names, you'll also find dozens of quirky local boutiques and bazaars worth seeking out. We've sifted through the best that the city has to offer and presented our pick of Manhattan's retail wonders below.

Practicalities

Opening hours in midtown Manhattan are roughly Monday to Saturday 9am to 6pm. Downtown shops (Soho, Tribeca, the East and West villages, the Lower East Side) tend to stay open later, at least until 8pm and sometimes until about midnight; bookstores especially are often open late. Most stores are open Sunday as well, but with abbreviated hours. Chinatown's shops and stalls are open all day, every day, while the stores that serve workers in the Financial District stick to nine-to-five office hours and are usually shuttered on Saturday and Sunday. These places excepted, expect retail establishments to be most crowded on weekends, especially in Soho and midtown.

Credit cards are widely accepted: even the smallest shops usually take American Express, MasterCard or Visa. A total 8.875 percent **sales tax** (which includes 4 percent state tax) will be added to your bill for all purchases; the only exceptions are for items of clothing and footwear under $110, which are tax-free.

The best places for browsing

If you'd rather browse than make a beeline for a specific store, listed below are the best areas in the city for a bit of ambling and window-shopping.

- The whole of Soho
- Lower East Side: Orchard and Ludlow streets
- East Village: 7th and 9th streets
- Meatpacking District: 14th Street between Eighth and Tenth avenues
- Lower Fifth: Fifth Avenue between 14th and 23rd streets
- Midtown: Fifth Avenue between 42nd and 60th streets
- Upper East Side: Madison Avenue between 60th and 80th streets

Shopping categories

Beauty and cosmetics

All department stores stock the main brands of beauty products (as does Century 21, often at a deep discount – see p.403), but if you're looking for hard-to-find cosmetics lines, here are the best options.

Aveda 233 Spring St, between Sixth Ave and Varick St ⓣ212/807-1492, ⓦwww.aveda.com. Subway C to Spring St. New Agey cosmetics company specializing in plant-extract-based shampoos, conditioners and skincare; some locations (call for more) also have a spa where you can sign up for pricey treatments. Mon–Fri 9am–9pm, Sat 9am–7pm, Sun 10am–6pm.

C.O. Bigelow Pharmacy 414 Sixth Ave, between W 8th and W 9th sts ⓣ212/473-7324, ⓦwww.bigelowchemists.com. Subway A, B, C, D, E, F, M to W 4th St; #1 to Christopher St. Established in 1882, C.O. Bigelow is one of the oldest pharmacies in the country – and that's exactly how it looks, with the original Victorian shopfittings still in place. Specializing in lesser-known and European beauty brands, this is the place to come for beauty and cosmetic items that you can't find elsewhere in the city. Mon–Fri 7.30am–9pm, Sat 8.30am–7pm, Sun 8.30am–5.30pm.

Kiehl's 109 Third Ave, between E 13th and E 14th sts ⓣ212/677-3171, ⓦwww.kiehls.com. Subway L to Third Ave. Decorated with aviation and motorcycle memorabilia, this 150-year-old pharmacy sells its own range of natural-ingredient-based classic creams, oils and so on. Known for giving out plenty of samples to customers, whether you're buying or not. Lots of celebs swear by this stuff, especially the patented Crème de Corps body lotion. Mon–Sat 10am–8pm, Sun 11am–6pm.

MAC 113 Spring St, between Greene and Mercer sts ⓣ212/334-4641, ⓦwww.maccosmetics.com. Subway #6 to Spring St. Also 175 Fifth Ave, at 22nd St, and several other locations. MAC is known for both its high-quality, non-animal-tested cosmetics and its HIV/AIDS fundraising (pick up a Viva Glam lipstick to donate). Quite popular with models and celebs. Daily 11am–7pm, Wed–Sat till 8pm.

Ray's Beauty Supply 721 Eighth Ave, at 45th St ⓣ212/757-0175, ⓦwww.raybeauty.com. Subway A, C, E to 42nd St. This ramshackle store supplies most of the city's hairdressers with their potions and props. Something of an "industry insider" place, but the public is welcome. The low prices make it worth a detour. Mon–Wed 8.30am–6pm, Thurs & Fri 8.30am–7pm, Sat 9am–5.15pm.

Ricky's 590 Broadway, between Houston and Prince sts ⓣ212-226-5552, ⓦwww.rickysnyc.com. Subway N, R to Prince St. Several other locations. New York's haven for the overdone, the brash and the OTT (think drag-diva favourites and plenty of lurid wigs). Stocks cool brands like Urban Decay and Tony & Tina as well as a house line of products. Daily 9am–10pm.

Sabon 93 Spring St, between Broadway and Mercer St ⓣ212/925-0742, ⓦsabonnyc.com. Subway N, R to Prince St; #6 to Spring St. Luxury body and bath fragrances, soaps and aromatic oils from Israel; friendly assistants help you try the products at the old-fashioned sink in the middle of the store. Mon–Sat 10am–10pm, Sun 11am–8.30pm.

Sephora 555 Broadway, between Prince and Spring sts ⓣ212/625-1309, ⓦwww.sephora.com. Subway N, R to Prince St. Also 597 Fifth Ave, at E 48th St ⓣ212/980-6534.

"Warehouse" of perfumes, make-up and body-care products all lined up alphabetically so everything's easy to find and you don't have to pester any salespeople. Call for additional locations. Mon–Sat 10am–8pm, Sun 11am–7pm.

Zitomer **969 Madison Ave, at E 76th ⓣ212/737-5561, ⓦwww.zitomer.com. Subway #6 to 77th St.** A venerable pharmacy that has transformed itself into a full-blown mini-department store, Zitomer serves the beauty and cosmetic needs of the Fifth Ave gentry. Stocked to the gills with every brand and item imaginable. Mon–Fri 9am–8pm, Sat 9am–7pm, Sun 10am–6pm.

Salons and spas

Astor Place Hair Designers **2 Astor Place, at Broadway ⓣ212/475-9854, ⓦwww.astorplacehairnyc.com. Subway #6 to Astor Place.** If you're caught short in the city and need a cheap haircut, try this local institution, a unisex barbershop with dozens of haircutters sprawled about three floors. Trims $14 and up. Mon & Sat 8am–8pm, Tues–Fri 8am–10pm, Sun 9am–6pm.

Bliss **568 Broadway, 2/F, between Houston and Prince sts ⓣ212/219-8970, ⓦwww.blissworld.com. Subway R to Prince St.** Top-notch spa with massage, facial, nail and wax services. There's a bevy of beauty potions waiting for you to purchase as you depart, including the spa's own popular lotions and the full line of Crème de la Mer skin products. There are two other spas at 12 W 57th St between Fifth and Sixth aves, and inside the *W Hotel* at 541 Lexington Ave at 49th St (use the number above for an appointment at any location). Mon–Fri 9am–9pm Sat 9.30am–6.30pm, Sun10am–6pm.

Halo Air Salt Room **133 W 22nd St, between Sixth and Seventh aves. ⓣ646/666-0554, ⓦwww.haloair.com. Subway F, M, #1 to 23rd St.** Ron Rofé's Dead Sea-inspired spa is worth a visit for the novelty factor alone; five luxurious rooms encased in Ukrainian salt, equipped with lounge chairs, movies and internet. The salt is supposed to help cleanse the body and aid breathing. $100/hr. Mon–Fri 9am–10pm, Sat & Sun 10am–8pm.

Jin Soon **56th E 4th St, between Second Ave and the Bowery ⓣ212/473-2047, ⓦwww.jinsoon.com. Subway #6 to Astor Place.** Small, soothing Japanese hand-and-foot spa. It's great for mani- and pedicures (has other branches at 23 Jones St in the West Village and 421 E 73rd St in the Upper East Side). Daily 11am–8pm, Sun till 7pm.

John Frieda **30 E 76th St, at Madison Ave ⓣ212/327-3400, ⓦwww.johnfrieda.com. Subway #6 to 77th St. Also 825 Washington St, between Gansevoort and Little W 12th sts ⓣ212/675-0001.** An excellent, highly rated (and quite expensive) hair salon that's also home to top celebrity stylists Luigi Murenu and Harry Josh. Mon & Sat 9am–6pm, Tues–Fri 8.30am–7pm.

Ling **191 Prince St, at Sullivan St ⓣ212/982-8833, ⓦlingskincare.com. Subway N, R to Prince St.** One of the city's most talked-about facial spas, located in the heart of Soho. Call for additional locations. Mon–Fri 10am–9pm, Sat 9.30am–9pm, Sun 11am–7pm.

Sally Hersberger **425 W 14th St, between Ninth and Tenth aves ⓣ212/206-8700, ⓦwww.sallyhershberger.com. Subway A, C, E, L to 14th St.** Stylist to stars like Sarah Jessica Parker, Sally Hersberger reigns supreme among New York's hair pros. She's in town about half the time, but her entire staff is trained in "the Hersberger method". Good spot for star-gazing. Tues–Fri 9am–7pm, Sat 9am–5pm.

Soho Sanctuary **119 Mercer St, between Prince and Spring sts ⓣ212/334-5550, ⓦwww.sohosanctuary.com. Subway N, R to Prince St.** One of the most enticing spas in the city, with a steam room, a sauna and a full range of services. Eminently relaxing, and women-only. Mon 3–9pm, Tues–Fri 10am–9pm, Sat 10am–8pm, Sun noon–6pm.

Books

New York is a paradise for book lovers. Despite the challenge of Amazon.com and the internet in general, there are still more independent booksellers here than in most other parts of America, with shops that run the gamut from clever and focused to quirky and expansive. Quick literary fixes can be easily taken care of, too – superstores like Barnes & Noble are omnipresent in New York.

General interest and new books

Book Culture 2915 Broadway at 114th St ⓣ646/403-3000, ⓦwww.booksite.com. Subway #1 to Cathedral Parkway (110th St). The new, main shop of the largest independent bookstore in the city (the first Book Culture, now mostly academic-oriented, remains at 536 112th St) boasts a fine selection of literary (especially international) fiction, children's books and much more. Mon–Fri 9am–11pm, Sat 10am–11pm, Sun 10am–10pm.

McNally Jackson 52 Prince St, between Mulberry and Lafayette sts ⓣ212/274-1160, ⓦwww.mcnallyjackson.com. Subway N, R to Prince St. This Canadian book chain has gained a foothold in the heart of Manhattan with its prime Soho location. Great service, and the staff here are friendly, too. Daily 10am–10pm, Sun till 9pm.

St Mark's Bookshop 31 Third Ave, at E 9th St ⓣ212/260-7853, ⓦwww.stmarksbookshop.com. Subway #6 to Astor Place. Founded in 1977, the best-known independent bookstore in the city offers a good selection of titles on contemporary art, politics, feminism, the environment and literary criticism, as well as more obscure subjects. Cool postcards, too, and stocked full of radical and art magazines. Mon–Sat 10am–midnight, Sun 11am–midnight.

Shakespeare & Co 939 Lexington Ave, between 68th and 69th sts ⓣ212/570-0201, ⓦwww.shakeandco.com (also 716 Broadway, at Washington Place ⓣ212/529-1330; and 137 E 23rd St, at Lexington Ave ⓣ212/505-2021 for course books only). Subway #6 to 68th St. New and used books, both paper and hardcover. Great for fiction and psychology. Mon–Fri 9am–8pm, Sat 10am–7pm, Sun 11am–6pm.

Three Lives & Co 154 W 10th St, at Waverly Place ⓣ212/741-2069, ⓦwww.threelives.com. Subway A, B, C, D, E, F, M to W 4th St; #1 to Christopher St. Excellent literary bookstore that has an especially good selection of works by and for women, as well as general titles. There's an excellent reading series in the autumn, which has previously hosted the likes of Maya Angelou and Peter Carey. Mon & Tues noon–8pm, Wed–Sat 11am–8.30pm, Sun noon–7pm.

Secondhand books

Argosy Bookstore 116 E 59th St, at Park Ave ⓣ212/753-4455, ⓦwww.argosybooks.com. Subway #4, #5, #6 to 59th St–Lexington Ave. Open since 1925 and unbeatable for rare books, Argosy also sells clearance books and titles of all kinds, though the shop's reputation means you may find mainstream works cheaper elsewhere. Mon–Fri 10am–6pm; Sept to mid-May also Sat 10am–5pm.

Housing Works Used Books Café 126 Crosby St, between Houston and Prince sts ⓣ212/334-3324, ⓦwww.housingworks.com. Subway B, D, F, M to Broadway–Lafayette; N, R to Prince St; #6 to Bleecker St. Excellent selection of very cheap and secondhand books. With a small espresso and snack bar and comfy chairs, it's a great place to spend an afternoon. Proceeds benefit AIDS charity. Mon–Fri 10am–9pm, Sat & Sun noon–7pm.

Strand Bookstore 828 Broadway, at E 12th St ⓣ212/473-1452, ⓦwww.strandbooks.com. Subway N, R, Q, L, #4, #5, #6 to Union Square. Yes, it's hot and crowded, and the staff seem to resent working there, but with "18 miles of books" and a stock of more than 2.5 million titles, this is the largest discount book operation in the city. There are recent review copies and new books for half-price in the basement; older books go for anything from 50¢. Mon–Sat 9.30am–10.30pm, Sun 11am–10.30pm.

Special-interest bookstores

Art and architecture

See also the excellent bookstores at the Met (p.161), MoMA (p.133), Whitney (p.177) and New Museum of Contemporary Art (p.88).

MoMA Design Store 81 Spring St, at Crosby St ⓣ646/613-1367, ⓦwww.momastore.org. Subway N, R to Prince St; #6 to Bleecker St. Contemporary art books galore. Mon–Sat 10am–8pm, Sun 11am–7pm.

Unoppressive, Non-Imperialist Bargain Books 34 Carmine St, between Bleecker and Bedford sts ⓣ212/229-0079, ⓦunoppressivebooks.blogspot.com. Subway A, B, C, D, E, F, M to W 4th St; #1 to Houston St. Arty overstock amongst a hodgepodge of travel guides, biographies, children's pop-up books and spiritual titles. Daily 11am–10pm, Fri & Sat till midnight.

Comics and sci-fi

Forbidden Planet 840 Broadway, at 13th St ⓣ212/473-1576, ⓦwww.fpnyc.com. Subway

#4, #5, #6, L, N, R, Q to 14th St/Union Square. Science fiction, fantasy, horror fiction, graphic novels and comics. Great for its large backlist of indie and underground comics, they also hawk T-shirts and the latest sci-fi toys and collectibles. Mon–Tues & Sun 10am–10pm, Wed 9am–midnight, Thurs–Sat 10am–midnight.

Jim Hanley's Universe 4 W 33rd St, between Fifth Ave and Broadway ⓣ212/268-7088, ⓦwww.jhuniverse.com. Subway B, D, F, M, N, Q, R to 34th St–Herald Square. Offers mainstream issues from the big leagues (DC, Marvel) as well as graphic novels, manga, small pressings and collectibles. Authors, illustrators and comic-related media types (Neil Gaiman, Mr. Tarantino, Guillermo Del Toro) have often stopped by to discuss their work. Staff are knowledgeable and try extra hard to please. Mon–Sat 9am–11pm, Sun 10am–9pm.

St Mark's Comics 11 St Mark's Place, between Second and Third aves ⓣ212/598-9439, ⓦwww.stmarkscomics.com. Subway #6 to Astor Place. Pilgrimage site for comic, manga and graphic-novel fans from all over the world, with plenty of rare memorabilia (T-shirts, action-figures) to enhance their huge stock of comics. Mon 10am–11pm, Tues–Sat 10am–1am, Sun 11am–11pm.

Crime and mystery

The Mysterious Bookshop 58 Warren St, at West Broadway ⓣ212/587-1011, ⓦwww.mysteriousbookshop.com. Subway #1, #2, #3 to Chambers St. The founder of this store started the Mysterious Press (now owned by Warner Books). The shop sells mysteries of every kind, from classic detectives to just-published titles, and also trades in some first editions and "Sherlockiana". Daily 11am–7pm.

Partners & Crime 44 Greenwich Ave, at Charles St ⓣ212/243-0440, ⓦwww.crimepays.com. Subway #1 to Christopher St. Crime novels. Also home to the W-Wow! Radio group (ⓣ212/462-3027), which performs classic 1940s radio scripts on the first Sat of every month (6pm & 8pm; tickets $7). Daily noon–9pm, Fri & Sat till 10pm, Sun till 7pm.

Foreign Language

Kinokuniya Bookstore 1073 Sixth Ave, between 40th and 41st sts ⓣ212/765-7766, ⓦwww.kinokuniya.com/ny. Subway B, D, F, M to 42nd St–Bryant Park. The largest Japanese bookstore in New York, with English books on Japan, too. Mon–Sat 10am–8pm, Sun 11am–7.30pm.

Rizzoli 31 W 57th St, between Fifth and Sixth aves ⓣ212/759-2424, ⓦwww.rizzoliusa.com. Subway F to 57th St. Manhattan branch of the prestigious Italian bookstore chain and publisher. They specialize in European publications, and have a good selection of foreign newspapers and magazines along with art books of all sorts. Mon–Fri 10am–7.30pm, Sat 10.30am–7pm, Sun 11am–7pm.

Russian Bookstore 21 174 Fifth Ave, between 22nd and 23rd sts ⓣ212/924-5477, ⓦwww.russianbookstore21.com. Subway N, R to 23rd St. All books, all in Russian. For curiosity's sake, worth a trip even for a non-speaker. Mon–Sat 11am–6pm.

Miscellaneous

Bluestockings 172 Allen St, between Stanton and Rivington sts ⓣ212/777-6028, ⓦbluestockings.com. Subway F to Lower East Side–Second Ave. New and used titles but only those authored by or related to women. Cosy, well-stocked, collective-style store in what was once a dilapidated crack house; nice FairTrade café, too. Daily 11am–11pm.

Books of Wonder 18 W 18th St, between Fifth and Sixth aves ⓣ212/989-3270, ⓦwww.booksofwonder.com. Subway #1, #2 to 18th St; F, M to 14th St; #4, #5, #6, N, Q, R to Union Square. A heavenly collection of kid lit. Mon–Sat 10am–7pm, Sun 11am–6pm.

Center for Book Arts 28 W 27th St, in between Broadway and Sixth Ave, 3rd floor ⓣ212/481-0295, ⓦwww.centerforbookarts.org. Subway N, R to 28th St. Not so much a bookstore as a space dedicated to the art of bookmaking. Hosts regular readings and workshops – fascinating stuff. Mon–Fri 10am–6pm, Sat 10am–4pm.

Complete Traveller Antiquarian Bookstore 199 Madison Ave, at E 35th St ⓣ212/685-9007, ⓦwww.ctrarebooks.com. Subway #6 to 33rd St. An extensive collection of rare travel tomes, including the entire Baedekers series, WPA Guides, old books on NYC and maps galore. You can also find other (non-travel) first pressings and vintage children's books here. Mon–Fri 9.30am–6pm, Sat 10am–6pm, Sun noon–5pm.

Drama Bookshop 250 W 40th St, between Seventh and Eighth aves ⓣ212/944-0595, ⓦwww.dramabookshop.com. Subway A, C, E to

42nd St. Theatre books, scripts and publications on all manner of drama-related subjects since 1917. Mon–Sat 11am–7pm, Thurs till 8pm with complimentary wine and cheese from 6pm.

Hue-Man Bookstore & Café 2319 Frederick Douglass Blvd, between 124th and 125th sts. ⓣ212/665-7400, ⓦwww.huemanbookstore.com. Subway A, B, C, D to 125th St. Harlem's best bookshop, crammed with all sorts of African-American, Caribbean and African lit – as well as magazines, regular books and a café. Mon–Sat 10am–8pm, Sun 11am–7pm.

Kitchen Arts & Letters 1435 Lexington Ave, between 94th and 95th sts ⓣ212/876-5550, ⓦwww.kitchenartsandletters.com. Subway #6 to 96th St. Cookbooks and books about food; run by a former culinary editor. Mon 1–6pm, Tues–Fri 10am–6.30pm, Sat 11am–6pm; closed Sat July & Aug.

The Old Print Shop 150 Lexington Ave, between 29th & 30th sts ⓣ212/683-3951, ⓦwww.oldprintshop.com. Subway #6 to 28th St. The place to find a great old map of a New York neighbourhood, a first-edition art book or a print from an old *Harper's Weekly*. June–Aug Mon–Thurs 9am–5pm, Fri 9am–4pm; Sept–May Tues–Fri 9am–5pm, Sat 9am–4pm.

Revolution Books 146 W 26th St, between Sixth and Seventh aves ⓣ212/691-3345, ⓦwww.revolutionbooksnyc.org. Subway #1 to 28th St. New York's major left-wing bookstore and contact point, with a wide range of political and cultural titles and periodicals. More significantly, a place for healthy discourse: almost every night, the store holds screenings, salons or other events (after official closing time). Daily noon–7pm.

Department stores

Barneys, Bergdorf Goodman and Saks Fifth Avenue are among the world's most famous (and most beautiful) **department stores** – each of their buildings is a landmark in itself. In general, the status of department stores in America is not what it once was; the last decades of the twentieth century were particularly tough, as specialty outlets swallowed up business. The department stores that have survived this transition, especially those in New York, have tweaked their offerings to provide fewer essentials and more luxuries (Macy's is a rare exception). Many of these stores offer in-house **discount cards** for foreign visitors – ask at the information desk.

Barneys New York 660 Madison Ave, at 61st St ⓣ212/826-8900, ⓦwww.barneys.com. Subway N, R to Fifth Ave–59th St. Barneys has been considered the trendiest New York department store for well over a decade now, and shows no sign of weakening. It's a temple to designer fashion, and the best place to find cutting-edge labels or next season's hot item. The Co-op section, focusing on younger styles, was such a hit that the powers that be opened several standalone **Barneys Co-op** stores (see website for details). Mon–Fri 10am–8pm, Sat 10am–7pm, Sun 11am–6pm.

Bergdorf Goodman 754 and 745 Fifth Ave, at 58th St ⓣ212/753-7300. Subway F to 57th St; N, R to Fifth Ave–59th St. This venerable department store caters to the city's wealthiest shoppers. Haute couture designers and salons fill both buildings, one for men, one for women, and it's the fairer of the sexes that get to shop within the

▲ Barney's New York

former Vanderbilt mansion on the east side of Fifth. Has exclusive rights to lines by Yves Saint Laurent and Chloé, among others. Mon–Fri 10am–8pm, Sat 10am–7pm, Sun noon–6pm.

Bloomingdale's Lexington Ave and 59th St (officially 1000 Third Ave) ⓣ212/705-2000, ⓦwww.bloomingdales.com. Subway N, R, #4, #5, #6 to Lexington Ave–59th St. Out-of-towners flock here for its famed "classiness", though local power-shoppers are more likely to view it as a bit of a frumpy has-been. It does still have the atmosphere of a large, bustling bazaar, packed with concessionaires offering perfumes and designer clothes. Mon, Tues & Thurs 10am–8.30pm, Wed, Fri & Sat 10am–10pm, Sun 11am–7pm.

Henri Bendel 712 Fifth Ave, between 55th and 56th sts ⓣ212/247-1100, ⓦwww.henribendel.com. Subway N, R to Fifth Ave–59th St. More gentle in its approach than the biggies, this store's refinement is thanks in part to its classic reuse of the Coty perfume building, with windows by René Lalique. There's an array of top-shelf make-up at street level and gorgeous designer clothing – with price tags certain to send your blood pressure soaring – upstairs. The powder rooms appear designed for royalty. Mon–Sat 10am–8pm, Sun noon–7pm.

Jeffrey 449 W 14th St, between Ninth and Tenth aves ⓣ212/206-1272, ⓦwww.jeffreynewyork.com. Subway A, C, E to 14th St. Opened in the 1990s, Jeffrey is a relative newcomer to New York's department-store scene. The all-white emporium is set squat in the middle of the city's cutting-edge Meatpacking District, and features offerings from trend-setting lines like Boudicca and Tess Giberson. Mon–Wed & Fri 10am–8pm, Thurs 10am–9pm, Sat 10am–7pm, Sun 12.30–6pm.

Macy's 151 W 34th St, on Broadway at Herald Square ⓣ212/695-4400 or 1-800/289-6229, ⓦwww.macys.com. Subway B, D, F, M, N, Q, R to 34th St–Herald Square. With two buildings, two million square feet of floor space and ten floors (four for women's garments alone), Macy's is, quite simply, the largest department store in the world. Given its size, it's not the hotbed of top fashion it ought to be: most merchandise is of mediocre quality. One highlight is The Cellar, the housewares department in the basement, arguably the best in the city. If you're not American, head to the visitor centre to receive a ten-percent discount card (bring your passport). Mon–Sat 10am–9.30pm, Sun 11am–8.30pm.

Saks Fifth Avenue 611 Fifth Ave, at 50th St ⓣ212/753-4000, ⓦwww.saks.com. Subway E, M to Fifth Ave–53rd St; B, D, F, M to 47–50 St–Rockefeller Center. Since 1924, the name Saks has been virtually synonymous with style. No less true today, the store has updated itself to carry the merchandise of all the big designers, while still retaining its reputation for quality. The ground floor can be a bit like Grand Central terminal as multiple salesgirls assault you with drive-by perfume sprays, but they stock top cosmetic lines (like Armani) that you can't find elsewhere in the city. Mon–Wed, Fri & Sat 10am–7pm, Thurs 10am–8pm, Sun noon–6pm.

Electronic and video equipment

Buying **electronic and video equipment** in New York can be a good deal, especially if you are visiting from Europe, where such merchandise is more expensive; make sure that appliances are compatible with your home country before handing over the cash. Tech-heads can brave the risky discount shopping on Sixth and Seventh avenues north of Times Square in the 50s for cameras, stereos and MP3 players, but it's much easier to head for the Apple stores (attractions in themselves), B&H or J&R, where merchandise is not only cheap but reliable as well.

Apple Store 103 Prince St, at Greene St ⓣ212/226-3126, ⓦwww.apple.com. Subway N, R to Prince St (other locations at 767 Fifth Ave, 401 W 14th St and 1981 Broadway). The original Apple gadget store in Manhattan gets extremely crowded, but the latest in laptops, iPads, iPhones and iPods are all here for as cheap as you'll get them anywhere – you can also play with the newest models. Head upstairs for technical support at the genius bar or sit in on one of the many tutorials in the theatre. Daily 9am–9pm, Sun till 7pm.

B&H Photo Video **420 Ninth Ave, between 33rd and 34th sts ⓣ212/444-6615 or 1-800/606-6969, ⓦwww.bhphotovideo.com. Subway A, C, E to 34th St.** For film, cameras and specialty equipment; knowledgeable sales staff will take the time to guide you through a buying decision. Excellent used-goods selection upstairs. Mon–Thurs 9am–7pm, Fri 9am–2pm, Sun 10am–6pm; closed Jewish holidays.

J&R Music and Computer World **15–23 Park Row, between Beekman and Ann sts ⓣ212/238-9000, ⓦwww.jr.com. Subway R to City Hall; #2, #3 to Park Place, #4, #5, #6 to Brooklyn Bridge–City Hall.** You'll find a good selection (for decent prices) of stereo and computer equipment at this strip of stores down by City Hall, as well as home appliances and CDs. If you can plug it in, they sell it here – and often at the cheapest prices in the city. Mon–Sat 9am–7.30pm, Sun 10.30am–6.30pm.

Fashion: accessories

Agent Provocateur **133 Mercer St, at Prince St ⓣ212/965-0229, ⓦwww.agentprovocateur.com. Subway N, R to Prince St.** New York outpost of the saucy, sexy, luxury lingerie line, co-owned by Joe Corre, son of avant-garde designer Vivienne Westwood. Think frills, bows and lashings of lace. Mon–Sat 11am–7pm, Sun noon–6pm.

Alain Mikli Optique **986 Madison Ave, between 76th and 77th sts ⓣ212/472-6085, ⓦwww.mikli.com. Subway #6 to 77th St.** The French king of eyewear. This is the *only* place to go for high-end fashionable frames. Mon–Wed & Fri 10.30am–6.30pm, Thurs 10am–7pm, Sat 10am–6pm, Sun noon–5pm.

Kate Spade **454 Broome St, at Mercer St ⓣ212/274-1991, ⓦwww.katespade.com. Subway N, R to Prince St; #6 to Spring St.** Boxy, high-quality fabric bags that were all the rage in the late 1990s. Get yourself one now that they're out of vogue and you may be doing yourself a favour – the "retro" Kate Spade craze is only a matter of time (and Kate knock-offs are still doing a steady trade on Canal Street). Mon–Sat 11am–7pm, Sun noon–6pm.

Mixona **262 Mott St, between Houston and Prince sts. Subway N, R to Prince St.** Gorgeous (and expensive) grabs for those with a fetish for undergarments that are both sexy and functional. Daily 11am–8.30pm, Sun till 7.30pm.

Robert Marc **551 Madison Ave, between 55th and 56th sts ⓣ212/319-2000, ⓦwww.robertmarc.com. Subway E, M to Fifth Ave–53rd St. Also at 400 Madison Ave, between E 47th &**

The Diamond District

The strip of 47th Street between Fifth and Sixth avenues is known as the **Diamond District** or **"Diamond Row"**. At street level are dozens of retail shops and more than twenty specialist marts known as "exchanges" – combined, they sell more jewellery than any other area in the world. There are separate dealers for different gems, gold and silver – even dealers who will string your beads for you, appraisers and "findings" stores where you can pick up the basic makings of do-it-yourself jewellery, like chains and earring posts. Some jewellers trade only among themselves; some sell retail; and others do business by appointment only. Most shops are open Monday to Saturday 10am to 5.30pm, though a few close on Friday afternoon and Saturday for religious reasons, and the standard vacation time is from the end of June to the second week in July.

It is very important that you shop armed with some information. Research what you are looking for and be as particular as possible. If at all feasible, it's always better to go to someone who has been specifically recommended to you. For a listing of all the district's vendors, shopping tips and the "Buyers Bill of Rights", visit ⓦwww.diamonddistrict.org.

If you want to get your sparklies **graded or appraised**, try the Gemological Institute of America at 580 Fifth Ave, 2nd floor (ⓣ1-800/366-8519), or the Universal Gemological Laboratory at 71 W 47th St, suite 204 (ⓣ212/921-3324).

E 48th sts; 436 West Broadway, between Prince and Spring sts; 386 Bleecker St, at Perry St; and three other locations in the Upper East Side. Exclusive New York distributor of frames by the likes of Lunor and Kirei Titan; also sells Retrospecs, restored antique eyewear from the 1890s to the 1940s. Very expensive and very hot.

Selima Optique 59 Wooster St, at Greene St ⓣ212/343-9490, ⓦwww.selimaoptique.com. Subway A, C, E to Canal St. Also 899 Madison, at E 72nd St; and 357 Bleecker St. Owner Selima Selaun stocks her own line of girly, groovy specs, alongside favourites from well-known designers like Dior and Kata. Mon–Sat 11am–8pm, Sun noon–6pm.

Fashion: jewellery

Karen Karch 240 Mulberry St, between Prince and Spring sts ⓣ212/965-9699, ⓦwww.karenkarch.com. Subway N, R to Prince St. One of the city's most exclusive jewellery stores, where one-of-a-kind items are displayed amid breezy surroundings on dollhouse furniture. Wed–Sat 1–7pm.

Me & Ro 241 Elizabeth St, between Houston and Prince sts ⓣ917/237-9215, ⓦwww.meandrojewelry.com. Subway B, D, F, M to Broadway–Lafayette; N, R to Prince St. The hottest, most distinctive jeweller in Manhattan, with tasteful modernist designs worth going out of your way for. Some items are quite expensive, but you can get really nice earrings here for a reasonable price. Mon–Sat 11am–7pm, Sun noon–6pm.

Tiffany & Co 727 Fifth Ave, at E 57th St. Subway N, R to Fifth Ave–59th St ⓣ212/755-8000, ⓦwww.tiffany.com. Even if you're just window-shopping, Tiffany's is worth a perusal, its soothing green marble and weathered wood interior best described by Truman Capote's fictional Holly Golightly: "It calms me down right away … nothing very bad could happen to you there." Mon–Sat 10am–7pm, Sun noon–6pm.

Fashion: clothing

New York is one of the major nerve centres of the global fashion industry, with the likes of Calvin Klein, Ralph Lauren, Donna Karan and a growing list of hot new designers. You'll also find boutiques for just about every major designer on the planet, with prices significantly lower than in European cities or Tokyo.

As such, **clothes shopping** here is a feast for any fashionista; if you are prepared to search the city with sufficient dedication, you can find just about anything. We've divided this section into four categories: **boutiques and trendy labels,** where you can pick up local big names or one-offs; **designer stores; discount stores,** where you can snag big names at deep discounts; and **vintage and thrift,** including the increasingly popular (and browse-worthy) resale or consignment stores, where owners sell off last season's barely worn outfits.

Boutiques and trendy labels

Brooklyn Industries 162 Bedford Ave, at N 8th St, Williamsburg ⓣ718/486-6464, ⓦwww.brooklynindustries.com. Subway L to Bedford Ave. Also in Soho, at 290 Lafayette St, between Prince & Houston; and 801 Broadway, between 11th & 12th sts; as well as four other locations in Brooklyn. Brooklyn chic in the form of hip vinyl bags and clothes (T-shirts, jackets and trousers for men and women). Founded by Lexy Funk in 1998, and still designer-owned. Daily 11am–9pm.

Calypso St Barth's 426 Broome St, between Crosby and Lafayette sts ⓣ212/941-6100, ⓦwww.calypso-celle.com. Subway #6 to Spring St. Forget black; colour is the name of the game at this outlet for the major chain. Vibrant fashions imbued with a rich hippie aesthetic – think string bikinis at $75 a pop. There are several other branches, specializing in jewellery and accessories, on the same block. Mon–Sat 11am–7pm, Sun noon–7pm.

Harlem Underground 20 E 125th St, between Fifth and Madison aves

Ⓣ212/987-9385, Ⓦwww.harlemunderground.com. Subway #4, #5, #6 to 125th St. Impress your friends with apparel from this hot Harlem label; cool T-shirts for men and women, featuring images from the world of hip-hop, reggae (Bob Marley) and yes, even Barack Obama.

Henry Lehr 9 Prince St, at Elizabeth St Ⓣ212/274-9921. Subway N, R to Prince St. A shopper's haven for T-shirts and a la mode jeans (men and women). Swing by as the season wanes for the best deals. Mon–Fri 11am–7pm, Sat noon–7pm, Sun noon–6pm.

Intermix 1003 Madison Ave, at E 77th St Ⓣ212/249-7858, Ⓦwww.intermixonline.com. Subway #6 to 77th St. Also at 125 Fifth Ave, at E 19th St Ⓣ212/533-9720; and 98 Prince St, between Mercer and Greene sts Ⓣ212/966-5303. Trendy boutiques for the working-girl fashionista, and a flat-out fun place to shop. A wide assortment of brands both high and low, and an admittedly confusing merchandise layout – they're called "intermix" for a reason. Mon–Sat 10am–7pm, Sun noon–6pm.

Inven.tory Soho 237 Lafayette St, at Spring St Ⓣ212/226-5292, Ⓦwww.inventorynyc.com. Subway #6 to Spring St. Inven.tory's store is essentially a curated sample sale (see p.404) made permanent; expect designer items at wholesale prices, serious shoppers and fabulous bargains. Mon–Sat noon–8pm, Sun 11am–7pm.

Kirna Zabête 96 Greene St, between Prince and Spring sts Ⓣ212/941-9656, Ⓦwww.kirnazabete.com. Subway N, R to Prince St. The best of the downtown shops, this is a concept store that stocks hand-picked highlights from designers such as Jason Wu, Rick Owens and Proenza Schouler. Mon–Sat 11am–7pm, Sun noon–6pm.

Matthew Williamson 415 W 14th St, at Washington St Ⓣ212/255-9881, Ⓦwww.matthewwilliamson.com. Subway A, C, E to 14th St. The first US boutique from the hip British designer, this glittering store is worth a look in itself, a perfect showcase for Williamson's colourful beadwork and patterns. Mon–Sat 11am–7pm, Sun 12.30–6pm.

Patricia Field 302 Bowery, between Bleecker and E Houston sts Ⓣ212/966-4066, Ⓦwww.patriciafield.com. Subway #6 to Bleecker St. Touted as the founder of Manhattan's most inventive clothing store, Pat Field was one of the first NYC vendors of "punk chic"; her recent renaissance came as the *tour de force* costumier behind Carrie Bradshaw's outfits in *Sex and the City*. This store has plenty of her wild designs at reasonable prices, as well as wacky accessories. Daily 11am–8pm, Fri & Sat till 9pm, Sun till 7pm.

Pookie & Sebastian 1069 Third Ave, at E 63rd St Ⓣ212/991-9636, Ⓦwww.pookieandsebastian.com. Subway F to Lexington Ave–63rd St. Home of preppy chic, with girly clothes, cutesy tops, designer denim, heaps of jewellery and assorted accessories. You, too, could be a Pookie Girl. Daily 11am–9pm, Sun till 7pm.

Ports 1961 3 Ninth Ave, at Gansevoort St Ⓣ212/917/475-1022, Ⓦwww.ports1961.com. Subway A, C, E to 14th St. Flagship of the much-loved brand established by Japanese designer Luke Tanabe in Canada in 1961. Featured in movies *Sex and the City* and *The Devil Wears Prada*. Mon–Sat 11am–7pm, Sun noon–6pm.

Scoop 1273–1277 Third Ave, at 73rd St Ⓣ212/535-5577, Ⓦwww.scoopnyc.com. Subway #6 to 77th St. Also at 473–475 Broadway, between Broome and Grand sts; and 430 W 14th St, in the West Village. Every season is cruise season at this lively fashion outpost for youngish Upper East Side girls. There's a bit of a bubblegum, Paris Hilton vibe to the place, but it's well stocked with the latest designs from a dozen different labels. Mon–Fri 11am–8pm, Sat 11am–7pm, Sun noon–6pm.

TG170 170 Ludlow St, between Houston and Stanton sts. Ⓣ212/995-8660, Ⓦwww.tg170.com. Subway F to Lower East Side–Second Ave. Terri Gillis's women's clothing boutique is a magnet for fashionistas hunting for independent and emerging local designers. Daily noon–8pm.

Top Shop 478 Broadway, at Broome St Ⓣ212/966-9555, Ⓦwww.topshopnyc.com. Subway N, R to Prince St, #6 to Spring St. Brits may be mildly amused, but America's first Top Shop attracted round-the-block lines when it opened in 2009 (Top Girl herself Kate Moss cut the ribbon). Regular collaborations with hip designers and affordable prices keep the punters coming back. Mon–Sat 10am–9pm, Sun 11am–8pm.

Triple 5 Soul 145 Bedford Ave, at N 9th St, Williamsburg Ⓣ718/599-5971, Ⓦtriple5usa.com. Subway L to Bedford Ave. The city's top skategear shop also stocks a healthy supply of popular men's & ladies' hip-hop gear.

Designer stores

We've listed all the outlets for the major **designer labels** – no big-name brand worth its cashmere would be without a Manhattan outpost, so the choice is enormous. As a general rule, internationally known design houses are concentrated uptown on Fifth Avenue in the 50s and on Madison Avenue in the 60s and 70s. The newer, younger designers are found downtown in Soho, Nolita, the East and West villages and Tribeca.

202 75 Ninth Ave, inside Chelsea Market, between 15th and 16th sts ⓣ212/421-7720, ⓦwww.nicolefarhi.com. Subway A, C, E to 14th St. Everything's understated and elegant, though the knitwear is the standout here, in designer Nicole Farhi's most recent venture mixing fashion and food. The front of the shop holds a café with tasty sandwiches and plates (and French toast on the weekend); it's a favourite place for fashionistas to refuel on black coffee. Mon–Fri 8.30am–11pm, Sat 9am–11pm, Sun 10am–4pm.

agnès b 13 E 16th St, between Fifth Ave and Broadway (men and women) ⓣ212/741-2585, ⓦusa.agnesb.com. Subway #4, #5, #6, L, N, R, Q, to 14th St–Union Square. Also 1063 Madison Ave, between 80th and 81st sts (women) ⓣ212/570-9333. Pared-down classic Parisian chic, all clean lines and fresh air, with unexpected bursts of colour. Mon–Sat 11am–7pm, Sun noon–6pm.

Alexander McQueen 417 W 14th St, between Ninth and Tenth aves ⓣ212/645-1797, ⓦwww.alexandermcqueen.com. Subway A, C, E to 14th St. Theatrical but flattering and well-cut clothes for women, though with the death of the namesake designer in early 2010, the label's future is somewhat unclear. A stablemate at the Gucci group, Stella McCartney, has a store a few doors down (see p.402). Mon–Sat 11am–7pm, Sun 12.30–6pm.

Anna Sui 113 Greene St, at Prince St ⓣ212/941-8406, ⓦwww.annasui.com. Subway N, R to Prince St. Funky, thrift-store-inspired clothes for girly girls from the popular American designer. Mon–Sat 11.30am–7pm, Sun noon–6pm.

Burberry 131 Spring St, at Greene St ⓣ212/925-9300, ⓦwww.burberry.com. Subway N, R to Prince St. Also at 9 E 57th St, at Fifth Ave ⓣ212/355-6314; and 444 Madison Ave. Their classic plaids and tweeds are still available, but these days they're on the back burner in favour of hot designer Christopher Bailey's more up-to-date offerings. Their women's coats are among the world's most sought-after. Mon–Sat 11am–7pm, Sun noon–6pm.

Calvin Klein 654 Madison Ave, at 60th St ⓣ212/292-9000, ⓦwww.calvinklein.com. Subway N, R to Fifth Ave–59th St. Sleek, minimalist shirts and suits from the New York-based master of classic American fashion. Mon–Wed, Fri & Sat 10am–6pm, Thurs 10am–7pm, Sun noon–6pm.

Chloé 850 Madison Ave, at 70th St ⓣ212/717-8220, ⓦwww.chloe.com. Subway #6 to 68th St. Industry watchers predicted the demise of this Paris-based line when Stella McCartney departed, but her former partner Phoebe Philo and now Hannah MacGibbon have this brand flying higher than ever with one stunning collection after another, including the hottest bag to come out in years (the Paddington). Mon–Sat 10am–6pm.

Christian Dior 21 E 57th St, at Madison Ave ⓣ212/931-2950, ⓦwww.dior.com. Subway N, R to Fifth Ave–59th St. John Galliano amps up the glamour here with his show-stopping designs and fad-producing handbags. Mon–Sat 10am–7pm, Sun noon–6pm.

Comme des Garçons 520 W 22nd St, at Tenth Ave ⓣ212/604-9200. Subway C, E to 23rd St. Japanese designer Rei Kawakubo's avant-garde line has a stunning showcase in this Chelsea store – worth stopping to see even if you don't plan on buying any clothes. Mon–Sat 11am–7pm, Sun noon–6pm.

DKNY 655 Madison Ave, at 60th St ⓣ212/223-3569, ⓦwww.dkny.com. Subway F to Lexington Ave–63rd St. Also at 420 W Broadway, between Spring and Prince sts ⓣ646/613-1100. Donna Karan's younger, cheaper line has two concept-store locations in the city, selling accessories and homewares for the "DKNY lifestyle" alongside clothes. Mon–Sat 11am–8pm, Sun noon–7pm.

Dolce & Gabbana 825 Madison Ave, at E 69th St ⓣ212/249-4100, ⓦwww.dolcegabbana.com. Subway #6 to 68th St. Both the diffusion and designer lines by this Italian duo offer studded, showy clothes – just make sure you're thin enough to slip into them. Mon–Wed & Fri–Sat 10am–6pm, Thurs 10am–7pm, Sun noon–5pm.

Donna Karan 819 Madison Ave, between E 69th and E 68th sts ⓣ1-866/240-4700, ⓦwww.donnakaran.com. Subway #6 to 68th St. The queen of New York fashion designs subtle clothes in understated shades guaranteed to flatter any figure. Mon–Wed, Fri & Sat 10am–6pm, Thurs 10am–7pm, Sun noon–5pm.

Giorgio Armani 760 Madison Ave, at 65th St ⓣ212/988-9191, ⓦwww.giorgioarmani.com. Subway #6 to 68th St. Also 410 West Broadway in Soho. Splash out on one of Armani's legendary deconstructed suits. Mon–Wed, Fri & Sat 10am–6pm, Thurs 10am–7pm.

Gucci 725 Fifth Ave, at 56th St ⓣ212/826-2600, ⓦwww.gucci.com. Subway E, M to Fifth Ave–53rd St. Also 840 Madison Ave, at 70th St ⓣ212/717-2619. Tom Ford may be gone, but his revamping of this classic label has had a lasting effect (his protégée Frida Giannini is the current creative director). Cutting-edge leather accessories and retro-cool clothes for a new generation. Mon–Sat 10am–8pm, Sun noon–6pm.

Hermès 691 Madison Ave, at 62nd St ⓣ212/751-3181, ⓦwww.hermes.com. Subway F to Lexington Ave–63rd St. More than just scarves for your mother and ties for your dad; check out the clothes designed by flamboyant Jean-Paul Gaultier. Mon–Wed, Fri & Sat 10am–6pm, Thurs 10am–7pm.

Isaac Mizrahi 23 East 67th St, at Madison Ave ⓣ212/288-8111, ⓦwww.isaacmizrahiny.com. Subway #6 to 68th St. First dedicated store for the much-loved Brooklyn-born designer (and ex-creative director of Liz Claiborne). Small but perfect showcase for the flamboyant and somewhat controversial designer. Mon–Fri 10am–6pm.

John Varvatos 122 Spring St, at Greene St ⓣ212/965-0700, ⓦwww.johnvarvatos.com. Subway N, R to Prince St, #6 to Spring St. Also at 315 Bowery, in the old CBGB space. Boxy though flattering casual wear and suits, plus the American designer's highly successful line of leather Converse sneakers. Mon–Sat 11am–7pm, Sun noon–6pm.

Marc Jacobs 163 Mercer St, between Houston and Prince sts ⓣ212/343-1490, ⓦwww.marcjacobs.com. Subway N, R to Prince St. Marc Jacobs rules the New York fashion world like a Cosmopolitan-sipping colossus. Women from all walks of life come here to blow the nest egg on his latest "it" bag or pair of boots. Check out his second line, Marc by Marc, at 403 Bleecker St, at 11th St (ⓣ212/924-0026). Mon–Sat 11am–7pm, Sun noon–6pm.

Marni 161 Mercer St, between Houston and Prince sts ⓣ212/343-3912, ⓦwww.marni.com. Subway N, R to Prince St. This relative newcomer from Milan has already been anointed "the new Prada" by fashion editors everywhere. The tops here are especially exquisite, with an emphasis on bright colours and unique patterns. Mon–Sat 11am–7pm, Sun noon–6pm.

Miu Miu 100 Prince St, at Greene St ⓣ212/334-5156, ⓦwww.miumiu.com. Subway N, R to Prince St. Miuccia Prada's fun, often bizarre, diffusion line (for women only). Mon–Wed 11am–7pm, Thurs–Sat 11am–8pm, Sun noon–7pm.

Paul Smith 108 Fifth Ave, at 16th St ⓣ212/627-9770, ⓦwww.paulsmith.co.uk. Subway F, L, M to 14th St. Excellent, sophisticated menswear from the iconic Britpop designer, often employing eccentric, eye-catching colour combinations. There's a good-value Paul Smith Sale Shop over in Williamsburg, at 280 Grand St. Mon–Wed, Fri & Sat 11am–7pm, Thurs 11am–8pm, Sun noon–6pm.

Polo Ralph Lauren 867 Madison Ave ⓣ212/606-2100 and Polo Sport Ralph Lauren 888 Madison Ave ⓣ212/434-8000, ⓦwww.ralphlauren.com; both between 71st and 72nd sts. Subway #6 to 68th St. The master of all things preppy: buy a blazer at the flagship and make like you're money. Mon–Wed 10am–7pm, Thurs 10am–8pm, Fri & Sat 10am–6pm, Sun noon–6pm.

Prada 575 Broadway, at Prince St ⓣ212/334-8888, ⓦwww.prada.com. Subway N, R to Prince St. The jaw-dropping flagship store designed by Rem Koolhaas is as much of a sight as Miuccia's deservedly famous clothes. Mon–Sat noon–8pm, Sun 11am–7pm.

Stella McCartney 429 W 14th St, at Tenth Ave ⓣ212/255-1556, ⓦwww.stellamccartney.com. Subway A, C, E to 14th St. More of the same stuff she produced at Chloé – uniforms for "it" girls slumming downtown. Mon–Sat 11am–7pm, Sun 12.30–6pm.

Versace 647 Fifth Ave, at 52nd St ⓣ212/317-0224, ⓦwww.versace.com. Subway E, M to Fifth Ave–53rd St. Loud, brassy, red-carpet-worthy clothes for those who like to enter a room with an exclamation mark. Mon–Sat 10am–7pm, Sun noon–6pm.

Yves Saint Laurent 3 E 57th St at Fifth Ave ⓣ212/988-3821, ⓦwww.ysl.com. Subway N, R to Fifth Ave–59th St. Sexy, oh-so-French separates for men and women. Mon–Wed,

Fri & Sat 10am–6pm, Thurs 10am–7pm, Sun noon–5pm.

Zero 33 Bleecker St, at Mott St ⓣ212/925-3849, ⓦzeromariacornejo.com. Subway #6 to Bleecker St. Also at 807 Greenwich St, at St Jane. Much-celebrated Chilean (but NYC-based) designer Maria Cornejo's Noho boutique features the best of her cutting-edge fashions, which tend toward a simple colour palette and some unconventional cuts. Daily 12.30–7.30pm, Sun till 6.30pm.

Discount stores

Century 21 22 Cortlandt St, between Broadway and Church St ⓣ212/227-9092, ⓦwww.c21store.com. Subway R to Cortlandt St or Rector St, #1 to Rector St, #4, #5 to Wall St. The granddaddy of designer discount department stores, where all the showrooms send their samples to be sold at the end of the season, usually at forty- to sixty-percent off retail prices – the richest pickings are in Jan and July. A limited number of dressing rooms, so buy what you want and return whatever doesn't fit. Mon–Wed 7.45am–9pm, Thurs & Fri 7.45am–9.30pm, Sat 10am–9pm, Sun 11am–8pm.

Loehmann's 101 Seventh Ave, between 16th and 17th sts ⓣ212/352-0856, ⓦwww.loehmanns.com. Subway #1 to 18th St. New York's best-known department store for designer clothes at knockdown prices, especially glamorous evening wear. No refunds and no exchanges after thirty days. Mon–Sat 9am–9pm, Sun 11am–7pm.

Syms Clothing 42 Trinity Place, at Rector St ⓣ212/797-1199, ⓦwww.syms.com. Subway R, #1 to Rector St. Also 400 Park Ave, at 54th St ⓣ212/317-8200. "Where the educated consumer is our best customer" – the stock's a bit stuffier than elsewhere, so plan on picking up a suit for work or a classic white blouse. Mon–Fri 8am–8pm, Sat 10am–6.30pm, Sun noon–5.30pm.

Vintage, secondhand and thrift stores

Aside from the standout shops we've listed below, there's a heavy concentration of thrift and vintage stores in the Lower East Side, especially around Ludlow and Rivington streets. Don't be surprised to find a famous designer (or one of their minions) rifling through the racks in this area – they're probably after inspiration for their next collection.

Amarcord 252 Lafayette St, between Prince and Spring sts ⓣ212/431-4161, ⓦamarcordvintagefashion.com. Subway N, R to Prince St, #6 to Spring St. Also 223 Bedford Ave, between N 4th and N 5th sts, Williamsburg (daily noon–8pm). This place is a real find. The owners make regular trips through their home country of Italy in search of discarded Dior, Gucci, Yves Saint Laurent and so forth from the 1940s onward. Things aren't too expensive, especially considering all the pieces are in mint condition. The Williamsburg store carries menswear. Daily noon–7.30pm, Sun till 7pm.

Andy's Chee-pees 18 W 8th St, between Fifth Ave and Sixth aves ⓣ212/420-5980, ⓦandyscheepees.com. Subway A, B, C, D, E, F, M to West 4th St. Also 37 St Mark's Place (near Second Ave). The place to go for those all-American bowling shirts, pump-attendant tees and beat-up denimwear. Mon–Thurs 11am–8pm, Fri & Sat 11am–9pm, Sun noon–8pm.

Beacon's Closet 88 N 11th St, between Berry St and Wythe Ave, Williamsburg, Brooklyn ⓣ718/486-0816, ⓦwww.beaconscloset.com. Subway L to Bedford Ave. Vast 5500-square-foot used-clothing paradise, specializing in modern fashions and vintage attire.

Buffalo Exchange 332 E 11th St, at Second Ave ⓣ212/260-9340, ⓦwww.buffaloexchange.com. Subway L to First Ave. Also 504 Driggs Ave in Williamsburg. US clothes exchange that started in Arizona in the 1970s; bring in your former threads for a trade-in or cash on the spot. Designer jeans, and a surprisingly high quality of men's and women's clothes grace the store. Mon–Sat 11am–6pm, Sun noon–7pm.

Domsey's 431 Broadway, at Hewes St, Williamsburg ⓣ718/384-6000. Subway J, M to Hewes St. This five-storey thrift store sells everything from boutique pieces to boot-camp salvage… by the pound! Plan to rifle ruthlessly; most of the offerings here are workaday basics from brands like Old Navy. Daily 9am–6pm.

Edith Machinist 104 Rivington St, at Ludlow St ⓣ212/979-9992. Subway F, J, M, Z to Delancey St–Essex St. Extremely popular with the trendy vintage set, this used-clothing emporium holds some amazing finds (particularly shoes) for those willing to sift through the massive stock. Mon–Fri 1–8pm, Sat & Sun noon–8pm.

Gabay's Outlet 225 First Ave, between E 13th and E 14th sts ⓣ212/254-3180, ⓦwww.gabaysoutlet.com. Subway L to First Ave. An East Village store crammed with remaindered merchandise (Marc Jacobs, YSL and the like) from midtown's department stores. Mon–Sat 10am–7pm, Sun 11am–7pm.

Housing Works Thrift Shop 143 W 17th St, between Sixth and Seventh aves ⓣ212/366-0820, ⓦwww.shophousingworks.com. Subway #1 to 18th St. Also 306 Columbus Ave, at 75th St ⓣ212/579-7566; 202 E 77th St, at Third Ave ⓣ212/772-8461; 157 East 23rd St; 730–732 Ninth Ave; and several other locations. Upscale thrift stores where you can find secondhand designer pieces in very good condition. All proceeds benefit Housing Works, an AIDS social-service organization. Mon–Fri 10am–7pm, Sat 10am–6pm, Sun noon–5pm.

INA 21 Prince St, between Mott and Elizabeth sts ⓣ212/334-9048, ⓦwww.inanyc.com. Subway N, R to Prince St. Designer resale shop usually crammed with end-of-season, barely worn pieces by hot designers. Fair prices make it by far the best secondhand store in the city. The men's store is next door at 19 Prince St (ⓣ212/334-2210). Daily noon–8pm, Sun 7pm.

Marmalade 172 Ludlow St, between Houston and Stanton sts ⓣ212/473-8070, ⓦwww.marmaladevintage.com. Subway F to Lower East Side–Second Ave. Fabulous vintage clothes from the 1940s to the 1990s, especially good for 1970s gear (including shoes and mink shawls). Prices are reasonable, and there are always some unique items. Daily noon–8.30pm.

Reminiscence 50 W 23rd St, between Fifth and Sixth aves ⓣ212/243-2292, ⓦwww.reminiscence.com. Subway F, M to 23rd St. Designed to evoke your memories of the 1980s everything-with-palm-trees phase. It carries funky new and used clothes for men and women – expect plenty of Hawaiian shirts, tie-string overalls and tube tops – in addition to period-relevant tchochkes. Mon–Sat 11am–7.30pm, Sun noon–7pm.

Resurrection 217 Mott St, at Spring St ⓣ212/625-1374, ⓦwww.resurrectionvintage.com. Subway F, M to 23rd St. Hands down the best high-end place for vintage clothing in the city, with first-class Pucci and Halston classics from the 60s to the 80s. The prices are very high, but it's still worth it just to check out the Pucci gowns and python Dior jackets. Mon–Sat 11am–7pm, Sun noon–7pm.

Screaming Mimi's 382 Lafayette St, at E 4th St ⓣ212/677-6464, ⓦwww.screamingmimis.com. Subway #6 to Bleecker St or Astor Place. One of the most well-established lower-end secondhand stores in Manhattan. Vintage clothes, including lingerie, bags, shoes and housewares, at reasonable prices. Mon–Sat noon–8pm, Sun 1–7pm.

Tokio 7 83 E 7th St, between First and Second aves ⓣ212/353-8443. Subway #6 to Astor Place. Attractive secondhand and vintage designer consignment items; known for its flashy, eccentric selection – think plenty of Gaultier, Moschino and McQueen – rather than boring, basic black. Daily noon–8pm.

What Comes Around Goes Around 351 W Broadway, between Broome and Grand sts ⓣ212/343-9303, ⓦwww.wcaga.com. Subway A, C, E to Canal St. Established and well-loved downtown vintage store. Popular with magazine stylists borrowing pieces for shoots. Mon–Sat 11am–8pm, Sun noon–7pm.

Sample sales

At the beginning of each fashion season, designers' and manufacturers' showrooms are still full of leftover merchandise from the previous season. These pieces are removed via informal sample sales, which kick off in October and run through March, though there are usually a few in April and May. You'll always save at least fifty percent off the retail price, though you may not be able to try on the clothes and you can never return them. Always take plenty of cash with you; some sales will not accept credit cards. The best way to find out what sales are coming up is to check the current issues of *Time Out New York* and *New York* magazine (see p.31). You can also sign up for the free regular emails issued by **Charlie Suisman's MUG** (ⓦwww.manhattanusersguide.com), **Clothing Line** (ⓦwww.clothingline.com) or **Daily Candy** (ⓦwww.dailycandy.com).

Zachary's Smile 317 Lafayette St, between Bleecker and Houston sts, ⓣ212/965-8248, ⓦwww.zacharyssmile.com. Subway B, D, F, M to Broadway–Lafayette. Also 9 Greenwich Ave, between Christopher and West 10th sts ⓣ212/965-8248. Blend of super cute, fun and classy vintage women's clothing, footwear and accessories. Daily noon–8pm, Sun till 7pm.

Fashion: shoes

Most department stores carry two or more shoe salons – one for less expensive brands and one for finer shoes. **Barneys** and **Loehmann's** are both known for their selection of high-end footwear, while the greatest concentration of bargain shoe shops can be found in the Village on West 8th Street, between University Place and Sixth Avenue, and on Broadway below West 8th Street.

Alife Rivington Club 158 Rivington St, at Clinton St ⓣ212/375-8128, ⓦwww.rivingtonclub.com. Subway F, J, M, Z to Delancey St–Essex St. Shrine to designer sneakers (trainers), with special-edition Nikes going for $900 as well as $150 sunglasses and other accessories for sale. The hip T-shirts are "just" $35. Daily noon–7pm, Sun till 6pm.

Camper 125 Prince St, at Wooster St ⓣ212/358-1842, ⓦwww.camper.com. Subway N, R to Prince St. Cult Spanish footwear with springy soles; some are based on eccentric takes on the bowling shoe. Mon–Sat 11am–8pm, Sun noon–6pm.

Jimmy Choo 645 Fifth Ave, at 51st St ⓣ212/593-0800, ⓦwww.jimmychoo.com. Subway E, M to Fifth Ave–53rd St. Popular British designer has a huge Manhattan following for his high-heeled, high-priced, high-quality shoes. Mon–Fri 10am–7pm, Sat 10am–6pm, Sun noon–5pm.

John Fluevog 250 Mulberry St, at Prince St ⓣ212/431-4484, ⓦwww.fluevog.com. Subway N, R to Prince St. Innovative designs for a walk about town – most styles are casual but quirky, with buckles or brightly coloured detailing. Mon–Sat 11am–8pm, Sun noon–6pm.

Jutta Neumann 355 E 4th St, between aves C and D ⓣ 212-982 7048, ⓦwww.juttaneumann-newyork.com. Subway F to Second Ave–Lower East Side. Her custom-designed, super-comfy sandals are all the rage downtown, and she also sells popular leather handbags. Mon–Fri noon–6pm, Sat 1–6pm.

Kenneth Cole 610 Fifth Ave, at 49th St ⓣ212/373-5800, ⓦwww.kennethcole.com. Subway E, M to Fifth Ave–53rd St. Classic and contemporary shoes and beautiful bags in excellent full-grain leather from another iconic NYC designer. Call for more locations. Mon–Sat 10am–8pm, Sun 11am–7pm.

Manolo Blahnik 31 W 54th St, at Fifth Ave ⓣ212/582-3007, ⓦwww.manoloblahnik.com. Subway E, M to Fifth Ave–53rd St. World-famous strappy stilettos – good for height (of fashion), hell for feet. The Spanish designer is more popular than ever thanks to Carrie Bradshaw and company in *Sex and the City*. Mon–Fri 10.30am–6pm, Sat 10.30am–5.30pm, Sun noon–5pm.

Sigerson Morrison 28 Prince St, at Mott St ⓣ212/219-3893, ⓦwww.sigersonmorrison.com. Subway N, R to Prince St. Kari Sigerson and Miranda Morrison make timeless, simple and elegant shoes for women. A required pilgrimage for shoe worshippers. The location just round the corner, Belle, 242 Mott St, at Prince St (ⓣ212/941-5244), stocks their popular line of handbags. Daily 8am–6pm.

Flea markets and craft fairs

New York **flea markets** are outstanding for funky and old clothes, collectibles, lingerie, jewellery and crafts; there's also any number of odd places – car parks, playgrounds or maybe just an extra-wide bit of pavement – where people set up to sell their wares, especially in spring and summer.

Antiques Garage Flea Market 112 W 25th St, between Sixth and Seventh aves ⓦwww.hellskitchenfleamarket.com. Subway C, E, #1 to 23rd St. Packed into a bi-level garage, vendors come to peddle all sorts of old knick-knacks, antique jewellery, framed items, toys, cigarette lighters and more. Sat & Sun 6.30am–5pm.

Brooklyn Flea Bishop Loughlin Memorial High School, 357 Clermont Ave, Fort Greene ⓣ212/243-5343, ⓦwww.brooklynflea.com. Subway G to Clinton–Washington aves, C to Lafayette Ave. The "flea" epithet is a bit of a misnomer, as this is as much a high-quality outdoor arts and crafts fair as secondhand fair, with two hundred stalls and superb artisan food thrown in. During the winter (Dec–March), the market moves indoors – check the website for locations. Sat & Sun 10am–5pm.

Green Flea Columbus Ave, between W 76th and W 77th St ⓣ212/239-3025, ⓦwww.greenfleamarkets.com. Subway #1 to 79th St. Two of the best and largest markets in the city: antiques and collectibles, desks and chests, textiles, vintage clothing, haberdashery and hot sauces, plus a farmers' market (Columbus location). Sun 10am–6pm, Nov–March till 5.30pm.

Hell's Kitchen Flea Market 39th St, between Ninth and Tenth aves ⓣ212/243-5343, ⓦwww.hellskitchenfleamarket.com. Subway A, C, E to 42nd St. Also at 26–37 & 112 W 25th St. This is the fastest-growing fair in New York, with 170 vendors selling regular and retro antiques, furniture, vintage clothes and bric-a-brac. Sat & Sun 10am–6pm.

Malcolm Shabazz Harlem Market 52 W 116th St, at Fifth Ave ⓣ212/987-8131. Subway #2, #3 to 116th St. Bazaar-like market, with an entrance marked by colourful fake minarets. A dazzling array of West African cloth, clothes, jewellery, masks, Ashanti dolls and beads. Also sells leather bags, music and Black Pride T-shirts. Daily 10am–8pm.

Food and drink

Food is a New York obsession – hence the proliferation of **gourmet groceries** and **specialty markets** across the city. For general snacking and late-night munchies, there's usually a 24-hour corner shop (referred to as a "bodega" by residents) within a few blocks' walk of anywhere.

Note that New York State's liquor-licensing laws mean that supermarkets and bodegas can only sell **beer**, and **wine and spirits** are only available in liquor stores. In either place, you'll need to be 21 to buy (and be able to prove it with a photo ID if asked). An added wrinkle is that the laws also preclude liquor-store owners from opening seven days a week, so most – though not all – are shut on Sundays.

Agata & Valentina 1505 First Ave, at 79th St ⓣ212/452-0690, ⓦwww.agatavalentina.com. Subway #6 to 77th St. The top gourmet grocer in town, with fresh pastas made on the premises, an enviable deli and cheese counter, a variety of pricey delicacies and an outstanding butcher. Daily 8am–8.30pm.

Alleva Dairy 188 Grand St, at Mulberry St ⓣ212/226-7990, ⓦwww.allevadairy.com. Subway J, Z, #6 to Canal St. Oldest Italian formaggiaio (cheesemonger) and grocery in America. Makes its own smoked mozzarella, provolone and ricotta. Daily 8.30am–6pm, Sun till 3pm.

Barney Greengrass 541 Amsterdam Ave, between W 86th and W 87th sts ⓣ212/724-4707, ⓦwww.barneygreengrass.com. Subway #1 to 86th St. "The Sturgeon King" is an Upper West Side smoked-fish institution, trading since 1908. You can sit down, or take your brunch makings to go. Tues–Sun 8am–6pm.

Chelsea Market 75 Ninth Ave, between W 15th and W 16th sts ⓣ212/243-6005, ⓦwww.chelseamarket.com. Subway A, C, E to 14th St. A complex of eighteen former industrial buildings, among them the old Nabisco Cookie Factory. A true smorgasbord of stores, including Amy's Bread, Bowery Kitchen Supply, the Fat Witch Bakery, Imports from Marrakech, The Green Table, Morimoto, the Ronnybrook Dairy, Lobster Place and the Manhattan Fruit Exchange. Mon–Fri 7am–8pm, Sat 7am–7pm, Sun 8am–6pm.

Dean & Deluca **560 Broadway, between Prince and Spring sts ⓣ212/226-6800, ⓦwww.deandeluca.com. Subway N, R to Prince St. Other locations throughout the city.** One of the original big neighbourhood food emporia. Beautiful quality fruit and veggies and top-notch prepared foods. Very chic, very Soho and not at all cheap. Mon–Fri 7am–8pm, Sat & Sun 8am–8pm.

Di Palo's Fine Foods **200 Grand St, at Mott St ⓣ212/226-1033, ⓦwww.dipaloselects.com. Subway B, D to Grand St.** Charming and authoritative family-run business since 1925 that sells some of the city's best ricotta, along with a fine selection of aged balsamic vinegars, oils and home-made pastas. Daily 9am–6.30pm, Sun till 4pm.

East Village Cheese Store **40 Third Ave, between E 9th and 10th sts. Subway N, R to 8th St; #6 to Astor Place.** The city's most affordable source for cheese; its front-of-the-store bins sell pungent blocks and wedges of the stuff starting at just 50¢. Daily 8.30am–6.30pm.

Economy Candy **108 Rivington St, between Essex and Ludlow sts ⓣ212/254-1832, ⓦwww.economycandy.com. Subway F, J, M, Z to Delancey St–Essex St.** A sweet shop on the Lower East Side, selling mountains of sweets, chocs, nuts and dried fruit at low prices. Mon–Fri & Sun 9am–6pm, Sat 10am–5pm.

Essex Street Market **120 Essex St, between Rivington and Delancey sts ⓣ212/388-0449, ⓦwww.essexstreetmarket.com. Subway F, J, M, Z to Delancey St–Essex St.** Here, a kosher fish market, Latino grocers, Saxelby Cheesemongers, Roni-Sue's Chocolates and a Chinese greenmarket all live under one roof, reflecting the diversity of the neighbourhood. Mon–Sat 8am–7pm.

Fairway **2127 Broadway, at 74th St ⓣ212/595-1888, ⓦwww.fairwaymarket.com. Subway #1, #2, #3 to 72nd St.** Long-established Upper West Side grocery that many locals find better value than the more famous Zabar's (see p.408). The operation has its own farm on Long Island, so the produce is always fresh, and the range in some items is enormous. Fantastic organic selection upstairs. Daily 8am–10pm.

Li-Lac **40 Eighth Ave at Jane St ⓣ212/924-2280, ⓦwww.li-lacchocolates.com. Subway A, C, E, L, #1, #2, #3 to 14th St.** Li-Lac's delicious chocolates have been handmade since 1923. One of the city's best treats for those with a sweet tooth – try the fresh fudge or hand-moulded Lady Liberties and Empire States. Daily noon–8pm, Sun till 6pm.

Mast Brothers Chocolate **105A N 3rd St, Williamsburg ⓣ718/388-2625, ⓦwww.mastbrotherschocolate.com. Subway L to Bedford Ave.** Once you've tried the handmade artisan chocolate here, you'll be utterly hooked; the delicate dark chocolate with almonds and sea salt is a mind-bending treat. The boys open their factory at the weekends, but you can also buy the choc at Murray's (see below). Quality comes at a price – it's around $9 a bar. Sat & Sun noon–8pm.

Murray's Cheese Shop **254 Bleecker St at Cornelia St ⓣ212/243-3289, ⓦwww.murrayscheese.com. Subway A, B, C, D, E, F, M to W 4th St; #1 to Christopher St.** More than three hundred fresh cheeses and excellent panini sandwiches, all served by a knowledgeable staff. Mon–Sat 8am–8pm, Sun 10am–7pm.

Porto Rico Importing Company **201 Bleecker St, between Sixth Ave and MacDougal St ⓣ212/477-5421, ⓦwww.portorico.com. Subway A, B, C, D, E, F, M to W 4th St.** An astounding 110 coffees (their specialty) and 140 varieties of tea on offer. The house blends are almost as good as many of the more expensive coffees. Mon–Fri 8am–9pm, Sat 9am–9pm, Sun noon–7pm.

▲ Murray's Cheese Shop

Rosenthal Wine Merchant 318 E 84 th St between First and Second aves ⓣ249-6650. Subway #4, #5, #6 to 86th St. There are lots of great and unusual wine shops in the city, perhaps none quite as particular as this: the storefront for a renowned importer who is all about terroir and small-scale wine growers. Tues–Fri 10am–6pm, Sat 10am–7pm.

Russ & Daughters 179 E Houston St, between Allen and Orchard sts ⓣ212/475-4880, ⓦwww.russanddaughters.com. Subway F to Lower East Side–Second Ave. The original Manhattan gourmet shop, set up in 1914 by Joel Russ (and his three daughters) to sate the appetites of homesick immigrant Jews, selling smoked fish, pickled vegetables, cheese and bagels with the finest lox anywhere. Mon–Fri 8am–8pm, Sat 9am–7pm, Sun 8am–5.30pm.

Sahadi's 187 Atlantic Ave, between Clinton and Court sts, Brooklyn Heights ⓣ718/624-4550, ⓦsahadis.com. Subway #4, #5 to Borough Hall. Fully stocked Middle Eastern grocery store selling everything from Iranian pistachios to creamy home-made hummus since 1948. Mon–Sat 9am–7pm.

Titan Foods 2556 31st St, between Astoria Blvd and 30th Ave, Queens ⓣ718/626-7771, ⓦwww.titanfood.com. Subway N to Astoria Blvd. Olympic-sized store for comestible Greek goods, including imported feta cheese, yogurt and stuffed grape leaves. Mon–Sat 8am–9pm, Sun 9am–8pm.

Warehouse Wines and Spirits 735 Broadway, between 8th St and Waverly Place ⓣ212/982-7770. Subway #6 to Astor Place. The top place to get a buzz for your buck, with a wide selection and frequent reductions on popular lines; *cava* and *prosecco* for $5–7, decent reds and whites for under $10.

Zabar's 2245 Broadway, at 80th St ⓣ212/787-2000, ⓦwww.zabars.com. Subway #1 to 79th St. Zabar's is still the city's pre-eminent gourmet shop. Choose from an astonishing variety of cheeses, olives, meats, salads, freshly baked breads and croissants and prepared dishes. Upstairs, shop for shiny kitchen and household implements to help you put it all together at home. Avoid weekend afternoons, when the tour buses pull up outside and turn the modest-sized store into Dante's seventh circle of hell. Mon–Fri 8am–7.30pm, Sat 8am–8pm, Sun 9am–6pm.

Music

The age of **music stores** is fading fast. Of the large chains, only J&R Music remains, as Virgin closed its doors in 2009. Nevertheless, many excellent **independent record stores** survive in pockets in the East and West villages, with particularly cheap used bargains available around St Mark's Place. Especially popular are small stores dedicated to various permutations of electronica, and venerable jazz-record stores with great LP selections that have been around for decades.

Academy 12 W 18th St, between Fifth and Sixth aves ⓣ212/242-3000, ⓦwww.academy-records.com. Subway F, M to 14th St. Also 415 E 12th St ⓣ212/780-9166; and 96 N 6th St, Brooklyn ⓣ718/218-8200. Used, rare and/or hard-to-find titles are the Academy's forte. Daily 11am–7pm.

Fat Beats 406 Sixth Ave, between W 8th and W 9th sts, 2nd floor ⓣ212/673-3883, ⓦwww.fatbeats.com. Subway A, B, C, D, E, F, M to W 4th St. The name says it all: it's *the* source for hip-hop on vinyl in New York City. Mon–Sat noon–9pm, Sun noon–6pm.

Generation Records 210 Thompson St, between Bleecker and W 3rd sts ⓣ212/254-1100, ⓦwww.generationrecords.com. Subway A, B, C, D, E, F, M to W 4th St. The focus here is on hardcore, metal and punk with some indie. New CDs and vinyl upstairs, used goodies downstairs. It also gets many of the imports the others don't have, plus fine bootlegs. Daily 11am–10pm, Fri & Sat till 11pm.

Halcyon 57 Pearl St, at Water St, DUMBO, Brooklyn ⓣ718/260-WAXY, ⓦwww.halcyonline.com. Subway F to York St. A trusted source for dance music, but offers stuff ranging from jazz to techno. It now carries drum & bass and import titles from defunct-yet-revered Lower East Side store Breakbeat Science, now an online-only operation. Radio shows, listening parties and a general air of music-nerd community make this a top pick. Daily noon–8pm, Tues & Thurs till 9pm, Sun till 6pm.

Greenmarkets

Several days each week, long before sunrise, hundreds of farmers from Long Island, the Hudson Valley and parts of Pennsylvania and New Jersey set out in trucks to transport their fresh-picked bounty to New York City, where they are joined by bakers, cheesemakers and other artisans at **greenmarkets**. These are run by the city authorities, roughly one to four days a week, and are busiest from June to September. Usually, you'll find apple cider, jams and preserves, flowers and plants, maple syrup, fresh meat and fish, pretzels, cakes and breads, herbs, honey – just about anything and everything produced in the rural regions around the city – not to mention occasional live-worm composts and basil ice cream.

To find the greenmarket nearest to you, call ⓣ212/788-7476 or visit ⓦwww.cenyc.org; the largest and most popular is held in Union Square, at E 17th Street and Broadway, year-round on Monday, Wednesday, Friday and Saturday from 8am to 6pm.

House of Oldies 35 Carmine St, between Bleecker St and Bedford St ⓣ212/243-0500, ⓦwww.houseofoldies.com. Subway A, B, C, D, E, F, M to W 4th St; #1 to Houston St. Just what the name says – oldies but goldies of all kinds from the 1950s to the 1970s. Vinyl only. Tues–Sat 10am–5pm.

J&R Music World 23 Park Row, at Beekman St ⓣ212/238-9000, ⓦwww.jr.com. Subway R to City Hall; #2, #3 to Park Place; #4, #5, #6 to Brooklyn Bridge–City Hall. Downtown's family-owned, home-grown music retailer, with a knowledgeable staff and reasonable prices. Check out the company's adjacent stores that offer computer equipment and electronics (see p.398). Mon–Sat 9am–7.30pm, Sun 10.30am–6.30pm.

Jazz Record Center 236 W 26th St, Room 804, between Seventh and Eighth aves ⓣ212/675-4480, ⓦwww.jazzrecordcenter.com. Subway #1 to 28th St. The place to come for rare or out-of-print jazz LPs from the dawn of recording through the bebop revolution, avant-jazz and beyond. They also have rare books, videos and memorabilia. Mon–Sat 10am–6pm.

Other Music 15 E 4th St, between Broadway and Lafayette St ⓣ212/477-8150, ⓦwww.othermusic.com. Subway #6 to Astor Place. This homespun place is an excellent spot for "alternative" CDs, both old and new, that can otherwise be hard to find. Stocking less indie on vinyl than it once did, and now leaning toward experimental and electronica, the store retains the same ever-friendly and knowledgeable staff. Daily noon–9pm, Sat till 8pm, Sun till 7pm.

Sound Fix 44 Berry St, between N 11th and N 12th sts, Williamsburg ⓣ718/388-8090, ⓦwww.soundfixrecords.com. Subway L to Bedford Ave. Friendly, well-stocked store, specializing in indie rock; the website features album reviews, and the store often hosts (free) in-store appearances and listening parties. Daily noon–9pm, Sun till 8pm.

Specialty stores

The shops below are either offbeat and interesting to visit, or sell useful items that are cheaper in New York than elsewhere.

ABC Carpet and Home 888 Broadway, at E 19th St ⓣ212/473-3000, ⓦwww.abchome.com. Subway N, R to 23rd St. Six floors of antiques and country furniture, knick-knacks, linens and, of course, carpets. The grandiose, museum-like setup is half the fun. Wander through to garner decorating ideas. Mon–Sat 10am–7pm, Sun 11am–6.30pm.

Brooklyn Women's Exchange 55 Pierrepont St, between Henry and Hicks sts, Brooklyn Heights ⓣ718/624-3435, ⓦwww.brooklyn-womens-exchange.org. Subway #2, #3 to Clark St. A crafts cooperative that dates back 150 years, the Exchange offers lots of handmade toys, clothes, bedding and so forth. Tues, Wed & Fri 11am–6pm, Thurs 11am–7pm, Sat & Sun 11am–5pm.

Charmingwall 191 W 4th St, between Sixth and Seventh aves ⓣ212/206-8235, ⓦwww.charmingwall.com. Subway A, B, C, D, E, F, M

to W 4th St. Gallery of quirky prints you can roll up and take home, from traditional paintings to comic characters. Daily noon–7pm.

Exit 9 64 Ave A, at E 4th St ⓣ212/228-0145, ⓦwww.shopexit9.com. Subway F to Lower East Side–Second Ave. Kooky emporium of kitsch, stocking soaps, bags, cards and various other offbeat goodies – great for last-minute gifts. Mon–Fri noon–8pm, Sat 11am–8pm, Sun noon–7pm.

FAO Schwartz 767 Fifth Ave, at 58th St ⓣ212/644-9400, ⓦwww.fao.com. Subway N, R to Fifth Ave–59th St. The classic New York toy store, with everything from a massive Barbie collection to a vintage Chevrolet pedal car that costs $1119. Even adults will be bowled over by the size, choice and quality of goods on offer. You can play with lots of them, too, before you buy. Mon–Thurs 10am–7pm, Fri & Sat 10am–8pm, Sun 11am–6pm.

Flight 001 96 Greenwich Ave, at 12th St ⓣ212/989-0001, ⓦwww.flight001.com. Subway A, C, E to 14th St. The best place for bags in the city, from Mandarina Duck to Freitag, plus a stylish selection of travel accessories (alarm clocks, candles, specialty mini-toiletries) and books. Mon–Sat 11am–8pm, Sun noon–6pm.

Kate's Paperie 72 Spring St, between Crosby and Lafayette sts ⓣ212/941-9816, ⓦwww.katespaperie.com. Subway #6 to Spring St. Any kind of paper you can imagine or want, including great handmade cards, albums and exotic notebooks. Mon–Sat 10am–8pm, Sun 11am–7pm.

Maxilla & Mandible 451 Columbus Ave, between 81st and 82nd sts ⓣ212/724-6173, ⓦmaxillaandmandible.com. Subway B, C to 81st St. Natural history made entertaining, with coyote skulls, butterflies (and scorpions) under glass, hollowed-out ostrich eggs, polished shells and anatomical charts. It's not just for show – the (background) staff consists largely of serious scientists. Perhaps not for the squeamish. Mon–Sat 11am–7pm.

Moss 150 Greene St, at Houston St ⓣ1-866/888-6677, ⓦwww.mossonline.com. Subway N, R to Prince St. By far the premier shop for top-quality designer home accessories and furniture. Owner Murry Moss is a design guru, and his playland of a store offers everything from wacky but expensive furniture (think sofas made from corrugated cardboard) to more affordable but still super-stylish salt and pepper shakers. Mon–Sat 11am–7pm.

Mxyplyzyk 125 Greenwich Ave, at 13th St ⓣ212/989-4300, ⓦwww.mxyplyzyk.com. Subway A, B, C to 14th St. Don't let the weird name put you off (for the record, it's pronounced "Mixee-plizz-ik", and is named for a character in a 1930s Superman comic); this is a housewares and gift shop, with sleek table-top and bath products as well as stationery, watches and sundries, wacky gadgets like slippers that clean floors, and kitsch cardboard moose heads. Mon–Sat 11am–7pm, Sun noon–6pm.

New York Yankees Clubhouse Shop 8 Fulton St, between Front and South sts ⓣ212/514-7182. Subway A, C, J, Z, #2, #3, #4, #5 to Fulton St. Also 393 Fifth Ave, between 36th and 37th sts ⓣ212/685-4693. In case you want that celebrated "NY" logo on your clothing, this South Street Seaport emporium has all things related to the legendary baseball team (2009 World Series winners). Mon–Sat 10am–9pm, Sun 11am–8pm.

Paper Presentation 23 W 18th St, between Fifth and Sixth aves ⓣ212/463-7035, ⓦwww.paperpresentation.com. Subway N, R to 23rd St. Perhaps the most comprehensive paperie in the city, with handmade and unique wrapping papers, stationery, fountain-pen ink, presentation folders, cards and gifts. Mon–Fri 9am–7pm, Sat 10am–6pm, Sun 11am–6pm.

Urban Archeology 143 Franklin St, between Hudson and Varick sts ⓣ212/431-4646, www.urbanarchaeology.com. Subway #1 to Franklin St. Sensational finds for the home from salvaged buildings, including lighting fixtures and old-fashioned plumbing. Mon–Thurs 8am–6pm, Fri 8am–5pm.

Utrecht Art Supplies 111 Fourth Ave, between 11th and 12th sts ⓣ212/777-5353, ⓦwww.utrechtart.com. Subway N, R, Q, L, #4, #5, #6 to Union Square. The brand has a forty-year hold on the NYC art market. Carries all manner of paints and brushes, printmaking supplies and drawing materials (charcoal to crayons), along with portfolios in which to carry the finished products. Mon–Sat 9am–7pm, Sun 11am–6pm.

Village Chess Shop 230 Thompson St, between W 3rd and Bleecker sts ⓣ212/475-8130, ⓦwww.chess-shop.com. Subway A, B, C, D, E, F, M to W 4th St. Every kind of chess set for every kind of pocketbook since 1972. Usually packed with people playing and contemplating their next move. Daily 11am–midnight.

Sporting goods

There are quite a number of sporting-goods outlets in the city – from cookie-cutter chain stores to mom-and-pop cycle shops to multistorey sneaker pleasure-domes. Check them out for merchandise as well as for their wealth of information about sports in and around the city.

Bicycle Renaissance 430 Columbus Ave, at 81st St ⓣ212/724-2350, ⓦwww.bicyclerenaissance.com. Subway B, C to 81st St. A classy place with competitive prices, custom-bike building and usually, same-day service. Specialized and Cannondale bikes, and Carrera and Pinarello frames in stock. Mon–Fri 10.30am–7pm, Sat & Sun 10am–5pm.

BLADES Board & Skate 156 W 72nd St, between Broadway and Columbus Ave ⓣ212/787-3911, ⓦwww.blades.com. Subway #1, #2, #3 to 72nd St. Also 659 Broadway, between Bleecker and 3rd sts ⓣ212/477-7074. Rent or buy roller-blades, skateboards and the like. Handy for Central Park.

Eastern Mountain Sports (EMS) 530 Broadway, at Spring St ⓣ212/966-8730, ⓦwww.ems.com. Subway N, R to Prince St, #6 to Spring St. Top-quality merchandise covering almost all outdoor sports, including skiing and kayaking. Mon–Sat 10am–9pm, Sun 11am–7pm.

Mason's Tennis Mart 56 E 53rd St, at Park Ave ⓣ212/755 5805, ⓦwww.masonstennis.com. Subway E, M to Fifth Ave–53rd St. New York's last remaining tennis specialty store – they let you try out all rackets. Mon–Fri 10am–7pm, Sat 10am–6pm, Sun noon–6pm.

NBA Store 666 Fifth Ave, at 53rd St ⓣ212/515-6221, ⓦwww.nba.com/nycstore. Subway E, M to Fifth Ave–53rd St. Basketball fans and players will find a treasure-trove of gear, balls and NBA memorabilia. Mon–Sat 10am–8pm, Sun 11am–6pm.

Niketown 6 E 57th St, at Fifth Ave ⓣ212/891-6453, ⓦwww.nike.com. Subway N, R to Fifth Ave-59th St. You can enter this five-floor sneaker temple through an atrium in Trump Tower, or through the front entry lined with basket-ball court hardwood. Then, you can join the masses and purchase Nike clothing and accessories at full price. Mon–Sat 10am–8pm, Sun 11am–7pm.

Paragon Sporting Goods 867 Broadway, at 18th St ⓣ212/255-8036, ⓦwww.paragonsports.com. Subway N, R, Q, L, #4, #5, #6 to Union Square. Family-owned, with three levels of general merchandise, stocking nearly everything you'll need for most sports. Mon–Sat 10am–8pm, Sun 11am–7pm.

Super Runners Shop 1337 Lexington Ave, at E 89th St ⓣ212/369-6010, ⓦwww.superrunnersshop.com. Subway #4, #5, #6 to 86th St. Five other locations in the city. Experienced runners work at all six locations; co-owner Gary Muhrcke won the first NYC Marathon in 1970. Mon–Wed & Fri 10am–7pm, Thurs 10am–9pm, Sat 10am–6pm, Sun noon–5pm.

31 Sports and outdoor activities

If measured by sheer number of teams and the coverage they are given, New York ranks as the number-one **sports** city in America. TV stations cover most regular-season games and all post-season games in the big four American team sports – **baseball**, **football**, **basketball** and **ice hockey**. Baseball is a vital part of New York culture; even tepid sports fans have some allegiance to either the Yankees or the Mets. Tickets can on occasion be hard to find (for certain games, impossible – it depends on what team is in town) and most don't come cheap. Nothing compares to the chill of the arena, the smell of the grass and the anxiety of pre-game introductions, but if you don't get a chance to see this slice of Americana in person, there are always **sports bars** – establishments with free-flowing beer, king-sized television screens and their own special kind of rabid fans (see the box on p.417 for listings).

Many **participatory activities** in the city are either free or fairly affordable and take place in all kinds of weather. New Yorkers are passionate about **jogging** – there are plenty of places to take a scenic run – and you can **swim** at local pools or borough beaches. However, even with the help of the Parks Department (Ⓣ311, Ⓦwww.nycgovparks.org) it can be hard to find facilities for some sports (like tennis), especially if you are not a city resident. To this end, many New Yorkers spend $40–100 (or more) a month to be members of private **health clubs**; you can usually get a free trial week at one of the major ones (the Ys, New York Sports Clubs, Crunch, etc), particularly if you use the address where you are staying in New York.

Baseball

In the early 1840s, the New York Knickerbocker Club played "base ball" near Madison Square in Manhattan, before moving to Elysian Fields, across the Hudson River in Hoboken, New Jersey. There, on June 26, 1846, they laid down the basic rules (the "Knickerbocker Rules") of the game of **baseball**, as it is played to this day.

For half a century, New York was home to three Major League Baseball (MLB) teams: the New York Giants and the Brooklyn Dodgers, who represented the National League, and the **New York Yankees**, who represented the American League. Additionally, in the years before MLB was integrated, the Negro League had several notable teams based in the city.

Minor-league baseball

Attending a **minor-league baseball game** is great fun. Not only do you get the chance to see up-and-coming players compete with those hanging on for one last shot at The Show, but the crowds are smaller, the seats are better and tickets much cheaper. The first new baseball franchise in New York in several decades debuted in 1999: the minor-league **Staten Island Yankees** (Ⓣ718/720-9265, Ⓦwww.siyanks.com; tickets $12–16), who play in the Class A New York–Penn League (June–Sept). They can be seen at the Richmond County Bank Ballpark at St George, within walking distance of the Staten Island ferry terminal.

After a 43-year absence, baseball returned to Brooklyn in 2001 in the form of the **Brooklyn Cyclones** (Ⓣ718/449-8497, Ⓦwww.brooklyncyclones.com; tickets $8–16), an affiliate of the Mets that play in the same New York–Penn League as the Staten Island Yankees. The beautiful, oceanside stadium is at the former Steeplechase Park in Coney Island.

The almost-decade between 1947 and 1956 was the golden age of baseball in New York, with a Yankees team first led by Joe DiMaggio, then by Mickey Mantle, steamrolling their opponents, and barrier-breaking heroes (not to mention great players) like Jackie Robinson and Roy Campanella playing for the Dodgers. This period ended abruptly in 1957, when the Giants and Dodgers bolted to California at the end of the season – though the city has mostly forgotten the Giants, old-time Brooklyn residents are still scarred by the loss of the Dodgers. New York was bereft of a National League franchise until the **Mets** arrived at the Polo Grounds in 1962, moving two years later to Shea Stadium and, most recently, to Citi Field, in Flushing, Queens.

The MLB **season** lasts for the better part of the year: Spring Training exhibition games occur (in Florida and Arizona) in March, the **regular season** runs from April to the end of September and the post-season series takes place in October.

New York Yankees

Reciting the achievements of the **Yankees** (also known as "The Bronx Bombers") over the decades can get tedious. They are the team with the most World Series titles (27 up until 2009) and they have been in the playoffs more than half of the past ninety seasons: an almost unheard-of success rate for major-league sports.

Their major rivals are the Boston Red Sox; the two have been among the better teams in the league in recent years, and bitter feelings can be traced back to 1920, when former Red Sox star pitcher Babe Ruth was traded to the Yankees. If you can get a ticket to see a game between the two, or a "Subway Series" tilt, when the Bombers face their cross-town adversaries, the Mets, in June interleague play, you won't be disappointed. For more on the Bombers, whose **new stadium** opened in 2009, see the box on p.256. For details on buying **tickets**, which start at $14 for the bleachers (the cheapest seats, with no shade) and range up to $300 for the best seats, see p.419.

New York Mets

The **Mets** have often been regarded as the ugly bridesmaids of the city. Despite intermittent success over the past decade or so, they seem to be best known for late-season collapses and poor free-agent signings; their last championship, in 1986 (one of two in their fifty-year history), feels awfully long ago. Still, they have some exciting young players, plenty of die-hard fans and an attractive new stadium, **Citi Field**, to showcase the team. For **tickets** (roughly $20–250), see p.418.

American football

The **National Football League (NFL) regular season** stretches from September until the end of December. New York's teams are the **Jets** and the **Giants**; both play at the just-completed **New Meadowlands Stadium**, which in 2010 replaced **Giants Stadium**, and is part of the Meadowlands Sports Complex in New Jersey. Tickets for both teams are always officially **sold out** well in advance, but you can often pick up tickets (legally) from secondary-broker websites such as Ⓦwww.ticketliquidator.com. Prices fluctuate according to supply and demand.

New York Giants

The **Giants** have a long and proud history dating back to the 1920s, having won four NFL and three Super Bowl championships; their most recent great moment came in 2008, when in a huge upset they defeated the previously unbeaten New England Patriots in Super Bowl XLII. Due to the length of the waiting list for season tickets (incredibly long), the **Giants** (Ⓣ201/935-8222, Ⓦwww.giants.com) actually encourage current ticket-holders to sell their unused seats to people farther down on the list; you have to join the waiting list (by mail) to have a shot at these tickets. For details on New Meadowlands Stadium and buying tickets ($85 and up), see p.418.

New York Jets

Founded in 1960 as part of the upstart American Football League, the **Jets** (Ⓣ973/549-4600, Ⓦwww.newyorkjets.com), originally known as the Titans, share New Meadowlands Stadium with the Giants (and have shared a stadium with them for 25 years). After some lean times (really, most of their existence), the team is on the move these days, led by boisterous coach Rex Ryan; they're still trying to get back to their first Super Bowl since 1969, when they beat the heavily favoured Baltimore Colts 16–7. As with the Giants, secondary websites offer the best deals on **tickets**, but they'll still be quite pricey (see p.418).

Professional basketball

The **National Basketball Association (NBA) regular season** begins in November and runs until the end of April. The two professional teams in the New York area are the **New York Knicks** (Knickerbockers), who play at Madison Square Garden, and the **New Jersey Nets**, whose current venue is the Izod Center at the Meadowlands Sports Complex in New Jersey, though the team has long-standing plans – finally about to be realized – to relocate to Brooklyn. There is also a women's professional team in New York, the WBNA **Liberty**; tickets to see them play are easier to come by.

New York Knicks

It's not easy being a **Knicks** (Ⓦwww.nba.com/knicks) fan, even though the venerable franchise is one of the most recognizable in any sport. Madison Square Garden is one of the ugliest structures in North America; their last championship win was way back in 1973; the team has had nine consecutive losing seasons since 2001; and after all that, tickets are expensive and virtually impossible to come by. There is a cautious sense of optimism, however, heading into 2010–11, with a new star in Amar'e Stoudemire on board.

For details on Madison Square Garden and buying tickets (cheapest seats $10–70, others can go up to the high hundreds), see p.418.

New Jersey Nets

The **Nets** (ⓦ www.nba.com/nets) began life in 1967 as the New Jersey Americans. Led by legendary Julius Erving (Dr J), they won two championships (1974 and 1976) playing on Long Island before joining the NBA. They had the worst season by a team in years in 2009–10, but that resulted in a high draft pick to join some promising young players. Nets tickets are easier to come by than for the Knicks, because of the comparative difficulty of getting to their New Jersey arena. This should change in 2012, when the Nets are scheduled to finally move to Brooklyn to play in the Barclay Center, currently under construction. For details on the Izod Center and buying tickets ($10–210), see Meadowlands p.418.

New York Liberty

The Women's National Basketball Association (WNBA) season opens when the NBA season ends and runs through the summer to its playoffs in September. The league jumped off in 1997, with the New York team, the **Liberty**, finishing as runners-up for the title; despite making the playoffs almost every year and appearing in four finals, the Liberty has yet to win the championship. Games are at Madison Square Garden, and prices low compared with those for the Knicks. You can usually get a ticket; call ⓣ 1-877/WNBA-TIX, go to ⓦ www.wnba.com/liberty, or pick some up at MSG. **Ticket prices**: $10–260.

College basketball

The **college basketball** season begins in November and ends with "March Madness", in which conference tournaments are followed by a 68-team tournament to select a national champion. The national tournament may be the most exciting, eagerly anticipated sporting event in the US.

Madison Square Garden (ⓣ 212/465-6741, ⓦ www.thegarden.com) hosts pre-season tournaments, the Big East Conference tournament and the semifinals and finals of the National Invitational Tournament. Metropolitan-area colleges pursuing hoop dreams include Columbia and St John's universities.

Ice hockey

There are two professional hockey teams in New York: the **Rangers**, who play at Madison Square Garden, and the **Islanders**, whose venue is the Nassau Coliseum

Street basketball

Free of the image-building and marketing that makes the NBA so superficial, and the by-the-books officiating of the NCAA, **street basketball** presents the game in its purest and, arguably, most attractive form. New York City is the capital of playground hoops, with a host of asphalt legends: Lew Alcindor (Kareem Abdul-Jabbar), Wilt Chamberlain, Julius Erving and Stephon Marbury are a few who have made it to the pros, though others who never made the transition, like Earl "The Goat" Manigault, were said to be just as skilled. If you want to play yourself, *Hoops Nation* by Chris Ballard is an invaluable guide to basketball courts in the five boroughs (and across the nation) and a useful primer in the etiquette of pickup ball; the courts in Rucker Park (155th St and Eighth Ave in Harlem) are the most celebrated. Scout out the next NBA superstar – or look for current ones dropping by for an off-season tune-up.

on Long Island. In addition, the **New Jersey Devils** play out at the Prudential Center in Newark. All three compete in the Atlantic Division of the Eastern Conference of the **National Hockey League (NHL)**. The **regular season** lasts throughout the winter and into early spring, when the playoffs take place.

New York Rangers

One of the six original NHL teams, the **Rangers** (Ⓣ212/465-6000, Ⓦwww.newyorkrangers.com) were founded in 1926 and won the Stanley Cup – awarded to the winner of the playoffs – three times in the following fifteen years. According to hockey lore, giddy from their 1940 playoff-finals victory over the Toronto Maple Leafs, the Madison Square Garden owners paid off their $3 million mortgage and celebrated by burning the deed in Lord Stanley's cup – an act of desecration that provoked a curse upon the franchise and its fans. The Rangers ended their 54-year championship drought in 1994, but this has been followed by another long period of mediocre performance.

Ticket prices: $40–254; for details on Madison Square Garden and buying tickets, see p.418.

New York Islanders

Founded in 1972, the **Islanders** (Ⓣ1-800/882-ISLES, Ⓦwww.newyorkislanders.com) were fortunate enough to string together their four Stanley Cups in consecutive years (1980–83) and thus qualify as a bona fide hockey dynasty. Since then, however, it's been mostly downhill.

Ticket prices: $19–120; for details on Nassau Coliseum and buying tickets, see p.418.

New Jersey Devils

The nomadic **New Jersey Devils** franchise (Ⓦwww.newjerseydevils.com) was founded in 1974 as the Kansas City Scouts and moved to New Jersey (after a brief stint as the Colorado Rockies in Denver) in 1982. A succession of mediocre seasons was interrupted when the Devils beat the heavily favoured Detroit Red Wings in four straight games to win the 1995 Stanley Cup. They regained the Cup in 2003, but lost it to the Philadelphia Flyers in the first round of the 2004 playoffs; since they, the team has regularly put together strong seasons but been disappointing in the playoffs.

Ticket prices: $19–349; for details on the Prudential Center and buying tickets, see p.418.

Soccer

The game of **soccer** (European football) continues to grow in popularity in America, thanks in part to the World Cup results and also the arrival of stars like Thierry Henry and David Beckham. Though soccer coverage is not as extensive in the US as it is abroad, it's not too hard to catch on TV and in sports bars (see box opposite).

The **New York Red Bulls** (Ⓣ201/583-7000, Ⓦwww.newyorkredbulls.com), who play at the new, purpose-built **Red Bull Arena**, in Harrison, New Jersey, are the metropolitan area's Major League Soccer representatives. The MLS **season** runs from April to November. **Ticket prices:** $22–50.

Horse racing

The two busiest **horse-racing** tracks in the area are the **Aqueduct Race Track** and the **Belmont Race Track**, both with thoroughbred racing.

Aqueduct (ⓣ718/641-4700, ⓦwww.nyra.com/index_aqueduct.html) in Ozone Park, Queens, has racing from October to April. **Belmont** (ⓣ516/488-6000, ⓦwww.nyra.com), in Elmont, Long Island, is home to the Belmont Stakes (June), one of the three races in which 3-year-olds compete for the **Triple Crown**. Belmont is open April to July and September to October. There's no charge for admission to Aqueduct; Belmont ranges from $2 to $7 (more for the Belmont Stakes). Valet parking costs $5 at Aqueduct, $6 at Belmont.

Off-track betting

To **place a bet** anywhere other than the track itself, find an **OTB (Off-Track Betting)** office. There are plenty around the city; call ⓣ212/221-5200 or check ⓦwww.nycotb.com for locations. You need an established account to place an internet or phone bet: to set one up, use the website or call ⓣ1-800/OTB-8118.

To watch racing in comfort, try *The Inside Track* (run by OTB) at 991 Second Ave on 53rd Street (ⓣ212/752-1940)

Sports bars

40/40 Club 6 W 25th St at Broadway ⓣ212/832-4040, ⓦthe4040club.com. Subway N, R to 23 rd St. Jay-Z's towering, two-level sports bar is probably the smartest place you'll ever watch the game, with six cream-coloured leather swing chairs suspended from the ceiling, Italian marble floors, and fifteen 60-inch LCD flat-screen TVs. After the game, the whole thing becomes a thumping R&B and hip-hop club. Mon–Fri 6pm–4am, Sat & Sun 4pm–4am.

The Central Bar 109 E 9th St, between Third and Fourth aves ⓣ212/529-5333, ⓦcentralbarnyc.com. Subway #6 to Astor Place; R to 8th St–NYU. Warm, friendly Irish bar showing European football alongside American games. Daily 11am–3/4am.

ESPN Zone 1472 Broadway, at W 42nd St ⓣ212/921-3776, ⓦespnzone.com/newyork. Subway N, Q, R, S, #1, #2, #3 to 42nd St–Times Square. ESPN-affiliated sports bar/restaurant, where you can catch the action from one of 278 screens (even in the bathroom), assuming you can get in. Mon–Thurs 11am–11pm, Fri 11am–midnight, Sat 9am–midnight, Sun 9am–11pm.

Kinsale Tavern 1672 Third Ave, at 93rd St ⓣ212/348-4370. Subway #6 to 96th St. Upper East Side Irish sports bar. Mon–Fri 11am–4am, Sat & Sun 8am–4am.

Nevada Smiths 74 Third Ave, between 11th and 12th sts ⓣ212/982-2591, ⓦwww.nevadasmiths.net. Subway #6 to Astor Place; N, #4, #5, #6 to Union Square–14th St. Possibly the top spot in Manhattan to watch soccer; many of the world's top clubs have ardent support groups that show up here regularly for games. Hours vary, but it opens a half-hour before gametime (anywhere from 7am to 2pm, depending on the day) and stays open until 4am.

Ship of Fools 1590 Second Ave, between 82nd and 83rd sts ⓣ212/570-2651, ⓦwww.shipoffoolsnyc.com. Subway #4, #5, #6 to 86th St. No matter what the game, the amiable owner at this Upper East Side postgrad hangout will try to put it up for you on one of their 48 satellite TVs (13 big ones), though American football is tops here. The bar grub is better than expected.

Stitch 247 37th St, between Seventh and Eighth aves ⓣ212/852-4826, ⓦwww.stitchnyc.com. A loud sports bar serving a mostly after-work commuter crowd, within stumbling distance of Madison Square Garden. Large plasma TV above the bar, with others scattered about. Decent pub fare and an upstairs lounge.

Woodwork 583 Vanderbilt Ave, at Dean St, Brooklyn ⓣ718/857-5777, ⓦwww.woodworkbk.com. Subway C to Clinton–Washington aves; B, Q to Seventh Ave; #2, #3 to Grand Army Plaza. Not your average sports bar, with some elegant food choices, small batch bourbons, a rustic decor and fidelity for the "beautiful game".

or OTB's two other tele-theatres, the *Winner's Circle*, at 515 Seventh Ave on 38th Street (ⓣ212/730-4900) and *The Yankee Clipper*, at 170 John St on Water Street (ⓣ212/269-4744), with food, drink, schmoozing and wagering on the premises.

Tennis

The **US Open Championships**, held each September at the National Tennis Center in Flushing Meadows–Corona Park, in Queens, is the top US tennis event of the year. Tickets go on sale the first week or two of June at the Tennis Center's box office (ⓣ718/760-6200, ⓦwww.usta.com; Mon–Fri 9am–5pm, Sat 10am–4pm). Promenade-level seats at the stadium cost $24–88 (better seats can cost several hundred dollars) for evening games, while day-passes start at $50; though big-name matches are frequently saved for the main stadium in the evening, it's plenty of fun to go during the day and wander to the outer courts, where you can get very close to the action. If events are sold out, keep trying up to the day of the event because corporate tickets are often returned.

Tickets and venues

Tickets for most sporting events can be booked ahead with a credit card through Ticketmaster (ⓣ1-866/448-7849 or 1-800/745-3000, ⓦwww.ticketmaster.com) and collected at the gate, though it's cheaper – and of course riskier for popular events – to try to pick up tickets on the night of the event. You can also call or go to the stadium's box office and buy advance tickets. If the box office has sold out, try one of the numerous internet brokers that sell **secondary tickets** (tickets that are resold by agencies or individuals); prices are set according to supply and demand, so can be cheaper or substantially more, depending on the importance of the game and the seats. Try ⓦwww.ticketliquidator.com, ⓦwww.stubhub.com or ⓦwww.razorgator.com.

Touting is illegal, and with the explosion of secondary websites, virtually redundant. If all else fails, simply catch the action on the big screen in a sports bar.

Citi Field 126th St and Roosevelt Ave, Willets Point, Queens ⓣ718/507-8499, ⓦmets.mlb.com. Subway #7 to Willets Point. The new home of the New York Mets takes its cues from old-fashioned stadiums like Ebbets Field. Box office Mon–Fri 9am–6pm, Sat, Sun & holidays 9am–5pm.

Madison Square Garden Seventh Ave, between 31st and 33rd sts ⓣ212/465-6741, ⓦwww.thegarden.com. Subway A, C, E, #1, #2, #3 to 34th St–Penn Station. Box office Mon–Fri 9am–6pm, Sat 10am–6pm.

Meadowlands Sports Complex containing both New Meadowlands Stadium and Izod Center, off routes 3, 17 and New Jersey Turnpike exit 16W, East Rutherford, New Jersey ⓣ201/935-8500, ⓦwww.meadowlands.com. Regular buses from Port Authority Bus Terminal on 42nd St and Eighth Ave. Izod Center box office Mon–Fri 11am–6pm; no official box office hours for New Meadowlands Stadium – contact the Giants, Jets or ticketmaster.

Nassau Veterans Memorial Coliseum 1255 Hempstead Turnpike, Uniondale, Long Island ⓣ516/794-9300, ⓦwww.nassaucoliseum.com. Not very accessible other than by car. If you don't have your own transportation, take the Long Island Railroad to Hempstead, then bus #N70, #N71 or #N72 from Hempstead bus terminal, one block away. Another option, which may be safer at night, is to catch the LIRR to Westbury and take a cab (5–10min ride) to the stadium. Box office Mon–Fri 9.30am–4.45pm.

Prudential Center 165 Mulberry St, between Edison Place and Lafayette St, Newark, NJ ⓣ973/757-6000 or 201/507-8900, ⓦwww.prucenter.com. The home of the New Jersey

Devils is just two blocks from Newark Penn Station, easily accessible by NJ Transit, Amtrak and PATH trains from Manhattan. Box office Mon–Fri 11am–6pm.

Yankee Stadium 161st St and River Ave, South Bronx ⓣ718/293-6000, ⓦyankees.mlb.com. Subway B, D, #4 to 161st St. New Yankee Stadium is right next door to where the old one was; get to the game early and visit Monument Park, where all the Yankee greats are memorialized. Box office Mon–Fri 9am–5pm, Sat 10am–4pm.

Participatory activities

Beaches

New York's **beaches** aren't worth a trip to the city in and of themselves, but they can be a cool summer escape from Manhattan. Most are only a MetroCard ride away.

Brooklyn

Brighton Beach Subway B, Q to Brighton Beach. Technically the same stretch as Coney Island Beach, but less crowded and populated mainly by the local Russian community. Boardwalk vendors and nearby cafés sell ethnic snacks.

Coney Island Beach Subway B, D, F, Q to Stillwell Ave. After Rockaway (see below), this is NYC's most popular bathing spot, jam-packed on summer weekends. The Atlantic here is only moderately dirty and there's a good, reliable onshore breeze.

Queens

Jacob Riis Park Subway #2, #5 to Flatbush Ave, then #Q35 bus. Good sandy stretches and very pristine. Some stretches on the eastern end are popular with gay men.

Rockaway Beach Subway A, C to any stop along the beach. Forget California: this seven-mile strip is where hundreds of thousands of New Yorkers come to get the best surf around – surf so good that the Ramones even wrote a song about it. Best beaches are at 9th St, 23rd St and from 80th to 118th sts.

Bicycling

New York has more than 100 miles of **cycle paths**; those in Central Park, Riverside Park, Hudson River Park and the East River Promenade are among the nicest. Three sources have done an excellent job of providing specific cycling routes and maps, laws and regulations, and other relevant info: the bike advocacy organization Transportation Alternatives (ⓣ212/629-8080, ⓦwww.transalt.org), which has some good maps; the New York City Department of City Planning (within ⓦnyc.gov), which has a wealth of information available as part of their BND (Bicycle Network Development) project; and ⓦwww.nycbikemaps.com, with extensive bike maps for all five boroughs, information on cycling events and links to other relevant sites. By law, you must wear a helmet when riding your bike on the street. Most bike stores rent bicycles by the day or hour. Refer to websites such as ⓦwww.bikenewyork.org for a list of rental shops.

Here are some clubs and resources for cycling enthusiasts:

Bicycle Habitat 244 Lafayette St ⓣ212/431-3315, ⓦbicyclehabitat.com. Subway B, D, F, M to Broadway–Lafayette; N, R to Prince St; #6 to Spring St. Known for an excellent repair service, they also offer rentals, tune-ups and advice. Mon–Thurs 10am–7pm, Fri 10am–6.30pm, Sat & Sun 10am–6pm.

Five Borough Bike Club ⓣ212/932-2300 ext 115, ⓦwww.5bbc.org. This club organizes rides throughout the year, including the Montauk Century, where riders can choose routes varying between 65 and 140 miles from New York to Montauk, Long Island.

New York Cycle Club ⓦwww.nycc.org. A 1400-member club that offers many rides and sponsors special events as well.

SBR 203 W 58th St between Seventh Ave and Broadway ⓣ212/399-3999, ⓦwww.sbrshop.com. Subway A, B, C, D, #1 to 59th St–Columbus Circle; N, R, Q to Seventh Ave–57th St. Besides gear (running and swimming too), they offer mechanical services and private coaching. Central Park Bike Tours, within the shop, rents out bikes by the hour or day ($20/$65). Mon–Sat 10am–7.30pm, Sun 11am–6pm.

Boating

Downtown Boathouse Hudson River Pier 40, Pier 96 (Clinton Cove) at 56th St, and 72nd St ⓣ212/229-2114, ⓦwww.downtownboathouse.org. Free kayaks and canoes available May–Oct weekends 9am–6pm (hours shorter at 72nd St); also weekdays 5–7pm at Piers 40 and 96.

Loeb Boathouse East Side of Central Park, between 74th and 75th sts ⓣ212/517-2233, ⓦwww.centralparknyc.org. Rowboats and kayaks for rent March–Oct, daily 10am–5pm. Rates are $12 for the first hour, $2.50 per additional 15 minutes, plus $20 deposit. Bikes for $9–15/hr.

Bowling

Brooklyn Bowl 61 Wythe Ave, between 11th and 12th sts, Williamsburg, Brooklyn ⓣ718/963-3369, ⓦwww.brooklynbowl.com. Subway L to Bedford Ave. As much a nightspot (see p.359) as a bowling alley, in a renovated industrial warehouse; upscale bar food by the Blue Ribbon group too. Lanes $20–25 per half-hour, $4 shoe rental. Mon–Thurs 6pm–2am, Fri 6pm–4am, Sat noon–4am, Sun noon–2am.

Leisure Time Bowl 625 Eighth Ave at 41st St, second floor in Port Authority ⓣ268-6909, ⓦwww.leisuretimebowl.com. Subway A, C, E, N, Q, R, #1, #2, #3, #7 to Times Square–42nd St. If you desire a strange location in which to bowl, look no further than this full-service, modern alley in Port Authority Bus Terminal. Mon–Thurs $7.50 per game per person before 5pm, $9.50 evenings; Sat & Sun $9.50; shoe rental $5. Mon–Wed 10am–midnight, Thurs 10am–2am, Fri 10am–3am, Sat 11am–3am, Sun 11am–11pm.

Fishing

Sometimes the amount of concrete in New York can make you forget that the city is actually surrounded by water, much of it teeming with fish. Call the New York State Department of Health's Environmental Health Information line (ⓣ1-800/458-1158) for

Central Park, Chelsea Piers and Hudson River Park

Central Park is, at 843 acres, the centre of the city's recreational life, from croquet to chess to soccer to socializing to sunning to swimming. Joggers, walkers and cyclists have the roads to themselves on weekdays 10am–3pm and 7–10pm and all day on weekends and holidays. It is not recommended that you hang out in the park too long after the sun goes down; at any rate, it is closed during the wee hours. To find out what is going on where and when, call ⓣ212/310-6600 or look at ⓦwww.centralparknyc.org. You can also pick up a calendar of events or directory in the park. See Chapter 13, "Central Park", for more information.

Chelsea Piers W 23rd St and the Hudson River (between 17th and 23rd sts) ⓣ212/336-6666, ⓦwww.chelseapiers.com. It features a year-round outdoor driving range, a track, the largest rock-climbing wall in the Northeast (as well as a smaller one for kids), basketball courts, a health club, indoor sand volleyball courts, bowling and more. You can also join the crew of the *Adirondack* and *Adirondack III*, two beautiful 78ft wooden schooners, which sail from Pier 62. During the two-hour sail of lower New York Harbor, passengers can take the wheel, help hoist the sails or just enjoy the surroundings. Boats operate May–Oct Wed 3.30pm, Thurs & Fri 1pm & 3.30pm, Sat 4.30pm, Sun 1pm, 2pm, 3.30pm, 4.30pm; $40, includes drinks; ⓣ646/336-5270, ⓦwww.sail-nyc.com.

Hudson River Park ⓣ212/533-7275, ⓦwww.hudsonriverpark.org. Twenty years in the planning, Hudson River Park is a massive redevelopment of the west-side waterfront from Battery Park to 59th St. The park links the Battery City Esplanade with Midtown, landscaping 550 acres of river, shoreline and old piers along the way; there's a free tennis court west of Tribeca/Soho and a skate park in the recently completed section of Pier 62 in Chelsea, among other sports facilities.

the latest tips on clean water and if you should toss your catch in the frying pan or back into the current.

Big City Fishing Pier 46 (West Village), Pier 84 (Midtown West) ⓣ212/627-2020. Hudson River Park Trust runs this free programme summer and early autumn weekends (until Oct), providing free fishing rods, reels and bait (as well as instruction) on a first-come, first-served basis, with a half-hour limit when others are waiting. Common species caught include American eel, striped bass, black sea bass, fluke and snapper – all fish are returned to the river at the end of the day.

Golf

Manhattan has no **public golf courses**, though there is a two-level driving range at Chelsea Piers (ⓣ212/336-6400). Recommended among those in the outer boroughs are the following, all of which are subject to low and generally standardized prices (if you don't have your own clubs, you can rent); full information is available at ⓦwww.nycparks.org. The fee for eighteen holes on weekdays before noon is $36, and $31 thereafter; the weekend rate is $44. Non-residents must pay an additional fee of $8. The biggest issue you'll face is pace of play; it's frequently slow once you're out on the links, with rounds of up to six hours possible.

Dyker Beach Golf Course 86th St and Seventh Ave, Dyker Heights, Brooklyn ⓣ718/836-9722. Subway R to 86th St. Often noted for its striking views of the Verrazano Narrows, Dyker is also one of the more convenient local courses, just a few blocks from the subway.

Flushing Meadows 100 Flushing Meadows Park, Flushing, Queens ⓣ718/271-8182. Subway #7 to Willets Point. The key here is the miniature golf course, a fun way to spend an evening with the family ($7.75 adults, $6.25 kids 12 and under); there's also a par-3 course ($14–17.75).

La Tourette 1001 Richmond Road, Staten Island ⓣ718/984-4400. An excellent all-round place to play a round, very well-kept, and with a driving range.

Van Cortlandt Park Golf Course Van Cortlandt Park S and Bailey Ave, Bronx ⓣ718/543-4595. The oldest 18-hole public golf course in the country.

Health and fitness: pools, gyms, and baths

You can join one of the city's **recreation centres** (ⓣ212/447-2020, ⓦwww.nycparks.org) for $50–75 per year (ages 18–54), $10 (seniors) or free (under 18). All have gym facilities; some hold fitness and other classes, and most have an indoor and/or outdoor pool.

Riverbank State Park W 145th St and Riverside Drive ⓣ212/694-3600. Beautiful facility built on top of a waste refinery in Harlem. Despite the strange location, it has great tennis courts, an outdoor track, an ice-skating rink (Nov–March) and several indoor facilities including a skating rink and Olympic-sized pool. Park admission is free; pool is $2, seniors and ages 5–15 $1. Daily 6am–11pm

Russian & Turkish Baths 268 E 10th St between First Ave and Ave A ⓣ212/674-9250, ⓦwww.russianturkishbaths.com. A neighbourhood landmark that's still going strong, with steam baths, sauna and an ice-cold pool, as well as a massage parlour and a restaurant. Free soap, towel, robe, slippers, etc. Admission $30, additional fee for massages and other extras. Mon, Tues, Thurs & Fri noon–10pm, Wed 10am–10pm, Sat 9am–10pm, Sun 8am–10pm; men only Thurs opening until 5pm & Sun opening until 2pm; women only Wed opening until 2pm; co-ed otherwise (shorts are mandatory).

Horse riding

Jamaica Bay Riding Academy 7000 Shore Parkway, Brooklyn ⓣ718/531-8949, ⓦwww.horsebackride.com. Trail riding, both Western and English, around the eerie landscape of Jamaica Bay. $37 for a guided 45min ride; lessons $85 for one hour.

Kensington Stables 51 Caton Place at E 8th St, Prospect Park, Brooklyn ⓣ718/972-4588, ⓦwww.kensingtonstables.com. Horses and classes available for rides along Prospect Park's 3.5-mile bridle path for $37/hr. Private lessons are $57/hr. Daily 10am–sunset.

Ice-skating

New York's freezing winter weather makes for good **ice-skating**. The best rinks are in Central and Prospect parks; don't try skating on a lake, as the ice can be deceptively thin.

New York City Marathon

Every year on the first Sunday in November 37,000 runners come to New York to run the **New York City Marathon**. Along with the competitors come the fans: on average, two million people turn out each year to watch the runners try to complete the 26.2-mile course, which starts in Staten Island, crosses the Verrazano Narrows Bridge and passes through all the other boroughs before ending in Central Park.

If you are a runner, you can try to take part, but beware: the competition is fierce before the race even starts. Not everyone who submits the necessary entry forms is chosen to participate; race veterans (who have run fifteen or more New York marathons), qualified New York Road Runners Club (NYRRC; ⓦwww.nyrrc.org) members who have completed at least nine official races during the calendar year, and those who have applied and been rejected for the last three NYC marathons receive guaranteed entry, which can also be (completely legitimately) procured for you by a travel agent in your home country. Applications must be sent before May 1 for that year's race (US lottery applications June 1), and you must be at least 18 years old on race day.

Lasker Rink 110th St, Central Park ⓣ212/534-7639, ⓦwww.centralparknyc.org. This lesser-known ice rink is at the northern end of the park, and is used as a pool in summer. Much cheaper than the Wollman Rink, though less accessible – both rinks are now owned by Donald Trump. Nov–March $6.25, under 12 $3.50, skate rental $5.50.

Rockefeller Center Ice Rink between 49th and 50th sts, off Fifth Ave ⓣ212/332-7654. Subway B, D, F, M to 47–50th St–Rockefeller Center. It's a quintessential New York scene, lovely to look at but with long queues and high prices. Oct–April $10–14, under 12 $7.50–8.50, rentals $8.

▲ Runners at the New York City Marathon

Sky Rink Pier 61 ⓣ212/336-6100, ⓦwww.chelseapiers.com. Subway C, E to 23rd St. Ice-skate year-round at this indoor rink at Chelsea Piers. Mon, Tues, Thurs & Fri 1.30–5.20pm, Sat & Sun 1–3.50pm; $13, youth $10.50, rentals $7.50.

Wollman Rink 62nd St, Central Park ⓣ212/439-6900, ⓦwww.wollmanskatingrink.com. Lovely rink, where you can skate to the marvellous, inspiring backdrop of the lower Central Park skyline – incredibly impressive at night. Oct–April Mon & Tues 10am–2.30pm, Wed & Thurs 10am–10pm, Fri & Sat 10am–11pm, Sun 10am–9pm; $10.25–14.75, under 12 $5.50–5.75, rentals $6.25. There's also a Wollman Rink in Brooklyn's Prospect Park ($5, under 15 $3, rental $6.50; ⓦwww.prospectpark.org).

Jogging and running

Jogging is still very much the number-one fitness pursuit in the city. The most popular venues are Central Park, Hudson River Park and the Battery City Esplanade. A favourite circuit in Central Park is the 1.57 miles around the reservoir; just make sure you jog in the right direction along with everyone else – counterclockwise. For company on your runs, contact the New York Road Runners Club (ⓣ212/860-4455, ⓦwww.nyrrc.org), which sponsors many races and fun runs per year.

Pool

Along with bars and nightclubs, a good option for an evening in Manhattan is to play **pool**, not only in dingy yet serious halls, but also in gleaming bars where well-heeled yuppies mix with the regulars. A number of sports, dive, and gay and lesbian bars have pool tables as well, though these are often much smaller than regulation size. Snooker fans will also find a few tables throughout the city.

Amsterdam Billiards 85 Fourth Ave, at E 11th St ⓣ212/995-0333, ⓦamsterdambilliardclub .com. Subway L, N, R, Q, #4, #5, #6 to Union Square–14th St. Very popular, upscale Union Square billiards club with 26 tables. They serve liquor and beer along with bar food. Mon–Fri noon–3am, Sat & Sun 11am–4am; $5.50–$9.50/hr.

Fat Cat 75 Christopher St, at Seventh Ave ⓣ212/675-6056, ⓦwww.fatcatmusic.org. Subway #1 to Christopher St–Sheridan Square. No gleaming pool hall this, but a somewhat dingy, fun subterranean space with ping pong, pool tables and a number of other gaming options, not to mention free live music that runs until very late. Tables 9¢/minute per person weekdays, 11¢/minute per person weekends. Mon–Thurs 2pm–5am, Fri & Sat noon–5am.

Tennis

There's not a great deal of court space in New York, so finding an affordable one can be tough. For information on all city courts, including those in Central Park (ⓣ212/360-8133; best to reserve ahead), go to ⓦwww.nyc .gov/parks; the ones at Prospect Park are nice as well (open year-round, with a bubble covering them in winter). You can reserve a court at either for $7 or just show up. Most city parks require a permit to play, which runs $100 for the year (seniors $20, under-18s $10), though you can buy one-off single sessions for $7. Hudson River Park has three courts that are free to all and work on a first-come, first-served basis (West St between Canal and Houston).

Yoga

New York is a great place to try **yoga** for the first time, with classes offered throughout the day at scores of locations. You'll find all difficulty levels and numerous styles; like much of the Western world, the ancient practice has a large following in fitness clubs where it tends to be regarded as just another gym class (with aerobic hybrids like Yogalates), though there are plenty of traditional forms like *jivamukti*, and classes where breathing is more important than how many calories you burn. Yoga studios will also be able to tell you where to practise martial arts and Pilates. If you intend to take a number of sessions, you may want to purchase a New York Yoga PassBook, an excellent deal at $75 for 350 sessions at name workshops throughout the city and suburbs (ⓣ212/808-0765, ⓦwww .health-fitness.org/ny.html). From spring until autumn, many outdoor classes are free; check *Time Out New York* magazine or websites such as ⓦnewyorkcityyoga.com for listings.

Om Yoga 826 Broadway (6th floor), between E 12th and E 13th sts ⓣ212/254-9642, ⓦwww .omyoga.com. Many classes for beginners, plus more advanced workshops. Includes meditation. $18 per session, $28 two introductory classes, $1 mat rental.

32

Parades, festivals and events

New York City takes its numerous **parades and festivals** extremely seriously. They are often political or religious in origin, but as in most of the world, whatever their official reason for existing, they are generally just an excuse for music, food and dance. Almost every large ethnic group in the city holds an annual get-together, often using Fifth Avenue as the main drag; in general, it is a big mistake to drive, take a taxi or ride the buses anywhere near these. In addition, the city also hosts numerous annual special **events**, everything from America's oldest dog show to the New York City Marathon, which can be fun to watch even if you don't know anyone taking part.

Chances are, your stay will coincide with at least one festive happening. For more details and exact dates of the events listed below, phone ⓣ1-800/NYC-VISIT or go to ⓦwww.nycgo.com. Also look at listings in the *Village Voice*'s "Voice Choices", *New York Magazine*'s "Agenda", *Time Out New York*'s "Around Town" sections, and in the *New York Times*' "Weekend Arts" section, published every Friday.

January

New York Jewish Film Festival Mid- to late Jan; ⓣ212/496-3809 or 875-5600, ⓦwww.filmlinc.com or www.thejewishmuseum.org. Screenings of complex, provocative Jewish films with an international bent, as well as some rare oldies. Most films are shown at Lincoln Center's Walter Reade Theater.

Lunar (Chinese) New Year Usually Jan or Feb; ⓦwww.explorechinatown.com. A noisy, joyful occasion celebrated for two weeks along and around Mott St in Lower Manhattan, as well as in Sunset Park in Brooklyn and Flushing in Queens. The chances of getting a meal without a reservation anywhere in Manhattan's Chinatown during this time are slim.

Martin Luther King Jr Day Tributes Third Mon; ⓣ718/636-4100, ⓦwww.bam.org. City-wide celebration honouring Dr King's contribution to civil rights and African-American heritage. The free talks and performances at the Brooklyn Academy of Music are the day's most notable occurrences.

Restaurant Week Late Jan to early Feb; also July ⓣ212/484-1200, ⓦwww.restaurantweek.com. For about ten weekdays, you can get prix-fixe three-course lunches at some of the city's finest establishments for $24.07, or three-course dinners for $35. This can be quite a savings at restaurants like *Aquavit* and *Nobu*, though the limited menus don't always show off the cuisine at its best, and you must make reservations months in advance for the most desirable places.

Street fairs

In various sections of the city on weekend afternoons in the spring, summer and autumn, **street fairs** close a stretch of several blocks to traffic to offer pedestrians T-shirts, curios and gut-busting snacks like sausage sandwiches and fried dough. Unfortunately, once you've seen one, you've seen them all, as the vendors are rarely neighbourhood-specific. You'll find the most local flavour at the raucously tacky **Feast of San Gennaro** (see p.428), which could be called the prototypical street fair. Heading to the outer boroughs often yields more character, too – you might happen across *lucha libre* (Mexican wrestling) along with the usual fare.

Street fairs are usually listed in *Time Out New York* and neighbourhood newspapers. Smaller **block parties**, sponsored by community groups rather than business organizations, are more intimate affairs, generally with one sidestreet closed to cars, kids performing, politicos popping in to shake hands and everyone taking part in a huge pot-luck meal. They're typically not advertised, however, so consider yourself lucky to stumble upon one.

February

Outsider Art Fair Early Feb; ⓣ212/777-5218, ⓦwww.sanfordsmith.com. Leading dealers of outsider, primitive, visionary and intuitive art exhibit their collections at the Mart, 7 W 34th St, at Fifth Ave. $50.

Westminster Kennel Club Dog Show Mid-Feb; ⓣ212/213-3165, ⓦwww.westminsterkennelclub.org. Second only to the Kentucky Derby as the oldest continuous sporting event in the country, this show at Madison Square Garden welcomes 2500 canines competing for best in breed, along with legions of fanatic dog-lovers.

March

St Patrick's Day Parade March 17; ⓣ212/484-1222, ⓦwww.saintpatricksdayparade.com. Based on an impromptu march through the Manhattan streets by Irish militiamen on St Patrick's Day in 1762, this parade is a draw for every Irish band and organization in the US and Ireland, and it's impressive for the sheer mobs of people – no cars or floats are allowed. Parade organizers have long prohibited gay and lesbian groups from marching, but they have a vocal presence on the sidelines. Starting around 11am at St Patrick's Cathedral on Fifth Ave and 44th St (following 8.30am Mass), it heads uptown to 86th St.

Greek Independence Day Parade Late March; ⓣ718/204-6500, ⓦwww.greekparade.org. Not as long or as boozy as St Pat's, more a patriotic nod to the old country from floats of pseudo-classically dressed Hellenes. When Independence Day (March 25) falls in the Orthodox Lent, the parade is shifted to April or May. It usually kicks off from 60th St and Fifth Ave and runs up to 79th St.

New Directors, New Films Late March to early April; ⓣ212/875-5638, ⓦwww.filmlinc.com. Lincoln Center and MoMA present this two-week series, one of the city's best, but rarely surrounded by hype. Films range from the next indie hits to obscure, never-to-be-seen-again works of genius, and the majority of the film-makers are from other countries. Tickets ($14) go on sale several weeks before the beginning of the festival, and films with a lot of buzz will sell out.

April

Easter Parade Easter Sun; ⓣ212/360-8111, ⓦwww.nycgovparks.org. Evoking the old fashion parade on the city's most stylish avenue, hundreds of people promenade up Fifth Ave, from 49th to 57th sts (10am–4pm) in elaborate, flower-bedecked Easter bonnets. These days, it's more like Halloween, with people using it as an excuse to dress up in wacky costumes.

Tribeca Film Festival Late April to early May; ⓣ212/941-2400, ⓦwww.tribecafilmfestival.org. Launched in 2002, this glitzy two-week fest presents an admirable mix of soon-to-be-blockbusters and indie work, including shorts and international films. Purchase tickets ($8; $16 after 6pm) well in advance.

May

Migrating Forms Early May; ⓣ212/505-5110, ⓦmigratingforms.org (new festival that grew out of the New York Underground Film Festival, which ended in 2008). Experimental video, fringy political documentaries, animated shorts and more at this catch-all, way-out-of-the-mainstream event at the Anthology Film Archives, 32 Second Ave, at 2nd St.

Affordable Art Fair Early May; ⓣ212/255-2003, ⓦwww.aafnyc.com. Four days of art sales for which everything is priced less than $10,000, held at 7 W New York, 7 W 34th St, near Fifth Ave (free).

Sakura Matsuri (Cherry Blossom Festival) Early May; ⓣ718/623-7200, ⓦwww.bbg.org. Music, art, dance, traditional fashion and sword-fighting demonstrations celebrate Japanese culture and the brief, sublime blossoming of the Brooklyn Botanic Garden's two hundred cherry trees. Free with garden admission.

Five Boro Bike Tour Early May; ⓣ212/932-2453, ⓦwww.bikenewyork.org. Cars are banished from the route of this 42-mile ride through all five boroughs, and some 30,000 cyclists take to the streets.

Ukrainian Festival Mid-May; ⓣ212/674-1615, ⓦwww.brama.com. This weekend festival (sponsored by St George Church) sees East 7th St – between Second and Third aves – filled with marvellous Ukrainian costumes,

Summer outdoor fun

Summer arts programmes are nice treats for those who stay in the city through the muggiest months. As most of these shows are free or at least very cheap, they're swarmed with fun-seeking New Yorkers – plan on arriving very early to stake out a picnic spot on the grass, and book tickets ahead when possible.

Bryant Park Summer Film Festival Mid-June to mid-Aug; ⓣ212/512-5700, ⓦwww.bryantpark.org. Each Monday night (8–9pm) picnickers watch classic films like *Breakfast at Tiffany's* on the lush lawn of Bryant Park. Get there very early and bring a blanket. Free.

Celebrate Brooklyn June–Aug; ⓣ718/855-7882, ⓦwww.bricartsmedia.org. One of New York's longest-running free music series, at the bandstand in Prospect Park; great Latin performances, among others.

Midsummer Night Swing July; ⓣ212/875-5766, ⓦwww.lincolncenter.org. In Lincoln Center's Damrosch Park, W 62nd St at Amsterdam Ave, every Tuesday to Saturday evenings, learn a different dance en masse each night to the rhythm of live swing, mambo, merengue, samba or country. Lessons at 6.30pm, music and dancing at 7.30pm.

New York Philharmonic June–Aug; ⓣ212/875-5656, ⓦwww.newyorkphilharmonic.org. See p.372.

River to River Festival June–Sept; ⓦwww.rivertorivernyc.com. Big-name performers in pop, World Music and dance take to the stage in Battery Park, the World Financial Center and elsewhere in Lower Manhattan. Free.

Rooftop Films May–Aug; ⓣ718/417-7362, ⓦwww.rooftopfilms.com. Set on factory roofs and in public parks in Brooklyn and Manhattan, this movie series offers nifty backdrops for watching hip indie shorts. $9

Shakespeare in the Park June–Aug; ⓣ212/539-8500, ⓦwww.publictheater.org. See p.159.

SummerStage June–Aug; ⓣ212/360-2777, ⓦwww.summerstage.org. See p.372.

folk music and dance, plus foods and traditional crafts such as egg-painting.

Salute to Israel Parade Late May or early June; ⓣ212/245-8200, ⓦwww.salutetoisrael.com. This celebration of Israeli independence attempts to display unity within New York's ideologically and religiously diverse Jewish community. On Fifth Ave, between 57th and 79th sts, rain or shine.

June

Museum Mile Festival First Tues evening; ⓣ212/606-2296, ⓦwww.museummilefestival.org. On Fifth Ave from 82nd to 105th sts. Nine museums, including the Museum of the City of New York, the Cooper Hewitt, the Guggenheim, the Neue Galerie and the Met, are open free 6–9pm, and the street is closed down for a massive block party.

American Crafts Festival Early June; ⓣ973/746-0091, ⓦwww.craftsatlincoln.org. Over two weekends in June, entertainment and food accompany four hundred juried displays at Lincoln Center. Free admission.

National Puerto Rican Day Parade Second Sun; ⓣ718/401-0404, ⓦwww.nationalpuertoricandayparade.org. The largest of several buoyant Puerto Rican celebrations in the city: seven hours of bands, flag-waving and baton-twirling from 44th to 86th sts on Fifth Ave, with an estimated two million people in attendance.

JVC Jazz Festival Mid-June; ⓣ212/501-1390, ⓦwww.festivalnetwork.com. The jazz world's top names appear at Carnegie Hall, *Le Poisson Rouge* and other venues around the city.

Mermaid Parade First Sat on or after June 21; ⓣ718/372-5159, ⓦwww.coneyisland.com. At this outstanding event, participants dress like mermaids, fish and other sea creatures, and saunter through Coney Island, led by assorted offbeat celebs. A Mermaid Ball with burlesque entertainment follows.

Pride Week Third or fourth week of June; ⓣ212/807-7433, ⓦwww.nycpride.org. The world's biggest lesbian, gay, bisexual and transgender Pride event kicks off with a rally in Bryant Park and ends with a march down Fifth Ave, a street fair in Greenwich Village and a huge last-night dance.

Dyke March Fourth Sat; ⓣ212/479-8520, ⓦdykemarchnyc.org. This technically illegal march rallies a diverse group of lesbian and bisexual women, from youngsters to topless grannies, at Bryant Park, to protest discrimination.

July

Independence Day July 4; ⓣ212/494-4495. The fireworks – above either the East River or Hudson River – are visible from all over Manhattan, but the best places to view them are along the waterfront (and Brooklyn or Jersey depending on which river is being used), starting at about 9pm.

Tap City Early July; ⓣ646/230-9564, ⓦwww.atdf.org. This week-long festival features hundreds of tap dancers who perform and give classes and workshops.

Asian American International Film Festival Mid-July; ⓣ212/989-1422, ⓦwww.asiancinevision.org. New films from Asia and the Asian diaspora, usually held at Chelsea Clearview Cinema, W 23rd St and Eighth Ave, or MOCA (see p.85). Tickets from $12.50.

Restaurant Week Mid-July. See p.424.

Festa del Giglio Mid-July; ⓣ718/384-0223, ⓦwww.olmcfeast.com. Since 1903, Havemeyer St between N 8th and N 11th sts in Williamsburg is taken over by this twelve-day Italian Catholic street festival ("Giglio" means lily), which culminates around July 16th, the feast day of Our Lady of Mount Carmel, with a procession of a giant wooden boat and a figure of St Paulinus on an 85-foot tower.

Mostly Mozart Late July to late Aug; ⓣ212/875-5766, ⓦwww.lincolncenter.org. More than forty concerts and Mozart-themed events at Lincoln Center, in the longest-running indoor summer festival in the US.

Washington Square Music Festival July; ⓣ212/252-3621, ⓦwww.washingtonsquaremusicfestival.org. Since 1953, a series of classical, jazz and big-band concerts, every Tues at 8pm, at this outdoor venue (rain space is NYU's Frederick Loewe Theater, 35 W 4th St). Free.

Antiques fairs

Antiques-lovers can find plenty of treasures in New York; these are only a few of the city's notable annual expos.

Winter Antiques Show Late Jan; ⓣ718/292-7392, ⓦwww.winterantiquesshow.com. Foremost American antiques show takes over the Park Avenue Armory, 643 Park Ave at 67th St, for one week; $20 per day.

Pier Antiques Show March & Nov; ⓣ212/255-0020, ⓦwww.stellashows.com. Largest metropolitan antiques fair, including vintage clothing, on Pier 94, Twelfth Ave at 55th St; $15 admission per day.

New York Antiquarian Book Fair Early April; ⓣ212/944-8291, ⓦwww.abaa.org. Collection of rare books, letters, drawings, etc, held at the Park Avenue Armory. Get free appraisals of up to five items on "Discovery Day"; $20 admission per day.

WFMU Record & CD Fair Late Oct; ⓣ201/521-1416 ext 225, ⓦwww.wfmu.org. Everything from ancient 78s to 1980s hip-hop is up for grabs in this celebration of vintage vinyl and CDs at the Metropolitan Pavilion, 125 W 18th St; $7 admission per day.

August

Harlem Week All month; ⓣ212/862-8473, ⓦharlemweek.com. What began as a week-long festival around Harlem Day on Aug 20 has stretched into a month of African, Caribbean and Latin performances, lectures and parties; some events in July, Sept and Oct, too.

Hong Kong Dragon Boat Festival First weekend in Aug; ⓣ718/767-1776, ⓦwww.hkdbf-ny.org. Flushing Meadows Corona Park is the site of this highly competitive race of 38-foot-long sculls; live entertainment, an arts and crafts market and a dumpling-eating contest round out the weekend.

New York International Fringe Festival Mid- to late Aug; ⓣ212/279-4488, ⓦwww.fringenyc.org. With more than two hundred companies performing at various downtown venues, this cutting-edge series is the biggest for performance art, theatre, dance, puppetry and more, offering the chance to see the hit shows before they move to bigger stages.

September

HOWL! Festival of East Village Arts Sept; ⓣ212/505-2225, ⓦwww.howlfestival.com. Eight days devoted to the Beats and other neighbourhood heroes, with an Allen Ginsberg Poetry Fest in and around Tompkins Square Park.

West Indian-American Day Parade and Carnival Labor Day; ⓣ718/467-1797, ⓦwww.wiadca.com. Brooklyn's largest parade, modelled after the carnivals of Trinidad and Tobago, features music, food, dance, floats with enormous sound systems and scores of steel-drum bands – not to mention more than a million attendees.

Broadway on Broadway Mid-Sept; ⓣ212/869-1890, ⓦwww.broadwayonbroadway.com. Free performances featuring songs by casts of the major Broadway musicals, culminating in a shower of confetti; held in Times Square.

Feast of San Gennaro Ten days in mid-Sept; ⓣ212/226-6427, ⓦwww.sangennaro.org. Since 1927, this festival has celebrated the patron saint of Naples along Mulberry St and its environs in Little Italy, with a cannoli-eating contest, midway games and tasty things to eat. In three parades (the largest is Sept 19, the saint's day), a San Gennaro statue is carried through the streets with donations pinned to his cloak.

African-American Day Parade Late Sept; ⓣ212/384-3080, ⓦwww.africanamericandayparade.org. Drum lines, step-dancers, politicians, the Boys Choir of Harlem,and other participants march through Harlem from 111th St and Adam Clayton Powell Jr Blvd to 142nd St, then east toward Fifth Ave, in the largest black parade in America.

DUMBO Art Under the Bridge Festival Late Sept; ⓣ718/694-0831, ⓦwww.dumboartfestival.org. More than two hundred resident artists show their work in open studios, bands perform and bizarre installations fill the streets in the stylish waterfront neighbourhood in Brooklyn.

New York Film Festival Late Sept to mid-Oct; ⓣ212/875-5600, ⓦwww.filmlinc.com. One of the world's leading film festivals unreels at Lincoln Center; tickets ($20) can be very hard to come by, as anticipated art hits get their debuts here.

October

Pulaski Day Parade First Sun in Oct; ⓦwww.pulaskiparade.org. Held on Fifth Ave (29th St to 53rd St from 12.30pm) since 1937 for the celebration of Polish heritage, beginning with Mass at St Patrick's Cathedral – it's named after the famous Polish general that fought for America in the Revolutionary War (he was killed in Charleston in 1779).

New Yorker Festival Early Oct; ⓦwww.newyorker.com/festival. Literary, music and film celebrities hobnob on stage with *New Yorker* editors, writers and cartoonists at this three-day festival, held at venues throughout the city. Tickets sell out quickly; sign up online for the Festival Wire to get advance notification of events by email.

Columbus Day Parade Second Mon; ⓣ212/249-9923, ⓦwww.columbuscitizensfd.org. On Fifth Ave between 49th and 79th sts, 35,000 marchers commemorate Italian-American heritage and the day America was put on the map. Parallel events celebrate the heritage of Native Americans and other indigenous peoples.

New York City Wine & Food Festival Mid-Oct; ⓦwww.nycwineandfoodfestival.com. The Food Network and *Food & Wine* magazine team up to present the city's biggest food festival, with big-name television and cookbook personalities giving talks and demonstrations and Meatpacking District restaurants hosting specially priced dinners. Tickets are expensive, but the proceeds go to charity.

Village Halloween Parade Oct 31; ⓦwww.halloween-nyc.com. In America's largest Halloween celebration, starting at 7pm on Sixth Ave at Spring St and making its way up to 23rd, you'll see spectacular costumes, giant puppets, bands and any other bizarre stuff New Yorkers can muster. Get there early for a good viewing spot; marchers (anyone in costume is eligible) line up at 6.30pm. (A tamer children's parade usually takes place earlier that day in Washington Square Park.)

Next Wave Festival Oct–Dec; ⓣ718/636-4100, ⓦwww.bam.org. Consistently excellent experimental arts festival at the Brooklyn Academy of Music, bringing the likes of Pina Bausch and Laurie Anderson to the stage in elaborate productions since 1981.

November

New York City Marathon First Sun; ⓣ212/423-2249, ⓦwww.ingnycmarathon.org. Some 37,000 runners from all over the world – from the champs to regular folks in goofy costumes – assemble for this high-spirited 26.2-mile run on city pavements through the five boroughs. One of the best places to watch is Central Park South, almost at the finish line.

Macy's Parade Inflation Eve

See Mickey Mouse and the other characters being inflated the night before **Macy's Thanksgiving Day Parade**. It's not as crowded as on parade day, and you can experience something not broadcast to every home in America. The giant nylon balloons are set up on West 77th and 81st streets between Central Park West and Columbus Avenue at the American Museum of Natural History. Wander around the feet of these giants and watch them gradually take shape.

Veterans Day Parade Nov 11; ⓣ212/693-1476 The United War Veterans sponsor this annual event on Fifth Ave from 23rd to 59th sts. Ceremony at 10.15am, salute and parade at 11am.

Macy's Thanksgiving Day Parade Thanksgiving Day; ⓣ212/494-4495, ⓦwww.macysparade.com. A made-for-TV extravaganza, with big corporate floats, dozens of marching bands from around the country and Santa Claus's first appearance of the season. Some two million spectators watch it along Central Park West from 77th St to Columbus Circle, and along Broadway down to Herald Square, 9am–noon.

Rockefeller Center Christmas Tree Lighting Late Nov; ⓣ212/632-3975, ⓦwww.rockefellercenter.com. Switching on the lights on the enormous tree in front of the ice rink begins the holiday season, in a glowing moment sure to warm even the most Grinch-like heart. The crowds, however, can be oppressive.

African Diaspora Film Festival Late Nov to early Dec; ⓣ212/864-1760, ⓦwww.nyadff.org. Films from throughout the world, by and about people of African descent, are shown at several Manhattan venues.

December

Hanukkah Celebrations Usually mid-Dec. During the eight nights of this Jewish feast, a menorah-lighting ceremony takes place at Brooklyn's Grand Army Plaza (ⓣ718/778-6000), and the world's largest menorah is illuminated on Fifth Ave near Central Park (ⓣ212/736-8400).

Kwanzaa Mid-Dec; ⓣ212/568-1645, ⓦwww.africanfolkheritagecircle.org. Celebrations city-wide, including a storytelling show by the African Folk Heritage Circle in Harlem.

New Year's Eve in Times Square Dec 31; ⓣ212/768-1560, ⓦwww.timessquarenyc.org. Several hundred thousand revellers party in the cold and well-guarded streets – a crowd-management nightmare, so take the subway and get where you're going early. Elsewhere in the city, you can choose from alcohol-free singles bashes, all-out clubbing, a four-mile midnight group run in Central Park or calmer activities, like meditation marathons.

33

Kids' New York

New York can be quite a wonderful place to bring **children**. Obvious attractions like museums, theatres, skyscrapers, ferry rides and all the diversions of Central Park will certainly thrill them, but a visit with kids may also give you reason to appreciate the simpler pleasures of the city, from watching street entertainers to introducing youngsters to strange foods and fascinating neighbourhoods like Chinatown. The city is full of high-calibre free events aimed at children, especially in the summer: puppet shows, garden plantings, cultural celebrations, park festivals and storytelling hours at local bookstores are all excellent ways to entertain. Many museums and theatres also feature specific children's programmes. Following are details on some attractions especially appealing to kids, but make sure to phone ahead for specific times, etc, to avoid any disappointment.

General advice

For a **listing** of what's available when you're in town, see the detailed NYC*kids*ARTS Cultural Calendar (free; Ⓦwww.nyckidsarts.org). *Time Out New York magazine* (and the extra-specialized *TONY Kids*), the *Village Voice* and websites such as Ⓦwww.gocitykids.com are also valuable resources. A solid directory of family-oriented events all around the city is available through NYC & Company, the convention and visitors' bureau, at 810 Seventh Ave, Third Floor, between 52nd and 53rd streets (Mon–Fri 8.30am–6pm, Sat & Sun 9am–5pm; Ⓣ212/484-1200, Ⓦwww.nycgo.com).

Once in the city, your main problem won't be finding stuff to do with your kids but transporting them. **Subways** are the fastest way to get around and are perfectly safe – as a bonus, children under 44 inches (112cm) ride free on the subway and buses when accompanied by an adult. Though some natives navigate the streets

Babysitting

The **Babysitters' Guild**, at 60 E 42nd St (daily 9am–9pm; Ⓣ212/682-0227, Ⓦwww.babysittersguild.com) offers childcare services with carefully selected staff, most of whom have teaching and nursing backgrounds. Fees (for one kid) are $25 an hour, four hours minimum, plus $4.50 to cover transportation ($10 after midnight), and "extra" children are $5 additional per hour. It's $5 extra for one of the multilingual sitters (sixteen foreign languages are represented in all). The organization is fully licensed and bonded. Book at least the night before, further ahead if you want to be absolutely safe.

Check Ⓦwww.gocitykids.com for many more childcare options.

and subway stairs with strollers, most prefer to keep infants and even toddlers conveniently contained in a backpack or front carrier. Indeed, many attractions do not accommodate strollers, though some will keep yours temporarily while you visit – call ahead for details. Most sights, restaurants and stores, however, are at the very least quite tolerant of children.

Finally, if all else fails, or if you want some quiet time to enjoy the city's more mature offerings, just hire a **babysitter** (see box, p.431).

Museums

You could spend an entire holiday just checking out the city's many **museums**, almost all of which contain something fascinating for kids. The following is a brief overview of the ones that tend to evoke special enthusiasm. See the appropriate Guide chapters for more details on these and other museums.

American Museum of Natural History and the Rose Center for Earth and Space

Central Park W at 79th St ⓣ212/769-5100, ⓦwww.amnh.org. Subway B, C to 81st St. Daily 10am–5.45pm, Rose Center until 8.45pm on first Fri of month. IMAX shows 10.30am–4.30pm, every hour on the half-hour daily 10.30am–4.30pm. Suggested donation $16, children 2–12 $9 (includes the Rose Center). Special exhibits and IMAX additional charge; combination packages available.

One of the best museums of its kind, this enormous complex is filled with fossils, meteorites, lots of stuffed animals and other natural objects (more than 34 million in all). Your first stop should be the Fossil Halls on the Fourth Floor, where you'll find towering dinosaur skeletons and interactive computer stations that are sure to please all ages.

Other halls are dedicated to more contemporary beasts: a full-scale herd of elephants dominates the Akeley Hall of African Mammals, a 94-foot-long blue whale hangs over the Milstein Hall of Ocean Life, and the Hall of Biodiversity offers a multimedia recreation of a Central African rainforest. In the winter, the Butterfly Conservatory is a sure bet for younger children. Weekends bring special events for families, including very young kids.

Just across from the Hall of Biodiversity lies the Rose Center for Earth and Space, which features the Space Theater, the Big Bang Theater (in which the beginning of the universe is recreated every half-hour) and the Cosmic Pathway, an evolutionary timeline.

Brooklyn Children's Museum

145 Brooklyn Ave, at St Mark's Ave ⓣ718/735-4400, ⓦwww.brooklynkids.org. Subway #3 to Kingston Ave. Wed–Fri 11am–5pm, Sat & Sun 10am–5pm, $7.50.

Founded in 1899, this was the world's first museum designed specifically for children. It's full of authentic ethnological, historical and technological artefacts with which kids can play, plus live animals, including a 17-foot-long Burmese python; kids of most ages should be more than adequately entertained.

Children's Museum of Manhattan

212 W 83rd St, between Broadway and Amsterdam Ave ⓣ212/721-1234, ⓦwww.cmom.org. Subway #1 to 86th St. Tues–Sun 10am–5pm, first Fri of month until 8pm; $10.

This participatory museum, founded in 1937, has five floors full of imaginative displays that involve a lot of clambering around. Older children can produce their own television shows in the Media Center, and exhibits often have a hip edge.

Children's Museum of the Arts

182 Lafayette St, between Broome and Grand sts ⓣ212/274-0986, ⓦwww.cmany.org. Subway #6 to Spring St. Wed & Fri–Sun noon–5pm, Thurs noon–6pm; $10, pay what you wish Thurs 4–6pm.

At this gallery, children are encouraged to look at different types of art and then create their own with paints, paper, clay, fabric, and other simple media. Holiday special events are particularly interesting – African mask-making for Kwanzaa, for example. Admission includes various dance, movie and music programmes on weekends.

Intrepid Sea, Air & Space Museum

Pier 86, W 46th St at Twelfth Ave ⓣ212/245-0072, ⓦwww.intrepidmuseum.org. Subway A, C, E to 42nd St. April–Sept Mon–Fri 10am–5pm, Sat & Sun 10am–6pm, Oct–March Tues–Sun 10am–5pm; $19.50, ages 3–17 $11.50.
Even non-military-minded kids will be impressed by the massive scale of this aircraft-carrier-cum-museum – not to mention the huge collection of airplanes and helicopters. The site, recently renovated, now includes a 15,000-sq-ft space for hands-on learning, in which children can climb a cargo net, experience (via computer) life on a ship and (for older kids or adults) simulate aircraft launches.

Museum of the City of New York

1220 Fifth Ave, at 103rd St ⓣ212/534-1672, ⓦwww.mcny.org. Subway #6 to 103rd St. Tues–Sun 10am–5pm; suggested donation $10, children 12 and under free.
The museum holds an extensive collection of toys, some 10,000 of them, such as antique dollhouses and the like; kids will also have fun identifying the city's landmarks, depicted in paintings in the picture gallery.

New York City Fire Museum

278 Spring St, between Hudson and Varick sts ⓣ212/691-1303, ⓦwww.nycfiremuseum.org. Subway C, E to Spring St; #1 to Houston St. Tues–Sat 10am–5pm, Sun 10am–4pm; suggested donation $7, kids under 12 $5.
A sure hit with the preschool crowd, this space pays pleasing homage to New York City's firefighters. On display are fire engines from yesteryear (horse-drawn and steam-powered), helmets, dog-eared photos and a host of motley objects on three floors of a former fire station. A neat and appealing display, even though it's not full of interactive doodahs.

New York Hall of Science

111th St, at 46th Ave, Flushing Meadows–Corona Park, Queens ⓣ718/699-0005, ⓦwww.nysci.org. Subway #7 to 111th St. April–June 9.30am–2pm, Fri 9.30am–5pm, Sat & Sun 10am–6pm; July & Aug Mon–Fri 9.30am–5pm, Sat & Sun 10am–6pm; Sept–March Tues–Thurs 9.30am–2pm, Fri 9.30am–5pm, Sat & Sun 10am–6pm; $11, children $8, free Sept–June Fri 2–5pm & Sun 10–11am.
Housed in a glowing blue tower built for the 1964–65 World's Fair, this is one of the top science museums in the country. A highlight is the giant, outdoor Science Playground (open April–Dec; an additional $4), where kids can clamber around as they learn about scientific principles. Located in Queens, the Hall of Science makes for a good day-trip combined with a visit to any of the attractions in Flushing–Corona Park: Queens Zoo, the nearby Queens Museum or the park itself.

New York Transit Museum

Old subway entrance at Schermerhorn St and Boerum Place, Brooklyn ⓣ718/694-1600, ⓦwww.mta.info/mta/museum. Subway #2, #3, #4, #5 to Borough Hall; A, C, F to Jay St–Borough Hall. Tues–Fri 10am–4pm, Sat & Sun noon–5pm; $5, children 3–17 $3. Also: Transit Museum Gallery and Store at Grand Central Terminal, open daily; free.
Housed in an abandoned 1930s subway station, this museum offers more than a hundred years of transportation memorabilia, including old subway cars and buses dating back to the turn of the nineteenth century. Frequent activities for kids include underground tours, workshops and an annual bus festival – all best for younger schoolkids (and there are usually plenty of them running around here). It's a quick hop on the subway, but if you don't want to go to Brooklyn, at least stop in to the museum's annexe at Grand Central in Manhattan, which has its own rotating exhibits.

South Street Seaport Museum

12 Fulton St ⓣ212/748-8600, ⓦwww.seany.org. Subway #2, #3, #4, #5 to Fulton St; A, C to Broadway–Nassau. Jan–March Fri–Sun 10am–5pm all galleries, also Mon 10am–5pm Schermerhorn Row Galleries only; April–Oct Tues–Sun 10am–6pm; $15, under 2 free.
South Street Seaport's dock is home to a small fleet of historic ships which kids are welcome to tour, including a nicely preserved 1893 fishing schooner, a merchant vessel with a towering mast and a hard-working harbour tugboat. With some

planning, you may even be able to go out on one of the crafts for a harbour tour (summers only). The museum building itself will seem staid in comparison to the boats.

Staten Island Children's Museum

Snug Harbor Cultural Center, 1000 Richmond Terrace, Staten Island ⓣ718/273-2060, ⓦwww.statenislandkids.org. June–Aug Tues–Sun 10am–5pm, Sept–May Tues–Sun noon–5pm; $6.

This is a good way to round off a trip on the Staten Island ferry; the #S40 bus runs from the ferry terminal. Expect, among other things, giant chess sets, a small-scale playhouse, a great exhibit about bugs that includes a human-size anthill and an outdoor play area on the water where kids can sail boats and learn about oysters.

Sights and entertainment

Brooklyn Botanic Garden

900 Washington Ave ⓣ718/623-7200, ⓦwww.bbg.org. Subway #2, #3 to Eastern Parkway. March–Oct Tues–Fri 8am–6pm, Sat & Sun 10am–6pm; Nov–Feb Tues–Fri 8am–4.30pm, Sat, & Sun 10am–4.30pm; $8, free Tues, Sat before noon, Nov–Feb weekdays.

This gorgeous landscape behind the Brooklyn Museum of Art is very child-friendly, with giant carp in the ponds and ducks to chase around. Kids will enjoy the City Farmers and KinderGarden programmes, and parents can drop in for the flower-arranging classes (dried and silk), garden tutorials, tours and yoga sessions. Families crowd the place for seasonal events like the Cherry Blossom Festival in late April.

Bronx Zoo

Bronx River Parkway at Fordham Rd ⓣ718/367-1010, ⓦwww.bronxzoo.org. Subway #2, #5 to East Tremont Ave. April–Oct Mon–Fri 10am–5pm, Sat & Sun 10am–5.30pm; Nov–March daily 10am–4.30pm; $15, children 3–12 $11. Pay what you wish on Wed, parking $10.

The largest urban zoo in America, with thrilling permanent exhibits – check out Wild Asia by monorail (May–Oct only), the lush rainforest of JungleWorld and the Congo Gorilla Forest. Kids can watch penguins being fed, get up close with Siberian tigers or ride a giant bug on an insect-themed carousel. Highly recommended for an all-day excursion, particularly in spring, when many baby animals are born. Be prepared for small additional fees once inside; check website for "bad weather bargains" and other specials.

Central Park

Central Park provides year-round, sure-fire entertainment for the younger set. In the summer it becomes one giant playground, with activities ranging from storytelling to rollerblading to boating. Highlights include the nature exhibits at Belvedere Castle, in mid-park at 79th St; the surprisingly fast Carousel, at 64th St, a vintage model salvaged from Coney Island (and recently restored); Central Park Zoo, Fifth Ave at 64th St, where youngsters will be delighted at the singing bronze animals on the musical clock at the entrance to the Tisch Children's Zoo; Loeb Boathouse, east side at 74th St, where you can rent rowboats; and ice-skating at Wollman Rink, east side at 63rd St (seasonal). For more detailed information on these and other sights, see Chapter 13, "Central Park".

New York Aquarium

Surf Ave at W 8th St, Coney Island, Brooklyn ⓣ718/265-FISH, ⓦwww.nyaquarium.com. Subway F, Q to W 8th St. June–Aug Mon–Fri 10am–6pm; weekends until 7pm; rest of the year closing times vary from 4.30pm to 5.30pm (opens at 10am); $17, children 3–12 $13.

Although it dates to 1896, the aquarium has very modern-looking exhibits dedicated to jellyfish and sea horses, along with 8000 other underwater animals. Open-air sea-lion shows and feedings – shark, penguin, sea otter and walrus – are held several times daily. This is also the site of the famous Coney Island boardwalk and amusement parks: older children and teens will find it a good spot to people-watch or enjoy the thrill of riding the Cyclone and the WonderWheel (see p.238).

New York Botanical Garden

Bronx River Parkway at Fordham Rd, Bronx (across from the Bronx Zoo) ⓣ718/817-8700, ⓦwww.nybg.org. Subway B, D, #4 to Bedford Park Blvd. Tues–Sun 10am–6pm, closes 5pm most of Jan & Feb; all-garden pass $20, children 2–12 $8, grounds-only $6, children 2–12 $1, parking $12.
One of America's foremost public gardens, with an enormous conservatory showcasing a rainforest and other types of ecosystems, plus the 12-acre Everett Children's Adventure Garden, which includes several mazes.

Sony Wonder Technology Lab

550 Madison Ave, at 56th St ⓣ212/833-8100, ⓦwww.sonywondertechlab.com. Subway #4, #5, #6 to 59th St–Lexington Ave; E to Fifth Ave. Tues–Sat 10am–5pm, Sun noon–5pm; free.
Sony's gee-whiz exhibit space emphasizes the marvels of the digital age, and although it's a bit corporate-slick, tech-minded kids will enjoy creating their own video games and trying out TV editing, among other computer-driven activities. This is a hugely popular attraction, so be sure to make reservations (you can do this up to three months in advance); same-day tickets are sometimes available as well.

Shops

Bank Street Bookstore 610 W 112th St, at Broadway ⓣ212/678-1654, ⓦwww.bankstreetbooks.com. Subway #1 to 110th St. The first floor of this store – affiliated with Bank Street College of Education – is filled with children's books and games, while the second floor is devoted to nonfiction books and educational materials. Frequent special events and afternoon story hours. Mon–Wed 11am–7pm, Thurs 10am–8pm, Fri & Sat 10am–6pm, Sun 11am–6pm.

Books of Wonder 18 W 18th St, between Fifth and Sixth aves ⓣ212/989-3270, ⓦwww.booksofwonder.com. Subway F, M to 14th St. Showpiece kids' bookstore, with a great Oz section, plus story hour on Sunday at 1pm and author appearances Saturday in the spring and autumn. Mon–Sat 10am–7pm, Sun 11am–6pm.

Dylan's Candy Bar 1011 Third Ave, at 60th St ⓣ646/735-0078, ⓦwww.dylanscandybar.com. Subway N, Q, R, #4, #5, #6 to 59th St–Lexington Ave. Kids will catch a sugar high just walking in the door of this stylish shop devoted to all things sweet. The selection is almost paralysing, with everything from a rainbow of gummy sweets to retro favourites like Charleston Chews. Mon–Thurs 10am–9pm, Fri & Sat 10am–11pm, Sun 11am–9pm.

F.A.O. Schwarz 767 Fifth Ave, at 58th St ⓣ212/644-9400, ⓦwww.fao.com. Subway N, Q, R to Fifth Ave. This multistorey toy emporium features an on-site ice-cream parlour, a whole wing dedicated to Lego and the legendary danceable floor piano featured in the 1988 film *Big*. Very popular (and very expensive), but a less frenzied experience than the plasticky Toys 'R' Us in Times Square. Mon–Thurs 10am–7pm, Fri & Sat 10am–8pm, Sun 11am–6pm.

Metropolitan Museum Store 15 W 49th St ⓣ212/332-1360, ⓦstore.metmuseum.org. Subway B, D, F, M to 47–50th St–Rockefeller Center. The third floor of the shop is devoted to arty children's toys, many of which highlight pieces in the museum's collection. Mon–Thurs, Sat & Sun 10am–7pm, Fri 10am–8pm.

Red Caboose 23 W 45th St, between Fifth and Sixth aves, lower level ⓣ212/575-0155, ⓦwww.theredcaboose.com. Subway B, D, F, M to 42nd St. A unique shop specializing in models, particularly trains and train sets. Mon–Fri 11am–7pm, Sat 11am–5pm.

CHECK Space Kiddets 26 E 22nd St, between Park Ave and Broadway ⓣ212/420-9878, ⓦwww.spacekiddets.com. Subway R, #6 to 23rd St. Show your baby's musical taste with a CBGB onesie or a David Bowie tee from this funky clothes shop that stocks infant to pre-teen sizes; vintage toys can be found at the shop around the block (46 E 21st St). Mon, Tues, Fri & Sat 10.30am–6pm, Wed & Thurs 10.30am–7pm, Sun 11am–5pm.

Tannen's Magic Studio 45 W 34th St, Suite 608, between Fifth and Sixth aves ⓣ212/929-4500, ⓦwww.tannens.com. Subway B, D, F, M to 34th St. Your kids will never forget a visit to the largest magic shop in the world, with nearly 8000 props, tricks, and magic sets. The staff is made up of magicians who perform free shows throughout the day. Mon–Fri 11am–6pm, Sat & Sun 10am–4pm.

Parks and playgrounds

Giving your kids a chance to let off some steam (preferably outdoors) is a necessity in the city, especially if your agenda includes somewhat confining activities like museums, shows and the odd nice restaurant. Aside from the obvious (Central Park and Prospect Park), consider places such as **Brooklyn Bridge Park** (see p.222), which – in addition to a new waterpark, roomy sandboxes and a giant slide, all at Pier 6 – has excellent views of the Brooklyn and Manhattan bridges, passing boats and the helipad across the water, and Madison Square Park (see p.124), with its playground, dog run, central fountain and, best of all, *Shake Shack*, for much-needed burgers and frozen custard. See ⓦwww.nycgovparks.org to find a complete list of playgrounds in the city's parks.

Theatre, circuses and other entertainment

The following is a highly selective roundup of **cultural activities** that might be of interest to children. As always, find out more by checking the listings in the *New York Times* (which publishes its calendar of youth activities in the arts section on Fri) and magazines such as *Time Out New York Kids*. Note too that the Brooklyn Museum and the Met, among other museums, often have events for children, as do many bookstores.

BAMfamily Brooklyn Academy of Music, 30 Lafayette Ave ⓣ718/636-4100, ⓦwww.bam.org. This periodic series presents public performances for families on weekends, as well as the international BAMkids Film Festival late Feb/early March.

Barnum & Bailey Circus Madison Square Garden ⓣ212/465-6741, ⓦwww.ringling.com. This large touring circus arrives in New York on a mile-long train in late March and stays for ten days. The real highlight is before the circus starts, when the elephants are escorted from the rail yards in Queens to the west side of Manhattan – usually around midnight, but the sight is worth staying up for. Keep an eye on local papers for the precise date and route. Tickets $15–155.

Big Apple Circus Lincoln Center ⓣ212/721-6500, ⓦwww.bigapplecircus.org. Small circus that performs in a tent in Damrosch Park next to the Met, from late Oct to mid-Jan. Tickets $40–90.

Manhattan Children's Theatre 52 White St ⓣ212/226-4085, ⓦwww.manhattanchildrenstheatre.org. $20, enquire for children's prices. Classic plays, fairy tales and musicals, plus some new works. Sat & Sun noon & 2pm.

New Victory Theater 209 W 42nd St, at Broadway ⓣ646/223-3010, ⓦwww.newvictory.org. The city's first theatre for families, located in a grand old renovated Times Square space, presents a rich mix of theatre, music, dance, storytelling, film and puppetry, in addition to pre- and post-performance workshops. Affordable shows (most tickets $12–35) run 1–2hr. In keeping with the cultural calendar that much of the city runs on, the theatre is dark (no performances) during the summer.

Streb Laboratory for Action Mechanics (S.L.A.M.) 51 N 1st St, Williamsburg, Brooklyn ⓣ718/384-6491, ⓦwww.streb.org. MacArthur-grant-winning choreographer Elizabeth Streb has developed a dynamic, physical dance style she calls Pop Action – go for one of the company's inspiring performances in its raw Brooklyn warehouse, or sign kids up for the week-long S.L.A.M. Summer Camps in July. The space also offers trampoline work, trapeze fun and basic tumbling; most classes are Tues–Thurs though it's open all week.

Trapeze School New York Hudson River Park at Canal St and 518 W 30th St ⓣ212/242-8769, ⓦnewyork.trapezeschool.com. Two-hour classes on the flying trapeze, for ages 6 and up, start at $69 (including a one-time $22 registration fee) and include an amazing view over the Hudson River from high atop the rig, as long as you're not at the indoor facility on 30th St of course. Parents must accompany children – but if this seems too daunting, you can just go sit in the park and watch the intrepid high-flyers practise their moves. Book well in advance.

Contexts

Contexts

History

To Europe she was America, to America she was the gateway of the earth. But to tell the story of New York would be to write a social history of the world.

H.G. Wells

Early days and colonial rule

Long before the arrival of European settlers, New York was inhabited by several Native American tribes; the **Algonquin** tribe was the largest and most populous in the area that is now New York City. Although descendants of the Algonquins and other tribes still live on Long Island's Shinnecock reservation, the appearance of Europeans in the sixteenth century essentially destroyed their settled existence.

Giovanni da Verrazano was the first explorer to discover Manhattan. An Italian in the service of French king Francis I, he had set out to find the Pacific's legendary Northwest Passage, but like his countryman Christopher Columbus, had been blown off-course into what would become New York Harbor in 1524. Verrazano returned to France to woo the court with tales of fertile lands and friendly natives, but it was nearly a century before the powers of Europe were tempted to follow him.

In 1609 **Henry Hudson**, an Englishman employed by the **Dutch East India Company**, landed at Manhattan, sailing his ship, the *Half-Moone*, upriver as far as Albany. Hudson found that the route did not lead to the Northwest Passage, which he, too, had been commissioned to discover – but in charting its course for the first time he gave his name to the mighty river. Returning home, Hudson was persuaded to embark on another expedition, this time under the British flag. He arrived in Hudson Bay in the dead of winter, the temperature below freezing and his mutinous crew doubting his ability as a navigator; he, his son and several loyal sailors were set adrift in a small boat on the icy waters where, presumably, they froze to death.

British fears that they had lost the upper hand in the newly discovered land proved justified when the Dutch established a trading post at the most northerly point on the river that Hudson had reached, **Fort Nassau**, and quickly seized the commercial advantage. In 1624, four years after the Pilgrims had sailed to Massachusetts, thirty families left Holland to become New York's first European settlers, most sailing up to Fort Nassau. But a handful – eight families in all – stayed behind on a small island they called Nut Island because of the many walnut trees there: today's Governors Island. The community slowly grew as more settlers arrived, and the little island became crowded; the **settlement of Manhattan**, taken from the Lenape word *Manna-Hata* meaning "Island of the Hills", began when families from Governors Island moved across the water.

The Dutch gave this new outpost the name **New Amsterdam**, and in 1626 the Dutch West India Company sent over **Peter Minuit** to govern the small community. Among his first, and certainly more politically adroit, moves was to buy the whole of Manhattan Island from the Native Americans for trinkets worth sixty guilders (the equivalent of $24, at least according to a nineteenth-century historian); the other side of this anecdote is whether the Native

Americans from whom Minuit "bought" the land had the same concept of permanent ownership as the Dutch.

As the colony slowly grew, a string of governors succeeded Minuit, the most famous of them **Peter Stuyvesant** or "Peg Leg Pete", a seasoned colonialist from the Dutch West Indies who'd lost his leg in a scrape with the Spanish. Under his leadership New Amsterdam doubled in size, population and fortifications, with an encircling wall (today's **Wall Street** follows its course) and a rough-hewn fort on what is now the site of the Customs House built to protect the settlement from the encroaching British. Stuyvesant also built himself a farm (a *bouwerij* in Dutch) nearby, giving Manhattan's Bowery district its name.

Meanwhile, the **British** were steadily and stealthily building up their presence to the north. They asserted that all of America's east coast, from New England to Virginia, was theirs, and in 1664 Colonel Richard Nicholls was sent to claim the lands around the Hudson for King Charles II. To reinforce his sovereignty, Charles sent along four warships and enough troops to land on Nut and Long islands. Angered by Stuyvesant's increasingly dictatorial leadership and the high taxes levied by the Dutch West India Company, the Dutch settlers refused to defend the colony against the British. Captain Nicholls' men took New Amsterdam, renamed it **New York** in honour of Charles II's brother, the Duke of York, and started what was to be a hundred-odd years of British rule, a period interrupted only briefly in 1673 when the Dutch once more gained, then lost, power in the region.

Revolution

By the 1750s the city had reached a population of 16,000, spread roughly as far north as Chambers Street. As the community grew, it also operated increasingly independently of the British, but England reasserted control in 1763, when France conceded sovereignty over most of explored North America. Within a year the British had riled colonists by imposing punitive taxes and requisitioning private dwellings and inns. Skirmishes between British soldiers and the insurrectionist **Sons of Liberty** culminated in January 1770 with the fatal stabbing of a colonist in New York City. A few weeks later, the **Boston Massacre** saw British troops open fire on taunting protesters, killing five and fanning the revolutionary flames.

New York did not play a large role in the **War of Independence**, due to several decisive defeats in the fall of 1776, first in Brooklyn in the vicinity of Prospect Park, then in Westchester County (the Bronx), with the British pushing the Americans ever northward. Though the Patriots were under the command of George Washington himself, the campaign was a disaster, ending with the routing of three thousand American troops at Fort Washington and the occupation of the city by the British for the remainder of the war.

Lord Cornwallis's **surrender** to the Americans in October 1783 marked the end of the Revolutionary War, and a month later New York was finally liberated. Washington – an infinitely sharper commander now than he was in the early days of the conflict – was there to celebrate, riding in triumphal procession down Canal Street and saying farewell to his officers at **Fraunces Tavern**, a facsimile of which stands at the end of Pearl Street. Soon after, New York became the fledgling nation's capital, and, on April 30, 1789, Washington its first president. The seat of the federal government was transferred to the District of Columbia a year later.

Immigration and civil war

In 1790 the first official census of Manhattan numbered the population around 33,000. Business and trade were steadily increasing, with the forerunner of the New York Stock Exchange created under a buttonwood tree on Wall Street in the early 1800s and a ferry service established between New York and Albany, and between Brooklyn and Manhattan, a few years later.

In 1825, the completion of the **Erie Canal** (running from the Hudson River across the state to the Great Lakes) opened up internal trade and increased demand for cheap labour. The first waves of **immigrants**, mainly **Irish** and **German**, began to arrive in the mid-nineteenth century, the former forced out by famine, the latter by the failed revolutions of 1848–49. Though traders grew wealthy, the city could not handle the arrival of so many people all at once: epidemics of yellow fever and cholera were common, exacerbated by poor water supplies, unsanitary conditions and the poverty of most of the newcomers, not least in the Lower East Side where two of the largest communities – **Italians** and **Eastern Europeans** (many of them Jewish) – shared one of the most notorious slum areas of its day.

When the **Civil War** broke out in 1861, New York sided with the Union (North) against the Confederates (South). While the city saw little hand-to-hand fighting, it was fertile ground for much of the liberal thinking that had informed the war. In 1863, an unjust **conscription law** provoked the draft riots, with impoverished New Yorkers (especially Irish immigrants) burning buildings, looting shops and lynching African-Americans; more than a thousand people were killed.

The late nineteenth century

After the Civil War, New York began to assume the mantle as the wealthiest and most influential city in the nation by dint of its skilled immigrant workers, distribution networks and financial resources. Broadway developed into the main thoroughfare, with grand hotels, restaurants and shops catering to the rich; newspaper editors **William Cullen Bryant** and **Horace Greeley** respectively founded the *Evening Post* and the *Tribune*; and the city became a magnet for intellectuals, with **Washington Irving** and **James Fenimore Cooper** among notable residents. **Cornelius Vanderbilt** controlled a vast shipping and railroad empire from here, and **J.P. Morgan**, the banking genius, was instrumental in organizing financial mergers, creating the nation's first major corporations.

The latter part of the nineteenth century was in many ways the city's golden age: elevated railways (**Els**) sprang up to transport people quickly and cheaply around the city; **Thomas Edison** lit the streets with his new electric lightbulb, powered by the nation's first commercial power plant, on Pearl Street; and in 1883, the **Brooklyn Bridge** was unveiled. In 1898, New York City – formerly just Manhattan – assumed its current size by officially incorporating Brooklyn, Staten Island, Queens and the part of Westchester County known as the Bronx.

All this expansion stimulated the city's cultural growth. **Walt Whitman** eulogized the city in his poems, and **Henry James** recorded its manners and mores in novels like *Washington Square*. Along Fifth Avenue, **Richard Morris Hunt** built palaces for the wealthy robber-barons who had plundered Europe's collections of fine art – collections that would eventually find their way into the newly opened **Metropolitan Museum**.

Turn-of-the-century development

In 1898, boosted by the first wave of Asian immigrants, New York's population topped three million for the first time, making it the largest city in the world. Nearly half its residents were foreign-born, with **Ellis Island**, the depot that processed arrivals, handling two thousand people a day. Many immigrants worked in sweatshops for the city's growing, notoriously exploitative garment industry. Although workers began to strike for better pay and conditions, it took the **Triangle Shirtwaist Factory** fire (see p.107) to rouse public and civic conscience; within months the state passed 56 factory-reform measures, and unionization spread through the city.

On the upside of New York's capitalist expansion, the early 1900s saw some of the city's wealth going into adventurous new architecture. In Soho classical facades were mass-produced from **cast iron**, and the **Flatiron Building** of 1902 announced the arrival of what was to become the city's trademark – the skyscraper. **Stephen Crane**, **Theodore Dreiser** and **Edith Wharton** all wrote stories about the city, and in 1913 the **Armory Exhibition** of paintings by Picasso, Duchamp and others caused a sensation. Skyscrapers pushed ever higher, and in 1913 a building that many consider the *ne plus ultra* of the genre, downtown's **Woolworth Building**, was completed. **Grand Central Terminal** also opened that year, celebrating New York as the gateway to the continent.

The war years and the Depression: 1914–45

As New York benefited from the trade and commerce generated by World War I, there was – perhaps surprisingly – little conflict between the various European communities crammed into the city, and few attacks on Germans.

Prohibition was passed in 1920 in an attempt to sober up the nation, but New York paid little heed. Under the helm of **Mayor Jimmy Walker**, who was quoted as saying, "No civilized man goes to bed the same day he wakes up", the city entered the Jazz Age. Writers as diverse as **Damon Runyon**, **F. Scott Fitzgerald** and **Ernest Hemingway** portrayed the excitement of the times, and musicians such as **George Gershwin** and **Benny Goodman** packed nightclubs with their new sound. Bootleg liquor ran freely in speakeasies all over town. The **Harlem Renaissance** soared to prominence with writers like **Langston Hughes** and **Zora Neale Hurston**, and music from **Duke Ellington**, **Cab Calloway** and **Billie Holiday**.

The **Wall Street Crash** of 1929, however, brought the party to an abrupt end. On October 24, known as **"Black Tuesday"**, sixteen million shares were traded in a panicked sell-off; five days later, the New York Stock Exchange collapsed, losing $125 million ($1.5 billion in today's dollars). Millions lost their savings; banks, businesses, and industries shut their doors. By 1932 approximately one in four New Yorkers was out of work, and shantytowns, known as "Hoovervilles" (after then-President Hoover, widely blamed for the Depression), had sprung up in Central Park to house the jobless and homeless.

Surprisingly, during this period three of New York's most beautiful skyscrapers were built – the **Chrysler Building** in 1930, the **Empire State** in 1931 (though it stood near-empty for years), and in 1932 the **Rockefeller Center** – but this impressive spate of construction was of little immediate help to those in Hooverville, Harlem or other depressed parts of the city. It fell to **Fiorello LaGuardia**, Jimmy

Walker's successor, to run the crisis-strewn city. He did so with stringent taxation, anti-corruption and social-spending programmes that won him the approval of the city's citizens. Simultaneously, President Roosevelt's **New Deal** supplied funds for roads, housing and parks, the latter undertaken by controversial Parks Commissioner **Robert Moses**. Under LaGuardia and Moses, the most extensive public-housing programme in the country was undertaken; the Triborough, Whitestone and Henry Hudson bridges were completed; fifty miles of new expressway and five thousand acres of new parks were designed and built; and, in 1939, the airport in Queens that still bears the legendary mayor's name was opened. That same year in Queens, New York hosted the **World's Fair**, in Flushing Meadows–Corona Park; the year-long event focused largely on technology and the future.

The country's entry into **World War II** in 1941 saw New York take on a top-secret role: the **Manhattan Project**, wherein scientists at Columbia University performed the experiments crucial to the creation of the first atomic weapon.

The postwar years to the 1960s

After World War II, New York regained its top-dog status in the fields of finance, art and communications, both in America and the world, its intellectual and creative community swollen by European refugees. The city was the obvious choice as the permanent home of the **United Nations Organization**: lured by Rockefeller-donated land on the east side of Manhattan, the UN started construction in 1947, instigating the rapid development of midtown Manhattan.

But even as the city, like the rest of the country, experienced a postwar boom, uniquely urban pressures were building. Immigrants from Puerto Rico and elsewhere in Latin America once more crammed East Harlem, the Lower East Side and other poor neighbourhoods, as did blacks from poor rural areas. Racial disturbances and riots started flaring up in what had for two hundred years been one of the more liberal of American cities. One response to the problem was a general exodus of the white middle classes – the **Great White Flight** as the media labelled it – out of New York. Between 1950 and 1970 more than a million families left the city. Things went from bad to worse during the 1960s with **race riots** in Harlem and Bedford-Stuyvesant in Brooklyn.

The **World's Fair** of 1964, again in Flushing Meadows, was a white elephant to boost the city's international profile, but on the streets the calls for civil liberties for blacks and withdrawal from Vietnam were, if anything, stronger than in most of the rest of the country. What few new buildings went up during this period seemed wilfully to destroy much of the best of earlier traditions. In particular, the eyesore that is **Madison Square Garden**, built over the old **Pennsylvania Station**, is still lamented as one of the city's worst architectural blunders.

The 1970s and 1980s

Manhattan reached **crisis point** in 1975 as companies, along with their employees, began leaving the city, lured by cheap land and low taxes in the suburbs. Even after municipal securities were sold, New York ran up a debt of millions of dollars. Essential services, long shaky due to underfunding, were ready to collapse. Ironically, the mayor who oversaw this fiasco, **Abraham Beame**, was an accountant.

Three things saved the city: the **Municipal Assistance Corporation**, which was formed to borrow the money the city could no longer get its hands on; the

1978 election of **Edward I. Koch** as mayor, a man whose tough talking helped reassure jumpy corporations; and, in a roundabout way, the plummeting of the dollar on the world currency market following the rise of oil prices in the 1970s. This last factor, combined with cheap transatlantic airfares, brought European tourists into the city en masse for the first time.

The city's slow reversal of fortunes coincided with the completion of two face-saving building projects: the former **World Trade Center** was a gesture of confidence by the Port Authority of New York and New Jersey, which financed it; and the 1977 construction of the **Citicorp** (now Citigroup) **Center** added modernity and prestige to its environs on Lexington Avenue. Meanwhile, the raucous nightlife scene that started in the mid-1970s was best exemplified by hotspot **Studio 54**, where drugs and illicit sex were the main events off the dancefloor.

The real-estate and stock markets boomed during the 1980s, ushering in another era of Big Money. A spate of construction gave the city more eye-catching, though not necessarily well-loved, architecture, notably **Battery Park City**, and master builder **Donald Trump** provided glitzy housing for the super-wealthy. The stock market dip in 1987 started yet another downturn, and Koch's popularity waned. In 1989, he lost the Democratic mayoral nomination to **David Dinkins**, a 61-year-old black ex-marine who went on to beat Republican Rudolph Giuliani, a hard-nosed US attorney, in a tightly contested election. Even before the votes were counted, though, pundits forecast that the city was beyond any mayoral healing.

New York slipped, hard and fast, into a **massive recession**: in 1989 the city's budget deficit ran at $500 million. Of the 92 companies that had made the city their base in 1980, only 53 remained, the others having moved to cheaper pastures; and one in four New Yorkers was officially classed as poor – a figure unequalled since the Depression. By the end of 1990, budget deficit was $1.5 billion.

The 1990s: the Giuliani years

Throughout 1991 the effects of these financial problems on the city's ordinary people became more and more apparent: homelessness increased; some public schools became no-go zones with armed police and metal detectors at the gates; and a garbage-workers' strike left piles of rubbish rotting on the streets. In 1993 New York, traditionally a Democratic city, wanted change and saw it in **Rudolph Giuliani** – the city's first Republican mayor in 28 years.

The voters were rewarded: Giuliani's first term ushered in a dramatic upswing in New York's prosperity. A *New York Times* article described 1995 as "the best year in recent memory for New York City". The pope even came to town and called New York "the capital of the world". Remarkable decreases in crime and a revitalized economy helped spur the tourism industry to some of its best years ever.

Giuliani emerged as a very proactive mayor and one quite happy to take credit for making the streets safer and city bureaucracy leaner. While he made enemies among progressives for gutting rent stabilization laws and providing massive tax-breaks to corporations for moving to or remaining in the city (even as he reduced payments to the poor), Giuliani was handily re-elected to a second term in 1997. The city's economy continued to grow, and a series of civic improvements, including the cleaning up of Times Square, the renovation of Grand Central Terminal and the influx of chain stores into Harlem ensued.

Several high-profile incidents involving shocking allegations of **police brutality** marred Giuliani's second term, but these issues would all be superseded by events that would shake not just the city but the whole country – and cause the locals to lean on Giuliani once more.

9/11 and beyond

As if the dot-com bust in the spring of 2001 wasn't hobbling enough, New York City was hit by the worst terrorist attack of the modern era on **September 11, 2001**. The story is now horribly familiar: two hijacked planes crashed into the Twin Towers of the World Trade Center, and, as the flaming fuel melted their steel frames, the towers collapsed. In all, 2750 people, including 343 firefighters, were killed in the catastrophe.

Over the next nine months, workers carted off 1.5 million tons of steel and debris, and by March 2002 the site was clear, well ahead of schedule (some would later ask if the job was perhaps done too quickly: several thousand Ground Zero workers continue to have chronic breathing problems as a result of not wearing ventilators and not following other environmental precautions at the site). So assured was his guidance throughout the ordeal that if Rudolph Giuliani had been able to run again, he most certainly would have won in a landslide. The law at the time, however, precluded him from running for a third term – he set his sights on the presidency instead – and so on January 1, 2002, businessman **Michael Bloomberg** replaced him as mayor.

Though he had no prior political experience, Bloomberg, also a Republican, proved himself an able leader, using his corporate know-how to shore up the city's shaky finances – the city ended the 2006 fiscal year with a $6.1 billion budget surplus – and reorganize the school system. One of the mayor's most controversial acts was to follow California's lead and **ban smoking** in bars, clubs and all restaurants in 2003. Bar owners, naturally, fought the move, but it turned out to be good for business. In 2004 Bloomberg handily won re-election to a second term, during which he signed a law banning "trans-fats" in New York restaurants, pushed through a plan to replace the city's 13,000 taxicabs with hybrid vehicles by 2012, and proposed a congestion pricing scheme to reduce traffic in Manhattan similar to the one in London. Only the last plan has met with significant resistance, mainly from upstate legislators and outer-boroughs commuters.

Not until the fall of 2007 did the economy begin to slump once more, as Wall Street registered heavy losses connected to the subprime mortgage crisis. The following year was a tough one for the city and some of its political figures. On Wall Street, investment banking giant **Bear Stearns** hit rock bottom in spring, to be bought out by JP Morgan, and **Lehman Brothers** declared bankruptcy in the autumn. The real-estate market finally began to cave in and numerous construction projects were put on hold due to lack of funds. The 2008 presidential election season ended up as a disappointment for both Giuliani and the state's junior senator, **Hillary Rodham Clinton**, who lost their bids for the Republican and Democratic nominations, respectively. Meanwhile, Bloomberg commissioned a poll to see if New Yorkers would consider abolishing term limits to allow him to run again as mayor. Despite approving of the mayor's work in office, New Yorkers wanted term limits to remain. Ignoring their wishes, Bloomberg pushed a change through the city council to allow him to stand for a third stint in the fall of 2009; he won a closer-than-expected vote over Comptroller William Thompson.

The following year the economy finally began to rebound, a spate of new hotels opened and construction sped up both on the buildings around the World Trade Center site and the long-awaited stadium in Brooklyn's Atlantic Yards. The city budget outlook, on the other hand, looked bleak: cutbacks in teaching jobs, MTA bus and subway routes, library hours and other services either took effect or were in the works. New York has, however, obviously weathered greater storms than this.

Books

Since the number of books about or set in New York is so vast, what follows is necessarily selective – use it as a place to begin further sleuthing. Most of the books listed are currently in print, but those that aren't should be available on websites such as ⓦwww.abebooks.com or ⓦwww.amazon.com. Titles that are out of print are marked "o/p". The ★ symbol indicates titles that are especially recommended.

Essays, memoirs and narrative nonfiction

Josh Alan Friedman *Tales of Times Square*. Expanded in 2007, the book chronicles activities on and around the square between 1978 and 1984, pornography's golden age, documenting a culture under siege by impresarios, pimps and 25-cent thrills.

William Grimes *Appetite City: A Culinary History of New York City*. The former *New York Times* restaurant critic engagingly traces the rise of the city's restaurants from way stations and early taverns to the glamour of today's celebrity-driven institutions.

Pete Hamill *Downtown: My Manhattan*. Former *Post* (and *Daily News*) editor Hamill is an authentic city voice. This isn't just his memoir of the island, though; it skilfully takes in centuries of New York characters and vanished settings along the way.

Phillip Lopate *Waterfront: A Walk Around Manhattan*. Somewhere between a guide, rumination and history, this book weaves personal observation of the city's waterfront today with its historical evolution – and works in a lot of salient quotes from literary types along the way.

Phillip Lopate (ed) *Writing New York*. A massive literary anthology of both fiction and nonfiction writings on the city, with selections by authors from Washington Irving to Tom Wolfe.

Federico García Lorca *Poet in New York*. The Andalusian poet and dramatist spent nine months in the city around the time of the 1929 Wall Street Crash. This collection of over thirty poems reveals his feelings on loneliness, greed, corruption, racism and mistreatment of the poor.

Frank McCourt *'Tis*. In the follow-up memoir to the phenomenon that was *Angela's Ashes*, McCourt relates life in NYC – concentrating on his time teaching in the public-school system – once he's left Ireland behind.

★ **Joseph Mitchell** *Up in the Old Hotel*. Mitchell's collected *New Yorker* essays are works of sober, if manipulative, genius, definitively chronicling NYC characters and situations with a reporter's precision and near-perfect style.

Jan Morris *Manhattan '45*. Morris's best piece of writing on Manhattan, reconstructing New York as it greeted returning GIs in 1945. Effortlessly written, fascinatingly anecdotal and marvellously warm about the city.

Georges Perec and Robert Bober *Ellis Island* (o/p). A brilliant, moving, original account of the "island of tears": part history, part meditation and part interviews. Some of the stories are heartbreaking (between 1892 and 1924 there were 3000 suicides on the island); the pictures even more so.

Suze Rotolo *A Freewheelin' Time: A Memoir of Greenwich Village in the Sixties*. Bob Dylan's formative years in the Village are recounted by his smart and sensitive girlfriend of four years, Suze Rotolo, who also talks about her own artistic pursuits and her family's devotion to communism.

History, politics and society

Herbert Asbury *The Gangs of New York*. First published in 1928, this fascinating telling of the seamier side of New York is essential reading. Full of historical detail, anecdotes and character sketches of crooks, the book describes New York mischief in all its incarnations and locales.

Edwin G. Burrows and Mike Wallace *Gotham: A History of New York City to 1898*. Enormous and encyclopedic in its detail, this is a serious history of the development of New York, with chapters on everything from its role in the Revolution to reform movements to its racial make-up in the 1820s.

Robert A. Caro *The Power Broker: Robert Moses and the Fall of New York*. Despite its imposing length, this brilliant and searing critique of New York City's most powerful twentieth-century figure is one of the most important books ever written about the city and its environs. Caro's book brings to light the megalomania and manipulation responsible for the creation of the nation's largest urban infrastructure.

George Chauncey *Gay New York: The Making of the Gay Male World 1890–1940*. Definitive, revealing account of the city's gay subculture.

Kenneth T. Jackson (ed) *The Enyclopedia of New York*. Massive, engrossing and utterly comprehensive guide to just about everything in the city. Did you know, for example, that Truman Capote's real name was Streckford Persons?

Roger Kahn *The Boys of Summer*. This account of the 1950s Brooklyn Dodgers by a Beat writer who covered them is considered one of the classic baseball reads.

David Levering Lewis *When Harlem Was in Vogue*. Much-needed account of the Harlem Renaissance, a brief flowering of the arts in the 1920s and 1930s that was suffocated by the dual forces of the Depression and racism.

Jonathan Mahler *Ladies and Gentlemen, the Bronx Is Burning: 1977, Baseball, Politics, and the Battle for the Soul of a City*. Incredible portrait of the city as it was in the late 1970s, weaving together Yankee Reggie Jackson's conflicts with manager Billy Martin, the duel between Mario Cuomo and Ed Koch, the birth of punk rock, the hunt for serial killer Son of Sam, the blackout and looting, and more.

Legs McNeil and Gillian McCain *Please Kill Me*. An oral history of punk music in New York, artfully constructed by juxtaposing snippets of interviews as if the various protagonists (artists, financiers, impresarios) were in a conversation. Sometimes hilarious, often quite bleak.

Dan Okrent *Great Fortune: The Epic of Rockefeller Center*. Everything you ever wanted to know about the construction of one of New York's cultural and architectural high-water marks: fascinating stories of the Rockefeller family, the designers, the art commissioned (and, in one case, removed) and much more.

Luc Sante *Low Life: Lures and Snares of Old New York*. This chronicle of the city's seamy side between 1840 and 1919 is a pioneering work. Full of outrageous details usually left out of conventional history, it reconstructs the day-to-day life of the urban poor, criminals and prostitutes with shocking clarity.

Russell Shorto *The Island at the Centre of the World*. Before New York was New York it was New Amsterdam; Shorto delivers a much-needed and highly readable account of this largely forgotten chapter in the city's history, using newly researched Dutch sources. Shorto's central thesis – that it was the freedom-loving and multicultural Dutch city that laid the roots of modern New York – is highly compelling.

Gay Talese *Fame and Obscurity*. Talese deftly presents interviews with New York City's famous (Sinatra, DiMaggio, etc) and its obscure (bums, chauffeurs, etc), offering not only a window into the heart of NYC, but that of human existence.

Jennifer Toth *Mole People*. A creepy sociological study of the people who live below NYC streets, in the dark reaches of the subway tunnel system. You may never again ride the subway without your face plastered to the window looking for signs of human life.

Art, architecture and photography

Lorraine Diehl *The Late Great Pennsylvania Station* (o/p). The anatomy of a travesty. How could a railroad palace, modelled after the Baths of Caracalla in Rome, stand for only fifty years before being destroyed? The pictures alone warrant the price.

Horst Hamann *New York Vertical*. This beautiful book pays homage to the New York skyscraper, and is filled with dazzling black-and-white vertical shots of Manhattan, accompanied by witty quotes from famous and obscure folk.

Jane Jacobs *The Death and Life of Great American Cities*. Landmark 1961 screed authored by Robert Moses' nemesis, and railing against urban over-planning.

David McCullough *Great Bridge: The Epic Story of the Building of the Brooklyn Bridge*. The story of the father-and-son Roebling team who fought the laws of gravity, sharp-toothed competitors and corrupt politicians to build a bridge that has withstood the test of time and become one of NYC's most noted landmarks.

Jacob Riis *How the Other Half Lives*. Photojournalism reporting on life in the Lower East Side at the end of the nineteenth century. Its original publication in 1890 awakened many to the plight of New York's poor.

Stern, Melins and Fishman/ Stern, Gilmartin and Massengale/ Stern, Gilmartin and Mellins/ Stern, Mellins and Fishman/Stern, Fishman and Tilove *New York 1880/1900/1930/1960/2000*. These five exhaustive tomes contain all you'll ever want or need to know about architecture and the organization of the city.

N. White, E. Willensky and F. Leadon (eds) *AIA Guide to New York*. The definitive contemporary guide to the city's architecture – witty, immensely informative and opinionated – and useful as an on-site reference; a new 2010 edition is available.

Other guides

Richard Alleman *The Movie Lover's Guide to New York*. More than two hundred listings of corners of the city with cinematic associations: TV and film locations, stars' childhood homes and final resting places, and more. Interestingly written, painstakingly researched.

Federal Writers' Project *The WPA Guide to New York City*. Originally written in 1939 and subsequently reissued, this detailed guide offers a fascinating look at life in New York City when the Dodgers played at Ebbetts Field, a trolley ride cost five cents and a room at the *Plaza* was $7.50. A surprising amount of description remains apt.

Rob Grader *The Cheap Bastard's Guide to New York City*. If the title doesn't immediately turn you off, this frequently updated guide is the book for you.

Eric Sanderson *Manahatta*. Get this for the illustrations, charts and maps if nothing else: it's a geographic, ecological history of the city that is bound to give you new perspectives on what Manhattan was before becoming such a densely populated island.

Fiction

Julia Alvarez *How the Garcia Girls Lost Their Accents*. Four Latina sisters are uprooted from their privileged life in the Dominican Republic to the Bronx in this compelling look at the modern immigrant experience.

Paul Auster *The New York Trilogy: City of Glass, Ghosts and The Locked Room*. Three Borgesian investigations into the mystery, madness, and murders of contemporary NYC.

James Baldwin *Another Country*. Baldwin's best-known novel, tracking the feverish search for meaningful relationships among a group of 1960s New York bohemians.

Lawrence Block *When the Sacred Ginmill Closes*. Tough to choose between Block's hard-hitting Matthew Scudder suspense novels, all set in the city; this might be the most compelling, with Hell's Kitchen, downtown Manhattan and far-flung parts of Brooklyn expertly woven into a dark mystery.

Truman Capote *Breakfast at Tiffany's*. Far sadder and racier than the movie, this novel is a rhapsody to New York in the early 1940s, tracking the dissolute youthful residents of an uptown apartment building and their movements about town.

Caleb Carr *The Alienist*. This 1896-set thriller evokes old New York to perfection. The heavy-handed psychobabble grates at times, but the story line (the pursuit of one of the first serial killers) is still involving. Best for its descriptions of New York as well as saliva-inducing details of meals at long-gone restaurants.

Michael Chabon *The Amazing Adventures of Kavalier and Clay*. A wartime fantasy of Jewish youths in Brooklyn and their fascination with all forms of escapism – magic, radio and, most important, comic strips.

Reed Farrel Coleman *Walking the Perfect Square*. Coleman's mysteries contain one of the genre's great (relatively) unknown creations: Brooklyn detective-cum-wine store operator Moe Prager, a very flawed protagonist. This, the first, flashes back between the late Seventies and late Nineties; the plot is involving enough but most importantly sets the scene for Prager's emotional development.

Stephen Crane *Maggie: A Girl of the Streets*. An 1893 melodrama about a girl growing up in a Lower East Side slum. Although luridly overdescribed, *Red Badge of Courage* author Crane was deservedly acclaimed for his ground-breaking naturalism; the fictional counterpart to Riis's work.

Don DeLillo *Underworld*. Following the fate of the baseball hit out of the park to win the 1951 pennant for the New York Giants, DeLillo's sprawling novel offers a counterhistory of twentieth-century America. His luminous prose is spellbinding even when the story feels faintly ridiculous.

Ralph Ellison *Invisible Man*. The definitive, if sometimes long-winded, novel of what it's like to be black and American, using Harlem and the 1950s race riots as a backdrop.

Paula Fox *Desperate Characters*. A depressing, engrossing drama about a faded marriage in 1960s Brooklyn, this slim book is exquisitely crafted and brilliantly observed.

Oscar Hijuelos *Our House in the Last World*. A warmly evocative novel of a Cuban immigrant's life in New York from before the war to the present day.

Chester Himes *The Crazy Kill*. Himes wrote violent, fast-moving and funny thrillers set in Harlem; this and *Cotton Goes to Harlem* are among the best.

Henry James *Washington Square*. Skilful and engrossing examination of the mores and strict social expectations of genteel New York society in the late nineteenth century.

Sue Kaufman *Diary of a Mad Housewife*. This is a classic dissection of 1960s New York, satirically chronicling the antics of a group of social climbers along with the disintegration of a marriage.

Jonathan Lethem *Motherless Brooklyn*. Brooklyn author sets this quirky suspense novel in Cobble Hill and its environs, where a Tourette's sufferer tries to track down his boss's killer. See also his subsequent *The Fortress of Solitude*, which treats childhood and gentrification with great wit and sensitivity, or *Chronic City*, a kind of send-up of Manhattan.

Alice McDermott *Charming Billy*. Billy is a poetry-loving drunkard from Queens, looking to bring his Irish love over to New York City. National Book Award winner.

Jay McInerney *Bright Lights, Big City*. A trendy, "voice of a generation" book when it came out in the 1980s, it made first-time novelist McInerney a household name. The story follows a struggling New York writer in his job as a fact-checker at an important literary magazine (a thinly disguised *New Yorker*), and from one cocaine-sozzled nightclub to another. Still amusing.

Emma McLaughlin and Nicola Kraus *The Nanny Diaries: A Novel*. A delicious and nimble comic novel, culled from the authors' own experiences nannying to the wealthy families of the Upper East Side; later made into an entertaining film with Scarlett Johansson.

Joseph O'Neill *Netherland*. Bringing together threads about friendship, marriage, cricket, the immigrant experience and 9/11, this literary novel, if at times overwritten, ranks as one of the more important and memorable New York stories of the past decade.

Dorothy Parker *Complete Stories*. Parker's tales are, at times, surprisingly moving, depicting New York in all its glories, excesses, and pretensions with perfect, searing wit.

Richard Price *Lush Life*. With perfect pitch for the language of the streets, Richard Price tells the sprawling story of the murder of a bartender on today's Lower East Side, a place where struggling writers, old Jewish immigrants, drug dealers, cops and club kids uneasily coexist.

Judith Rossner *Looking for Mr Goodbar*. A disquieting book, tracing the life – and eventual demise – of a female teacher in search of love in volatile and permissive 1970s New York.

Henry Roth *Call It Sleep*. Roth's novel traces the awakening of a small immigrant child to the realities of life among the slums of the Jewish Lower East Side. Read more for the evocations of childhood than the social comment.

Paul Rudnick *Social Disease*. Hilarious, often incredible send-up of Manhattan night-owls. Very New York, very funny.

J.D. Salinger *The Catcher in the Rye*. Salinger's gripping novel of adolescence, following Holden Caulfield's sardonic journey of discovery through the streets of New York. A classic.

Hubert Selby, Jr *Last Exit to Brooklyn*. When first published in Britain in 1966, this novel was tried on charges of obscenity. Even now it's a disturbing read, evoking the sex, immorality, drugs, and violence of Brooklyn in the 1960s with fearsome clarity.

Betty Smith *A Tree Grows in Brooklyn*. A classic, and rightly so – a courageous Irish girl learns about family, life and sex against a vivid prewar Brooklyn backdrop. Totally absorbing.

Rex Stout *The Doorbell Rang*. Stout's Nero Wolfe is perhaps the most intrinsically "New York" of all the literary detectives based in the city, a larger-than-life character who, with the help of his dashing assistant, Archie Goodwin, solves crimes from the comfort of his sumptuous midtown brownstone. Wonderfully evocative of the city in the 1940s and 1950s.

Colm Toibin *Brooklyn*. Another immigrant story, this time via Ireland to 1950s Brooklyn; a methodical, literary work that rewards your patience and persistence.

Jess Walter *The Zero*. This dark, hallucinatory and probing satire, set just after 9/11, may set your head spinning like that of its protagonist – who endures memory loss, a self-inflicted gunshot wound and an unusual mission for which he has no idea why he's on.

Lauren Weisberger *The Devil Wears Prada*. A satirical snapshot of New York's cut-throat magazine world, this *roman à clef* from *Vogue* editor Anna Wintour's former assistant is pleasant enough, but the film version with Meryl Streep is even better.

Edith Wharton *Age of Innocence*. A withering, deftly drawn picture of New York high society at the turn of the twentieth century and how rigid social convention keeps two sensitive, ill-fated lovers apart. See also Wharton's astounding *House of Mirth* and her classic stories *Old New York*.

Tom Wolfe *Bonfire of the Vanities*. Set all around New York City, this sprawling novel skewers 1980s status-mongers to great effect.

New York on film

With its skyline and rugged facades, its mean streets and swanky avenues, its electric energy and edgy attitude, New York City is a natural-born movie star. From the silent era's cautionary tales of young lovers ground down by the metropolis, through the smoky location-shot *noirs* of the 1940s, right through to the Lower East Side and Brooklyn indies of the past few decades, New York has probably been the most filmed city on earth.

What follows is a selection not just of the best New York movies but the most New York of New York movies – movies that capture the city's atmosphere, pulse and style; movies that celebrate its diversity or revel in its misfortunes; and movies that, if nothing else, give you a pretty good idea of what you're going to get before you get there.

Ten New York classics

Breakfast at Tiffany's (*Blake Edwards, 1961*). The most charming and cherished of New York movie romances, starring Audrey Hepburn as party girl Holly Golightly. Hepburn and George Peppard run up and down each other's fire escapes and skip along Fifth Avenue, taking in the New York Public Library and that jewellery store.

Do the Right Thing (*Spike Lee, 1989*). Set over 24 hours on the hottest day of the year in Brooklyn's Bed-Stuy – a day on which the melting pot reaches boiling point – Spike Lee's colourful, stylish masterpiece moves from comedy to tragedy to compose an epic song of New York.

King Kong (*Merian C. Cooper and Ernest B. Schoedsack, 1933*). *King Kong* paints a vivid picture of Depression-era Manhattan, and gives us the city's most indelible movie image: King Kong straddling the Empire State Building and swatting at passing planes.

Manhattan (*Woody Allen, 1979*). This black-and-white masterpiece, one of the truly great eulogies to the city, details the self-absorptions, lifestyles and romances of middle-class intellectuals, to the tune of a Gershwin soundtrack.

On the Town (*Gene Kelly and Stanley Donen, 1949*). Three sailors get 24 hours' shore leave in NYC and fight over whether to see the sights or chase the girls. Starring Gene Kelly, Frank Sinatra and Ann Miller flashing her legs in the Museum of Natural History, this was the first musical taken out of the studios and onto the streets. Smart, cynical and satirical with a bunch of terrific numbers.

On the Waterfront (*Elia Kazan, 1954*). Few images of New York are as unforgettable as Marlon Brando's rooftop pigeon coop at dawn and those misty views of the New York Harbor (actually shot just over the river in Hoboken), in this unforgettable story of long-suffering longshoremen and union racketeering.

Shadows (*John Cassavetes, 1960*). Cassavetes' debut film is a New York movie *par excellence*: a New Wave melody about jazz musicians, young love and racial prejudice, shot with bebop verve and jazzy passion in Central Park, Greenwich Village and even the MoMA sculpture garden.

Sweet Smell of Success (*Alexander Mackendrick, 1957*). Broadway as a nest of vipers. Gossip columnist Burt Lancaster and sleazy press-agent Tony Curtis eat each other's tails in this snappy, cynical study of showbiz corruption. Shot on location and mostly at night, in steely black and white. Times Square and the Great White Way never looked so alluring.

Taxi Driver (*Martin Scorsese, 1976*). A long night's journey into day by the great chronicler of the city's dark side. Scorsese's New York is hallucinatorily seductive and thoroughly repellent in this superbly unsettling study of obsessive outsider Travis Bickle (Robert De Niro).

West Side Story (*Robert Wise and Jerome Robbins, 1961*). Sex, singing and Shakespeare in a hyper-cinematic Oscar-winning musical (via Broadway) about rival street gangs.

Ten films about modern New York

The 25th Hour (*Spike Lee, 2002*). Lee stacks his film (based on an excellent first novel by David Benioff) with an impressive cast, headed by Ed Norton as a drug dealer on the last day before he goes to prison, ricocheting round between friends and lovers. Bleak but gripping.

Bad Lieutenant *(Abel Ferrara, 1992)*. Nearly every movie by Ferrara, from *Driller Killer* to *The Funeral*, deserves a place in a list of great New York movies, but this, above all, seems his own personal Manhattan: a journey through the circles of Hell with Harvey Keitel as a depraved Dante.

The Cruise *(Bennett Miller, 1998)*. A documentary portrait of a true New York eccentric, Timothy "Speed" Levitch, a Dostoyevskian character with a baroque flair for language and an encyclopedic knowledge of local history, who takes puzzled tourists on guided "cruises" around the city, on which he rails against the tyranny of the grid plan and rhapsodizes about "the lascivious voyeurism of the tour bus".

The Devil Wears Prada (*David Frankel, 2006*). A delicious turn by Meryl Streep as an Anna Wintour-clone propels this story of a young woman who arrives in the city with high journalistic ambitions but can only find work at a glamorous fashion magazine (a thinly disguised *Vogue*); based on a popular novel (see p.451).

In America *(Jim Sheridan, 2003)*. Sheridan and his two daughters wrote this autobiographical tale of an immigrant Irish family arriving in New York in the 1980s, and even in its bleakest moments, the tenderness and intimacy of the story is enchanting.

Kids *(Larry Clark, 1995)*. An overhyped but affecting portrait of a group of amoral, though supposedly typical, teenagers hanging out on the Upper East Side, in Washington Square Park, and in the Carmine Street swimming pool on one muggy, mad day.

Roger Dodger *(Dylan Kidd, 2002)*. A self-important advertising exec (Campbell Scott) takes his nephew (Jesse Eisenberg) on an alcohol-fuelled tour of the city in search of sex, plumbing the depths of his own depravity. Extremely witty, if hard to watch.

Six Degrees of Separation *(Fred Schepisi, 1993)*. Brilliant, enthralling adaptation of John Guare's acclaimed play which uses the story – a young black man (Will Smith) turns up at a rich Upper East Side apartment claiming to be the son of Sidney Poitier – as a springboard for an examination of the great social and racial divides of the city.

Smoke *(Wayne Wang, 1995)*. A clever, beguiling film scripted by novelist Paul Auster, which connects a handful of stories revolving around Harvey Keitel's Brooklyn cigar store. A companion film, *Blue in the Face*, has a looser, more improvisational feel.

Unmade Beds (*Nicholas Barker, 1998*). This poignant, occasionally hilarious and beautifully stylized documentary about four single New Yorkers looking for love in the personal columns, visualizes the city as one endless Edward Hopper painting, full of lonely souls biding time in rented rooms.

Ten films about New York's past

The Age of Innocence (*Martin Scorsese, 1993*). The upper echelons of New York society in the 1870s brought gloriously to life. Though Scorsese restricts most of the action to drawing rooms and ballrooms, look out for the breathtaking matte shot of a then-undeveloped Upper East Side.

Basquiat (*Julian Schnabel, 1996*). Haunting portrait of the artist as a young (doomed) man, rising from spray-painting graffiti and living in a box in a Lower East Side park to taking the New York art world by storm in the early 1980s. David Bowie plays a sensitive Andy Warhol.

The Crowd (*King Vidor, 1928*). "You've got to be good in that town if you want to beat the crowd." A young couple try to make it in the big city but are swallowed up and spat out by the capitalist machine. A bleak vision of New York in the 1920s, and one of the great silent films.

The Godfather Part II (*Francis Ford Coppola, 1974*). Flashing back to the early life of Vito Corleone, Coppola's great sequel recreated the Italian immigrant experience at the turn of the century, portraying Corleone quarantined at Ellis Island and growing up tough on the meticulously recreated streets of Little Italy.

The Last Days of Disco (*Whit Stillman, 1998*). About the most unlikely setting for Stillman's brand of square WASPy talkfests would be the bombastic glittery bacchanals that were *Studio 54* in its late-1970s heyday, which is what makes this far more enjoyable than the same season's overly literal and melodramatic *54* (*Mark Christopher, 1998*).

Little Fugitive (*Morris Engel and Ruth Orkin, 1953*). A Brooklyn 7-year-old, tricked into believing he has killed his older brother, takes flight to Coney Island where he spends a day and a night indulging in all its previously forbidden pleasures. This beautifully photographed time capsule of 1950s Brooklyn influenced both the American indie scene and the French New Wave.

Man on Wire (*James Marsh, 2008*). This documentary on Philippe Petit's astounding tightrope walk between the Twin Towers in 1974 is illuminating both about the feat and the character of the man behind it.

Pollock (*Ed Harris, 2000*). From a cramped Manhattan apartment to the barren nature of the Hamptons, abstract artist Jackson Pollock drips on canvases and battles his wife (Oscar-winner Marcia Gay Harden), fame and drink. Harris is powerful in the title role.

Radio Days (*Woody Allen, 1987*). Woody contrasts reminiscences of his loud, vulgar family in 1940s Rockaway with reveries of the golden days of radio and the glamour of Times Square.

Summer of Sam (*Spike Lee, 1999*). The dark summer of 1977 – the summer of the "Son of Sam" killings, a blistering heatwave, power black-outs, looting, arson and the birth of punk – provides the perfect backdrop for Lee's sprawling tale of paranoia and betrayal in an Italian–American enclave of the Bronx.

Ten New York comedies

Annie Hall (*Woody Allen, 1977*). Oscar-winning autobiographical comic romance, which flits from reminiscences of Alvy Singer's childhood living beneath the Coney Island Cyclone, to life and love in uptown Manhattan, is a valentine both to ex-lover co-star Diane Keaton and to the city. Simultaneously clever, bourgeois and very winning.

Elf (*Jon Favreau, 2003*). A Will Ferrell-vehicle with an actual heart, in which a young orphan mistakenly gets carried off to the North Pole, is brought up as an elf, then goes as an adult to Manhattan to find his real father. Dad (James Caan) works in the Empire State Building; the romantic interest (Zooey Deschanel) works at Gimbel's; and the climactic scenes take place in and around Central Park.

The Out-of-Towners (*Arthur Hiller, 1969*). If you have any problems getting into town from the airport take solace from the fact that they can be nothing compared to those endured by Jack Lemmon and Sandy Dennis – for whom everything that can go wrong does go wrong – in Neil Simon's frantic comedy.

Quick Change (*Howard Franklin and Bill Murray, 1990*). The "change" is cash stolen from a bank. The "quick" of the title is ironic: though the robbery was easy, it's fleeing the city that proves difficult, as Bill Murray and his cohorts are delayed by cops, other crooks and regular, eccentric New Yorkers. One of Murray's best efforts.

The Royal Tenenbaums (*Wes Anderson*, 2001). Filmed in numerous places around the city, especially Harlem (the family house is on Convent Avenue), *Tenenbaums* is an exceptionally well-acted, darkly comic take on a dysfunctional family full of child prodigies.

The Seven Year Itch (*Billy Wilder, 1955*). When his wife and kid vacate humid Manhattan, Mitty-like pulp editor Tom Ewell is left guiltily leching over the innocent TV-toothpaste temptress upstairs – Marilyn Monroe, at her most wistfully comic. The sight of her pushing down her billowing skirt as she stands on a subway grating (at Lexington Ave and 52nd St) is one of the era's and the city's most resonant movie images.

So This is New York (*Richard Fleischer, 1948*). A bomb on its initial release, this rarely shown but edgy and innovative comedy plants three Midwesterners amongst the sharpies and operators of 1930s New York. The voiceover by star Henry Morgan (an Indiana salesman thoroughly unimpressed by the big city) is sublimely sarcastic.

The Squid and the Whale (*Noah Baumbach, 2005*). A sometimes-uncomfortable but quite funny and resonant coming-of-age story in Park Slope, Brooklyn; the title refers to an exhibit from the Natural History Museum.

Stranger than Paradise (*Jim Jarmusch, 1984*). Only the first third of this, the original slacker indie, is set in New York, but its portrayal of Lower East Side lethargy is hilariously spot-on. The film's downtown credentials – John Lurie is a jazz saxophonist with the Lounge Lizards, Richard Edson used to drum for Sonic Youth and Jarmusch himself is an East Village celebrity – are impeccable.

Tootsie (*Sidney Pollack, 1982*). Tired of being rejected in audition after audition, a struggling actor (comic turn for Dustin Hoffman) dons a wig and woman's attire to win a prize role on an afternoon soap. Great script, with a memorable scene set in the *Russian Tea Room*.

Ten New York nightmares

The Addiction (*Abel Ferrara, 1995*). A simple trip home from the college library turns into a living nightmare for Lili Taylor when she's bitten by a vampiric streetwalker on Bleecker Street and transformed into a blood junkie cruising the East Village for fresh kill.

After Hours (*Martin Scorsese, 1985*). Yuppie computer programmer Griffin Dunne inadvertently ends up on a nightlong odyssey into the Hades of downtown New York, a journey that goes from bad to worse to awful as he encounters every kook south of 14th Street. Amazing footage of pre-gentrified Soho.

American Psycho (*Mary Harron, 2000*). This stylized adaptation of the Bret Easton Ellis novel succeeds largely due to Christian Bale, pulling off some blacker-than-black comedy in his role as a securities trader consumed by designer labels, the ladder of success and Huey Lewis lyrics.

Escape from New York (*John Carpenter, 1981*). In the then-not-too-distant future (1997, in fact), society has given up trying to solve the problems of Manhattan and has walled it up as a lawless maximum-security prison from which Kurt Russell has to rescue the hijacked US president. Ludicrous but great fun.

The Lost Weekend (*Billy Wilder, 1945*). Alcoholic Ray Milland is left alone in the city with no money and a desperate thirst. The film's most famous scene is his long trek up Third Avenue (shot on location) trying to hawk his typewriter to buy booze, only to find all the pawn shops closed for Yom Kippur.

Marathon Man (*John Schlesinger, 1976*). Innocent, bookish Dustin Hoffman runs for his life all over Manhattan after he's dragged into a conspiracy involving old Nazis and tortured with dental instruments. ("Is it safe?") Shot memorably around the Central Park Reservoir and Zoo, Columbia University, the Diamond District and Spanish Harlem.

Requiem for a Dream (*Darren Aronofsky, 2000*). A jagged and harrowing adaptation of Hubert Selby's novel about a band of junkies' descent into insanity amid their cold, grey Coney Island surroundings.

Rosemary's Baby (*Roman Polanski, 1968*). Mia Farrow and John Cassavetes move into their dream New York apartment and think they have problems with nosy neighbours – but that's just until Farrow gets pregnant and hell, literally, breaks loose. Arguably the most terrifying film ever set in the city.

The Taking of Pelham One Two Three (*Joseph Sargent, 1974*). Just when you thought it was safe to get back on the subway. A gang of mercenary hoods hijacks a train on its way through midtown and threatens to start killing one passenger per minute if their million-dollar ransom is not paid within the hour.

The Warriors (*Walter Hill, 1979*). The Coney Island Warriors ride to the Bronx for a meeting with all of New York's gangs; when the organizer is killed, the Warriors are unjustly blamed and have to navigate their way back to their home turf. Old-school subway graffiti, distinctive gang costumes and a pervading sense of nighttime paranoia all contribute to this original cult film.

Ten walks down the mean streets

American Gangster (*Ridley Scott, 2007*). Russell Crowe is utterly convincing as the New York detective trying to bring down drug kingpin Frank Lucas (Denzel Washington), who built a heroin empire in the 1970s by mixing violence and family values. Washington's a bit too sweet to shoot a rival point-blank on a crowded pavement, but the directing is first-rate.

A Bronx Tale (*Robert De Niro, 1993*). An overlooked film with depth and heart. In a 1960s Bronx, Calogero witnesses a traffic accident and its aftermath at the hands of a local gangster, Sonny (Chazz Palminteri). Over the next several years, his loyalties to his bus-driver father (De Niro) are tested as he is seduced by Sonny's glamorous world. Great soundtrack.

The French Connection (*William Friedkin, 1971*). Plenty of heady Brooklyn atmosphere in this sensational Oscar-winning cop thriller starring Gene Hackman, whose classic car-and-subway chase takes place under the Bensonhurst Elevated Railroad.

Gangs of New York (*Martin Scorsese, 2002*). Sprawling, overlong but impressive historical yarn, detailing the bitter immigrant rivalries and gang warfare that dogged early Manhattan settlement.

Goodfellas (*Martin Scorsese, 1990*). Vibrant and nuanced tale, based on the true story of a mob turncoat; another in a fine series of Scorsese New York stories. Seduced by the allure of the Mafia from a young age, Brooklyn native Henry Hill (a fine Ray Liotta) recounts 25 years of crime, his rise through the ranks, and decision to turn on his brethren.

Mean Streets (*Martin Scorsese, 1973*). Scorsese's brilliant breakthrough film breathlessly follows small-time hood Harvey Keitel and his volatile, harum-scarum buddy Robert De Niro around a vividly portrayed Little Italy before reaching its violent climax.

Midnight Cowboy (*John Schlesinger, 1969*). The odd love story between Jon Voight's bumpkin hustler and Dustin Hoffman's touching urban creep Ratso Rizzo plays out against both the seediest and swankiest of New York locations. The only X-rated film to receive an Oscar for Best Picture.

Naked City (*Jules Dassin, 1948*). A crime story that views the city with a documentarist's eye. Shot on actual locations, it follows a police manhunt for a ruthless killer all over town toward an unforgettable chase through the Lower East Side and a shoot-out on the Williamsburg Bridge.

Prince of the City (*Sidney Lumet, 1981*). Lumet is a die-hard New York director, and this is his New York epic. A corrupt narcotics detective turns federal informer to assuage his guilt, and Lumet takes us from drug busts in Harlem to the cops' suburban homes on Long Island, to federal agents' swanky pads overlooking Central Park.

Superfly (*Gordon Parks Jr, 1972*). Propelled by its ecstatic Curtis Mayfield score, this blaxploitation classic about one smooth-looking drug dealer's ultimate score is best seen today for its mind-boggling fashion excess and almost documentary-like look at the Harlem bars, streets, clubs and diners of thirty-odd years ago. Also see Parks' *Shaft*, released a year earlier.

Five New York song and dance mov(i)es

42nd Street (*Lloyd Bacon, 1933*). One of the best films ever made about Broadway – though the film rarely ventures outside the theatre. Starring Ruby Keeler as the young chorus girl who has to replace the ailing leading lady: she goes on stage an unknown and, well, you know the rest.

A Great Day in Harlem (*Jean Bach, 1994*). A unique jazz documentary that spins many tales around the famous Art Kane photograph for which the cream of New York's jazz world assemble on the steps of a Harlem brownstone one August morning in 1958. Using home-movie footage of the event and present-day interviews, Bach creates a wonderful portrait of a golden age.

Guys and Dolls (*Joseph L. Mankiewicz, 1955*). *The* great Broadway musical shot entirely on soundstages and giving as unlikely a picture of Times Square hoodlums (all colorfully suited sweetie-pies) as was ever seen. And a singing and dancing Marlon Brando to boot.

New York, New York (*Martin Scorsese, 1977*). Scorsese's homage to the grand musicals of postwar Hollywood, reimagined for the post-Vietnam era.

Saturday Night Fever (*John Badham, 1977*). What everybody remembers is the tacky glamour of flared white pantsuits and mirror-balled discos, but *Saturday Night Fever* is actually a touching and believable portrayal of working-class youth in the 1970s, Italian-American Brooklyn and the road to Manhattan.

Travel store

Travel

Andorra The Pyrenees, Pyrenees & Andorra Map, Spain
Antigua The Caribbean
Argentina Argentina, Argentina Map, Buenos Aires, South America on a Budget
Aruba The Caribbean
Australia Australia, Australia Map, East Coast Australia, Melbourne, Sydney, Tasmania
Austria Austria, Europe on a Budget, Vienna
Bahamas The Bahamas, The Caribbean
Barbados Barbados DIR, The Caribbean
Belgium Belgium & Luxembourg, Bruges DIR, Brussels, Brussels Map, Europe on a Budget
Belize Belize, Central America on a Budget, Guatemala & Belize Map
Benin West Africa
Bolivia Bolivia, South America on a Budget
Brazil Brazil, Rio, South America on a Budget
British Virgin Islands The Caribbean
Brunei Malaysia, Singapore & Brunei [1 title], Southeast Asia on a Budget
Bulgaria Bulgaria, Europe on a Budget
Burkina Faso West Africa
Cambodia Cambodia, Southeast Asia on a Budget, Vietnam, Laos & Cambodia Map [1 Map]
Cameroon West Africa
Canada Canada, Pacific Northwest, Toronto, Toronto Map, Vancouver
Cape Verde West Africa
Cayman Islands The Caribbean
Chile Chile, Chile Map, South America on a Budget
China Beijing, China, Hong Kong & Macau, Hong Kong & Macau DIR, Shanghai
Colombia South America on a Budget
Costa Rica Central America on a Budget, Costa Rica, Costa Rica & Panama Map
Croatia Croatia, Croatia Map, Europe on a Budget
Cuba Cuba, Cuba Map, The Caribbean, Havana
Cyprus Cyprus, Cyprus Map
Czech Republic The Czech Republic, Czech & Slovak Republics, Europe on a Budget, Prague, Prague DIR, Prague Map
Denmark Copenhagen, Denmark, Europe on a Budget, Scandinavia
Dominica The Caribbean
Dominican Republic Dominican Republic, The Caribbean
Ecuador Ecuador, South America on a Budget
Egypt Egypt, Egypt Map
El Salvador Central America on a Budget
England Britain, Camping in Britain, Devon & Cornwall, Dorset, Hampshire and The Isle of Wight [1 title], England, Europe on a Budget, The Lake District, London, London DIR, London Map, London Mini Guide, Walks In London & Southeast England
Estonia The Baltic States, Europe on a Budget
Fiji Fiji
Finland Europe on a Budget, Finland, Scandinavia
France Brittany & Normandy, Corsica, Corsica Map, The Dordogne & the Lot, Europe on a Budget, France, France Map, Languedoc & Roussillon, The Loire, Paris, Paris DIR, Paris Map, Paris Mini Guide, Provence & the Côte d'Azur, The Pyrenees, Pyrenees & Andorra Map
French Guiana South America on a Budget
Gambia The Gambia, West Africa
Germany Berlin, Berlin Map, Europe on a Budget, Germany, Germany Map
Ghana West Africa
Gibraltar Spain
Greece Athens Map, Crete, Crete Map, Europe on a Budget, Greece, Greece Map, Greek Islands, Ionian Islands
Guadeloupe The Caribbean
Guatemala Central America on a Budget, Guatemala, Guatemala & Belize Map
Guinea West Africa
Guinea-Bissau West Africa
Guyana South America on a Budget
Holland see The Netherlands
Honduras Central America on a Budget
Hungary Budapest, Europe on a Budget, Hungary
Iceland Iceland, Iceland Map
India Goa, India, India Map, Kerala, Rajasthan, Delhi & Agra [1 title], South India, South India Map
Indonesia Bali & Lombok, Southeast Asia on a Budget
Ireland Dublin DIR, Dublin Map, Europe on a Budget, Ireland, Ireland Map
Israel Jerusalem
Italy Europe on a Budget, Florence DIR, Florence & Siena Map, Florence & the best of Tuscany, Italy, The Italian Lakes, Naples & the Amalfi Coast, Rome, Rome DIR, Rome Map, Sardinia, Sicily, Sicily Map, Tuscany & Umbria, Tuscany Map, Venice, Venice DIR, Venice Map
Jamaica Jamaica, The Caribbean
Japan Japan, Tokyo
Jordan Jordan
Kenya Kenya, Kenya Map
Korea Korea
Laos Laos, Southeast Asia on a Budget, Vietnam, Laos & Cambodia Map [1 Map]
Latvia The Baltic States, Europe on a Budget
Lithuania The Baltic States, Europe on a Budget
Luxembourg Belgium & Luxembourg, Europe on a Budget
Malaysia Malaysia Map, Malaysia, Singapore & Brunei [1 title], Southeast Asia on a Budget
Mali West Africa
Malta Malta & Gozo DIR
Martinique The Caribbean
Mauritania West Africa
Mexico Baja California, Baja California, Cancún & Cozumel DIR, Mexico, Mexico Map, Yucatán, Yucatán Peninsula Map
Monaco France, Provence & the Côte d'Azur
Montenegro Montenegro
Morocco Europe on a Budget, Marrakesh DIR, Marrakesh Map, Morocco, Morocco Map,
Nepal Nepal
Netherlands Amsterdam, Amsterdam DIR, Amsterdam Map, Europe on a Budget, The Netherlands
Netherlands Antilles The Caribbean
New Zealand New Zealand, New Zealand Map

DIR: Rough Guide **DIRECTIONS** for short breaks

Available from all good bookstores

Nicaragua Central America on a Budget
Niger West Africa
Nigeria West Africa
Norway Europe on a Budget, Norway, Scandinavia
Panama Central America on a Budget, Costa Rica & Panama Map, Panama
Paraguay South America on a Budget
Peru Peru, Peru Map, South America on a Budget
Philippines The Philippines, Southeast Asia on a Budget,
Poland Europe on a Budget, Poland
Portugal Algarve DIR, The Algarve Map, Europe on a Budget, Lisbon DIR, Lisbon Map, Madeira DIR, Portugal, Portugal Map, Spain & Portugal Map
Puerto Rico The Caribbean, Puerto Rico
Romania Europe on a Budget, Romania
Russia Europe on a Budget, Moscow, St Petersburg
St Kitts & Nevis The Caribbean
St Lucia The Caribbean
St Vincent & the Grenadines The Caribbean
Scotland Britain, Camping in Britain, Edinburgh DIR, Europe on a Budget, Scotland, Scottish Highlands & Islands
Senegal West Africa
Serbia Montenegro Europe on a Budget
Sierra Leone West Africa
Singapore Malaysia, Singapore & Brunei [1 title], Singapore, Singapore DIR, Southeast Asia on a Budget
Slovakia Czech & Slovak Republics, Europe on a Budget
Slovenia Europe on a Budget, Slovenia
South Africa Cape Town & the Garden Route, South Africa, South Africa Map
Spain Andalucía, Andalucía Map, Barcelona, Barcelona DIR, Barcelona Map, Europe on a Budget, Ibiza & Formentera DIR, Gran Canaria DIR, Madrid DIR, Lanzarote & Fuerteventura DIR Madrid Map, Mallorca & Menorca, Mallorca DIR, Mallorca Map, The Pyrenees, Pyrenees & Andorra Map, Spain, Spain & Portugal Map, Tenerife & La Gomera DIR
Sri Lanka Sri Lanka, Sri Lanka Map
Suriname South America on a Budget
Sweden Europe on a Budget, Scandinavia, Sweden
Switzerland Europe on a Budget, Switzerland
Taiwan Taiwan
Tanzania Tanzania, Zanzibar
Thailand Bangkok, Southeast Asia on a Budget, Thailand, Thailand Map, Thailand Beaches & Islands
Togo West Africa
Trinidad & Tobago The Caribbean, Trinidad & Tobago
Tunisia Tunisia, Tunisia Map
Turkey Europe on a Budget, Istanbul, Turkey, Turkey Map
Turks and Caicos Islands The Bahamas, The Caribbean
United Arab Emirates Dubai DIR, Dubai & UAE Map [1 title]
United Kingdom Britain, Devon & Cornwall, Edinburgh DIR England, Europe on a Budget, The Lake District, London, London DIR, London Map, London Mini Guide, Scotland, Scottish Highlands & Islands, Wales, Walks In London & Southeast England
United States Alaska, Boston, California, California Map, Chicago, Colorado, Florida, Florida Map, The Grand Canyon, Hawaii, Los Angeles, Los Angeles Map, Los Angeles and Southern California, Maui DIR, Miami & South Florida, New England, New England Map, New Orleans & Cajun Country, New Orleans DIR, New York City, NYC DIR, NYC Map, New York City Mini Guide, Oregon & Washington, Orlando & Walt Disney World® DIR, San Francisco, San Francisco DIR, San Francisco Map, Seattle, Southwest USA, USA, Washington DC, Yellowstone & the Grand Tetons National Park, Yosemite National Park
Uruguay South America on a Budget
US Virgin Islands The Bahamas, The Caribbean
Venezuela South America on a Budget
Vietnam Southeast Asia on a Budget, Vietnam, Vietnam, Laos & Cambodia Map [1 Map],
Wales Britain, Camping in Britain, Europe on a Budget, Wales
First-Time Series FT Africa, FT Around the World, FT Asia, FT Europe, FT Latin America
Inspirational guides Earthbound, Clean Breaks, Make the Most of Your Time on Earth, Ultimate Adventures, World Party
Travel Specials Camping in Britain, Travel with Babies & Young Children, Walks in London & SE England

ROUGH GUIDES Don't Just Travel

Computers Cloud Computing, FWD this link, The Internet, iPhone, iPods & iTunes, Macs & OS X, Website Directory
Film & TV American Independent Film, British Cult Comedy, Comedy Movies, Cult Movies, Film, Film Musicals, Film Noir, Gangster Movies, Horror Movies, Sci-Fi Movies, Westerns
Lifestyle Babies & Toddlers, Brain Training, Food, Girl Stuff, Green Living, Happiness, Men's Health, Pregnancy & Birth, Running, Saving & Selling Online, Sex, Weddings
Music The Beatles, The Best Music You've Never Heard, Blues, Bob Dylan, Book of Playlists, Classical Music, Heavy Metal, Jimi Hendrix, Led Zeppelin, Nirvana, Opera, Pink Floyd, The Rolling Stones, Soul and R&B, Velvet Underground, World Music
Popular Culture Anime, Classic Novels, Conspiracy Theories, Crime Fiction, The Da Vinci Code, Graphic Novels, Hidden Treasures, His Dark Materials, Hitchhiker's Guide to the Galaxy, The Lost Symbol, Manga, Next Big Thing, Shakespeare, True Crime, Tutankhamun, Unexplained Phenomena, Videogames
Science The Brain, Climate Change, The Earth, Energy Crisis, Evolution, Future, Genes & Cloning, The Universe, Weather

NOTES

Small print and Index

A Rough Guide to Rough Guides

Published in 1982, the first Rough Guide – to Greece – was a student scheme that became a publishing phenomenon. Mark Ellingham, a recent graduate in English from Bristol University, had been travelling in Greece the previous summer and couldn't find the right guidebook. With a small group of friends he wrote his own guide, combining a highly contemporary, journalistic style with a thoroughly practical approach to travellers' needs.

The immediate success of the book spawned a series that rapidly covered dozens of destinations. And, in addition to impecunious backpackers, Rough Guides soon acquired a much broader and older readership that relished the guides' wit and inquisitiveness as much as their enthusiastic, critical approach and value-for-money ethos.

These days, Rough Guides include recommendations from shoestring to luxury and cover more than 200 destinations around the globe, including almost every country in the Americas and Europe, more than half of Africa and most of Asia and Australasia. Our ever-growing team of authors and photographers is spread all over the world, particularly in Europe, the US and Australia.

In the early 1990s, Rough Guides branched out of travel, with the publication of Rough Guides to World Music, Classical Music and the Internet. All three have become benchmark titles in their fields, spearheading the publication of a wide range of books under the Rough Guide name.

Including the travel series, Rough Guides now number more than 350 titles, covering: phrasebooks, waterproof maps, music guides from Opera to Heavy Metal, reference works as diverse as Conspiracy Theories and Shakespeare, and popular culture books from iPods to Poker. Rough Guides also produce a series of more than 120 World Music CDs in partnership with World Music Network.

Visit www.roughguides.com to see our latest publications.

Rough Guide credits

Text editors: James Rice, Keith Drew
Layout: Pradeep Thapliyal
Cartography: Karobi Gogoi, Ashutosh Bharti
Picture editor: Sarah Cummins
Production: Rebecca Short
Proofreader: Karen Parker
Cover design: Nicole Newman, Dan May, Jess Carter
Photographers: Greg Roden, Susannah Sayler, Angus Oborn, Curtis Hamilton
Editorial: **London** Andy Turner, Edward Aves, Alice Park, Lucy White, Jo Kirby, James Smart, Natasha Foges, Róisín Cameron, Emma Beatson, Emma Gibbs, Kathryn Lane, Monica Woods, Mani Ramaswamy, Harry Wilson, Lucy Cowie, Lara Kavanagh, Alison Roberts, Eleanor Aldridge, Ian Blenkinsop, Joe Staines, Matthew Milton, Tracy Hopkins; **Delhi** Madhavi Singh, Jalpreen Kaur Chhatwal
Design & Pictures: **London** Scott Stickland, Dan May, Diana Jarvis, Mark Thomas, Nicole Newman, Emily Taylor; **Delhi** Umesh Aggarwal, Ajay Verma, Jessica Subramanian, Ankur Guha, Sachin Tanwar, Anita Singh, Nikhil Agarwal, Sachin Gupta
Production: Liz Cherry, Louise Daly, Erika Pepe
Cartography: **London** Ed Wright, Katie Lloyd-Jones; **Delhi** Rajesh Chhibber, Rajesh Mishra, Animesh Pathak, Jasbir Sandhu, Swati Handoo, Deshpal Dabas, Lokamata Sahu
Online: **London** Faye Hellon, Jeanette Angell, Fergus Day, Justine Bright, Clare Bryson, Aine Fearon, Adrian Low, Ezgi Celebi; **Delhi** Amit Verma, Rahul Kumar, Narender Kumar, Ravi Yadav, Debojit Borah, Rakesh Kumar, Ganesh Sharma, Shisir Basumatari
Marketing & Publicity: **London** Liz Statham, Jess Carter, Vivienne Watton, Anna Paynton, Rachel Sprackett, Laura Vipond; **New York** Katy Ball; **Delhi** Aman Arora
Digital Travel Publisher: Peter Buckley
Reference Director: Andrew Lockett
Operations Assistant: Becky Doyle
Operations Manager: Helen Atkinson
Publishing Director (Travel): Clare Currie
Commercial Manager: Gino Magnotta
Managing Director: John Duhigg

Publishing information

This twelfth edition published January 2011 by
Rough Guides Ltd,
80 Strand, London WC2R 0RL
11, Community Centre, Panchsheel Park, New Delhi 110017, India
Distributed by the Penguin Group
Penguin Books Ltd,
80 Strand, London WC2R 0RL
Penguin Group (USA)
375 Hudson Street, NY 10014, USA
Penguin Group (Australia)
250 Camberwell Road, Camberwell, Victoria 3124, Australia
Penguin Group (NZ)
67 Apollo Drive, Mairangi Bay, Auckland 1310, New Zealand
Rough Guides is represented in Canada by Tourmaline Editions Inc. 662 King Street West, Suite 304, Toronto, Ontario M5V 1M7
Cover concept by Peter Dyer.
Typeset in Bembo and Helvetica to an original design by Henry Iles.
Printed in Singapore

480pp includes index
A catalogue record for this book is available from the British Library
ISBN: 978-1-848365-902

1 3 5 7 9 8 6 4 2

Help us update

We've gone to a lot of effort to ensure that the twelfth edition of **The Rough Guide to New York City** is accurate and up-to-date. However, things change – places get "discovered", opening hours are notoriously fickle, restaurants and rooms raise prices or lower standards. If you feel we've got it wrong or left something out, we'd like to know, and if you can remember the address, the price, the hours, the phone number, so much the better.

Please send your comments with the subject line "**Rough Guide New York City Update**" to ⓔmail@uk.roughguides.com. We'll credit all contributions and send a copy of the next edition (or any other Rough Guide if you prefer) for the very best emails.

Find more travel information, connect with fellow travellers and book your trip on ⓦwww.roughguides.com

SMALL PRINT

Acknowledgements

Stephen Keeling wishes to thank: Anna Catchpole, Yuien Chin, Debra Harris, Andrew Luan, Victor Ozols, Gordon Polatnick, Neal Shoemaker, Kate Stober, Thatiana Wilkinson, fellow author Andrew Rosenberg, James Rice and Keith Drew for their fine editing and Tiffany Wu, whose love and support made this book possible.

Andrew Rosenberg wishes to thank: his co-author Stephen Keeling; James Rice and Keith Drew for their tireless editorial work; Mani Ramaswamy and Martin Dunford for the opportunity; the Rough Guiders who worked on maps, pictures and typesetting; Larry Burnett for his contributions to "Gay New York City", and everyone else who helped out or contributed along the way, including but not limited to: JD Dickey, Andy Young, Mark Fass, Tomoko Kawamoto, Heidi Riegler, James Vanderberg, Brandon Rivard, Alanna Schindewolf, Gus Matsukawa, Christina Tzortzinis, Lois Rosebrooks, Tiffany Pak, Anna Catchpole, Marisa Picker, Nicole Grzywacz and, for the love, company and support, Melanie and Jules.

Readers' letters

Thanks to all the readers who have taken the time to write in with comments and suggestions (and apologies if we've inadvertently omitted or misspelt anyone's name):

Leah Ammon, Cathy Guppey, Richard Koss, Ranjit Madgavkar, Sheryn Omeri

Photo credits

All photography by Greg Roden, Susannah Sayler, Angus Oborn or Curtis Hamilton © Rough Guides except the following::

Introduction

Manhattan skyline © Narvikk/Istock

Things not to miss

02 Lincoln Center fountain courtesy of Jon Ortner/Lincoln Center
03 New York Yankees versus New York Mets © Ray Stubblebine/Reuters/Corbis
08 Halloween, New York © Franz-Marc Frei/Corbis
10 Staten Island Ferry © Onne van der Wal/Corbis
11 Rockefeller Center, GE Building with a statue by Paul Manship showing Prometheus © Ludovic Maisant/Hemis/Corbis
14 Peace Fountain at Cathedral of St John The Divine © Philip Scalia/Alamy

New York architecture colour section

New York City at dusk © Andy Selinger/Alamy

Ethnic New York colour section

Signs in Little Italy © Pietro Scozzari/Photolibrary
Abyssinian Church choir © Thos Robinson/Getty Images
Greek Independence Day © Ramin Talaie/Corbis
Chinese New Year © Ramin Talaie/Corbis

Black and whites

p.204 Harlem Brownstones © Ambient Images Inc/Alamy

Index

Map entries are in colour.

ROUGH GUIDES

SMALL PRINT

B

C

D

INDEX

N

O

P

Q

R

S

U

V

W

Y

Z

Map symbols

maps are listed in the full index using coloured text

Chapter boundary
State boundary
Borough/county boundary
Interstate
US highway
State highway
Pedestrianized street
Footpath
Tunnel
River
Ferry route
Railway
Peak
International airport
Gate
Subway station
Point of interest
Gardens
Golf course
Parking
Bridge
Boat
Lighthouse
Hospital
Post office
Tourist office
Internet access
Monument
Restaurant
Synagogue
Buddhist temple
Mosque
Church
Stadium
Building
Cemetery
Park/forest
Beach

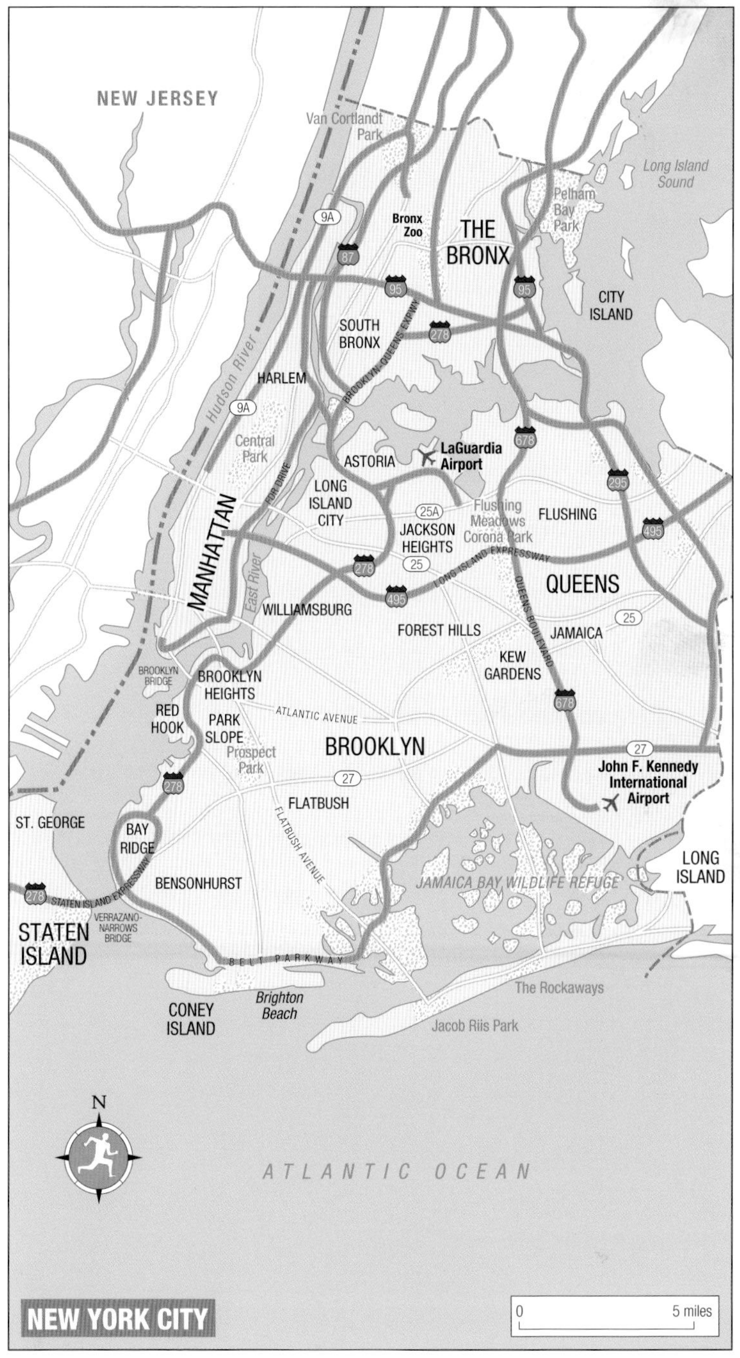
NEW JERSEY
Van Cortlandt Park
Long Island Sound
Pelham Bay Park
9A
Bronx Zoo
THE BRONX
87
95
95
CITY ISLAND
SOUTH BRONX
278
BROOKLYN-QUEENS EXPWY
Hudson River
HARLEM
9A
Central Park
LaGuardia Airport
678
ASTORIA
295
FDR DRIVE
LONG ISLAND CITY
25A
Flushing Meadows Corona Park
FLUSHING
495
MANHATTAN
JACKSON HEIGHTS
25
LONG ISLAND EXPRESSWAY
278
East River
QUEENS
495
WILLIAMSBURG
QUEENS BOULEVARD
25
FOREST HILLS
JAMAICA
KEW GARDENS
BROOKLYN BRIDGE
BROOKLYN HEIGHTS
678
RED HOOK
ATLANTIC AVENUE
PARK SLOPE
BROOKLYN
27
Prospect Park
John F. Kennedy International Airport
278
27
FLATBUSH
ST. GEORGE
FLATBUSH AVENUE
BAY RIDGE
LONG ISLAND
BENSONHURST
JAMAICA BAY WILDLIFE REFUGE
278
STATEN ISLAND EXPRESSWAY
VERRAZANO-NARROWS BRIDGE
STATEN ISLAND
BELT PARKWAY
The Rockaways
Brighton Beach
CONEY ISLAND
Jacob Riis Park
N
ATLANTIC OCEAN
NEW YORK CITY
0
5 miles

Metropolitan Transportation Authority
MTA New York City Subway
with bus and railroad connections
Key
The subway operates 24 hours a day, but not all lines operate at all times. The map depicts morning to evening weekday service. For more information, call our Travel Information Center (6AM to 10PM) at 718-330-1234. Non-English-speaking customers call 718-330-4847 (6AM to 10PM).
visit www.mta.info
To show service more clearly, geography on this map has been modified.
© 2010 Metropolitan Transportation Authority
June 2010
Rush hour line extension
Accessible station
Bus or AIRTRAIN to airport
Police
Full time service
Part time service
Station Name
Terminal
Local service only
All trains stop (local and express service)
Normal service
Additional express service
Free subway transfer
Free out-of-system subway transfer (excluding single-ride ticket)
Bus to airport
Commuter rail service
Service Note
The subway map depicts weekday service. Service differs by time of day and is sometimes affected by construction. Overhead directional signs on platforms show weekend, evening, and late night service.
This information is also available on mta.info: click on "Maps" in the top menu bar, then select "Individual Subway Line Maps."
For construction-related service changes, click on "Planned Service Changes" in the top menu bar. This information is also at station entrances and on platform columns of affected lines.
Hudson River
Harlem River
MANHATTAN
175 St
168 St A·C·1
163 St Amsterdam Av C
157 St 1
155 St C
155 St B·D
145 St 1
145 St A·B·C·D
137 St City College 1
135 St B·C
125 St 1
125 St A·B·C·D
M60 LaGuardia Airport
116 St Columbia University 1
116 St B·C
Cathedral Pkwy (110 St) 1
Cathedral Pkwy (110 St) B·C
103 St 1
103 St B·C
96 St 1·2·3
96 St B·C
86 St 1
86 St B·C
81 St–Museum of Natural History B·C
79 St 1
72 St 1·2·3
72 St B·C
66 St Lincoln Center 1
59 St Columbus Circle A·B·C·D·1
7 Av B·D·E
57 St-7 Av N·Q·R
57 St F
5 Av/59 St N·Q·R
Harlem 148 St 3
145 St 3
135 St 2·3
125 St 2·3
116 St 2·3
Central Park North (110 St) 2·3
167 St 4
167 St B·D
161 St Yankee Stadium B·D·4
149 St–Grand Concourse 2·4·5
138 St–Grand Concourse 4·5
3 Av–149 St 2·5
Jackson Av 2·5
Prospect Av 2·5
Intervale Av 2·5
Simpson St 2·5
Hunts Point Av 6
Longwood Av 6
3 Av 138 St 6
Brook Av 6
125 St 4·5·6
116 St 6
110 St 6
103 St 6
96 St 6
86 St 4·5·6
77 St 6
68 St Hunter College 6
Lexington Av/63 St F
Lexington Av/59 St N·Q·R
59 St 4·5·6
Lexington Av/53 St E·M
Roosevelt Island F
21 St Queensbridge F
Queensboro Plaza N·Q·7
23 St-Ely Av E·M
Queens Plaza E·M·R
Broadway N·Q
36 Av N·Q
39 Av N·Q
36 St M·R
33 St-Rawson 7
40 St Lowery St 7
46 St Bliss St 7
52 St 7
Woodside 61 St 7
69 St 7
Jackson Hts Roosevelt Av E·F·M·R·7
LGA Airport
WASHINGTON HEIGHTS
HARLEM
EAST HARLEM
MOTT HAVEN
THE HUB
UPPER WEST SIDE
UPPER EAST SIDE
WEST SIDE
LONG ISLAND CITY
RANDALLS ISLAND
ROOSEVELT ISLAND
RIVERBANK STATE PARK
CENTRAL PARK
METROPOLITAN MUSEUM OF ART
ROBERT F KENNEDY BRIDGE
QUEENSBORO BRIDGE
TRAMWAY
Amtrak
LIRR

Port Authority Bus Terminal A·C·E
Times Sq-42 St N·Q·R·S·1·2·3·7
42 St Bryant Pk B·D·F·M
5 Av 7
Grand Central 42 St S·4·5·6·7·Metro-North
Vernon Blvd Jackson Av 7
Hunters Point Av 7·LIRR
34 St Penn Station A·C·E·LIRR
34 St Penn Station 1·2·3·LIRR
34 St Herald Sq B·D·F M·N·Q·R
33 St 6
28 St 1
28 St N·R
28 St 6
23 St C·E
23 St 1
23 St F·M
23 St N·R
23 St 6
18 St 1
14 St-Union Sq L·N·Q·R·4·5·6
3 Av L
1 Av L
8 Av L
6 Av L
14 St A·C·E
14 St 1·2·3
14 St F·M
8 St-NYU N·R
Astor Pl 6
W 4 St Wash Sq A·B·C·D·E·F·M
Christopher St Sheridan Sq 1
Bleecker St 6
B'way-Lafayette St B·D·F·M
2 Av F
Houston St 1
Prince St N·R
Spring St C·E
Spring St 6
Delancey St Essex St F·J·M·Z
Canal St 1
Canal St A·C·E
Canal St J·N·Q R·Z·6
Bowery J·Z
Grand St B·D
East Broadway F
Franklin St 1
Chambers St A·C
Chambers St 1·2·3
Park Place 2·3
City Hall R
Chambers St J·Z
Brooklyn Bridge City Hall 4·5·6
World Trade Center E
Fulton St Broadway-Nassau A·C·J·Z 2·3·4·5
Cortlandt St R northbound service only
Cortlandt St 1
Wall St 4·5
Wall St 2·3
Rector St 1
Rector St R
Broad St J·Z
Bowling Green 4·5
Whitehall St South Ferry R
South Ferry 1
York St F
High St A·C
Jay St Borough Hall A·C·F
Court St R
Clark St 2·3
Borough Hall 2·3·4·5
Hoyt St 2·3
Lawrence St R
DeKalb Av B·Q·R
Fulton St G
Nevins St 2·3·4·5
Hoyt Schermerhorn A·C·G
Bergen St F·G
Carroll St F·G
Smith 9 Sts F·G
Atlantic Av-Pacific St D·N·R·LIRR
Union St R
4 Av-9 St F·G·R
Prospect Av R
Lafayette Av C
Atlantic Av B·Q·2·3·4·5·LIRR
Bergen St 2·3
Grand Army Plaza 2·3
Eastern Pkwy Brooklyn Museum 2·3
7 Av B·Q
Park Pl S
Franklin Av C·S
Clinton Washington Avs C
Clinton Washington Avs G
Classon Av G
Bedford Nostrand Avs G
Myrtle Willoughby Avs G
Flushing Av G
7 Av F·G
15 St Prospect Park F·G
Marcy Av J·M·Z
Hewes St J·M
Broadway G
Lorimer St J·M
Flushing Av J·M
Myrtle Av J·M·Z
Greenpoint Av G
Nassau Av G
Bedford Av L
Lorimer St L
Metropolitan Av G
Graham Av L
Grand St L
Montrose Av L
Morgan Av L
Jefferson St L
LINCOLN TUNNEL
QUEENS MIDTOWN TUNNEL
HOLLAND TUNNEL
BROOKLYN-BATTERY TUNNEL
WILLIAMSBURG BRIDGE
MANHATTAN BRIDGE
BROOKLYN BRIDGE
East River
JAVITS CENTER
CHELSEA
GREENWICH VILLAGE
TRIBECA
SOHO
NOHO
LITTLE ITALY
CHINATOWN
EAST VILLAGE
LOWER EAST SIDE
EAST RIVER PARK
WASHINGTON SQUARE PARK
FINANCIAL DISTRICT
BATTERY PARK CITY
WTC Site
ELLIS ISLAND
LIBERTY ISLAND
GOVERNORS ISLAND
Staten Island Ferry
summer only
NJTransit • Amtrak
PATH
GREENPOINT
WILLIAMSBURG
NAVY YARD
DUMBO
FORT GREENE
FORT GREENE PARK
BROOKLYN HEIGHTS
NEW YORK TRANSIT MUSEUM
CARROLL GARDENS
RED HOOK
PARK SLOPE
PROSPECT PARK
BROOKLYN BOTANIC GARDEN
BEDFORD-STUYVESANT
CALVARY CEMETERY
MASPETH
QUEENS
BROOKLYN
Long Island City
LONG ISLAND EXPWY

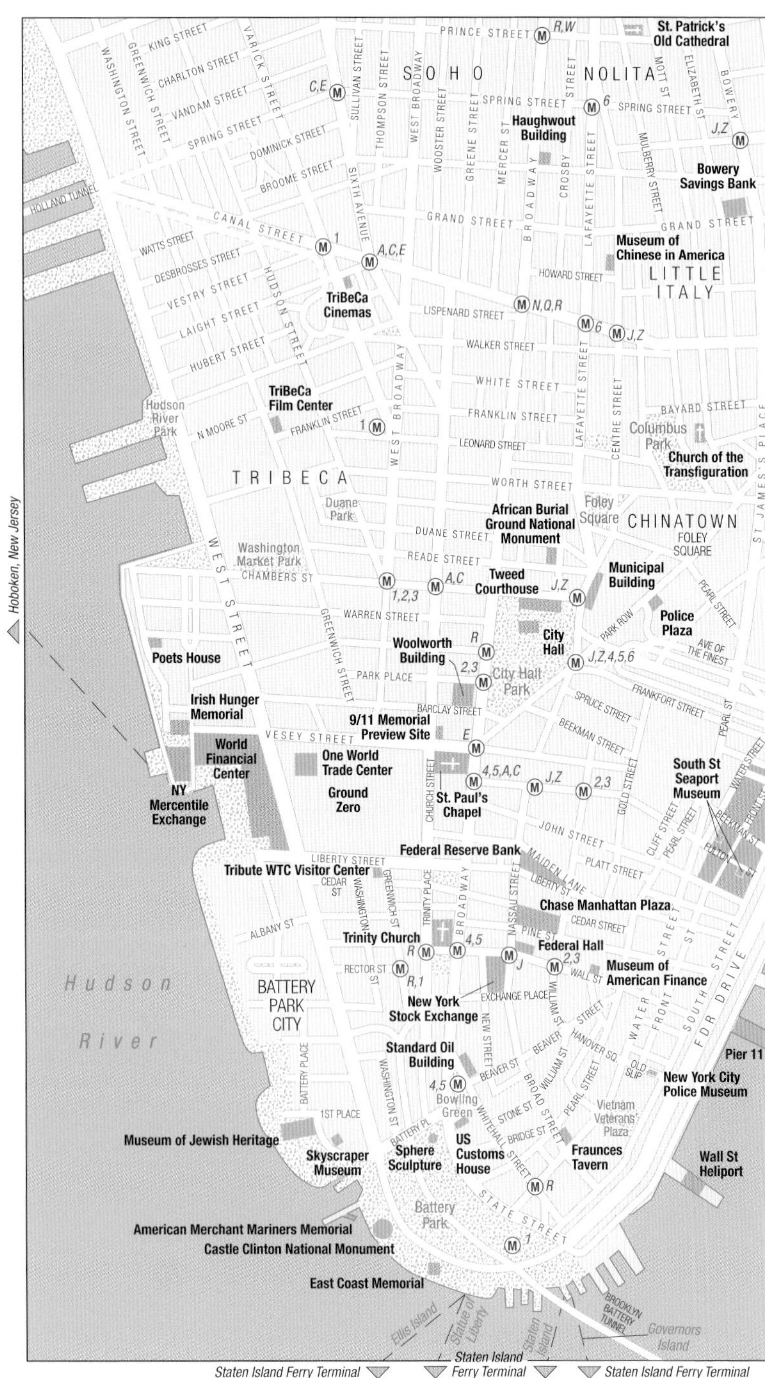

PRINCE STREET
R,W
St. Patrick's Old Cathedral
KING STREET
CHARLTON STREET
VANDAM STREET
SPRING STREET
DOMINICK STREET
BROOME STREET
WASHINGTON STREET
GREENWICH STREET
VARICK STREET
C,E
SULLIVAN STREET
THOMPSON STREET
WEST BROADWAY
WOOSTER STREET
GREENE STREET
MERCER ST
BROADWAY
CROSBY
LAFAYETTE STREET
STREET
MOTT ST
ELIZABETH ST
BOWERY
S O H O
NOLITA
SPRING STREET
6
Haughwout Building
J,Z
MULBERRY STREET
Bowery Savings Bank
HOLLAND TUNNEL
CANAL STREET
1
SIXTH AVENUE
A,C,E
GRAND STREET
GRAND STREET
Museum of Chinese in America
WATTS STREET
DESBROSSES STREET
VESTRY STREET
LAIGHT STREET
HUBERT STREET
HUDSON STREET
HOWARD STREET
LITTLE ITALY
TriBeCa Cinemas
LISPENARD STREET
N,Q,R
6
J,Z
WALKER STREET
WHITE STREET
TriBeCa Film Center
FRANKLIN STREET
FRANKLIN STREET
BAYARD STREET
Hudson River Park
N MOORE ST
1
WEST BROADWAY
LEONARD STREET
Columbus Park
CENTRE STREET
Church of the Transfiguration
ST JAMES S PLACE
TRIBECA
WORTH STREET
Duane Park
African Burial Ground National Monument
Foley Square
CHINATOWN
FOLEY SQUARE
DUANE STREET
Washington Market Park
READE STREET
CHAMBERS ST
WEST STREET
1,2,3
A,C
Tweed Courthouse
J,Z
Municipal Building
PEARL STREET
WARREN STREET
GREENWICH STREET
Police Plaza
PARK ROW
City Hall
R
Woolworth Building
J,Z,4,5,6
AVE OF THE FINEST
Poets House
2,3
PARK PLACE
City Hall Park
FRANKFORT STREET
Irish Hunger Memorial
BARCLAY STREET
SPRUCE STREET
PEARL ST
9/11 Memorial Preview Site
BEEKMAN STREET
VESEY STREET
E
World Financial Center
One World Trade Center
CHURCH STREET
4,5,A,C
J,Z
2,3
GOLD STREET
South St Seaport Museum
WATER STREET
NY Mercentile Exchange
Ground Zero
St. Paul's Chapel
JOHN STREET
CLIFF STREET
PEARL STREET
BEEKMAN ST
FRONT ST
FULTON ST
Federal Reserve Bank
MAIDEN LANE
LIBERTY STREET
Tribute WTC Visitor Center
LIBERTY ST
PLATT STREET
CEDAR ST
WASHINGTON
GREENWICH ST
TRINITY PLACE
BROADWAY
NASSAU STREET
Chase Manhattan Plaza
CEDAR STREET
ALBANY ST
PINE ST
Trinity Church
R
4,5
Federal Hall
J
2,3
Museum of American Finance
RECTOR ST
R,1
WALL ST
Hudson River
BATTERY PARK CITY
EXCHANGE PLACE
New York Stock Exchange
WILLIAM ST
WATER STREET
FRONT STREET
SOUTH STREET
FDR DRIVE
NEW STREET
HANOVER SQ.
Standard Oil Building
BEAVER
Pier 11
BATTERY PLACE
WASHINGTON ST
BEAVER ST
BROAD STREET
OLD SLIP
New York City Police Museum
4,5
Bowling Green
1ST PLACE
STONE ST
PEARL STREET
Vietnam Veterans Plaza
BATTERY PL
BRIDGE ST
Museum of Jewish Heritage
Skyscraper Museum
Sphere Sculpture
US Customs House
Fraunces Tavern
Wall St Heliport
WHITEHALL STREET
R
STATE STREET
Battery Park
American Merchant Mariners Memorial
1
Castle Clinton National Monument
East Coast Memorial
BROOKLYN BATTERY TUNNEL
Ellis Island
Statue of Liberty
Staten Island
Governors Island
Staten Island Ferry Terminal
Hoboken, New Jersey

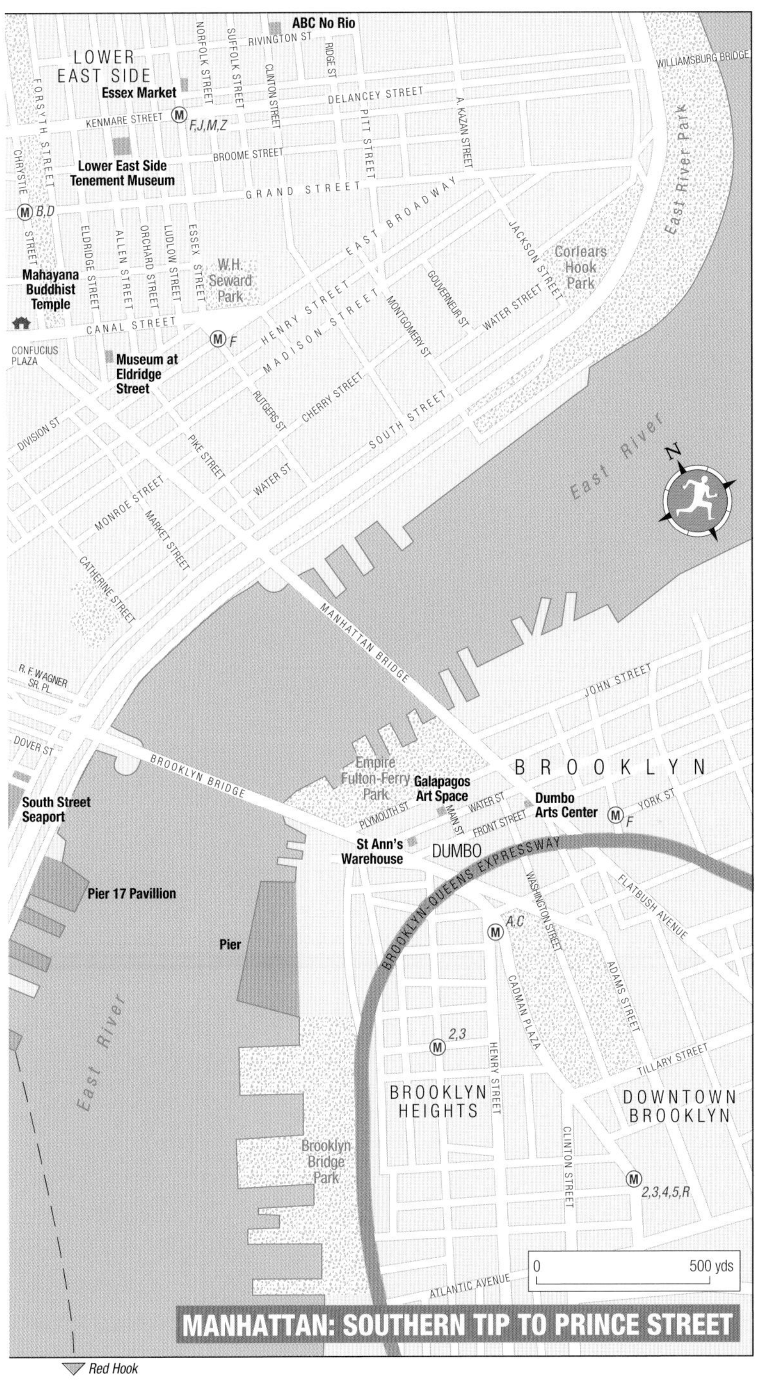

ABC No Rio
RIVINGTON ST
LOWER EAST SIDE
Essex Market
NORFOLK STREET
SUFFOLK STREET
CLINTON STREET
RIDGE ST
WILLIAMSBURG BRIDGE
DELANCEY STREET
KENMARE STREET
F,J,M,Z
PITT STREET
A. KAZAN STREET
FORSYTH STREET
CHRYSTIE STREET
BROOME STREET
Lower East Side Tenement Museum
GRAND STREET
East River Park
B,D
EAST BROADWAY
ELDRIDGE STREET
ALLEN STREET
ORCHARD STREET
LUDLOW STREET
ESSEX STREET
JACKSON STREET
Corlears Hook Park
W.H. Seward Park
Mahayana Buddhist Temple
GOUVERNEUR ST
WATER STREET
HENRY STREET
MADISON STREET
MONTGOMERY ST
CANAL STREET
F
CONFUCIUS PLAZA
Museum at Eldridge Street
RUTGERS ST
CHERRY STREET
SOUTH STREET
DIVISION ST
PIKE STREET
East River
N
WATER ST
MONROE STREET
MARKET STREET
CATHERINE STREET
MANHATTAN BRIDGE
R. F. WAGNER SR. PL.
JOHN STREET
DOVER ST
BROOKLYN BRIDGE
Empire Fulton-Ferry Park
Galapagos Art Space
BROOKLYN
Dumbo Arts Center
YORK ST
South Street Seaport
PLYMOUTH ST
WATER ST
MAIN ST
FRONT STREET
F
St Ann's Warehouse
DUMBO
BROOKLYN-QUEENS EXPRESSWAY
Pier 17 Pavillion
WASHINGTON STREET
FLATBUSH AVENUE
4,C
Pier
CADMAN PLAZA
ADAMS STREET
East River
2,3
HENRY STREET
TILLARY STREET
BROOKLYN HEIGHTS
DOWNTOWN BROOKLYN
CLINTON STREET
Brooklyn Bridge Park
2,3,4,5,R
0
500 yds
ATLANTIC AVENUE
MANHATTAN: SOUTHERN TIP TO PRINCE STREET
Red Hook

Intrepid Sea, Air & Space Museum
Circle Line Ferry
LINCOLN TUNNEL
TO N.J.
N.J.
HELL'S KITCHEN
Discovery Times Square Exposition
International Center of Photography
Algonquin Hotel
NY Yacht Club
Harvard Club
General Society of Mechanics & Tradesmen
TIMES SQUARE
Bryant Park
New York Public Library
Port Authority Bus Terminal
Jacob Javits Convention Center
GARMENT DISTRICT
Macy's
HERALD SQUARE
Empire State Building
GREELEY SQUARE
Pennsylvania Station
General Post Office
Madison Square Garden
Marble Collegiate Church
Church of the Transfiguration
FIT Museum
Museum of Sex
Chelsea Park
(Park under construction)
Madison Square Park
London Terrace Gardens
Chelsea Hotel
Flatiron Building
General Theological Seminary
CHELSEA
Chelsea Piers
High Line
Rubin Museum of Art
Chelsea Market
Hudson River
Forbes Galleries
First Presbyterian Church
Church of the Ascension
MEATPACKING DISTRICT
Jefferson Market Courthouse
ABINGDON SQUARE
WEST VILLAGE
SHERIDAN SQUARE
Washington Square Park
Judson Memorial Church
Center for Architecture
Hudson River Park
SOHO
0 500 yds
N

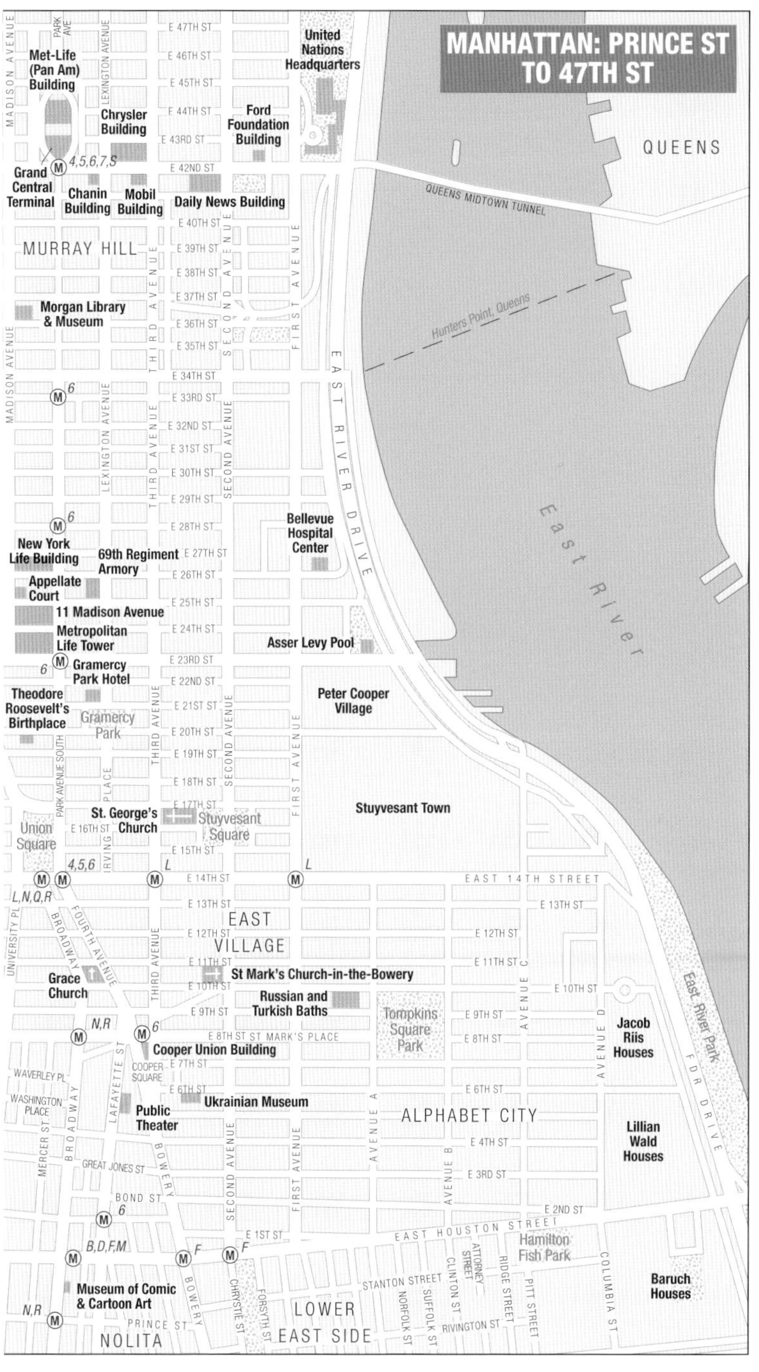

MANHATTAN: PRINCE ST TO 47TH ST
QUEENS
QUEENS MIDTOWN TUNNEL
Hunters Point, Queens
East River
EAST RIVER DRIVE
East River Park
FDR DRIVE
United Nations Headquarters
Ford Foundation Building
Met-Life (Pan Am) Building
Chrysler Building
Grand Central Terminal
Chanin Building
Mobil Building
Daily News Building
4,5,6,7,S
MURRAY HILL
Morgan Library & Museum
Bellevue Hospital Center
New York Life Building
69th Regiment Armory
Appellate Court
11 Madison Avenue
Metropolitan Life Tower
Asser Levy Pool
Gramercy Park Hotel
Theodore Roosevelt's Birthplace
Gramercy Park
Peter Cooper Village
Stuyvesant Town
St. George's Church
Stuyvesant Square
Union Square
4,5,6
L,N,Q,R
L
EAST VILLAGE
EAST 14TH STREET
Grace Church
St Mark's Church-in-the-Bowery
Russian and Turkish Baths
Tompkins Square Park
Jacob Riis Houses
N,R
6
Cooper Union Building
COOPER SQUARE
ST MARK'S PLACE
Ukrainian Museum
Public Theater
ALPHABET CITY
Lillian Wald Houses
EAST HOUSTON STREET
Hamilton Fish Park
Baruch Houses
B,D,F,M
F
Museum of Comic & Cartoon Art
LOWER EAST SIDE
NOLITA
MADISON AVENUE
PARK AVE
LEXINGTON AVENUE
THIRD AVENUE
SECOND AVENUE
FIRST AVENUE
PARK AVENUE SOUTH
IRVING PLACE
UNIVERSITY PL
BROADWAY
FOURTH AVENUE
LAFAYETTE ST
BOWERY
MERCER ST
WAVERLEY PL
WASHINGTON PLACE
GREAT JONES ST
BOND ST
PRINCE ST
CHRYSTIE ST
FORSYTH ST
AVENUE A
AVENUE B
AVENUE C
AVENUE D
STANTON STREET
NORFOLK ST
SUFFOLK ST
CLINTON ST
ATTORNEY STREET
RIDGE STREET
PITT STREET
RIVINGTON ST
COLUMBIA ST
E 47TH ST
E 46TH ST
E 45TH ST
E 44TH ST
E 43RD ST
E 42ND ST
E 40TH ST
E 39TH ST
E 38TH ST
E 37TH ST
E 36TH ST
E 35TH ST
E 34TH ST
E 33RD ST
E 32ND ST
E 31ST ST
E 30TH ST
E 29TH ST
E 28TH ST
E 27TH ST
E 26TH ST
E 25TH ST
E 24TH ST
E 23RD ST
E 22ND ST
E 21ST ST
E 20TH ST
E 19TH ST
E 18TH ST
E 17TH ST
E 16TH ST
E 15TH ST
E 14TH ST
E 13TH ST
E 12TH ST
E 11TH ST
E 10TH ST
E 9TH ST
E 8TH ST
E 7TH ST
E 6TH ST
E 4TH ST
E 3RD ST
E 2ND ST
E 1ST ST

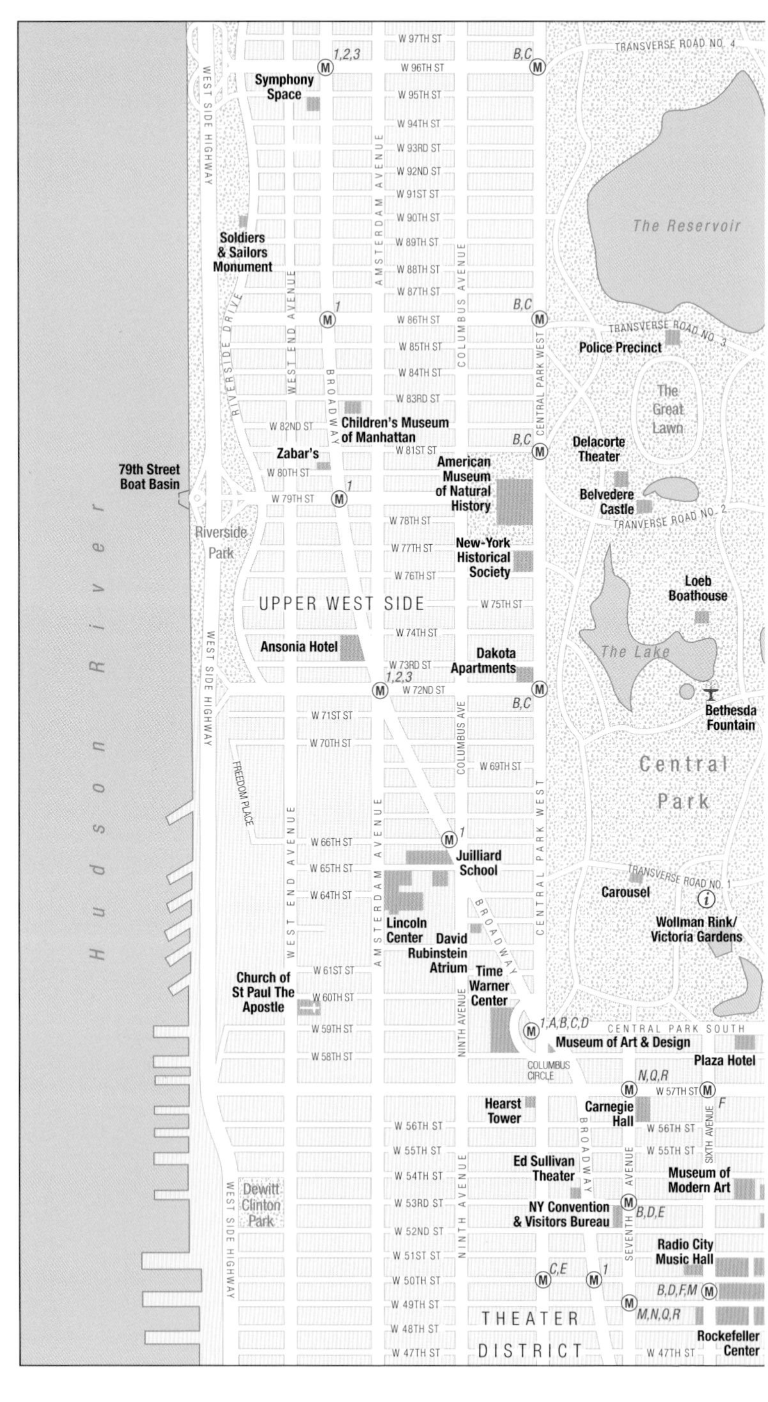
Hudson River
Symphony Space
Soldiers & Sailors Monument
79th Street Boat Basin
Riverside Park
Children's Museum of Manhattan
Zabar's
American Museum of Natural History
New-York Historical Society
UPPER WEST SIDE
Ansonia Hotel
Dakota Apartments
The Reservoir
Police Precinct
The Great Lawn
Delacorte Theater
Belvedere Castle
Loeb Boathouse
The Lake
Bethesda Fountain
Central Park
Carousel
Wollman Rink/ Victoria Gardens
Juilliard School
Lincoln Center
David Rubinstein Atrium
Time Warner Center
Church of St Paul The Apostle
Museum of Art & Design
Plaza Hotel
Columbus Circle
Hearst Tower
Carnegie Hall
Ed Sullivan Theater
Museum of Modern Art
NY Convention & Visitors Bureau
Radio City Music Hall
Rockefeller Center
Dewitt Clinton Park
THEATER DISTRICT
West Side Highway
Riverside Drive
Freedom Place
West End Avenue
Broadway
Amsterdam Avenue
Columbus Avenue
Central Park West
Ninth Avenue
Seventh Avenue
Sixth Avenue
Central Park South
Transverse Road No. 4
Transverse Road No. 3
Tranverse Road No. 2
Transverse Road No. 1
W 97th St
W 96th St
W 95th St
W 94th St
W 93rd St
W 92nd St
W 91st St
W 90th St
W 89th St
W 88th St
W 87th St
W 86th St
W 85th St
W 84th St
W 83rd St
W 82nd St
W 81st St
W 80th St
W 79th St
W 78th St
W 77th St
W 76th St
W 75th St
W 74th St
W 73rd St
W 72nd St
W 71st St
W 70th St
W 69th St
W 66th St
W 65th St
W 64th St
W 61st St
W 60th St
W 59th St
W 58th St
W 57th St
W 56th St
W 55th St
W 54th St
W 53rd St
W 52nd St
W 51st St
W 50th St
W 49th St
W 48th St
W 47th St
1,2,3
B,C
1
1,A,B,C,D
N,Q,R
F
B,D,E
C,E
B,D,F,M
M,N,Q,R

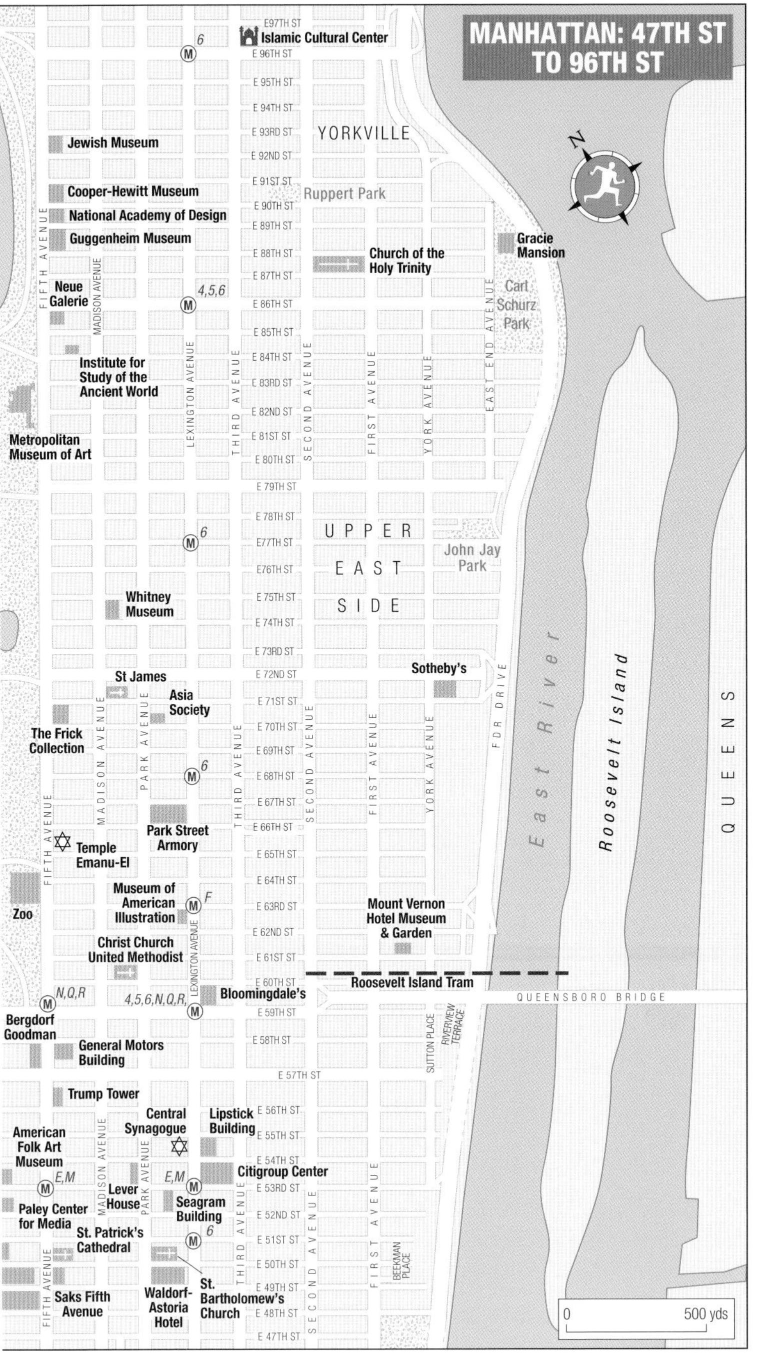
MANHATTAN: 47TH ST TO 96TH ST
Islamic Cultural Center
YORKVILLE
Ruppert Park
Jewish Museum
Cooper-Hewitt Museum
National Academy of Design
Guggenheim Museum
Church of the Holy Trinity
Gracie Mansion
Carl Schurz Park
Neue Galerie
Institute for Study of the Ancient World
Metropolitan Museum of Art
UPPER EAST SIDE
John Jay Park
Whitney Museum
Sotheby's
St James
Asia Society
The Frick Collection
Park Street Armory
Temple Emanu-El
Museum of American Illustration
Zoo
Mount Vernon Hotel Museum & Garden
Christ Church United Methodist
Roosevelt Island Tram
Bloomingdale's
QUEENSBORO BRIDGE
Bergdorf Goodman
General Motors Building
Trump Tower
Central Synagogue
Lipstick Building
American Folk Art Museum
Citigroup Center
Lever House
Seagram Building
Paley Center for Media
St. Patrick's Cathedral
St. Bartholomew's Church
Saks Fifth Avenue
Waldorf-Astoria Hotel
East River
Roosevelt Island
QUEENS
FIFTH AVENUE
MADISON AVENUE
PARK AVENUE
LEXINGTON AVENUE
THIRD AVENUE
SECOND AVENUE
FIRST AVENUE
YORK AVENUE
EAST END AVENUE
FDR DRIVE
SUTTON PLACE
RIVERVIEW TERRACE
BEEKMAN PLACE
E97TH ST
E 96TH ST
E 95TH ST
E 94TH ST
E 93RD ST
E 92ND ST
E 91ST ST
E 90TH ST
E 89TH ST
E 88TH ST
E 87TH ST
E 86TH ST
E 85TH ST
E 84TH ST
E 83RD ST
E 82ND ST
E 81ST ST
E 80TH ST
E 79TH ST
E 78TH ST
E77TH ST
E76TH ST
E 75TH ST
E 74TH ST
E 73RD ST
E 72ND ST
E 71ST ST
E 70TH ST
E 69TH ST
E 68TH ST
E 67TH ST
E 66TH ST
E 65TH ST
E 64TH ST
E 63RD ST
E 62ND ST
E 61ST ST
E 60TH ST
E 59TH ST
E 58TH ST
E 57TH ST
E 56TH ST
E 55TH ST
E 54TH ST
E 53RD ST
E 52ND ST
E 51ST ST
E 50TH ST
E 49TH ST
E 48TH ST
E 47TH ST
6
4,5,6
6
6
F
N,Q,R
4,5,6,N,Q,R,
E,M
E,M
6
N
0
500 yds

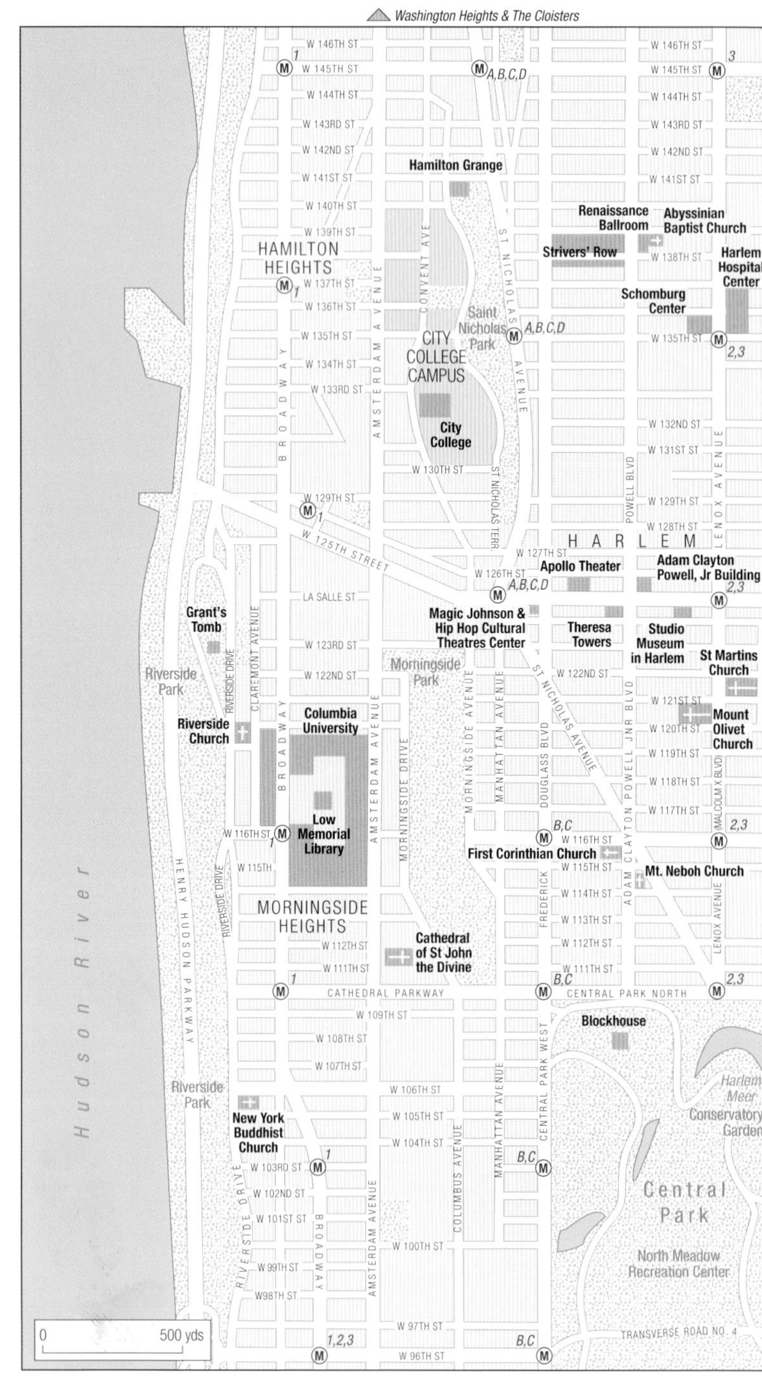
Washington Heights & The Cloisters
W 146TH ST
W 145TH ST
W 144TH ST
W 143RD ST
W 142ND ST
W 141ST ST
W 140TH ST
W 139TH ST
W 138TH ST
W 137TH ST
W 136TH ST
W 135TH ST
W 134TH ST
W 133RD ST
W 132ND ST
W 131ST ST
W 130TH ST
W 129TH ST
W 128TH ST
W 127TH ST
W 126TH ST
W 125TH STREET
LA SALLE ST
W 123RD ST
W 122ND ST
W 121ST ST
W 120TH ST
W 119TH ST
W 118TH ST
W 117TH ST
W 116TH ST
W 115TH
W 115TH ST
W 114TH ST
W 113TH ST
W 112TH ST
W 111TH ST
CATHEDRAL PARKWAY
CENTRAL PARK NORTH
W 109TH ST
W 108TH ST
W 107TH ST
W 106TH ST
W 105TH ST
W 104TH ST
W 103RD ST
W 102ND ST
W 101ST ST
W 100TH ST
W 99TH ST
W98TH ST
W 97TH ST
W 96TH ST
TRANSVERSE ROAD NO. 4
HAMILTON HEIGHTS
Hamilton Grange
CITY COLLEGE CAMPUS
City College
Saint Nicholas Park
CONVENT AVE
AMSTERDAM AVENUE
BROADWAY
ST NICHOLAS AVENUE
ST NICHOLAS TERR.
Renaissance Ballroom
Abyssinian Baptist Church
Strivers' Row
Harlem Hospital Center
Schomburg Center
POWELL BLVD
LENOX AVENUE
HARLEM
Apollo Theater
Adam Clayton Powell, Jr Building
Magic Johnson & Hip Hop Cultural Theatres Center
Theresa Towers
Studio Museum in Harlem
St Martins Church
Mount Olivet Church
Grant's Tomb
Riverside Park
RIVERSIDE DRIVE
CLAREMONT AVENUE
Riverside Church
Columbia University
Low Memorial Library
Morningside Park
MORNINGSIDE DRIVE
MORNINGSIDE AVENUE
MANHATTAN AVENUE
DOUGLASS BLVD
ADAM CLAYTON POWELL JNR BLVD
(MALCOLM X BLVD)
First Corinthian Church
Mt. Neboh Church
FREDERICK
MORNINGSIDE HEIGHTS
Cathedral of St John the Divine
HENRY HUDSON PARKWAY
Hudson River
Blockhouse
Harlem Meer
Conservatory Garden
New York Buddhist Church
COLUMBUS AVENUE
CENTRAL PARK WEST
Central Park
North Meadow Recreation Center
A,B,C,D
B,C
1,2,3
2,3
1
3
0
500 yds

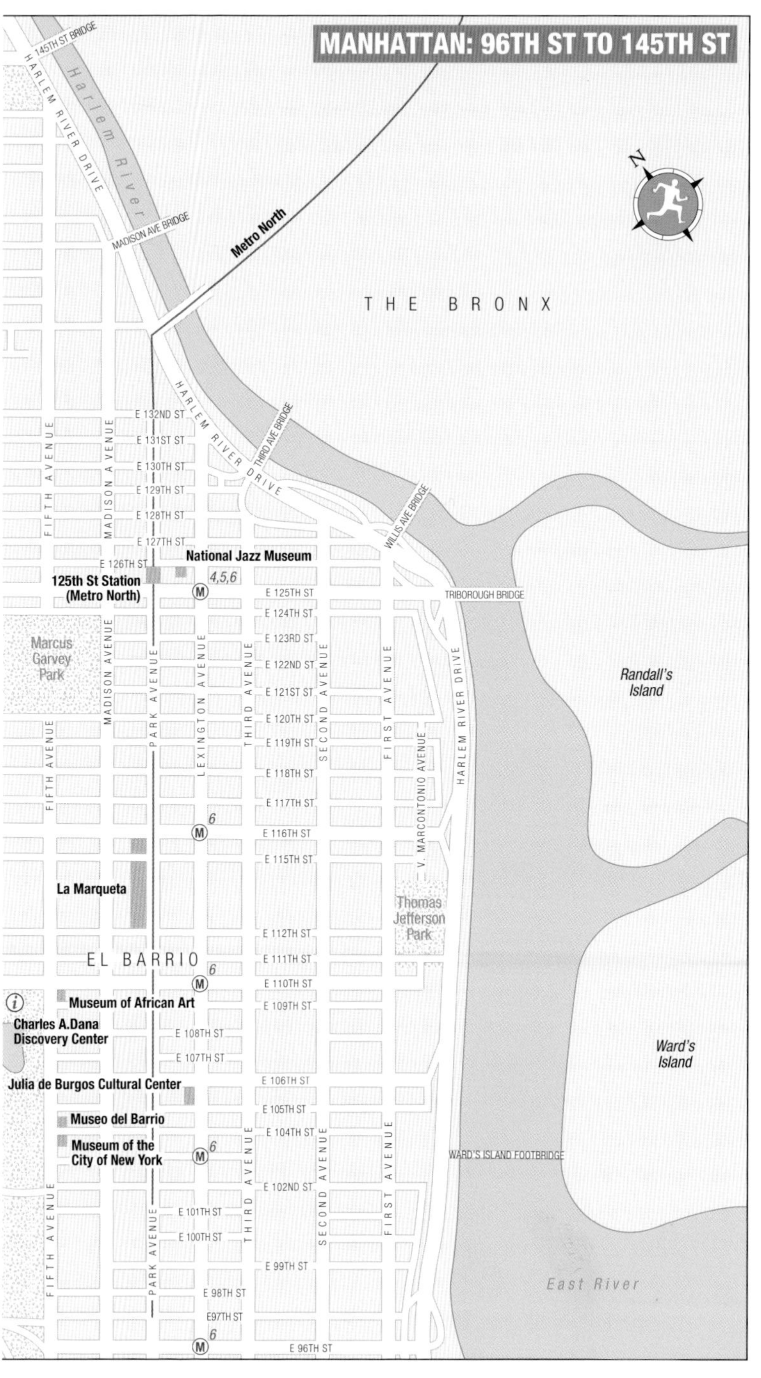
MANHATTAN: 96TH ST TO 145TH ST
145TH ST BRIDGE
HARLEM RIVER DRIVE
Harlem River
MADISON AVE BRIDGE
Metro North
THE BRONX
THIRD AVE BRIDGE
WILLIS AVE BRIDGE
TRIBOROUGH BRIDGE
Randall's Island
Ward's Island
WARD'S ISLAND FOOTBRIDGE
East River
National Jazz Museum
125th St Station (Metro North)
4,5,6
Marcus Garvey Park
La Marqueta
EL BARRIO
Thomas Jefferson Park
Museum of African Art
Charles A.Dana Discovery Center
Julia de Burgos Cultural Center
Museo del Barrio
Museum of the City of New York
FIFTH AVENUE
MADISON AVENUE
PARK AVENUE
LEXINGTON AVENUE
THIRD AVENUE
SECOND AVENUE
FIRST AVENUE
V. MARCONTONIO AVENUE
E 132ND ST
E 131ST ST
E 130TH ST
E 129TH ST
E 128TH ST
E 127TH ST
E 126TH ST
E 125TH ST
E 124TH ST
E 123RD ST
E 122ND ST
E 121ST ST
E 120TH ST
E 119TH ST
E 118TH ST
E 117TH ST
E 116TH ST
E 115TH ST
E 112TH ST
E 111TH ST
E 110TH ST
E 109TH ST
E 108TH ST
E 107TH ST
E 106TH ST
E 105TH ST
E 104TH ST
E 102ND ST
E 101TH ST
E 100TH ST
E 99TH ST
E 98TH ST
E97TH ST
E 96TH ST

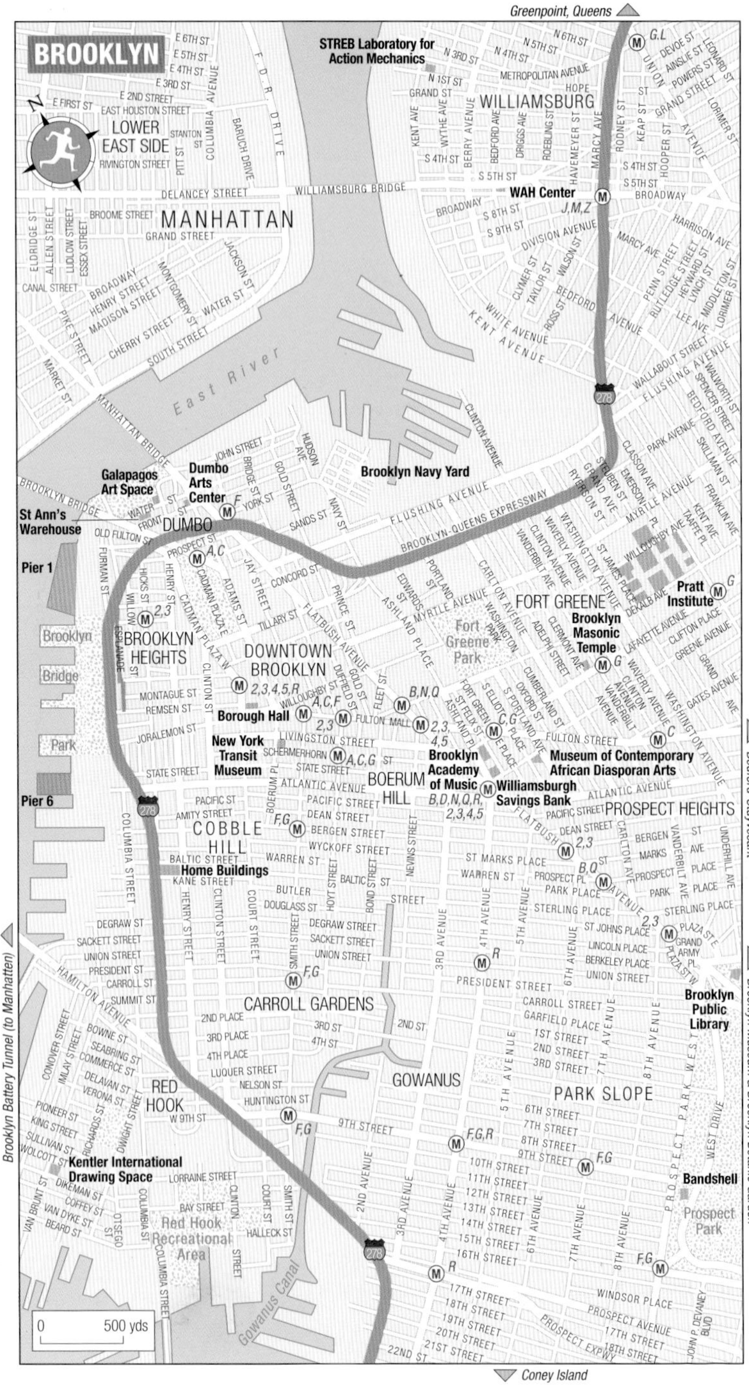

BROOKLYN
Greenpoint, Queens
STREB Laboratory for Action Mechanics
WILLIAMSBURG
LOWER EAST SIDE
MANHATTAN
WAH Center
East River
Brooklyn Navy Yard
Galapagos Art Space
Dumbo Arts Center
St Ann's Warehouse
DUMBO
Pier 1
BROOKLYN HEIGHTS
Brooklyn Bridge Park
DOWNTOWN BROOKLYN
Borough Hall
New York Transit Museum
FORT GREENE
Fort Greene Park
Pratt Institute
Brooklyn Masonic Temple
Brooklyn Academy of Music
Williamsburgh Savings Bank
Museum of Contemporary African Diasporan Arts
BOERUM HILL
PROSPECT HEIGHTS
Pier 6
COBBLE HILL
Home Buildings
Bedford-Stuyvesant
Brooklyn Battery Tunnel (to Manhatten)
CARROLL GARDENS
Brooklyn Public Library
Brooklyn Museum & Brooklyn Botanic Garden
RED HOOK
GOWANUS
PARK SLOPE
Kentler International Drawing Space
Bandshell
Red Hook Recreational Area
Prospect Park
Gowanus Canal
0 500 yds
Coney Island